History of Law

Compiled by
Karyn Lavender

Scribbles

Year of Publication 2018

ISBN : 9789387513020

Book Published by

Scribbles

(An Imprint of Alpha Editions)

email - alphaedis@gmail.com

Produced by: PediaPress GmbH
Limburg an der Lahn
Germany
http://pediapress.com/

Contents

Preface

Legal history or the history of law is the study of how law has evolved and why it changed. Legal history is closely connected to the development of civilisations and is set in the wider context of social history. Among certain jurists and historians of legal process, it has been seen as the recording of the evolution of laws and the technical explanation of how these laws have evolved with the view of better understanding the origins of various legal concepts; some consider it a branch of intellectual history. Twentieth century historians have viewed legal history in a more contextualised manner more in line with the thinking of social historians. They have looked at legal institutions as complex systems of rules, players and symbols and have seen these elements interact with society to change, adapt, resist or promote certain aspects of civil society. Such legal historians have tended to analyse case histories from the parameters of social science inquiry, using statistical methods, analysing class distinctions among litigants, petitioners and other players in various legal processes. By analysing case outcomes, transaction costs, number of settled cases they have begun an analysis of legal institutions, practices, procedures and briefs that give us a more complex picture of law and society than the study of jurisprudence, case law and civil codes can achieve.

Maat

Maat	
Goddess of Truth and Justice	

Maat was both the goddess and the personification of truth and justice. Her ostrich feather represents truth.

Major cult center	All ancient Egyptian cities
Symbol	the ostrich feather
Consort	Thoth (in some accounts)
Parents	Ra

Maat or **Ma'at** (Egyptian *m3't*) refers to both the ancient Egyptian concepts of truth, balance, order, harmony, law, morality, and justice, and the personification of these concepts as a goddess regulating the stars, seasons, and the actions of both mortals and the deities, who set the order of the universe from chaos at the moment of creation. Her ideological opposite was Isfet, meaning injustice, chaos, violence or to do evil.

Pronunciation

Cuneiform texts indicate that the word *m3't* was pronounced /múʔʕa/ during the New Kingdom period, having lost the feminine ending *t*. Sound shifts from *u* to *e* later produced the cognate Coptic word ⲙⲉⲉ/ⲙⲉ "truth, justice".

History

The earliest surviving records indicating that Maat is the norm for nature and society, in this world and the next, were recorded during the Old Kingdom,

Figure 1: *Winged Maat*

the earliest substantial surviving examples being found in the Pyramid Texts of Unas (ca. 2375 BCE and 2345 BCE).

Later, as a goddess in other traditions of the Egyptian pantheon, where most goddesses were paired with a male aspect, her masculine counterpart was Thoth, as their attributes are similar. In other accounts, Thoth was paired off with Seshat, goddess of writing and measure, who is a lesser known deity.

After her role in creation and continuously preventing the universe from returning to chaos, her primary role in Egyptian mythology dealt with the weighing of souls (also called the weighing of the heart) that took place in the underworld, Duat.[1] Her feather was the measure that determined whether the souls (considered to reside in the heart) of the departed would reach the paradise of afterlife successfully.

Pharaohs are often depicted with the emblems of Maat to emphasise their role in upholding the laws of the Creator.

As a principle

Maat represents the ethical and moral principle that every Egyptian citizen was expected to follow throughout their daily lives. They were expected to act with honor and truth in manners that involve family, the community, the nation, the environment, and the gods.

Maat as a principle was formed to meet the complex needs of the emergent Egyptian state that embraced diverse peoples with conflicting interests. The development of such rules sought to avert chaos and it became the basis of Egyptian law. From an early period the King would describe himself as the "Lord of Maat" who decreed with his mouth the Maat he conceived in his heart.

The significance of Maat developed to the point that it embraced all aspects of existence, including the basic equilibrium of the universe, the relationship between constituent parts, the cycle of the seasons, heavenly movements, religious observations and fair dealings, honesty and truthfulness in social interactions.

The ancient Egyptians had a deep conviction of an underlying holiness and unity within the universe. Cosmic harmony was achieved by correct public and ritual life. Any disturbance in cosmic harmony could have consequences for the individual as well as the state. An impious King could bring about famine or blasphemy blindness to an individual.[2] In opposition to the right order expressed in the concept of Maat is the concept of *Isfet*: chaos, lies and violence.[3]

In addition to the importance of the Maat, several other principles within ancient Egyptian law were essential, including an adherence to tradition as opposed to change, the importance of rhetorical skill, and the significance of achieving impartiality, and "righteous action". In one Middle Kingdom (2062 to c. 1664 BCE) text the Creator declares "*I made every man like his fellow*". Maat called the rich to help the less fortunate rather than exploit them, echoed in tomb declarations: "*I have given bread to the hungry and clothed the naked*" and "*I was a husband to the widow and father to the orphan*".

To the Egyptian mind, Maat bound all things together in an indestructible unity: the universe, the natural world, the state, and the individual were all seen as parts of the wider order generated by Maat.

A passage in the Instruction of Ptahhotep presents Ma'at as follows:

Ma'at is good and its worth is lasting.

It has not been disturbed since the day of its creator,

whereas he who transgresses its ordinances is punished.

It lies as a path in front even of him who knows nothing.

Wrongdoing has never yet brought its venture to port.

It is true that evil may gain wealth but the strength of truth is that it lasts;

a man can say: "It was the property of my father."

Figure 2: *Maat wearing feather of truth*

The law

There is little surviving literature that describes the practice of ancient Egyptian law. Maat was the spirit in which justice was applied rather than the detailed legalistic exposition of rules (as found in Mosaic law of the 1st millennium BCE; but see the 42 negative confessions, below). Maat represented the normal and basic values that formed the backdrop for the application of justice that had to be carried out in the spirit of truth and fairness. From the 5th dynasty (c. 2510–2370 BCE) onwards the Vizier responsible for justice was called the *Priest of Maat* and in later periods judges wore images of Maat.

Later scholars and philosophers also would embody concepts from the wisdom literature, or Sebayt. These spiritual texts dealt with common social or professional situations and how each was best to be resolved or addressed in the spirit of Maat. It was very practical advice, and highly case-based, so that few specific and general rules could be derived from them.

During the Greek period in Egyptian history, Greek law existed alongside Egyptian law. The Egyptian law preserved the rights of women who were allowed to act independently of men and own substantial personal property and in time this influenced the more restrictive conventions of the Greeks and Romans. When the Romans took control of Egypt, the Roman legal system which existed throughout the Roman Empire was imposed in Egypt.

Scribes

Scribes held prestigious positions in ancient Egyptian society in view of their importance in the transmission of religious, political and commercial information.[4]

Thoth was the patron of scribes who is described as the one "who reveals Maat and reckons Maat; who loves Maat and gives Maat to the doer of Maat".[5] In texts such as the Instruction of Amenemope the scribe is urged to follow the precepts of Maat in his private life as well as his work.[6] The exhortations to live according to Maat are such that these kinds of instructional texts have been described as "Maat Literature".[7]

As a goddess

Goddess Maat[8,9]
in hieroglyphs

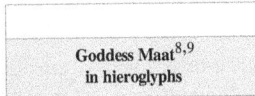

Maat was the goddess of harmony, justice, and truth represented as a young woman, sitting or standing, holding a *was* scepter, the symbol of power, in one hand and an *ankh*, the symbol of eternal life, in the other. Sometimes she is depicted with wings on each arm or as a woman with an ostrich feather on her head. The meaning of this emblem is uncertain, although the god Shu, who in some myths is Maat's brother, also wears it.[10] Depictions of Maat as a goddess are recorded from as early as the middle of the Old Kingdom (c. 2680 to 2190 BCE).[11]

The sun-god Ra came from the primaeval mound of creation only after he set his daughter Maat in place of Isfet (chaos). Kings inherited the duty to ensure Maat remained in place and they with Ra are said to "live on Maat", with Akhenaten (r. 1372–1355 BCE) in particular emphasising the concept to a degree that, John D. Ray asserts, the kings contemporaries viewed as intolerance and fanaticism.[12] Some kings incorporated Maat into their names, being referred to as *Lords of Maat*, or *Meri-Maat* (*Beloved of Maat*).

Maat had an invaluable role in the ceremony of the Weighing of the Heart. (See below: "The Weighing of the Heart").

Temples

The earliest evidence for a dedicated temple is in the New Kingdom (c. 1569 to 1081 BCE) era, despite the great importance placed on Maat. Amenhotep III commissioned a temple in the Karnak complex, whilst textual evidence indicates that other temples of Maat were located in Memphis and at Deir el-Medina.[13] The Maat temple at the Karnak complex was also used by courts to meet regarding the robberies of the royal tombs during the rule of Ramesses IX.

The afterlife

The Weighing of the Heart

In the Duat, the Egyptian underworld, the hearts of the dead were said to be weighed against her single "Feather of Ma'at", symbolically representing the concept of Maat, in the *Hall of Two Truths*. This is why hearts were left in Egyptian mummies while their other organs were removed, as the heart (called "ib") was seen as part of the Egyptian soul. If the heart was found to be lighter or equal in weight to the feather of Maat, the deceased had led a virtuous life and would go on to Aaru. Osiris came to be seen as the guardian of the gates of Aaru after he became part of the Egyptian pantheon and displaced Anubis in the Ogdoad tradition. A heart which was unworthy was devoured by the goddess Ammit and its owner condemned to remain in the Duat.

The weighing of the heart, pictured on papyrus in the Book of the Dead typically, or in tomb scenes, shows Anubis overseeing the weighing and the lioness Ammit seated awaiting the results so she could consume those who failed. The image would be the vertical heart on one flat surface of the *balance scale* and the vertical Shu-feather standing on the other balance scale surface. Other traditions hold that Anubis brought the soul before the posthumous Osiris who performed the weighing. While the heart was weighed the deceased recited the 42 Negative Confessions as the Assessors of Maat looked on.

In funerary texts (*The Book of Coming Forth by Day* and on tomb inscriptions)

Egyptians were often entombed with funerary texts in order to be well equipped for the afterlife as mandated by Egyptian burial customs. These often served to guide the deceased through the afterlife, and the most famous one is the *Book of the Dead* or *Papyrus of Ani* (known to the ancient Egyptians as *The Book of Coming Forth by Day*). The lines of these texts are often collectively called the "Forty-Two Declarations of Purity". These declarations varied somewhat from tomb to tomb as they were tailored to the individual, and so cannot be

Figure 3: *Weighing of the Heart Book of the Dead writ-*
ten on papyrus showing the "Weighing of the Heart" in the
Duat using the feather of Maat as the measure in balance

considered a canonical definition of Maat. Rather, they appear to express each tomb owner's individual practices in life to please Maat, as well as words of absolution from misdeeds or mistakes, made by the tomb owner in life could be declared as not having been done, and through the power of the written word, wipe particular misdeed from the afterlife record of the deceased. Many of the lines are similar, however, and paint a very unified picture of Maat.

The doctrine of Maat is represented in the declarations to Rekhti-merti-f-ent-Maat and the 42 Negative Confessions listed in the Papyrus of Ani. The following are translations by E. A. Wallis Budge.

42 Negative Confessions (*Papyrus of Ani*)

From the *Papyrus of Ani*.

1. I have not committed sin.
2. I have not committed robbery with violence.
3. I have not stolen.
4. I have not slain men and women.
5. I have not stolen grain.
6. I have not purloined offerings.
7. I have not stolen the property of the gods.
8. I have not uttered lies.
9. I have not carried away food.
10. I have not uttered curses.
11. I have not committed adultery.

12. I have made none to weep.
13. I have not eaten the heart [i.e., I have not grieved uselessly, or felt remorse].
14. I have not attacked any man.
15. I am not a man of deceit.
16. I have not stolen cultivated land.
17. I have not been an eavesdropper.
18. I have slandered [no man].
19. I have not been angry without just cause.
20. I have not debauched the wife of any man.
21. I have not debauched the wife of [any] man. (repeats the previous affirmation but addressed to a different god).
22. I have not polluted myself.
23. I have terrorized none.
24. I have not transgressed [the Law].
25. I have not been wroth.
26. I have not shut my ears to the words of truth.
27. I have not blasphemed.
28. I am not a man of violence.
29. I am not a stirrer up of strife (or a disturber of the peace).
30. I have not acted (or judged) with undue haste.
31. I have not pried into matters.
32. I have not multiplied my words in speaking.
33. I have wronged none, I have done no evil.
34. I have not worked witchcraft against the King (or blasphemed against the King).
35. I have never stopped [the flow of] water.
36. I have never raised my voice (spoken arrogantly, or in anger).
37. I have not cursed (or blasphemed) God.
38. I have not acted with evil rage.
39. I have not stolen the bread of the gods.
40. I have not carried away the khenfu cakes from the spirits of the dead.
41. I have not snatched away the bread of the child, nor treated with contempt the god of my city.
42. I have not slain the cattle belonging to the god.

Assessors of Ma'at

"The Assessors of Ma'at" are the 42 deities listed in the *Papyrus of Nebseni*, to whom the deceased make the Negative Confession in the *Papyrus of Ani*.[14] They represent the 42 united nomes of Egypt, and are called "the hidden Maati gods, who feed upon Maat during the years of their lives;" i.e., they are the righteous minor deities who deserve offerings. As the deceased follows the set formula of Negative Confessions, he addresses each god directly and mentions the nome of which the god is a patron, in order to emphasize the unity of the nomes of Egypt.

References

Bibliography

- Black, James Roger. *"The Instruction of Amenemope: A Critical Edition and Commentary–Prolegomenon and Prologue"*, Dissertation University of Wisconsin-Madison, 2002[15]
- Budge, E. A. Wallis. *The Egyptian Book of the Dead: (The Papyrus of Ani) Egyptian Text Transliteration and Translation*. New York: Dover Publications, 1967. Originally published in 1895.
- Budge, E. A. Wallis. *The Gods of the Egyptians: Studies in Egyptian Mythology — Volume 1*. New York: Dover Publications, 1969. Originally published in 1904.
- Collier, Mark and Manly, Bill. *How to Read Egyptian Hieroglyphs: Revised Edition*. Berkeley: University of California Press, 1998.
- Faulkner, Raymond. *The Egyptian Book of the Dead*. San Francisco: Chronicle Books, 1994. ISBN 0-8118-6489-8
- Mancini, Anna. *Maat Revealed: Philosophy of Justice in Ancient Egypt*. New York: Buenos Books America, 2004.
- Strudwick, Helen. (2006). *The Encyclopedia of Ancient Egypt*. Singapore: De Agostini UK.
- *Journey through the afterlife, Ancient Egyptian Book of the Dead* edited by John H. Taylor (the British Museum Press 2010. London ISBN 0-7141-1989-X)

Further reading

- Assmann, Jan (1990). *Ma'at: Gerechtigkeit und Unsterblichkeit im Alten Ägypten* (in German). C.H. Beck Verlag. ISBN 3406346677.
- Menu, Bernadette (2005). *Maât: L'ordre juste du monde* (in French). Editions Michalon. ISBN 2841862836.

Babylonian law

The ancient Near East

Regions and states

Fertile Crescent
Mesopotamia
- Akkadian Empire
- Assyria
- Babylonia
- Neo-Assyrian Empire
- Neo-Babylonian Empire
- Sumer

Egypt
- Ancient Egypt

Persia
- Achaemenid Empire
- Elam
- Medes

Anatolia
- Hittites
- Hurrians
- Neo-Hittite states
- Urartu

The Levant
- Ancient Israel
- Phoenicia

Archaeological periods

- Chronology
- Bronze Age
- Bronze Age collapse
- Iron Age

Languages

- Akkadian

- Aramaic

- Assyriology

- Cuneiform script

- Elamite

- Hebrew

- Hittite

- Hurrian

- Phoenician

- Sumerian

- Urartian

Literature

- Babylonian
- Hittite texts
- Sumerian

Mythology

- Babylonian
- Hittite
- Mesopotamian
- Egyptian

Other topics

- Cradle of civilization
- Assyrian law
- Babylonian astronomy
- Babylonian law
- Babylonian mathematics
- Cuneiform law
- History of the Middle East
- $\underline{v}$
- $\underline{t}$
- $\underline{e}^{16}$

Babylonian law is a subset of cuneiform law that has received particular study, owing to the singular extent of the associated archaeological material that has been found for it. So-called "contracts" exist in the thousands, including a great variety of deeds, conveyances, bonds, receipts, accounts, and most important of all, actual legal decisions given by the judges in the law courts. Historical inscriptions, royal charters and rescripts, dispatches, private letters and the general literature afford welcome supplementary information. Even grammatical and lexicographical texts contain many extracts or short sentences bearing on law and custom. The so-called "Sumerian Family Laws" are preserved in this way.

Other cultures involved with ancient Mesopotamia shared the same common laws and precedents, extending to the form of contacts that Kenneth Kitchen has studied and compared to the form of contracts in the Bible with particular note to the sequence of blessings and curses that bind the deal. The Maxims of Ptahhotep and Sharia Law,[17] also include certifications for professionals like doctors, lawyers and skilled craftsmen which prescribe penalties for malpractice very similar to the code of Hammurabi.

The discovery of the now-celebrated Code of Hammurabi (hereinafter simply termed "the Code") has made possible a more systematic study than could have resulted from just the classification and interpretation of other material. Fragments of other Ancient codes exist and have been published, but there still remain many points whereof evidence is still lacking. There survive legal texts from the earliest writings through the Hellenistic period, but evidence on a particular point may be very full for one period and almost entirely lacking for another. The Code forms the backbone of most reconstructions. Fragments of it recovered from Assur-bani-pal's library at Nineveh and later Babylonian copies show that it was studied, divided into chapters, entitled *Ninu ilu sirum* from its incipit (opening words), and recopied for fifteen hundred years or more.

Much Babylonian legal precedent remained in force, even through the Persian, Greek and Parthian conquests, which had little effect on private life in Babylonia; and it survived to influence Romans. The laws and customs that preceded the Code may be called "early"; that of the Neo-Babylonian empire (as well as the Persian, Greek, etc.), "late". The law of Assyria was derived from the Babylonian, but it conserved early features long after they had disappeared elsewhere.

History

Tribal influence

The early history of Mesopotamia is the story of a struggle for supremacy between the cities. A metropolis demanded tribute and military support from its subject cities but left their local cults and customs unaffected. City rights and usages were respected by kings and conquerors alike. When the ancient Semitic-speaking peoples settled in the cities of Mesopotamia, their tribal customs passed over into city law.

As late as the accession of Assur-bani-pal and Shamash-shum-ukin, we find the Babylonians appending to their city laws that groups of aliens to the number of twenty at a time were free to enter the city; that foreign women, once married to Babylonian husbands, could not be enslaved; and that not even a dog that entered the city could be put to death untried.Wikipedia:Citation needed

The population of Babylonia was multi-ethnic from early times, and intercommunication between the cities was incessant. Every city had a large number of resident aliens. This freedom of intercourse must have tended to assimilate custom. It was, however, reserved for the genius of Hammurabi to make Babylon his metropolis and weld together his vast empire by a uniform system of law.

Hammurabi's Code

By Hammurabi's time, almost all trace of tribal custom had already disappeared from the law of the Code. It is state law—self-help, blood-feud, and marriage by capture, are all absent; though code of family solidarity, district responsibility, ordeal, and the *lex talionis* (an eye for an eye), are primitive features that remain. The king is a benevolent autocrat, easily accessible to all his subjects, both able and willing to protect the weak against the highest-placed oppressor. The royal power, however, can only pardon when private resentment is appeased. Judges are strictly supervised, and appeal is allowed. The whole land is covered with feudal holdings, masters of the levy, police, etc. There is a regular postal system. The *pax Babylonica* is so assured that private individuals do not hesitate to ride in their carriage from Babylon to the coast of the Mediterranean. The position of women is free and dignified.

The Code did not merely embody contemporary custom or conserve ancient law. It is true that centuries of law-abiding and litigious habitude had accumulated, in the temple archives of each city, vast stores of precedent in ancient deeds and records of judicial decisions and that intercourse had assimilated city custom. The universal habit of writing, and perpetual recourse to written contract, further modified primitive custom and ancient precedent.

If the parties themselves could agree to the terms, the Code as a rule left them free to make contracts. Their deed of agreement was drawn up in the temple by a notary public and confirmed with an oath "by god and the king." It was publicly sealed and witnessed by professional witnesses, as well as by collaterally interested parties. The manner in which it was executed may have been sufficient guarantee that its stipulations were not impious or illegal. Custom or public opinion doubtlessly ensured that the parties would not agree to "wrong". If a dispute arose, the judges dealt first with the contract. They might not sustain it, but if the parties did not dispute it, they were free to observe it. The judges' decision might, however, be appealed. Many contracts contain the proviso that in case of future dispute, the parties would abide by "the decision of the king." The Code made known, in a vast number of cases, what that decision would be, and many cases of appeal to the king were returned to the judges with orders to decide in accordance with it. The Code itself was carefully and logically arranged, its sections arranged by subject matter. Nevertheless, the order is not that of modern scientific treatises, so a somewhat different order than either is most convenient for our purpose.

See also: English translation of Hammurabi's Code[18]

Three classes

Part of a series on
Slavery

- <u>v</u>
- <u>t</u>
- <u>e</u>[19]

The Code contemplates the whole population as falling into three classes: the *amelu*, the *mushkenu* and the *ardu*.

The *amelu* was originally a patrician, a man from an elite family, possessed of full civil rights, whose birth, marriage and death were registered. He had aristocratic privileges and responsibilities, and the right to exact retaliation for corporal injuries, but was liable to a heavier punishment for crimes and misdemeanours, higher fees and fines. To this class belonged the king and court, the higher officials, the professions and craftsmen. Over time, the term became a mere courtesy title—already in the Code, when status is not concerned, it is used to denote anyone. There was no property qualification, nor does the term appear to be racial.

It is most difficult to characterize the *mushkenu* exactly. The term in time came to mean "a beggar", and that meaning has passed through Aramaic and Hebrew into many modern languages; but though the Code does not regard him as necessarily poor, he may have been landless. He was free but had to accept monetary compensation for corporal injuries, paid smaller fees and fines, and even paid less offerings to the gods. He inhabited a separate quarter of the city. There is no reason to regard him as specially connected with the court, as a royal pensioner, nor as forming the bulk of the population. The rarity of any references to him in contemporary documents makes further specification conjectural.

The *ardu* was a slave, his master's chattel, and formed a very numerous class. He could acquire property and even own other slaves. His master clothed and fed him and paid his doctor's fees, but took all compensation paid for injury done to him. His master usually found him a slave girl for a wife (the children were then born slaves), often set him up in a house (with farm or business) and simply took an annual rent of him. Otherwise, he might marry a free woman (the children were then free), who might bring him a dower that his master could not touch, and at his death, one-half of his property passed to his master as his heir. He could acquire his freedom by purchase from his master, or might be freed and dedicated to a temple, or even adopted, when he became an *amelu* and not a *mushkenu*. Slaves were recruited by purchase abroad, from captives taken in war, or by freemen degraded for debt or crime. A slave often ran away; if caught, the captor was bound to restore him to his master, and the Code fixes a reward of two shekels that the owner must pay the captor. It was about one-tenth of the average value of a slave. To detain or harbour a slave was punishable by death. So was aiding him to escape the city gates. A slave bore an identification mark, removable only by a surgical operation, that later consisted of his owner's name tattooed or branded on the arm. On the other hand, on the great estates in Assyria and its subject provinces there were many serfs, mostly of subject race, settled captives, or quondam slaves; tied to the soil they cultivated and sold with the estate, yet capable of possessing land and property of their own. There is little trace of serfs in Babylonia, unless the *mushkenu* is really a serf.

Citizens tenants of gods

The god of a city was originally considered the owner of its land, which encircled it with an inner ring of irrigable arable land and an outer fringe of pasture; the citizens were his tenants. The god and his vice regent, the king, had long ceased to disturb tenancy and were content with fixed dues *in naturalia*, stock, money or service.

One of the earliest monuments records the purchase by a king of a large estate for his son, paying a fair market price and adding a handsome honorarium to the many owners, in costly garments, plate, and precious articles of furniture. The Code recognizes complete private ownership of land but apparently extends the right to hold land to votaries and merchants; but all land sold was subject to its fixed charges. The king, however, could free land from these charges by charter, which was a frequent way of rewarding those who deserved well of the state.

It is from these charters that we learn of the obligations lying upon land. The state demanded men for the army and the *corvée*, as well as dues in kind. A certain area was bound to provide a bowman, together with his linked pikeman (who bore the shield for both), and to furnish them with supplies for the campaign. This area was termed a "bow" as early as the 8th century BC, but the practice goes back much earlier. Later, a horseman was also due from certain areas. A man was only bound to serve a certain number of times, but the land still had to find a man annually. This service was usually discharged by slaves and serfs, but the *amelu* (and perhaps the *mushkenu*) also went to war. The bows were grouped together in tens and hundreds. The *corvée* was less regular. Special liabilities also lay upon riparian owners to repair canals, bridges, quays, etc. The letters of Hammurabi often deal with claims to exemption. Religious officials and shepherds in charge of flocks were exempt from military duty.

The state claimed certain proportions of all crops, stock, etc. The king's messengers could commandeer any subject's property, giving a receipt. Further, every city had its own octroi duties, customs, ferry dues, highway and water rates. The king had long ceased to be owner of the land, if he ever was. He had his own royal estates, his private property, and dues from all his subjects. The higher officials had endowments and official residences.

The Code regulates the feudal position of certain classes. They held an estate from the king, consisting of a house, a garden, a field, stock, and a salary, on condition of personal service on the king's errand. They could not delegate the service, on penalty of death. When ordered abroad, they could nominate a capable son to hold the benefice and carry on the duty. If there was no capable son, the state put in a *locum tenens* but granted one-third to the wife to maintain herself and her children. The fief was otherwise inalienable; it could not be sold, pledged, exchanged, sublet, devised or diminished. Other land was leased from the state. Ancestral estate was strictly tied to the family. If a holder would sell, the family kept the right of redemption, and there seems to have been no time limit to its exercise.

Temple

The temple occupied a most important position. It received income from its estates, from tithes and other fixed dues, as well as from the sacrifices (a customary share) and other offerings of the faithful—vast amounts of all sorts of naturalia, besides money and permanent gifts. The larger temples had many officials and servants.

Originally, perhaps, each town clustered round one temple, and each head of family had a right to minister there and share its receipts. As the city grew, the right to so many days a year at one shrine (or its gate) descended within certain families and became a kind of property that could be pledged, rented or shared within the family, but not alienated. Despite all these demands, the temples became great granaries and storehouses and were also the city archives. The temple had its responsibilities. If a citizen was captured by the enemy and could not ransom himself, the temple of his city must do so. To the temple came the poor farmer to borrow seed, grain, or supplies for harvesters, etc.—advances that he repaid without interest.

The king's power over the temple was not proprietary, but administrative. He might borrow from it, but repaid like other borrowers. The tithe seems to have been considered the rent due to the god for his land. It is not clear that all lands paid tithe; perhaps only such as once had a special connection with the temple.

The Code deals with a class of persons devoted to the service of a god, as vestals or hierodules. The vestals were vowed to chastity, lived together in a great nunnery, were forbidden to enter a tavern, and, together with other votaries, had many privileges.

Property law

The Code recognizes many ways of disposing of property: sale, lease, barter, gift, dedication, deposit, loan, or pledge, all of which were matters of contract. Sale was the delivery of a purchase (in the case of real estate, symbolized by a staff, a key, or deed of conveyance) in return for purchase money, receipts being given for both. Credit, if given, was treated as a debt, and secured as a loan by the seller to be repaid by the buyer, for which he gave a bond.

The Code only allows claims substantiated by documents, or in some cases the oath of witnesses. Saving contracts and receipts thus assumed a vital importance in Babylon - in fact it could literally be a matter of life or death. A buyer had to be sure of the seller's title. If he bought (or received on deposit) property from even a minor or a slave without witnessing contracts, he would be executed as a thief (§7). If purchased goods were stolen and the rightful owner reclaimed them, he had to prove his purchase by producing the seller and the deed of sale, or witnesses to it; otherwise, he would be adjudged a thief and die. If he proved his purchase, he had to give up the property but could pursue a remedy against the seller or, if the seller had died, could reclaim fivefold from his estate.

A man who bought a slave abroad might find that he had previously been stolen or captured from Babylonia; he would then have to restore him to his former owner without recompense. If he bought property belonging to a feudal holding, or to a ward in Chancery, he had to return it as well as forfeit what he paid for it. He could repudiate the purchase of a slave attacked by the *bennu* sickness within a month (later, a hundred days) and could hold a newly purchased female slave for three days "on approval". A defect of title, or an undisclosed liability, would invalidate a sale at any time.

Leasing

Landowners frequently cultivated their land themselves, but could also employ a husbandman, or rent it. The husbandman was bound to carry out proper cultivation, raise an average crop, and leave the field in good tilth. In case the crop failed, the Code fixed a statutory return. Land might be leased at a fixed rent, where the Code stipulates that accidental loss fell on the tenant. If leased on profit-sharing terms, the landlord and tenant shared the loss proportionally to their stipulated share of profit. If the tenant paid his rent and kept the land in good tilth, the landlord could not interfere nor forbid subletting.

Wasteland could be leased for reclamation, the tenant being rent-free for three years and paying a stipulated rent in the fourth year. If the tenant neglected to reclaim the land, the Code stipulated that he must hand it over in good tilth and set a statutory rent. Gardens or plantations were leased in the same ways and under the same conditions; but for date groves, four years' free tenure was allowed.

The metayer system was common, especially on temple lands. The landlord found land, labour, oxen for ploughing and working the watering machines, carting, threshing or other implements, grain seed, rations for the workmen and fodder for the cattle. The tenant, or steward, usually had other land of his own. If he stole the seed, rations or fodder, the Code stipulated that his fingers be cut off. If he appropriated or sold the implements, or impoverished or sublet the cattle, he was heavily fined and in default of payment, might be condemned to be torn to pieces by the cattle on the field. Rent was determined by contract.

Irrigation was essential for farming in this region. If the irrigator neglected to repair his dike or left his runnel open and caused a flood, he had to make good the damage done to his neighbours' crops or be sold with his family to pay the cost. The theft of a watering machine, water-bucket or other agricultural implement was heavily fined.

Houses were usually leased for the year, but also for longer terms, rent being paid in advance, half-yearly. The contract generally specified that the house be in good repair, and the tenant was bound to keep it so. The woodwork, including doors and door frames, was removable, and the tenant might bring and take away his own. The Code stipulated that if the landlord re-entered before the term was up, he must remit a fair proportion of the rent. Land could be leased for the purpose of building houses or other buildings on it, the tenant being rent-free for eight or ten years; after which the building came into the landlord's possession.

Hired labour

Despite the multitude of slaves, hired labour was often needed, especially at harvest. This was a matter of contract, and the employer, who usually paid in advance, might demand a collateral against fulfillment of the work. Cattle were hired for ploughing, working the watering machines, carting, threshing, etc. The Code fixed a statutory wage for sowers, ox-drivers, field-labourers, and hire for oxen, asses, etc.

There were many herds and flocks. The flocks were committed to a shepherd, who gave receipt for them and took them out to pasture. The Code fixed his wage. He was responsible for all care, must restore ox for ox, sheep for sheep and must breed them satisfactorily. Any dishonest use of the flock had to be repaid tenfold, but loss due to disease or wild beasts fell upon the owner. The shepherd made good all loss due to his own neglect. If he let the flock feed on a field of crops, he had to pay damages fourfold; if he turned them into standing crops when they ought to have been folded, he paid twelvefold.

Debt

In commerce, payment in kind was still common, though contracts usually stipulated cash, naming the currency expected—that of Babylon, Larsa, Assyria, Carchemish, etc. The Code stipulated, however, that a debtor must be allowed to pay in produce according to a statutory scale. If a debtor had neither money nor crops, the creditor must not refuse goods.

Debt was secured on the debtor's own person. Distraint on a debtor's grain was forbidden by the Code; not only must the creditor return it, but his illegal action forfeited his claim altogether. An unwarranted seizure for debt was fined, as was the distraint of a working ox.

If a debtor were seized for debt, he could nominate as *mancipium*, or hostage to work off the debt, his wife, child, or slave. The creditor could only hold a wife or child three years as *mancipium*. If the *mancipium* died a natural death while in the creditor's possession, no claim could lie against the latter; but if he was the cause of death by cruelty, he had to give son for son, or pay for a slave. He could sell a slave-hostage, but not a slave-girl who had borne her master children; she had to be redeemed by her owner.

The debtor could also pledge his property and in contracts, often pledged a field, house or crop. The Code stipulated, however, that the debtor must take the crop himself and pay the creditor from its yield. If the crop failed, payment was deferred, and no interest could be charged for that year. If the debtor did not cultivate the field himself, he had to pay for its cultivation, but if the field was already cultivated, he must harvest it himself and pay his debt from the crop. If the cultivator did not get a crop, this would not cancel his contract.

Pledges were often made where the intrinsic value of the article was equivalent to the amount of the debt; but antichretic pledge was more common, where the profit of the pledge was a set-off against the interest of the debt. The whole property of a debtor might be pledged as collateral for payment of a debt, without any of it passing through the hands of the creditor. Personal guarantees were often given in Babylon that the debtor would repay, or the guarantor become liable himself.

Trade

Trade was very extensive. A common procedure was for a merchant to entrust his goods or money to a traveling agent, who sought a market for his goods. The caravans travelled far beyond the limits of the empire.

The Code insisted that the agent should inventory and give a receipt for all that he received. No claim could be made for anything not so entered. Even if the agent made no profit, he was bound to return double what he had received; if he made poor profit, he had to make up the deficiency; but he was not responsible for loss by robbery or extortion on his travels. On his return, the lending merchant must give him a receipt for what was handed over to him. Any false entry or claim on the agent's part was penalised threefold; on the lending merchant's part, sixfold. In normal cases, profits were divided according to contract, usually equally.

A considerable amount of forwarding (advancing wares to the agent up front) was done by the caravans. The carrier gave a receipt for the consignment, took all responsibility, and exacted a receipt upon delivery. If he defaulted, he paid fivefold. He was usually paid in advance. Deposit, especially warehousing of grain, was charged for at one-sixtieth. The warehouse man took all risks and paid double for all shortage, but no claim could be made unless he had given a properly witnessed receipt.

Water traffic on the Euphrates and canal system was early on, quite considerable. Ships, whose tonnage was estimated by the amount of grain they could carry, were continually hired for the transport of all kinds of goods. The Code fixes the price for shipbuilding and insists on the builder's giving a year's guarantee of seaworthiness. It also fixes the rate of hire for ship and crew. The captain was responsible for the freight and the ship; he had to replace all loss. Even if he refloated the ship, he had to pay a fine of half its value for sinking it. In the case of collision, the boat under way was responsible for damages to the boat at anchor.

The Code also regulated the liquor traffic—fixing a fair price for beer and forbidding the connivance of the tavern keeper (a female) at disorderly conduct or treasonable assembly, under pain of death. She was required to take the offenders to the palace—implying an efficient and accessible police system.

Payment through a banker or by written draft against deposit was frequent. Bonds to pay were treated as negotiable. Interest was rarely charged on advances by the temple or wealthy landowners for pressing needs, but this may have been part of the metayer system. The borrowers may have been tenants. Interest was charged at very high rates for overdue loans of this kind. Merchants (and even temples in some cases) made ordinary business loans, charging from 20% to 30%.

Family law

Marriage

Marriage retained the form of purchase, but was essentially a contract to be husband and wife together. The marriage of young people was usually arranged between their relatives—the groom's father the bride-price, which, with other gifts, the suitor ceremonially presented to the bride's father. This bride-price was usually then handed over by her father to the bride upon her marriage, and so returned into the bridegroom's possession, along with her dowry, which was her portion of the family's inheritance as a daughter.

The bride-price varied greatly, according to the status of the parties, but surpassed the price of a slave. The Code stipulated that if the father did not give the suitor his daughter after accepting the suitor's gifts, he must return the gifts. The bride-price had to be returned even if the father reneged on the marriage contract because of slander of the suitor on the part of the suitor's friend, and the Code stipulated that the slanderer should not marry the girl (and thus would not profit from his slander). Conversely, if a suitor changed his mind, he forfeited the presents.

The dowry might include real estate, but generally consisted of personal effects and household furniture. It remained the wife's for life, descending to her children, if any; otherwise returning to her family, when the husband could deduct the bride-price if it had not been given to her, or return it if it had.

The marriage ceremony included joining hands and the bridegroom uttering a formula of acceptance, such as, "I am the son of nobles, silver and gold shall fill thy lap, thou shalt be my wife, I will be thy husband. Like the fruit of a garden I will give thee offspring." The ceremony must be performed by a freeman.

The marriage contract—without which, the Code ruled that the woman was no wife—usually stated the consequences to which each party was liable for repudiating the other. These by no means necessarily agree with the Code. Many other conditions might also be inserted: such as that the wife should act as maidservant to her mother-in-law or to a first wife.

The married couple formed a single unit in terms of external responsibility, especially for debt. The man was responsible for debts contracted by his wife, even before her marriage, as well as for his own; but he could use her as a *mancipium* (see above). Hence the Code allowed a proviso to be inserted in the marriage contract, that the wife should not be seized for her husband's pre-nuptial debts; but stipulated that then he was not responsible for her pre-nuptial debts, and, in any case, that both together were responsible for all debts contracted after marriage. A man might make his wife a settlement by deed of gift, which gave her a life interest in part of his property, and he might reserve to her the right to bequeath it to a favorite child; but she could in no case leave it to her family. Although married, she always remained a member of her father's house—she is rarely named wife of A, but usually daughter of B, or mother of C.

Divorce

Divorce was the husband's option, but he had to restore the dowry, and if the wife had borne him children, she had custody of them. He then had to assign her the income from property, as well as goods to maintain herself and their children until they grew up. She shared equally with their children in the allowance (and apparently in his estate at his death) and was free to marry again. If she had no children, he returned her dowry to her and paid her a sum equivalent to the bride-price, or a mina of silver if there had been none. The latter is the forfeit usually named in the contract for his repudiation of her.

If the husband could show that his wife had been a bad wife, the Code allowed him to send her away, while he kept the children as well as her dowry; or he could degrade her to the position of a slave in his own house, where she would have food and clothing. The wife might bring an action against her husband for cruelty and neglect and, if she proved her case, obtain a judicial separation, taking her dowry with her. No other punishment fell on the man. If she did not prove her case, but was proved to be a bad wife, she was drowned.

If the wife was left without maintenance during an involuntary absence of her husband (called to war, etc.), she could cohabit with another man, but must return to her husband when he came back, the children of the second union remaining with their own father. If she had maintenance, a breach of the marriage tie was adultery. Willful desertion by, or exile of, the husband dissolved the marriage without penalty to the wife. If he returned, she was not required or even permitted to return to him.

Widowhood

A widow took her husband's place in the family—living in his house and bringing up the children. She could only remarry with judicial consent, where the judge inventoried the deceased's estate and handed it over to her and her new husband in trust for the children. They could not alienate a single utensil.

If she did not remarry, she lived on in her husband's house and, when the children had grown up, took a child's share in the division of his estate. She retained her dowry and any settlement deeded to her by her husband. This property would come down to her children on her death. If she had remarried, all her children would share equally in her dowry, but the first husband's estate fell only to his children, or to her selection among them, if so empowered.

Childbearing

Monogamy was the rule, and a childless wife might give her husband a maid to bear him children, who were then reckoned hers. She remained mistress of her maid, and might degrade her to slavery again for insolence, but could not sell her if she had borne her husband children. If the wife did this, the Code did not allow the husband to take a concubine; but if she did not, he could do so. The concubine was a co-wife, though not of the same rank; the first wife had no power over her. A concubine was a free woman, often dowered for marriage, and her children were legitimate and lawful heirs. She could only be divorced on the same conditions as a wife.

If a wife became a chronic invalid, the husband was bound to maintain her in the home they had made together, unless she preferred to take her dowry and return to her father's house; but he was free to remarry. Again, the children of the new wife were legitimate and lawful heirs.

There was no hindrance to a man having children by a slave girl. These children were free, and their mother then could not be sold, though she might be pledged, and she became free upon her master's death. Her children could be legitimized by their father's acknowledgment before witnesses and were often adopted. They then ranked equally in sharing their father's estate; but if not adopted, the wife's children divided and took first choice.

Temple priests were not supposed to have children, yet they could marry and often did. The Code contemplated that such a wife would give a husband a maid, as above.

Free women might marry slaves and still be dowered for the marriage. The children were free, and at the slave's death, the wife took her dowry and half of what she and her husband had acquired in wedlock for self and children; the master taking the other half, as his slave's heir.

A father had control over his children until their marriage. He had a right to their labor in return for their keep. He might hire them out and receive their wages, pledge them for debt, or even sell them outright. Mothers had the same rights in the absence of the father; elder brothers, when both parents were dead. A father had no claim on his married children for support, but they retained the right to inherit on his death.

The daughter was not only in her father's power to be given in marriage, but he might dedicate her to the service of a god as a vestal or a hierodule or give her as a concubine. She had no choice in these matters, often decided in her childhood. An adult daughter might wish to become a votary, perhaps in preference to an uncongenial marriage, and it seems that her father could not refuse her wish.

In all these cases, the father might dower her. If he did not, on his death the brothers were obligated to do so, giving her a full child's share if a wife, a concubine or a vestal, but one-third of a child's share if she were a hierodule or a Marduk priestess. The latter had the privilege of exemption from state dues and absolute disposal of her property. All other daughters had only a life interest in their dowry, which reverted to their family if childless or went to their children if they had any. A father might, however, execute a deed granting a daughter power to leave her property to a favorite brother or sister.

A daughter's estate was usually managed for her by her brothers, but if they dissatisfied her, she could appoint a steward. If she married, her husband then managed it. Sons also appear to have received their share on marriage, but then did not always leave their father's house; they might bring their wives there. This was usual in child marriages.

Adoption

Adoption was very common, especially when the father (or mother) was child-less or had seen all his children grow up and marry away. The child was then adopted to care for the parents' old age. This was done by contract, which usu-ally specified what the parent had to leave and what maintenance was expected. The natural children, if any, were usually consenting parties to an arrangement that cut off their expectations. In some cases they even acquired the estate for the adopted child who was to relieve them of care. If the adopted child failed to carry out the filial duty, the contract was annulled in the law courts. Slaves were often adopted, and if they proved unfilial, were reduced to slavery again.

A craftsman often adopted a son to learn the craft. He profited by the son's labour. If he failed to teach his son the craft, that son could prosecute him and get the contract annulled. This was a form of apprenticeship, and it is not clear whether the apprentice had any filial relation.

A man who had adopted a child, and afterwards married and had a family of his own, could dissolve the contract and must give the adopted child one-third of a child's share in goods, but no real estate. Property could only descend through his legitimate family. Vestals frequently adopted daughters, usually other vestals, to care for them in their old age.

Adoption had to be with consent of the natural parents, who usually executed a deed making over the child, who thus ceased to have any claim upon them. But vestals, hierodules, certain palace officials and slaves had no rights over their children and could raise no objection. Orphans and illegitimate children had no parents to object. Ingratitude by adopted children was severely frowned on by the law: if the adopted child of a prostitute abandoned his foster parents and returned to his biological father's house, his eye was torn out. If an adopted child rejected his foster parents, claiming they were not his mother and father, his tongue was torn out. An adopted child was a full heir; the contract might even assign him the position of eldest son. Usually, he was residuary legatee.

Inheritance

All legitimate children shared equally in the father's estate on his death, reservation being made of a bride-price for an unmarried son, dower for a daughter, or property deeded to favourite children by the father. There was no birthright attaching to the position of eldest son, but he usually acted as executor and, after considering what each had already received, equalized the shares. He even made grants in excess to the others from his own share.Wikipedia:Please clarify If there were two widows with legitimate issue, both families shared equally in the father's estate, until later times, when the first family took two-thirds. Daughters, in the absence of sons, had sons' rights. Children also shared their own mother's property, but had no share in that of a stepmother.

A father could disinherit a son in early times without restriction, but the Code insisted upon judicial consent, and that only for repeated unfilial conduct. In early times, the son who denied his father had his front hair shorn and a slave-mark put on him and could be sold as a slave; while the son who denied his mother had his front hair shorn, was driven round the city as an example and expelled from his home, but not degraded to slavery.

Adultery

Adultery was punished with the death of both parties by drowning; but if the husband was willing to pardon his wife, the king might intervene to pardon the paramour. For incest between mother and son, both were burned to death; with a stepmother, the man was disinherited; with a daughter, the man was exiled; with a daughter-in-law, he was drowned; with a son's fiancée, he was fined.

A wife who for her lover's sake procured her husband's death was gibbeted. A betrothed girl seduced by her prospective father-in-law took her dowry and returned to her family and was free to marry as she chose.

Punishment

In the criminal code, the ruling principle was the *lex talionis*. Eye for eye, tooth for tooth, limb for limb was the penalty for assault upon an *amelu*. A sort of symbolic retaliation was the punishment for the offender, seen in cutting off the hand that struck a father or stole a trust; in cutting off the breast of a wet nurse who switched the child entrusted to her for another; in the loss of the tongue that denied father or mother (in Elamite contracts, the same penalty was inflicted for perjury); in the loss of the eye that pried into forbidden secrets. The loss of the surgeon's hand that caused loss of life or limb, or the brander's hand that obliterated a slave's identification mark, are very similar. The slave who struck a freeman or denied his master lost an ear, the organ of hearing and symbol of obedience. A person who brought another into danger of death by false accusation was punished by death. A perjurer was punished by the same penalty the perjurer sought to bring upon another.

The death penalty was freely rendered for theft and other crimes in this section of the Code: for theft involving entering a palace or temple treasury, for illegal purchase from a minor or slave, for selling stolen goods or receiving the same, for common theft in the open (in lieu of multiple-fold restoration) or receiving the same, for false claim to goods, for kidnapping, for assisting or harbouring fugitive slaves, for detaining or appropriating the same, for brigandage, for fraudulent sale of drink, for not reporting criminal conspiracy in one's tavern, for delegation of personal service and refusing to pay the delegate or not sending the delegate, for misappropriating the levy, for harming or robbing one of the king's captains, for causing the death of a house owner through bad construction. The manner of death is not specified for these cases.

This death penalty was also set for conduct that placed another in danger of death. The form of death penalty was specified for the following cases: gibbeting: for burglary (on the spot where crime was committed), later also for encroaching on the king's highway, for getting a slave-brand obliterated, for procuring a husband's death; burning: for incest with own mother, for a vestal entering or opening a tavern, for looting a house on fire (thrown into the fire); drowning: for adultery, rape of a betrothed maiden, bigamy, bad conduct as a wife, seduction of a daughter-in-law.

A curious extension of the *lex talionis* isWikipedia:Citation needed the death of a creditor's son for his father's having caused the death of a debtor's son as *mancipium*; of a builder's son for his father's causing the death of a house owner's son by bad construction; the death of a man's daughter because her father caused the death of another man's daughter.

Contracts naturally do not usually touch on criminal matters as the above, but marriage contracts do specify death by strangling, drowning, precipitation from a tower or pinnacle of the temple, or by the iron sword, for a wife's repudiation of her husband. We are quite without evidence as to the executioner in all these cases.

Exile was inflicted for incest with a daughter; disinheritance for incest with a stepmother, or for repeated unfilial conduct. Sixty strokes of an ox-hide scourge were awarded for a brutal assault on a superior, both being *amelu*. Branding (perhaps the equivalent of degradation to slavery) was the penalty for slander of a married woman or vestal. Permanent deprivation of office fell upon the corrupt judge. Enslavement befell the extravagant wife and unfilial children. Imprisonment was common, but is not mentioned in the Code.

The commonest of all penalties was a fine. This is awarded by the Code for corporal injuries to a *mushkenu* or to a slave (paid to his master), for damages done to property, or for breach of contract. The restoration of goods appropriated, illegally bought, or damaged by neglect, was usually accompanied by a fine, giving it the form of multiple restoration. This might be double, treble, fourfold, fivefold, sixfold, tenfold, twelvefold, or even thirtyfold, according to the enormity of the offence.

The Code recognized the importance of intent. A man who killed another in a quarrel must swear he did not do so intentionally and was then only fined according to the rank of the deceased. The Code does not say what would be the penalty of murder, but death is so often awarded where death is caused, that we can hardly doubt that the murderer was put to death. If the assault only led to injury and was unintentional, the assailant in a quarrel had to pay the doctor's fees. A brander, induced to remove a slave's identification mark, could swear to his ignorance and was free. The owner of an ox that gored a man on the street was only responsible for damages if the ox was known by him to be vicious—even if it caused death. If the *mancipium* died a natural death under the creditor's hand, the creditor was free. In ordinary cases, a person was not responsible for accident or if they exercised more than proper care. Poverty excused bigamy on the part of a deserted wife.

On the other hand, carelessness and neglect were severely punished, as in the case of the unskillful physician, if it led to loss of life or limb, his hands were cut off; a slave had to be replaced, the loss of his eye paid for by half his value; a veterinary surgeon who caused the death of an ox or donkey paid quarter value; a builder whose careless workmanship caused death lost his life or paid for it by the death of his child, replaced slave or goods and in any case, had to rebuild the house or make good any damages due to defective building and repair the defect as well. The boat builder had to make good any defect of construction or damage due to it for a year's warranty.

Throughout the Code, respect is paid to evidence. Suspicion was not enough. The criminal must be taken in the act, e.g. the adulterer, etc. A man could not be convicted of theft unless the goods were found in his possession.

In the case of a lawsuit, the plaintiff proffered his own plea. There is no trace of professional advocates, but the plea had to be in writing, and the notary doubtlessly assisted in the drafting of it. The judge saw the plea, called the other parties before him, and sent for the witnesses. If these were not at hand, he might adjourn the case for their subpoena, specifying a time for up to six months. Pledges might be made to produce the witnesses on a fixed day.

The more important cases, especially those involving life and death, were tried by a bench of judges. With the judges were associated a body of elders who shared in the decision, but whose exact function is not yet clear. Agreements, declarations and non-contentious cases were usually witnessed by one judge and twelve elders.

Parties and witnesses were put on oath. The penalty for false witness was usually the punishment that would have been awarded the victim if convicted. In matters beyond human knowledge, such as the guilt or innocence of an alleged practitioner of magic or a suspected wife, the ordeal by water was used. The accused jumped into the sacred river, and the innocent swam while the guilty drowned. The accused could clear himself by taking an oath if the only knowledge available was his own. The plaintiff could swear to his loss by brigands, the price paid for a slave purchased abroad, or the sum due to him; but great stress was laid on the production of written evidence. It was a serious thing to lose a document. The judges might be satisfied of its existence and terms by the affidavit of the witnesses to it and then issue an order that whenever found, it should be submitted. The clay tablets of contracts that were annulled were broken. The court might even travel to view the property and take with them the sacred symbols with which oaths were made.

Court decisions were set in writing, sealed and witnessed by the judges, the elders, witnesses, and a scribe. Women might act in all these capacities. The parties swore an oath, included in the document, to observe its stipulations. Each party received a copy, and one was kept by the scribe to be stored in the archives.

Appeal to the king was allowed and is well attested. The judges at Babylon seem to have formed a superior court to those of provincial towns, but a defendant might elect to answer the charge before the local court and refuse to plead at Babylon.

Finally, it may be noted that many immoral acts, such as the use of false weights, lying, etc., that could not be brought into court are severely denounced in the Omen Tablets as likely to bring the offender into "the hand of God" as opposed to "the hand of the king".

References

- ⓘ This article incorporates text from a publication now in the public domain: Chisholm, Hugh, ed. (1911). "Babylonian Law". *Encyclopædia Britannica*. **3** (11th ed.). Cambridge University Press. pp. 115–121. As of March 2017[20], this Wikipedia article is almost entirely a copy of the Encyclopædia Britannica article; if additional text is added, the EB text should be specifically attributed. The Encyclopædia Britannica article cites the following bibliography:
  - Contracts in general: Julius Oppert and Joachim Menant, *Documents juridiques de l'Assyrie et de la Chaldée* (Paris, 1877)
  - J. Kohler and F. E. Peiser, *Aus dem babylonischen Rechtsleben* (Leipzig, 1890 if.)
  - F. E. Peiser, *Babylonische Verträge* (Berlin, 1890), *Keilinschriftliche Actenstücke* (Berlin, 1889)
  - Bruno Meissner, *Beiträge zur altbabylonischen Privatrecht* (Leipzig, 1893)
  - F. E. Peiser, *Texte juristischen und geschäftlichen Inhalts*
  - Vol. iv. of Schrader's *Keilinschriftliche Bibliothek* (Berlin, 1896)
  - Claude Hermann Walter Johns, *Assyrian Deeds and Documents relating to the Transfer of Property* (3 vols., Cambridge, 1898)
  - H. Radau, *Early Babylonian history* (New York, 1900)
  - C. H. W. Johns, *Babylonian and Assyrian Laws, Contracts and Letters* (Edinburgh, 1904). For editions of texts and the innumerable articles in scientific journals, see the bibliographies and references in the above works.
  - "The Code of Hammurabi", *Editio princeps* by Vincent Scheil in tome iv. of the *Textes Elamites-Semitiques of the Mémoires de la délégation en Perse* (Paris, 1902)
  - H. Winckler, "Die Gesetze Hammurabis Konigs von Babylon um 2250v. Chr." *Der alte Orient*, iv. Jahrgang, Heft 4
  - D. H. Müller, *Die Gesetze Hammurabis* (Vienna, 1903)
  - J. Kohler and F. E. Peiser, *Hammurabis Gesetz* (Leipzig, 1904)
  - R. F. Harper, *The Code of Hammurabi, King of Babylon about 2250 BC* (Chicago, 1904)
  - S. A. Cook, *The Laws of Moses and the Code of Hammurabi* (London, 1903)

External links

- Avalon Project at Yale[21]

Ancient Greek law

Ancient Greek law consists of the laws and legal institutions of Ancient Greece.

The existence of certain general principles of law is implied by the custom of settling a difference between two Greek states, or between members of a single state, by resorting to external arbitration. The general unity of Greek law shows mainly in the laws of inheritance and adoption, in laws of commerce and contract, and in the publicity uniformly given to legal agreements.[22]

While its older forms can be studied by the laws of Gortyn, its influence can be traced in legal documents preserved in Egyptian papyri and it may be recognized as a consistent whole in its ultimate relations to Roman law in the eastern provinces of the Roman empire, with scholars in the discipline of comparative law comparing Greek law with both Roman law and the primitive institutions of the Germanic nations.[22]

Historical Sources

There is no systematic collection of Greek laws, thus the knowledge the earliest notions of the subject is derived from the Homeric poems. The works of Theophrastus' 'On the Laws', included a recapitulation of the laws of various barbaric as well as of the Grecian states, yet only a few fragments of it remain.[22]

Figure 4: *The Aristotelian Constitution of the Athenians, now in the British Library (Oxyrhynchus Papyrus 131)*

Athens

Incidental illustrations of the Athenian law are found in the *Laws* of Plato, who describes it without exercising influence on its actual practice.Wikipedia:Citation needed Aristotle criticized Plato's *Laws* in his Politics, in which he reviews the work of certain early Greek lawgivers. The treatise on the Constitution of Athens includes an account of the jurisdiction of the various public officials and of the mechanics of the law courts, and thus enables historians to dispense with the second-hand testimony of grammarians and scholiasts who derived their information from that treatise.[22]

Other evidence for ancient Athenian law comes from statements made in the extant speeches of the Attic orators, and from surviving inscriptions.[22]

Procedural laws

Athens

Historians consider the Ancient Athenian law broadly procedural and concerned with the administration of justice rather than substantive.[23] Athenian laws are typically written in the form where if an offense is made, then the offender will be punished according to said law,[24] thus they are more concerned with the legal actions which should be undertaken by the prosecutor, rather than strictly defining which acts are prosecutable.[25] Often, this would have resulted in juries having to decide whether the offense said to have been committed was in fact a violation of the law in question.[26]

Development of Ancient Greek law

Athens

One of the earliest dateable events in Athenian history is the creation of the Draconian law code, c.620 BC. We know little about Draco and the code, with the homicide law being the only one known due to it surviving the Solonian reforms. The law seems to have distinguished between premeditated and involuntary homicide, and provided for the reconciliation of the killer with the family of the dead man. The homicide law of Draco was still in force in the fourth century. Though the rest of the code is unknown, it was by Athenian tradition known to have been very harsh.

The Athenian law codes set forth by Draco were completely reformed by Solon, who was the archon of Athens c.593 BC. Solon's reforms included the cancellation of debts and reforms to land ownership, as well as the abolition of slavery for those who were born Athenian.[27] However, attributing specific

legal innovations and reforms to Solon and his successors is notoriously difficult because there was a tendency in ancient Athens to ascribe laws to Solon
irrespective of the date of enactment.[28]

Courts and judicial system

Along with the official enforcement of the law in the courts in the Grecian
states, justice and social cohesion were collectively enforced by society at
large.[29] with informal collective justice often being targeted at elite offenders.

Athens

Ancient Greek courts were cheap and run by laypeople. Court officials were
paid little, if anything, and most trials were completed within a day, with private
cases done even quicker. There were no court officials, no lawyers, and no
official judges. A normal case consisted of two litigants, arguing if an unlawful
act had been committed. The jury would decide whether the accused was
guilty, and should he be guilty, what the punishment will be. In Athenian
courts, the jury tended to be made of the common people, whereas litigants
were mostly from the elites of society.

In the Athenian legal system, the courts have been seen as a system for settling
disputes and resolving arguments, rather than enforcing a coherent system of
rules, rights and obligations. The Prytaneion court was responsible for trial-
ing random residents, animals, and inanimate objects for homicide, and it is
assumed that it was in order to ensure that Athens was free of blood-guilt for
the crime.

The Athenian court system was dominated by men. The jury was all-male,[30]
and it has been argued that the Athenian court seemed to have been remarkably
unwilling to allow any female presence in the civic space of the lawcourt itself.

Public and private cases

In Ancient Athens, there were two types of lawsuit. Public prosecutions, or
graphai, were heard by juries of 501 or more, increasing in increments of 500
jurors, while private suits, or *dikai*, were heard by 201 or 401 jurors, depending
on the amount of money at stake.[31] Juries were made up of men selected from
a panel of 6,000 volunteers, who were selected annually and were required to
be full citizens, aged over 30.[32] Juries were paid a small fee from the time of
Pericles, which may have led to disproportionate numbers of poor and elderly
citizens working on juries.[33]

Oratory

Athens

In the Athenian legal system, there were no professional lawyers, though well-known speechwriters such as Demosthenes composed speeches which were delivered by, or on behalf of others. These speechwriters have been described as being as close as a function of a modern lawyer as the Athenian legal system would permit.

It has been argued that the rhetorical and performative features evident in surviving Classical Athenian law court speeches are evidence that Athenian trials were essentially rhetorical struggles which were generally unconcerned with the strict applicability of the law.[34] It is also said that orators constructing stories played a much more significant role in Athenian court cases than those of the modern day, due to the lack of modern forensic and investigatory techniques which might provide other sources of evidence in the Athenian courtroom.[35]

References

- ⓦ This article incorporates text from a publication now in the public domain: Sandys, John Edwin (1911). "Greek Law". In Chisholm, Hugh. *Encyclopædia Britannica*. **12** (11th ed.). Cambridge University Press. pp. 501–507. This describes the topic in more procedural detail, and has a large set of citations.
- Carey, Christopher (1998). "The Shape of Athenian Laws". *The Classical Quarterly*. **48** (1). doi: 10.1093/cq/48.1.93[36].
- Andrewes, A. "The Growth of the Athenian State". In Boardman, John; Hammond, N.G.L. *The Cambridge Ancient History Volume III, Part 3: The Expansion of the Greek World, Eighth to Sixth Centuries B.C.* ISBN 0-521-23447-6.
- Forsdyke, Sara (2008). "Street Theatre and Popular Justice in Ancient Greece: Shaming, Stoning, and Starving Offenders Inside and Outside the Courts". *Past and Present*. **201**.
- Gagarin, Michael (2003). "Telling Stories in Athenian Law". *Transactions of the American Philological Association (1974–)*. **133** (2). doi: 10.1353/apa.2003.0015[37].
- Hamel, Debra (2003). *Trying Neaira: The True Story of a Courtesan's Scandalous Life in Ancient Greece*. New Haven & London: Yale University Press.

Book of Leviticus

Tanakh (Judaism)

Old Testament (Christianity)

Bible portal

- v
- t
- e[38]

The **Book of Leviticus** (/lɪˈvɪtɪkəs/) is the third book of the Torah and the third book of the Old Testament. The book addresses all the people of Israel (1:2) though some passages specifically address the priests (6:8). Most of its chapters (1–7, 11–27) consist of God's speeches to Moses which he is commanded to repeat to the Israelites. This takes place within the story of the Israelites' Exodus after they escaped Egypt and reached Mt. Sinai (Exodus 19:1). The Book of Exodus narrates how Moses led the Israelites in building the Tabernacle (Exodus 35–40) based on God's instructions (Exodus 25–31). Then in Leviticus, God tells the Israelites and their priests how to make offerings in the Tabernacle and how to conduct themselves while camped around the holy tent sanctuary. Leviticus takes place during the month or month-and-a-half between the completion of the Tabernacle (Exodus 40:17) and the Israelites' departure from Sinai (Numbers 1:1, 10:11).

The instructions of Leviticus emphasize ritual, legal and moral practices rather than beliefs. Nevertheless, they reflect the world view of the creation story in Genesis 1 that God wishes to live with humans. The book teaches that faithful performance of the sanctuary rituals can make that possible, so long as the people avoid sin and impurity whenever possible. The rituals, especially the sin and guilt offerings, provide the means to gain forgiveness for sins (Leviticus 4–5) and purification from impurities (Leviticus 11–16) so that God can continue to live in the Tabernacle in the midst of the people.[39]

Name

The English name Leviticus comes from the Latin *Leviticus,* which is in turn from the Greek Greek Λευιτικόν, *Leuitikon.* The Greek expression is in turn a variant of the rabbinic Hebrew *torat kohanim,* "law of priests."

In Hebrew the book is called *Vayikra* (Hebrew: וַיִּקְרָא), from the first word of the book, *Vayikra,* "He [God] called."

Authorship

The traditional view is that Leviticus was compiled by Moses, or that the material in it goes back to his time, but internal clues suggest that the book developed much later in Israel's history and was completed either near the end of the Kingdom of Judah in the late seventh century BC or in the exilic and post-exilic period of the sixth and fifth centuries BC. Scholars debate whether it was written primarily for Jewish worship in exile that centered on reading or preaching,[40,41] or was aimed instead at worshipers at temples in Jerusalem and Samaria,[42] but they are practically unanimous that the book had a long period of growth, and that although it includes some material of considerable antiquity, it reached its present form in the Persian period (538–332 BC).[43]

Structure

(The outlines provided by commentaries are similar, though not identical; compare those of Wenham, Hartley, Milgrom, and Watts)[44,45,46,47]

I. Laws on sacrifice (1:1–7:38)

    A. Instructions for the laity on bringing offerings (1:1–6:7)

        1–5. The types of offering: burnt, cereal, peace, purification, reparation (or sin) offerings (ch. 1–5)

    B. Instructions for the priests (6:1–7:38)

        1–6. The various offerings, with the addition of the priests' cereal offering (6:1–7:36)

        7. Summary (7:37–38)

II. Institution of the priesthood (8:1–10:20)

    A. Ordination of Aaron and his sons (ch. 8)

    B. Aaron makes the first sacrifices (ch. 9)

    C. Judgement on Nadab and Abihu (ch. 10)

III. Uncleanliness and its treatment (11:1–15:33)

    A. Unclean animals (ch. 11)

    B. Uncleanliness caused by childbirth (ch. 12)

    C. Unclean diseases (ch. 13)

    D. Cleansing of diseases (ch. 14)

    E. Unclean discharges (ch. 15)

IV. Day of Atonement: purification of the tabernacle from the effects of uncleanliness and sin (ch. 16)

V. Prescriptions for practical holiness (the Holiness Code, chs. 17–26)

    A. Sacrifice and food (ch. 17)

    B. Sexual behaviour (ch. 18)

    C. Neighbourliness (ch.19)

    D. Grave crimes (ch. 20)

    E. Rules for priests (ch. 21)

    F. Rules for eating sacrifices (ch. 22)

    G. Festivals (ch.23)

    H. Rules for the tabernacle (ch. 24:1–9)

    I. Blasphemy (ch. 24:10–23)

    J. Sabbatical and Jubilee years (ch. 25)

    K. Exhortation to obey the law: blessing and curse (ch. 26)

VI. Redemption of votive gifts (ch. 27)

Figure 5: *Vaikro – Book of Leviticus, Warsaw edition, 1860, page 1*

Summary

Chapters 1–5 describe the various sacrifices from the sacrificers' point of view, although the priests are essential for handling the blood. Chapters 6–7 go over much the same ground, but from the point of view of the priest, who, as the one actually carrying out the sacrifice and dividing the "portions", needs to know how this is to be done. Sacrifices are to be divided between God, the priest, and the offerers, although in some cases the entire sacrifice is a single portion consigned to God—i.e., burnt to ashes.[48]

Chapters 8–10 describe the consecration by Moses of Aaron and his sons as the first priests, the first sacrifices, and God's destruction of two of Aaron's sons for ritual offenses. The purpose is to underline the character of altar priest-hood (i.e., those priests empowered to offer sacrifices to God) as an Aaronite privilege, and the responsibilities and dangers of their position.[49]

With sacrifice and priesthood established, chapters 11–15 instruct the lay people on purity (or cleanliness). Eating certain animals produces uncleanliness, as does giving birth; certain skin diseases (but not all) are unclean, as are certain conditions affecting walls and clothing (mildew and similar conditions);

and genital discharges, including female menses and male gonorrhea, are unclean. The reasoning behind the food rules are obscure; for the rest the guiding principle seems to be that all these conditions involve a loss of "life force", usually but not always blood.[50]

> **❝**   **❞**
> If a man's hair falls out from his head, he is bald; he is clean.
>
> — Leviticus 13:40

51

Leviticus 16 concerns the Day of Atonement. This is the only day on which the High Priest is to enter the holiest part of the sanctuary, the holy of holies. He is to sacrifice a bull for the sins of the priests, and a goat for the sins of the laypeople. A second goat is to be sent into the desert to "Azazel", bearing the sins of the whole people. Azazel may be a wilderness-demon, but its identity is mysterious.[52]

Chapters 17–26 are the Holiness code. It begins with a prohibition on all slaughter of animals outside the Temple, even for food, and then prohibits a long list of sexual contacts and also child sacrifice. The "holiness" injunctions which give the code its name begin with the next section: penalties are imposed for the worship of Molech, consulting mediums and wizards, cursing one's parents and engaging in unlawful sex. Priests are instructed on mourning rituals and acceptable bodily defects. Blasphemy is to be punished with death, and rules for the eating of sacrifices are set out; the calendar is explained, and rules for sabbatical and Jubilee years set out; and rules are made for oil lamps and bread in the sanctuary; and rules are made for slavery. The code ends by telling the Israelites they must choose between the law and prosperity on the one hand, or, on the other, horrible punishments, the worst of which will be expulsion from the land.[53]

Chapter 27 is a disparate and probably late addition telling about persons and things dedicated to the Lord and how vows can be redeemed instead of fulfilled.[54]

Composition

The majority of scholars have concluded that the Pentateuch received its final form during the Persian period (538–332 BC).[55] Nevertheless, Leviticus had a long period of growth before reaching that form.

The entire book of Leviticus is composed of Priestly literature.[56] Most scholars see chapters 1–16 (the Priestly code) and chapters 17–26 (the Holiness code)

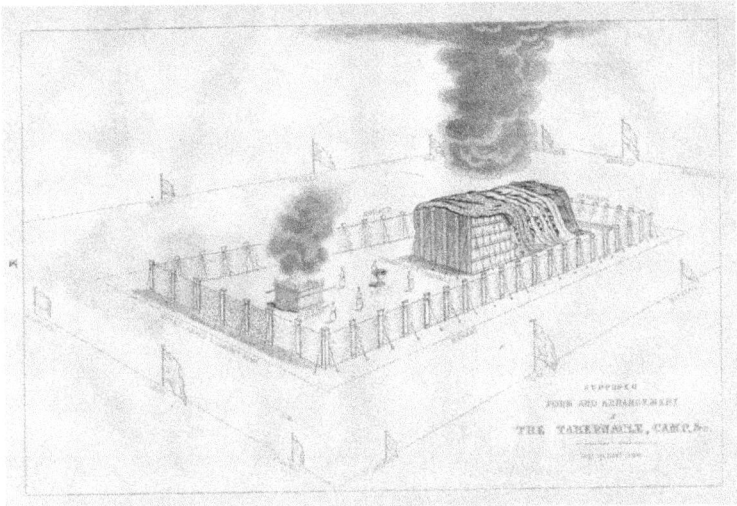

Figure 6: *The Tabernacle and the Camp (19th Century drawing)*

as the work of two related schools, but while the Holiness material employs the same technical terms as the Priestly code, it broadens their meaning from pure ritual to the theological and moral, turning the ritual of the Priestly code into a model for the relationship of Israel to God: as the tabernacle is made holy by the presence of the Lord and kept apart from uncleanliness, so He will dwell among Israel when Israel is purified (made holy) and separated from other peoples.[57] The ritual instructions in the Priestly code apparently grew from priests giving instruction and answering questions about ritual matters; the Holiness code (or H) used to be regarded as a separate document later incorporated into Leviticus, but it seems better to think of the Holiness authors as editors who worked with the Priestly code and actually produced Leviticus as we now have it.[58]

The En-Gedi Scroll, a burnt text that was excavated from an ancient Synagogue in Ein Gedi in 1970, and has been carbon dated to the late 5th century AD, was recently discovered to contain verses from the second chapter of Leviticus, making it the oldest piece of the Torah ever discovered after the Dead Sea Scrolls. The text was unreadable until analyzed with a micro CT scanner that was then used to recreate a 3D image of the scroll. It is the first Torah scroll to be found in an ancient Synagogue.

Figure 7: *The Scapegoat (1854 painting by William Holman Hunt)*

Themes

Sacrifice and ritual

Many scholars argue that the rituals of Leviticus have a theological meaning concerning Israel's relationship with its God. Jacob Milgrom was especially influential in spreading this view. He maintained that the priestly regulations in Leviticus expressed a rational system of theological thought. The writers expected them to be put into practice in Israel's temple, so the rituals would express this theology as well, as well as ethical concern for the poor.[59] Milgrom also argued that the book's purity regulations (chaps. 11–15) are based in ethical thinking.[60] Many other interpreters have followed Milgrom in exploring the theological and ethical implications of Leviticus's regulations (e.g. Marx, Balentine), though some have questioned how systematic they really are.[61] Ritual, therefore, is not a series of actions undertaken for their own sake, but a means of maintaining the relationship between God, the world, and humankind.[62]

Kehuna (Jewish Priesthood)

The main function of the priests is service at the altar, and only the sons of Aaron are priests in the full sense.[63] (Ezekiel also distinguishes between altar-priests and lower Levites, but in Ezekiel the altar-priests are called sons of Zadok instead of sons of Aaron; many scholars see this as a remnant of struggles between different priestly factions in First Temple times, resolved by the Second Temple into a hierarchy of Aaronite altar-priests and lower-level Levites, including singers, gatekeepers and the like).[64]

In chapter 10, God kills Nadab and Abihu, the oldest sons of Aaron, for offering "strange incense". Fortunately, Aaron has two sons left. Commentators have read various messages in the incident: a reflection of struggles between priestly factions in the post–Exilic period (Gerstenberger); or a warning against offering incense outside the Temple, where there might be the risk of invoking strange gods (Milgrom). In any case, the sanctuary has been polluted by the bodies of the two dead priests, leading into the next theme, holiness.[65]

Uncleanliness and purity

Ritual purity is essential for an Israelite to be able to approach Yahweh and remain part of the community. Uncleanliness threatens holiness;[66] Chapters 11–15 review the various causes of uncleanliness and describe the rituals which will restore cleanliness;[67] cleanliness is to be maintained through observation of the rules on sexual behaviour, family relations, land ownership, worship, sacrifice, and observance of holy days.[68]

Yahweh dwells with Israel in the holy of holies. All of the priestly ritual is focused on Yahweh and the construction and maintenance of a holy space, but sin generates impurity, as do everyday events such as childbirth and menstruation; impurity pollutes the holy dwelling place. Failure to ritually purify the sacred space could result in God leaving, which would be disastrous.[69]

Atonement

Through sacrifice the priest "makes atonement" for sin and the offerer is forgiven (but only if God accepts the sacrifice—forgiveness comes only from God).[70] Atonement rituals involve blood, poured or sprinkled, as the symbol of the life of the victim: the blood has the power to wipe out or absorb the sin.[71] The role of atonement is reflected structurally in two-part division of the book: chapters 1–16 call for the establishment of the institution for atonement, and chapters 17–27 call for the life of the atoned community in holiness.[72]

Holiness

The consistent theme of chapters 17–26 is the repeated phrase, "Be holy, for I the Lord your God am holy." Holiness in ancient Israel had a different meaning than in contemporary usage: it might have been regarded as the "god-ness" of God, an invisible but physical and potentially dangerous force.[73] Specific objects, or even days, can be holy, but they derive holiness from being connected

Figure 8: *The Blasphemer (ink and watercolor, circa 1800, by William Blake)*

with God—the seventh day, the tabernacle, and the priests all derive their holiness from God.[74] As a result, Israel had to maintain its own holiness in order to live safely alongside God.[75]

The need for holiness is directed to the possession of the Promised Land (Canaan), where the Jews will become a holy people: "You shall not do as they do in the land of Egypt where you dwelt, and you shall not do as they do in the land of Canaan to which I am bringing you...You shall do my ordinances and keep my statutes...I am the Lord, your God" (ch. 18:3).[76]

Subsequent tradition

Leviticus, as part of the Torah, became the law book of Jerusalem's Second Temple as well as of the Samaritan temple. Evidence of its influence was found among the Dead Sea Scrolls, which included fragments of seventeen manuscripts of Leviticus dating from the third to the first centuries BC.[77] Many other Qumran scrolls cite the book, especially the Temple Scroll and 4QMMT.

Leviticus's instructions for animal offerings have not been observed by Jews or Christians since the first century AD. Because of the destruction of the temple in Jerusalem in 70 AD, Jewish worship has focused on prayer and the study of Torah. Nevertheless, Leviticus constitutes a major source of Jewish law

Figure 9: *The Sacrifice of the Old Covenant (painting by Peter Paul Rubens)*

and is traditionally the first book taught to children in the Rabbinic system of education. There are two main Midrashim on Leviticus—the halakhic one (Sifra) and a more aggadic one (Vayikra Rabbah).

The New Testament, particularly the Epistle to the Hebrews, uses ideas and images from Leviticus to describe Christ as the high priest who offers his own blood as a sin offering. Therefore, Christians do not make animal offerings either, as Gordon Wenham summarized: "With the death of Christ the only sufficient "burnt offering" was offered once and for all, and therefore the animal sacrifices which foreshadowed Christ's sacrifice were made obsolete."[78]

Christians generally have the view that the New Covenant supersedes (i.e., replaces) the Old Testament's ritual laws, which includes many of the rules in Leviticus. Christians therefore have usually not observed Leviticus' rules regarding diet, purity, and agriculture, but have used its passage on homosexuality as their justification for their views against same-sex marriage. Christian teachings have differed, however, as to where to draw the line between ritual and moral regulations.[79]

Contents according to Judaism's weekly Torah portions

For detailed contents see:

- *Vayikra, on Leviticus 1–5: Laws of the sacrifices*
- *Tzav, on Leviticus 6–8: Sacrifices, ordination of the priests*
- *Shemini, on Leviticus 9–11: Tabernacle consecrated, alien fire, dietary laws*
- *Tazria, on Leviticus 12–13: Childbirth, skin disease, clothing*
- *Metzora, on Leviticus 14–15: Skin disease, infected houses, genital discharges*
- *Acharei Mot, on Leviticus 16–18: Yom Kippur, centralized offerings, sexual practices*
- *Kedoshim, on Leviticus 19–20: Holiness, penalties for transgressions*
- *Emor, on Leviticus 21–24: Rules for priests, holy days, lights and bread, a blasphemer*
- *Behar, on Leviticus 25–25: Sabbatical year, debt servitude limited*
- *Bechukotai, on Leviticus 26–27: Blessings and curses, payment of vows*

Bibliography

Translations of Leviticus

- Leviticus[80] at Bible gateway

Commentaries on Leviticus

- Balentine, Samuel E (2002). *Leviticus*[81]. Westminster John Knox Press. ISBN 9780664237356.
- Bamberger, Bernard Jacob The Torah: A Modern Commentary (1981), ISBN 0-8074-0055-6
- Gerstenberger, Erhard S (1996). *Leviticus: A Commentary*[82]. Westminster John Knox Press. ISBN 9780664226732.
- Gorman, Frank H (1997). *Divine presence and community: a commentary on the Book of Leviticus*[83]. Eerdmans. ISBN 9780802801104.
- Grabbe, Lester (1998). "Leviticus". In John Barton. *Oxford Bible Commentary*[84]. Oxford University Press. ISBN 9780198755005.
- Hartley, John E. (1992). *Leviticus*[85]. Word. ISBN 0849902037.
- Houston, Walter J (2003). "Leviticus". In James D. G. Dunn, John William Rogerson. *Eerdmans Bible Commentary*[86]. Eerdmans. ISBN 9780802837110.

- Kleinig, John W (2004). *Leviticus*[87]. Concordia Publishing House. ISBN 9780570063179.
- Levine, Baruch A. (1989). *JPS Torah Commentary: Leviticus*[88]. Jewish Publication Society.
- Milgrom, Jacob (1998–2001). *Leviticus 1–16, Leviticus 17–22, Leviticus 23–27*[89]. New Haven: Yale.
- Milgrom, Jacob (2004). *Leviticus: A Book of Ritual and Ethics*[90]. Minneapolis: Fortress. ISBN 9781451410150.
- Watts, James W. (2013). *Leviticus 1–10*[91]. Leuven: Peeters. ISBN 9042929847.
- Wenham, Gordon (1979). *The book of Leviticus*[92]. Eerdmans. ISBN 9780802825223.

General

- Balentine, Samuel E (1999). *The Torah's Vision of Worship*[93]. Fortress Press. ISBN 9781451418088.
- Bandstra, Barry L (2004). *Reading the Old Testament: An Introduction to the Hebrew Bible*[94]. Wadsworth. ISBN 9780495391050.
- Brueggemann, Walter (2002). *Reverberations of Faith: A Theological Handbook of Old Testament themes*[95]. Westminster John Knox. ISBN 9780664222314.
- Campbell, Antony F; O'Brien, Mark A (1993). *Sources of the Pentateuch: Texts, Introductions, Annotations*[96]. Fortress Press. ISBN 9781451413670.
- Clines, David A (1997). *The Theme of the Pentateuch*[97]. Sheffield Academic Press. ISBN 9780567431967.
- Davies, Philip R; Rogerson, John W (2005). *The Old Testament World*[98]. Liturgical Press. ISBN 9780664230258.
- Dawes, Gregory W (2005). *Introduction to the Bible*[99]. Liturgical Press. ISBN 9780814628355.
- Gilbert, Christopher (2009). *A Complete Introduction to the Bible*[100]. Paulist Press. ISBN 9780809145522.
- Grabbe, Lester (2006). "The priests in Leviticus". In Rolf Rendtorff, Robert A. Kugler. *The Book of Leviticus: Composition and Reception*[101]. Brill. ISBN 9789004126343.
- Knierim, Rolf P (1995). *The Task of Old Testament Theology: Substance, Method, and Cases*[102]. Eerdmans. ISBN 9780802807151.
- Kugler, Robert; Hartin, Patrick (2009). *An Introduction to the Bible*[103]. Eerdmans. ISBN 9780802846365.
- Levine, Baruch (2006). "Leviticus: Its Literary History and Location in Biblical Literature". In Rolf Rendtorff, Robert A. Kugler. *The Book of Leviticus: Composition and Reception*[101]. Brill. ISBN 9789004126343.

- Marx, Alfred (2006). "The Theology of the Sacrifice according to Leviticus 1–7". In Rolf Rendtorff, Robert A. Kugler. *The Book of Leviticus: Composition and Reception*[101]. Brill. ISBN 9789004126343.
- McDermott, John J (2002). *Reading the Pentateuch: A Historical Introduction*[104]. Pauline Press. ISBN 9780809140824.
- Newsom, Carol Ann (2004). *The Self as Symbolic Space: Constructing Identity and Community at Qumran*[105]. BRILL. ISBN 9789004138032.
- Nihan, Christophe (2007). *From Priestly Torah to Pentateuch: A Study in the Composition of the Book of Leviticus*[106]. Tuebingen: Mohr Siebeck. ISBN 9783161492570.
- Rodd, Cyril S (2001). *Glimpses of a Strange Land: Studies in Old Testament Ethics*[107]. T&T Clark. ISBN 9780567087539.
- Rogerson, J.W (1991). *Genesis 1–11*[108]. T&T Clark. ISBN 9780567083388.
- Van Seters, John (1998). "The Pentateuch". In Steven L. McKenzie, Matt Patrick Graham. *The Hebrew Bible Today: An Introduction to Critical Issues*[109]. Westminster John Knox Press. ISBN 9780664256524.
- Ska, Jean-Louis (2006). *Introduction to Reading the Pentateuch*[110]. Eisenbrauns. ISBN 9781575061221.
- Watts, James W. (2007). *Ritual and Rhetoric in Leviticus: From Sacrifice to Scripture*[111]. New York: Cambridge. ISBN 9780521871938.
- Wenham, Gordon (2003). *Exploring the Old Testament: The Pentateuch*. SPCK.

External links

Wikisourcehas original text related to this article:
Leviticus (Bible)

Wikimedia Commons has media related to *Book of Leviticus*.

Wikiquote has quotations related to: *Book of Leviticus*

Online versions of Leviticus:
- Hebrew:
  - Leviticus - Mikraot Gedolot Haketer - online edition[112], Menachem Cohen, Bar Ilan University (Hebrew)

- Leviticus at Mechon-Mamre[113] (Jewish Publication Society translation)
- Leviticus (The Living Torah)[114] Rabbi Aryeh Kaplan's translation and commentary at Ort.org
- Vayikra—Levitichius (Judaica Press)[115] translation [with Rashi's commentary] at Chabad.org
- ויקרא *Vayikra*—Leviticus[116] (Hebrew—English at Mechon-Mamre.org)
- Christian translations:
  - The Book of Leviticus, Douay Rheims Version, with Bishop Challoner Commentaries[117]
  - *Online Bible* at GospelHall.org[118] (King James Version)
  - *Online Audio and Classic Bible* at Bible-Book.org[119] (King James Version)
  - *oremus Bible Browser*[120] (New Revised Standard Version)
  - *oremus Bible Browser*[121] (*Anglicized* New Revised Standard Version)
  - ◀◉ *Leviticus*[122] public domain audiobook at LibriVox Various versions

Related article:

- Book of Leviticus article[123] (Jewish Encyclopedia)
- The Literary Structure of Leviticus[124] (chaver.com)

Brief introduction

- Leviticus[125]

Book of Leviticus **Pentateuch**		
Preceded by **Exodus**	**Hebrew Bible**	Succeeded by **Numbers**
	Christian Old Testament	

Hittite laws

The **Hittite laws** have been preserved on a number of Hittite cuneiform tablets
found at Hattusa (CTH 291-292, listing 200 laws). Copies have been found
written in Old Hittite as well as in Middle and Late Hittite, indicating that they
had validity throughout the duration of the Hittite Empire (ca. 1650–1100
BCE).

The corpus

The laws are formulated as case laws; they start with a condition, and a ruling
follows, e.g. *"If anyone tears off the ear of a male or female slave, he shall
pay 3 shekels of silver"*. The laws show an aversion to the death penalty, the
usual penalty for serious offenses being enslavement to forced labour. They
are preserved on two separate tablets, each with approximately 200 clauses,
the first categorised as being 'of a man'; the second 'of a vine'; a third set may
have existed.

The laws may be categorised into eight groups of similar clauses. These are
separated for the most part by two types of seemingly orphaned clauses: Sacral
or incantatory clauses, and afterthoughts.

These eight main groups of laws were:

- I Aggression and assault: Clauses 1 - 24
- II Marital relationships: Clauses 26 - 38
- III Obligations and service - TUKUL: Clauses 39 - 56
- IV Assaults on property and theft: Clauses 57 - 144
- V Contracts and prices: Clauses 145 - 161
- VI Sacral matters: Clauses 162 - 173
- VII Contracts and tariffs: Clauses 176 - 186
- VIII Sexual relationships - HURKEL: Clauses 187 - 200
    - Including the criminalisation of bestiality (except with horses and
      mules).[126] The death penalty was a common punishment among sex-
      ual crimes.

The Hittite laws were kept in use for some 500 years, and many copies show
that, other than changes in grammar, what might be called the 'original edition'
with its apparent disorder, was copied slavishly; no attempt was made to 'tidy
up' by placing even obvious afterthoughts in a more appropriate position.

This corpus and the classification scheme is based on findings arising out of a
Master of Arts degree taken at the University of Queensland by N H Dewhirst,
supervised by Dr Trevor Bryce in 2004.

Figure 10: *A Hittite tablet found at Hattusa, believed to be a legal deposition.*

Changes were apparently made to penalties at least twice: firstly, the *kara – kinuna* changes, which generally reduced the penalties found in a former, but apparently unpreserved, 'proto-edition'; and secondly, the 'Late Period' changes to penalties in the already-modified Old Hittite version.[127]

Modern editions

The laws were first fully published by Bedřich Hrozný in 1922. Johannes Friedrich published a new edition in 1959 and the latest critical edition was published by Harry Hoffner in 1997.

External links

• The Code of the Nesilim, c. 1650-1500 BCE (Excerpts)[128]

Literature

• E. Neu, StBoT 26 (1983)
• Harry Angier Hoffner Jr., *The Laws of the Hittites: a Critical Edition* (DMOA 23) – Leiden, New York, Köln 1997

Ostracism

Ostracism (Greek: ὀστρακισμός, *ostrakismos*) was a procedure under the Athenian democracy in which any citizen could be expelled from the city-state of Athens for ten years. While some instances clearly expressed popular anger at the citizen, ostracism was often used preemptively. It was used as a way of neutralizing someone thought to be a threat to the state or potential tyrant. It has been called an "honourable exile" by scholar P. J. Rhodes.[129] The word "ostracism" continues to be used for various cases of social shunning.

Procedure

The name is derived from the *ostraka* (singular *ostrakon*, ὄστρακον), referring to the pottery shards that were used as voting tokens. Broken pottery, abundant and virtually free, served as a kind of scrap paper (in contrast to papyrus, which was imported from Egypt as a high-quality writing surface, and was thus too costly to be disposable).

Each year the Athenians were asked in the assembly whether they wished to hold an ostracism. The question was put in the sixth of the ten months used for state business under the democracy (January or February in the modern Gregorian Calendar). If they voted "yes", then an ostracism would be held two months later. In a section of the agora set off and suitably barriered,[130] citizens gave the name of those they wished to be ostracised to a scribe, as many of them were illiterate, and they then scratched the name on pottery shards, and deposited them in urns. The presiding officials counted the *ostraka* submitted and sorted the names into separate piles. The person whose pile contained the most *ostraka* would be banished, provided that an additional criterion of a quorum was met, about which there are two principal sources:

- According to Plutarch,[131] the ostracism was considered valid if the total number of votes cast was at least 6,000.
- According to a fragment of Philochorus,[132] the "winner" of the ostracism must have obtained at least 6,000 votes.

Plutarch's evidence for a quorum of 6,000, on *a priori* grounds a necessity for ostracism also per the account of Philochorus, accords with the number required for grants of citizenship in the following century and is generally preferred.

The person nominated had ten days to leave the city. If he attempted to return, the penalty was death. Notably, the property of the man banished was not confiscated and there was no loss of status. After the ten years, he was allowed to return without stigma. It was possible for the assembly to recall an ostracised person ahead of time; before the Persian invasion of 479 BC, an amnesty was declared under which at least two ostracised leaders—Pericles' father Xanthippus and Aristides 'the Just'—are known to have returned. Similarly, Cimon, ostracised in 461 BC, was recalled during an emergency.[133]

Distinction from other Athenian democratic processes

Ostracism was crucially different from Athenian law at the time; there was no charge, and no defence could be mounted by the person expelled. The two stages of the procedure ran in the reverse order from that used under almost any trial system — here it is as if a jury are first asked *"Do you want to find someone guilty?"*, and subsequently asked *"Whom do you wish to accuse?"*. Equally out of place in a judicial framework is perhaps the institution's most peculiar feature: that it can take place at most once a year, and only for one person. In this it resembles the Greek *pharmakos* or scapegoat — though in contrast, *pharmakos* generally ejected a lowly member of the community.

A further distinction between these two modes (and one not obvious from a modern perspective) is that ostracism was an automatic procedure that required no initiative from any individual, with the vote simply occurring on the wish of the electorate — a diffuse exercise of power. By contrast, an Athenian trial needed the initiative of a particular citizen-prosecutor. While prosecution often led to a counterattack (or was a counterattack itself), no such response was possible in the case of ostracism as responsibility lay with the polity as a whole. In contrast to a trial, ostracism generally reduced political tension rather than increased it.

Although ten years of exile would have been difficult for an Athenian to face, it was relatively mild in comparison to the kind of sentences inflicted by courts; when dealing with politicians held to be acting against the interests of the people, Athenian juries could inflict very severe penalties such as death, unpayably large fines, confiscation of property, permanent exile and loss of citizens' rights through *atimia*. Further, the elite Athenians who suffered ostracism were rich or noble men who had connections or *xenoi* in the wider Greek world and who, unlike genuine exiles, were able to access their income in Attica from abroad. In Plutarch, following as he does the anti-democratic line common in elite sources, the fact that people might be recalled early appears to be another example of the inconsistency of majoritarianism that was characteristic of Athenian democracy. However, ten years of exile usually resolved whatever had prompted the expulsion. Ostracism was simply a pragmatic measure; the concept of serving out the full sentence did not apply as it was a preventative measure, not a punitive one.

One curious window on the practicalities of ostracism comes from the cache of 190 ostraka discovered dumped in a well next to the acropolis.[134] From the handwriting they appear to have been written by fourteen individuals and bear the name of Themistocles, ostracised before 471 BC and were evidently meant for distribution to voters. This was not necessarily evidence of electoral fraud (being no worse than modern voting instruction cards), but their being dumped in the well may suggest that their creators wished to hide them. If so, these ostraka provide an example of organized groups attempting to influence the outcome of ostracisms. The two-month gap between the first and second phases would have easily allowed for such a campaign.Wikipedia:Citation needed

There is another interpretation, however, according to which these ostraka were prepared beforehand by enterprising businessmen who offered to them for sale to citizens who could not easily inscribe the desired names for themselves or who simply wished to save time.[135]

The two-month gap is a key feature in the institution, much as in elections under modern liberal democracies. It first prevented the candidate for expulsion being chosen out of immediate anger, although an Athenian general such as Cimon would have not wanted to lose a battle the week before such a second vote. Secondly, it opened up a period for discussion (or perhaps agitation), whether informally in daily talk or public speeches before the Athenian assembly or Athenian courts. *[136] In this process a consensus, or rival consensuses, might emerge. Further, in that time of waiting, ordinary Athenian citizens must have felt a certain power over the greatest members of their city; conversely, the most prominent citizens had an incentive to worry how their social inferiors regarded them.

Period of operation

Ostracism was not in use throughout the whole period of Athenian democracy (circa 506–322 BC), but only occurred in the fifth century BC. The standard account, found in Aristotle's Constitution of the Athenians 22.3,[137] attributes the establishment to Cleisthenes, a pivotal reformer in the creation of the democracy. In that case ostracism would have been in place from around 506 BC. The first victim of the practice, however, was not expelled until 487 BC — nearly twenty years later. Over the course of the next sixty years some twelve or more individuals followed him. The list may not be complete, but there is good reason to believe the Athenians did not feel the need to eject someone in this way every year. The list of known ostracisms runs as follows:

• 487 Hipparchos son of Charmos, a relative of the tyrant Peisistratos

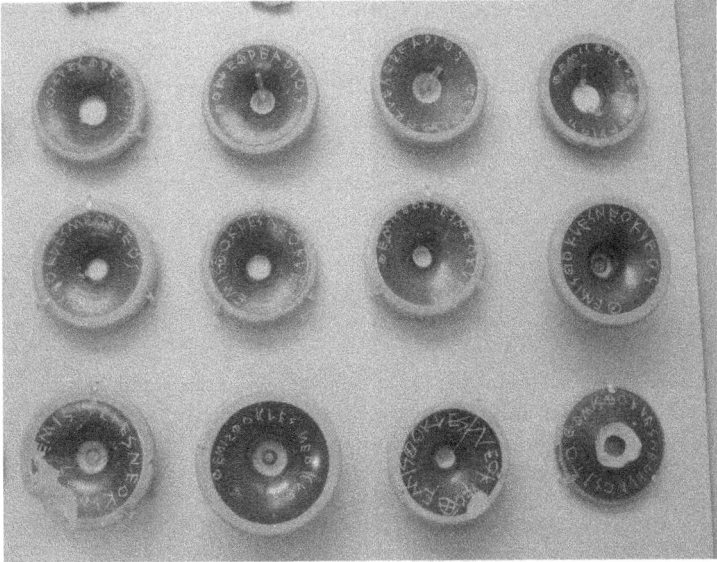

Figure 11: *Ostraca from 482 BC*

- 486 Megacles son of Hippocrates; Cleisthenes' nephew (possibly ostracised twice[138])
- 485 Kallixenos nephew of Cleisthenes and head of the Alcmaeonids at the time (not known for certain)Wikipedia:Citation needed
- 484 Xanthippus son of Ariphron; Pericles' father
- 482 Aristides son of Lysimachus
- 471 Themistocles son of Neocles (last possible year)
- 461 Cimon son of Miltiades
- 460 Alcibiades son of Kleinias (possibly ostracised twice)
- 457 Menon son of Meneclides [less certain]
- 442 Thucydides son of Melesias
- 440s Callias son of Didymos [less certain]
- 440s Damon son of Damonides [less certain]
- 416 Hyperbolus son of Antiphanes (±1 year)

Around twelve thousand political ostraka have been excavated in the Athenian agora and in the Kerameikos. Wikipedia:Citation needed The second victim, Cleisthenes' nephew Megacles, is named by 4647 of these, but for a second undated ostracism not listed above. The known ostracisms seem to fall into three distinct phases: the 480s BC, mid-century 461–443 BC and finally the years 417–415: this matches fairly well with the clustering of known expulsions, although Themistocles before 471 may count as an exception. This suggests that ostracism fell in and out of fashion.[139]

The last known ostracism was that of Hyperbolos in circa 417 BC. There is no sign of its use after the Peloponnesian War, when democracy was restored after the oligarchic coup of the Thirty had collapsed in 403 BC. However, while ostracism was not an active feature of the 4th-century version of democracy, it remained; the question was put to the assembly each year, but they did not wish to hold one.

Purpose

Because ostracism was carried out by thousands of people over many decades of an evolving political situation and culture, it did not serve a single monolithic purpose. Observations can be made about the outcomes, as well as the initial purpose for which it was created.

The first rash of people ostracised in the decade after the defeat of the first Persian invasion at Marathon in 490 BC were all related or connected to the tyrant Peisistratos, who had controlled Athens for 36 years up to 527 BC. After his son Hippias was deposed with Spartan help in 510 BC, the family sought refuge with the Persians, and nearly twenty years later Hippias landed with their invasion force at Marathon. Tyranny and Persian aggression were paired threats facing the new democratic regime at Athens, and ostracism was used against both.

Tyranny and democracy had arisen at Athens out of clashes between regional and factional groups organised around politicians, including Cleisthenes. As a reaction, in many of its features the democracy strove to reduce the role of factions as the focus of citizen loyalties. Ostracism, too, may have been intended to work in the same direction: by temporarily decapitating a faction, it could help to defuse confrontations that threatened the order of the State.

In later decades when the threat of tyranny was remote, ostracism seems to have been used as a way to decide between radically opposed policies. For instance, in 443 BC Thucydides son of Melesias (not to be confused with the historian of the same name) was ostracised. He led an aristocratic opposition to Athenian imperialism and in particular to Pericles' building program on the acropolis, which was funded by taxes created for the wars against Persia. By expelling Thucydides the Athenian people sent a clear message about the direction of Athenian policy.[140] Similar but more controversial claims have been made about the ostracism of Cimon in 461 BC.

The motives of individual voting citizens cannot, of course, be known. Many of the surviving ostraka name people otherwise unattested. They may well be just someone the submitter disliked, and voted for in moment of private spite. As such, it may be seen as a secular, civic variant of Athenian curse tablets, studied in scholarly literature under the Latin name *defixiones*, where small dolls were wrapped in lead sheets written with curses and then buried, sometimes stuck through with nails for good measure.

In one anecdote about Aristides, known as "the Just", who was ostracised in 482, an illiterate citizen, not recognising him, came up to ask him to write the name Aristides on his ostrakon. When Aristides asked why, the man replied it was because he was sick of hearing him being called "the Just".[141] Perhaps merely the sense that someone had become too arrogant or prominent was enough to get someone's name onto an ostrakon. Ostracism rituals could have also been an attempt to dissuade people from covertly committing murder or assassination for intolerable or emerging individuals of power so as to create an open arena or outlet for those harboring primal frustrations and urges or political motivations. The solution for murder, in Gregory H. Padowitz's theory, would then be "ostracism" which would ultimately be beneficial for all parties – the unfortunate individual would live and get a second chance and society would be spared the ugliness of feuds, civil war, political jams and murder.

Fall into disuse

The last ostracism, that of Hyperbolos in or near 417 BC, is elaborately narrated by Plutarch in three separate *lives*: Hyperbolos is pictured urging the people to expel one of his rivals, but they, Nicias and Alcibiades, laying aside their own hostility for a moment, use their combined influence to have him ostracised instead. According to Plutarch, the people then become disgusted with ostracism and abandoned the procedure forever.

In part ostracism lapsed as a procedure at the end of the fifth century because it was replaced by the *graphe paranomon*, a regular court action under which a much larger number of politicians might be targeted, instead of just one a year as with ostracism, and with greater severity. But it may already have come to seem like an anachronism as factional alliances organised around important men became increasingly less significant in the later period, and power was more specifically located in the interaction of the individual speaker with the power of the assembly and the courts. The threat to the democratic system in the late 5th century came not from tyranny but from oligarchic coups, threats of which became prominent after two brief seizures of power, in 411 BC by "the Four Hundred" and in 404 BC by "the Thirty", which were not dependent on single powerful individuals. Ostracism was not an effective defence against the oligarchic threat and it was not so used.

Analogues

Other cities are known to have set up forms of ostracism on the Athenian model, namely Megara, Miletos, Argos and Syracuse. In the last of these it was referred to as *petalismos*, because the names were written on olive leaves. Little is known about these institutions. Furthermore, pottery shards identified as *ostraka* have been found in Chersonesos Taurica, leading historians to the conclusion that a similar institution existed there as well, in spite of the silence of the ancient records on that count.[142]

A similar modern practice is the recall election, in which the electoral body removes its representation from an elected officer. It is interesting to note that unlike under modern voting procedures, the Athenians did not have to adhere to a strict format for the inscribing of *ostraka*. Many extant *ostraka* show that it was possible to write expletives, short epigrams or cryptic injunctions beside the name of the candidate without invalidating the vote.[143] For example:

- Kallixenes, son of Aristonimos, "the traitor"
- Archen, "lover of foreigners"
- Agasias, "the donkey"
- Megacles, "the adulterer"

Modern usage

The social psychologist Kipling Williams has written extensively on ostracism as a modern phenomenon. Williams defines ostracism as "any act or acts of ignoring and excluding of an individual or groups by an individual or a group".[144] Williams suggests that the most common form of ostracism in a modern context is refusing to communicate with a person. By refusing to communicate with a person, that person is effectively ignored and excluded.[145] The advent of the internet has made ostracism much easier to engage in, and conversely much more difficult to detect, with Williams and others describing this online ostracism as "cyberostracism". In email communication, in particular, it is relatively easy for a person or organization to ignore and exclude a specific person, through simply refusing to communicate with the person. Karen Douglas thus describes "unanswered emails" as constituting a form of cyberostracism,[146] and similarly Eric Wesselmann and Kipling Williams describe "ignored emails" as a form of cyberostracism.[147]

Williams and his colleagues have charted responses to ostracism in some five thousand cases, and found two distinctive patterns of response. The first is increased group-conformity, in a quest for re-admittance; the second is to become more provocative and hostile to the group, seeking attention rather than acceptance.[148]

Whistleblowing

Research suggests that ostracism is a common reprisal strategy used by organizations in response to whistleblowing. Kipling Williams, in a survey on US whistleblowers, found that 100% reported post-whistleblowing ostracism.[149] Alexander Brown similarly found that post-whistleblowing ostracism is a common response, and indeed describes ostracism as form of "covert" reprisal, as it is normally so difficult to identify and investigate.[150]

Qahr and ashti

Qahr and Ashti is a culture-specific Iranian form of personal shunning, most frequently of another family member.[151] Qahr and ashti are described by Dr. Kambiz Behzadi[152] as:

> *Qahr (to not be on speaking terms with someone) and ashti (to make up) represent a complex culture-specific fusion of emotional dynamics, cognitive evaluations, and behavioral tendencies, which codes both negative and 'distancing' emotions and initiates a set of social actions and gestures that lead to amelioration of that emotional state.*

While modern Western concepts of ostracism are based upon enforcing conformity within a societally-recognized group,[153] Iranian Qahr is a private (batin), family-oriented affair of conflict or display of anger[154] that is never disclosed to the public at large, as to do would be a breach of social etiquette.[155]

In the Islamic Republic of Iran, the husband only has the right to show *qahr* towards his wife, the wife does not have this right to show qahr towards her husband,[156] as the husband's family rank is that of Head of Household while the wife has a much lower family ranking.[157] She may practice qahr only towards others of equal or lower status.

Qahr is avoidance of a lower-ranking family member who has committed a perceived insult. It is one of several ritualized social customs of Iranian culture.[158]

Gozasht, an Iranian word meaning 'tolerance, understanding and a desire or willingness to forgive'[159] is an essential componant of Qahr and Ashti for both psychological needs of closure and cognition, as well as a culturally accepted source for practicing necessary religious requirements of *tawbah (repentance, see Koran 2:222)*[160][161] and *du'a* (supplication).[162]

Notes

^ Oration IV of Andocides purports itself to be speech urging the ostracism of Alcibiades in 415 BC, but it is probably not authentic.

^ The second ostracisms of Megacles and of Alcibiades son of Kleinias are reported only by Lysias in the quoted passage – no other ancient author refers to them. Thus, Lysias's report is regarded as probably spurious by many modern historians.

References

Additional ancient

From Aristotle Constitution of the Athenians:

- Athenian Constitution 22[163]

From Philochorus, *Atthis*

- Fragment 30[164]

From Plutarch's 'Lives':

- Life of Pericles 11–12[165]
- Life of Pericles 14[166]
- Life of Aristides 7[167]
- Life of Cimon 17[168]
- Life of Alcibiades 13[169]
- Life of Nicias 11[170]
- A list[171], differing slightly from that given above, of known ostracisms and many of the key Greek passages translated, from John Paul Adams's site at CSU Northridge.

Note that the ancient sources on ostracism are mostly 4th century or much later and often limited to brief descriptions such as notes by lexicographers. Most of the narrative and analytical passages of any length come from Plutarch writing five centuries later and with little sympathy for democratic practices. There are no contemporary accounts that can take one into the experiences of participants: a dense account of Athenian democracy can only be made on the basis of the much fuller sources available in the 4th century, especially the Attic orators, after ostracism had fallen into disuse. Most of such references are a 4th-century memory of the institution.

Additional modern

- (1996). "Ostracism". *Oxford Classical Dictionary, 3rd edition*. Oxford. ISBN 0-19-860165-4.
- Mabel Lang, (1990). *Ostraka*, Athens. ISBN 0-87661-225-7.
- Eugene Vanderpool, (1970). *Ostracism at Athens*, Cincinnati. ISBN 3-11-006637-8
- Rudi Thomsen, (1972). *The Origins of Ostracism, A Synthesis*, Copenhagen.
- P.J. Rhodes, (1994). "The Ostracism of Hyberbolus", *Ritual, Finance, Politics: Athenian Democratic Accounts presented to David Lewis* p. 85-99, editors. Robin Osborne, Simon Hornblower, (Oxford). ISBN 0-19-814992-1.
- Mogens Herman Hansen, (1987). *The Athenian Democracy in the age of Demosthenes*, Oxford. ISBN 0-8061-3143-8.
- Josiah Ober, (1989), "Mass and Elite in Democratic Athens: Rhetoric", *Ideology and the Power of the People*, Princeton University Press. ISBN 0-691-02864-8.
- Igor E. Surikov, (2006), "Остракизм в Афинах", Языки Славянских Культур. ISBN 5-9551-0136-5 (Russian, with English summary)

External links

Wikimedia Commons has media related to *Greek ostraka*.

- Ostracism - Ancient History Encyclopedia[172]
- Livius[173], Ostracism[174] by Jona Lendering

Manusmriti

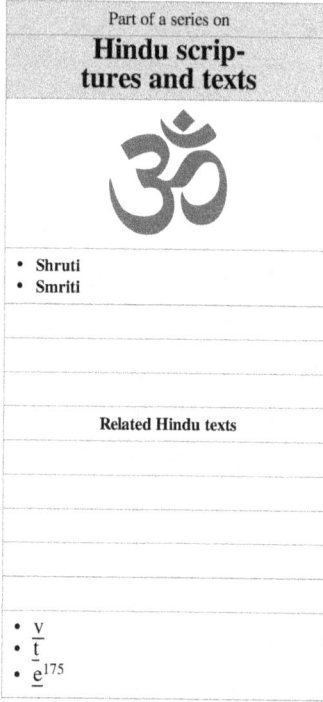

The *Manusmṛti* (Sanskrit: मनुस्मृति), also spelled as ***Manusmriti***,[176] is an ancient legal text among the many *Dharmaśāstras* of Hinduism.[177] It was one of the first Sanskrit texts translated during the British rule of India in 1794, by Sir William Jones, and used to formulate the Hindu law by the colonial government.[178]

Over fifty manuscripts of the *Manusmriti* are now known, but the earliest discovered, most translated and presumed authentic version since the 18th century has been the "Calcutta manuscript with Kulluka Bhatta commentary". Modern scholarship states this presumed authenticity is false, and the various manuscripts of Manusmriti discovered in India are inconsistent with each other, and within themselves, raising concerns of its authenticity, insertions and interpolations made into the text in later times.

The metrical text is in Sanskrit, is variously dated to be from the 2nd century BCE to 3rd century CE, and it presents itself as a discourse given by Manu (Svayambhuva) and Bhrigu on dharma topics such as duties, rights, laws, conduct, virtues and others. The text's fame spread outside India, long before the colonial era. The medieval era Buddhistic law of Myanmar and Thailand are also ascribed to Manu,[179,180] and the text influenced past Hindu kingdoms in Cambodia and Indonesia.[181]

Manusmriti is also called the *Mānava-Dharmaśāstra* or *Laws of Manu*.

Nomenclature

The title *Manusmriti* is a relatively modern term and a late innovation, probably coined because the text is in a verse form. The over fifty manuscripts discovered of the text, never use this title, but state the title as *Manava Dharmasastra* (Sanskrit: मानवधर्मशास्त्र) in their colophons at the end of each chapter. In modern scholarship, these two titles refer to the same text.[182]

Chronology

Eighteenth-century philologists Sir William Jones and Karl Wilhelm Friedrich Schlegel assigned *Manusmriti* to the period of around 1250 BCE and 1000 BCE respectively, which from later linguistic developments is untenable due to the language of the text which must be dated later than the late Vedic texts such as the Upanishads which are themselves dated a few centuries ago around 500BC. Later scholarship, shifted the chronology of the text to between 200 BCE and 200 CE.[183,184] Olivelle adds that numismatics evidence, and the mention of gold coins as a fine, suggest that text may date to the 2nd or 3rd century CE.[185]

Most scholars consider the text a composite produced by many authors put together over a long period. Olivelle states that the various ancient and medieval Indian texts claim revisions and editions were derived from the original text with 100,000 verses and 1,080 chapters. However, the text version in modern use, according to Olivelle, is likely the work of a single author or a chairman with research assistants.

Manusmriti, Olivelle states, was not a new document, it drew on other texts, and it reflects "a crystallization of an accumulated knowledge" in ancient India. The root of theoretical models within Manusmriti rely on at least two shastras that pre-date it: *artha* (statecraft and legal process), and *dharma* (an ancient Indian concept that includes duties, rights, laws, conduct, virtues and others discussed in various Dharmasutras older than Manusmriti).[186] Its contents can be traced to *Kalpasutras* of the Vedic era, which led to the development of *Smartasutras* consisting of *Grihyasutras* and *Dharmasutras*.[187] The foundational texts of Manusmriti include many of these sutras, all from an era preceding the common era. Most of these ancient texts are now lost, and only four of have survived: the law codes of *Apastamba*, *Gautama*, *Baudhayana* and *Vasishtha*.[188]

Structure

The modern version of the text has been subdivided into twelve *Adhyayas* (chapters), but the original text had no such division.[189] The text covers different topics, and is unique among ancient Indian texts in using "transitional verses" to mark the end of one subject and the start of the next. The text can be broadly divided into four, each of different length. and each further divided into subsections:

1. Creation of the world
2. Source of dharma
3. The dharma of the four social classes
4. Law of karma, rebirth and final liberation

The text is composed in metric *Shlokas* (verses), in the form of a dialogue between an exalted teacher and disciples who are eager to learn about the various aspects of dharma.[190] The first 58 verses are attributed by the text to Manu, while the remaining more than two thousand verses are attributed to his student Bhrigu. Olivelle lists the subsections as follows:[191]

Creation of the world

The *Sarvasya Sambhavah* (Origin, creation of the World) section has one hundred nineteen verses, describing how the world was created out of complete darkness, the cosmic egg, the cyclic nature of time and all existence.[192]

Sources of the law

The *Dharmasya Yonih* (Sources of the Law) has twenty-four verses, and one transition verse. These verses state what the text considers as the proper and just sources of law:

वेदोऽखिलो धर्ममूलं स्मृतिशीले च तद्विदाम् । आचारश्चैव साधूनामात्मनस्तुष्टिरेव च ॥

Translation 1: The whole Veda is the (first) source of the sacred law, next the tradition and the virtuous conduct of those who know the (Veda further), also the customs of holy men, and (finally) self-satisfaction (Atmana santushti).[193]
Translation 2: The root of the religion is the entire Veda, and (then) the tradition and customs of those who know (the Veda), and the conduct of virtuous people, and what is satisfactory to oneself.[194]

—*Manusmriti 2.6*

वेद: स्मृति: सदाचार: स्वस्य च प्रियमात्मन: । एतच्चतुर्विधं प्राहु: साक्षाद् धर्मस्य लक्षणम् ॥

Translation 1: The Veda, the sacred tradition, the customs of virtuous men, and one's own pleasure, they declare to be the fourfold means of defining the sacred law.

Translation 2: The Veda, tradition, the conduct of good people, and what is pleasing to oneself – they say that is four fold mark of religion.

—*Manusmriti 2.12*

This section of Manusmriti, like other Hindu law texts, includes fourfold sources of *Dharma*, states Levinson, which include *Atmana santushti* (satisfaction of one's conscience), *Sadachara* (local norms of virtuous individuals), *Smriti* and *Sruti*.[195,196]

Dharma of the four Varnas

- 3.1 Rules Relating to Law (2.25 – 10.131)

    - 3.1.1 Rules of Action in Normal Times (2.26 – 9.336)

        - 3.1.1.1 Fourfold Dharma of a Brahmin (2.26 – 6.96) (contains the longest section of Manusmriti, 3.1, called *dharmavidhi*)

        - 3.1.1.2 Rules of Action for a King (7.1 – 9.324) (contains 960 verses, includes description of institutions and officials of state, how officials are to be appointed, tax laws, rules of war, the role and limits on the power of the king, and long sections on eighteen grounds for litigation, including those related to non-delivery under contract, breach of contract, non-payment of wages, property disputes, inheritance disputes, humiliation and defamation, physical assault, theft, violence of any form, injury, sexual crimes against women, public safety, and others; the section also includes rules of evidence, rules on interrogation of witnesses, and the organization of court system)[197]

        - 3.1.1.3 Rules of Action for Vaiśyas and Śūdras (9.326 – 9.335) (shortest section, eight rules for Vaishyas, two for Shudras, but some applicable laws to these two classes are discussed generically in verses 2.26 – 9.324)[198]

    - 3.1.2 Rules of Action in Times of Adversity (10.1 – 11.129) (contains revised rules on the state machinery and four varnas in the times of war, famine or other emergencies)[199]

- 3.2 Rules Relating to Penance (11.1 – 11.265) (includes rules of proportionate punishment; instead of fines, incarceration or death, discusses penance or social isolation as a form of punishment for certain crimes)

The verses 6.97, 9.325, 9.336 and 10.131 are transitional verses. Olivelle notes instances of likely interpolation and insertions in the notes to this section, in both the presumed vulgate version and the critical edition.[200]

Determination of Karmayoga

The verses 12.1, 12.2 and 12.82 are transitional verses. This section is in a different style than the rest of the text, raising questions whether this entire chapter was added later. While there is evidence that this chapter was extensively redacted over time, however it is unclear whether the entire chapter is of a later era.

- 4.1 Fruits of Action (12.3-81) (section on actions and consequences, personal responsibility, action as a means of moksha – the highest personal bliss)[201]
- 4.2 Rules of Action for Supreme Good (12.83-115) (section on karma, duties and responsibilities as a means of supreme good)

The closing verses of Manusmriti declares,

> एवं यः सर्वभूतेषु पश्यत्यात्मानमात्मना *UNIQ-nowiki-0-2b539e9a3aa42eb6-QINU*
>
> *He who thus recognizes in his individual soul (Self, Atman), the universal soul that exists in all beings,*
>
> *becomes equal-minded towards all, and enters the highest state, Brahman.*
>
> —*Manusmriti 12.125, Calcutta manuscript with Kulluka Bhatta commentary*[202,203]

Contents

The structure and contents of the Manusmriti suggest it to be a document predominantly targeted at the Brahmins (priestly class) and the Kshatriyas (king, administration and warrior class). The text dedicates 1,034 verses, the largest portion, on laws for and expected virtues of Brahmins, and 971 verses for Kshatriyas.[204] The statement of rules for the Vaishyas (merchant class) and the Shudras (artisans and working class) in the text is extraordinarily brief. Olivelle suggests that this may be because the text was composed to address the balance "between the political power and the priestly interests", and because of the rise in foreign invasions of India in the period it was composed.[205]

On virtues and outcast

Manusmriti lists and recommends virtues in many verses. For example, verse 6.75 recommends non-violence towards everyone and temperance as key virtues,[206,207] while verse 10.63 preaches that all four varnas must abstain from injuring any creature, abstain from falsehood and abstain from appropriating property of others.[208,209]

Similarly, in verse 4.204, states Olivelle, some manuscripts of Manusmriti list the recommended virtues to be, "compassion, forbearance, truthfulness, non-injury, self-control, not desiring, meditation, serenity, sweetness and honesty" as primary, and "purification, sacrifices, ascetic toil, gift giving, vedic recitation, restraining the sexual organs, observances, fasts, silence and bathing" as secondary.[210] A few manuscripts of the text contain a different verse 4.204, according to Olivelle, and list the recommended virtues to be, "not injuring anyone, speaking the truth, chastity, honesty and not stealing" as central and primary, while "not being angry, obedience to the teacher, purification, eating moderately and vigilance" to desirable and secondary.

In other discovered manuscripts of *Manusmriti*, including the most translated Calcutta manuscript, the text declares in verse 4.204 that the ethical precepts under Yamas such as Ahimsa (non-violence) are paramount while Niyamas such as Ishvarapranidhana (contemplation of personal god) are minor, and those who do not practice the *Yamas* but obey the *Niyamas* alone become an outcast.[211,212]

On personal choices, behaviors and morals

Manusmriti has numerous verses on duties a person has towards himself and to others, thus including moral codes as well as legal codes.[213] This is similar to, states Olivelle, the modern contrast between informal moral concerns to birth out of wedlock in the developed nations, along with simultaneous legal protection for children who are born out of wedlock.

Personal behaviors covered by the text are extensive. For example, verses 2.51-2.56, recommend that a monk must go on his begging round, collect almsfood and present it to his teacher first, then eat. One should revere whatever food one gets and eat it without disdain, states Manusmriti, but never overeat, as eating too much harms health.[214] In verse 5.47, the text states that work becomes without effort when a man contemplates, undertakes and does what he loves to do and when he does so without harming any creature.[215]

Numerous verses relate to the practice of meat eating, how it causes injury to living beings, why it is evil, and the morality of vegetarianism. Yet, the text balances its moral tone as an appeal to one's conscience, states Olivelle.

For example, verse 5.56 as translated by Olivelle states, "there is no fault in eating meat, in drinking liquor, or in having sex; that is the natural activity of creatures. Abstaining from such activity, however, brings great rewards."[216]

On women's rights

Manusmriti offers an internally inconsistent and conflicting perspective on women's rights. The text, for example, declares that a marriage cannot be dissolved by a woman or a man, in verse 8.101-8.102.[217] Yet, the text, in other sections, allows either to dissolve the marriage. For example, verses 9.72-9.81 allow the man or the woman to get out of a fraudulent marriage or an abusive marriage, and remarry; the text also provides legal means for a woman to remarry when her husband has been missing or has abandoned her.[218]

It preaches chastity to widows such as in verses 5.158-5.160, opposes a woman marrying someone outside her own social class as in verses 3.13-3.14.[219] In other verses, such as 2.67-2.69 and 5.148-5.155, Manusmriti preaches that as a girl, she should obey and seek protection of her father, as a young woman her husband, and as a widow her son; and that a woman should always worship her husband as a god.[220] In verses 3.55-3.56, Manusmriti also declares that "women must be honored and adorned", and "where women are revered, there the gods rejoice; but where they are not, no sacred rite bears any fruit".[221,222] Elsewhere, in verses 5.147-5.148, states Olivelle, the text declares, "a woman must never seek to live independently".[223]

Simultaneously, states Olivelle, the text presupposes numerous practices such a marriages outside varna, such as between a Brahmin man and a Shudra woman in verses 9.149-9.157, a widow getting pregnant with a child of a man she is not married to in verses 9.57-9.62, marriage where a woman in love elopes with her man, and then grants legal rights in these cases such as property inheritance rights in verses 9.143-9.157, and the legal rights of the children so born.[224] The text also presumes that a married woman may get pregnant by a man other than her husband, and dedicates verses 8.31-8.56 to conclude that the child's custody belongs to the woman and her legal husband, and not to the man she got pregnant with.[225,226]

Manusmriti provides a woman with property rights to six types of property in verses 9.192-9.200. These include those she received at her marriage, or as gift when she eloped or when she was taken away, or as token of love before marriage, or as gifts from her biological family, or as received from her husband subsequent to marriage, and also from inheritance from deceased relatives.[227]

Flavia Agnes states that Manusmriti is a complex commentary from women's rights perspective, and the British colonial era codification of women's rights

based on it for Hindus, and from Islamic texts for Muslims, picked and emphasized certain aspects while it ignored other sections.[228] This construction of
personal law during the colonial era created a legal fiction around Manusmriti's
historic role as a scripture in matters relating to women in South Asia.[229]

On statecraft and rules of war

Chapter 7 of the Manusmriti discusses the duties of a king, what virtues he
must have, what vices he must avoid. In verses 7.54 - 7.76, the text identifies
precepts to be followed in selecting ministers, ambassadors and officials, as
well as the characteristics of well fortified capital. Manusmriti then lays out
the laws of just war, stating that first and foremost, war should be avoided by
negotiations and reconciliations. If war becomes necessary, states Manusmriti, a soldier must never harm civilians, non-combatants or someone who has
surrendered, that use of force should be proportionate, and other rules. Fair
taxation guidelines are described in verses 7.127 to 7.137.[230],[231]

Authenticity and inconsistencies in various manuscripts

Patrick Olivelle, credited with a 2005 translation of Manusmriti published by
the Oxford University Press, states the concerns in postmodern scholarship
about the presumed authenticity and reliability of Manusmriti manuscripts. He
writes (abridged),

> *The MDh [Manusmriti] was the first Indian legal text introduced to the*
> *western world through the translation of Sir William Jones in 1794. (...)*
> *All the editions of the MDh, except for Jolly's, reproduce the text as found*
> *in the [Calcutta] manuscript containing the commentary of Kulluka. I have*
> *called this as the "vulgate version". It was Kulluka's version that has been*
> *translated repeatedly: Jones (1794), Burnell (1884), Buhler (1886) and*
> *Doniger (1991). (...)*
>
> *The belief in the authenticity of Kulluka's text was openly articulated by*
> *Burnell (1884, xxix): 'There is then no doubt that the textus receptus,*
> *viz., that of Kulluka Bhatta, as adopted in India and by European scholars,*
> *is very near on the whole to the original text." This is far from the truth.*
> *Indeed, one of the great surprises of my editorial work has been to discover*
> *how few of the over fifty manuscripts that I collated actually follow the*
> *vulgate in key readings.*

> —*Patrick Olivelle, Manu's Code of Law (2005)*[232]

Other scholars point to the inconsistencies and have questioned the authenticity of verses, and the extent to which verses were changed, inserted or interpolated into the original, at a later date. Sinha, for example, states that less than half, or only 1,214 of the 2,685 verses in Manusmriti, may be authentic. Further, the verses are internally inconsistent.[233] Verses such as 3.55-3.62 of Manusmriti, for example, glorify the position of women, while verse such as 9.3 and 9.17 do the opposite.[234] Other passages found in Manusmriti, such as those relating to Ganesha, are modern era insertions and forgeries.

Nelson in 1887, in a legal brief before the Madras High Court of British India, had stated, "there are various contradictions and inconsistencies in the Manu Smriti itself, and that these contradictions would lead one to conclude that such a commentary did not lay down legal principles to be followed but were merely recommendatory in nature."[235] Mahatma Gandhi remarked on the observed inconsistencies within Manusmriti as follows,

> *I hold Manusmriti as part of Shastras. But that does not mean that I swear by every verse that is printed in the book described as Manusmriti. There are so many contradictions in the printed volume that, if you accept one part, you are bound to reject those parts that are wholly inconsistent with it. (...) Nobody is in possession of the original text.*
>
> —*Mahatma Gandhi, An Adi-Dravida's Difficulties*[236]

Commentaries

There are numerous classical commentaries on the *Manusmṛti* written in the medieval period.

Bhāruci

Bhāruci is the oldest known commentator on the *Manu Smṛti*. Kane places him in the late 10th or early 11th century,[237] Olivelle places him in the 8th century,[238] and Derrett places him between 600-800 CE.[239] From these three opinions we can place Bhāruci anywhere from the early 7th century CE to the early 11th century CE. Bhāruci's commentary, titled *Manu-sastra-vivarana*, has far fewer number of verses than the Kullūka-Calcutta vulgate version in circulation since the British colonial era, and it refers to more ancient texts that are believed to be lost. It is also called *Raja-Vimala*, and J Duncan M Derrett states Bharuci was "occasionally more faithful to his source's historical intention" than other commentators.[240]

Medhātithi

Medhātithi commentary on *Manu Smṛti* has been widely studied. Scholars such as Buhler, Kane, and Lingat believe he was from north India, likely the Kashmir region. His commentary on Manusmriti is estimated to be from 9th to 11th century.[241]

Govindarāja

Govindarāja's commentary, titled *Manutika*, is an 11th-century commentary on Manusmriti, referred to by *Jimutavahana* and *Laksmidhara*, and was plagiarized by Kullūka, states Olivelle.

Kullūka

Kullūka's commentary, titled *Manvarthamuktavali*, along with his version of the *Manusmrti* manuscript has been "vulgate" or default standard, most studied version, since it was discovered in 18th-century Calcutta by the British colonial officials. It is the most reproduced and famous, not because, according to Olivelle, it is the oldest or because of its excellence, but because it was the lucky version found first. The Kullūka commentary dated to be sometime between the 13th to 15th century, adds Olivelle, is mostly a plagiary of Govindaraja commentary from about the 11th century, but with Kullūka's criticism of Govindaraja.[242]

Nārāyana

Nārāyana's commentary, titled *Manvarthavivrtti*, is probably from the 14th century and little is known about the author. This commentary includes many variant readings, and Olivelle found it useful in preparing a critical edition of the Manusmriti text in 2005.

Nandana

Nandana was from south India, and his commentary, titled *Nandini*, provides a useful benchmark on Manusmriti version and its interpretation in the south.

Others

Other known medieval era commentaries on Manusmriti include those by Sarvajnanarayana, Raghavananda and Ramacandra.[243]

Significance and role in history

In ancient and medieval India

Scholars doubt Manusmriti was ever administered as law text in ancient or medieval Hindu society. David Buxbaum states, "in the opinion of the best contemporary orientalists, it [Manusmriti] does not, as a whole, represent a set of rules ever actually administered in Hindustan. It is in great part an ideal picture of that which, in the view of a Brahmin, ought to be law".[244]

Donald Davis writes, "there is no historical evidence for either an active propagation or implementation of Dharmasastra [Manusmriti] by a ruler or any state – as distinct from other forms of recognizing, respecting and using the text. Thinking of Dharmasastra as a legal code and of its authors as lawgivers is thus a serious misunderstanding of its history".[245] Other scholars have expressed the same view, based on epigraphical, archeological and textual evidence from medieval Hindu kingdoms in Gujarat, Kerala and Tamil Nadu, while acknowledging that Manusmriti was influential to the South Asian history of law and was a theoretical resource.[246,247]

In British India

Prior to the British colonial rule, Sharia (Islamic law) for Muslims in South Asia had been codified as *Fatawa-i Alamgiri*, but laws for non-Muslims – such as Hindus, Buddhists, Sikhs, Jains, Parsis – were not codified during the 600 years of Islamic rule. With the arrival of the British colonial officials, Manusmriti played a historic role in constructing a legal system for non-Muslims in South Asia and early Western perceptions about the ancient and medieval Indian society.

In the 18th century, the earliest British of the East India Company acted as agents of the Mughal emperor. As the British colonial rule took over the political and administrative powers in India, it was faced with various state responsibilities such as legislative and judiciary functions.[248] The East India Company, and later the British Crown, sought profits for its British shareholders through trade as well as sought to maintain effective political control with minimal military engagement. The administration pursued a path of least resistance, relying upon co-opted local intermediaries that were mostly Muslims and some Hindus in various princely states. The British exercised power by avoiding interference and adapting to law practices as explained by the local intermediaries. The existing legal texts for Muslims, and resurrected Manusmriti manuscript thus helped the colonial state sustain the pre-colonial religious and political law and conflicts, well into the late nineteenth century. The colonial policy on the system of personal laws for India, for example, was expressed by Governor-General Hastings in 1772 as follows,

That in all suits regarding inheritance, marriage, caste and other religious usages or institutions, the law of the Koran with respect to Mahometans [Muslims], and those of the Shaster with respect to Gentoos [Hindus] shall be invariably be adhered to.

— Warren Hastings, August 15, 1772

For Muslims of India, the British accepted sharia as the legal code for Muslims, based on texts such the *al-Sirjjiyah* and *Fatawa-i Alamgiri* written under sponsorship of Aurangzeb.[249,250,251] For Hindus and other non-Muslims such as Buddhists, Sikhs, Jains, Parsis and Tribal people, this information was unavailable. The substance of Hindu law, was derived by the British colonial officials from Manusmriti, and it became the first Dharmasastra that was translated in 1794. The British colonial officials, for practice, attempted to extract from the Dharmaśāstra, the English categories of law and religion for the purposes of colonial administration.[252,253]

The British colonial officials, however, mistook the Manusmriti as codes of law, failed to recognize that it was a commentary on morals and law and not a statement of positive law. The colonial officials of the early 19th century also failed to recognize that Manusmriti was one of many competing Dharmasastra texts, it was not in use for centuries during the Islamic rule period of India. The officials resurrected Manusmriti, constructed statements of positive law from the text for non-Muslims, in order to remain faithful to its policy of using sharia for the South Asian Muslim population.[254,255] Manusmriti, thus played a role in constructing the Anglo-Hindu law, as well as Western perceptions about ancient and medieval era Hindu culture from the colonial times.[256] Abdullahi Ahmed An-Na'im states the significance and role of Manusmriti in governing India during the colonial era as follows (abridged),

The [British] colonial administration began the codification of Hindu and Muslim laws in 1772 and continued through the next century, with emphasis on certain texts as the authentic "sources" of the law and custom of Hindus and Muslims, which in fact devalued and retarded those dynamic social systems. The codification of complex and interdependent traditional systems froze certain aspects of the status of women, for instance, outside the context of constantly evolving social and economic relations, which in effect limited or restricted women's rights. The selectivity of the process, whereby colonial authorities sought the assistance of Hindu and Muslim religious elites in understanding the law, resulted in the Brahminization and Islamization of customary laws [in British India]. For example, the British orientalist scholar William Jones translated the key texts Al Sirjjiyah in 1792 as the Mohammedan Law of Inheritance, and Manusmriti in 1794 as the Institutes of Hindu Law or the Ordinances of Manu. In

short, British colonial administrators reduced centuries of vigorous de-
velopment of total ethical, religious and social systems to fit their own
preconceived European notions of what Muslim and Hindu "law" should
be.

—*Abdullahi Ahmed An-Na'im, Islam and the Secular State: Negotiating*
the Future of Sharia

Outside India

The *Dharma-sastras*, particularly Manusmriti, states Anthony Reid, were
"greatly honored in Burma (Myanmar), Siam (Thailand), Cambodia and Java-
Bali (Indonesia) as the defining documents of the natural order, which kings
were obliged to uphold. They were copied, translated and incorporated into
local law code, with strict adherence to the original text in Burma and Siam,
and a stronger tendency to adapt to local needs in Java (Indonesia)".[257,258,259]
The medieval era derived texts and Manusmriti manuscripts in Southeast Asia
are, however, quite different than the "vulgate" version that has been in use
since its first use in British India. The role of then extant Manusmriti as a historic foundation of law texts for the people of Southeast Asia has been very
important, states Hooker.

Comparison with other dharmasastras

Along with Manusmriti (*Manava Dharmasastra*), ancient India had between
eighteen and thirty six competing *Dharma-sastras*, states John Bowker. Many
of these texts have been lost completely or in parts, but they are referred to in
other ancient Indian texts suggesting that they were influential in some regions
or time. Of the numerous jurisprudence-related commentaries and Smriti
texts, after Manu Smriti and other than the older Dharma Sutras, Yajnavalkya
Smriti has attracted the attention of many scholars, followed by Narada Smriti
and Parashara Smriti (the oldest Dharma-smriti).[260] Evidence suggests that
Yajnavalkya Smriti, state Ghose and other scholars, was the more referred to
text than Manu Smriti, in matters of governance and practice. This text, of
unclear date of composition, but likely to be a few centuries after Manusmriti,
is more "concise, methodical, distilled and liberal".[261] According to Jois,

Regarding the 18 titles of law, Yajnavalkya follows the same pattern as
in Manu with slight modifications. On matters such as women's rights
of inheritance and right to hold property, status of Sudras, and criminal
penalty, Yajnavalkya is more liberal than Manu. (...) He deals exhaus-
tively on subjects like creation of valid documents, law of mortgages, hy-
pothecation, partnership and joint ventures.

—M Rama Jois, Legal and Constitutional History of India[262]

Jois suggests that the Yajnavalkya Smriti text liberal evolution may have been influenced by Buddhism in ancient India. The Yajnavalkya text is also different from Manu text in adding chapters to the organization of monasteries, land grants, deeds execution and other matters. The Yajnavalkya text was more referred to by many Hindu kingdoms of the medieval era, as evidenced by the commentary of 12th-century Vijñāneśvara, titled *Mitakshara*.[263]

Modern reception

Views on Manusmriti have varied among Indian leaders. Ambedkar (left) burnt it in 1927, while Gandhi (right) found it a mix of lofty as well as contradictory teachings. Gandhi suggested a critical reading, and rejection of parts that were contrary to ahimsa.

The *Manusmrti* has been subject to appraisal and criticism.[264] Among the notable Indian critics of the text in the early 20th century was Dr. B. R. Ambedkar, who held Manusmriti as responsible for caste system in India. In protest, Ambedkar burnt *Manusmrti* in a bonfire on December 25, 1927.[265] While Dr. Babasaheb Ambedkar condemned Manusmriti, Mahatma Gandhi opposed the book burning. The latter stated that while caste discrimination was harmful to spiritual and national growth, it had nothing to do with Hinduism and its texts such as Manusmriti. Gandhi argued that the text recognizes different callings and professions, defines not one's rights but one's duties, that all work from that of a teacher to a janitor are equally necessary, and of equal status. Gandhi considered Manusmriti to include lofty teachings but a text with inconsistency and contradictions, whose original text is in no one's possession. He recommended that one must read the entire text, accept those parts of Manusmriti which are consistent with "truth and ahimsa (non-injury or non-violence to others)" and the rejection of other parts.[266]

The Manu Smriti was one of the first Sanskrit texts studied by the European philologists. It was first translated into English by Sir William Jones. His version was published in 1794.[267] This interest in its translation was encouraged by British administrative requirements, which they believed to be legal codes. In fact, states Romila Thapar, these were not codes of law but social and ritual texts.[268]

A Louis Jacolliot translation of the Calcutta version of "Law of Manu" was reviewed by Friedrich Nietzsche. He commented on it both favorably and unfavorably:

> He deemed it "an incomparably spiritual and superior work" to the Christian Bible, observed that "the sun shines on the whole book" and attributed its ethical perspective to "the noble classes, the philosophers and warriors, [who] stand above the mass."[269] Nietzsche does not advocate a caste system, states David Conway, but endorses the political exclusion conveyed in the Manu text.[270] Nietzsche considered Manu's social order as far from perfect, but considers the general idea of a caste system to be natural and right, and stated that "caste-order, order of rank is just a formula for the supreme law of life itself", a "natural order, lawfulness par excellence".[271,272] According to Nietzsche, states Julian Young, "Nature, not Manu, separates from each other: predominantly spiritual people, people characterized by muscular and temperamental strength, and a third group of people who are not distinguished in either way, the average". He wrote that 'To prepare a book of law in the style of Manu means to give a people the right to become master one day, to become perfect, - to aspire to the highest art of life.'

> The Law of Manu was also criticized by Nietzsche. He, states Walter Kaufmann, "denounces the way in which the 'Law of Manu' dealt with the outcastes, saying that there is nothing that outrages our feelings more ... ."[273] Neitzsche wrote, "these regulations teach us enough, in them we find for once Aryan humanity, quite pure, quite primordial, we learn that the concept of pure blood is the opposite of a harmless concept."[274]

In his book *Revolution and Counter-Revolution in India*, leader B. R. Ambedkar asserted that Manu Smriti was written by a sage named Brigu during the times of Pushyamitra of Sangha in connection with social pressures caused by the rise of Buddhism.[275] However, historian Romila Thapar considers these claims to be exaggerations. Thapar writes that archaeological evidence casts doubt on the claims of Buddhist persecution by Pushyamitra.[276] Support of the Buddhist faith by the Shungas at some point is suggested by an epigraph on the gateway of Bharhut, which mentions its erection "during the supremacy of the Shungas"[277] Hinduism does not evangelize.[278]

Pollard et al. state that the code of Manu was derived to answer questions on how men could rebuild their societies following a series of floods.Wikipedia:Verifiability Swami Dayananda Saraswati, the founder of Arya Samaj, held the text to be authentic and authoritative.[279] Other admirers of the text have included Annie Besant.

Friedrich Nietzsche is noted to have said "Close the Bible and open the Manu Smriti. It has an affirmation of life, a triumphing agreeable sensation in life and that to draw up a lawbook such as Manu means to permit oneself to get the upper hand, to become perfection, to be ambitious of the highest art of living."[280] Contra Nietzsche, W.A. Borody has coined the phrase "sublimation-transmogrification logic" to describe the 'state of mind' lying behind the ethical teaching of the Manu Smṛti—a 'state of mind' that would have found Nietzsche's concept of the Dionysian Übermensch abhorrent, and a 'state of mind' or 'voice' that has always been radically contested within India's various philosophical and religious traditions.

Editions and translations

- *The Institutes of Hindu Law: Or, The Ordinances of Manu*[281], Calcutta: Sewell & Debrett, 1796.
- Translation by G. Bühler (1886). *Sacred Books of the East: The Laws of Manus (Vol. XXV)*. Oxford. Available online as The Laws of Manu[282]
- Olivelle, Patrick (2004). *The Law Code of Manu*. New York: OUP. ISBN 0192802712.
- Olivelle, Patrick (2005). *Manu's Code of Law: A Critical Edition and Translation of the Mānava-Dharmaśāstra*. Oxford: Oxford University Press. ISBN 0-195-17146-2.
- Pranjivan Harihar Pandya (ed.), *Manusmriti; With a commentary called Manvarth Muktavali by Kullooka Bhatt*, Bombay, 1913.
- J.I. Shastri (ed.), *Manusmriti with Kullukabhatta Commentary* (1972-1974), reprinted by Motilal Banarsidass, ISBN 9788120807662.
- Ramacandra Varma Shastri, *Manusmṛti: Bhāratīya ācāra-saṃhitā kā viśvakośa*[283], Śāśvata Sāhitya Prakāśana, 1997.

References

- Jha, Ganganath (1920). *Manusmṛti with the Manubhāṣya of Med-hātithi*[284]. Motilal Banarsidass Publishers. ISBN 81-208-1155-0.
- Flood, Gavin (1996). *An Introduction to Hinduism*. Cambridge: Cambridge University Press. ISBN 0-521-43878-0.
- Hopkins, Thomas J. (1971). *The Hindu Religious Tradition*. Belmont, California: Wadsworth Publishing Company.
- Koenraad Elst: Manu as a Weapon against Egalitarianism. Nietzsche and Hindu Political Philosophy, in: Siemens, Herman W. / Roodt, Vasti (Hg.): Nietzsche, Power and Politics. Rethinking Nietzsche's Legacy for Political Thought, Berlin / New York 2008, 543-582.
- Keay, John (2000). *India: A History*. New York: Grove Press. ISBN 0-8021-3797-0.
- Kulke, Hermann; Rothermund, Dietmar (1986). *A History of India*. New York: Barnes & Noble. ISBN 0-88029-577-5.
- Thapar, Romila (2002). *Early India: From the Origins to AD 1300*. Berkeley, California: University of California Press. ISBN 0-520-24225-4.
- ⊚ Herbermann, Charles, ed. (1913). "The Laws of Manu". *Catholic Encyclopedia*. New York: Robert Appleton Company.
- Olivelle, Patrick (2010). "Dharmasastra: A Literary History". In Lubin, Timothy; Krishnan, Jayanth; Davis, Jr. Donald R. *Law and Hinduism: An Introduction*. Cambridge University Press. ISBN 9780521716260.

External links

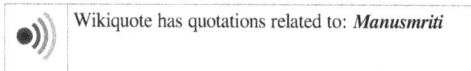

	Wikiquote has quotations related to: *Manusmriti*

Yājñavalkya Smṛti

Part of a series on

Hindu scrip-
tures and texts

ॐ

* **Shruti**
* **Smriti**

Related Hindu texts

* v
* t
* e[285]

The *Yajnavalkya Smriti* (IAST: *Yājñavalkya Smṛti*) is one of the many Dharma-related texts of Hinduism composed in Sanskrit. It is dated to between the 3rd to 5th-century CE, and belongs to the Dharmasastras tradition.[286] The text was composed after the Manusmriti, but like it and Naradasmriti, the text was composed in *shloka* (poetic meter) style.[287] The legal theories within the *Yajnavalkya Smriti* are presented in three books, namely *achara-kanda* (customs), *vyavahara-kanda* (judicial process) and *prayascitta-kanda* (crime and punishment, penance).[288]

The text is the "best composed" and systematic specimen of this genre, with large sections on judicial process theories, one which had greater influence in medieval India's judiciary practice than Manusmriti.[289,290,291] It later became influential in the studies of legal process in ancient and medieval India, during the colonial British India, with the first translation published in German in 1849.[292] The text is notable for its differences in legal theories from Manusmriti, for being more liberal and humane, and for extensive discussions on evidence and judiciousness of legal documents.[293]

Date

The text most likely dates to the Gupta period, between roughly the 3rd and 5th centuries of the common era. There is some debate as to whether it is to be placed in the earlier or later part of that time span.[294] Patrick Olivelle suggests the likely date may be in the 4th to 5th-century CE.[286]

Arguments for particular dating are based on the concise, sophisticated vocabulary found throughout the text and on the use of certain terms such as *nāṇaka* (a coin), and references to Greek astrology (which has been known in India since the 2nd century; see Yavanajataka). The argument arises when considerations are made as to who was exchanging the *nāṇaka* and when the level of Greek thought which the author understood is brought into question.[295]

Author

— *Yajnavalkya Smriti 2.84*[296]

The text is named after the revered Vedic sage Yajnavalkya who appears in many major Upanishads of Hinduism as well as other influential texts such as the Yoga Yajnavalkya.[297] However, the text was composed more than a millennium after his life, It was attributed to him because the text is a SMRITI. A smriti is a form of knowledge that is passed from one generation to other orally. Rishi Yajnavalkya had formed all these ideas and had then passed it down the line. That is why the text has been attributed to him.[297]

The text was likely composed in the Mithila region of historic India (in and around modern Bihar).[293]

Structure

The text is in classical Sanskrit, and is organized in three books. These are *achara-kanda* (368 verses), *vyavahara-kanda* (307 verses) and *prayascitta-kanda* (335 verses).[288,291] The *Yājñavalkya Smṛti* consists of a cumulative total of 1,010 ślokas (verses), and its presentation is methodical, clear and concise instead of the poetic "literary beauty" found in Manusmriti according to Robert Lingat.[291]

Ludo Rocher states that this treatise, like others in Dharmasastras genre, is a scholarly tradition on Dharma rather than a Law book, as understood in the western languages.[298] In contrast, Robert Lingat states that the text is closer to presenting legal philosophy and a transition from being Dharma speculations found in earlier Dharma-related texts.[298]

Content

The text is laid out as a frame story in which the sages of Mithila approach
Yājñavalkya and ask him to teach them dharma.[299] The text opens its reply
by reverentially mentioning ancient Dharma scholars, and asserting in verses
1.4-5 that the following each have written a Dharmasastra (most of these are
lost to history) – Manu, Atri, Visnu, Harita, Yajnavalkya, Ushanas, Angiras, Yama, Apastamba, Samvarta, Katyayana, Brihaspati, Parashara, Vyasa,
Samkha, Likhita, Daksha, Gautama, Shatatapa and Vashistha.[300] The rest of
the text is Yājñavalkya's theories on dharma, presented under Ācāra (proper
conduct), Vyavahāra (criminal law) and Prāyaścitta (expiation).

The *Yajnavalkya Smriti* extensively quotes the Manu Smriti and other Dharma-
texts, sometimes directly paraphrasing passages from these, often reducing
earlier views into a compendium and offering an alternate legal theory. There
are influential differences from the Manu Smriti and earlier Dharma texts, especially with regard to statecraft, the primary of attested documentary evidence in legal process, and in jurisprudence.[301]

— *Yajnavalkya Smriti 3.82*[302]

1. Pioneered the structure which was adopted in future dharmaśāstric discourse:[303] Wikipedia:Citing sources#What information to include

   a) Divided dharma into fairly equally weighted categories of:

   - Ācāra (proper conduct)
   - Vyavahāra (legal procedure)
   - Prāyaścitta (penance)

   b) Subdivided these three further by specific topics within the major subject
   heading.

2. Documentary evidence as the highest foundation of Legal Procedure:

   Yājñavalkya portrayed evidence as hierarchical, with attested documents
   receiving the highest consideration, followed by witnesses, and finally ordeals (five types of verifiable testimony).[304,305]

3. Restructured the Courts:[306] Wikipedia:Citing sources#What information to
   include

   Yājñavalkya distinguished between courts appointed by the king and those
   which were formed by communities of intermediate groups. He then portrayed these courts as a part of a system of hierarchical appeals.

4. Changed the placement of the discussion of Ascetic Orders:

   Forest hermits and renouncers are discussed within the section regarding
   penance (prāyaścitta). In previous texts, description of ascetics followed

the discussion of Brahmins and framed them in opposition to householder Brahmins. The placement of ascetic orders within penance remained in subsequent texts following the general acceptance of the Yājñavalkya Smṛti.

5. Focused on Mokṣa:

Increased attention was given to a description of Mokṣa, dwelling on meditation and the transience of the worldly body. There is even an in-depth, technical discourse based on a medical treatise of the time.

Commentary

Five medieval era *bhasya* (review and commentaries) on *Yajnavalkya Smrti* have survived into the modern era. These are by Visvarupa (*Bālakrīḍā*, 750-1000 CE), Vijanesvara (*Mitaksara*, 11th or 12th century, most studied, from the Varanasi school), Apararka (*Apararka-nibandha*, 12th-century, from the Kashmir school), Sulapani (*Dipakalika*, 14th or 15th century) and Mitramisra (*Viramitrodaya*, 17th-century).

Influence

The legal theories in this text were likely very influential in medieval India, because its passages and quotes are found inscribed in every part of India, and these inscriptions are dated to be from around 10th to 11th century CE.[307,308] The text is also widely commented upon, and referenced in popular works such as the 5th-century *Panchatantra*.[307] The text is profusely quoted in chapters 253-258 of the extant manuscripts of the Agni Purana, and in chapters 93-106 of the Garuda Purana.[308]

References

Bibliography

* Mandagadde Rama Jois (1984). *Legal and Constitutional History of India: Ancient legal, judicial, and constitutional system*[309]. Universal Law Publishing. ISBN 978-81-7534-206-4.
* Robert Lingat (1973). *The Classical Law of India (Translated by J Duncan M Derrett)*[310]. University of California Press. ISBN 978-0-520-01898-3.
* Timothy Lubin; Donald R. Davis Jr; Jayanth K. Krishnan (2010). *Hinduism and Law: An Introduction*[311]. Cambridge University Press. ISBN 978-1-139-49358-1.

- John Mayne (1991). *A treatise on Hindu law and usage*[312]. Stevens and Haynes, London (Reprinted by Motilal Banarsidass). OCLC 561697663[313].
- Patrick Olivelle (2006). *Between the Empires: Society in India 300 BCE to 400 CE*[314]. Oxford University Press. ISBN 978-0-19-977507-1.
- Patrick Olivelle (1999). *Dharmasutras: The Law Codes of Ancient India*[315]. Oxford University Press. ISBN 978-0-19-283882-7.
- Patrick Olivelle (2005). *Manu's Code of Law*[316]. Oxford University Press. ISBN 978-0-19-517146-4.
- Ludo Rocher (2014). *Studies in Hindu Law and Dharmaśāstra*[317]. Anthem Press. ISBN 978-1-78308-315-2.
- Winternitz, Maurice (1986). *History of Indian Literature*. Motilal Banarsidass Publ. ISBN 81-208-0056-7.
- Nath Dutt, Manmatha (2005). *Yajnavalkyasmrti: Sanskrit Text, English Translation, Notes, Introduction and Index of Verses*. New Delhi: Parimal Publications. ISBN 81-7110-273-5.

External links

- Yájnavalkya Smriti with Vijnanesvara commentary, Book 1 of 3[318] SC Vidyarnava (1918), English translation
- Yájnavalkya Smriti with Vijnanesvara commentary[319] (Sanskrit manuscript)

Arthashastra

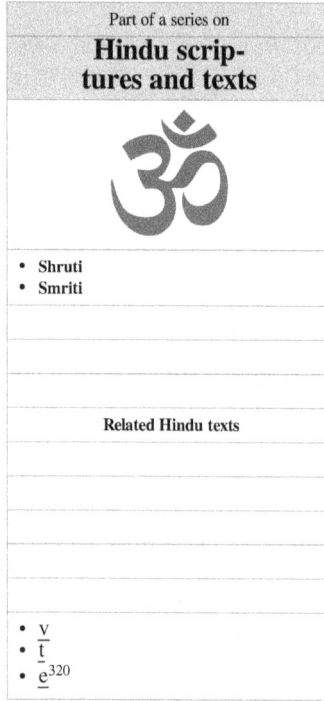

Part of a series on

Hindu scrip-
tures and texts

ॐ

- **Shruti**
- **Smriti**

Related Hindu texts

- <u>v</u>
- <u>t</u>
- <u>e</u>[320]

The **Arthashastra** (IAST: *Arthaśāstra*) is an ancient Indian treatise on state-craft, economic policy and military strategy, written in Sanskrit.[321,322] Likely to be the work of several authors over centuries,[323] Kautilya, also identified as Vishnugupta and Chanakya, is traditionally credited as the author of the text.[324,325] The latter was a scholar at Takshashila, the teacher and guardian of Emperor Chandragupta Maurya.[326] However, scholars have questioned this identification.[327,328]

Composed, expanded and redacted between the 2nd century BCE and 3rd century CE,[329] the Arthashastra was influential until the 12th century, when it disappeared. It was rediscovered in 1905 by R. Shamasastry, who published it in 1909. The first English translation was published in 1915.

The title "Arthashastra" is often translated to "the science of politics",[330] but the book *Arthashastra* has a broader scope. It includes books on the nature of government, law, civil and criminal court systems, ethics, economics, markets and trade, the methods for screening ministers, diplomacy, theories on war, nature of peace, and the duties and obligations of a king.[331,332,333] The text incorporates Hindu philosophy,[334] includes ancient economic and cultural details on agriculture, mineralogy, mining and metals, animal husbandry, medicine, forests and wildlife.[335]

The *Arthashastra* explores issues of social welfare, the collective ethics that hold a society together, advising the king that in times and in areas devastated by famine, epidemic and such acts of nature, or by war, he should initiate public projects such as creating irrigation waterways and building forts around major strategic holdings and towns and exempt taxes on those affected.[336] The text was influential on other Hindu texts that followed, such as the sections on king, governance and legal procedures included in Manusmriti.[337]

History of the manuscript

The text was considered lost by colonial era scholars, until a manuscript was discovered in 1905.[338] A copy of the Arthashastra in Sanskrit, written on palm leaves, was presented by a Tamil Brahmin from Tanjore to the newly opened Mysore Oriental Library headed by Benjamin Lewis Rice. The text was identified by the librarian Rudrapatnam Shamasastry as the Arthashastra. During 1905-1909, Shamasastry published English translations of the text in installments, in journals *Indian Antiquary* and *Mysore Review*.[338,339]

During 1923-1924, Julius Jolly and Richard Schmidt published a new edition of the text, which was based on a Malayalam script manuscript in the Bavarian State Library. In the 1950s, fragmented sections of a north Indian version of Arthashastra were discovered in form of a Devanagari manuscript in Gujarat. A new edition based on this manuscript was published by Muni Jina Vijay in 1959. In 1960, R. P. Kangle published a critical edition of the text, based on all the available manuscripts.[339] Numerous translations and interpretations of the text have been published since then.[338]

The text is an ancient treatise written in 1st millennium BCE Sanskrit, coded, dense and can be interpreted in many ways, with English and Sanskrit being grammatically and syntactically different languages.[340] It has been called, by Patrick Olivelle—whose translation was published in 2013 by Oxford University Press—as the "most difficult translation project I have ever undertaken", parts of the text are still opaque after a century of modern scholarship, and the translation of Kautilya's masterpiece intrigue and political text remains unsatisfactory.[340]

Authorship, date of writing, and structure

The authorship and date of writing are unknown, and there is evidence that
the surviving manuscripts are not original and have been modified in their history but were most likely completed in the available form between 2nd-century
BCE to 3rd-century CE.[341] Olivelle states that the surviving manuscripts of the
Arthashastra are the product of a transmission that has involved at least three
major overlapping divisions or layers, which together consist of 15 books, 150
chapters and 180 topics.[342] The first chapter of the first book is an ancient table
of contents, while the last chapter of the last book is a short 73 verse epilogue
asserting that all thirty two *Yukti* – elements of correct reasoning methods –
were deployed to create the text.[342]

—*Arthashastra* Books 2.10, 6-7, 10[343]

A notable structure of the treatise is that while all chapters are primarily prose,
each transitions into a poetic verse towards its end, as a marker, a style that is
found in many ancient Hindu Sanskrit texts where the changing poetic meter
or style of writing is used as a syntax code to silently signal that the chapter
or section is ending.[342] All 150 chapters of the text also end with a colophon
stating the title of the book it belongs in, the topics contained in that book (like
an index), the total number of titles in the book and the books in the text.[342]
Finally, the *Arthashastra* text numbers it 180 topics consecutively, and does
not restart from one when a new chapter or a new book starts.[342]

The division into 15, 150 and 180 of books, chapters and topics respectively
was probably not accidental, states Olivelle, because ancient authors of major Hindu texts favor certain numbers, such as 18 Parvas in the epic Mahabharata.[344] The largest book is the second, with 1,285 sentences, while the
smallest is eleventh, with 56 sentences. The entire book has about 5,300 sentences on politics, governance, welfare, economics, protecting key officials and
king, gathering intelligence about hostile states, forming strategic alliances,
and conduct of war, exclusive of its table of contents and the last epilogue-
style book.[344]

Chronology

Olivelle states that the oldest layer of text, the "sources of the Kauṭilya", dates
from the period 150 BCE – 50 CE. The next phase of the work's evolution,
the "Kauṭilya Recension", can be dated to the period 50–125 CE. Finally, the
"Śāstric Redaction" (i.e., the text as we have it today) is dated period 175–300
CE.[341] Detailed examination of astronomical data and place-names suggests
that the work was composed in present-day Gujarat and northern Maharashtra.[341]

Author(s)

It identifies its author by the names "Kauṭilya" and "Vishnugupta" (Viṣṇugupta),[345] both names that are traditionally identified with Chanakya (Cāṇakya) (c. 350–283 BCE).

Stylistic differences within some sections of the surviving manuscripts suggest that it likely includes the work of several authors over the centuries. There is no doubt, states Olivelle, that "revisions, errors, additions and perhaps even subtractions have occurred" in Arthashastra since its final redaction in 300 CE or earlier.[346] The identification of Kauṭilya with the Mauryan minister Chanakya came later.[341]

Translation of the title

Different scholars have translated the word "arthashastra" in different ways.

- R.P. Kangle: "Artha is the sustenance or livelihood of men, and Arthaśāstra is the science of the means to Artha"[347] "science of politics";
- A.L. Basham: a "treatise on polity"[348]
- D.D. Kosambi: "science of material gain"
- G.P. Singh: "science of polity"
- Roger Boesche: "science of political economy"
- Patrick Olivelle: "science of politics"[330]

Artha (prosperity, wealth, purpose, meaning, economic security) is one of the four aims of human life in Hinduism (Puruṣārtha),[349] the others being dharma (laws, duties, rights, virtues, right way of living),[350] kama (pleasure, emotions, sex) and moksha (spiritual liberation).[351] Śāstra is the Sanskrit word for "rules" or "science".

Organization

Arthashastra is divided into 15 book titles, 150 chapters and 180 topics, as follows:[352]

Title	English	Title	English
Raja	King	*Yuvaraja*	Crown prince
Senapati	Chief, armed forces	*Parishad*	Council
Nagarika	Town manager	*Pauravya vaharika*	City overseer
Mantri	Minister	*Karmika*	Works officer
Samnidhatr	Treasurer	*Karmantika*	Director, factories
Antapala	Frontier commander	*Antar vimsaka*	Head, guards

Dauvarika	Chief guard	Gopa	Revenue officer
Purohita	Chaplain	Karanika	Accounts officer
Prasastr	Administrator	Nayaka	Commander
Upayukta	Junior officer	Pradeshtri	Magistrate
Sunyapala	Regent	Adhyaksha	Superintendent

1. On the Subject of Training, 21 chapters, Topics 1-18
2. On the Activities of Superintendents,
   36 chapters, Topics 19-56 (Largest book)
3. On Justices, 20 chapters, Topics 57-75
4. Eradication of Thorns, 13 chapters, Topics 76-88
5. On Secret Conduct, 6 chapters, Topics 89-95
6. Basis of the Circle, 2 chapters, Topics 96-97
7. On the Sixfold Strategy, 18 chapters, Topics 98-126
8. On the Subject of Calamities, 5 chapters, Topics 127-134
9. Activity of a King preparing to March into Battle,
   7 chapters, Topics 135-146
10. On War, 6 chapters, Topics 147-159
11. Conduct toward Confederacies, 1 chapter, Topics 160-161
12. On the Weaker King, 5 chapters, Topics 162-170
13. Means of Capturing a Fort, 5 chapters, Topics 171-176
14. On Esoteric Practices, 4 chapters, Topics 177-179
15. Organization of a Scientific Treatise, 1 chapter, Topic 180

Contents

The need for law, economics and government

The ancient Sanskrit text opens, in chapter 2 of Book 1 (the first chapter is table of contents), by acknowledging that there are a number of extant schools with different theories on proper and necessary number of fields of knowledge, and asserts they all agree that the science of government is one of those fields.[353] It lists the school of *Brihaspati*, the school of *Usanas*, the school of *Manu* and itself as the school of *Kautilya* as examples.[354]

— Kautilya, *Chanakya Sutra 1-6*[355]

The school of *Usanas* asserts, states the text, that there is only one necessary knowledge, the science of government because no other science can start or survive without it.[353] The school of *Brihaspati* asserts, according to Arthashastra, that there are only two fields of knowledge, the science of government and the science of economics (*Varta*[356]</ref> of agriculture, cattle and trade) because all other sciences are intellectual and mere flowering of the temporal life of man.[353] The school of *Manu* asserts, states Arthashastra, that there are three fields of knowledge, the Vedas, the science of government and the science of economics (*Varta* of agriculture, cattle and trade) because these three support each other, and all other sciences are special branch of the Vedas.[353]

The Arthashastra then posits its own theory that there are four necessary fields of knowledge, the Vedas, the *Anvikshaki* (philosophy of *Samkhya, Yoga* and *Lokayata*),[357]</ref> the science of government and the science of economics (*Varta* of agriculture, cattle and trade). It is from these four that all other knowledge, wealth and human prosperity is derived.[353] The Kautilya text thereafter asserts that it is the Vedas that discuss what is Dharma (right, moral, ethical) and what is Adharma (wrong, immoral, unethical), it is the *Varta* that explain what creates wealth and what destroys wealth, it is the science of government that illuminates what is *Nyaya* (justice, expedient, proper) and *Anyaya* (unjust, inexpedient, improper), and that it is *Anvishaki* (philosophy)[358] that is the light of these sciences, as well as the source of all knowledge, the guide to virtues, and the means to all kinds of acts.[353,359] He says of government in general:

> *Without government, rises disorder as in the Matsya nyayamud bhavayati (proverb on law of fishes). In the absence of governance, the strong will swallow the weak. In the presence of governance, the weak resists the strong.*[360,361]

Raja (king)

The best king is the *Raja-rishi*, the sage king.[362]

The *Raja-rishi* has self-control and does not fall for the temptations of the senses, he learns continuously and cultivates his thoughts, he avoids false and flattering advisors and instead associates with the true and accomplished elders, he is genuinely promoting the security and welfare of his people, he enriches and empowers his people, he practices ahimsa (non-violence against all living beings), he lives a simple life and avoids harmful people or activities, he keeps away from another's wife nor craves for other people's property.[362,363] The greatest enemies of a king are not others, but are these six: lust, anger, greed, conceit, arrogance and foolhardiness.[362,358] A just king gains the loyalty of his people not because he is king, but because he is just.[362,364]

Officials, advisors and checks on government

Book 1 and Book 2 of the text discusses how the crown prince should be trained and how the king himself should continue learning, selecting his key *Mantri* (ministers), officials, administration, staffing of the court personnel, magistrates and judges.[365]

Topic 2 of the Arthashastra, or chapter 5 of Book 1, is dedicated to the continuous training and development of the king, where the text advises that he maintain a counsel of elders, from each field of various sciences, whose accomplishments he knows and respects.[366] Topic 4 of the text describes the process of selecting the ministers and key officials, which it states must be based on king's personal knowledge of their honesty and capacity.[367] Kautilya first lists various alternate different opinions among extant scholars on how key government officials should be selected, with *Bharadvaja* suggesting honesty and knowledge be the screen for selection, *Kaunapadanta* suggesting that heredity be favored, *Visalaksha* suggesting that king should hire those whose weaknesses he can exploit, *Parasara* cautioning against hiring vulnerable people because they will try to find king's vulnerability to exploit him instead, and yet another who insists that experience and not theoretical qualification be primary selection criterion.[367]

Kautilya, after describing the conflicting views on how to select officials, asserts that a king should select his *Amatyah* (ministers and high officials) based on the capacity to perform that they have shown in their past work, the character and their values that is accordance with the role.[368] The *Amatyah*, states Arthashastra, must be those with following *Amatya-sampat*: well trained, with foresight, with strong memory, bold, well spoken, enthusiastic, excellence in their field of expertise, learned in theoretical and practical knowledge, pure of character, of good health, kind and philanthropic, free from procrastination, free from ficklemindedness, free from hate, free from enmity, free from anger, and dedicated to dharma.[369,370] Those who lack one or a few of these characteristics must be considered for middle or lower positions in the administration, working under the supervision of more senior officials.[369] The text describes tests to screen for the various *Amatya-sampat*.[369]

The Arthashastra, in Topic 6, describes checks and continuous measurement, in secret, of the integrity and lack of integrity of all ministers and high officials in the kingdom.[371] Those officials who lack integrity must be arrested. Those who are unrighteous, should not work in civil and criminal courts. Those who lack integrity in financial matters or fall for the lure of money must not be in revenue collection or treasury, states the text, and those who lack integrity in sexual relationships must not be appointed to *Vihara* services (pleasure grounds).[372] The highest level ministers must have been tested and

Figure 12: *Chanakya portrait in 1915 Shamasastry's Arthashastra translation.*

have successfully demonstrated integrity in all situations and all types of allurements.[372,373]

Chapter 9 of Book 1 suggests the king to maintain a council and a *Purohit* (chaplain, spiritual guide) for his personal counsel. The *Purohit* claims the text must be one who is well educated in the Vedas and its six *Angas*.[369]

Causes of impoverishment, lack of motivation and disaffection among people

The Arthashastra, in Topic 109, Book 7 lists the causes of disaffection, lack of motivation and increase in economic distress among people. It opens by stating that wherever "good people are snubbed, and evil people are embraced" distress increases.[374] Wherever officials or people initiate unprecedented violence in acts or words, wherever there is unrighteous acts of violence, disaffection grows. When the king rejects the Dharma, that is "does what ought not to be done, does not do what ought to be done, does not give what ought to be given, and gives what ought not to be given", the king causes people to worry and dislike him.[374,375]

Anywhere, states *Arthashastra* in verse 7.5.22, where people are fined or punished or harassed when they ought not to be harassed, where those that should be punished are not punished, where those people are apprehended when they ought not be, where those who are not apprehended when they ought to, the king and his officials cause distress and disaffection.[374] When officials engage in thievery, instead of providing protection against robbers, the people are impoverished, they lose respect and become disaffected.[374]

A state, asserts *Arthashastra* text in verses 7.5.24 - 7.5.25, where courageous activity is denigrated, quality of accomplishments are disparaged, pioneers are harmed, honorable men are dishonored, where deserving people are not rewarded but instead favoritism and falsehood is, that is where people lack motivation, are distressed, become upset and disloyal.[374]

In verse 7.5.33, the ancient text remarks that general impoverishment relating to food and survival money destroys everything, while other types of impoverishment can be addressed with grants of grain and money.[374]

Civil, criminal law and court system

— Arthashastra 3.1[376,377]

Book 3 of the Arthashastra, states Trautmann, is dedicated to civil law, including sections relating to economic relations of employer and employee, partnerships, sellers and buyers.[378] Book 4 is a treatise on criminal law, where the king or officials acting on his behalf, take the initiative and start the judicial process against acts of crime, because the crime is felt to be a wrong against the people of the state. This system, states Trautman is similar to European system of criminal law, rather than other historic legal system, because in the European (and Arthashastra) system it is the state that initiates judicial process in cases that fall under criminal statutes, while in the latter systems the aggrieved party initiates a claim in the case of murder, rape, bodily injury among others.

The ancient text stipulates that the courts have a panel of three *pradeshtri* (magistrates) for handling criminal cases, and this panel is different, separate and independent of the panel of judges of civil court system it specifies for a Hindu kingdom. The text lays out that just punishment is one that is in proportion to the crime in many sections starting with chapter 4 of Book 1,[379,380] and repeatedly uses this principle in specifying punishments, for example in Topic 79, that is chapter 2 of Book 4.[381] Economic crimes such as conspiracy by a group of traders or artisans is to be, states the Arthashastra, punished with much larger and punitive collective fine than those individually, as conspiracy causes systematic damage to the well being of the people.[382]

Marriage laws

The text discusses marriage and consent laws in Books 3 and 4. It asserts, in chapter 4.2, that a girl may marry any man she wishes,[383]</ref>[384]</ref> three years after her first menstruation, provided that she does not take her parent's property or ornaments received by her before the marriage. However, if she marries a man her father arranges or approves of, she has the right to take the ornaments with her.[385]

In chapter 3.4, the text gives the right to a woman that she may remarry anyone if she wants to, if she has been abandoned by the man she was betrothed to, if she does not hear back from him for three menstrual periods, or if she does hear back and has waited for seven menses.[386,387]

The chapter 2 of Book 3 of Arthashastra legally recognizes eight types of marriage. The bride is given the maximum property inheritance rights when the parents select the groom and the girl consents to the selection (Brahma marriage), and minimal if bride and groom marry secretly as lovers (Gandharva marriage) without the approval of her father and her mother.[388] However, in cases of Gandharva marriage (love), she is given more rights than she has in Brahma marriage (arranged), if the husband uses the property she owns or has created, with husband required to repay her with interest when she demands.[389]

Wildlife and forests

Arthashastra states that forests be protected and recommends that the state treasury be used to feed animals such as horses and elephants that are too old for work, sick or injured.[390] However, Kautilya also recommends that wildlife that is damaging crops should be restrained with state resources. In Topic 19, chapter 2, the text suggests:

> *The king should grant exemption [from taxes]*
>
> *to a region devastated by an enemy king or tribe,*
>
> *to a region beleaguered by sickness or famine.*
>
> *He should safeguard agriculture*
>
> *when it is stressed by the hardships of fines, forced labor, taxes, and animal herds*
>
> *when they are harassed by thieves, vicious animals, poison, crocodiles or sickness*
>
> *He should keep trade routes [roads] clear*
>
> *when they are oppressed by anyone, including his officers, robbers or frontier commanders*

when they are worn out by farm animals

The king should protect produce, forests, elephants forests, reservoirs and mines

established in the past and also set up new ones.   UNIQ-ref-0-2b539e9a3aa42eb6-QINU

In topic 35, the text recommends that the "Superintendent of Forest Produce" appointed by the state for each forest zone be responsible for maintaining the health of the forest, protecting forests to assist wildlife such as elephants (*hastivana*), but also producing forest products to satisfy economic needs, products such as Teak, Palmyra, Mimosa, Sissu, Kauki, Sirisha, Catechu, Latifolia, Arjuna, Tilaka, Tinisa, Sal, Robesta, Pinus, Somavalka, Dhava, Birch, bamboo, hemp, Balbaja (used for ropes), Munja, fodder, firewood, bulbous roots and fruits for medicine, flowers.[391] The *Arthashastra* also reveals that the Mauryas designated specific forests to protect supplies of timber, as well as lions and tigers, for skins.Wikipedia:Citation needed

Mines, factories and superintendents

The Arthashastra dedicates Topics 30 through 47 discussing the role of government in setting up mines and factories,[392] gold and precious stone workshops,[393] commodities,[394] forest produce,[395] armory,[396] standards for balances and weight measures,[397] standards for length and time measures,[397] customs,[398] agriculture,[399] liquor,[399] abattoirs and courtesans,[400] shipping,[401] domesticated animals such as cattle, horses and elephants along with animal welfare when they are injured or too old,[402] pasture land,[403] military preparedness[404] and intelligence gathering operations of the state.[405]

On spying, propaganda and information

— Arthashastra 11.1[406]

The Arthashastra dedicates many chapters on the need, methods and goals of secret service, and how to build then use a network of spies that work for the state. The spies should be trained to adopt roles and guises, to use coded language to transmit information, and be rewarded by their performance and the results they achieve, states the text.[407]

The roles and guises recommended for *Vyanjana* (appearance) agents by the Arthashastra include ascetics, forest hermits, mendicants, cooks, merchants, doctors, astrologers, consumer householders, entertainers, dancers, female agents and others.[408] It suggests that members from these professions should be sought to serve for the secret service.[409] A prudent state, states the text, must expect that its enemies seek information and are spying inside its territory and spreading propaganda, and therefore it must train and reward double agents to gain identity about such hostile intelligence operations.[410]

The goals of the secret service, in Arthashastra, was to test the integrity of government officials, spy on cartels and population for conspiracy, to monitor hostile kingdoms suspected of preparing for war or in war against the state, to check spying and propaganda wars by hostile states, to destabilize enemy states, to get rid of troublesome powerful people who could not be challenged openly.[411,412] The spy operations and its targets, states verse 5.2.69 of Arthashastra, should be pursued "with respect to traitors and unrighteous people, not with respect to others".[413]

On war and peace

The Arthashastra dedicates Book 7 and 10 to war, and considers numerous scenarios and reasons for war. It classifies war into three broad types – open war, covert war and silent war.[414] It then dedicates chapters to defining each type of war, how to engage in these wars and how to detect that one is a target of covert or silent types of war.[415] The text cautions that the king should know the progress he expects to make, when considering the choice between waging war and pursuing peace.[416] The text asserts:

> When the degree of progress is the same in pursuing peace and waging war, peace is to be preferred. For, in war, there are disadvantages such as losses, expenses and absence from home.[417]

Kautilya, in the Arthashastra, suggests that the state must always be adequately fortified, its armed forces prepared and resourced to defend itself against acts of war. Kautilya favors peace over war, because he asserts that in most situations, peace is more conducive to creation of wealth, prosperity and security of the people.[418] Arthashastra defines the value of peace and the term peace, states Brekke, as "effort to achieve the results of work undertaken is industry, and absence of disturbance to the enjoyment of the results achieved from work is peace".[419]

All means to win a war are appropriate in the Arthashastra, including assassination of enemy leaders, sowing discord in its leadership, engagement of covert men and women in the pursuit of military objectives and as weapons of war, deployment of accepted superstitions and propaganda to bolster one's own troops or to demoralize enemy soldiers, as well as open hostilities by deploying kingdom's armed forces. After success in a war by the victorious just and noble state, the text argues for humane treatment of conquered soldiers and subjects.

The Arthashastra theories are similar with some and in contrast to other alternate theories on war and peace in the ancient Indian tradition. For example, states Brekke, the legends in Hindu epics preach heroism qua heroism which is in contrast to Kautilya suggestion of prudence and never forgetting the four Hindu goals of human life, while Kamandaki's *Nitisara*, which is similar to Kautilya's *Arthashastra*, is among other Hindu classics on statecraft and foreign policy that suggest prudence, engagement and diplomacy, peace is preferable and must be sought, and yet prepared to excel and win war if one is forced to.[420]

On regulations and taxes

The Arthashastra discusses a mixed economy, where private enterprise and state enterprise frequently competed side by side, in agriculture, animal husbandry, forest produce, mining, manufacturing and trade.[421] However, royal statutes and officials regulated private economic activities, some economic activity was the monopoly of the state, and a superintendent oversaw that both private and state owned enterprises followed the same regulations.[421] The private enterprises were taxed.[421] Mines were state owned, but leased to private parties for operations, according to chapter 2.12 of the text.[422] The Arthashastra states that protecting the consumer must be an important priority for the officials of the kingdom.[423]

—Stocking the Treasury, *Arthashastra* 5.2.70[424,413]

Arthashastra stipulates restraint on taxes imposed, fairness, the amounts and how tax increases should is implemented. Further, state Waldauer et al., the text suggests that the tax should be "convenient to pay, easy to calculate, inexpensive to administer, equitable and non-distortive, and not inhibit growth.[425] Fair taxes build popular support for the king, states the text, and some manufacturers and artisans, such as those of textiles, were subject to a flat tax.[424] The Arthashastra states that taxes should only be collected from ripened economic activity, and should not be collected from early, unripe stages of economic activity.[424] Historian of economic thought Joseph Spengler notes:

> *Kautilya's discussion of taxation and expenditure gave expression to three Indian principles: taxing power [of state] is limited; taxation should not be felt to be heavy or exclusive [discriminatory]; tax increases should be graduated.*[426]

Agriculture on privately owned land was taxed at the rate of 16.67%, but the tax was exempted in cases of famine, epidemic, and settlement into new pastures previously uncultivated and if damaged during a war.[427] New public projects such as irrigation and water works were exempt from taxes for five years, and major renovations to ruined or abandoned water works were granted

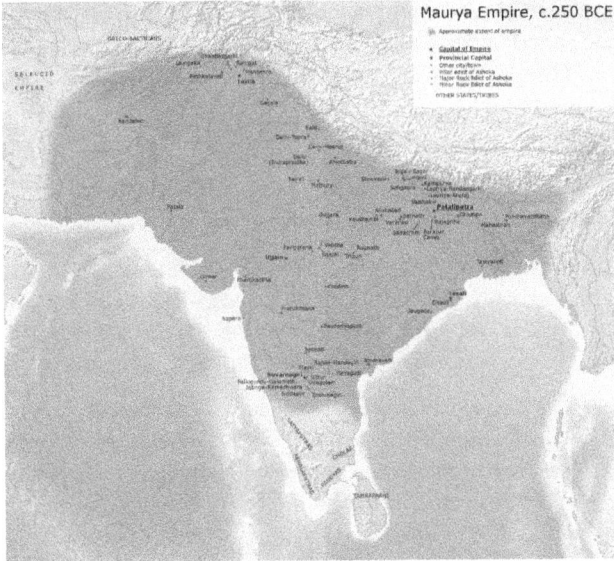

Figure 13: *Maurya Empire in Kautilya's time*

tax exemption for four years.[428] Temple and *gurukul* lands were exempt from taxes, fines or penalties.[429] Trade into and outside the kingdom's borders was subject to toll fees or duties.[430] Taxes varied between 10% to 25% on industrialists and businessmen, and it could be paid in kind (produce), through labor, or in cash.[431]

Translations and scholarship

The text has been translated and interpreted by Shamashastry, Kangle, Trautmann and many others.[432] Recent translations or interpretations include those of Patrick Olivelle[432] and McClish.

Influence and reception

Scholars state that the Arthashastra was influential in Asian history. Its ideas helped create one of the largest empires in South Asia, stretching from the borders of Persia to Bengal on the other side of the Indian subcontinent, with its capital Pataliputra twice as large as Rome under Emperor Marcus Aurelius.

Kautilya's patron Chandragupta Maurya consolidated an empire which was inherited by his son Bindusara and then his grandson Ashoka. With the progressive secularization of society, and with the governance-related innovations contemplated by the *Arthashastra*, India was "prepared for the reception of the great moral transformation ushered in by Ashoka", and the spread of Buddhist, Hindu and other ideas across South Asia, East Asia and southeast Asia.[433,434]

Comparisons to Machiavelli

In 1919, a few years after the newly discovered Arthashastra manuscript's translation was first published, Max Weber stated:

> *Truly radical "Machiavellianism", in the popular sense of that word, is classically expressed in Indian literature in the Arthashastra of Kautilya (written long before the birth of Christ, ostensibly in the time of Chandragupta): compared to it, Machiavelli's The Prince is harmless.*[435]

More recent scholarship has disagreed with the characterization of *Arthashastra* as "Machiavellianism".[436,437] In Machiavelli's *The Prince*, the king and his coterie are single-mindedly aimed at preserving the monarch's power for its own sake, states Paul Brians for example, but in the *Arthashastra*, the king is required "to benefit and protect his citizens, including the peasants". Kautilya asserts in Arthashastra that, "the ultimate source of the prosperity of the kingdom is its security and prosperity of its people", a view never mentioned in Machiavelli's text. The text advocates "land reform", states Brians, where land is taken from landowners and farmers who own land but do not grow anything for a long time, and given to poorer farmers who want to grow crops but do not own any land.

Arthashastra declares, in numerous occasions, the need for empowering the weak and poor in one's kingdom, a sentiment that is not found in Machiavelli; Arthashastra, states Brians, advises "the king shall provide the orphans, the aged, the infirm, the afflicted, and the helpless with maintenance [welfare support]. He shall also provide subsistence to helpless women when they are carrying and also to the children they give birth to".[390] Elsewhere, the text values not just powerless human life, but even animal life and suggests in Book 2 that horses and elephants be given food, when they become incapacitated from old age, disease or after war.[390]

Welfare state but totalitarianism

Roger Boesche, who relied entirely on the 1969 translation by Kangle for his analysis of Arthashastra,[438]</ref> and who criticized an alternate 1992 translation by Rangarajan,[390] has called the Arthashastra as "a great political book of the ancient world".[439] He interprets that the 1st millennium BCE text is grounded more like the Soviet Union and China where the state envisions itself as driven by the welfare of the common good, but operates an extensive spy state and system of surveillance.[440] This view has been challenged by Thomas

Trautmann, who asserts that a free market and individual rights, albeit a regulated system, are proposed by Arthashastra.[441] Boesche is not summarily critical and adds:

> *Kautilya's Arthashastra depicts a bureaucratic welfare state, in fact some kind of socialized monarchy, in which the central government administers the details of the economy for the common good...In addition, Kautilya offers a work of genius in matters of foreign policy and welfare, including key principles of international relations from a realist perspective and a discussion of when an army must use cruel violence and when it is more advantageous to be humane.*[442]

Scholars disagree on how to interpret the document. Kumud Mookerji states that the text may be a picture of actual conditions in Kautilya's times.[443] In contrast, Sastri, as well as Romila Thapar, quotes Brians, caution that the text, regardless of which translation is considered, must be seen as a normative document of strategy and general administration under various circumstances, but not as description of existing conditions.[443] Other scholars such as Burton Stein concur with Thapar and Sastri, however, Bhargava states that given Kautilya was the prime minister, one must expect that he implemented the ideas in the book.[443]

Free market state with guaranteed human rights

Thomas Trautmann states that the *Arthashastra* in chapter 3.9 does recognize the concept of land ownership rights and other private property, and requires king to protect that right from seizure or abuse. This makes it unlike Soviet Union and China model of citizen's private property rights. There is no question, states Trautmann, that people had a power to buy and sell land. However, adds Trautmann, this does not mean that Kautilya was advocating a capitalistic free market economy. Kautilya requires that the land sale be staggered and grants certain buyers automatic "call rights", which is not free market. The Arthashastra states that if someone wants to sell land, the owner's kins, neighbors and creditors have first right of purchase in that order, and only if they do not wish to buy the land for a fair competitive price, others and strangers can bid to buy. Further, the price must be announced in front of witnesses, recorded and taxes paid, for the buy-sale arrangement to deemed recognized by the state. The "call rights" and staggered bid buying is not truly a free market, states Trautmann.[444]

The text dedicates Book 3 and 4 to economic laws, and a court system to oversee and resolve economic, contracts and market-related disputes.[445] The text also provides a system of appeal where three *dharmastha* (judges) consider contractual disputes between two parties, and considers profiteering and false claims to dupe customers a crime. The text, states Trautmann, thus anticipates market exchange and provides a framework for its functioning.

Book on strategy anticipating all scenarios

— Jan Gonda[446]

More recent scholarship presents a more nuanced reception for the text.[447] Paul Brians states that the scope of the work is far broader than earlier much publicized perceptions indicate, and in the treatise can also be found compassion for the poor, for servants and slaves, and for women.

The text, states Sihag, is a treatise on how a state should pursue economic development and it emphasized "proper measurement of economic performance", and "the role of ethics, considering ethical values as the glue which binds society and promotes economic development".[448] Kautilya in Arthashastra, writes Brians, "mixes the harsh pragmatism for which he is famed with compassion for the poor, for slaves, and for women. He reveals the imagination of a romancer in imagining all manner of scenarios which can hardly have been commonplace in real life".

Realism

India's former National Security Adviser, Shiv Shankar Menon, states: "Arthashastra is a serious manual on statecraft, on how to run a state, informed by a higher purpose, clear and precise in its prescriptions, the result of practical experience of running a state. It is not just a normative text but a realist description of the art of running a state". The text is useful, according to Menon, because in many ways "the world we face today is similar to the world that Kautilya operated in". He recommended reading of the book for broadening the vision on strategic issues.

In popular culture

* Mentioned in season 5 episode 22 of the TV show *Blue Bloods*
* The novel *Chanakya's Chant* by Ashwin Sanghi
* The novel *Blowback* by Brad Thor

References

Bibliography

- Boesche, Roger (2002), *The First Great Political Realist: Kautilya and His Arthashastra*, Lanham: Lexington Books, ISBN 0-7391-0401-2
- Kangle, R. P. (1969), *Kautilya Arthashastra, 3 vols*, Motilal Banarsidass (Reprinted 2010), ISBN 978-8120800410
- Mabbett, I. W. (April 1964). "The Date of the Arthaśāstra". *Journal of the American Oriental Society*. **84** (2): 162–169. JSTOR 597102[449]. doi: 10.2307/597102[450].
- Olivelle, Patrick (2013), *King, Governance, and Law in Ancient India: Kauṭilya's Arthaśāstra*[451], Oxford UK: Oxford University Press, ISBN 978-0199891825, retrieved 2016-02-20
- Rangarajan, L.N. (1992), *Kautilya: The Arthashastra*, Penguin Classics, ISBN 0-14-044603-6
- Rao, Velcheru; Subrahmanyam, Sanjay (2013), "Notes on Political Thought in Medieval and Early Modern South India", in Richard M. Eaton; Munis D. Faruqui; David Gilmartin; Sunil Kumar, *Expanding Frontiers in South Asian and World History: Essays in Honour of John F. Richards*[452], Cambridge University Press, pp. 164–199, ISBN 978-1-107-03428-0, retrieved 2016-02-20
- Trautmann, Thomas R. (1971), *Kauṭilya and the Arthaśāstra: A Statistical Investigation of the Authorship and Evolution of the Text*, Leiden: E.J. Brill
- *Arthashastra-Studien*, Dieter Schlingloff, Wiener Zeitschrift für die Kunde Süd- und Ostasiens, vol. 11, 1967, 44-80 + Abb. 1a-30, ISSN 0084-0084.
- Ratan Lal Basu and Raj Kumar Sen, *Ancient Indian Economic Thought, Relevance for Today*, ISBN 81-316-0125-0, Rawat Publications, New Delhi, 2008

External links

- The full text of *Arthashastra* at Wikisource (First English translation, 1915 by R Shamasastry)
- *Arthashastra* (English)[453] (Another archive of 1915 R Shamasastry translation)

Dharmaśāstra

Part of a series on

Hindu scrip-
tures and texts

ॐ

- Shruti
- Smriti

Related Hindu texts

- v
- t
- e[454]

Dharmaśāstra (Sanskrit: धर्मशास्त्र) is a genre of Sanskrit texts, and refers to the treatises (shastras) of Hinduism on dharma. There are many Dharmashastras, variously estimated to be 18 to about 100, with different and conflicting points of view.[455,456]</ref> Each of these texts exist in many different versions, and each is rooted in Dharmasutras texts dated to 1st millennium BCE that emerged from Kalpa (Vedanga) studies in the Vedic era.[457,458]

The textual corpus of Dharmaśāstra were composed in poetic verses,[459] are part of the Hindu Smritis,[460] constituting divergent commentaries and treatises on duties, responsibilities and ethics to oneself, to family and as a member of society.[461,462] The texts include discussion of ashrama (stages of life), varna (social classes), purushartha (proper goals of life), personal virtues and duties such as ahimsa (non-violence) against all living beings, rules of just war, and other topics.[463,464]

Dharmaśāstra became influential in modern colonial India history, when they were formulated by early British colonial administrators to be the law of the land for all non-Muslims (Hindus, Jains, Buddhists, Sikhs) in India, after Sharia was already accepted as the law for Muslims in colonial India.[465]

Figure 14: *Copy of a royal land grant, recorded on copper plate, made by Chalukya King Tribhuvana Malla Deva in 1083*

History

The Dharmashastras are based on ancient Dharmasūtras texts, which themselves emerged from the literary tradition of the Vedas (Rig, Yajur, Sāma, and Atharva) composed in 2nd millennium BCE to the early centuries of the 1st millennium BCE. These Vedic branches split into various other schools (*shakhas*) possibly for a variety of reasons such as geography, specialization and disputes.[466] Each Veda is further divided into two categories namely the Samhitā which is a collection of mantra verses and the Brahmanas which are prose texts that explain the meaning of the Samhita verses. The Brāhmaṇa layer expanded and some of the newer esoteric speculative layers of text were called Aranyakas while the mystical and philosophical sections came to be called the Upanishads.[467] The Vedic basis of Dharma literature is found in the Brahmana layer of the Vedas.

Towards the end of the vedic period, after the middle of the 1st millennium BCE, the language of the Vedic texts composed centuries earlier grew too archaic to the people of that time. This led to the formation of Vedic Supplements called the Vedangas which literally means 'limbs of the Veda'. The

Vedangas were ancillary sciences that focused on understanding and interpreting the Vedas composed many centuries earlier, and included Shiksha (phonetics, syllable), Chandas (poetic metre), Vyakarana (grammar, linguistics), Nirukta (etymology, glossary), Jyotisha (timekeeping, astronomy), and Kalpa (ritual or proper procedures). The Kalpa Vedanga studies gave rise to the Dharma-sutras, which later expanded into Dharma-shastras.[468]

The Dharmasutras

The Dharmasutras were numerous, but only four texts have survived into the modern era.[469] The most important of these texts are the sutras of Apastamba, Gautama, Baudhayana, and Vasistha. These extant texts cite writers and refer opinions of seventeen authorities, implying that a rich Dharmasutras tradition existed prior to when these texts were composed.[470,471]

The extant Dharmasutras are written in concise sutra format,[472] with a very terse incomplete sentence structure which are difficult to understand and leave much to the reader to interpret.[469] The Dharmasastras are derivative works on the Dharmasutras, using a shloka (four 8-syllable verse style chandas poetry, Anushtubh meter), which are relatively clearer.[469,459]

The Dharmasutras can be called the guidebooks of dharma as they contain guidelines for individual and social behavior, ethical norms, as well as personal, civil and criminal law.[469] They discuss the duties and rights of people at different stages of life like studenthood, householdership, retirement and renunciation. These stages are also called ashramas. They also discuss the rites and duties of kings, judicial matters, and personal law such as matters relating to marriage and inheritance. However, Dharmasutras typically did not deal with rituals and ceremonies, a topic that was covered in the Shrautasutras and Grihyasutras texts of the Kalpa (Vedanga).[469]

Style of Composition

The hymns of Rgveda are one of the earliest texts composed in verse. The Brāhmaṇa which belongs to the middle vedic period followed by the vedāṇga are composed in prose. The basic texts are composed in an aphoristic style known as the *sutra* which literally means thread on which each aphorism is strung like a pearl.[473]

The Dharmasūtras are composed in sutra style and were part of a larger compilation of texts, called the Kalpasūtras which give an aphoristic description of the rituals, ceremonies and proper procedures. The Kalpasutras contain three sections, namely the Śrautasūtras which deal with vedic ceremonies, Gṛhyasūtras which deal with rites of passage rituals and domestic matters, and Dharmasūtras which deal with proper procedures in one's life. The Dharmasūtras of Āpastamba and Baudhāyana form a part of larger Kalpasutra texts, all of which has survived into the modern era.

The *sūtra* tradition ended around the beginning of the common era and was followed by the poetic octosyllable verse style called the *śloka*. The verse style was used to compose the Dharmaśāstras such as the Manusmriti, the Hindu epics, and the Puranas.

The age of Smṛtis that ended around the second half of the first millennium CE was followed by that of commentaries around the 9th century called *nibandha*. This legal tradition consisted of commentaries on earlier Dharmasūtras and Smritis.

Authorship and Dates

About 20 Dharmasutras are known, some surviving into the modern era just as fragments of their original.[474] Four Dharmasūtras have been translated into English, and most remain in manuscripts.[474] All carry the names of their authors, but it is still difficult to determine who these real authors were.

The extant Dharmasūtra texts are listed below:

1. *Apastamba (450–350 BCE) this Dharmasūtra forms a part of the larger Kalpasūtra of Apastamba. It contains 1,364 sutras.*[475]
2. *Gautama (600–200 BCE) although this Dharmasūtra comes down as an independent treatise it may have once formed a part of the Kalpasūtra, linked to the Samaveda.*[476] *It is likely the oldest extant Dharma text, and originated in what is modern Maharashtra-Gujarat.*[477] *It contains 973 sutras.*[478]
3. *Baudhāyana (500–200 BCE) this Dharmasūtra like that of Apastamba also forms a part of the larger Kalpasūtra. It contains 1,236 sutras.*[475]
4. *Vāsiṣṭha (300–100 BCE) this Dharmasūtra forms an independent treatise and other parts of the Kalpasūtra, that is Shrauta- and Grihya-sutras are missing.*[474] *It contains 1,038 sutras.*[475]

The Dharmasūtra of Āpastamba and Baudhayana form a part of the Kalpasūtra but it is not easy to establish whether they were historical authors of these texts or whether these texts were composed within certain institutions attributed to their names. Moreover, Gautama and Vasiṣṭha are ancient sages related to specific vedic schools and therefore it is hard to say whether they were historical authors of these texts.[479] The issue of authorship is further complicated by the fact that apart from Āpastamba the other Dharmasūtras have various alterations made at later times.[479]

— *Vasishtha Dharmasutra 30.1*[480]

There is uncertainty regarding the dates of these documents due to lack of evidence concerning these documents. Kane has posited the following dates for the texts, for example, though other scholars disagree: Gautama 600 BCE to 400 BCE, Āpastamba 450 BCE to 350 BCE, Baudhāyana 500 BCE to 200 BCE, and Vasiṣṭha 300 BCE to 100 BCE.[481] Patrick Olivelle suggests that Apastamba Dharmasutra is the oldest of the extant texts in Dharmasutra genre and one by Gautama second oldest, while Robert Lingat suggests that Gautama Dharmasutra is the oldest.[482,477]

There is confusion regarding the geographical provenance of these documents. According to Bühler and Kane, Āpastamba came from South India probably from a region corresponding to modern Andhra Pradesh.[483] Baudhāyana also came from south although evidence regarding this is weaker than that of Āpastamba.[483] Gautama likely came from western region, nearer to the northwestern region to which Pāṇini belonged, and one which corresponds to where Maratha people in modern India are found.[476] Nothing can be said about Vasiṣṭha due to lack of any evidence.[484]

Scholars have varied opinions about the chronology of these documents. Regarding the age of Āpastamba and Gautama there are opposite conclusions. According to Bühler and Lingat Āpastamba is younger than Baudhāyana. Vasiṣṭha is surely a later text.[484]

Literary structure

The structure of these Dharmasūtras primarily addresses the Brahmins both in subject matter and the audience.[485] The Brahmins are the creators and primary consumers of these texts.[485] The subject matter of Dharmasūtras is *dharma*. The central focus of these texts is how a Brahmin male should conduct himself during his lifetime.[485] The text of Āpastamba which is best preserved has a total of 1,364 sūtras out of which 1,206 (88 per cent) are devoted to the Brahmin, whereas only 158 (12 per cent) deals with topics of general nature.[486] The structure of the Dharmasūtras begin with the vedic initiation of a young boy followed by entry into adulthood, marriage and responsibilities of adult life that includes adoption, inheritance, death rituals and ancestral offerings.[486] According to Olivelle, the reason Dharmasutras introduced vedic initiation was to make the individual subject to Dharma precepts at school, by making him a 'twice born' man, because children were considered exempt from Dharma precepts in the vedic tradition.[486]

The structure of Dharmasūtra of Āpastamba begins with the duties of the student, then describes householder duties and rights such as inheritance, and ends with administration of the king.[487] This forms the early structure of the Dharma texts. However, in the Dharmasūtras of Gautama, Baudhāyana and Vasiṣṭha some sections such as inheritance and penance are reorganized, and moved from householder section to king-related section.[487] Ollivelle suggests that these changes may be because of chronological reasons where civil law increasingly became part of the king's administrative responsibilities.[487]

The meaning of Dharma

Dharma is a concept which is central not only in Hinduism (Brahmanical traditions) but also in Jainism and Buddhism.[488] The term means a lot of things and has a wide scope of interpretation.[488] The fundamental meaning of *Dharma* in Dharmasūtras, states Olivelle is diverse, and includes accepted norms of behavior, procedures within a ritual, moral actions, righteousness and ethical attitudes, civil and criminal law, legal procedures and penance or punishment, and guidelines for proper and productive living.[489]

The term Dharma also includes social institutions such as marriage, inheritance, adoption, work contracts, judicial process in case of disputes, as well personal choices such as meat as food and sexual conduct.[490]

The source of Dharma: scriptures or empiricism

The source of *dharma* was a question that loomed in the minds of Dharma text writers, and they tried to seek "where guidelines for Dharma can be found?"[491] They sought to define and examine vedic injunctions as the source of Dharma, asserting that like the Vedas, *Dharma* is not of human origin.[491] This worked for rituals-related rules, but in all other matters this created numerous interpretations and different derivations.[491] This led to documents with various working definitions, such as dharma of different regions (*deshadharma*), of social groups (*jatidharma*), of different families (*kuladharma*).[491] The authors of Dharmasutras and Dharmashastra admit that these *dharmas* are not found in the Vedic texts, nor can the behavioral rules included therein be found in any of the Vedas.[491] This led to the incongruity between the search for legal codes and dharma rules in the theological versus the reality of epistemic origins of dharma rules and guidelines.[491]

The Hindu scholar Āpastamba, in a Dharmasutra named after him (~400 BCE), made an attempt to resolve this issue of incongruity. He placed the importance of the Veda scriptures second and that of *samayacarika* or mutually agreed and accepted customs of practice first.[492] Āpastamba thus proposed that scriptures alone cannot be source of Law (dharma), and dharma has an empirical nature.[492] Āpastamba asserted that it is difficult to find absolute sources of law, in ancient books or current people, states Patrick Olivelle with, "The Righteous (dharma) and the Unrighteous (adharma) do not go around saying, 'here we are!'; Nor do gods, Gandharvas or ancestors declare, 'This is righteous and that is unrighteous'."[492] Most laws are based on agreement between the Aryas, stated Āpastamba, on what is right and what is wrong.[492]

Laws must also change with ages, stated Āpastamba, a theory that became known as *Yuga dharma* in Hindu traditions.[493] Āpastamba also asserted in verses 2.29.11–15, states Olivelle, that "aspects of dharma not taught in Dharmasastras can be learned from women and people of all classes".[494]

Āpastamba used a hermeneutic strategy that asserted that the Vedas once contained all knowledge including that of ideal Dharma, but parts of Vedas have been lost.[493] Human customs developed from the original complete Vedas, but given the lost text, one must use customs between good people as a source to infer what the original Vedas might have stated the Dharma to be.[493] This theory, called the 'lost Veda' theory, made the study of customs of good people as a source of dharma and guide to proper living, states Olivelle.[493]

— *Gautama Dharmasutras 13.2–13.6*[495,496]

The sources of *dharma* according to Gautama Dharmasutra are three: the Vedas, the Smriti (tradition), acāra (the practice) of those who know the Veda. These three sources are also found in later Dharmashastra literature.[493] Baudhāyana Dharmasutra lists the same three, but calls the third as śiṣṭa (शिष्ट, literally polite cultured people)[497]</ref> or the practice of cultured people as the third source of dharma.[493] Both Baudhāyana Dharmasutra and Vāsiṣṭha Dharmasutra make the practices of śiṣṭa as a source of dharma, but both state that the geographical location of such polite cultured people does not limit the usefulness of universal precepts contained in their practices.[493] In case of conflict between different sources of dharma, Gautama Dharmasutra states that the Vedas prevail over other sources, and if two Vedic texts are in conflict then the individual has a choice to follow either.[498]

The nature of Dharmasūtras is normative, they tell what people ought to do, but they do not tell what people actually did.[499] Some scholars state that these sources are unreliable and worthless for historical purposes instead to use archaeology, epigraphy and other historical evidence to establish the actual legal codes in Indian history. Olivelle states that the dismissal of normative texts is unwise, as is believing that the Dharmasutras and Dharmashastras texts present a uniform code of conduct and there were no divergent or dissenting views.[499]

The Dharmaśāstras

Written after the Dharmasūtras, these texts use a metered verse and are much more elaborate in their scope than Dharmasutras.[500] The word *Dharmaśāstras* never appears in the Vedic texts, and the word *śāstra* itself appears for the first time in Yaska's *Nirukta* text.[501] Katyayana's commentary on Panini's work (∼3rd century BCE), has the oldest known single mention of the word *Dharmaśāstras*.[501]

The extant Dharmaśāstras texts are listed below:

1. *The Manusmriti (∼ 2nd to 3rd century CE)[502,503] is the most studied and earliest metrical work of the Dharmaśāstra textual tradition of Hinduism.[504] The medieval era Buddhistic law of Myanmar and Thailand are also ascribed to Manu,[505,506] and the text influenced past Hindu kingdoms in Cambodia and Indonesia.[507]*

2. *The Yājñavalkya Smṛti (∼ 4th to 5th-century CE)[502] has been called the "best composed" and "most homogeneous"[608] text of the Dharmaśāstra tradition, with its superior vocabulary and level of sophistication. It may have been more influential than Manusmriti as a legal theory text.[509,510]*

3. *The Nāradasmṛti (∼ 5th to 6th-century CE)[502] has been called the "juridical text par excellence" and represents the only Dharmaśāstra text which deals solely with juridical matters and ignoring those of righteous conduct and penance.[511]*

4. *The Viṣṇusmṛti (∼ 7th-century CE)[502] is one of the latest books of the Dharmaśāstra tradition in Hinduism and also the only one which does not deal directly with the means of knowing dharma, focusing instead on the bhakti tradition.[512]*

In addition, numerous other Dharmaśāstras are known,[513,514]</ref> partially or indirectly, with very different ideas, customs and conflicting versions.[515] For example, the manuscripts of Bṛhaspatismṛti and the Kātyāyanasmṛti have not been found, but their verses have been cited in other texts, and scholars have made an effort to extract these cited verses, thus creating a modern reconstruction of these texts.[516] Scholars such as Jolly and Aiyangar have gathered some 2,400 verses of the lost Bṛhaspatismṛti text in this manner.[516] Brihaspati-smriti was likely a larger and more comprehensive text than Manusmriti,[516] yet both Brihaspati-smriti and Katyayana-smriti seem to have been predominantly devoted to judicial process and jurisprudence.[517] The writers of Dharmasastras acknowledged their mutual differences, and developed a "doctrine of consensus" reflecting regional customs and preferences.[518]

Of the four extant Dharmasastras, Manusmriti, Yajnavalkyasmriti and Naradasmriti are the most important surviving texts.[519] But, states Robert Lingat, numerous other Dharmasastras whose manuscripts are now missing, have enjoyed equal authority.[519] Between the three, the Manusmriti became famous during the colonial British India era, yet modern scholarship states that other Dharmasastras such as the Yajnavalkyasmriti appear to have played a greater role in guiding the actual Dharma.[520] Further, the Dharmasastras were open texts, and they underwent alterations and rewriting through their history.[521]

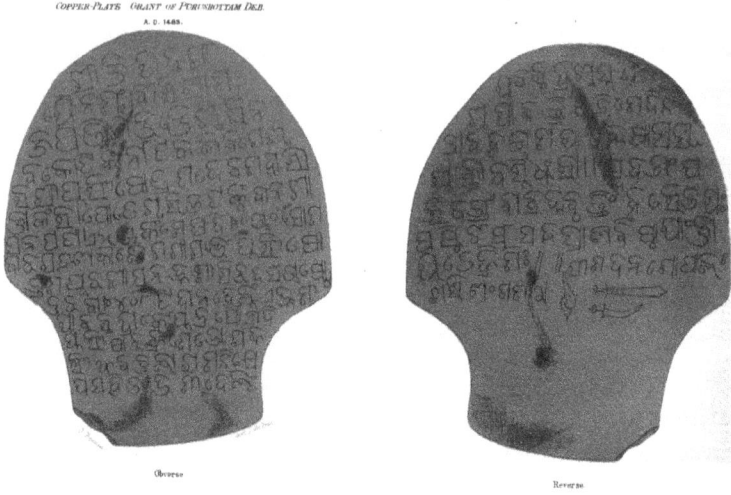

Figure 15: *A facsimile of an inscription in Oriya script on a copper plate recording a land grant made by Rāja Purushottam Deb, king of Odisha, in the fifth year of his reign (1483). Land grants made by royal decree were protected by law, with deeds often being recorded on metal plates*

Contents of Dharmasutras and Dharmaśāstra

All Dharma, in Hindu traditions, has its foundation in the Vedas.[467] The Dharmashastra texts enumerate four sources of Dharma – the precepts in the Vedas, the tradition, the virtuous conduct of those who know the Vedas, and approval of one's conscience (Atmanastushti, self satisfaction).[522]

The Dharmashastra texts include conflicting claims on the sources of dharma. The theological claim therein asserts, without any elaboration, that Dharma just like the Vedas are eternal and timeless, the former is directly or indirectly related to the Vedas.[523] Yet these texts also acknowledge the role of Smriti, customs of polite learned people, and one's conscience as source of dharma.[522,523] The historical reality, states Patrick Olivelle, is very different than the theological reference to the Vedas, and the dharma taught in the Dharmaśāstra has little to do with the Vedas.[523] These were customs, norms or pronouncements of the writers of these texts that were likely derived from evolving regional ethical, ideological, cultural and legal practices.[524]

The Dharmasutra and Dharmaśāstra texts, as they have survived into the modern era, were not authored by a single author. They were viewed by the ancient and medieval era commentators, states Olivelle, to be the works of many authors.[525] Robert Lingat adds that these texts suggest that "a rich literature on dharma already existed" before these were first composed.[526] These texts were revised and interpolated through their history because the various text manuscripts discovered in India are inconsistent with each other, and within themselves, raising concerns of their authenticity.[527,528,529]

The Dharmaśāstra texts present their ideas under various categories such as Acara, Vyavahara, Prayascitta and others, but they do so inconsistently.[530] Some discuss Acara but do not discuss Vyavahara, as is the case with *Parasara-Smriti* for instance,[531] while some solely discuss Vyavahara.[517]

Ācāra

Ācāra (आचार) literally means "good behavior, custom".[532,533] It refers to the normative behavior and practices of a community, conventions and behaviors that enable a society and various individuals therein to function.[534,535]

Vyavahāra

Vyavahāra (व्यवहार) literally means "judicial procedure, process, practice, conduct".[536,537] The due process, honesty in testimony, considering various sides, was justified by Dharmashastra authors as a form of Vedic sacrifice, failure of the due process was declared to be a sin.[538,539]

The Vyavahara sections of Dharma texts included chapters on duties of a king, court system, judges and witnesses, judicial process, crimes and penance or punishment.[537] However, the discussions and procedures in different Dharmasutra and Dharmashastra texts diverge significantly.[537]

Some Dharmaśāstra texts such as that attributed to Brihaspati, are almost entirely Vyavahāra-related texts. These were probably composed in the common era, around or after 5th-century of 1st millennium.[517]

Prāyaścitta

Prāyaścitta (प्रायश्चित्त) literally means "atonement, expiation, penance".[540,541] Prāyaścittas are asserted by the Dharmasutra and Dharmashastra texts as an alternative to incarceration and punishment,[541] and a means of expiating bad conduct or sin such as adultery by a married person.[542] Thus, in the Apastambha text, a willing sexual act between a male and female is subject to penance, while rape is covered by harsher judicial punishments, with a few texts such as Manusmriti suggesting public punishments in extreme cases.[541]

Those texts that discuss Prāyaścitta, states Robert Lingat, debate the intent and thought behind the improper act, and consider penance appropriate when the "effect" had to be balanced, but "cause" was unclear.[543] The roots of this theory are found in the Brahmana layer of text in the Samaveda.[544]

Secondary works

The Dharmasutras and Dharmasastras attracted secondary works called commentaries (Bhashya) would typically interpret and explain the text of interest, accept or reject the ideas along with reasons why.[545]

Commentaries (*bhasya*) on Dharmasastras

Dharmasas-tra	Author of Commentary
Manu-smriti	Bhāruci (600–1050 CE),[546] Medhātithi (820–1050 CE),[547] Govindarāja (11th-century),[548] Kullūka (1200–1500 CE),[548] Narayana (14th-century),[548] Nandana,[548] Raghavananda,[548] Ramacandra[548]
Yajnavalkya Smriti	Visvarupa (750–1000 CE), Vijanesvara (11th or 12th century, most studied), Apararka (12th-century), Sulapani (14th or 15th century), Mitramisra (17th-century)
Narada-smriti	Kalyāṇbhaṭṭa (based on Asahaya's work)
Visnu-smriti	Nandapaṇḍita

Another category of secondary literature derived from the Dharmasutras and Dharmasastras were the digests (*nibandhas*, sometimes spelled *nibhandas*). These arose primarily because of the conflict and disagreements on a particular subject across the various Dharma texts. These digests attempted to reconcile, bridge or suggest a compromise guideline to the numerous disagreements in the primary texts, however the digests in themselves disagreed with each other even on basic principles. Geographically, the medieval era digest writers came from many different parts of South Asia, such as Assam, Bengal, Bihar, Gujarat, Kashmir, Karnataka, Maharashtra, Odisha, Tamil Nadu, and Uttar Pradesh. The oldest surviving digest on Dharma texts is *Krityakalpataru*, from early 12th-century, by Lakshmidhara of Kannauj in north India, belonging to the Varanasi school.

The digests were generally arranged by topic, referred to many different Dharmasastras for their contents. They would identify an idea or rule, add their comments, then cite contents of different Dharma texts to support or explain their view.

Digests (*nibhandas*) on Dharmasastras

Subject	Author of Digests
General	Lakṣmīdhara (1104–1154 CE), Devaṇṇa-bhaṭṭan (1200 CE), Pratāparuda-deva (16th-century),[549] Nīlakaṇṭha (1600–1650), Dalpati (16th-century), Kashinatha (1790)
Inheritance	Jīmūtavāhana, Raghunandana
Adoption	Nanda-paṇḍita (16th–17th century)[550]
King's duties	Caṇḍeśvara, Ṭoḍar Mal (16th century, sponsored by the Mughal emperor Akbar)
Judicial process	Caṇḍeśvara (14th century), Kamalākara-bhatta (1612), Nīlakaṇṭha (17th century), Mitra-miśra (17th century)

Women jurists

A few notable historic digests on Dharmasastras were written by women. These include Lakshmidevi's *Vivadachandra* and Mahadevi Dhiramati's *Danavakyavali*. Lakshmidevi, state West and Bühler, gives a latitudinarian views and widest interpretation to *Yajnavalkya Smriti*, but her views were not widely adopted by male legal scholars of her time. The scholarly works of Lakshmidevi were also published with the pen name *Balambhatta*, and are now considered classics in legal theories on inheritance and property rights, particularly for women.

Dharma texts and the schools of Hindu philosophy

The Mimamsa school of Hindu philosophy developed textual hermeneutics, theories on language and interpretation of Dharma, ideas which contributed to the Dharmasutras and Dharmasastras.[551] The Vedanga fields of grammar and linguistics – Vyakarana and Nirukta – were the other significant contributors to the Dharma-text genre.[551]

Mimamsa literally means the "desire to think", states Donald Davis, and in colloquial historical context "how to think, interpret things, and the meaning of texts".[551] In the early portions of the Vedas, the focus was largely on the rituals; in the later portions, largely on philosophical speculations and the spiritual liberation (moksha) of the individual.[551] The Dharma-texts, over time and each in its own way, attempted to present their theories on rules and duties of individuals from the perspective of a society, using the insights of hermeneutics and on language developed by Mimamsa and Vedanga.[551,552] The Nyaya school of Hindu philosophy, and its insights into the theories on logic and reason, contributed to the development of and disagreements between the Dharmasastra texts, and the term *Nyaya* came to mean "justice".[553,554]

Influence

Dharmaśāstras played an influential role in modern era colonial India history, when they were used as the basis for the law of the land for all non-Muslims (Hindus, Jains, Buddhists, Sikhs).

In 18th century, the earliest British of the East India Company acted as agents of the Mughal emperor. As the British colonial rule took over the political and administrative powers in India, it was faced with various state responsibilities such as legislative and judiciary functions.[555] The East India Company, and later the British Crown, sought profits for its British shareholders through trade as well as sought to maintain effective political control with minimal military engagement. The administration pursued a path of least resistance, relying upon co-opted local intermediaries that were mostly Muslims and some Hindus in various princely states. The British exercised power by avoiding interference and adapting to law practices as explained by the local intermediaries. The colonial policy on the system of personal laws for India, for example, was expressed by Governor-General Hastings in 1772 as follows,

> That in all suits regarding inheritance, marriage, caste and other religious usages or institutions, the law of the Koran with respect to Mahometans, and those of the Shaster [Dharmaśāstra] with respect to Gentoos shall be invariably be adhered to.

— Warren Hastings, August 15, 1772

For Muslims of India, the Sharia or the religious law for Muslims was readily available in al-Hidaya and Fatawa-i Alamgiri written under the sponsorship of Aurangzeb. For Hindus and other non-Muslims such as Buddhists, Sikhs, Jains, Parsis and Tribal people, this information was unavailable. The British colonial officials extracted from the Dharmaśāstra, the legal code to apply on non-Muslims for the purposes of colonial administration.[556,557]

The Dharmashastra-derived laws for non-Muslim Indians were dissolved after India gained independence, but Indian Muslim Personal Law (Shariat) Application Act of 1937 continued to be the personal and family law for Indian Muslims. For non-Muslims, a non-religious uniform civil code was passed by Indian parliament in the 1950s, and amended by its elected governments thereafter, which has since then applied to all non-Muslim Indians.

Major English Translations

1. Best for beginners

- Olivelle, Patrick. 1999. *Dharmasūtras: The Law Codes of Āpastamba, Gautama, Baudhāyana, and Vāsiṣṭha*. New York: Oxford UP.
- Olivelle, Patrick. 2004. *The Law Code of Manu*[558]. New York: Oxford UP.

2. Other major translations

- Kane, P.V. (ed. and trans.) 1933. *Kātyāyanasmṛti on Vyavahāra (Law and Procedure)*. Poona: Oriental Book Agency.
- Lariviere, Richard W. 2003. *The Nāradasmṛti*. 2nd rev. ed. Delhi: Motilal Banarsidass.
- Rocher, Ludo. 1956. *Vyavahāracintāmani: a digest on Hindu legal procedure*. Gent.

3. Early translations with full-text online

- Jha, Ganganath (trans.), Manusmṛti with the Manubhāṣyya of Medhātithi[559], including additional notes, 1920.
- Bühler, Georg (trans.), The Laws of Manu[560], SBE Vol. 25, 1886.
- Bühler, Georg (trans.), The Sacred Laws of the Āryas[561], SBE Vol. 2, 1879 [Part 1: Āpastamba and Gautama]
- Bühler, Georg (trans.), The Sacred Laws of the Āryas[562], SBE Vol. 14, 1882 [Part 2: Vāsiṣṭha and Baudhāyana]
- Jolly, Julius (trans.), The Institutes of Viṣṇu[563], SBE Vol. 7, 1880.
- Jolly, Julius (trans.), The Minor Law-Books[564], SBE Vol. 33. Oxford, 1889. [contains both *Bṛhaspatismṛti* and *Nāradasmṛti*]

References

Bibliography

- Donald R. Davis, Jr (2010). *The Spirit of Hindu Law*[565]. Cambridge University Press. ISBN 978-1-139-48531-9.
- Mandagadde Rama Jois (1984). *Legal and Constitutional History of India: Ancient legal, judicial, and constitutional system*[566]. Universal Law Publishing. ISBN 978-81-7534-206-4.
- Kane, P.V. (1973). *History of DharmaŚāstra*. Poona: Bhandarkar Oriental research Institute.
- Translation by Richard W. Lariviere (1989). *The Nāradasmṛti*. University of Philadelphia.

- Flood, Gavin (1996). *An Introduction to Hinduism*. Cambridge: Cambridge University Press. ISBN 0-521-43878-0.
- Timothy Lubin; Donald R. Davis Jr; Jayanth K. Krishnan (2010). *Hinduism and Law: An Introduction*[567]. Cambridge University Press. ISBN 978-1-139-49358-1.
- Robert Lingat (1973). *The Classical Law of India*[568]. University of California Press. ISBN 978-0-520-01898-3.
- Patrick Olivelle (1999). *Dharmasutras: The Law Codes of Ancient India*[569]. Oxford University Press. ISBN 978-0-19-283882-7.
- Patrick Olivelle (2005). *Manu's Code of Law*[570]. Oxford University Press. ISBN 978-0-19-517146-4.
- Patrick Olivelle (2006). *Between the Empires: Society in India 300 BCE to 400 CE*[571]. Oxford University Press. ISBN 978-0-19-977507-1.
- Ludo Rocher (2008). Gavin Flood, ed. *The Blackwell Companion to Hinduism*[572]. John Wiley & Sons. ISBN 978-0-470-99868-7.

External links

- Various Dharma Shastras Vol 1[573], MN Dutt (Translator), Hathi Trust
- Various Dharma Shastras Vol 2[574], MN Dutt (Translator), Hathi Trust
- The Cooperative Annotated Bibliography of Hindu Law and Dharmaśāstra[575]
- Alois Payer's Dharmaśāstra Site (in German, with copious extracts in English)[576]
- "Maharishi University of Management – Vedic Literature Collection"[577] A Sanskrit reference to the texts of all 18 Smritis.

Classical Hindu law

Part of a series on

Hinduism

- **Hindu**
- **History**

- **Glossary of Hinduism terms**
- ॐ *Hinduism portal*

- <u>v</u>
- <u>t</u>
- <u>e</u>[578]

Classical Hindu law is a category of Hindu law (dharma) in traditional Hinduism, taken to begin with the transmittance of the Vedas and ending in 1772 with the adoption of "A Plan for the Administration of Justice in Bengal" by the Bengal government.[579] Law during the classical period was theologically based on the dharmasastra, and dharma which was traditionally delineated by "learned people" or scholars of the Vedas.[580] However, in reality, classical Hindu law was diverse in practice, varying between locations, vocational groups, and castes. Thus, the common source of classical Hindu law was the community and, therefore, laws on a whole were highly decentralized and diverse.[581] These laws were dictated by various corporate groups such as merchant leaders, heads of caste, and kings, and because of the diverse leadership, these laws were particular to a set place.[582] Records of classical Hindu law can be found in the Manu Smriti and other smṛti literature; although, actual court records during this time period are rare.

Sources

Classical Hindu law was theologically based on the Dharmasastras. Traditionally these texts established the rules of dharma which could be found through
three sources. Theologically the most important source for dharma was from
the śruti or Veda because it was acknowledged to be of divine origin. If one
could not find a particular idea in the Vedas, the Dharmasutras instructed him
or her to consult the next source of authority: smṛti followed then by ācāra and
in some cases ātmatuṣṭi.[583]

> *The Law is set forth in the Vedas and the Traditional Texts. When these do
> not address an issue, the practice of cultured people becomes authoritative.*
> (VaDh 1.4-5)

However, ācāra was the law that was conveyed in actual practice.[584]

Śruti

Śruti is a section of texts that are learned through hearing and are synonymous
with the Vedas.[585] Originally transmitted to ancient Rishis by way of cosmic
vibration, the texts are considered the highest form of revelation.[586] Because
of their divine origin, the texts were passed orally through the generations by
a select group of people who were granted the power to interpret the texts
into more tangible laws. Although the texts themselves contain no specific law
codes or rules, they are the claimed source for all classical Hindu Laws.[587]
These texts contain the four Vedas and the supplementary commentary associated with them.

Smṛti

Smriti, defined as tradition, is the second source of dharma and specifically
refers to the written texts which cite the traditions of lawful virtuous people.
These texts include the Dharmasastras.[588] Smriti refers to the collections of
acara or customary law wherein learning takes place. Smriti is the testimony
of people who know the Vedas and is considered as the secondary Veda. Unlike Sruti, revelation, Smriti is based on memory; specifically those of sages
who transmit their memories of traditions onto men as a means of passing
down their wisdom. Smriti also represents the complete set of sacred literature: the six Vedangas, the epics (the Mahabharata and the Ramayana) and
the Puranas.[589]

Ācāra

Ācāra is the third source of dharma and refers to the community norms and standards of a particular social group.[590] Traditionally, according to the dharmasastras, these standards are derived from the actions of those so fully learned in the Vedas that all their actions are aligned with Vedic teaching.[591] Such actions are looked towards for example in times when information regarding a particular instance is not found within śruti and smṛti literature. Although theologically the Vedas or śruti literature should be the primary source for information regarding Hindu law, in reality, ācāra provided the basis for the working system of law during the classical period.[592] Along with this shift away from laws directly resulting from the Vedas came the normalization of leaders whose actions are considered ācāra yet are not Vedic scholars. Over time, merchant leaders, heads of caste, and community leaders became the true sources of ācāra and therefore, also became the primary source for rulings within the Hindu law tradition.[593]

Ātmatuṣṭi

Atmatusti is defined as being what is pleasing to oneself and is considered by some to be the fourth source of dharma.[594] However, only the law codes of Manu and Yājñavalkya cite atmatusti as the fourth source of law.[595] Most scholars do not recognize atmatusti as a source of dharma within Hindu Law because it does not have the same authority as sruti, smriti, and acara. Atmatusti is used as a last resort where a person may only use it if the first three legitimate sources do not address the issue in question.[596]

Classical Hindu Law in Practice

Administration

Classical Hindu law in practice originates from community, not a state polity. In this way, particular groups of society began to gain influence in the creation and administration of law. Primary corporate groups, Kingships, and Brahmins were the factions, which conveyed Hindu jurisprudence in practice. Corporate groups were responsible for legislating law through the conception of social norms;[597] kingships were responsible for the administration of punishment and the worldly Hindu system; and Brahmins were responsible for ritual, penance, and the maintenance of a spiritual Hindu system.[598]

Judicial Procedure

Evidence of Judicial Procedure in ancient India was mostly derived from classical Hindu law and religious texts like the Vedas. The King was made to be the ultimate law authority within a court. Ordeals the divine methods of proof and Oaths for simple cases were used to help in the decision making process. While ultimately basing the decision from the basis of different texts like Manu, Yājñavalkya,Dharmaśāstras, Sastras and Smrtis.

References

- Coburn, Thomas B. 1984. *Scripture" in India: Towards a Typology of the Word in Hindu Life*. Journal of the American Academy of Religion, Vol. 52, No. 3.
- Davis, Jr. Donald R. Forthcoming. *The Spirit of Hindu Law*.
- Davis, Jr. Donald R. 2005. *Intermediate Realms of Law: Corporate Groups and Rulers in Medieval India* JESHO
- Hacker, Paul. 2006. *Dharma in Hinduism*. Journal of Indian Philosophy 34:5
- Jho, Chakradhar. 1986. *History and Sources of Law in Ancient India*. New Delhi: Ashish Publishing House.
- Lingat, Robert. 1973. *The Classical Law of India*. Trans. J. Duncan M. Derrett. Berkeley: University of California Press.
- Olivelle, Patrick. 2004. *The Law Code of Manu*. New York: Oxford University Press.
- Rocher, Rosane. Forthcoming *The Creation of Anglo-Hindu Law* LHI

Classical Hindu law in practice

Classical Hindu law in practice originates from community, not a state polity. In this way, particular groups of society began to gain influence in the creation and administration of law. Primary corporate groups, Kingships, and Brahmins were the factions, which conveyed Hindu jurisprudence in practice. Corporate groups were responsible for legislating law through the conception of social norms;[599] kingships were responsible for the administration of punishment and the worldly Hindu system; and Brahmins were responsible for ritual, penance, and the maintenance of a spiritual Hindu system.[600]

Administration of Classical Hindu Law

Corporate groups

Corporate groups in medieval India included, but were not limited to, merchants, traders, religious specialists, soldiers, agriculturalists, pastoralists, and castes. These groups held legal prominence in classical Indian society because the primary authority and responsibility for law at the time came from the community, not a state polity. Particularly, early Dharmasūtra (dharmasutra) texts, beginning in about the 2nd BC, recognized a full-fledged theology surrounding the household institution.[601] The texts viewed households and families as the archetype of community, "an exemplary institution of religious and legal reflection of Hindu jurisprudence". Thus, Hindu jurisprudence portrayed the household, not the state, as the primary institution of law. Connectedly, the household is the institution to which Hindu law is most applied. For example, the texts are most explicit in reference to quotidian household acts such as eating, bathing, creating a family, etc. The focus on the household and other local institutions helped to identify the shared goals and goods within society which are inherent to Hindu law. Furthermore, small-scale communities such as the household were more effective in imposing the acceptance of common values and core ideas.

Because of the social implication revolving around the importance of the household and the community in the creation and administration of law, Hindu law jurisprudentially subordinated state law to the law of castes and life-stages (varnasramadharma). In this manner, each caste and life-stage was responsible for highly localized occupations. –

Table 1. Dharmas of the Castes, showing the subordinate place of political rulership

I. Brahmin

    a. six occupations – teaching and studying the Veda, offering and officiating at sacrifices, giving and accepting gifts (MDh10.74-75)

II. Kṣatriya

    a. three occupations – studying the Veda, offering sacrifices, and giving gifts (MDh 10.77, 79)

    b. special dharmas = rājadharma, the dharma of a ruler (MDh 10.79-80)

        1. protection of the people (MDh 7.144; YS 1.323, 335)

        2. promulgation of the law of castes and life-stages (MDh 7.24, 35; 8.41, 390-91, 410-418; YS 1.361; NS 12.117, 18.5)

        3. punishment of the wicked (MDh 7.14-31; YS 1.338, 354-359)

  4. adjudication of disputes

III. Vaiśya

  a. three occupations – studying the Veda, offering sacrifices, and giving gifts (MDh 10.78-79)

  b. special dharmas (MDh 9.326-333; 10.79-80)

   1. trade

   2. animal husbandry

   3. agriculture

IV. Śūdra

  a. special dharma – "obedient service to distinguished Brahmin house-holders who are learned in the Veda" (MDh 9.334)

Although the household and family were central to corporate groups' influence, medieval India was a time of political integration over larger and larger core areas.[602] During the time, corporate groups showed increased importance in the creation and administration of law. Such influence came with the development of corporate groups as intermediary tools. These intermediate-corporate groups exercised influence in two main ways:

1. they moderate legal influences of both "highly local sources (villages, families, etc)" and "elite-level political rulers", which promotes pragmatic conflict resolution and the circulation of legal standards for specific groups, and
2. they reconcile legal norms that influence local and regional customary law with esoteric Brahminical dialogue of Dharmaśāstra which establish "viable ideologies" that respect both customary and textual law.[603]

Corporate groups also created their own laws and systems of jurisprudence. Specifically, the concept of ācāra in the Hindu legal texts (i.e. the Dharmaśāstra) legitimized these localized laws. Ācāra allowed localized corporate groups to create their own laws, especially in the situations where Hindu legal texts were vague, ambiguous, or completely silent. In particular, ācāra of specific corporate groups plays out in practice as "norms accepted and imposed by the leaders of various social institutions". The key to the legitimization of these norms created and accepted by the leaders of corporate groups is the concept of the 'good person' in ācāra. This principal allows for the dissemination of sastric and Vedic control over practice through the mediation of experts who are learned in the texts. Through this, the Dharmaśāstra is connected to real life in a "mediate" way.[604] Ācāra is also recognized and validated in a legal sense through the device of paribhāṣā, which deemed the conventional rules of ācāra as technical supplementary refinements of the rules of the śāstra.

Kingships

The dharmasastras, starting with Manu, first addressed the function of the king pertaining to the administration of Hindu law. These texts define the king as 'he who has been anointed.' Many scholars interpret anointment as the celebration of coronation rites, and thus believe that the ceremony is necessary to invest the king with supreme authority. Although no rules lay down why or how a particular individual fits to qualify as king, Manu VII.2 indicates that only a Kṣatriya has the right to kingship. Some assume this is because the Kṣatriya possessed the force necessary to obtain obedience. However, interpreters of other dharmasastras, dispute this qualifying trait.[605] The king was considered to have a divine nature, but not because of birth or immortality. Rather, the king encompassed god-likeness through exercising the royal function, which the texts say the gods created. This royal function is the source of the king's authority. The royal function vests the king with the power of command (kṣatra) and the mission to protect the people and give them the guarantee of security.[606] The sastras delineate the royal function to be the king's dharma (rājadharma). Aside from physical protection from the harmful in and outside of king's jurisdiction, rājadharma protects and permits his subjects' dharma to flourish. In this way, the king's dharma encompasses all dharma since each individual's performance of his or her personal duties is dependent on the protection secured by the king. Because of this interconnectedness between rājadharma and individual dharma (swadharma) "the salvation of the king depends on his subjects, just as the salvation of the subjects depend on the king". The king's spiritual happiness depends on his subjects, for he suffers the consequences of their sins and profits from the merits they acquire. This relation applies vice versa as well.

Punishment and justice

The royal function gives two main privileges: the right to tax and the right to punish (daṇḍa), and they are benefits outlined solely for the king. Only the king may use punishment to secure the execution of his orders. Due to his ability to punish, the king possesses an unlimited power on the temporal plane, and he may do whatever he wishes. Narada says, "whatever the king does is justified: such is the rule." Furthermore, the execution of punishment ensures justice within the king's jurisdiction, and thus the king is the sole judge of the means needed to accomplish his mission of justice. In this vein, he may act as he deems necessary for justice. Moreover, exercising the royal function to maintain justice is equivalent to the celebration of a sacrifice, which keeps the king pure no matter what actions he must commit to bring a culprit to justice. However, although a king is always justified on a temporal plane, he would suffer the consequences of poor actions in his next lives.

Punishment falls under royal authority because it pertains to accomplishing true justice—a concept only the king can judge. Thus, where there is textual silence, kings are responsible for administrating trials (vyavahāra) of criminal law as well as administering punishment (daṇḍa) for criminal acts. King's judge trials other than criminal cases too, except when parties do not wish to appear before him. When parties do not wish to bring a complaint to the king, individuals and corporate groups conduct their own trials. In these cases, although corporate groups such as castes and vocational sects have their own jurisdiction (which came from customary origins) they are still in the king's control. The king exercises this control through the recognition of a corporate group's particular jurisprudence. Recognition is important because the king's court is the only jurisdiction Dharmasastras identifies, thus the king's acceptance of other courts transfers sastric meaning to the particular jurisdictions. The king also employs danda when the Dharmasastra gives more than one penalty for a crime or when texts are contradictory. He is a source of last resort on questions of both fact and law, but once the king passes judgment it is not up for review.

Lawmaking

Kings were not very active in legislating especially for the reason that Hindu legal texts always preceded the authority of the king. In this way, kings were limited in their ability to make laws on conduct because the Veda already out-lined dharma. Judgments made by the king were never law, but considered orders. These orders did not change laws or give new interpretations to texts but merely secured order and peace to the king's jurisdiction. More reason-ably, the king was an administrator rather than a legislator. As an administra-tor, the king maintained peace between his subjects rather than made laws. In addition, royal authority did allow the king to divide tasks of administration amongst ministers and to define the scope and the powers of each ministry. Davis further attributes the lack of royal legislation or edict to the social con-text presumed by Hindu jurisprudence (i.e. the subordination of the state to the household). In this way, "the state is jurisprudentially part of the household dharma of the ruler"[607]

Brahminical jurisprudence

The Brahmin was an integral part of the administration of classical Hindu law. For Gautama, the Brahmins and the king sustain the divine order of the world, the Brahmins with their council and the king by punishment. In this way, dharma cannot come to fruition without the two castes' cooperation. The Brah-min's opinion is the only counterbalance to the king's authority in society, and because of this, the texts say that the king cannot make a decision without the advice of a Brahmin. For this reason, Brahmins have a right to participate in the court of justice. Additionally, when a king cannot preside over a case him-self, a Brahmin must be appointed to take his place. The Brahmin not only gives advice on the administration of justice but also in affairs of the state. "Brahmin is master when the question is one of ritual and of penance. But his scope extends in reality over all the field of royal activity, as much on its po-litical side as on its religious". The superiority of the Brahmin is not attached to their birth (varna) but to the fact that they are devoted to the study of the Veda, and thus are qualified to instruct other people. Because of this devotion to the Veda, the Brahmin is more closely in line with the divine than the king. Thus, Gautama says, the king is the master of all with the exception of the Brahmin. Such high ranking in the classical Hindu law system is apparent in that Brahmin's are exempt from taxes, and may own land (something that is reserved for only kings and Brahmins).

Judicial practices of Classical Hindu Law

There are no references of Judicial procedure in early Vedic times but there was a frequent mention of the term Rta implying that there was a divine cosmic order by which the universe was regulated. The idea of Dharma seems to have developed from Rta, since Dharma later became the word commonly used in ancient India to designate law. The Rig Veda provides little evidence of civil law. In ancient India Dharma had a religious basis and was enforced by religious threat. It changed not by the will of the king but the evolution of social custom usages and practices.[608] During the Brahmana period, the process of giving punishments to culprits was formed and for this reason law-assistants were appointed. The full Judicial procedure came into light during the composition of the Dharmaśāstras and Smrtis. King figures appeared as the highest judicial authority with a network of courts established under him. The courts consisted of ten members King, Pravivaka, the Sabhyas, the Ganika (accountant), the Lekhaka (Clerk) and court inspector.

- **Kings** at the center of the court, facing the east- Sabhyas and Pradvivka on his right facing the north side, bench clerk on the left accountant opposite the bench clerk facing west. The King acted as the supreme judge and had the final decision issued under his signature and seal.
- **Pradvivakas and Sabhyas-** assist the king in arriving at the truth and giving correct judgment.
- **Sabhyas** seven, five or three in number—selected for their knowledge of the law and they had to advise the king on laws applicable to the case. Including only the people well versed in the Vedic lore and civil law.
- **Bench clerk** wrote down the pleading made orally in the case.
- **Accountant** made calculation of money involved in the suits.

- **Sadhyapala** preserved the order in the court, execute its decrees and see to the attendance of parties and witnesses.

The decision of a case in ancient India was based on eight sources according to brahmanical law givers. These sources are the three Pramanas (possession, documents, and witnesses) logical inference, the usages of the country, sapathas (oaths and ordeals), the kings edict and admission of the litigants.[609] If there were cases where no possessions, documents and recourse can be provided the decision of the King became the ultimate authority.

Four parts of a trial—

- Pratijna - plaint or complaint
- Uttaram — answer of written statement
- Kriya — Trial
- Nirnaya — Decision according to Yajnavalkya

Ordeals

Ordeals also referred to as Divya were divine methods of proof. They decided what cannot be or is not to be decided by human means of proof. The general rule stated by Yājñavalkya, Narada, Brahaspati, Katyayana is that ordeals are to be retorted to only if there is no human evidence or circumstantial evidence available.[610] Different kinds of ordeals are mentioned at different places, Manu gives only two ordeals i.e. holding of fire and plunging in water. Yet Yājñavalkya and Vishnu give a list of five, namely balance, fire, water, poison, consecrate water. Narada gives seven different types of ordeals, i.e. ordeal by balance, fire, water, poison, libration, rice, hot piece of gold. Though there has been evidence found that shows the practice of only two ordeals i.e. ordeal by rice and ordeal by sacred libation. They show up in the sources from ancient Kashmir. In the final decisions by the King human modes of proof ruled over divine modes of proof. Ordeals were only used in extraordinary circumstances. There are also more restrictions on who can perform what type of ordeal. Ordeals were generally performed in the presence of King, the judge, learned Brahmans and the public. The place and time where the ordeals could be performed also held importance. They were usually administered either at dawn or in the forenoon or sometimes even late at night. Sunday was the preferred day to administer them. They usually took place at places like temple, royal gate, public place where four roads meet and the hall of justice. The chief judge by the order of the King had to conduct all the rites like a sacrificial priest. The chief judge and the Sodhya had to take religious dips, observe a fast and convoke all deities.

Four major ordeals

- **Ordeal of balance** (Tula, Dhata)—mostly given to women, minors and old or disabled people. The person performing the ordeal was twice weighed on a balance. If the person weighed lighter than the previous weight they were considered innocent; if they were heavier the second time they were considered guilty.
- **Ordeal of fire** (Agni)—A hot ball of iron had to be carried across a certain distance in the palm of the hand using pipul leaves. If the hand did not end up getting burnt the person was declared innocent. If the hand was burnt the person was found guilty.
- **Ordeal of water** (Salila)—The person had to dive into a river and keep themselves under water, while at the same time an arrow was also shot into the water and was brought back by a fleet runner. If the person stayed under water till that time and no body part was visible then the person was considered innocent. If the person floated back up again before the arrow was retrieved or a body part other than the top of the head became visible the person was found guilty.
- **Ordeal of Poison** (Visa)—the person had to take a certain quantity of poison and was monitored for any reactions for a certain time period. If there was no visible effect of the poison the person was considered innocent.

Other types of ordeals included ordeals mentioned in the Smrtis like the ordeal of sacred libation in which an image of a deity was washed in holy water and the accused had to drink that water. If within a certain time period a misfortune occurred in his life he was found to be guilty. Ordeal of rice grains, ordeal of heated piece of gold, ordeal by ploughshare, ordeal by lot also existed within various texts. Ordeals played a significant part in the judicial administration of ancient India, even though they were not really rational and couldn't really detect guilt. As pointed out in Medhatithi ordeals were like magic and were meant to scare the guilty party and come out with the truth.

Oaths

Oaths are an affirmation of truth which can be liable to punishment for perjury if the statement given turns out to be false. Manu recommended that when human proofs failed Sapatha or oath could be applied in search of the truth.[611] According to the Smrti oaths were intended to be used in simple cases, while ordeals were used only in serious cases. A person making an oath was to swear on his near and dear ones. He might touch the head or feet of a Brahman or his wife or his son, or the feet of an image of a deity or take sacred grass or sesamum, silver, gold, earth, fire, water according as the value of the disputed property. The waiting period on the oaths was one, three, five or more days depending on the nature of the accusation. There is a great amount of sanctity attached to Oaths as explained in Manu that if a man swears on an oath falsely even in a small matter will be lost in this world as well as the next.

References

* Das, Sukla. "Judicial Administration." *Crime and Punishment in Ancient India*. 1st ed. New Delhi: Abhinav Publications, 1977
* Davis, Jr. Donald R. *Intermediate Realms of Law: Corporate Groups and Rulers in Medieval India* JESHO (2005)
* Davis, Jr. Donald R. *The Spirit of Hindu Law* Forthcoming
* Kaul, Anjali. *Administration of Law and Justice in Ancient India*. 1st ed. New Delhi: Sarup & Sons, 1993
* Lingat, Robert. 1973. *The Classical Law of India*. Trans. J. Duncan M. Derrett. Berkeley: University of California Press ISBN 978-1882239085
* Olivelle, Patrick. 2004. *The Law Code of Manu*. New York: Oxford University Press

Hindu law

Part of a series on
Hinduism
• **Hindu** • **History**
• **Glossary of Hinduism terms** • ॐ *Hinduism portal*
• v • t • e[612]

Hindu law, as a historical term, refers to the code of laws applied to Hindus, Buddhists, Jains and Sikhs in British India.[613,614] Hindu law, in modern scholarship, also refers to the legal theory, jurisprudence and philosophical reflections on the nature of law found in ancient and medieval era Indian texts. It is one of the oldest known jurisprudence theories in the world.

Hindu tradition, in its surviving ancient texts, does not express the law in the canonical sense of *ius* or of *lex*. The ancient term in Indian texts is Dharma, which means more than a code of law. The term "Hindu law" is a colonial construction,[615] and emerged after the colonial rule arrived in South Asia, and when in 1772 it was decided by British colonial officials, that European common law system would not be implemented in India, that Hindus of India would be ruled under their "Hindu law" and Muslims of India would be ruled under "Muslim law" (Sharia).[616]

Prior to the British colonial rule, Muslim law was codified as *Fatawa-i Alamgiri*, but laws for non-Muslims – such as Hindus, Buddhists, Sikhs, Jains, Parsis – were not codified during the 601 years of Islamic rule. The substance of Hindu law implemented by the British was derived from a Dharmaśāstra named Manusmriti, one of the many treatises (śāstra) on *Dharma*. The British, however, mistook the Dharmaśāstra as codes of law and failed to recognise that these Sanskrit texts were not used as statements of positive law until the British colonial officials chose to do so.[617] Rather, Dharmaśāstra contained jurisprudence commentary, i.e., a theoretical reflection upon practical law, but not a statement of the law of the land as such.[618] Scholars have also questioned the authenticity and the corruption in the Manusmriti manuscript used to derive the colonial era Hindu law.

In colonial history context, the construction and implementation of Hindu law and Islamic law was an attempt at "legal pluralism" during the British colonial era, where people in the same region were subjected to different civil and criminal laws based on the religion of the plaintiff and defendant.[619] Legal scholars state that this divided the Indian society, and that Indian law and politics have ever since vacillated between "legal pluralism - the notion that religion is the basic unit of society and different religions must have different legal rights and obligations" and "legal universalism – the notion that individuals are the basic unit of society and all citizens must have uniform legal rights and obligations". In modern India, Hindus and other non-Muslims in India favor legal universalism that is based not on any Hindu text but on parliamentary laws, however Muslims favor legal pluralism with sharia as the source of marriage, divorce and inheritance laws for Muslims in India.[620,621]

Terminology and nomenclature

In Hinduism, law is discussed as a subset of *dharma* which signifies behaviors that are considered in accord with *rta*, the order that makes life and universe possible,[622]</ref> and includes duties, rights, laws, conduct, virtues and "right way of living".[623] The concept of *Dharma* includes Hindu law.[624]

In ancient texts of Hinduism, the concept of dharma incorporates the principles of law, order, harmony, and truth. It is explained as the necessary law of life and equated to *satya* (Sanskrit: सत्यं, truth), in hymn 1.4.14 of Brhadaranyaka Upanishad, as follows:

धर्म: तस्माद्धर्मात् परं नास्त्य् अथो अबलीयान् बलीयाँसमाशंसते धर्मेण यथा राज्ञैवम् । यो वै स धर्म: सत्यं वै तत् तस्मात्सत्यं वदन्तमाहुर् धर्मं वदतीति धर्मं वा वदन्तँ सत्यं वदतीत्य् एतद्ध्येवैतदुभयं भवति ।।

Nothing is higher than Dharma. The weak overcomes the stronger by Dharma, as over a king. Truly that Dharma is the Truth (Satya); Therefore, when a man speaks the Truth, they say, "He speaks the Dharma"; and if he speaks Dharma, they say, "He speaks the Truth!" For both are one.

—*Brihadaranyaka Upanishad, 1.4.xiv*[625]

Related terms?

In ancient Hindu jurisprudence texts, a number of Sanskrit words refer to aspects of law. Some of these include *Niyama* (Sanskrit: नियम, rule or law), *Nyaya* (न्याय, legal proceeding, judicial sentence), *Yuktata* (युक्तता, justice),[626] *Samya* (साम्य, equality and impartiality in law), *Vidhi* (विधि, precept or rule), *Vyavastha* (व्यवस्था, agreement, arrangement or regulation), *Sambhasa* (सम्भाषा, contract or mutual engagement), *Prasamvida-patra* (प्रसंविदा-पत्र, written contract),[627] *Vivadayati* (विवादयति,[628] litigate or dispute), *Adhivakta* (अधिवक्ता, lawyer), *Nyayavadi* (न्यायवादी, male lawyer), *Nyayavadani* (न्यायवादिनी, female lawyer), *Nyayadata* (न्यायदाता, judge), *Danda* (दण्ड, punishment, penalty or fine), among others.[629,630]

Classical Hindu law

John Mayne, in 1910, wrote that the classical Hindu law has the oldest pedigree of any known system of jurisprudence.[631] Mayne noted that while being ancient, the conflicting texts on almost every question presents a great difficulty in deciding what the classical Hindu law was. As more literature emerges, and is translated or interpreted, Mayne noted that the conflict between the texts on every matter of law has multiplied, and that there is a lack of consensus between the Western legal scholars resident in India.

Ludo Rocher states that Hindu tradition does not express law in the sense of *ius* nor of *lex*. The term "Hindu law" is a colonial construction, and emerged when the colonial rule arrived in South Asia, and when in 1772 it was decided by British colonial officials in consultation with Mughal rulers, that European common law system would not be implemented in India, that Hindus of India would be ruled under their "Hindu law" and Muslims of India would be ruled under sharia (Muslim law). However, Hindu law were neither mentioned, nor in use, nor codified, during the 600 years of Islamic rule of India. An attempt was then to find any old surviving Sanskrit text that mentioned elements of law, and this is how Western editors and translators arrived at the equation that "dharma shastra equals lawbook, code or Institute", states Rocher.

Scholars such as Derrett, Menski and others have repeatedly asked whether and what evidence there is that the Dharmasastras were the actual legal authority before and during the Islamic rule in India?[632,633] They have also questioned whether the Dharmasastras contain "precepts" or "recommendations", that is whether the jurisprudence mentioned in Dharmasastras was actually ever used in disputes in Indian society?[634] Early scholars during the British colonial rule such as John Mayne suggested that it is probable that Dharma-smriti text reflect the "practical administration of law", at least before the arrival of Islam in India.[635] However, most later scholars state that Dharma texts of Hinduism are "purely or mostly concerned with moral and religious norms which have some but not a very close relationship to legal practice".[636] A few scholars have suggested that the Dharma-related Smritis such as Manusmriti, Naradasmriti and Parashara Smriti do not embody the Hindu law but are commentaries and scholarly notes on more ancient authoritative legal texts that have been lost or yet to be found.

Classical Hindu law, states Donald Davis, "represents one of the least known, yet most sophisticated traditions of legal theory and jurisprudence in world history. Hindu jurisprudential texts contain elaborate and careful philosophical reflections on the nature of law and religion. The nature of Hindu law as a tradition has been subject to some debate and some misunderstanding both within and especially outside of specialist circles."

In South India, temples were intimately involved in the administration of law.[637]

Sources of Dharma

Śruti have been considered as the authority in the Hindu Dharma.[638] (Note: This differentiation between epistemic and deontic authority is true for all Indian religions)</ref> The *Smritis*, such as Manusmriti, Naradasmriti and Parashara Smriti, contribute to the exposition of the Hindu Dharma but are considered less authoritative than *Śrutis* (the Vedic corpus that includes early Upanishads).[639,640]</ref> The root texts of ancient Hindu jurisprudence and law are the *Dharma-sūtras*. These express that Shruti, Smriti and Achara are sources of jurisprudence and law. The precedence of these sources is declared in the opening verses of each of the known, surviving Dharma-sūtras. For example,

> *The source of Dharma is the Veda, as well as the tradition [Smriti], and practice of those who know the Veda. – Gautama Dharma-sūtra 1.1-1.2*
>
> *The Dharma is taught in each Veda, in accordance with which we will explain it. What is given in the tradition [Smriti] is the second, and the conventions of cultured people are the third. – Baudhayana Dharma-sūtra 1.1.1-1.1.4*
>
> *The Dharma is set forth in the vedas and the Traditional Texts [Smriti]. When these do not address an issue, the practice of cultured people becomes authoritative. – Vāsiṣṭha Dharma-sūtra 1.4-1.5*
>
> *—Translated by Donald Davis, The Spirit of Hindu Law*[641]

The *Smritis*, such as Manusmriti, Naradasmriti, Yajnavalkya Smrti and Parashara Smriti, expanded this definition, as follows,

वेदोऽखिलो धर्ममूलं स्मृतिशीले च तद्विदाम् । आचारश्चैव साधूनामात्मनस्तुष्टिरेव च ॥

> *Translation 1: The whole Veda is the (first) source of the sacred law, next the tradition and the virtuous conduct of those who know the (Veda further), also the customs of holy men, and (finally) self-satisfaction (Atmanastushti).*[642]
>
> *Translation 2: The root of the religion is the entire Veda, and (then) the tradition and customs of those who know (the Veda), and the conduct of virtuous people, and what is satisfactory to oneself.*[643]
>
> *—Manusmriti 2.6*

वेद: स्मृति: सदाचार: स्वस्य च प्रियमात्मन: । एतच्चतुर्विधं प्राहु: साक्षाद् धर्मस्य लक्षणम् ॥

> *Translation 1: The Veda, the sacred tradition, the customs of virtuous men, and one's own pleasure, they declare to be the fourfold means of defining the sacred law.*
>
> *Translation 2: The Veda, tradition, the conduct of good people, and what is pleasing to oneself – they say that is four fold mark of religion.*
>
> *—Manusmriti 2.12*

As a source of *Dharma*, only three of the four types of texts in the Vedas have behavioral precepts. Lingat notes (abridged),

> *For the Hindu all belief takes its source and its justification in the Vedas [Śruti]. Consequently every rule of dharma must find its foundation in the Veda. Strictly speaking, the Samhitas do not even include a single*

precept which could be used directly as a rule of conduct. One can find there only references to usage which falls within the scope of dharma. By contrast, the Brahmanas, the Aranyakas and the Upanishads contain numerous precepts which propound rules governing behavior.

—Robert Lingat[644]

Bilimoria states the role of *Shruti* in Hindu Dharma has been inspired by "the belief in a higher natural cosmic order (*Rta* succeeded later by the concept *Dharma*) that regulates the universe and provides the basis for its growth, flourishing and sustenance – be that of the gods, human beings, animals and eco-formations".[645]

Levinson states that the role of *Shruti* and *Smriti* in Hindu law is as a source of guidance, and its tradition cultivates the principle that "the facts and circumstances of any particular case determine what is good or bad". The later Hindu texts include fourfold sources of *Dharma*, states Levinson, which include *Atmanastushti* (satisfaction of one's conscience), *Sadachara* (local norms of virtuous individuals), *Smriti* and *Sruti*.[195,646,647]

Lawyers in classical Hindu Law

While texts on ancient Hindu law have not survived, texts that confirm the existence of the institution of lawyers in ancient India have. The Sanskrit text *Vivadarnavasetu*, in Chapter 3, for example, states,

If the plaintiff or defendant have any excuse for not attending the court, or for not pleading their own cause, or, on any other account, excuse themselves, they shall, at their own option, appoint a person as their lawyer; if the lawyer gains the suit, his principal also gains; if the lawyer is cast, his principal is cast also.

In a cause where the accusation is for murder, for a robbery, for adultery, for (...), the principals shall plead and answer in person; but a woman, a minor, an insane, or a person lacking mental competency may be represented by a lawyer.

—Vivadarnavasetu, Classical Hindu Law Process

Punishment in classical Hindu Law

Ancient texts of the Hindu tradition formulate and articulate punishment.[648] These texts from the last 2500 years, states Terence Day,[649] imply or recognize key elements in their theories of fair punishment: (1) the texts set a standard of Right, in order to define a violation that warrants punishment; (2) they discuss the possibility of a violation thereby defining a wrongdoing; (3) they discuss a theory of responsibility and assignability of a wrongdoing; (4) the texts discuss degrees of guilt, and therewith the form and severity of punishment must match the transgression; (5) they discuss approved and authorized forms of punishments and how these may be properly administered. The goal of punishment, in Hindu law, has been retributive and reformative.[650] Hindu law, states Sarkar, developed the theory of punishment from its foundational theory of what it believed was necessary for the prosperity of the individual and a collection of individuals, of state and non-state.

There are wide variations in the statement of crime and associated punishment in different texts.[651] Some texts, for example discuss punishment for crimes such as murder, without mentioning the gender, class or caste of the plaintiff or defendant, while some discuss and differentiate the crime based on gender, class or caste. It is unclear, states Terence Day, whether these were part of the original, because the stylistic, structural and substantive evidence such as inconsistencies between versions of different manuscripts of the same text suggest changes and corruption of the original texts.[652]

Outside India

Ancient Hindu legal texts and traditions arrived in parts of Southeast Asia (Cambodia, Java, Bali, Malaysia, Thailand, and Burma) as trade grew and as part of a larger culture sharing in ancient Asia.[653] In each of these regions, Hindu law fused with local norms and practices, giving rise to legal texts (Āgamas such as the Kuṭāra-Mānawa in Java, and the Buddhist-influenced Dhammasattas/Dhammathats of Burma and Thailand)[654] as well as legal records embodied (as in India) in stone and copper-plate inscriptions.[655]

Anglo-Hindu law

In 18th century, the earliest British of the East India Company acted as agents of the Mughal emperor. As the British colonial rule took over the political and administrative powers in India, it was faced with various state responsibilities such as legislative and judiciary functions.[656] The East India Company, and later the British Crown, sought profits for its British shareholders through trade as well as sought to maintain effective political control with minimal military engagement. The administration pursued a path of least resistance, relying upon co-opted local intermediaries that were mostly Muslims and some Hindus in various princely states. The British exercised power by avoiding interference and adapting to law practices as explained by the local intermediaries.[657] The colonial state thus sustained what were essentially pre-colonial religious and political law and conflicts, well into the late nineteenth century. The colonial policy on the system of personal laws for India, for example, was expressed by Governor-General Hastings in 1772 as follows,

> *That in all suits regarding inheritance, marriage, caste and other religious usages or institutions, the law of the Koran with respect to Mahometans, and those of the Shaster with respect to Gentoos shall be invariably be adhered to.*

— *Warren Hastings, August 15, 1772*

For Muslims of India, the code of Muslim law was readily available in al-Hidaya and Fatawa-i Alamgiri written under sponsorship of Aurangzeb. For Hindus and other non-Muslims such as Buddhists, Sikhs, Jains, Parsis and Tribal people, this information was unavailable. The British colonial officials, for practice, attempted to extract from the Dharmaśāstra, the English categories of law and religion for the purposes of colonial administration.[658,659]

The early period of Anglo-Hindu Law (1772–1828) was structured along the lines of Muslim law practice. It included the extracted portions of law from one Dharmaśāstra by British colonial government appointed scholars (especially Jones, Henry Thomas Colebrooke, Sutherland, and Borrodaile) in a manner similar to Islamic al-Hidaya and Fatawa-i Alamgiri.[660,661,662] It also included the use of court pandits in British courts to aid British judges in interpreting Shastras just like Qadis (Maulavis) for interpreting the Islamic law.

The arrival of William Bentinck as the Governor-General of British India in 1828, marked a shift towards universal civil code, whose administration emphasized same law for all human beings, individualism and equal treatment to help liberate, empower and end social practices among Hindus and Muslims of India that had received much public coverage in Britain through the publications of Christian missionaries and individuals such as Thomas Macaulay.

Governor-General Dalhousie, in 1848, extended this trend and stated his policy that the law must "treat all natives much the same manner". Over time, between 1828-1855, a series of British parliamentary acts were passed to revise the Anglo-Hindu and Anglo-Muslim laws, such as those relating to the right to religious conversion, widow remarriage, and right to create wills for inheritance. In 1832, the British colonial government abolished accepting religious fatwa as a source of law. In 1835, the British began creating a criminal code that would replace the existing criminal code which was a complex conflicting mixture of laws derived from Muslim texts (Quran) and Hindu texts (Shastras), and this common criminal code was ready by 1855. These changes were welcomed by Hindu law reform movement, but considered abrogating religion-defined rules within the Muslim law. The changes triggered discontent, call for jihad and religious war, and became partly responsible for the 1857 Indian revolt against the British rule.[663,664]

In 1864, after the East India Company was dissolved and India became a formal part of the British Empire, Anglo-Hindu law entered into a second phase (1864–1947), one in which British colonial courts in India relied less on the Muslim Qadis and Hindu Pandits for determining the respective religious laws, and relied more on a written law. A universal criminal code in India, that did not discriminate between people based on their religion, was adopted for the first time in 1864.[665] It was expanded to include a universal procedural and commercial code by 1882, which overruled pre-existing Anglo-Hindu and Anglo-Muslim laws.[666] However, the personal laws for Muslims remained sharia-based, while the Anglo-Hindu law was enacted independent of any text on matters such as marriage, divorce, inheritance and the Anglo-Hindu law covered all Hindus, Jains, Sikhs and Buddhists in India.[667] In 1872, the British crown enacted the Indian Christian Marriage Act which covered marriage, divorce and alimony laws for Indian Christians of all denominations except the Roman Catholics.[668]

The development of legal pluralism, that is separate law based on individual's religion was controversial in India, from the very start.

Modern Hindu law

After the independence of India from the colonial rule of Britain in 1947, India adopted a new constitution in 1950.[669] Most of the legal code from the colonial era continued as the law of the new nation, including the personal laws contained in Anglo-Hindu law for Hindus, Buddhists, Jains and Sikhs, the Anglo-Christian law for Christians, and the Anglo-Muslim law for Muslims. Article 44 of the 1950 Indian constitution mandates a uniform civil code, eliminating all religion-based civil laws including Hindu law, Christian law and Muslim law throughout the territory of India. However, while Hindu law has since been amended to be independent of ancient religious texts, the Article 44 of the Indian constitution has remained largely ignored in matters of Muslim law, by successive Indian governments since 1950.

An amendment to the constitution (42nd Amendment, 1976) formally inserted the word *secular* as a feature of the Indian republic.[670] However, unlike the Western concept of secularism which separates religion and state, the concept of secularism in India means acceptance of religious laws as binding on the state, and equal participation of state in different religions.[671,672]

Since the early 1950s, India has debated whether legal pluralism should be replaced with legal universalism and a uniform civil code that does not differentiate between people based on their religion. This debate remains unresolved. The Quran-based Indian Muslim Personal Law (Shariat) Application Act of 1937 remains the law of land of modern India for Indian Muslims, while parliament-based, non-religious uniform civil code passed in mid-1950s applies to Indians who are Hindus (which includes Buddhists, Jains, Sikhs, Parsees), as well as to Indian Christians and Jews. In 1955, India revised its Hindu Marriage Act and it applied to all Hindus, Buddhists, Jains and Sikhs; scholars contest whether the law applies to cases where the either the husband or wife is Hindu, Buddhist, Jain or Sikh, and the other is a Christian or Muslim.[673]

References

Sources

- Creese, Helen. 2009a. Old Javanese legal traditions in pre-colonial Bali. *Bijdragen tot de Taal-, Land- en Volkenkunde* 165(2/3): 241–290.
- Creese, Helen. 2009b. "Judicial processes and legal authority in pre-colonial Bali." *Bijdragen tot de Taal-, Land- en Volkenkunde* 165(4): 515–550.
- Davis, Jr., Donald R. (2005). "Intermediate Realms of Law: Corporate Groups and Rulers in Medieval India". *Journal of the Economic and Social History of the Orient*. Brill. **48** (1): 92–117. JSTOR 25165079[674].
- Davis, Jr., Donald R. "Dharma in Practice: Ācāra and Authority in Medieval Dharmaśāstra". *Journal of Indian Philosophy*. Springer. **32** (5): 813–830. doi: 10.1007/s10781-004-8651-4[675].
- Davis, Jr. Donald R. 1999. " Recovering the Indigenous Legal Traditions of India: Classical Hindu Law in Practice in Late Medieval Kerala[676]," *Journal of Indian Philosophy* 27 (3): 159–213.
- Davis, Jr. Donald R. 2010. *The Spirit of Hindu Law*. Cambridge University Press.
- Derrett, J. Duncan M. 1968. *Religion, Law, and the State in India*. London: Faber & Faber.
- Dhavan, Rajeev. 1992. "Dharmaśāstra and Modern Indian Society: A Preliminary Exploration." *Journal of the Indian Law Institute* 34 (4): 515–540.
- Fuller, C.J. 1988. "Hinduism and Scriptural Authority in Modern Indian Law." *Comparative Studies in Society and History*. 30:2, 225–248.

- Hacker, Paul. 2006, Dharma in Hinduism[677], Journal of Indian Philosophy 34:5.
- Hooker, M.B., ed. 1986. *The Laws of South-East Asia. Volume 1: The pre-modern texts.* Singapore: Butterworth & Co.
- Jain, M.P. 1990. *Outlines of Indian Legal History.* 5th Ed, Nagpur, Wadhwa & Co.
- Jha, Ganganath (trans.), Manusmṛti with the Manubhāṣyya of Medhātithi[678], including additional notes, 1920.
- Lariviere, Richard W. 2003. *The Nāradasmrti.* crit. ed. and trans. Delhi: Motilal Banarsidass.
- Lariviere, Richard W. 1997. "Dharmaśāstra, Custom, 'Real Law,' and 'Apocryphal' Smrtis." In: *Recht, Staat, und Verwaltung im klassischen Indien*, ed. Bernhard Kölver. Munich: R. Oldenbourg, 97–110.
- Lariviere, Richard W. 1996. "Law and Religion in India." *Law, Morality, and Religion: Global Perspectives*, ed. Alan Watson. Berkeley: University of California, 75–94.
- Lingat, Robert. 1973. *The Classical Law of India.* trans. J.D.M. Derrett. Berkeley: Univ of California Press.
- Lubin, Timothy. 2007. "Punishment and Expiation: Overlapping Domains in Brahmanical Law,"[679] *Indologica Taurinensia* 33: 93–122.
- Lubin, Timothy. 2010. "Indic Conceptions of Authority." In: *Hinduism and Law: An Introduction*, ed. T. Lubin, D.R. Davis, Jr., and J.K. Krishnan. Cambridge: Cambridge University Press, 37–53.
- Lubin, Timothy. 2012. "Legal Diglossia: Modeling Discursive Practices in Premodern Indic Law." In: *Bilingual Discourse and Cross-cultural Fertilisation: Sanskrit and Tamil in Mediaeval India*, ed. Whitney Cox and Vincenzo Vergiani (Paris/Pondicherry: École française d'Extrême-Orient), pp. 411–455.
- Lubin, Timothy, Donald R. Davis, Jr., and Jayanth K. Krishnan, eds. 2010. *Hinduism and Law: An Introduction.* Cambridge: Cambridge University Press.
- Menski, Werner. 2003. *Hindu Law: Beyond Tradition and Modernity.* Delhi: Oxford UP.
- Olivelle, Patrick. 2004a. "The Semantic History of Dharma in the Middle and late Vedic Periods." *Journal of Indian Philosophy* 32 (5): 491–511.
- Olivelle, Patrick. 2004b. *The Law Code of Manu.* New York: Oxford UP.
- Olivelle, Patrick. 2000. *Dharmasūtras: The Law Codes of Āpastamba, Gautama, Baudhāyana, and Vasistha.* Delhi: Motilal Banarsidass.
- Rangaswami Aiyangar, K.V. 1941. *Rājadharma.* Adyar: Adyar Library.
- Rocher, Ludo. 1978. " Hindu Conceptions of Law[680]", *Hastings Law Journal*, 29:6, 1283–1305.

- Rocher, Ludo. 1972. "Hindu Law and Religion: Where to draw the line?" *Malik Ram Felicitation* Volume, ed. S.A.J. Zaidi. New Delhi, 167–194.
- Rocher, Ludo. 1956. *Vacaspati Misra: Vyavaharacintamani. A digest on Hindu legal procedure*. Crit. Ed., with Introduction, Annotated Translation, and Appendices. Ghent University.
- Rocher, Rosane. 2010. "The Creation of Anglo-Hindu Law." In: *Hinduism and Law: An Introduction*, ed. T. Lubin, D.R. Davis, Jr., and J.K. Krishnan. Cambridge: Cambridge University Press, 78–88.
- Solanki, Gopika. 2011. "Adjudication in Religious Family Laws: Cultural Accommodation, Legal Pluralism and Gender Equality in India".Cambridge and New York: Cambridge University Press.
- Washbrook, David A. 1981. " Law, State, and Agrarian Society in Colonial India[681]", *Modern Asian Studies*. 15:3, 649–721.
- Wezler, Albrecht. 2004. "Dharma in the Veda and the Dharmaśāstras." Journal of Indian Philosophy 32 (5): 629–654.

Further reading

- Davis, Jr. Donald R. 2010. *The Spirit of Hindu Law* (Cambridge: Cambridge University Press, 2010), ISBN 978-0521877046
- Lubin, Timothy, Donald R. Davis, Jr., and Jayanth K. Krishnan, eds. *Hinduism and Law: An Introduction* (Cambridge: Cambridge University Press, 2010), ISBN 978-0521716260

Anglo-Indian law

- J. Duncan M. Derrett, "The Administration of Hindu Law by the British," *Comparative Studies in Society and History,* 4.1 (November 1961).

Modern Hindu law

- N.R. Raghavachariar, *Hindu Law- Principles and Precedents*, 12th Edition (Madras).
- Satyajeet A. Desai, *Mulla's Principles of Hindu Law*. 17th ed. 2 Vol. (New Delhi: Butterworths, 1998).
- Paras Diwan and Peeyushi Diwan, *Modern Hindu Law*. 10th ed. (Allahabad: Allahabad Law Agency, 1995).
- Ranganath Misra, *Mayne's Treatise on Hindu Law and Usage*. 15th ed. (New Delhi: Bharat Law House, 2003).
- Werner Menski, *Hindu Law: Beyond Tradition and Modernity* (Delhi: Oxford University Press, 2003).
- Gopika Solanki, "Adjudication in Religious Family Laws: Cultural Accommodation, Legal Pluralism and Gender equality in India" (Cambridge and New York: Cambridge University Press, 2011).

External links

- JDM Derrett (1961), The administration of Hindu law by the British[682], Comparative Studies in Society and History, 4(1), pages 10–52
- KLS Rao (1998), Practitioners of Hindu Law: Ancient and Modern[683] Fordham Law Review
- William Hay Macnaghten, *Principles and Precedents of Hindu Law - Mitakshara*[684], p. PA109, at Google Books Rules of Judicial Proceedings and Rules of Evidence in 11th century CE India, Harvard Law School
- Donald Davis Jr (2007), Hinduism as a Legal Tradition[685], Journal of the American Academy of Religion, Oxford University Press, 75(2), pages 241–267

Traditional Chinese law

Traditional Chinese law refers to the laws, regulations and rules used in China up to 1911, when the last imperial dynasty fell. It has undergone continuous development since at least the 11th century BC. This legal tradition is distinct from the common law and civil law traditions of the West – as well as Islamic law and classical Hindu law – and to a great extent, is contrary to the concepts of contemporary Chinese law. It incorporates elements of both Legalist and Confucian traditions of social order and governance.

To Westerners, perhaps the most striking feature of the traditional Chinese criminal procedure is that it was an inquisitorial system where the judge, usually the district magistrate, conducts a public investigation of a crime, rather than an adversarial system where the judge decides between attorneys representing the prosecution and defense. "The Chinese traditionally despised the role of advocate and saw such people as parasites who attempted to profit from the difficulties of others. The magistrate saw himself as someone seeking the truth, not a partisan for either side."[686]

Two traditional Chinese terms approximate "law" in the modern Western sense. The first, *lü* (律), means primarily "norm" or "model". The second, *fa* (法), is usually rendered as "statute".

History

Early development

The laws of the aristocratic societies of early China put substantial emphasis on maintaining the distinct ranks and orders among the nobles, in addition to controlling the populace. As a result, *li* (禮), meaning ritual and etiquette, governed the conduct of the nobles whilst *xing* (刑), rules of punishment, governed the commoners and slaves.

The early rulers of the Zhou Dynasty issued or enforced laws that already exemplified the values of a primogeniture regime, most notable of which is filial piety. The earliest document on law in China that is generally regarded as authentic is the *Kang Gao* (康誥), a set of instructions issued by King Wu of Zhou to a younger prince for the government of a fief. The Kang Gao is a chapter of the Book of Documents.

During the 6th century BC, several of the independent states into which the Zhou kingdom had fragmented codified their penal laws and inscribed them on bronze cauldrons. For example, at least two codifications from the state of Zheng survive, from 536 BC and 504 BC - the first on cauldrons and the second on bamboo. And the codes of Wei, drafted by Li Kui, are also notable. Such codification was part of the process by which rulers attempted to make more effective the central administration of the state. They attracted criticism from orthodox statesmen, including Confucius, on the basis that they eroded the distinction between the "noble" and the "base".

The Five Punishments dated from this time.

Legalism and Qin

In 221 BC, the state of Qin finally obtained supremacy over its rivals and founded the Qin Dynasty. One of the reasons for its success was the adoption, on the advice of Lord Shang Yang, of far-reaching penal and administrative codes in the 4th century BC. The laws imposed severe punishments for failure to comply with duties imposed by the state and on the whole punished all alike. During this stage, law was marked by a purely Legalist spirit, hostile to the moral values advocated by the Confucian school.

The Legalist school, as represented by such thinkers as Han Fei Zi, insisted that the ruler must always rely on penal law and the imposition of heavy punishments as the main instrument of government. At the same time, moral considerations and social standing should be rigorously excluded. Another hallmark of Legalist thinking was that there should be equality before the law. On the question of legislative technique, the Legalists stressed that the rules enacted by the ruler for punishment of offences should be clear, intelligible to the ordinary people, and properly communicated to them.

Multiple corporal punishments were implemented by the Qin, such as death by boiling, chariots, beating, and permanent mutilation in the form of tattooing and castration. People who committed crimes were also sentenced to hard labor for the state.

Legalism survived in a diluted form after the Han Dynasty succeeded the Qin. It was recognised that there was a need for complex penal and administrative codes that enabled the emperor to govern the country through a hierarchy of ministers and officials, all ultimately responsible to him. Imperial legal systems all retained the original Legalist insistence that the powers of officials be defined in detail and that punishments be prescribed for transgressions, whether inadvertent or not. Han law-makers took account of Confucian values and introduced rules designed to implement them.

By 167 BC the law had changed so that castration itself was not used to punish, instead, it became an optional replacement for execution.

Tang Code

This process continued throughout the Han and later dynasties, culminating in the Tang Dynasty. Ch'ü T'ung-tsu has shown that the "Confucianisation" of Chinese law was a slow process and that the amalgamation of the Confucian views of society with the law codes was completed only in the great Tang Code of CE 624. The code is regarded as a model of precision and clarity in terms of drafting and structure.

The original Tang Code was promulgated in 624, by the founding Emperor (Gaozu) of the Tang Dynasty. It would become in modern times the earliest fully preserved legal code in the history of Chinese law. It was endowed with a commentary, known as Tanglu Shuyi, incorporated in 653, the fourth year of the reign of Perpetual Splendour, as part of the Tang Code of Perpetual Splendour.

The Tang Code was based on the Code of Northern Zhou (Bei Zhou Lu, 557-581), promulgated 89 years earlier in 564, which was in turn based on the earlier, less comprehensive and less elaborate Code of Cao Wei (Cao Wei Lu, 220-265) and the Code of Western Jin (Xi Jin Lu, 265-317) promulgated almost four centuries earlier in 268.

Confucian attitudes place low reliance on law and punishment for maintaining social order. Evidence of this can be found in the Aspiration (Zhi) section of the 200-volume Old Book on Tang (Jiu Tang Shu), a magnum opus of Tang historiography. The history classic was compiled under official supervision in

945 during the Late Jin Dynasty (Hou Jin, 936-946) of the era of Five Generations (Wudai, 907-960), some three centuries after the actual events. A single chapter on Punishment and Law (Xingfa) is placed last after seven chapters on Rites (Liyi), after which come four chapters on Music (Yinyue), three chapters on the Calendar (Li), two on Astronomy and Astrology (Tianwen), one on Physics (Wuheng), four on Geography (Dili), three on Hierarchy of Office (Zhiguan), one on Carriages and Costume (Yufu), two on Sutras and Books (Jingji), two on Commodities (Chihuo) and finally one single chapter on Punishment and Law, in that order.

The Confucian Code of Rites (Liji), not law, is expected to be the controlling document on civilised behaviour. In the Confucian world view, rule of law is applied only to those who have fallen beyond the bounds of civilised behaviour. Civilised people are expected to observe proper rites. Only social outcasts are expected to have their actions controlled by law. Thus the rule of law is considered a state of barbaric primitiveness, prior to achieving the civilised state of voluntary observation of proper rites. What is legal is not necessarily moral or just.

Under the supervision of Tang Confucian minister Fang Xuanling, 500 sections of ancient laws were compiled into 12 volumes in the Tang Code, titled:

Vol 1: Term and es (Mingle)
Vol 2: Security and Forbiddance (Weijin)
Vol 3: Office and Hierarchy (Zhizhi)
Vol 4: Domestic Matters and Marriage (Huhun)
Vol 5: Stables and Storage (Jiuku)
Vol 6: Impeachment and Promotion (Shanxing)
Vol 7: Thievery and Robbery (Zeidao)
Vol 8: Contest and Litigation (Dousong)
Vol 9: Deceit and Falsehood (Zhawei)
Vol 10: Miscellaneous Regulation (Zalu)
Vol 11: Arrest and Escape (Buwang)
Vol 12: Judgment and Imprisonment (Duanyu)

The Tang Code lists the five forms of corporal punishment for serfs as:

1. Flogging (Chinese: 笞 ; pinyin: *chī*)
2. Caning (Chinese: 杖 ; pinyin: *zhàng*)
3. Imprisonment (Chinese: 徒 ; pinyin: *tú*)
4. Exile (Chinese: 流 ; pinyin: *liú*)
5. Death (Chinese: 死 ; pinyin: *sǐ*)

Leniency is applied according to the Eight Deliberations:

1. Blood relation

2. Motive for the crime
3. Virtue of the culprit
4. Ability of the culprit
5. Past merits
6. Nobility status
7. Friendship
8. Diligent character

Confucianism in its revised form (Neo-Confucianism) continued to be the state orthodoxy under the Song, Ming and Qing dynasties. This ensured that the Confucian foundations of the Tang code were retained, and in some respects they were even strengthened. By the time of the Qing dynasty however, the mass of legislation had increased to such an extent that it was doubtful whether even officials could adequately master the complex distinctions it came to contain.

Varieties of law

Traditional Chinese law can be divided into the "official" law and "unofficial law". The "official law" emanates from the authority of the emperor. The doctrine of separation of powers was unknown in China until the 20th century. In particular, judicial and administrative functions were performed by magistrates rather than by separate persons. The emperor delegated many of his administrative and judicial powers to his officials while reserving for himself the legislative function.

Official law may itself be divided into two main components: penal law and administrative law. The former prescribed punishments for certain behaviour, and the latter defined the duties of the officials.

By contrast, "unofficial" law was the customary law of the people, rules that developed in localities or in merchant guilds for the handling of matters of common concern. Neither of the standard words for law - *fa* (法) or *lü* (律) - was ever applied to rules of this kind.

Of these varieties only penal law has been systematically studied by Western scholars. The complexity of the Chinese administrative system has made it difficult for Western students to acquire a general familiarity with the legal principles that govern it. The study of unofficial law has also been limited due in part to the fact that the data are contained in such a variety of source materials, most extremely difficult to access. The lack of access to source material gave earlier scholars, both Chinese and Western, the mistaken impression that Imperial China did not have a system of civil law.

Penal law

The centrepiece of the penal law is the "code of punishments" issued by each dynasty at its inception. Although fragments of laws survive from the Qin and Han, the first surviving complete code was the Kaihuang Code developed during the Sui Dynasty and adopted by later dynasties including the Tang in 653. This code provided the model for all the later traditional penal codes through its definition of the Five Punishments and Ten Abominations. Only the Mongol Yuan Dynasty failed to issue a penal code, but the collections of legal materials from that dynasty still show the strong influence of the Tang code.

The penal codes contain only rules that prescribe punishments for specific offences, rules that define generally the allocation of punishment, or those that establish principles of interpretation. Each offence was allocated a specific punishment. The task of the magistrate was to identify the proper name of the offence disclosed by the facts. Determination of the correct punishment automatically followed.

The penal code was seen as indispensable part of government rules, yet punishments were still to be humane. The mutilating punishments that had characterised earlier law were no longer used by the 8th century. The five regular punishments established by the Tang code were, in descending order of severity: death, life exile, penal servitude (forced labour), beating with a heavy stick, or beating with a light stick. They remained the regular punishments until the closing years of the Qing.

The penal codes were divided into a "General Principles" and a "Specific Offences" section. Each dynasty retained the same basic content, though the Ming and Qing codes introduced some variation in the classification of offences. The Tang and Song codes consisted of a number of articles (律), many of which were adopted, sometimes without alteration, by the Ming and Qing codes. Once the articles of the code had been established at the beginning of the dynasty, there was a reluctance on the part of the founding emperor or his successors to change them.

Consequently, to deal with the problem of changing circumstances, the Ming started the practice of adding substatutes (例) to the code. The practice grew extensively under the Qing, with the result that, by the end of the 19th century, the penal code had lost something of its internal coherence and become an unwieldy instrument. Substatutes tended to be more specific and detailed than articles. Explanatory commentaries were added to the penal codes. The most authoritative were those approved by the throne for inclusion in the code. These often themselves contained rules not found in the articles or substatutes.

In cases where no ambiguous article or substatute could be invoked, previous decisions by the Board of Punishments might function as "precedents".

Some rules in the penal codes, especially those relating to civil matters, were obsolete or not enforced. Jean Escarra, has suggested that the penal law as a whole was intended to function as a guide to model conduct and not as a set of enforceable rules. Whilst this view has largely been rejected, it is clear that many of the enforced rules on family relationships were retained on account of their symbolic value.

After the Han period, all rules of a code which were not *lü* were called *ling* (ordinances) and *ge* (rulings), sometimes *shi* (models), and often *zhi* (decrees).

Administrative law

Administrative law was well developed in China very early; most of its basic framework being laid by the Zhou Dynasty. In the administrative structure, the emperor was supreme and hence above the law. He could make the law, override existing laws, and upset administrative decisions taken in his name. Yet, although autocratic, the very existence of the complex bureaucratic machinery constituted a check on his arbitrary exercise of power.

On occasion he might modify a capital sentence referred to him by the central judicial agencies for his approval, but he always did so with reference to the facts of the particular case and explained in his edict the reasons for the change he had made. Sometimes he would even accept a remonstrance by his officials that the change was not proper and accept that he had to act in conformity with the existing law.

Civil law

Customary law, dealt with what in the West is termed private law or civil law. In particular, it comprises rules governing matters of contract and property. In contrast with Western systems in which civil law preceded criminal law, in traditional Chinese law, the reverse was true. From the provisions of the penal code, magistrates could either derive principles of civil law either directly, if a matter was in stated in the penal code such as matters regarding such as that regarding debt and usury, dealings with land, the borrowing and pledging of property, and the sale of goods in markets, or indirectly reading into a criminal statute a basis for a private civil suit.

Although the stereotypical view of Chinese magistrates was that they were reluctant to intervene as arbiters in any kind of civil dispute, more recent studies have argued that most of a magistrate's work involved the settlement of civil disputes. In this view, the reluctance of magistrates to take on case work had to do largely with the fact that the Chinese civil administration was small, and that the workload on magistrates was very large. Moreover, scholars in the early 21st century, such as Philip Huang （黃宗智）, have argued that the traditional Chinese system of justice was fair, efficient, and frequently used in the settlement of disputes.

Use of property was divided into topsoil (*tianpi*) and subsoil (*tiangu*) rights. Landlords with subsoil rights had a permanent claim to the property if they paid taxes and received official seals from the government, but did not have rights to actively use the land. Instead, those with topsoil rights paid the subsoil landlord a fixed rent (or part of the proceeds of what was produced on the land) for not only the right to farm and live on the land, but the right to independently sell or lease the topsoil rights to another party. So as long as another party held topsoil rights, the party holding subsoil did not have right to actively use the land or evict the topsoil owner. Land, like other forms of property, was seen as being held collectively by the family and not individuals within the family. Another concept in imperial Chinese property rights was *dianmai* (典賣 /典賣), more commonly known as *huomai* (活賣 /活卖), or conditional sales of property that allowed the seller (i.e., his family) to buy back the land at the original price (without interest). The assumption was that land, having been held by a family for generations, should stay with the same family. From the Sui dynasty onwards, women could not hold property directly and, for land to stay in the same family, it had to pass between male heirs following the rule of primogeniture.

Procedure

Suspects and criminals were arrested by the county police or the posthouse chiefs who were subordinate to the county chief of police. One important principle of traditional Chinese law was that a person could not be convicted of a crime without a confession. Because a confession was required for a conviction and sentence the use of torture was often used to elicit such a confession. A common tool was the bastinado, applied to the buttocks and thighs.

During the Qin and Han, local magistrates were fully authorised to apply the full scale of punishments, including the death penalty.

In principle all criminal cases, whatever their gravity, were heard first in the court of the district in which the facts occurred. The magistrate investigated the facts, determined guilt or innocence, and then proposed the sentence for the offence as prescribed by the code. Whenever a sentence of greater severity than a beating was applicable, it was necessary to forward the case to the next superior court in the hierarchy, that of the prefect, for rehearing. The prefect's decision was final only in cases of penal servitude. Cases of exile or death were automatically reviewed by the provincial governor. All homicide cases and all cases attracting the death sentence were sent to the capital for review by the highest judicial tribunal, the Board of Punishments. No sentence of death could be implemented, except in extreme circumstances, without express approval from the emperor himself.

Moral values and the law

In contrast to the Legalists, the Confucian view of law was always centred on morality. Xun Zi, an early Confucian thinker, saw the necessity for legislation, but emphasised equally the importance of virtue on the part of the legislator and judiciary. There was a conviction that maintenance of the Confucian moral prescriptions through the apparatus of the state was essential for the preservation of a civilised society. Encouragement of the virtue of filial piety helped to strengthen the related duty of respect and submission to imperial authority.

The codes signal their moral orientation by placing right at the beginning of the "General Principles" section a description of the offences known as the "Ten Abominations". These offences were regarded as the most abhorrent. As the official commentary of the Qing code states: "persons guilty of any of the Ten Abominations destroy human bonds (倫), rebel against Heaven (天), go against reason (理), and violate justice (義)."

Law-making and legal reasoning

Where a new piece of legislation was being considered, care would be taken to assess its relationship to the existing law.

General characteristics

Equality before law was never officially accepted as a legal principle and as a legal practice. For example, the system of exemption of eight categories or persons from criminal prosecution (*ba yi*) and the system of exemption from punishment by giving up official positions (*guandang*) are formally recognised legal device.

Unlike in the West, where secular and religious powers co-existed and fostered a tradition of pluralism, the traditional Chinese legal system, as a tool of the sovereign, has never encountered strong counterparts, and therefore never tolerated the existence of any alien powers and legal rules other than those of the emperor. From a socio-cultural standpoint, however, it is interesting to note that while in the West, individuals have typically been intrinsically seen as linked to a single religious tradition (that is, a strong division traditionally existed between rival denominations, or between Christianity and Judaism), in Chinese culture, people have been able to simultaneously be adherents of Buddhism, Taoism, and Confucianism, or some combination of these.

In contrast to many other peoples, the Chinese never attributed their laws to a divine lawgiver. The same is true for the rule which governed the whole of life, and which therefore might legitimately be called "laws"; no divine origin is found for *li* (rules of correct behaviour) either.

Further reading

- Bodde, Derk, "Basic concepts of Chinese law: The genesis and evolution of legal thought in traditional China," *Essays on Chinese civilisation*, ed. Charles Le Blanc and Dorothy Borei. Princeton: Princeton University Press, 1981.
- Ch'ü T'ung-tsu, *Law and society in traditional China*. Paris and The Hague: Mouton, 1961.
- Escarra, Jean. *Le droit chinois: conception et évolution. Institutions législatives et judicaires. Science et enseignement*. Pekin: Henri Veitch, 1936.
- Huang, Philip, *Civil Justice in China: Representation and Practice in the Qing*. Stanford, California, Stanford University Press, 1996.
- Jiang, Yonglin (2011). *The Mandate of Heaven and The Great Ming Code (Asian Law Series)*[687]. University of Washington Press. ISBN 0295990651. Retrieved 24 April 2014.

Early Chinese law

- Hulsewé, Anthony F. P. "The Legalist and the laws of Ch'in," *Leyden studies in Sinology*, ed. W. L. Idema. Leiden: E. J. Brill, 1981.
- Hulsewé, Anthony F. P. *Remnants of Han Law*. Vol. 1. Leiden: E.J. Brill, 1955
- Hulsewé, Anthony F. P. *Remnants of Ch'in Law: An annotated translation of the Ch'in legal and administrative rules of the 3rd century B.C. discovered in Yünmeng Prefecture, Hu-pei Province in 1975*. Vol. 1. Leiden: E.J. Brill, 1985
- Uchida Tomoo (内田智雄), *Kanjo keishō shi* (漢書刑法志). Kyoto: Dōshishia University, 1958.

External links

- Chinese Law Codes[688]
- China - The Legal System[689]
- Ancient Chinese Theories of Control[690]
- Main Codes of Ancient China[691]

Tang Code

Part of a series on
Chinese Legalism

法

- v
- t
- e[692]

The *Tang Code* (Chinese: 唐律 ; pinyin: *Táng lǜ*) was a penal code that was established and used during the Tang Dynasty in China. Supplemented by civil statutes and regulations, it became the basis for later dynastic codes not only in China but elsewhere in East Asia. The Code synthesized Legalist and Confucian interpretations of law. Created in 624 and modified in 627 and 637, it was promulgated in 652 with 502 articles in 12 sections and enhanced with a commentary (the *Tánglǜ shūyì* 唐律疏議) in 653.[693] Considered as one of the greatest achievements of traditional Chinese law, the Tang Code is also the earliest Chinese Code to have been transmitted to the present in its complete form.[694]

Origin and context

The Tang code took its roots in the code of the Northern Zhou (564) dynasty, which was itself based on the earlier codes of the Cao-Wei and Western Jin (268).[695] Aiming to smooth the earlier laws and reduce physical punishments (such as mutilations) in order to appease social tensions in the newly pacified Tang territories, it was created in AD 624 at the request of Emperor Gaozu of Tang. After further revisions in 627 and 637 under Emperor Taizong, the code was completed by commentaries in 653, under Gaozong.

Organization and system of punishments

Tang Code[696]

Section	Name
I	General definitions and rules
II	Laws relating to passing into or through forbidden places (imperial palaces, town gates, walls, frontier posts)
III	Offences committed by officials in the exercise of their functions
IV	Laws concerning peasant families (lands, taxes, marriages)
V	Laws related to state stud-farms and storehouses
VI	Laws relating to the raising of troops
VII	Offences against the person and against property
VIII	Offences committed in the course of brawls
IX	Forgery and counterfeiting
X	Various laws of a special character
XI	Laws concerning the apprehension of guilty persons
XII	Laws relating to the administration of justice

French historian and sinologist Jacques Gernet has called the *Tang Code* "an admirable composition of faultless logic in spite of its size and complexity." The American sinologists Wallace Johnson and Denis C. Twitchett described it as "a very rational system of justice" in which "both the accuser and the officials involved had to be careful lest they themselves face punishment".[697] The *Tang Code* contained more than 500 articles divided into twelve large sections (see right-side table).

The penalty for an offence was determined according to two factors:

- **Offence** : The Tang Code clearly associated each offence with a penalty.

- **Relational position** : For relatives, this position was measured by the
kind and duration of mourning that had to be observed for each degree of
kinship. Relations outside the family were defined according to positions
in a social hierarchy capped by the emperor himself. In this hierarchy,
officials were higher than ordinary men, who were themselves superior to
persons of servile status. For instance, a slave committing a crime against
his master was punished more severely than if an ordinary person had
committed the same crime. The same offence committed by the master
against his slave, on the other hand, resulted in a *lower* penalty than the
same crime committed by a common person.

The local magistrate acted as examiner and sometimes as investigator, but his
final role in legal cases was to determine the proper penalty for the offense that
had been committed: he had to fix the nature of the offense as defined by the
code, and to increase or reduce the associated penalty depending on the social
relation between offender and victim.

The historically famous *wuting* 五聽 "five hearings" was a Chinese technique
for eliciting the facts of a case. While questioning a witness, the magistrate
would look closely for five kinds of behavior: "the person's statements, expression, breathing, reaction to the words of the judge, and eyes. Through
careful observation, it was thought that the experienced magistrate could arrive at a knowledge of whether the person was, in fact, telling the truth."[698]

If a magistrate was unable to decide a case on the basis of evidence and witness testimony, he could seek the permission of higher officials to use judicial
torture. The accused could be beaten no more than 200 blows in up to three
interrogations held at least twenty days apart. But when the accused was able
to withstand the full amount of torture without making a confession, the magistrate would use the same torture on the accuser. If the tortured accuser admitted making a false accusation, he would receive the same punishment that
would have been inflicted upon the accused had this latter been convicted.[699]

The offence modulated according to the degree of social relation determined
the final penalty which could range from flagellation using a rattan and bastinado with a bamboo stick, to penal labour, exile with penal labour, and death
by strangulation (garrote) or decapitation.

Interesting facts

- The code imposed two years of forced labor on any private household
found in possession of such works as the *Luoshu Square* or the *Yellow
River Map*, which are used in *Yijing* and *Fengshui* divination. The practice was preserved in the legal practice until the Song dynasty.

- Specific rules governed the application of judicial torture. The only instrument permitted was the *xunqiuzhang* 訊囚杖 "interrogation stick", which was approximately 40 inches long and .32[700] and .22 inches wide at the large and small ends respectively. The magistrate himself would be punished if other means were used to try to force a confession.[701]

Bibliography

- Gernet, Jacques (1996), *A History of Chinese Civilization*[702] (Second ed.), Cambridge, England: Cambridge University Press, pp. 801 pages, ISBN 9780521497817 Originally published in French as *Le monde chinois*.
- Johnson, Wallace, trans. (1979), *The Tang Code: Volume One: General Principles*. Princeton: Princeton University Press.
- Johnson, Wallace and Denis Twitchett (1993), "Criminal Procedure in T'ang China", *Asia Major* 3rd series, 6.2, 113-146.

Great Qing Legal Code

The **Great Qing Legal Code** (or **Great Ching Legal Code**),[703] also known as the **Qing Code** (**Ching Code**) or, in Hong Kong law, as the *Ta Tsing Leu Lee* (大清律例), was the legal code of the Qing empire (1644–1912). The code was based on the Ming legal system, which was kept largely intact. Compared to the Ming code which had no more than several hundred statutes and sub-statutes, the Qing code contained 1,907 statutes from over 30 times of revisions between 1644 and 1912.

The Qing code was the last legal code of imperial China. By the end of Qing dynasty, it was the only legal code enforced in China for nearly 270 years. Even with the fall of imperial Qing in 1912, the Confucian philosophy of social control enshrined in the Qing code remain influential in the German-based system of the Republic of China, and later, the Soviet-based system of the People's Republic of China.

Nature of the Code

Ta Tsing Leu Lee contains 4 parts: constitutional statement (Faat , 法), details legal statement (Luet, 律), executive order (Ling, 令) and case (Laai, 例).

Constitutional statement: The legal statements approved by the founder of dynasty, generally about the basic policies of the dynasty and the structure of state, which are almost impossible to be modified.

Details legal statement: The common legal statements.

Executive order: The executive orders declared by the emperor.

Case: The imperial government collects and publishes selected cases periodically.

The traditional Chinese law was largely in place by Qing dynasty. The process of amalgamation of Confucian views and law codes was considered complete by the *Tang Code* of AD 624. The code was regarded as a model of precision and clarity in terms of drafting and structure. Confucianism in revised form (Neo-Confucianism) continued to be the state orthodoxy under the Song, Ming and Qing dynasty. Throughout the centuries the Confucian foundations of the *Tang Code* were retained with even some aspects strengthened.

During the Qing dynasty, criminal justice was based on an extremely detailed criminal code. One element of the traditional Chinese criminal justice system is the notion that criminal law has a moral purpose, one of which is to get the convicted to repent and see the error of his ways. In the traditional Chinese legal system, a person could not be convicted of a crime unless he has confessed. This often led to the use of torture, in order to extract the necessary confession. These elements still influence modern Chinese views toward law. All death sentences were reported to the capital and required the personal approval of the emperor.

There was no civil code separate from the criminal code, which led to the now discredited belief that traditional Chinese law had no civil law. More recent studies have demonstrated that most of the magistrates' legal work was in civil disputes, and that there was an elaborate system of civil law which used the criminal code to establish torts.

The *Qing Code* was in form exclusively a criminal code. Its statutes throughout stated as prohibitions and restrictions, and the violation of which was subjected to a range of punishments by a legalist state. In practice, however, large sections of the code and its sub-statutes dealt with matters that would properly be characterised as civil law. The populace made extensive use (perhaps a third of all cases) of the local magistrate courts to bring suits or threaten to sue on a whole range of civil disputes, characterized as "minor matters" in the *Qing Code*. Moreover, in practice, magistrates frequently tempered the application of the code by taking prevalent local custom into account in their decisions. Filed complaints were often settled among the parties before they received a formal court hearing, sometimes under the influence of probable action by the court.

Qing Code and the West

The *Great Qing Legal Code* was the first written Chinese work directly translated into English.[704] The translation, known as *Fundamental Laws of China* was completed by Sir George Thomas Staunton in 1810. It was the first time the Qing code had been translated into a European language. The French translation was published in 1812.

The translation played an important role for Europeans to gain insights into the Chinese legal system. Due to the increased competition among European powers in the 18th century AD, understanding of the Chinese legal foundation was crucial to gain profitable trading access into China. Even though the *Qing Code* was in form exclusively a criminal code, the British were able to use it to their advantage to resolve trading obstacles and resistance, such as those resulting from the First and Second Opium Wars. It was this fundamental understanding of the Chinese legal code that made it possible for Britain to devise a number of unequal treaties geared to their advantageWikipedia:Citation needed.

In the late Qing dynasty there was a concerted effort to establish legal codes based on European models. Because of the German victory in the Franco-Prussian War and because Japan was used as the model for political and legal reform, the adopted law code were modelled closely on that of Germany.

The end of the Qing Code and its remaining influence

In the early 20th century AD, with the advent of the "Constitutional Movement", the imperial government was forced by various pressures to quickly modernise its legal system. While the Qing Code remained law, it was qualified and supplemented in quick succession by the *Outline of the Imperial Constitution* of 1908 and the *Nineteen Important Constitutional Covenants* of 1911 AD, as well as various specialist laws, such as the *Great Qing Copyright Code* in 1910 AD.

In 1912 AD the collapse of Qing dynasty ended 268 years of its imperial rule over China and 2000 years of imperial history came to an end. The Qing court was replaced by the Republic of China government. While some parts of the Qing Code and other late Qing statutes were adopted for "temporary application" by the Beiyang Government of the Republic of China, as a general law position the Qing Code ceased to have effect *de jure* due to the dissolution of the Qing state.

Republic of China

The newly founded Republic of China adopted the existing German-based legal codesWikipedia:Please clarify, but these codes were not immediately put into practice. Following the overthrow of the Qing dynasty in 1912 AD, China came under the control of rival warlords and had no government strong enough to establish a legal code to replace the Qing code. Finally in 1927 AD, Chiang Kai-shek's Kuomintang government attempted to develop Western-style legal and penal systems. Few of the KMT codes, however, were implemented nationwide. Although government leaders were striving for a Western-inspired system of codified law, the traditional Chinese preference for collective social sanctions over impersonal legalism hindered constitutional and legal development. The spirit of the new laws never penetrated to the grass-roots level or provided hoped-for stability. Ideally, individuals were to be equal before the law, but this premise proved to be more rhetorical than substantive.

Law in the Republic of China on Taiwan today is based on the German-based legal system carried to Taiwan by the Kuomintang. The influence of the Qing Code manifests itself in the form of an exceptionally detailed penal code, with a large number of offences punishable by death. For example, in addition to the offence of piracy, there are also *piracy causing grievous bodily harm* (punishable by death or life imprisonment pursuant to Section 3 of Article 333 of the *Criminal Code of the Republic of China* (中華民國刑法)), as well as *piracy causing death* and *piracy with arson, rape, kidnapping or murder* (both entail mandatory death penalty pursuant to Section 3 of Article 333 and Article 334 of the *Criminal Code*). One legacy from those bygone era is the offence of *murder of a family member* (e.g. patricide and matricide). The offense entails life imprisonment or death pursuant to Section 1 of Article 272 of the *Criminal Code*, even for minors under 18 years old until abolition on July 1, 2006 of Section 2 of Article 63 of the *Criminal Code* that would permit life imprisonment or death penalty against minors committing crimes under Section 1 of Article 272.

People's Republic of China

In the People's Republic of China, while the legal system was, and to some extent still is, based on socialist law, it incorporates certain aspects of the Qing Code, most notably the notion that offenders should be shamed into repentance - hence the now notorious practice of parading condemned criminals in public - and the idea of using law as the means of controlling social mores. Wikipedia:Citation needed.

Hong Kong

In Hong Kong, after the colonization by the British Empire in 1841, the Great Qing Legal Code remained in force for the local Chinese population. Until the end of the 19th Century AD, Chinese offenders were still executed by decapitation, whereas the British would be put to death by hanging. Even deep into the 20th Century and well after the fall of the Qing dynasty in China, Chinese men in Hong Kong could still practice polygamy by virtue of the Qing Code—a situation that was ended only with the passing of the Marriage Reform Ordinance 1970 (Cap.178) which came into force on 7 October 1971. Therefore, the Great Qing Legal Code was actually enforced in some form for a total of 327 years, from 1644 AD to 1971 AD.

Because there are still existing alive concubines married before the Marriage Reform Ordinance (Cap.178), and their rights (of inheritance, and the inheritance rights of their sons and daughters) are respected by the Hong Kong legal system (even after the 1997 handover), the Great Qing Legal Code is still admissible in evidence when handling legal cases with history dated back before 1971.

References

- ⓒ *This article incorporates text from* Life among the Chinese: with characteristic sketches and incidents of missionary operations and prospects in China, *by Robert Samuel Maclay, a publication from 1861 now in the public domain in the United States.*

Further reading

- Bodde, Derk, and Clarence Morris, eds. *Law in Imperial China: Exemplified by 190 Ch'ing dynasty Cases.* Cambridge, MA: Harvard University Press, 1967.
- Jones, William C. *The Great Qing Code.* Oxford: Clarendon Press; New York: Oxford University Press, 1994.

External links

> Chinese Wikisourcehas original text related to this article: 大清律例

- The Qing Code[705], Wallace Johnson, ed.
- Gray, John Henry (1878). Gregor, William Gow, ed. *China, a history of the laws, manners and customs of the people, ed. by W.G. Gregor*[706]. London: MACMILLAN AND CO. Retrieved 24 April 2014.
- Gray, John Henry (1878). Gregor, William Gow, ed. *China: A History of the Laws, Manners, and Customs of the People, Volume 1*[707]. London: Macmillan and Company. Retrieved 24 April 2014.

Yassa

Yasser (alternatively: *Yasa, Yasaq, Jazag, Zasag*, Mongolian: Их засаг, *Yehe Zasag*) was a secret written code of law created by Genghis Khan. The word Yassa translates into "order" or "decree". It was the *de facto* law of the Mongol Empire even though the "law" was kept secret and never made public. The Yassa seems to have its origin as decrees issued in war times. Later, these decrees were codified and expanded to include cultural and life-style conventions. By keeping the Yassa secret, the decrees could be modified and used selectively. It is believed that the Yassa was supervised by Genghis Khan himself and his stepbrother Shihihutag who was then high judge (in Mongolian: *улсын их заргач*) of the Mongol Empire.[708] Genghis Khan appointed his second son Chagatai (later Chagatai Khan) to oversee the execution of the laws.

Overview

The Yassa decrees were thought to be comprehensive and specific, although no Mongolian scroll or codex has been found. There are records of excerpts among many chronicles including Makrizi, Vartang, and ibn Batuta, among others. Moreover, copies may have been discovered in Korea as well. The absence of any physical document is historically problematic. Historians are left with secondary sources, conjecture and speculation, which describes much of the content of this overview. Historical certainty about the Yassa is weak compared to the much older Code of Hammurabi 18th century BCE or the Edicts of Ashoka, 3rd century BCE. The latter were carved for all to see on stone plinths, 12 to 15 meters high, which were located throughout Ashoka's empire (today's India, Nepal, Pakistan, and Afghanistan). The Yassa, thought to be written in the Uigur Mongolian script and scribed on scrolls, was preserved in secret archives and known only to and read only by the royal family. Beyond being a code of laws, the Yassa may have included philosophical, spiritual, and mystical elements, and thus may have been thought of as a quasi-sacred or magic text.

The exoteric aspect of Yassa outlined laws for various members of the Mongol community such as soldiers, officers, and doctors. The Yassa aimed at three things: obedience to Genghis Khan, a binding together of the nomad clans, and the merciless punishment of wrongdoing. It concerned itself with people, not property. Unless a man actually confessed, he was not judged guilty. The purpose of many decrees was probably to eliminate social and economic disputes among the Mongols and future allied peoples. Among the rules were no stealing of livestock from other people, sharing food with travelers, no abduction of women from other families, and no defection among soldiers. It represented a day-to-day set of rules for people under Mongol control that was strictly enforced.

The Yassa also addressed and reflected Mongol cultural and lifestyle norms. Death via beheading was the most common punishment save for when the offender was of noble blood, in which case the offender was killed without shedding blood. Even minor offenses were punishable by death. For example, a soldier would be put to death if he did not pick up something that fell from the person in front of him. Those favored by the Khan were often given preferential treatment within the system of law and were allowed several chances before being punished.

As Genghis Khan had set up an institution that ensured complete religious freedom, people under his rule were free to worship as they pleased, as long as the laws of the Yassa were observed.

Conjectural laws

Many sources provide conjectures about the actual laws of the Yassa. The Yassa was so influential that other cultures appropriated and adapted portions of it, or reworked it for ends of negative propaganda. (For instance, the number of offenses for which the death penalty was given was famous among contemporaries of the Yassa.) However, Harold Lamb's *Genghis Khan: The Emperor of All Men* quotes a translation by François Pétis de la Croix. Although unable to come upon a complete list of the laws, he compiled several from Persian and Arabic chroniclers, Fras Rubruquis, and Giovanni da Pian del Carpine, among other sources. Those laws are listed here:

1. "It is ordered to believe that there is only one God, creator of heaven and earth, who alone gives life and death, riches and poverty as pleases Him—and who has over everything an absolute power, a different version states that there was liberty to worship God in whatever way suitable (Plantagenet Somerset Fry).

2. He [Chingis-Khan] ordered that all religions were to be respected and that no preference was to be shown to any of them. All this he commanded in order that it might be agreeable to Heaven. {al-Makrizi}

3. Leaders of a religion, lawyers, physicians, scholars, preachers, monks, persons who are dedicated to religious practice, the Muezzin (this latter appearing to be from the later period of Khubilai Khan unless this was further translated there had been no specific reference made to any Muezzin and cities including mosques were levelled), physicians and those who bathe the bodies of the dead are to be freed from public charges. {Al-Makrizi}

4. It is forbidden under penalty of death that anyone, whoever he be, shall be proclaimed emperor unless he has been elected previously by the princes, khans, officers, and other Mongol nobles in a general council.

5. Forbidden to ever make peace with a monarch, a prince or a people who have not submitted. [It is apparent they presented certain proposals to the different states or kingdoms that existed that they should participate with them.]

6. The ruling that divides men of the army into tens, hundreds, thousands, and ten thousands is to be maintained. He put leaders, (princes/bogatyrs/ generals/noyans) at the head of the troops and appointed commanders of thousands, hundreds, and tens. {al-Makrizi} This arrangement serves to raise an army in a short time, and to form the units of commands.

7. The moment a campaign begins, each soldier must receive his arms from the hand of the officer who has them in charge. The soldier must keep them in good order, and have them inspected by his officer before a battle. He ordered his successors to personally examine the troops and their armament before going to battle, to supply the troops with everything they needed for the campaign and to survey everything even to needle and thread, and if any of the soldiers lacked a necessary thing that soldier was to be punished. {al-Makrizi}

8. Forbidden, under death penalty, to pillage the enemy before the general commanding gives permission; but after this permission is given the soldier must have the same opportunity as the officer, and must be allowed to keep what he has carried off, provided he has paid his share to the receiver for the emperor.

9. He ordered that soldiers be punished for negligence; and hunters who let an animal escape during a community hunt he ordered to be beaten with

sticks and in some cases to be put to death. {Mirhond or Mirkhwand} (may appear excluded from some accounts, can be a more restricted Siberian-originating practice, but seems genuine).

10. To keep the men of the army exercised, a great hunt shall be held every winter. On this account, it is forbidden any man of the empire to kill from the month of March to October, deer, bucks, roe-bucks, hares, wild ass and some birds.

11. Forbidden, to cut the throats of animals slain for food; When an animal is to be eaten, its feet must be tied, its belly ripped open and its heart squeezed in the hand until the animal dies; then its meat may be eaten; but if anyone slaughter an animal after the Mohammedan fashion, he is to be himself slaughtered. {al-Makrizi} [Women were not supposed to slaughter animals this way, possibly due to being weaker, there is no prohibition in the Yassa.]

12. It is permitted to eat the blood and entrails of animals though this was forbidden before now.

13. Every man who does not go to war must work for the empire, without reward, for a certain time.

14. The man in whose possession a stolen horse is found must return it to its owner and add nine horses of the same kind: if he is unable to pay this fine, his children must be taken instead of the horses, and if he have no children, he himself shall be slaughtered like a sheep. {al-Makrizi} In the versions where the provisions appear the method of execution is likened to sheep therefore as in accordance it may be presumed with the law for the slaughter of animals [it is unclear in another version as of when their bodies should be cut in two parts] For lesser thefts the punishment shall be, according to the value of the thing stolen, a number of blows of a staff-seven, seventeen, twenty-seven, up to seven hundred. But this bodily punishment may be avoided by paying nine times the worth of the thing stolen. [Another older version mentions no punishment for thefts under the value mentioned, it is not so specified.]

15. No subject of the empire may take a Mongol for servant or slave. Every man, except in rare cases, must join the army.

16. Whoever gives food or clothing to a captive without the permission of his captor is to be put to death. {al-Makrizi}

17. Whoever finds a runaway slave or captive and does not return him to the person to whom he belongs is to be put to death.{al-Makrizi} The word translated as "slave" means "captive taken for labor", the opponents of the Mongols were usually regarded by them as facing a punishment for resisting the universal principles/the Mongol system, or what it aspired to via its codes and measures, the concept was passed on also to their descendants, based on concepts of sedentary populations who degrade the people and

criminal tribes, criminal already often simply by their concept of resisting to the above-referred Mongol system, the word is "bo´ol", linked to
modern "boolt", band for tying, "booch" (ch as in chaver in Hebrew) is
in the modern Mongolian both associated with the type of binding and
process used in capture as a verb where it is translated as meaning "slave".
However other lands differ in meaning of "slave" though allied.

18. The law required the payment of a bride price. Though not mentioned
in other sources, it may be that this is a dowry reference, given that the
bride price is usually a custom restricted to specific Mongol tribes (but
that may have appeared later). This may have been practiced earlier, while
Chinggis Khan himself had never followed this custom, nor is it much
(if at all) referred to in the Nuvs Tobchaan Mongolyn. The bride price
might have been considered as a useful deterrent to trade in women, or
simply a modernizing experimental inversion from a dowry; however,
the Tatar neighbors traded in women (which was prohibited it is reported
by the Yassa) and that marriage between the first and second degrees
of kinship is forbidden. A man may marry two sisters, or have several
concubines; however, under Buddhism and shamanism there was a progressive tendency for a marriage ceremony. Some Buddhist forms revived
some casualty without marriage. The women should attend to the care
of property, buying and selling at their pleasure, specifically in another
version "Os Mongóis" by a Portuguese publisher of summarized histories
of culture, the law is quoted as defining trade as their sphere, there is no
exclusion from military participation, but this was reported more popular
among Tatars as according to Islamic law which was only possible to
follow via Sufism. Men should occupy themselves only with hunting and
war.

19. Children born of a concubine are to be considered as legitimate, and
receive their share of the heritage according to the disposition of it made
by the father. The distribution of property is to be carried out on the basis
of the senior son receiving more than the junior, the younger son inherit-
ing the household of the father. The seniority of children depends upon
the rank of their mother; one of the wives must always be the senior, this
being determined chiefly by the time of her marriage. After the death of
his father, a son may dispose of the father's wives, all except his mother;
he may marry them or give them in marriage to others. All except the
legal heirs are strictly forbidden to make use of any of the property of the
deceased. {Vermadsky}

20. An adulterer is to be put to death without any regard as to whether he is
married or not. {al-Makrizi} The Yasa prescribes these rules: to love one
another, not to commit adultery, not to steal, not to give false witness, not
to be a traitor, and to respect old people and beggars. Whoever violates

these commands is put to death. {Mahak'ia] Here are the laws of God which they call Iasax which were given to them [g288]: first, that they love one another; second, that they not commit adultery; not steal; not bear false witness; not betray anyone; and that they honor the aged and the poor. And should perpetrators of such crimes be found among them, they should be killed." {Grigor of Akanc}

21. If two families wish to be united in marriage and have only young children, the marriage of these children is allowed, if one be a boy and the other a girl. If the children are dead, the marriage contract may still be drawn up.

22. It is forbidden to bathe or wash garments in running water during thunder.

23. Whoever intentionally lies, or practices sorcery, or spies upon the behavior of others, or intervenes between the two parties in a quarrel to help the one against the other is also to be put to death. [al-Makrizi] (Intentional liars being included in this section in one of the versions however it is not as definable in practice, and may refer to methodical lying which also appears in areas of earlier Asiatic influence in Europe, but becomes particularly defined together with a Germanic version which may have legal undertones, and a Latin practicality, it is a version intended to cause grievous harm to people and damage them and further particularly as a means of sabotage, but this is not completely clear. It can also have an aspect of those who practice lying with frivolous purposes.)

24. Officers and chieftains who fail in their duty, or do not come at the summons of the Khan are to be slain, especially in remote districts. If their offense be less grave, they must come in person before the Khan."

25. Whoever is guilty of sodomy is also to be put to death [al-Makrizi]

26. Urinating in water or ashes is punishable by death. [al-Makrizi]

27. It was forbidden to wash clothing until completely worn out. [al-Makrizi]

28. He forbade his people to eat food offered by another until the one offering the food tasted of it himself, even though one be a prince and the other a captive; he forbade them to eat anything in the presence of another without having invited him to partake of the food; he forbade any man to eat more than his comrades, and to step over a fire on which food was being cooked or a dish from which people were eating. [al-Makrizi]

29. One may not dip their hands into water and must instead use a vessel for the drawing of water. [al-Makrizi]

30. When the wayfarer passes by a group of people eating, he must eat with them without asking for permission, and they must not forbid him in this. [al-Makrizi]

31. It was forbidden to show preference to a sect, or to put emphasis on a word. When talking to someone, do not speak to them with a title, calling them by their name. This applies to even the Khan himself. [al-Makrizi]

32. At the beginning of each year, all the people must present their daughters to the Khan so he may choose some of them for himself and his children. [al-Makrizi]

- Also that minors not higher than a cart wheel may not be killed in war.
- Also abduction of women and sexual assault and or abuse of women was forbidden punishable by death.
- In cases of murder (punishment for murder) one could ransom himself by paying fines which were: for a Mohammedan - 40 golden coins (Balysh); and for a Chinese - one donkey. [Mirhod or Mirkhwand]
- The Khan established a postal system so that he might quickly learn about events of the empire.
- He ordered his son Chagatai to see that the Yasa was observed. [al-Makrizi]

Verkhovensky reports that the Yassa begins with an exhortation to honor men of all nations based on their virtues. This pragmatic admonition is borne out by the ethnic mixture created by Genghis Khan in the Mongolian medieval army for purpose of unity (Ezent Gueligen Mongolyn), the United Mongol Warriors. The origin of the word Mongol, "mong", means "brave". Thus, at the time, it may have meant as much an army of "the brave", as an army from or made up of people from Mongolia.

- Genghis Khan consulted teachers of religions, such as imáms and probably rabbis and Christian priests, in compiling his law codex.

After Genghis Khan

Ogedei Khan, the 3rd son of Genghis Khan and the second Great Khan, proclaimed the Great Yassa as an integral body of precedents, confirming the continuing validity of his father's commands and ordinances while adding his own. Ogedei codified rules of dress, conduct of the kurultais, the military council. His two immediate successors followed the tradition of the Yassa.

The Mongols in various parts of the empire began to add laws more appropriate to their area.

Present day influence

In the modern Turkish language (as used presently in Turkey), the word "law" is *yasa*, and the adjective "legal" is *yasal*. The word for a constitution, including the Constitution of Turkey, is *Anayasa* ("mother-law").

Etymology

The word "Yasa" or "Yassa" is existent in both Mongolic and Turkic languages. It is believed that the word comes from the Mongolian verb "zas-" or "yas-" which means "to set in order". "Tsereg zasakh" is a phrase commonly found in old Mongolian texts like the Secret History that means "to set the soldiers in order" in the sense of rallying the soldiers before a battle. The supreme executive body of the present-day Mongolian government is called the "Zasag-in gazar" which means the "place of Zasag", the "place of order". Zasag during the Qing dynasty referred to native provincial governors in Mongolia. The local office called Zasag-in gazar served as a court of the first instance and included secretaries and other officials. The verb "zasaglakh" means "to govern" in Mongolian. The Turkic verb "yas-" which means "to spread", probably originated in Uighur Turkic and was firstly used by Uighur Turks.[709]

References

- Lamb, Harold (1927). *Genghis Khan: The Emperor of All Men*. Garden City Publishing.
- Vernadsky, George: "The Mongols and Russia," Yale University Press, 1953, page 102
- Vernadsky, George: "The Scope and Content of Chingis Khan's Yasa." Printed in Harvard Journal of Asiatic Studies, Volume 3, 1938, pages 337-360
- Akner, Grigor of, History of the Nation of Archers, previously attributed to Maghak'ia the Monk. The Armenian text with English translation by Robert Blake and Richard Frye printed in vol. 12 of the Harvard Journal of Asiatic Studies #3-4 (1949) pp. 269–443
- Bar Hebraeus (Abul-Faraj), Makhtbhanuth Zabhne, Chronicon, the second portion, Chronicon Ecclesiasticum. The current edition of the Chronicon Ecclesiasticum is by Jean Baptiste Abbeloos and Thomas Joseph Lamy, Syriac text, Latin translation.

- Gibb, H.A.R. trans. and ed. (1958), The Travels of Ibn Baṭṭūṭa, A.D. 1325–1354 (Volumes 1-3), London: Hakluyt Society. Gibb, H.A.R.; Beckingham, C.F. trans. and eds. (1994), The Travels of Ibn Baṭṭūṭa, A.D. 1325–1354 (Volume 4), London: Hakluyt Society, ISBN 978-0-904180-37-4.
- Areveltsi, Vardan(or Vardang), Havakumn Patmutsyun (Historical Compilation) at the Matenadaran in Yerevan, Armeni
- Mirhond (or Mirkhwand (byname of Muḥammad Ibn Khāvandshāh Ibn Maḥmūd), Rowzat oṣ-ṣafā' (Eng. trans. begun as History of the Early Kings of Persia, 1832
- Maqrizi (byname of Taqi al-Din Abu al-Abbas Ahmad ibn 'Ali ibn 'Abd al-Qadir ibn Muhammad al-Maqrizi (1364 – 1442), The History of the Ayyubit and Mameluke Rulers, translated into French by E Quatremére (2 vols. Paris, 1837-1845)
- Ayalon, D. "The Great *Yasa* of Chingiz Khan: a re-examination." A, *Studia Islamica* 33 (1971): 97-140.
- Morgan, D.O. "The 'Great *Yasa* of Chingiz Khan' and Mongol law in the Ilkhanate." *Bulletin of the School of Oriental and African Studies* 49/1 (1986): 163-176.

External links

- The Yasa of Chingis Khan. A code of honor, dignity, and excellence[710]
- Yasa: The law of the People[711]
- Nişanyan - Türkçe Etimolojik Sözlük[712]

Legal history of the Catholic Church

Part of a series on the

Jurisprudence of Catholic canon law

Catholicism portal

- v
- t
- e[713]

The **legal history of the Catholic Church** is the history of the oldest continuously functioning legal system in the West,[714] much later than Roman law but predating the evolution of modern European civil law traditions. The history of Latin canon law can be divided into four periods: the *jus antiquum*, the *jus novum*, the *jus novissimum* and the *Code of Canon Law*.[715] In relation to the Code, history can be divided into the *jus vetus* (all law before the Code) and the *jus novum* (the law of the Code, or *jus codicis*). Eastern canon law developed separately.

Latin canon law

Jus Antiquum

The most ancient collections of canonical legislation are certain very early Apostolic documents, known as the Church Orders: for instance, the *Didache ton dodeka apostolon* or "Teaching of the Twelve Apostles", which dates from the end of the first or the beginning of the 2nd century; the Apostolic Church-Ordinance; the *Didascalia*, or "Teaching of the Apostles"; the Apostolic Canons and Apostolic Constitutions. These collections have never had any official value, no more than any other collection of this first period. However, the Apostolic Canons and, through it, the Apostolic Constitutions, were influential for a time in that later collections would draw upon these earliest sources of Church law.[716]

It was in the East, after Constantine I's Edict of Milan of toleration (313), that arose the first systematic collections. We cannot so designate the chronological collections of the canons of the councils of the 4th and 5th centuries (314-451); the oldest systematic collection, made by an unknown author in 535, has not come down. The most important collections of this epoch are the *Synagoge kanonon*, or the collection of John the Scholastic (Joannes Scholasticus), compiled at Antioch about 550, and the Nomocanons, or compilations of civil laws affecting religious matters (*nomos*) and ecclesiastical laws (*kanon*). One such mixed collection is dated in the 6th century and has been erroneously attributed to John the Scholastic; another of the 7th century was rewritten and much enlarged by the schismatical ecumenical patriarch Photius (883).

In the Western Church one collection of canons, the *Collectio Dionysiana*, exercised an influence far beyond the limits of the country in which it was composed. This collection was the work of Dionysius Exiguus, who compiled several collections that now go under the name *Dionysiana*. Dionysius appears to have done most of his work shortly after the year 600.[717] His collections contain his own Latin translation of the canons of the ancient third-, fourth- and fifth-century councils, excerpts from a (probably) confected collection of African canons (which Dionysius calls the *Registrum ecclesiae Carthaginensis*), and a collection of (38) papal letters (*Epistolæ decretales*) dating from the reign of Pope Siricius (384-398) to that of Anastasius II (died 498). The influence of this Italian collection grew enormously during the seventh and eighth centuries, especially in England and France. It was continuously enlarged and modified, the most famous modification being a version supposedly send by Pope Adrian I to Charlemagne in 774 and therefore known today as the *Collectio Dionysio-Hadriana*.

Besides the *Dionysiana* Italy also produced two 5th-century Latin translations of the Greek synods known as the *Corpus canonum Africano-Romanum* and

Collectio prisca, both of which are now lost though large portions of them survive in two very large Italian collections known as the *Collectio canonum Quesnelliana* and *Collectio canonum Sanblasiana* respectively. In Italy was also produced a popular fifth-century collection of forgeries known today as the *Symmachean forgeries*. Africa possessed a late fourth-century collection known as the *Breviarium Hipponense* as well as an early fifth-century collection known as the *Codex Apiarii causae*; also the *Breviatio canonum*, or digest of the canons of the councils by Fulgentius Ferrandus (died c. 546), and the *Concordia canonum* of Cresconius Africanus, an adaptation of the *Dionysiana* (about 690). In Gaul many important collections were produced, like the collection known today as the *Concilium Arelatense secundum* and, at the beginning of the 6th century, the *Statuta Ecclesiæ antiqua*, erroneously attributed to Africa. Also from Gaul/France are the collections known today as the *Collectio canonum quadripartita* and the *Libri duo de synodalibus causis* composed by Regino of Prüm. Gaul/France also produced two immensely important collections known as the *Collectio canonum vetus Gallica* (compiled in Lyons about 600) and the *Collectio canonum Dacheriana* (about 800), the latter so called from the name of its editor, Luc d'Achéry. The *Collectio canonum Hibernensis* or Irish collection of canons, compiled in the 8th century, influenced both England, Gaul and (though much later) Italy.[718] Unlike almost every other region, England never produced a 'national' collection, though English personnel played an important role in copying and disseminating Irish and Italian collections in Germany and France.[719] Around the year 700 there developed in either England or Germany a collection of penitential canons attributed to Theodore of Tarsus, Archbishop of Canterbury (died 690). This collection marked a major advance in the development of penitential-canonical collections, which had already been in development for centuries especially within the Irish church. Collection like the one attributed to Theodore were known as *penitentials*, and were often rather short and simple, most likely because they were meant as handbooks for the use of confessors. There were many such books circulating in Europe from the seventh to the eleventh century, each penitential containing rules indicating exactly how much penance was required for which sins. In various ways these penitentials, mainly Insular in origin, came to affect the larger canon law collections in development on the continent.[720]

Iberia (i.e. Spain) possessed the *Capitula Martini*, compiled about 572 by Martin, Bishop of Braga (in Portugal), and the immense and influential *Collectio Hispana* dating from about 633, attributed in the 9th century to St. Isidore of Seville. In the 9th century arose several apocryphal collections, viz. those of Benedictus Levita, of Pseudo-Isidore (also Isidorus Mercator, Peccator, Mercatus), and the *Capitula Angilramni*. An examination of the controversies which these three collections give rise to will be found elsewhere (see False

Decretals). The Pseudo-Isidorian collection, the authenticity of which was for a long time admitted, has exercised considerable influence on ecclesiastical discipline, without however modifying it in its essential principles. Among the numerous collections of a later date, we may mention the *Collectio Anselmo dedicata*, compiled in Italy at the end of the 9th century, the *Libellus de ecclesiasticis disciplinis* of Regino of Prum (died 915); the *Collectarium canonum* of Burchard of Worms (died 1025); the collection of the younger St. Anselm of Lucca, compiled towards the end of the 11th century; the *Collectio trium partium*, the *Decretum* and the *Panormia* of Yves of Chartres (died 1115 or 1117); the *Liber de misericordia et justitia* of Algerus of Liège, who died in 1132; the Collection in 74 Titles — all collections which Gratian made use of in the compilation of his *Decretum*

Jus Novum

The period of canonical history known as the *Jus Novum* ("new law") or *middle period* covers the time from Gratian to the Council of Trent (mid-12th century–16th century).

The spurious conciliar canons and papal decrees were gathered together into collections, both unofficial and official. In the year 1000, there was no book that had attempted to summarized the whole body of canon law, to systematize it in whole or in part.[721] There were, however, many collections of the decrees of councils and great bishops. These collections usually only had regional force and were usually organized chronologically by type of document (e.g. letters of popes, canons of councils, etc.), or occasionally, by general topic. Before the late 11th century, canon law was highly decentralized, depending on many different codifications and sources, whether of local councils, ecumenical councils, local bishops, or of the Bishops of Rome.

The first truly systematic collection was assembled by the Camaldolese monk Gratian in the 11th century, commonly known as the *Decretum Gratiani* ("Gratian's Decree") but originally called *The Concordance of Discordant Canons*[722] (*Concordantia Discordantium Canonum*). Canon law greatly increased from 1140 to 1234. After that it slowed down, except for the laws of local councils (an area of canon law in need of scholarship), and secular laws supplemented.[723] In 1234 Pope Gregory IX promulgated the first official collection of canons, called the *Decretalia Gregorii Noni* or *Liber Extra*. This was followed by the *Liber Sextus* (1298) of Boniface VIII, the *Clementines* (1317) of Clement V, the *Extravagantes Joannis XXII* and the *Extravagantes Communes*, all of which followed the same structure as the *Liber Extra*. All these collections, with the *Decretum Gratiani*, are together referred to as the *Corpus Juris Canonici*. After the completion of the *Corpus Juris Canonici*, subsequent papal legislation was published in periodic volumes called *Bullaria*.

Johannes Gratian was a monk who taught theology at a monastery in Bologna.[724] He produced a comprehensive and *comprehensible* collection of canon law. He resolved contradictions and discrepancies in the existing law.[725] In the 1140s his work became the dominant legal text.[726] The papacy appreciated and approved the *Decretum* of Gratian. The *Decretum* formed the core of the body of canon law upon which a greater legal structure was built.Wikipedia:Please clarify Before Gratian there was no "jurisprudence of canon law" (system of legal interpretation and principles). Gratian is the founder of canonical jurisprudence, which merits him the title "Father of Canon Law".[727]

> *'The combination of logical, moral, and political elements contributed to a systematization that was quite different from a merely doctrinal or dogmatic analysis of legal rules, however complex and however coherent. The canon law as a system was more than rules; it was a process, a dialectical process of adapting rules to new situations. This was inevitable if only because of the limits imposed upon its jurisdiction, and the consequent competition which it faced from the secular legal systems that coexisted with it.'*[728]

In the thirteenth century, the Roman Church began to collect and organize its canon law, which after a millennium of development had become a complex and difficult system of interpretation and cross-referencing. The official collections were the *Liber Extra* (1234) of Pope Gregory IX, the *Liber Sextus* (1298) of Boniface VIII and the *Clementines* (1317), prepared for Clement V but published by John XXII. These were addressed to the universities by papal letters at the beginning of each collection, and these texts became textbooks for aspiring canon lawyers. In 1582 a compilation was made of the Decretum, Extra, the Sext, the Clementines and the *Extravagantes* (that is, the decretals of the popes from Pope John XXII to Pope Sixtus IV).

Jus Novissimum

After the Council of Trent, an attempt to secure a new official collection of church laws was made about 1580, when Gregory XIII charged three cardinals with the task. The work continued during the pontificate of Sixtus V, was accomplished under Clement VIII and was printed (Rome, 1598) as: "Sanctissimi Domini nostri Clementis papæ VIII Decretales", sometimes also "Septimus liber Decretalium". This collection, never approved either by Clement VIII or by Paul V, was edited (Freiburg, 1870) by Sentis. In 1557 the Italian canonist Paul Lancelottus attempted unsuccessfully to secure from Paul IV, for the four books of his "Institutiones juris canonici" (Rome, 1563), an authority equal to that which its model, the "Institutiones" of Emperor Justinian, once enjoyed in the Roman Empire. A private individual, Pierre Mathieu of Lyons, also wrote a "Liber Septimus Decretalium", inserted in the appendix to the Frankfort (1590) edition of the "Corpus Juris Canonici". This work was put on the Index.

Jus Codicis

Pio-Benedictine law

At the First Vatican Council several bishops asked for a new codification of the canon law, and after that several canonists attempted to compile treatises in the form of a full code of canonical legislation, e.g. de Luise (1873), Pillet (1890), Pezzani (1894), Deshayes (1894), Collomiati (1898–1901). Pius X determined to undertake this work by his decree "Arduum sane munus" (19 March 1904), and named a commission of cardinals to compile a new "Corpus Juris Canonici" on the model of the codes of civil law. The 1917 *Codex Iuris Canonici* (CIC, Code of Canon Law) was the first instance of a new code completely re-written in a systematic fashion, reduced to a single book or "codex" for ease of use. It took effect on 29 May 1918. It had 2,414 canons.

Johanno-Pauline law

In 1959, Pope John XXIII announced, together with his intention to call the Second Vatican Council and a Synod of the Diocese of Rome, that the 1917 Code would be completely revised.[729],[730] In 1963, the commission appointed to undertake the task decided to delay the project until the Council had been concluded. After Vatican II closed in 1965, it became apparent that the Code would need to be revised in light of the documents and theology of Vatican II. After decades of discussion and numerous drafts, the project was nearly complete upon the death of Paul VI in 1978. The work was completed in the pontificate of Pope John Paul II. The revision was promulgated by the apostolic constitution "Sacrae Disciplinae Leges" on 25 January 1983, taking effect on 27 November 1983. The subjects of the *Codex Iuris Canonici* (CIC, Code of Canon Law) are the world's 1.2 billion Catholics of what the Code itself calls the Latin Church. It has 7 books and 1,752 canons.

Oriental canon law

Distinct from the canonical tradition of the Latin Church is the tradition of the Eastern Catholic Churches. The earliest Oriental canon law collections were called nomocanons, which were collections of both canon and civil law.

In the early twentieth century, when Eastern Churches began to come back to full communion with the Holy See, Pope Benedict XV created the Sacred Congregation for the Oriental Church in order to preserve the rights and traditions of the Eastern Catholic Churches.

Since the early twentieth century, Oriental canon law had been in the process of codification. Some of these Oriental canon law reforms were promulgated by Pope Pius XII. The codification effort culminated with the Pope John Paul II's 1990 promulgation of the *Codex Canonum Ecclesiarum Orientalium* (CCEO, Code of Canons of the Eastern Churches) which incorporates certain differences in the hierarchical, administrative, and judicial *fora* for the 23 *sui juris* particular Eastern Catholic Churches, which were each encouraged to issue codes of particular law peculiar to each church, so that all of the Catholic Church's canon law would be codified.

Timeline

Jus antiquum

- From the apostolic period, the Church used different collections of law but development of a single collection which could be used in all courts did not develop until the Middle Ages.
- 1059—Nicolas II decrees that Cardinals have the right of electing the pope.[731]

Jus novum

- The books of the Corpus Juris Canonici were derived from Gratian's work Decretum Gratiani and were integrated with papal decretals written from 1200 to 1500.
- 1210—Innocent III promulgates the *Compilatio tertia* (compiled by Petrus Beneventanus)
- 1225—Honorius III promulgates the *Compilatio quinta* (compiled by Tancredus of Bologna
- 1234—Gregory IX promulgates the *Decretals* (compiled by St. Raymond of Peñafort)
- 1298—Boniface VIII published a similar code on 3 March 1298, called the *Liber Sextus* (codified by a commission of legal scholars)[732]
- 1317—John XXII added to it the last official collection of Canon law, the "Liber Septimus Decretalium", better known under the title of "Constitutiones Clementis V", or simply "Clementinæ", on 25 October 1317
- 1319—John XXII promulgated his *Extravagantes* in August 1319

Jus novissimum

- 1566—Pius V begins a project to unify the collection of law. He wanted to ensure the use of authentic and reliable versions of the *libri legales* so that the administration of justice did not depend on the version of Gratian that a particular canonical court used. He assembled a committee of great canon law scholars who became known as the Correctores Romani. The Correctores were guided by Antonio Agustín of Spain. Pope Pius V did not live to see this project to completion.
- 1582 — Gregory XIII orders republication of the entire *Corpus Iuris Canonici* as compiled at the time[733] (enforced until 1917)

Jus codicis

- 1904—Pius X appoints a commission to compile a code of canon law for the Latin Church
- 1917—Benedict XV promulgates a complete code, the 1917 Code of Canon Law (Latin: *Codex Iuris Canonici*)[734]
- 1918—The 1917 Code comes into legal effect
- 1959, 25 January[735]—John XXIII announces that the 1917 Code would be completely revised.
- 1963, March 28—The "Pontifical Commission for the Revision of the Code of Canon Law" is established.
- 1963, November 12—It is decided to postpone the work of revising the 1917 Code until the end of Vatican II.
- 1965, November 20—Paul VI inaugurates the work of the Pontifical Commission for the Revision of the Code of Canon Law
- 1983—John Paul II promulgates the 1983 Code of Canon Law,[736] abrogating the Code of 1917.[737]
- 1990—John Paul II promulgates the *Code of Canons of the Eastern Churches* (Latin: *Codex Canonum Ecclesiarum Orientalium*)
- 1998—John Paul II promulgates the motu proprio *Ad Tuendam Fidem*, amending certain canons of the 1983 CIC and the 1990 CCEO.[738]
- 2009—Benedict XVI promulgates the motu proprio *Omnium in Mentem*, amending certain canons of the 1983 CIC and the 1990 CCEO.[739]
- 2015—Pope Francis reforms the matrimonial processes dealing with declaring the nullity of marriage, promulgating the motu proprio *Mitis Iudex Dominus Iesus* amending the 1983 Code of Canon Law, and the motu proprio *Mitis et misericors Iesus* amending the Code of Canons of the Eastern Churches[740]

References

Bibliography

- Berman, Harold J. *Law and Revolution: The Formation of the Western Legal Tradition (Cambridge, Mass. Harvard University Press, 1983) ISBN 0-674-51776-8*
- Coriden, James A., Thomas J. Green, Donald E. Heintschel (editors). *The Code of Canon Law: A Text and Commentary* (New York: Paulist Press, 1985). Commissioned by the Canon Law Society of America.

Canon law of the Catholic Church

Part of a series on the

**Jurisprudence of
Catholic canon law**

▒ Catholicism portal

- v
- t
- e[741]

The **canon law of the Catholic Church** (Latin: *jus canonicum*)[742] is the system
of laws and legal principles made and enforced by the hierarchical authorities
of the Church to regulate its external organization and government and to order
and direct the activities of Catholics toward the mission of the Church.[743] It
was the first modern Western legal system[744] and is the oldest continuously
functioning legal system in the West, while the unique traditions of Oriental
canon law govern the 23 Eastern Catholic particular churches *sui iuris*.

Positive ecclesiastical laws, based directly or indirectly upon immutable divine law or natural law, derive formal authority in the case of universal laws
from promulgation by the supreme legislator—the Supreme Pontiff—who possesses the totality of legislative, executive, and judicial power in his person,[745]
while particular laws derive formal authority from promulgation by a legislator inferior to the supreme legislator, whether an ordinary or a delegated
legislator. The actual subject material of the canons is not just doctrinal or
moral in nature, but all-encompassing of the human condition. It has all the
ordinary elements of a mature legal system: laws, courts, lawyers, judges,[746]
a fully articulated legal code for the Latin Church[747] as well as a code for the
Eastern Catholic Churches, principles of legal interpretation,[748] and coercive
penalties.[749] It lacks civilly-binding force in most secular jurisdictions. Those
who are versed and skilled in canon law, and professors of canon law, are
called **canonists**[750] (or colloquially, **canon lawyers**).[751] Canon law as a sacred
science is called **canonistics**.

The jurisprudence of canon law is the complex of legal principles and traditions within which canon law operates, while the philosophy, theology, and
fundamental theory of canon law are the areas of philosophical, theological,
and legal scholarship dedicated to providing a theoretical basis for canon law
as legal system and as true law.

Definitions

The term "canon law" (*jus canonicum*) was only regularly used from the
twelfth century onwards.[752] The term *jus ecclesiasticum*, by contrast, referred
to the secular law, whether imperial, royal, or feudal, that dealt with relations
between the state and the Catholic Church. The term *corpus juris canonici*
was used to denote canon law as legal system beginning in the thirteenth century.[753]

Other terms sometimes used synonymously with *jus canonicum* include *jus
sacrum*, *jus ecclesiasticum*, *jus divinum*, and *jus pontificium*.[754]

Ecclesiastical positive law is the positive law that emanates from the legislative power of the Catholic Church in order to govern its members in accordance with the Gospel of Jesus Christ.[755] Fernando della Rocca used the term "ecclesiastical-positive law" in contradistinction to *civil*-positive law, in order to differentiate between the human legislators of church and state, all of which issue "positive law" in the normal sense.[756]

Examples of ecclesiastical positive law are fasting during the liturgical season of Lent, and religious workers (monks, nuns, etc.) requiring permission from their superiors to publish a book.[757]

Etymology of "canon"

The word "canon" comes from the Greek *kanon*, which in its original usage denoted a straight rod, was later used for a measuring stick, and eventually came to mean a rule or norm.[758] In 325, when the first ecumentical council, Nicaea I, was held, *kanon* started to obtain the restricted juridical denotation of a law promulgated by a synod or ecumenical council, as well as that of an individual bishop.

Legal history and codification

Latin canon law

The Catholic Church has the oldest continuously functioning legal system in the West, much later than Roman law but predating the evolution of modern European civil law traditions. What began with rules ("canons") adopted by the Apostles at the Council of Jerusalem in the first century has developed into a highly complex legal system encapsulating not just norms of the New Testament, but some elements of the Hebrew (Old Testament), Roman, Visigothic, Saxon, and Celtic legal traditions. As many as 36 collections of canon law are known to have been brought into existence before 1150.[759]

The history of Latin canon law can be divided into four periods: the *jus antiquum*, the *jus novum*, the *jus novissimum* and the *Codex Iuris Canonici*.[760] In relation to the Code, history can be divided into the *jus vetus* (all law before the Code) and the *jus novum* (the law of the Code, or *jus codicis*).

The Oriental canon law of the Eastern Catholic Churches, which had developed some different disciplines and practices, underwent its own process of codification, resulting in the Codex Canonum Ecclesiarum Orientalium promulgated in 1990 by Pope John Paul II.[761]

St. Raymond of Penyafort (1175–1275), a Spanish Dominican priest, is the patron saint of canonists,[762] due to his important contributions to canon law in codifying the *Decretales Gregorii IX*. Other saintly patrons include St. Ivo of Chartres and the Jesuit St. Robert Bellarmine.Wikipedia:Citation needed

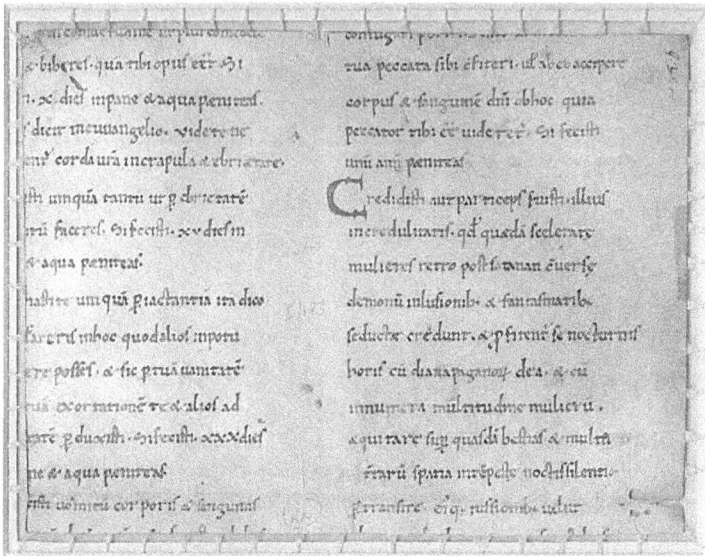

Figure 16: *Image of pages from the Decretum of Burchard of Worms, the 11th-century book of canon law.*

Jus Antiquum

The period of canonical history known as the *Jus Antiquum* ("ancient law") extends from the foundation of the Church to the time of Gratian (mid-12th century). This period can be further divided into three periods: the time of the apostles to the death of Pope Gelasius I (A.D. 496), the end of the 5th century to the spurious collection of the 9th century, and the last up to the time of Gratian (mid-12th century).[763]

In the Early Church, the first canons were decreed by bishops united in "Ecumenical" councils (the Emperor summoning all of the known world's bishops to attend with at least the acknowledgement of the Bishop of Rome) or "local" councils (bishops of a region or territory). Over time, these canons were supplemented with decretals of the Bishops of Rome, which were responses to doubts or problems according to the maxim, *"Roma locuta est, causa finita est"* ("Rome has spoken, the case is closed"). A common misconception, the Catholic Encyclopedia links this saying to St Augustine who actually said something quite different: *"jam enim de hac causa duo concilia missa sunt ad sedem apostolicam; inde etiam rescripta venerunt; causa finita est"* (which roughly translate to: "there are two councils, for now this matter as brought to the Apostolic See, whence also letters are come to pass, the case was finished") in response to the heretical Pelagianism of the time.

Figure 17: *Gratian,*
the "Father of Canon Law"

In the first millennium of the Roman Church, the canons of various ecumenical and local councils were supplemented with decretals of the popes; these were gathered together into collections.

Jus Novum

The period of canonical history known as the *Jus Novum* ("new law") or *middle period* covers the time from Gratian to the Council of Trent (mid-12th century–16th century).

The spurious conciliar canons and papal decrees were gathered together into collections, both unofficial and official. In the year 1000, there was no book that had attempted to summarized the whole body of canon law, to systematize it in whole or in part.[764] The first truly systematic collection was assembled by the Camaldolese monk Gratian in the 11th century, commonly known as the *Decretum Gratiani* ("Gratian's Decree") but originally called *The Concordance of Discordant Canons*[765] (*Concordantia Discordantium Canonum*). Before Gratian there was no "jurisprudence of canon law" (system of legal interpretation and principles). Gratian is the founder of canonical jurisprudence, which merits him the title "Father of Canon Law".[766] Gratian also had an enormous influence on the history of natural law in his transmission of the ancient doctrines of natural law to Scholasticism.[767]

Canon law greatly increased from 1140 to 1234. After that it slowed down, except for the laws of local councils (an area of canon law in need of scholarship), and secular laws supplemented.[768] In 1234 Pope Gregory IX promulgated the first official collection of canons, called the *Decretalia Gregorii Noni* or *Liber Extra*. This was followed by the *Liber Sextus* (1298) of Boniface VIII, the *Clementines* (1317) of Clement V, the *Extravagantes Joannis XXII* and the *Extravagantes Communes*, all of which followed the same structure as the *Liber Extra*. All these collections, with the *Decretum Gratiani*, are together referred to as the *Corpus Juris Canonici*. After the completion of the *Corpus Juris Canonici*, subsequent papal legislation was published in periodic volumes called *Bullaria*.

In the thirteenth century, the Roman Church began to collect and organize its canon law, which after a millennium of development had become a complex and difficult system of interpretation and cross-referencing. The official collections were the *Liber Extra* (1234) of Pope Gregory IX, the *Liber Sextus* (1298) of Boniface VIII and the *Clementines* (1317), prepared for Clement V but published by John XXII. These were addressed to the universities by papal letters at the beginning of each collection, and these texts became textbooks for aspiring canon lawyers. In 1582 a compilation was made of the Decretum, Extra, the Sext, the Clementines and the *Extravagantes* (that is, the decretals of the popes from Pope John XXII to Pope Sixtus IV).

Jus Novissimum

The third canonical period, known as the *Jus Novissimum* ("newest law"), stretches from the Council of Trent to the promulgation of the 1917 Code of Canon Law which took legal effect in 1918. The start of the *Jus Novissimum* is not universally agreed upon, however. Dr. Edward N. Peters argues that the *Jus Novissimum* actually started with the *Liber Extra* of Gregory IX in 1234.[769]

Jus Codicis

The fourth period of canonical history is that of the present day, initiated by the promulgation of the 1917 Code of Canon Law on 27 May 1917.[770] It is sometimes referred to as the *Jus Codicis* ("law of the code") or, in comparison with all law before it, the *Jus Novum* ("new law"). From time to time, the Pontifical Council for Legislative Texts issues authentic interpretations regarding the code. The pope occasionally amends the text of the codes.

Figure 18: *Pietro Cardinal Gasparri, Architect of the 1917 Code of Canon Law*

Pio-Benedictine law

By the 19th century, the body of canonical legislation included some 10,000 norms. Many of these were difficult to reconcile with one another due to changes in circumstances and practice. The situation impelled Pope St. Pius X to order the creation of the first Code of Canon Law, a single volume of clearly stated laws. Under the aegis of the Cardinal Pietro Gasparri, the Commission for the Codification of Canon Law was completed under Benedict XV, who promulgated the Code on 27 May 1917, effective on 29 May 1918. The work having been begun by Pius X, it was sometimes called the "Pio-Benedictine Code" but more often the 1917 Code to distinguish it from the later 1983 Code which replaced it. In its preparation, centuries of material was examined, scrutinized for authenticity by leading experts, and harmonized as much as possible with opposing canons and even other codes, from the Code of Justinian to the Napoleonic Code.

Johanno-Pauline law

In the succeeding decades, some parts of the 1917 Code were retouched, especially under Pope Pius XII. In 1959, Pope John XXIII announced, together with his intention to call the Second Vatican Council a Synod of the Diocese of Rome, that the 1917 Code would be completely revised.[771,772] In 1963, the commission appointed to undertake the task decided to delay the project until the Council had been concluded. After the Second Ecumenical Council of the Vatican (Vatican II) closed in 1965, it became apparent that the Code would need to be revised in light of the documents and theology of Vatican II. When work finally began, almost two decades of study and discussion on drafts of the various sections were needed before Pope John Paul II could promulgate the revised edition, which came into force on 27 November 1983,[773] having been promulgated via the apostolic constitution *Sacrae Disciplinae Leges* of 25 January 1983. Containing 1752 canons,[774] it is the law currently binding on the Latin Church.

This edition is referred to as the 1983 Code of Canon Law to distinguish it from the 1917 Code. Like the preceding edition, it applies to Roman Catholics of the Latin Church.[775]

Oriental canon law

For Eastern Catholics two sections of Oriental canon law had already, under Pope Pius XII, been put in the form of short canons. These parts were revised as part of the application of Pope John XXIII's decision to carry out a general revision of the Church's canon law; as a result a distinct Code for members of the Eastern Catholic Churches came into effect for the first time on 1 October 1991 (Apostolic Constitution *Sacri Canones* of 18 October 1990). The *Code of Canons of the Eastern Churches*, as it is called, differs from the Latin *1983 Code of Canon Law* in matters where Eastern and Latin traditions diverge, such as terminology, discipline concerning hierarchical offices and administration of the sacraments.

Jurisprudence of canon law

The institutions and practices of canon law paralleled the legal development of much of Europe, and consequently both modern civil law and common law[776,777] bear the influences of canon law. Much of the legislative style was adapted from that of Roman Law especially the Justinianic *Corpus Juris Civilis*.[778,779] After the 'fall' of the Roman Empire and up until the revival of Roman Law in the 11th century canon law served as the most important unifying force among the local systems in the Civil Law tradition.[780] The Catholic Church developed the inquisitorial system in the Middle Ages.[781] The canonists introduced into post-Roman Europe the concept of a higher law of ultimate justice, over and above the momentary law of the state.[782]

The primary canonical sources of law are the 1983 Code of Canon Law,[783] the Code of Canons of the Eastern Churches, and *Pastor Bonus*.[784] Other sources include apostolic constitutions, *motibus propriis*, particular law, and—with the

Figure 19: *Portrayal of a meeting of the Roman Rota*

approbation of the competent legislator—custom. A law must be promulgated for it to have legal effect.[785] A later and contrary law obrogates an earlier law.

Canonists have formulated interpretive rules of law for the magisterial (non-legislatorial) interpretation of canonical laws. An authentic interpretation is an official interpretation of a statute issued by the statute's legislator, and has the force of law.[786]

Philosophy, theology, and fundamental theory of canon law

Although canonical jurisprudential theory generally follows the principles of Aristotelian-Thomistic legal philosophy, Thomas Aquinas never explicitly discusses the place of canon law in his *Treatise on Law*[787] However, Aquinas himself was influenced by canon law.[788] While many canonists apply the Thomistic definition of law (*lex*) to canon law without objection, some authors dispute the applicability of the Thomistic definition to canon law, arguing that its application would impoverish ecclesiology and corrupt the very supernatural end of canon law.[789]

In the decades following the Second Vatican Council, many canonists called for a more theological, rather than philosophical, conception of canon law,[790]

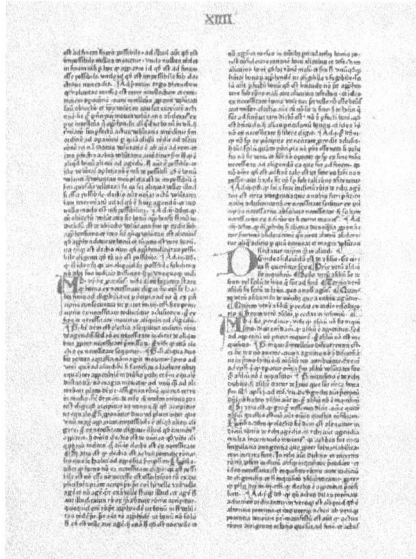

Figure 20: *Summa theologica, Pars secunda, prima pars. (copy by Peter Schöffer, 1471)*

acknowledging the "triple relationship between theology, philosophy, and canon law".[791] Some authors conceive of canon law as *essentially* theological and the discipline of canon law as a theological subdiscipline, but Msgr. Carlos José Errázuriz contends that "in a certain sense, all postconciliar canonical scholarship has shown a theological concern in the widest sense, that is, a tendency to determine more clearly the place of the juridical in the mystery of the Church."

The fundamental theory of canon law is a discipline covering the basis of canon law in the very nature of the church.[792] Fundamental theory is a newer discipline that takes as is object "the existence and nature of what is juridical in the Church of Jesus Christ."[793] The discipline seeks to better explain the nature of law in the church and engages in theological discussions in post-conciliar Catholicism[794] and seeks to combat "postconciliar antijuridicism".[795]

Canonistics, faculties, and institutes

The academic degrees in canon law are the J.C.B. (*Juris Canonici Baccalaureatus*, Bachelor of Canon Law, normally taken as a graduate degree), J.C.L. (*Juris Canonici Licentiatus*, Licentiate of Canon Law) and the J.C.D. (*Juris Canonici Doctor*, Doctor of Canon Law), and those with a J.C.L. or higher are usually called "canonists" or "canon lawyers". Because of its specialized nature, advanced degrees in civil law or theology are normal prerequisites for the study of canon law. Canon law as a field is called **Canonistics**.

Canon law and Church office

Under the 1983 Code of Canon Law, all seminary students are required to take courses in canon law.[796] Some ecclesiastical officials are required to have the doctorate (JCD) or at least the licentiate (JCL) in canon law in order to fulfill their functions: judicial vicars;[797] judges;[798] promoters of justice;[799] defenders of the bond; canonical advocates.[800] In addition, vicars general and episcopal vicars are to be doctors, or at least licensed in canon law or theology.[801] Ordinarily, bishops are to have an advanced degree (doctorate or at least licentiate) in scripture, theology, or canon law.[802]

Faculties and institutes of canon law

Number	University	Name of entity	City	Country
1	Catholic University of West Africa	Higher Institute of Canon Law	Abidjan	Ivory Coast
2	Catholic University of Central Africa	Autonomous Department of Canon Law	Yaoundé	Cameroon
3	Catholic University of Congo	Faculty of Canon Law	Kinshasa	Democratic Republic of the Congo
4	Saint Paul University	Faculty of Canon Law	Ottawa	Canada
5	Pontifical University of Mexico	Faculty of Canon Law	Mexico City	Mexico
6	The Catholic University of America	School of Canon Law	Washington, D.C.	USA
7	Pontifical Catholic University of Argentina	Faculty of Canon Law of Saint Turibius of Mongrovejo	Buenos Aires	Argentina
8	Pontifical Institute of Canon Law	Pontifical Higher Institute of Canon Law	Rio de Janeiro	Brazil
9	Pontifical Faculty of Theology of Our Lady of the Assumption	Institute of Canon Law of Fr Dr. Giuseppe Benito Pegoraro	São Paulo	Brazil
10	Pontifical Xavierian University	Faculty of Canon Law	Bogotá	Colombia

11	St. Peter's Pontifical Institute of Theology	Centre of Canon Law Studies	Bangalore	India
12	Dharmaram Vidya Kshetram	Institute of Oriental Canon Law	Bangalore	India
13	Sagesse High School	Faculty of Canon Law	Beirut	Lebanon
14	University of Santo Tomas	Faculty of Canon Law	Manila	Philippines
15	Katholieke Universiteit Leuven	Faculty of Canon Law	Leuven	Belgium
16	Université catholique de Louvain	Faculty of Canon Law	Louvain-la-Neuve	Belgium
17	Academy of Canon Law		Brno	Czech Republic
18	Institut Catholique de Paris	Faculty of Canon Law	Paris	France
19	University of Strasbourg	Institute of Canon Law	Strasbourg	France
20	Catholic University of Toulouse	Faculty of Canon Law	Toulouse	France
21	Ludwig Maximilian University of Munich	Institute of Canon Law of Klaus Mörsdorf	Munich	Germany
22	University of Münster	Faculty of Canon Law	Münster	Germany
23	Pázmány Péter Catholic University	Institute of Canon Law	Budapest	Hungary
24	St Patrick's College	Faculty of Canon Law	Maynooth	Ireland
25	Pontifical Gregorian University	Faculty of Canon Law	Vatican City	Vatican City
26	Pontifical Lateran University	Faculty of Canon Law	Vatican City	Vatican City
27	Pontifical University of Saint Thomas Aquinas, *Angelicum*	Faculty of Canon Law	Rome	Italy
28	Pontifical University Antonianum	Faculty of Canon Law	Rome	Italy
29	Pontifical Urbaniana University	Faculty of Canon Law	Vatican City	Vatican City
30	Salesian Pontifical University	Faculty of Canon Law	Rome	Italy
31	Pontifical Oriental Institute	Faculty of Oriental Canon Law	Vatican City	Vatican City
32	Pontifical University of the Holy Cross	Faculty of Canon Law	Vatican City	Vatican City
33	Studium Generale Marcianum	Faculty of Canon Law of St Pius X	Venice	Italy

34	Pontifical University of John Paul II	Faculty of Canon Law	Kraków	Poland
35	John Paul II Catholic University of Lublin	Faculty of Law, Canon Law and Administration	Lublin	Poland
36	University of Warmia and Mazury in Olsztyn	Faculty of Theology	Olsztyn	Poland
37	Cardinal Stefan Wyszyński University in Warsaw	Faculty of Canon Law	Warsaw	Poland
38	Catholic University of Portugal	Higher Institute of Canon Law	Lisbon	Portugal
39	Comillas Pontifical University	Faculty of Canon Law	Madrid	Spain
40	Ecclesiastical University St Damasus	Faculty of Canon Law	Madrid	Spain
41	University of Navarre	Faculty of Canon Law	Pamplona	Spain
42	Pontifical University of Salamanca	Faculty of Canon Law	Salamanca	Spain
43	Valencia Catholic University Saint Vincent Martyr	Faculty of Canon Law	Valencia	Spain

Related terms

- Apostolic Administrator
- Apostolic vicariate
- Benefice
- Bishop (Catholic Church)
- Canon Episcopi
- Catholic Church hierarchy
- Confirmation of bishops
- Consanguinity

- Devil's advocate
- Ecclesiastical court
- Epiclesis
- Oratory
- Particular church

- Prefecture
- Prelate
- Privilege (canon law)
- Rector
- Religious law
- Roman Catholic (term)
- Secular clergy
- Sede vacante
- Simony
- Team of priests *in solidum*
- Territorial abbot

Footnotes

Bibliography

Arranged alphabetically by author.

- Aquinas, Thomas. "St. Thomas Aquinas: *Summa Theologiæ*, Volume 28: Law and Political Theory (Ia2æ. 90-97); Latin text. English translation, Introduction, Notes, Appendices & Glossary [by] Thomas Gilby O.P.", Blackfriars (Cambridge: Eyre and Spottiswoode Limited, 1966).
- Berman, Harold J., *Law and Revolution: The Formation of the Western Legal Tradition* (Cambridge, MA: Harvard University Press, 1983).
- Benedict XVI, Pope. *Address of His Holiness Benedict XVI for the Inauguration of the Judicial Year of the Tribunal of the Roman Rota*, Clementine Hall, 21 January 2012. https://w2.vatican.va/content/benedict-xvi/en/speeches/2012/january/documents/hf_ben-xvi_spe_20120121_rota-romana.html Accessed 29 March 2016.
- Caparros, Ernest. *Exegetical Commentary on the Code of Canon Law, Volume I: Prepared under the Responsibility of the Martín de Azpilcueta Institute, Faculty of Canon Law, University of Navarre* (Chicago, Illinois: Midwest Theological Forum, 2004) Edited by Ángel Marzoa, Jorge Miras and Rafael Rodríguez-Ocaña (English language edition General editor: Ernest Caparros; Review coordinator: Patrick Lagges).
- Della Rocca, Fernando, *Manual of Canon Law* (Milwaukee: The Bruce Publishing Company, 1959) translated by Rev. Anselm Thatcher, O.S.B.
- Errázuriz M., Carlos José. *Justice in the Church: A Fundamental Theory of Canon Law* (Montreal: Wilson & Lefleur Ltée, 2009) trans. Jean Gray in collaboration with Michael Dunnigan.
- Friedman, Lawrence M. *American Law: An Introduction* (New York: W.W. Norton & Company, 1984).
- Glendon, Mary Anne, Michael Wallace Gordon, Christopher Osakwe, *Comparative Legal Traditions: Text, Materials and Cases (American Casebook Series)* (St. Paul, MN: West Publishing Co., 1985).
- Jordan, William Chester. *The Penguin History of Europe: Europe in the High Middle Ages* (London: Penguin Books, 2002).
- McCormick, Anne O'Hare. *Vatican Journal: 1921-1954* (New York: Farrar, Straus and Cudahy, 1957).
- Mylne, Robert Scott. *The Canon Law* (Published by Forgotten Books 2013; originally published 1912). PIBN 1000197046.
- Orsy, Ladislas. *Towards a Theological Conception of Canon Law* (essay published in Jordan Hite, T.O.R., & Daniel J. Ward, O.S.B., *Readings, Cases, Materials in Canon Law: A Textbook for Ministerial Students, Revised Edition* (Collegeville, MN: The Liturgical Press, 1990).
- Peters, Dr. Edward N., translator, *The 1917 or Pio-Benedictine Code of Canon Law: in English Translation with Extensive Scholarly Apparatus* (Ignatius Press, 2001)
- Peters, Dr. Edward N., JD, JCD, Ref. Sig. Ap., *CanonLaw.info*[803]

- Rommen, Heinrich A. *The Natural Law: A Study in Legal and Social History and Philosophy* (St Louis: B. Herder Book Co., 1947 [1959]) translated by Thomas R. Hanley, O.S.B.
- Wormser, René A., *The Story of the LAW and the Men Who Made It—From the Earliest Times to the Present: Revised and Updated Edition of* The Law (New York: Simon and Schuster, 1962).
- *Black's Law Dictionary, 5th Edition* (St. Paul, MN: West Publishing Co., 1979).
- *Catechism of the Catholic Church*[804] at Vatican.va
- *1983 Code of Canon Law* (1983 CIC)[805] at Vatican.va. Publication details: Latin-English Edition, New English Translation; Prepared under the auspices of the Canon Law Society of America, Washington, DC 20064.

External links

> Wikisourcehas the text of the 1913 Catholic Encyclopediaarticle *Canon Law*.

- *Sacrea Disciplinae Leges*[806] (Document establishing the 1983 Code of Canon Law)
- Norms of current canon law[807] (Table of canonical norms which are currently in force)
- Canon Law Wiki[808] (Notes, Commentary, Discussion, Papers & Bibliography on Canon Law)

Texts and translations of Codes of Canon Law

With referenced concordances

- Codex Iuris Canonici (1983)[809] (in Latin)
- Code of Canon Law (1983)[805] (Translation by Canon Law Society of America – via *vatican.va*. Includes 1998 modification of canons 750 and 1371.)
- Code of Canon Law (1983)[810] (Translation by the Canon Law Society of Great Britain and Ireland, assisted by the Canon Law Society of Australia and New Zealand and the Canadian Canon Law Society)
- Codex canonum ecclesiarum orientalium (1990)[811] (in Latin)
- "Code of canons of Oriental Churchs" (1990)[812] (Translation by Canon Law Society of America)
- Codex Iuris Canonici (1917)[813] (in Latin) (Abrogated by 1983 Code of Canon Law)

Without concordances

- Code de 1917[814] (in French) (Abrogated by 1983 Code of Canon Law)

Sharia

Part of a series on
Islam

- اللّٰه **Islam portal**

- v
- t
- e[815]

Part of the Politics series

Basic forms of government

Power structure

Separation

- Associated state
- Dominion
- Chiefdom

Federalism

- Federation
- Confederation
- Devolution

Integration

- Empire
- Hegemony
- Unitary state

Administrative division

Power source

Democracy
power of many
• Direct • Representative • Semi • *others*
Oligarchy
power of few
• Aristocracy • Military junta • Plutocracy • Stratocracy • Timocracy • Theocracy • Kritarchy • Particracy
Autocracy
power of one
• Despotism • Illiberal democracy • Semi-authoritarian • Dictatorship
Hybrids
• Anocracy

Power ideology
Monarchy vs. Republic
socio-political ideologies
• Absolute • Constitutional • Directorial • Legalist • Parliamentary • Semi-presidential • Presidential
Authoritarian vs. Libertarian
socio-economic ideologies
• Capitalism • Colonialism • Communism • Distributism • Feudalism • Socialism
Anarchism vs. Statism
civil-liberties ideologies
• Anarchy • Minarchy • Totalitarianism
Global vs. Local
geo-cultural ideologies
• Central • City-state • National unity • World

Politics portal

- v
- t
- e[816]

Sharia, **Sharia law**, or **Islamic law** (Arabic: شريعة (IPA: [ʃaˈriːʕa])) is the religious law forming part of the Islamic tradition. It is derived from the religious precepts of Islam, particularly the Quran and the Hadith. In Arabic, the term *sharīʿah* refers to God's immutable divine law and is contrasted with *fiqh*, which refers to its human scholarly interpretations.[817,818] The manner of its application in modern times has been a subject of dispute between Muslim traditionalists and reformists.

Traditional theory of Islamic jurisprudence recognizes four sources of sharia: the Quran, *sunnah* (authentic hadith), *qiyas* (analogical reasoning), and *ijma* (juridical consensus).[819] Different legal schools—of which the most prominent are Hanafi, Maliki, Shafi'i, Hanbali and Jafari—developed methodologies for deriving sharia rulings from scriptural sources using a process known as *ijtihad*.[817] Traditional jurisprudence distinguishes two principal branches of law, *ʿibādāt* (rituals) and *muʿāmalāt* (social relations), which together comprise a wide range of topics.[818] Its rulings assign actions to one of five categories: mandatory, recommended, neutral, abhorred, and prohibited.[817,818] Thus, some areas of sharia overlap with the Western notion of law while others correspond more broadly to living life in accordance with God's will.[817]

Historically, sharia was interpreted by independent jurists (muftis). Their legal opinions (fatwas) were taken into account by ruler-appointed judges who presided over *qāḍī's* courts, and by *maẓālim* courts, which were controlled by the ruler's council and administered criminal law.[817,818] Ottoman rulers achieved additional control over the legal system by promulgating their own legal code (*qanun*) and turning muftis into state employees.[817] Non-Muslim (dhimmi) communities had legal autonomy, except in cases of interconfessional disputes, which fell under jurisdiction of qadi's courts.[817]

In the modern era, sharia-based criminal laws were widely replaced by statutes inspired by European models.[817,820] Judicial procedures and legal education in the Muslim world were likewise brought in line with European practice.[817] While the constitutions of most Muslim-majority states contain references to sharia, its classical rules were largely retained only in personal status (family) laws.[817] Legislative bodies which codified these laws sought to modernize them without abandoning their foundations in traditional jurisprudence.[817,821] The Islamic revival of the late 20th century brought along calls by Islamist movements for full implementation of sharia, including reinstatement of *hudud* corporal punishments, such as stoning.[817,821] In some cases, this resulted in traditionalist legal reform,[822,823] </ref> while other countries witnessed juridical reinterpretation of sharia advocated by progressive reformers.[817,821,824]

The role of sharia has become a contested topic around the world. Attempts to impose it on non-Muslims have caused intercommunal violence in Nigeria[825,826] and may have contributed to the breakup of Sudan.[817] Some Muslim-minority countries in Asia (such as Israel), Africa, and Europe recognize the use of sharia-based family laws for their Muslim populations.[827,828] Some jurisdictions in North America have passed bans on use of sharia, framed as restrictions on religious or foreign laws. There are ongoing debates as to whether sharia is compatible with secular forms of government, human rights, freedom of thought, and women's rights.[829]

Etymology and usage

Contemporary usage

The word *sharī'ah* is used by Arabic-speaking peoples of the Middle East to designate a prophetic religion in its totality.[830] For example, *sharī'at Mūsā* means law or religion of Moses and *sharī'atu-nā* can mean "our religion" in reference to any monotheistic faith.[830] Within Islamic discourse, *šarī'ah* refers to religious regulations governing the lives of Muslims.[830] For many Muslims, the word means simply "justice", and they will consider any law that promotes justice and social welfare to conform to sharia.[817]

Jan Michiel Otto distinguishes four senses conveyed by the term *sharia* in religious, legal and political discourse:[831]

- *Divine, abstract sharia*: God's plan for mankind and the norms of behavior which should guide the Islamic community. Muslims of different perspectives agree in their respect for the abstract notion of sharia, but they differ in how they understand the practical implications of the term.
- *Classical sharia*: the body of rules and principles elaborated by Islamic jurists during the first centuries of Islam.
- *Historical sharia(s)*: the body of rules and interpretations developed throughout Islamic history, ranging from personal beliefs to state legislation and varying across an ideological spectrum. Classical sharia has often served as a point of reference for these variants, but they have also reflected the influences of their time and place.
- *Contemporary sharia(s)*: the full spectrum of rules and interpretations that are developed and practiced at present.

A related term *al-qānūn al-islāmī* (القانون الإسلامي, Islamic law), which was borrowed from European usage in the late 19th century, is used in the Muslim world to refer to a legal system in the context of a modern state.[832]

Etymology

The primary range of meanings of the Arabic word *šarī'ah*, derived from the root *š-r-ʕ*, is related to religion and religious law.[830] The lexicographical tradition records two major areas of use where the word *šarī'ah* can appear without religious connotation.[833] In texts evoking a pastoral or nomadic environment, the word and its derivatives refer to watering animals at a permanent waterhole or to the seashore, with special reference to animals who come there.[833] Another area of use relates to notions of stretched or lengthy.[833] This range of meanings is cognate with the Hebrew *sara'* and is likely to be the origin of the meaning "way" or "path".[833] Both these areas have been claimed to have given rise to aspects of the religious meaning.[833]

Some scholars describe the word *šarī'ah* as an archaic Arabic word denoting "pathway to be followed" (analogous to the Hebrew term Halakhah ["The Way to Go"]),[834] or "path to the water hole" and argue that its adoption as a metaphor for a divinely ordained way of life arises from the importance of water in an arid desert environment.[835]

Use in religious texts

In the Quran, *šarī'ah* and its cognate *šir'ah* occur once each, with the meaning "way" or "path".[830] The word *šarī'ah* was widely used by Arabic-speaking Jews during the Middle Ages, being the most common translation for the word *torah* in the 10th century Arabic Old Testament known as Saʿadya Gaon.[830] A similar use of the term can be found in Christian writers.[830] The Arabic expression *Sharī'at Allāh* (شريعة الله "God's Law") is a common translation for תורת אלוהים ('God's Law' in Hebrew) and νόμος τοῦ θεοῦ ('God's Law' in Greek in the New Testament [Rom. 7: 22]).[836] In Muslim literature, *šarī'ah* designates the laws or message of a prophet or God, in contrast to *fiqh*, which refers to a scholar's interpretation thereof.[837]

Historical origins

According to the traditional Muslim view, the emergence of Islamic jurisprudence (*fiqh*) goes back to the lifetime of the Islamic prophet Muhammad.[817,818] In this view, his companions and followers took what he did and approved of as a model (sunnah) and transmitted this information to the succeeding generations in the form of hadith.[817,818] These reports led first to informal discussion and then systematic legal thought, articulated with greatest success in the eighth and ninth centuries by the master jurists Abu Hanifah, Malik ibn Anas, Al-Shafi'i, and Ahmad ibn Hanbal, who are viewed as the founders of the Hanafi, Maliki, Shafi'i, and Hanbali legal schools (*madhhabs*) of Sunni jurisprudence.[818]

Figure 21: *Juristic exchange between Abu Dawood and Ibn Hanbal. One of the oldest literary manuscripts of the Islamic world, dated October 879.*

Modern historians have presented alternative theories of the formation of fiqh.[817,818] At first Western scholars accepted the general outlines of the traditional account.[838] An influential revisionist hypothesis was advanced by Ignac Goldziher and elaborated by Joseph Schacht in the mid-20th century.[818] Schacht argued that the hadith reflected local practices of early Muslim communities and their chains of transmission were extended back to Muhammad's companions at a later date, when it became accepted that legal norms must be formally grounded in scriptural sources.[818] In his view, the real architect of Islamic jurisprudence was al-Shafi'i, who formulated this and other elements of classical legal theory in his work *al-risala*.[818,838] Both these accounts gave rise to objections, and modern historians generally adopt more cautious, intermediate positions.[838]

While the origin of hadith remains a subject of scholarly controversy, it is generally accepted that early Islamic jurisprudence developed out of a combination of administrative and popular practices shaped by the religious and ethical precepts of Islam.[839,817,840] It continued some aspects of pre-Islamic laws and customs of the lands that fell under Muslim rule in the aftermath of the early conquests and modified other aspects, aiming to meet the practical need of establishing Islamic norms of behavior and adjudicating disputes arising in the early Muslim communities.[841] Juristic thought gradually developed in study circles, where independent scholars met to learn from a local master and discuss religious topics.[841,842] At first, these circles were fluid in their membership, but with time distinct regional legal schools crystallized around shared sets of methodological principles.[842,817] As the boundaries of the schools became clearly delineated, the authority of their doctrinal tenets came to be vested in a master jurist from earlier times, who was henceforth identified as the school's founder.[842,817] In the course of the first three centuries of Islam, all legal schools came to accept the broad outlines of classical legal theory, according to which Islamic law had to be firmly rooted in the Quran and hadith.[817,843]

Traditional jurisprudence (*fiqh*)

Fiqh is traditionally divided into the fields of *uṣūl al-fiqh* (lit. the roots of fiqh), which studies the theoretical principles of jurisprudence, and *furū' al-fiqh* (lit. the branches of fiqh), which is devoted to elaboration of rulings on the basis of these principles.[818,844]

Principles of jurisprudence (*uṣūl al-fiqh*)

Classical jurists held that human reason is a gift from God which should be exercised to its fullest capacity.[845] However, they believed that use of reason alone is insufficient to distinguish right from wrong, and that rational argumentation must draw its content from the body of transcendental knowledge revealed in the Quran and through the sunnah of Muhammad.[845]

Traditional theory of Islamic jurisprudence elaborates how scriptures should be interpreted from the standpoint of linguistics and rhetoric.[818] It also comprises methods for establishing authenticity of hadith and for determining when the legal force of a scriptural passage is abrogated by a passage revealed at a later date.[818] In addition to the Quran and sunnah, the classical theory of Sunni fiqh recognizes two other sources of law: juristic consensus (*ijma'*) and analogical reasoning (*qiyas*).[839] It therefore studies the application and limits of analogy, as well as the value and limits of consensus, along with other methodological principles, some of which are accepted by only certain legal schools.[818] This interpretive apparatus is brought together under the rubric of ijtihad, which refers to a jurist's exertion in an attempt to arrive at a ruling on a particular question.[818] The theory of Twelver Shia jurisprudence parallels that of Sunni schools with some differences, such as recognition of reason (*'aql*) as a source of law in place of *qiyas* and extension of the notion of sunnah to include traditions of the imams.[846]

Sources of sharia

- *Quran*: In Islam, the Quran is considered to be the most sacred source of law.[847] Classical jurists held its textual integrity to be beyond doubt on account of it having been handed down by many people in each generation, which is known as "recurrence" or "concurrent transmission" (*tawātur*).[839,847] Only several hundred verses of the Quran have direct legal relevance, and they are concentrated in a few specific areas such as inheritance, though other passages have been used as a source for general principles whose legal ramifications were elaborated by other means.[817,847]

- *Hadith*: The body of hadith provides more detailed and practical legal guidance, but it was recognized early on that not all of them were authentic.[817,847] Early Islamic scholars developed a methodology for evaluating their authenticity by assessing trustworthiness of the individuals listed in their transmission chains.[847] These criteria narrowed down the vast corpus of prophetic traditions to several thousand "sound" hadiths, which were collected in several canonical compilations.[847] The hadiths which enjoyed concurrent transmission were deemed unquestionably authentic; however, the vast majority of hadiths were handed down by only one or a few transmitters and were therefore seen to yield only probable knowledge.[848,839] The uncertainty was further compounded by ambiguity of the language contained in some hadiths and Quranic passages.[847] Disagreements on the relative merits and interpretation of the textual sources allowed legal scholars considerable leeway in formulating alternative rulings.[817]

- *Consensus (ijma)* could in principle elevate a ruling based on probable evidence to absolute certainty.[849,817] This classical doctrine drew its authority from a series of hadiths stating that the Islamic community could never agree on an error.[849] This form of consensus was technically defined as agreement of all competent jurists in any particular generation, acting as representatives of the community.[849,817,850] However, the practical difficulty of obtaining and ascertaining such an agreement meant that it had little impact on legal development.[849,817] A more pragmatic form of consensus, which could be determined by consulting works of prominent jurists, was used to confirm a ruling so that it could not be reopened for further discussion.[817] The cases for which there was a consensus account for less than 1 percent of the body of classical jurisprudence.[849]

- *Analogical reasoning (qiyas)* : Qiyas is used to derive a ruling for a situation not addressed in the scripture by analogy with a scripturally based rule.[839] In a classic example, the Quranic prohibition of drinking wine is extended to all intoxicating substances, on the basis of the "cause" (*'illa*) shared by these situations, which in this case is identified to be intoxication.[839] Since the cause of a rule may not be apparent, its selection

Figure 22: *Turkish mufti (17th century Spanish drawing)*

commonly occasioned controversy and extensive debate.[851] Twelver Shia jurisprudence does not recognize the use of qiyas, but relies on reason (*'aql*) in its place.[844]

Ijtihad

The classical process of ijtihad combined these generally recognized principles with other methods, which were not adopted by all legal schools, such as *istihsan* (juristic preference), *istislah* (consideration of public interest) and *istishab* (presumption of continuity).[839] A jurist who is qualified to practice ijtihad is known as a *mujtahid*.[840] The use of independent reasoning to arrive at a ruling is contrasted with *taqlid* (imitation), which refers to following the rulings of a mujtahid.[840] By the beginning of the 10th century, development of Sunni jurisprudence prompted leading jurists to state that the main legal questions had been addressed and the scope of ijtihad was gradually restricted.[840,852] From the 18th century on, leading Muslim reformers began calling for abandonment of taqlid and renewed emphasis on ijtihad, which they saw as a return to the vitality of early Islamic jurisprudence.[852]

Decision types (*aḥkām*)

Sharia rulings fall into one of five categories known as "the five decisions" (*al-aḥkām al-khamsa*): mandatory (*farḍ* or *wājib*), recommended (*mandūb* or *mustaḥabb*), neutral (*mubāḥ*), reprehensible (*makrūh*), and forbidden (*ḥarām*).[817,844] It is a sin or a crime to perform a forbidden action or not to perform a mandatory action.[817] Reprehensible acts should be avoided, but they are not considered to be sinful or punishable in court.[817,853] Avoiding reprehensible acts and performing recommended acts is held to be subject of reward in the afterlife, while allowed actions entail no judgement from God.[817,853] Jurists disagree on whether the term *ḥalāl* covers the first three or the first four categories.[817] The legal and moral verdict depends on whether the action is committed out of necessity (*ḍarūra*).[817]

Aims of sharia and public interest

Maqāṣid (aims or purposes) of sharia and *maṣlaḥa* (welfare or public interest) are two related classical doctrines which have come to play an increasingly prominent role in modern times.[854,855,856] They were first clearly articulated by al-Ghazali (d. 1111), who argued that *maslaha* was God's general purpose in revealing the divine law, and that its specific aims was preservation of five essentials of human well-being: religion, life, intellect, offspring, and property.[857] Although most classical-era jurists recognized *maslaha* and *maqasid* as important legal principles, they held different views regarding the role they should play in Islamic law.[854,856] Some jurists viewed them as auxiliary rationales constrained by scriptural sources and analogical reasoning.[854,858] Others regarded them as an independent source of law, whose general principles could override specific inferences based on the letter of scripture.[854,859] While the latter view was held by a minority of classical jurists, in modern times it came to be championed in different forms by prominent scholars who sought to adapt Islamic law to changing social conditions by drawing on the intellectual heritage of traditional jurisprudence.[854,839,855] These scholars expanded the inventory of *maqasid* to include such aims of sharia as reform and women's rights (Rashid Rida); justice and freedom (Mohammed al-Ghazali); and human dignity and rights (Yusuf al-Qaradawi).[854]

Branches of law

Part of a series on
Islamic jurisprudence *(fiqh)*
Islamic studies

- v̲
- t̲
- e̲[860]

The domain of *furū' al-fiqh* (lit. branches of fiqh) is traditionally divided into
'ibādāt (rituals or acts of worship) and *mu'āmalāt* (social relations).[818,840]
Many jurists further divided the body of substantive jurisprudence into "the
four quarters", called rituals, sales, marriage and injuries.[861] Each of these
terms figuratively stood for a variety of subjects.[861] For example, the quarter
of sales would encompass partnerships, guaranty, gifts, and bequests, among
other topics.[861] Juristic works were arranged as a sequence of such smaller
topics, each called a "book" (*kitab*).[818,861] The special significance of ritual
was marked by always placing its discussion at the start of the work.[818,861]

Some historians distinguish a field of Islamic criminal law, which combines
several traditional categories.[817,862,844] Several crimes with scripturally prescribed punishments are known as *hudud*.[817] Jurists developed various restrictions which in many cases made them virtually impossible to apply.[817] Other
crimes involving intentional bodily harm are judged according to a version of
lex talionis that prescribes a punishment analogous to the crime (*qisas*), but the
victims or their heirs may accept a monetary compensation (*diya*) or pardon
the perpetrator instead; only *diya* is imposed for non-intentional harm.[817,862]
Other criminal cases belong to the category of *ta'zīr*, where the goal of punishment is correction or rehabilitation of the culprit and its form is largely left
to the judge's discretion.[817,862] In practice, since early on in Islamic history,
criminal cases were usually handled by ruler-administered courts or local police using procedures which were only loosely related to sharia.[818,862]

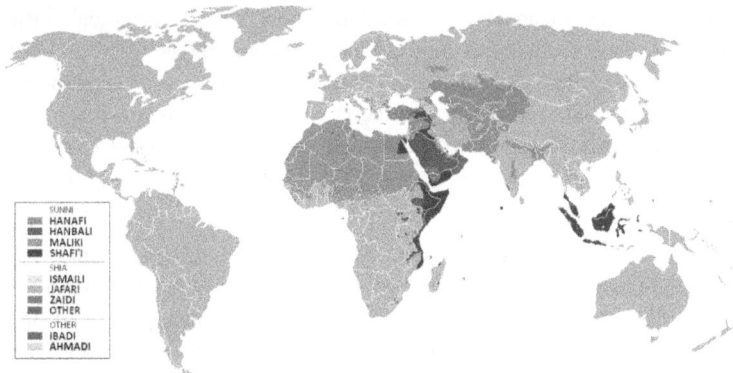

Figure 23: *Predominant madhhab by region of the Muslim world*

The two major genres of *furū'* literature are the *mukhtasar* (concise summary of law) and the *mabsut* (extensive commentary).[818] *Mukhtasars* were short specialized treatises or general overviews that could be used in a classroom or consulted by judges.[818,817,863] A *mabsut*, which usually provided a commentary on a *mukhtasar* and could stretch to dozens of large volumes, recorded alternative rulings with their justifications, often accompanied by a proliferation of cases and conceptual distinctions.[818,863] The terminology of juristic literature was conservative and tended to preserve notions which had lost their practical relevance.[818] At the same time, the cycle of abridgement and commentary allowed jurists of each generation to articulate a modified body of law to meet changing social conditions.[863] Other juristic genres include the *qawā'id* (succinct formulas meant to aid the student remember general principles) and collections of fatwas by a particular scholar.[817]

Schools of law

The main Sunni schools of law (*madhhabs*) are the Hanafi, Maliki, Shafi'i and Hanbali madhhabs.[840] They emerged in the ninth and tenth centuries and by the twelfth century almost all jurists aligned themselves with a particular madhhab.[864] These four schools recognize each other's validity and they have interacted in legal debate over the centuries.[864,840] Rulings of these schools are followed across the Muslim world without exclusive regional restrictions, but they each came to dominate in different parts of the world.[864,840] For example, the Maliki school is predominant in North and West Africa; the Hanafi school in South and Central Asia; the Shafi'i school in Lower Egypt, East Africa, and Southeast Asia; and the Hanbali school in North and Central Arabia.[864,840,817] The first centuries of Islam also witnessed a number of short-lived Sunni madhhabs.[818] The Zahiri school, which is commonly identified as extinct, continues to exert influence over legal thought.[818,840,864] The development of Shia legal schools occurred along the lines of theological differences and resulted in formation of the Twelver, Zaidi and Ismaili madhhabs, whose differences from Sunni legal schools are roughly of the same order as the differences among Sunni schools.[818,817] The Ibadi legal school, distinct from Sunni and Shia madhhabs, is predominant in Oman.[840]

The transformations of Islamic legal institutions in the modern era have had profound implications for the madhhab system.[864] Legal practice in most of the Muslim world has come to be controlled by government policy and state law, so that the influence of the madhhabs beyond personal ritual practice depends on the status accorded to them within the national legal system.[864] State law codification commonly utilized the methods of *takhayyur* (selection of rulings without restriction to a particular madhhab) and *talfiq* (combining parts of different rulings on the same question).[864] Legal professionals trained in modern law schools have largely replaced traditional ulema as interpreters of the resulting laws.[864] Global Islamic movements have at times drawn on different madhhabs and at other times placed greater focus on the scriptural sources rather than classical jurisprudence.[864] The Hanbali school, with its particularly strict adherence to the Quran and hadith, has inspired conservative currents of direct scriptural interpretation by the Salafi and Wahhabi movements.[864] Other currents, such as networks of Indonesian ulema and Islamic scholars residing in Muslim-minority countries, have advanced liberal interpretations of Islamic law without focusing on traditions of a particular madhhab.[864]

Part of a series on:
Islamism

Politics portal   Islam portal

- v
- t
- e[865]

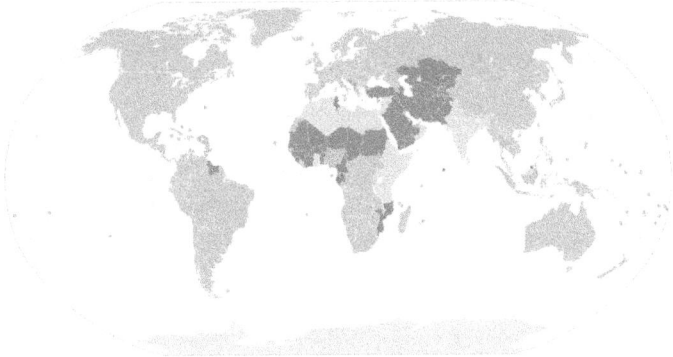

Figure 24:
Use of sharia by country:
Sharia plays no role in the judicial system.
Sharia applies to Muslim's personal law.
Sharia applies in full, including criminal law.
Regional variations in the application of sharia.

Social context

From the 9th century onward, the power to interpret law in traditional Islamic societies was in the hands of the scholars (ulema). This separation of powers served to limit the range of actions available to the ruler, who could not easily decree or reinterpret law independently and expect the continued support of the community. Through succeeding centuries and empires, the balance between the ulema and the rulers shifted and reformed, but the balance of power was never decisively changed.[866] Over the course of many centuries, imperial, political and technological change, including the Industrial Revolution and the French Revolution, ushered in an era of European world hegemony that gradually included the domination of many of the lands which had previously been ruled by Islamic empires.[867,868] At the end of the Second World War, the European powers found themselves too weakened to maintain their empires as before.[869] The wide variety of forms of government, systems of law, attitudes toward modernity and interpretations of sharia are a result of the ensuing drives for independence and modernity in the Muslim world.[870,871]

Application

Application by country

Most Muslim-majority countries incorporate sharia at some level in their legal framework, with many calling it the highest law or the source of law of the land in their constitution.[872] Most use sharia for personal law (marriage, divorce, domestic violence, child support, family law, inheritance and such matters).[873] Elements of sharia are present, to varying extents, in the criminal justice system of many Muslim-majority countries. Saudi Arabia, Yemen, Brunei, Qatar, Pakistan, United Arab Emirates, Iraq, Iran, Afghanistan, Sudan and Mauritania apply the code predominantly or entirely while it applies in some parts of Indonesia.[874,875]

Most Muslim-majority countries with sharia-prescribed hudud punishments in their legal code do not prescribe it routinely and use other punishments instead. The harshest sharia penalties such as stoning, beheading and other forms of the death penalty are enforced with varying levels of consistency.

Since the 1970s, most Muslim-majority countries have faced vociferous demands from their religious groups and political parties for immediate adoption of sharia as the sole, or at least primary, legal framework. Some moderates and liberal scholars within these Muslim countries have argued for limited expansion of sharia.[876]

With the growing Muslim immigrant communities in Europe, there have been reports in some media of "no-go zones" being established where sharia law reigns supreme. However, there is no evidence of the existence of "no-go zones", and these allegations are sourced from anti-immigrant groups falsely equating low-income neighborhoods predominantly inhabited by immigrants as "no-go zones". In England, the Muslim Arbitration Tribunal makes use of sharia family law to settle disputes, though this limited adoption of sharia is controversial.[877,878]

Enforcement

Sharia is enforced in Islamic nations in a number of ways, including *mutaween* (police enforcement) and *hisbah*. mutaween (Arabic: المطوعين، مطوعية *muṭawwi'īn, muṭawwi'iyyah*)[879] are the government-authorized or government-recognized religious police (or clerical police) of Saudi Arabia. Elsewhere, enforcement of Islamic values in accordance with sharia is the responsibility of the *Polisi Perda Syariah Islam* in Aceh province of Indonesia,[880] the Committee for the Propagation of Virtue and the Prevention of Vice (Gaza Strip) in parts of Palestine, and the Basiji Force in Iran.

Figure 25: *Official from the Taliban beating a woman in Afghanistan for violating local interpretation of sharia.*[881,882]

Hisbah (Arabic: حسبة‎ *ḥisb(ah)*, or hisba) is a historic Islamic doctrine which means "accountability".[883] Hisbah doctrine holds that it is a religious obligation of every Muslim that he or she report to the ruler (Sultan, government authorities) any wrong behavior of a neighbor or relative that violates sharia or insults Islam. The doctrine states that it is the divinely sanctioned duty of the ruler to intervene when such charges are made, and coercively "command right and forbid wrong" in order to keep everything in order according to sharia.[884,885,886] Al-Jama'a al-Islamiyya (considered a terrorist organization) suggest that enforcement of sharia under the Hisbah doctrine is the sacred duty of all Muslims, not just rulers.

The doctrine of Hisbah in Islam may allow a Muslim to accuse another Muslim, ex-Muslim or non-Muslim for beliefs or behavior that harms Islamic society. This principle has been used in countries such as Egypt, Pakistan and others to bring blasphemy charges against apostates.[887] For example, in Egypt, sharia was enforced on the Muslim scholar Nasr Abu Zayd, through the doctrine of Hisbah for apostasy. Similarly, in Nigeria, after twelve northern Muslim-majority states such as Kano adopted a sharia-based penal code between 1999 and 2000, hisbah became the allowed method of sharia enforcement where Muslim citizens could police compliance of moral order based on sharia. In Aceh province of Indonesia, Islamic vigilante activists have invoked

Figure 26: *Shariah Court in Malacca, Malaysia.*

Hisbah doctrine to enforce sharia on fellow Muslims as well as demanding that non-Muslims respect sharia. Hisbah has been used in many Muslim majority countries to enforce sharia restrictions on blasphemy and criticism of Islam over internet and social media.[888,889]

Legal and court proceedings

Sharia judicial proceedings have significant differences from other legal traditions, including those in both common law and civil law. Sharia courts traditionally do not rely on lawyers; plaintiffs and defendants represent themselves. Trials are conducted solely by the judge, and there is no jury system. There is no pre-trial discovery process, and no cross-examination of witnesses. Unlike common law, judges' verdicts do not set binding precedents[890] under the principle of *stare decisis*,[891] and unlike civil law, sharia is left to the interpretation in each case and has no formally codified universal statutes.[892]

The rules of evidence in sharia courts also maintain a distinctive custom of prioritizing oral testimony.[893] Witnesses, in a sharia court system, must be faithful, that is Muslim.[894] Male Muslim witnesses are deemed more reliable than female Muslim witnesses, and non-Muslim witnesses considered unreliable and receive no priority in a sharia court.[895,896] In civil cases in some countries, a Muslim woman witness is considered half the worth and reliability than a Muslim man witness. In criminal cases, women witnesses are unacceptable in stricter, traditional interpretations of sharia, such as those found in Hanbali madhhab.

Criminal cases

A confession, an oath, or the oral testimony of Muslim witnesses are the main evidence admissible, in sharia courts, for hudud crimes, that is the religious crimes of adultery, fornication, rape, accusing someone of illicit sex but failing to prove it, apostasy, drinking intoxicants and theft.[897,898,899,900] Testimony must be from at least two free Muslim male witnesses, or one Muslim male and two Muslim females, who are not related parties and who are of sound mind and reliable character. Testimony to establish the crime of adultery, fornication or rape must be from four Muslim male witnesses, with some fiqhs allowing substitution of up to three male with six female witnesses; however, at least one must be a Muslim male.[901] Forensic evidence (*i.e.*, fingerprints, ballistics, blood samples, DNA etc.) and other circumstantial evidence is likewise rejected in hudud cases in favor of eyewitnesses, a practice which can cause severe difficulties for women plaintiffs in rape cases.

Muslim jurists have debated whether and when coerced confession and coerced witnesses are acceptable.Wikipedia:Citation needed In the Ottoman Criminal Code, the executive officials were allowed to use torture only if the accused had a bad reputation and there were already indications of his guilt, such as when stolen goods were found in his house, if he was accused of grievous bodily harm by the victim or if a criminal during investigation mentioned him as an accomplice. Confessions obtained under torture could not be used as a ground for awarding punishment unless they were corroborated by circumstantial evidence.

Civil cases

Quran 2:282[902] recommends written financial contracts with reliable witnesses, although there is dispute about equality of female testimony.

Marriage is solemnized as a written financial contract, in the presence of two Muslim male witnesses, and it includes a brideprice (Mahr) payable from a Muslim man to a Muslim woman. The brideprice is considered by a sharia court as a form of debt. Written contracts are paramount in sharia courts in the matters of dispute that are debt-related, which includes marriage contracts. Written contracts in debt-related cases, when notarized by a judge, is deemed more reliable.

In commercial and civil contracts, such as those relating to exchange of merchandise, agreement to supply or purchase goods or property, and others, oral contracts and the testimony of Muslim witnesses triumph over written contracts. Sharia system has held that written commercial contracts may be forged.[903,904] Timur Kuran states that the treatment of written evidence in religious courts in Islamic regions created an incentive for opaque transactions, and the avoidance of written contracts in economic relations. This led to a continuation of a "largely oral contracting culture" in Muslim nations and communities.[905]

In lieu of written evidence, oaths are accorded much greater weight; rather than being used simply to guarantee the truth of ensuing testimony, they are themselves used as evidence. Plaintiffs lacking other evidence to support their claims may demand that defendants take an oath swearing their innocence, refusal thereof can result in a verdict for the plaintiff.[906] Taking an oath for Muslims can be a grave act; one study of courts in Morocco found that lying litigants would often "maintain their testimony 'right up to the moment of oath-taking and then to stop, refuse the oath, and surrender the case."[907] Accordingly, defendants are not routinely required to swear before testifying, which would risk casually profaning the Quran should the defendant commit perjury; instead oaths are a solemn procedure performed as a final part of the evidence process.Wikipedia:Citation needed

Diya

In classical jurisprudence monetary compensation for bodily harm (*diya* or blood money) is assessed differently for different classes of victims. For example, for Muslim women the amount was half that assessed for a Muslim man.[908] *Diya* for the death of a free Muslim man is twice as high as for Jewish and Christian victims according to the Maliki and Hanbali madhhabs and three times as high according to Shafi'i rules. Several legals schools assessed *diya* for Magians (*majus*) at one-fifteenth the value of a free Muslim male.[909]

Modern countries which incorporate classical *diya* rules into their legal system treat them in different ways. The Pakistan Penal Code modernized the Hanafi doctrine by eliminating distinctions between Muslims and non-Muslims. In Iran, *diya* for non-Muslim victims professing one of the faiths protected under the constitution (Jews, Christians, and Zoroastrians) was made equal to *diya* for Muslims in 2004, though according to a 2006 US State Department report, the penal code still discriminates against other religious minorities and women. According to Human Rights Watch and the US State Department, in Saudi Arabia Jewish or Christian male plaintiffs are entitled to half the amount a Muslim male would receive, while for all other non-Muslim males the proportion is one-sixteenth.[910,911,912]

Support and opposition

Support

A 2013 survey based on interviews of 38,000 Muslims, randomly selected
from urban and rural parts in 39 countries using area probability designs,
by the Pew Forum on Religion and Public Life found that a majority—in
some cases "overwhelming" majority—of Muslims in a number of countries
support making sharia the law of the land, including Afghanistan (99%),
Iraq (91%), Niger (86%), Malaysia (86%), Pakistan (84%), Morocco (83%),
Bangladesh (82%), Egypt (74%), Indonesia (72%), Jordan (71%), Uganda
(66%), Ethiopia (65%), Mali (63%), Ghana (58%), and Tunisia (56%). In
Muslim regions of Southern-Eastern Europe and Central Asia, the support is
less than 50%: Russia (42%), Kyrgyzstan (35%), Tajikistan (27%), Kosovo
(20%), Albania (12%), Turkey (12%), Kazakhstan (10%), Azerbaijan (8%).
Regarding specific averages, in South Asia, Sharia had 84% favorability rat-
ing among the respondents; in Southeast Asia 77%; in the Middle-East/North
Africa 74%; in Sub-Saharan Africa 64%; in Southern-Eastern Europe 18%;
and in Central Asia 12%.

However, while most of those who support implementation of sharia favor
using it in family and property disputes, fewer supported application of severe
punishments such as whippings and cutting off hands, and interpretations of
some aspects differed widely. According to the Pew poll, among Muslims
who support making sharia the law of the land, most do not believe that it
should be applied to non-Muslims. In the Muslim-majority countries surveyed
this proportion varied between 74% (of 74% in Egypt) and 19% (of 10% in
Kazakhstan), as percentage of those who favored making sharia the law of the
land.[913] Polls demonstrate that for Egyptians, the 'Shariah' is associated with
notions of political, social and gender justice.[914]

In 2008, Rowan Williams, the archbishop of Canterbury, has suggested that
Islamic and Orthodox Jewish courts should be integrated into the British legal
system alongside ecclesiastical courts to handle marriage and divorce, subject
to agreement of all parties and strict requirements for protection of equal rights
for women. His reference to the sharia sparked a controversy. Later that year,
Nicholas Phillips, then Lord Chief Justice of England and Wales, stated that
there was "no reason why sharia principles [...] should not be the basis for mediation or other forms of alternative dispute resolution." A 2008 YouGov poll
in the United Kingdom found 40% of Muslim students interviewed supported
the introduction of sharia into British law for Muslims.[915] Michael Broyde,
professor of law at Emory University specializing in alternative dispute resolution and Jewish law,[916] has argued that sharia courts can be integrated into
the American religious arbitration system, provided that they adopt appropriate institutional requirements as American rabbinical courts have done.

Figure 27: *A public demonstration calling*
for Sharia law in Maldives, September 2014

Extremism

Fundamentalists, wishing to return to basic Islamic religious values and law, have in some instances imposed harsh sharia punishments for crimes, curtailed civil rights and violated human rights. Extremists have used the Quran and their own particular version of sharia to justify acts of war and terror against Muslim as well as non-Muslim individuals and governments, using alternate, conflicting interpretations of sharia and their notions of jihad.[917,918]

The sharia basis of arguments advocating terrorism is controversial. According to Bernard Lewis, "[a]t no time did the classical jurists offer any approval or legitimacy to what we nowadays call terrorism"[919] and the terrorist practice of suicide bombing "has no justification in terms of Islamic theology, law or tradition".[920] In the modern era the notion of jihad has lost its jurisprudential relevance and instead gave rise to an ideological and political discourse. For al-Qaeda ideologues, in jihad all means are legitimate, including targeting Muslim non-combatants and the mass killing of non-Muslim civilians. According to these interpretations, Islam does not discriminate between military and civilian targets, but rather between Muslims and nonbelievers, whose blood can be legitimately spilled.

Some scholars of Islam, such as Yusuf al-Qaradawi and Sulaiman Al-Alwan, have supported suicide attacks against Israeli civilians, arguing that they are army reservists and hence should be considered as soldiers, while Hamid bin Abdallah al-Ali declared that suicide attacks in Chechnya were justified as a "sacrifice".[921] Many prominent Islamic scholars, including al-Qaradawi himself, have issued condemnations of terrorism in general terms. For example, Abdul-Aziz ibn Abdullah Al ash-Sheikh, the Grand Mufti of Saudi Arabia has stated that "terrorizing innocent people [...] constitute[s] a form of injustice that cannot be tolerated by Islam", while Muhammad Sayyid Tantawy, Grand Imam of al-Azhar and former Grand Mufti of Egypt has stated that "attacking innocent people is not courageous; it is stupid and will be punished on the Day of Judgment".[922,923]

Opposition

In the Western world, sharia has been called a source of "hysteria", "more controversial than ever", the one aspect of Islam that inspires "particular dread". On the Internet, "dozens of self-styled counter-jihadis" emerged to campaign against sharia law, describing it in strict interpretations resembling those of Salafi Muslims. Also, fear of sharia law and of "the ideology of extremism" among Muslims reportedly spread to mainstream conservative Republicans in the United States. Former House Speaker Newt Gingrich won ovations calling for a federal ban on sharia law. The issue of "liberty versus Sharia" was called a "momentous civilisational debate" by right-wing pundit Diana West. In 2008 in Britain, the future Prime Minister (David Cameron) declared his opposition to "any expansion of Sharia law in the UK." In Germany, in 2014, the Interior Minister (Thomas de Maizière) told a newspaper (*Bild*), "Sharia law is not tolerated on German soil."

Some countries and jurisdictions have explicit bans on sharia law. In Canada, for example, sharia law has been explicitly banned in Quebec by a 2005 unanimous vote of the National Assembly,[924] while the province of Ontario allows family law disputes to be arbitrated only under Ontario law. In the U.S., opponents of Sharia have sought to ban it from being considered in courts, where it has been routinely used alongside traditional Jewish and Catholic laws to decide legal, business, and family disputes subject to contracts drafted with reference to such laws, as long as they do not violate secular law or the U.S. constitution. After failing to gather support for a federal law making observing Sharia a felony punishable by up to 20 years in prison, anti-Sharia activists have focused on state legislatures. By 2014, bills aimed against use of Sharia have been introduced in 34 states and passed in 11. These bills have generally referred to banning foreign or religious law in order to thwart legal challenges.

According to Jan Michiel Otto, Professor of Law and Governance in Developing Countries at Leiden University, "[a]nthropological research shows that people in local communities often do not distinguish clearly whether and to

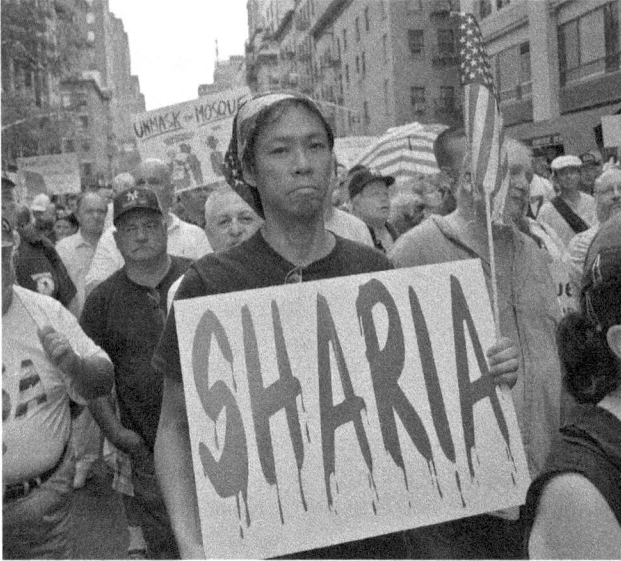

Figure 28: *A protester opposing the Park51 project, carries an anti-sharia sign.*

what extent their norms and practices are based on local tradition, tribal custom, or religion. Those who adhere to a confrontational view of sharia tend to
ascribe many undesirable practices to sharia and religion overlooking custom
and culture, even if high-ranking religious authorities have stated the opposite."[925]

Criticism

Compatibility with democracy

Ali Khan states that "constitutional orders founded on the principles of sharia
are fully compatible with democracy, provided that religious minorities are
protected and the incumbent Islamic leadership remains committed to the right
to recall".[926] Other scholars say sharia is not compatible with democracy,
particularly where the country's constitution demands separation of religion
and the democratic state.

Courts in non-Muslim majority nations have generally ruled against the implementation of sharia, both in jurisprudence and within a community context,
based on sharia's religious background. In Muslim nations, sharia has wide
support with some exceptions.[927] For example, in 1998 the Constitutional
Court of Turkey banned and dissolved Turkey's Refah Party on the grounds

that "Democracy is the antithesis of Sharia", the latter of which Refah sought to introduce.

On appeal by Refah the European Court of Human Rights determined that "sharia is incompatible with the fundamental principles of democracy".[928] Refah's sharia-based notion of a "plurality of legal systems, grounded on religion" was ruled to contravene the European Convention for the Protection of Human Rights and Fundamental Freedoms. It was determined that it would "do away with the State's role as the guarantor of individual rights and freedoms" and "infringe the principle of non-discrimination between individuals as regards their enjoyment of public freedoms, which is one of the fundamental principles of democracy".[929]

Human rights

Several major, predominantly Muslim countries have criticized the Universal Declaration of Human Rights (UDHR) for its perceived failure to take into account the cultural and religious context of non-Western countries. Iran declared in the UN assembly that UDHR was "a secular understanding of the Judeo-Christian tradition", which could not be implemented by Muslims without trespassing the Islamic law.[930] Islamic scholars and Islamist political parties consider 'universal human rights' arguments as imposition of a non-Muslim culture on Muslim people, a disrespect of customary cultural practices and of Islam. In 1990, the Organisation of Islamic Cooperation, a group representing all Muslim majority nations, met in Cairo to respond to the UDHR, then adopted the Cairo Declaration on Human Rights in Islam.[931]

Ann Elizabeth Mayer points to notable absences from the Cairo Declaration: provisions for democratic principles, protection for religious freedom, freedom of association and freedom of the press, as well as equality in rights and equal protection under the law. Article 24 of the Cairo declaration states that "all the rights and freedoms stipulated in this Declaration are subject to the Islamic *shari'a*".

In 2009, the journal *Free Inquiry* summarized the criticism of the Cairo Declaration in an editorial: "We are deeply concerned with the changes to the Universal Declaration of Human Rights by a coalition of Islamic states within the United Nations that wishes to prohibit any criticism of religion and would thus protect Islam's limited view of human rights. In view of the conditions inside the Islamic Republic of Iran, Egypt, Pakistan, Saudi Arabia, the Sudan, Syria, Bangladesh, Iraq, and Afghanistan, we should expect that at the top of their human rights agenda would be to rectify the legal inequality of women, the suppression of political dissent, the curtailment of free expression, the persecution of ethnic minorities and religious dissenters – in short, protecting their citizens from egregious human rights violations. Instead, they are worrying about protecting Islam."[932]

H. Patrick Glenn states that sharia is structured around the concept of mutual obligations of a collective, and it considers individual human rights as potentially disruptive and unnecessary to its revealed code of mutual obligations. In giving priority to this religious collective rather than individual liberty, the Islamic law justifies the formal inequality of individuals (women, non-Islamic people).[933] Bassam Tibi states that sharia framework and human rights are incompatible. Abdel al-Hakeem Carney, in contrast, states that sharia is misunderstood from a failure to distinguish *sharia* from *siyasah* (politics).

Freedom of speech

The Cairo Declaration on Human Rights in Islam conditions free speech with sharia law: Article 22(a) of the Declaration states that "Everyone shall have the right to express his opinion freely in such manner as would not be contrary to the principles of the Shariah."

Blasphemy in Islam is any form of cursing, questioning or annoying God, Muhammad or anything considered sacred in Islam.[934,935] The sharia of various Islamic schools of jurisprudence specify different punishment for blasphemy against Islam, by Muslims and non-Muslims, ranging from imprisonment, fines, flogging, amputation, hanging, or beheading.[936,937] In some cases, sharia allows non-Muslims to escape death by converting and becoming a devout follower of Islam.[938]

Blasphemy, as interpreted under sharia, is controversial.[939] Muslim nations have petitioned the United Nations to limit "freedom of speech" because "unrestricted and disrespectful opinion against Islam creates hatred".[940] Other nations, in contrast, consider blasphemy laws as violation of "freedom of speech",[941] stating that freedom of expression is essential to empowering both Muslims and non-Muslims, and point to the abuse of blasphemy laws, where hundreds, often members of religious minorities, are being lynched, killed and incarcerated in Muslim nations, on flimsy accusations of insulting Islam.[942,943]

Freedom of thought, conscience and religion

According to the United Nations' Universal Declaration of Human Rights, every human has the right to freedom of thought, conscience and religion; this right includes freedom to change their religion or belief. Sharia has been criticized for not recognizing this human right. According to scholars of Islamic law, the applicable rules for religious conversion under sharia are as follows:

• If a person converts to Islam, or is born and raised as a Muslim, then he or she will have full rights of citizenship in an Islamic state.

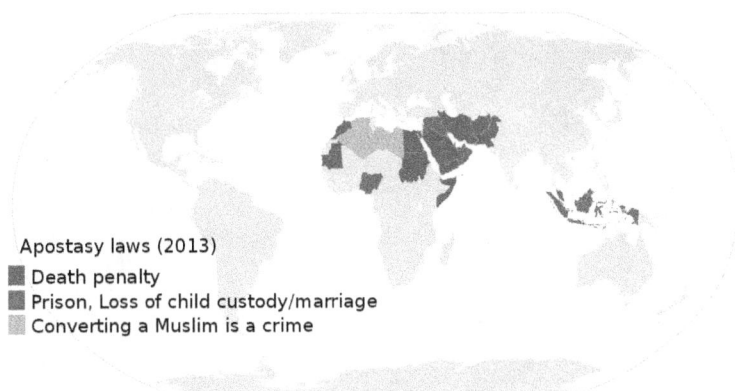

Apostasy laws (2013)
■ Death penalty
■ Prison, Loss of child custody/marriage
▨ Converting a Muslim is a crime

Figure 29: *Countries that criminalize apostasy from Islam as of 2013.*
Some Muslim countries impose the death penalty or a prison sentence
for apostasy from Islam, or ban non-Muslims from proselytizing .[944]

- Leaving Islam is a sin and a religious crime. Once any man or woman is officially classified as Muslim, because of birth or religious conversion, he or she will be subject to the death penalty if he or she becomes an apostate, that is, abandons his or her faith in Islam in order to become an atheist, agnostic or to convert to another religion. Before executing the death penalty, sharia demands that the individual be offered one chance to return to Islam.
- If a person has never been a Muslim, and is not a kafir (infidel, unbeliever), he or she can live in an Islamic state by accepting to be a dhimmi, or under a special permission called *aman*. As a dhimmi or under aman, he or she will suffer certain limitations of rights as a subject of an Islamic state, and will not enjoy complete legal equality with Muslims.
- If a person has never been a Muslim, and is a kafir (infidel, unbeliever), sharia demands that he or she should be offered the choice to convert to Islam and become a Muslim; if he or she rejects the offer, he or she may become a dhimmi. Failure to pay the tax may lead the non-Muslim to either be enslaved, killed or ransomed if captured.

According to sharia theory, conversion of disbelievers and non-Muslims to Islam is encouraged as a religious duty for all Muslims, and leaving Islam (apostasy), expressing contempt for Islam (blasphemy), and religious conversion of Muslims is prohibited.[945] Not all Islamic scholars agree with this interpretation of sharia theory. In practice, as of 2011, 20 Islamic nations had laws declaring apostasy from Islam as illegal and a criminal offense. Such laws

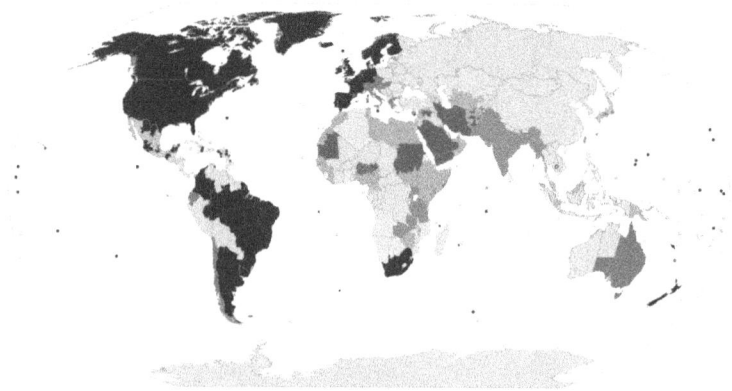

Figure 30:
Same-sex intercourse illegal:
Death penalty
Up to life in prison
Imprisonment
Unenforced penalty

are incompatible with the UDHR's requirement of freedom of thought, conscience and religion.[946] In another 2013 report based on international survey of religious attitudes, more than 50% of Muslim population in 6 out of 49 Islamic countries supported death penalty for any Muslim who leaves Islam (apostasy). However it is also shown that the majority of Muslims in the 43 nations surveyed did not agree with this interpretation of sharia.

Some scholars claim sharia allows religious freedom because a sharia verse teaches, "there is no compulsion in religion." Other scholars claim sharia recognizes only one proper religion, considers apostasy as sin punishable with death, and members of other religions as kafir (infidel);[947] or hold that sharia demands that all apostates and kafir must be put to death, enslaved or be ransomed.Wikipedia:Verifiability[948,949,950] Yet other scholars suggest that sharia has become a product of human interpretation and inevitably leads to disagreements about the "precise contents of the Shari'a." In the end, then, what is being applied is not sharia, but what a particular group of clerics and government decide is sharia. It is these differing interpretations of sharia that explain why many Islamic countries have laws that restrict and criminalize apostasy, proselytism and their citizens' freedom of conscience and religion.[951]

LGBT rights

Homosexual intercourse is illegal under sharia law, though the prescribed penalties differ from one school of jurisprudence to another. For example, some Muslim-majority countries impose the death penalty for acts perceived as sodomy and homosexual activities: Iran, Saudi Arabia, and in other Muslim-majority countries such as Egypt, Iraq, and the Indonesian province of Aceh, same-sex sexual acts are illegal, and LGBT people regularly face violence and discrimination.

Women

Domestic violence

Many claim sharia law encourages domestic violence against women, when a husband suspects *nushuz* (disobedience, disloyalty, rebellion, ill conduct) in his wife. Other scholars claim wife beating, for *nashizah*, is not consistent with modern perspectives of the Quran.

One of the verses of the Quran relating to permissibility of domestic violence is Surah 4:34.[952] Sharia has been criticized for ignoring women's rights in domestic abuse cases. Musawah, CEDAW, KAFA and other organizations have proposed ways to modify sharia-inspired laws to improve women's rights in Islamic nations, including women's rights in domestic abuse cases.

Personal status laws and child marriage

Shari'a is the basis for personal status laws in most Islamic majority nations. These personal status laws determine rights of women in matters of marriage, divorce and child custody. A 2011 UNICEF report concludes that sharia law provisions are discriminatory against women from a human rights perspective. In legal proceedings under sharia law, a woman's testimony is worth half of a man's before a court.

Except for IranWikipedia:Citation needed, LebanonWikipedia:Citation needed and BahrainWikipedia:Citation needed which allow child marriagesWikipedia:Citation needed, the civil code in Islamic majority countries do not allow child marriage of girls. However, with sharia personal status laws, sharia courts in all these nations have the power to override the civil code. The religious courts permit girls less than 18 years old to marry. As of 2011, child marriages are common in a few Middle Eastern countries, accounting for 1 in 6 of all marriages in Egypt and 1 in 3 marriages in Yemen. UNICEF and other studies state that the top five nations in the world with highest observed child marriage rates – Niger (75%), Chad (72%), Mali (71%), Bangladesh (64%), Guinea (63%) – are Islamic-majority countries where the personal laws for Muslims are sharia-based. In his Cairo speech, President Obama spoke out against child marriage.

Rape is considered a crime in all countries, but sharia courts in Bahrain, Iraq, Jordan, Libya, Morocco, Syria and Tunisia in some cases allow a rapist to escape punishment by marrying his victim, while in other cases the victim who complains is often prosecuted with the crime of *Zina* (adultery).

Women's right to property and consent

Sharia grants women the right to inherit property from other family members, and these rights are detailed in the Quran.[953]   A woman's inheritance is unequal and less than a man's, and dependent on many factors.[Quran 4:12[954]] For instance, a daughter's inheritance is usually half that of her brother's.[Quran 4:11[955]]

Until the 20th century, Islamic law granted Muslim women certain legal rights, such as the right to own property received as Mahr (brideprice) at her marriage. However, Islamic law does not grant non-Muslim women the same legal rights as the few it did grant Muslim women. Sharia recognizes the basic inequality between master and women slave, between free women and slave women, between Believers and non-Believers, as well as their unequal rights.[956,957] Sharia authorized the institution of slavery, using the words *abd* (slave) and the phrase *ma malakat aymanukum* ("that which your right hand owns") to refer to women slaves, seized as captives of war.[958] Under Islamic law, Muslim men could have sexual relations with female captives and slaves.[959]

Slave women under sharia did not have a right to own property or to move freely.[960,961] Sharia, in Islam's history, provided a religious foundation for enslaving non-Muslim women (and men), but allowed for the manumission of slaves. However, manumission required that the non-Muslim slave first convert to Islam. A non-Muslim slave woman who bore children to her Muslim master became legally free upon her master's death, and her children were presumed to be Muslims like their father, in Africa and elsewhere.

Starting with the 20th century, Western legal systems evolved to expand women's rights, but women's rights under Islamic law have remained tied to the Quran, hadiths and their fundamentalist interpretation as sharia by Islamic jurists.

Parallels with Western legal systems

Elements of Islamic law have parallels in western legal systems. As example, the influence of Islam on the development of an international law of the sea can be discerned alongside that of the Roman influence.

Makdisi states Islamic law also parallels the legal scholastic system in the West, which gave rise to the modern university system. He writes that the triple status of *faqih* ("master of law"), *mufti* ("professor of legal opinions") and *mudarris* ("teacher"), conferred by the classical Islamic legal degree, had its equivalents in the medieval Latin terms *magister*, *professor* and *doctor*, respectively, although they all came to be used synonymously in both East and West. Makdisi suggests that the medieval European doctorate, *licentia docendi* was modeled on the Islamic degree *ijazat al-tadris wa-l-ifta'*, of which it is a word-for-word translation, with the term *ifta'* (issuing of fatwas) omitted. He also argues that these systems shared fundamental freedoms: the freedom of a professor to profess his personal opinion and the freedom of a student to pass judgement on what he is learning.

There are differences between Islamic and Western legal systems. For example, sharia classically recognizes only natural persons, and never developed the concept of a legal person, or corporation, i.e., a legal entity that limits the liabilities of its managers, shareholders, and employees; exists beyond the lifetimes of its founders; and that can own assets, sign contracts, and appear in court through representatives. Interest prohibitions imposed secondary costs by discouraging record keeping and delaying the introduction of modern accounting. Such factors, according to Timur Kuran, have played a significant role in retarding economic development in the Middle East.[962]

References

Sources

- An-Na'im, Abdullahi Ahmed. " Islamic Foundations of Religious Human Rights[963]" in *Religious Human Rights in Global Perspective: Religious Perspectives*. John Witte Jr. & Johan D. van der Vyver eds. (1996). Springer Publishing ISBN 978-9041101778.
- Brown, Jonathan A. C. (2009). "Maṣlaḥah"[964]. In John L. Esposito. *The Oxford Encyclopedia of the Islamic World*. Oxford: Oxford University Press. (Subscription required (help)).
- Calder, Norman; Hooker, Michael Barry (2007). "Sharī'a"[965]. In P. Bearman, Th. Bianquis, C.E. Bosworth, E. van Donzel, W.P. Heinrichs. *Encyclopaedia of Islam*. **9** (2nd ed.). Brill. pp. 321–26.

- Calder, Norman (2009). "Law. Legal Thought and Jurisprudence"[966]. In John L. Esposito. *The Oxford Encyclopedia of the Islamic World*. Oxford: Oxford University Press.
- Duderija, Adis (2014). Adis Duderija, ed. *Contemporary Muslim Reformist Thought and Maqāṣid cum Maṣlaḥa Approaches to Islamic Law: An Introduction*. Maqasid al-Shari'a and Contemporary Reformist Muslim Thought: An Examination. Springer.
- Gleave, R.M. (2012). "Maḵāṣid al-Sharīʻa"[967]. In P. Bearman, Th. Bianquis, C.E. Bosworth, E. van Donzel, W.P. Heinrichs. *Encyclopaedia of Islam* (2nd ed.). Brill. doi: 10.1163/1573-3912_islam_SIM_8809[968]. (Subscription required (help)).
- Glenn, H. Patrick (2014). *Legal Traditions of the World – Sustainable Diversity in Law* (5th edition), Oxford University Press, ISBN 978-0199669837.
- Hallaq, Wael B. (2009). *An Introduction to Islamic Law*. Cambridge University Press.
- Harnischfeger, Johannes (2008). *Democratization and Islamic Law – The Sharia Conflict in Nigeria*. Frankfurt; New York City: Campus Verlag and Chicago: University of Chicago Press (distributor). ISBN 978-3-593-38256-2.
- Horrie, Chris; Chippindale, Peter (1991). *What Is Islam? A Comprehensive Introduction*. Virgin Books. ISBN 0-7535-0827-3.
- Hussin, Iza (2014). "Sunni Schools of Jurisprudence"[969]. In Emad El-Din Shahin. *The Oxford Encyclopedia of Islam and Politics*. Oxford University Press. doi:10.1093/acref:oiso/9780199739356.001.0001/acref-9780199739356-e-0416 (inactive 2017-09-12). (Subscription required (help)).
- Jokisch, Benjamin (2015). "Origins of and Influences on Islamic law"[970]. In Anver M. Emon and Rumee Ahmed. *The Oxford Handbook of Islamic Law*. Oxford: Oxford University Press. doi:10.1093/oxfordhb/9780199679010.001.0001/oxfordhb-9780199679010-e-12 (inactive 2017-09-12). (Subscription required (help)).
- Khadduri, Majid (1955). *War and Peace in the Law of Islam*. Baltimore: Johns Hopkins. OCLC 647084498[971].
- Kamali, Mohammad Hashim (1999). John Esposito, ed. *Law and Society*. The Oxford History of Islam. Oxford University Press (Kindle edition).
- Khadduri, Majid; Liebesny, Herbert J., eds. (1955). *Law in the Middle East*. Middle East Institute. OCLC 578890367[972].
- Lapidus, Ira M. (2014). *A History of Islamic Societies*. Cambridge University Press (Kindle edition). ISBN 978-0-521-51430-9.

- Mayer, Ann Elizabeth (2009). "Law. Modern Legal Reform"[973]. In John L. Esposito. *The Oxford Encyclopedia of the Islamic World*. Oxford: Oxford University Press.
- Opwis, Felicitas (2007). Abbas Amanat, Frank Griffel, eds. *Islamic Law and Legal Change: The Concept of Maslaha in Classical and Contemporary Legal Theory*. Shari'a: Islamic Law in the Contemporary Context. Stanford University Press (Kindle edition).
- Otto, Jan Michiel (2008). *Sharia and National Law in Muslim Countries: Tensions and Opportunities for Dutch and EU Foreign Policy*[974] (PDF). Amsterdam University Press. ISBN 978-90-8728-048-2.
- Otto, Jan Michiel, ed. (2010). *Sharia Incorporated: A Comparative Overview of the Legal Systems of Twelve Muslim Countries in Past and Present*. Leiden University Press. ISBN 978-94-0060-017-1.
- Rabb, Intisar A. (2009). "Law. Civil Law & Courts"[975]. In John L. Esposito. *The Oxford Encyclopedia of the Islamic World*. Oxford: Oxford University Press.
- Rabb, Intisar A. (2009b). "Fiqh"[976]. In John L. Esposito. *The Oxford Encyclopedia of the Islamic World*. Oxford: Oxford University Press. doi: 10.1093/acref/9780195305135.001.0001/acref-9780195305135-e-1150 (inactive 2017-09-12). (Subscription required (help)).
- Rabb, Intisar A. (2009c). "Ijtihād"[977]. In John L. Esposito. *The Oxford Encyclopedia of the Islamic World*. Oxford: Oxford University Press. doi:10.1093/acref/9780195305135.001.0001/acref-9780195305135-e-0354 (inactive 2017-09-12). (Subscription required (help)).
- Schneider, Irene (2014). "Fiqh"[978]. In Emad El-Din Shahin. *The Oxford Encyclopedia of Islam and Politics*. Oxford University Press. doi: 10.1093/acref:oiso/9780199739356.001.0001/acref-9780199739356-e-0171 (inactive 2017-09-12). (Subscription required (help)).
- Vikør, Knut S. (2014). "Sharī'ah"[979]. In Emad El-Din Shahin. *The Oxford Encyclopedia of Islam and Politics*. Oxford University Press.
- Ziadeh, Farhat J. (2009). "Uṣūl al-fiqh"[980]. In John L. Esposito. *The Oxford Encyclopedia of the Islamic World*. Oxford: Oxford University Press. doi:10.1093/acref/9780195305135.001.0001/acref-9780195305135-e-0831 (inactive 2017-09-12). (Subscription required (help)).
- Ziadeh, Farhat J. (2009b). "Law. Sunnī Schools of Law"[966]. In John L. Esposito. *The Oxford Encyclopedia of the Islamic World*. Oxford: Oxford University Press.
- Ziadeh, Farhat J. (2009c). "Criminal Law"[981]. In John L. Esposito. *The Oxford Encyclopedia of the Islamic World*. Oxford: Oxford University Press.

Further reading

* Ali, Abdullah Yusuf (2000). *The Holy Qur'an* (Translated by Abdullah Yusuf Ali). Ware, Hertfordshire, England: Wordsworth Editions. ISBN 978-1-85326-782-6. A popular translation of the Quran.
* Coulson, Noel J. (1964). *A History of Islamic Law*. Edinburgh: Edinburgh U.P.
* Elliesie, Hatem (2014): *Binnenpluralität des Islamischen Rechts: Diversität religiöser Normativität rechtsdogmatisch- und methodisch betrachtet*[982], SFB Governance Working Paper Series, Collaborative Research Center 700 „Governance in Areas of Limited Statehood", No. 54, ISSN 1863-6896[983].
* Hallaq, Wael B. (2009). *An Introduction to Islamic Law*. Cambridge: Cambridge U.P. ISBN 978-0-52167-873-5
* Hussain, Jamila (2011). *Islam: Its Law and Society* (3rd edition). Annandale, N.S.W., Australia: The Federation Press. ISBN 1-86287-499-9. OCLC 742018517[984]. A modern discourse on Sharia law.
* Khan, Muhammad Muhsin (1996). *The English Translation of Ṣaḥīḥ Al Bukhārī with the Arabic Text*. Alexandria, Va.: Al-Saadawi Publications. ISBN 978-1-881963-59-2. OCLC 35673415[985]. The complete translation (in nine volumes) of a popular Sunni collection of hadith.
* Mahmassani, Maher (2014). *Islam in Retrospect: Recovering the Message*. Olive Branch Pr. ISBN 1566569222.
* Mahmassani, Sobhi (1961). *The Philosophy of Jurisprudence in Islam*, translated by Farhat J. Ziadeh. Leiden: Brill.
* Mahmassani, Sobhi (1966). *The Principles of International Law in the Light of Islamic Doctrine*, publications of The Hague Academy of International Law, Leiden.
* Potz, Richard (2011). *Islamic Law and the Transfer of European Law*[986]. Mainz: European History Online, Institute of European History. Retrieved: November 28, 2011.
* Nuh Ha Mim Keller (ed., trans.), *Reliance of the Traveller: Classic Manual of Islamic Sacred Law*, Amana Publications, revised edition 1997, ISBN 9780-915957-72-9
* Schacht, Joseph (1964). *An Introduction to Islamic Law*. Oxford: Clarendon
* Schacht, Joseph (1950). *The Origins of Muhammadan Jurisprudence*. Oxford: Clarendon

External links

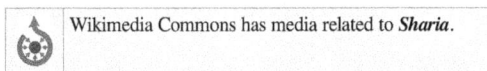

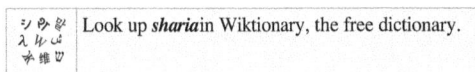

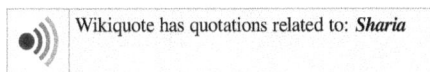

Wikimedia Commons has media related to *Sharia*.

Look up *sharia* in Wiktionary, the free dictionary.

Wikiquote has quotations related to: *Sharia*

- *Islamic law*[987] – in *The Oxford Dictionary of Islam*, via Oxford Islamic Studies Online
- *Sharia* by Knut S. Vikør[979] – In *The Oxford Encyclopedia of Islam and Politics*, via Bridging Cultures, National Endowment for the Humanities & George Mason University
- *Law* by Norman Calder et al[966] – In *The Oxford Encyclopedia of the Islamic World*, via Oxford Islamic Studies
- UNAA site on sharia in Muslim Countries[988] – United Nations
- Sharia Law in the International Legal Sphere[989] – Yale University
- Private Arrangements: 'Recognizing Sharia' in Britain[990] – anthropologist John R. Bowen explains the working of Britain's sharia courts in a *Boston Review* article
- Division of Inheritance According to Qur'an[991]
- "Explanation of "The Reward of the Omnipotent""[992] is a manuscript, in Arabic, from the late 19th or early 20th century about Sharia

Fiqh

Fiqh	
Arabic	فقه
Romanization	Fiqh
Literal meaning	"deep understanding" "full comprehension"

Part of a series on
Islamic jurisprudence **(*fiqh*)**
Islamic studies
• <u>v</u> • <u>t</u> • <u>e</u>993

Part of a series on
Islam
الله

- ٱللّٰه **Islam portal**
- v
- t
- e[994]

Fiqh (/fɪk/; Arabic: فقه [fɪqh]) is Islamic jurisprudence.[995] While *sharia* is believed by Muslims to represent divine law as revealed in the Quran and the *Sunnah* (the teachings and practices of the Islamic prophet Muhammad), *fiqh* is the human understanding of the *sharia—sharia* expanded and developed by interpretation (*ijtihad*) of the Quran and *Sunnah* by Islamic jurists (*ulama*) and implemented by the rulings (*fatwa*) of jurists on questions presented to them. Thus conceptually, whereas *sharia* is considered immutable and infallible, *fiqh* is considered fallible and changeable. *Fiqh* deals with the observance of rituals, morals and social legislation in Islam. In the modern era, there are four prominent schools (*madh'hab*) of *fiqh* within Sunni practice, plus two (or three) within Shi'a practice. A person trained in *fiqh* is known as a *faqīh* (plural *fuqaha*).[996]

Figuratively, *fiqh* means knowledge about Islamic legal rulings from their sources. Thus the figurative definition of *fiqh* is taken from its literal one in the sense that deriving religious rulings from their sources necessitates the *mujtahid* (an individual who exercises *ijtihad*) to have a deep understanding in the different discussions of jurisprudence. A *faqīh* must look deep down into a matter and not suffice himself with just the apparent meaning, and a person who only knows the appearance of a matter is not qualified as a *faqīh*.

On the studies of *fiqh*, it is traditionally divided into *Uṣūl al-fiqh* (principles of Islamic jurisprudence, lit. the roots of fiqh), the methods of legal interpretation and analysis, and *Furū' al-fiqh* (lit. the branches of fiqh), the elaboration of rulings on the basis of these principles.[997,998] *Furū' al-fiqh* is the product of the application of *Uṣūl al-fiqh* and the total product of human efforts at understanding the divine will. A *hukm* (plural *aḥkām*) is a particular ruling in a given case.

Etymology

The word *fiqh* is an Arabic term meaning "deep understanding" or "full comprehension". Technically it refers to the body of Islamic law extracted from detailed Islamic sources (which are studied in the principles of Islamic jurisprudence) and the process of gaining knowledge of Islam through jurisprudence. The historian Ibn Khaldun describes *fiqh* as "knowledge of the rules of God which concern the actions of persons who own themselves bound to obey the law respecting what is required (*wajib*), sinful (*haraam*), recommended

(*mandūb*), disapproved (*makrūh*) or neutral (*mubah*)".[999] This definition is
consistent amongst the jurists.

In Modern Standard Arabic, *fiqh* has come to mean jurisprudence in general,
be it Islamic or secular. It is thus possible to speak of Chief Justice John Roberts
as an expert in the common law *fiqh* of the United States, or of Egyptian legal
scholar Abd El-Razzak El-Sanhuri as an expert in the civil law *fiqh* of Egypt.

History

The history of Islamic juriprudence is "customarily divided into eight periods".[1000]

- the first period ending with the death of Muhammad in 11 AH.
- second period "characterized by personal interpretations" of the canon by
  the *Sahabah* or companions of Muhammad, lasting until 50 A.H.
- from 50 AH until the early second century AH there was competition
  between a "a traditionalist approach to jurisprudence" in western Arabia
  where Islam was revealed and a "rationalist approach in Iraq".
- the "golden age of classical Islamic jurisprudence" from the "early second
  to the mid-fourth century when the eight "most significant" schools of
  Sunni and Shi'i jurisprudence emerged."
- from the mid-fourth century to mid-seventh AH Islamic jurisprudence
  was "limited to elaborations within the main juristic schools".
- the "dark age" of Islamic jurisprudence stretched from the fall of Baghdad
  in the mid-seventh AH (1258 CE) to 1293 AH/1876 CE.
- In 1293 AH (1876 CE) the Ottomans codified Hanafi jurisprudence in the
  Majallah el-Ahkam-i-Adliya. Several "juristic revival movements" influenced by "exposure to Western legal and technological progress" followed
  until the mid-20th century CE. Muhammad Abduh and Abd El-Razzak
  El-Sanhuri were products of this era.
- The most recent era has been that of the "Islamic revival", which has been
  "predicated on rejection of Western social and legal advances" and the
  development of specifically Islamic states, social sciences, economics, and
  finance.

The formative period of Islamic jurisprudence stretches back to the time of the
early Muslim communities. In this period, jurists were more concerned with
issues of authority and teaching than with theory and methodology.[1001]

Progress in theory and methodology happened with the coming of the early
Muslim jurist Muhammad ibn Idris ash-Shafi'i (767–820), who codified the
basic principles of Islamic jurisprudence in his book *ar-Risālah*. The book
details the four roots of law (Qur'an, Sunnah, *ijma*, and *qiyas*) while specifying that the primary Islamic texts (the Qur'an and the hadith) be understood

according to objective rules of interpretation derived from scientific study of the Arabic language.[1002]

Secondary sources of law were developed and refined over the subsequent centuries, consisting primarily of juristic preference (*istihsan*), laws of the previous prophets (*shara man qablana*), continuity (*istishab*), extended analogy (*maslaha mursala*), blocking the means (*sadd al-dhari'ah*), custome *urf* and saying of a companion (*qawl al-sahabi*).[1003]

Diagram of early scholars

The Quran set the rights,, the responsibilities and the rules for people and for societies to adhere to, like not dealing in interest. Muhammad then provided an example, which is recorded in the hadith books, showing people how he practically implemented these rules in a society. After the passing of Muhammad, there was a need for jurists, to decide on new legal matters where there is no such ruling in the Quran or the Hadith, example of Islamic prophet Muhammad regarding a similar case.

In the years proceeding Muhammad, the community in Madina continued to use the same rules. People were familiar with the practice of Muhammad and therefore continued to use the same rules.

The scholars appearing in the diagram below were taught by Muhammad's companions, many of whom settled in Madina. Muwatta by Malik ibn Anas was written as a consensus of the opinion, of these scholars. The Muwatta by Malik ibn Anas quotes 13 hadiths from Imam Jafar al-Sadiq.[1004]

Much of the knowledge we have about Muhammad is narrated through Aisha the wife of Muhammad, also a renowned scholar of her time. Aisha raised and taught her nephew Qasim ibn Muhammad ibn Abu Bakr after her brother Muhammad ibn Abu Bakr was killed by the Syrians.

Qasim ibn Muhammad ibn Abu Bakrs mother was from Alis family and Qasims daughter Farwah bint al-Qasim was married to Muhammad al-Baqir and was the mother of Jafar al-Sadiq. Therefore, Qasim ibn Muhammad ibn Abu Bakr was the grand son of Abu Bakr the first caliph and the grand father of Jafar al-Sadiq whose views the twelver Shias follow. The twelver Shia do not accept Abu Bakr as the first caliph but do accept his great grand son Jafar al-Sadiq.

Aishas also taught her nephew Urwah ibn Zubayr. He then taught his son Hisham ibn Urwah, who was the main teacher of Malik ibn Anas whose views many Sunni follow and also taught Jafar al-Sadiq. Qasim ibn Muhammad ibn Abu Bakr, Hisham ibn Urwah and Muhammad al-Baqir taught Zayd ibn Ali, Jafar al-Sadiq, Abu Hanifa, and Malik ibn Anas.

Imam Jafar al-Sadiq, Imam Abu Hanifa and Malik ibn Anas worked together in Al-Masjid an-Nabawi in Medina. Along with Qasim ibn Muhammad ibn Abu Bakr, Muhammad al-Baqir, Zayd ibn Ali and over 70 other leading jurists and scholars.

Al-Shafi'i was taught by Malik ibn Anas. Ahmad ibn Hanbal was taught by Al-Shafi'i. Muhammad al-Bukhari travelled every where collecting hadith and his father Ismail ibn Ibrahim was a student of Malik ibn Anas

---

- $\underline{v}$
- $\underline{t}$
- $\underline{e}^{1005}$

Early Islamic scholars

In the books actually written by these original jurists and scholars, there are very few theological and judicial differences between them. Imam Ahmad rejected the writing down and codifying of the religious rulings he gave. They knew that they might have fallen into error in some of their judgements and stated this clearly. They never introduced their rulings by saying, "Here, this judgement is the judgement of God and His prophet." There is also very little text actually written down by Jafar al-Sadiq himself. They all give priority to the Qur'an and the Hadith (the practice of Muhammad). They felt that the Quran and the Hadith, the example of Muhammad provided people with almost everything they needed. "This day I have perfected for you your religion and completed My favor upon you and have approved for you Islam as religion" Quran 5:5.

These scholars did not distinguish between each other. They were not Sunni or Shia. They felt that they were following the religion of Abraham as described in the Quran "Say: Allah speaks the truth; so follow the religion of Abraham, the upright one. And he was not one of the polytheists" (Qur'an 3:95).

Most of the differences are regarding Sharia laws devised through Ijtihad where there is no such ruling in the Quran or the Hadiths of Islamic prophet Muhammad regarding a similar case. As these jurists went to new areas, they were pragmatic and continued to use the same ruling as was given in that area during pre-Islamic times, if the population felt comfortable with it, it was just and they used Ijtihad to deduce that it did not conflict with the Quran or the Hadith. As explained in the Muwatta by Malik ibn Anas. This made it easier for the different communities to integrate into the Islamic State and assisted in the quick expansion of the Islamic State.

To reduce the divergence, ash-Shafi'i proposed giving priority to the Qur'an and the Hadith (the practice of Muhammad) and only then look at the consensus of the Muslim jurists (*ijma*) and analogical reasoning (*qiyas*). This then resulted in jurists like Muhammad al-Bukhari dedicating their lives to the collection of the correct Hadith, in books like Sahih al-Bukhari. Sahih translates as authentic or correct. They also felt that Muhammad's judgement was more impartial and better than their own.

These original jurists and scholars also acted as a counterbalance to the rulers. When they saw injustice, all these scholars spoke out against it. As the state expanded outside Madina, the rights of the different communities, as they were constituted in the Constitution of Medina still applied. The Quran also gave additional rights to the citizens of the state and these rights were also applied. Ali, Hassan and Hussein ibn Ali gave their allegiance to the first three caliphs because they abided by these conditions. Later Ali the fourth caliph wrote in a letter "I did not approach the people to get their oath of allegiance but they came to me with their desire to make me their Amir (ruler). I did not extend my hands towards them so that they might swear the oath of allegiance to me but they themselves extended their hands towards me".[1006] But later as fate would have it (Predestination in Islam) when Yazid I, an oppressive ruler took power, Hussein ibn Ali the grand son of Muhammad felt that it was a test from God for him and his duty to confront him. Then Abd Allah ibn al-Zubayr, Qasim ibn Muhammad ibn Abu Bakrs cousin confronted the Umayyad rulers after Hussein ibn Ali was betrayed by the people of Kufa and killed by Syrian Roman Army now under the control of the Yazid I the Umayyad ruler.[1007] Abd Allah ibn al-Zubayr then took on the Umayyad's and expelled their forces from Hijaz and Iraq. But then his forces were depleted in Iraq, trying to stop the Khawarij. The Ummayad's then moved in. After a lengthy campaign, on his last hour Abd Allah ibn al-Zubayr asked his mother Asma' bint Abu Bakr the daughter of Abu Bakr the first caliph for advice. Asma' bint Abu Bakr replied to her son, she said: "You know better in your own self, that if you are upon the truth and you are calling towards the truth go forth, for people more honourable than you have been killed and if you are not upon the truth, then what an evil son you are and you have destroyed yourself and those who are with you. If you say, that if you are upon the truth and you will be killed at the hands of others, then you will not truly be free". Abd Allah ibn al-Zubayr left and was later also killed and crucified by the Syrian Roman Army now under the control of the Umayyads and led by Hajjaj. Muhammad ibn Abi Bakr the son of Abu Bakr the first caliph and raised by Ali the fourth caliph was also killed by the Ummayads.[1008] Aisha then raised and taught his son Qasim ibn Muhammad ibn Abu Bakr who later taught his grandson Jafar al-Sadiq.

During the early Ummayad period, there was more community involvement. The Quran and Muhammad's example was the main source of law after which

Figure 31: *Legal systems of the world*

the community decided. If it worked for the community, was just and did not conflict with the Quran and the example of Muhammad, it was accepted. This made it easier for the different communities, with Roman, Persian, Central Asia and North African backgrounds to integrate into the Islamic State and that assisted in the quick expansion of the Islamic State. The scholars in Madina were consulted on the more complex judicial issues. The Sharia and the official more centralized schools of fiqh developed later, during the time of the Abbasids.[1009]

Components

The sources of *fiqh* in order of importance are

1. the Qur'an
2. Hadith
3. Ijma, i.e. collective reasoning and consensus amongst authoritative Muslims of a particular generation, and its interpretation by Islamic scholars.
4. Qiyas, i.e. analogy which is deployed if *Ijma* or historic collective reasoning on the issue is not available.

The Qur'an gives clear instructions on many issues, such as how to perform the ritual purification (*wudu*) before the obligatory daily prayers (*salat*), but on other issues, some Muslims believe the Qur'an alone is not enough to make things clear. For example, the Qur'an states one needs to engage in daily prayers (*salat*) and fast (*sawm*) during the month of Ramadan but Muslims believe they need further instructions on how to perform these duties. Details about these issues can be found in the traditions of Muhammad, so Qur'an and Sunnah are in most cases the basis for (*Shariah*).

Some topics are without precedent in Islam's early period. In those cases, Muslim jurists (*Fuqaha*) try to arrive at conclusions by other means. Sunni jurists use historical consensus of the community (*Ijma*); a majority in the modern era also use analogy (*Qiyas*) and weigh the harms and benefits of new topics (*Istislah*), and a plurality utilizes juristic preference (*Istihsan*). The conclusions arrived at with the aid of these additional tools constitute a wider array of laws than the Sharia consists of, and is called **fiqh**. Thus, in contrast to the *sharia*, *fiqh* is not regarded as sacred and the schools of thought have differing views on its details, without viewing other conclusions as sacrilegious. This division of interpretation in more detailed issues has resulted in different schools of thought (*madh'hab*).

This wider concept of **Islamic jurisprudence** is the source of a range of laws in different topics that guide Muslims in everyday life.

Component categories

Islamic jurisprudence (*fiqh*) covers two main areas:

1. Rules in relation to actions, and,
2. Rules in relation to circumstances surrounding actions.

These types of rules can also fall into two groups:

1. Worship (Ibadaat)
2. Dealings & Transactions (with people) (Mu'amalaat)

Rules in relation to actions (*'amaliyya* — عملية) or "decision types" comprise:

1. Obligation (*fardh*)
2. Recommendation (*mustahabb*)
3. Permissibility (*mubah*)
4. Disrecommendation (*makrooh*)
5. Prohibition (*haraam*)

Rules in relation to circumstances (*wadia'*) comprise:

1. Condition (*shart*)
2. Cause (*sabab*)
3. Preventor (*mani*)
4. Permit / Enforced (*rukhsah, azeemah*)
5. Valid / Corrupt / Invalid (*sahih, fasid, batil*)
6. In time / Deferred / Repeat (*adaa, qadaa, i'ada*)

Methodologies of jurisprudence

The modus operandi of the Muslim jurist is known as *usul al-fiqh* ("principles of jurisprudence").

There are different approaches to the methodology used in jurisprudence to derive Islamic law from the primary sources. The main methodologies are those of the Sunni, Shi'a and Ibadi denominations. While both Sunni and Shi'ite are divided into smaller sub-schools, the differences among the Shi'ite schools is considerably greater. Ibadites only follow a single school without divisions.

Fatawa

While using court decisions as legal precedents and case law are central to Western law, the importance of the institution of fatawa (non-binding answers by Islamic legal scholars to legal questions) has been called "central to the development" of Islamic jurisprudence.[1010] This is in part because of a "vacuum" in the other source of Islamic law, *qada'* (legal rulings by state appointed Islamic judges) after the fall of the last caliphate the Ottoman Empire. While the practice in Islam dates back to the time of Muhammad, according to at least one source (Muhammad El-Gamal), it is "modeled after the Roman system of *responsa*," and gives the questioner "decisive primary-mover advantage in choosing he question and its wording."

Arguments for and against reform

Each school (*madhhab*) reflects a unique *al-urf* or culture (a cultural practice that was influenced by traditions), that the classical jurists themselves lived in, when rulings were made. Some suggest that the discipline of *isnad*, which developed to validate *hadith* made it relatively easy to record and validate also the rulings of jurists. This, in turn, made them far easier to imitate (*taqlid*) than to challenge in new contexts. The argument is, the schools have been more or less frozen for centuries, and reflect a culture that simply no longer exists. Traditional scholars hold that religion is there to regulate human behavior and nurture people's moral side and since human nature has not fundamentally changed since the beginning of Islam a call to modernize the religion is essentially one to relax all laws and institutions.

Early *shariah* had a much more flexible character, and some modern Muslim scholars believe that it should be renewed, and that the classical jurists should lose special status. This would require formulating a new fiqh suitable for the modern world, e.g. as proposed by advocates of the Islamization of knowledge, which would deal with the modern context. This modernization is opposed by most conservative *ulema*. Traditional scholars hold that the laws are contextual and consider circumstance such as time, place and culture, the

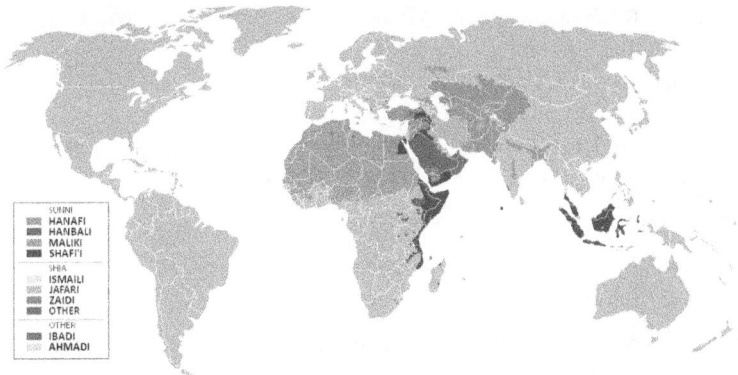

Figure 32: *Map of the Muslim world with the main madh'habs.*

principles they are based upon are universal such as justice, equality and respect. Many Muslim scholars argue that even though technology may have advanced, the fundamentals of human life have not.

Fields of jurisprudence

- Criminal
- Economics
- Etiquette
- Hygienical
- Inheritance
- Marital
- Military
- Political
- Theological

Schools of jurisprudence

There are several schools of fiqh thought (Arabic: مذهب *maḍhab*; pl. مذاهب *maḍāhib*)

The schools of Sunni Islam are each named by students of the classical jurist who taught them. The Sunni schools (and where they are commonly found) are

- Hanafi (Turkey, the Balkans, Central Asia, Indian subcontinent, China and Egypt)
- Maliki (North Africa, West Africa and several of the Arab states of the Persian Gulf)

- Shafi'i (Kurdistan, Indonesia, Malaysia, Egypt, East Africa, Yemen, Somalia and southern parts of India)
- Hanbali (Saudi Arabia) see Wahhabism
- Zahiri (minority communities in Morocco and Pakistan)
- Qurtubi No longer exists
- Laythi No longer exists but there are a few texts left of it.

The schools of Shia Islam comprise:

- Ja'fari (Twelver Shia: Iran, Iraq, Lebanon, etc.)
- Zaydi (Yemen)

Entirely separate from both the Sunni and Shia traditions, Khawarij Islam has evolved its own distinct school.

- Ibadi (Oman)

These schools share many of their rulings, but differ on the particular hadiths they accept as authentic and the weight they give to analogy or reason (qiyas) in deciding difficulties.

Possible links with Western law

A number of important legal institutions were developed by Muslim jurists during the classical period of Islam, known as the Islamic Golden Age. One such institution was the *Hawala*, an early informal value transfer system, which is mentioned in texts of Islamic jurisprudence as early as the 8th century. *Hawala* itself later influenced the development of the agency in common law and in civil laws such as the *aval* in French law and the *avallo* in Italian law. The "European commenda" (Islamic *Qirad*) used in European civil law may have also originated from Islamic law.

The *Waqf* in Islamic law, which developed during the 7th–9th centuries, bears a notable resemblance to the trusts in the English trust law. For example, every *Waqf* was required to have a *waqif* (settlor), *mutawillis* (trustee), *qadi* (judge) and beneficiaries. The trust law developed in England at the time of the Crusades, during the 12th and 13th centuries, was introduced by Crusaders who may have been influenced by the *Waqf* institutions they came across in the Middle East.

The Islamic *lafif* was a body of twelve members drawn from the neighbourhood and sworn to tell the truth, who were bound to give a unanimous verdict, about matters "which they had personally seen or heard, binding on the judge, to settle the truth concerning facts in a case, between ordinary people, and obtained as of right by the plaintiff." The only characteristic of the English jury which the Islamic *lafif* lacked was the "judicial writ directing the jury to be summoned and directing the bailiff to hear its recognition." According to Professor John Makdisi, "no other institution in any legal institution studied to date shares all of these characteristics with the English jury." It is thus likely that the concept of the *lafif* may have been introduced to England by the Normans, who conquered both England and the Emirate of Sicily, and then evolved into the modern English jury.

Several other fundamental common law institutions may have been adapted from similar legal institutions in Islamic law and jurisprudence, and introduced to England by the Normans after the Norman conquest of England and the Emirate of Sicily, and by Crusaders during the Crusades. In particular, the "royal English contract protected by the action of debt is identified with the Islamic *Aqd*, the English assize of novel disseisin is identified with the Islamic *Istihqaq*, and the English jury is identified with the Islamic *lafif*." Other English legal institutions such as "the scholastic method, the licence to teach", the "law schools known as Inns of Court in England and *Madrasas* in Islam" and the "European commenda" (Islamic *Qirad*) may have also originated from Islamic law. The methodology of legal precedent and reasoning by analogy (*Qiyas*) are also similar in both the Islamic and common law systems. These influences have led some scholars to suggest that Islamic law may have laid the foundations for "the common law as an integrated whole".

References

- Doi, Abd ar-Rahman I., and Clarke, Abdassamad (2008). *Shari'ah: Islamic Law*. Ta-Ha Publishers Ltd., ISBN 978-1-84200-087-8 (hardback)
- Cilardo, Agostino, "Fiqh, History of", in *Muhammad in History, Thought, and Culture: An Encyclopedia of the Prophet of God* (2 vols.), Edited by C. Fitzpatrick and A. Walker, Santa Barbara, ABC-CLIO, 2014, Vol I, pp. 201–206.
- El-Gamal, Mahmoud A. (2006). *Islamic Finance : Law, Economics, and Practice*[1011] (PDF). Cambridge University Press.
- Gaudiosi, Monica M (April 1988). "The Influence of the Islamic Law of Waqf on the Development of the Trust in England_ The Case of Merton College". *University of Pennsylvania Law Review*. The University of Pennsylvania Law Review. **136** (4): 1231–1261. JSTOR 3312162[1012]. doi: 10.2307/3312162[1013].
- Levy, Reuben (1957). *The Social Structure of Islam*. UK: Cambridge University Press. ISBN 978-0-521-09182-4.
- Makdisi, John A. (June 1999). "The Islamic Origins of the Common Law". *North Carolina Law Review*. **77** (5): 1635–1739.

Further reading

- Potz, Richard, Islamic Law and the Transfer of European Law[1014], European History Online, Mainz: Institute of European History, 2011. (Retrieved 28 November 2011.)

Islamic ethics

<table>
<tr><td align="center">Part of a series on
Islam</td></tr>
<tr><td align="center">الله</td></tr>
<tr><td></td></tr>
<tr><td></td></tr>
<tr><td></td></tr>
<tr><td></td></tr>
<tr><td></td></tr>
<tr><td align="center">• الله Islam portal</td></tr>
<tr><td>• <u>v</u>
• <u>t</u>
• <u>e</u>[1015]</td></tr>
</table>

Islamic ethics (أَخْلاق إسلامية), defined as "good character," historically took shape gradually from the 7th century and was finally established by the 11th century. It was eventually shaped as a successful amalgamation of the Qur'anic teachings, the teachings of the Sunnah of Muhammad, the precedents of Islamic jurists (see Sharia and Fiqh), the pre-Islamic Arabian tradition, and non-Arabic elements (including Persian and Greek ideas) embedded in or integrated with a generally Islamic structure. Although Muhammad's preaching produced a "radical change in moral values based on the sanctions of the new religion and the present religion, and fear of God and of the Last Judgment", the tribal practice of Arabs did not completely die out. Later Muslim scholars expanded the religious ethic of the Qur'an and Hadith in immense detail.

Foundational motifs

The foundational source in the gradual codification of Islamic ethics was the Muslim understanding and interpretations of the Qur'an and practices of Muhammad. Its meaning has always been in context of active submission to God (Arabic: Allah), performed by the community in unison. The motive force in Islamic ethics is the notion that every human being is called to "command the good and forbid the evil" in all spheres of life. Muslims understand the role of Muhammad as attempting to facilitate this submission. Another key factor in the field of Islamic ethics is the belief that mankind has been granted the faculty to discern God's will and to abide by it. This faculty most crucially involves reflecting over the meaning of existence. Therefore, regardless of their environment, humans are believed to have a moral responsibility to submit to God's will and to follow Islam (as demonstrated in the Qur'an, [Quran 7:172[1016]]).

This natural inclination is, according to the Qur'an, subverted by mankind's focus on material success: such focus first presents itself as a need for basic survival or security, but then tends to manifest into a desire to become distinguished amongst one's peers. Ultimately, the focus on materialism, according to the Islamic texts, hampers with the innate reflection as described above, resulting in a state of *jahiliyya* or "heedlessness." Muslims believe that Muhammad, like other prophets in Islam, was sent by God to remind human beings of their moral responsibility, and challenge those ideas in society which opposed submission to God. According to Kelsay, this challenge was directed against five main characteristics of pre-Islamic Arabia:

1. The division of Arabs into varying tribes (based upon blood and kinship). This categorization was confronted by the ideal of a unified community based upon Islamic piety, an *"ummah;"*
2. The acceptance of the worship of a multitude of deities besides Allah - a view challenged by strict Islamic monotheism, which dictates that Allah has no partner in worship nor any equal;
3. The trait of *muruwwa* (manliness), which Islam discouraged, instead emphasizing on the traits of humility and piety;
4. The focus on achieving fame or establishing a legacy, which was replaced by the concept that mankind would be called to account before God on the day of resurrection;
5. The reverence of and compliance with ancestral traditions, a practice challenged by Islam — which instead assigned primacy to submitting to God and following revelation.

These changes lay in the reorientation of society as regards to identity and life of the Muslim belief, world view, and the hierarchy of values. From the viewpoint of subsequent generations, this caused a great transformation in the society and moral order of life in the Arabian Peninsula. For Muhammad, although pre-Islamic Arabia exemplified "heedlessness," it was not entirely without merit. Muhammad approved and exhorted certain aspects of the Arab pre-Islamic tradition, such as the care for one's near kin, for widows, orphans, and others in need and for the establishment of justice. However, these values would be re-ordered in importance and placed in the context of strict monotheism.

Moral commandments

In the 17th chapter, "Al-Israa" ("The Night Journey"), verses [Quran 17:22[1017]], the Qur'an provides a set of moral stipulations which are "among the (precepts of) wisdom, which thy Lord has revealed to thee" that can be reasonably categorised as ten in number. According to S. A. Nigosian, Professor of religious studies at the University of Toronto, these resemble the Ten Commandments in the Bible and "represents the fullest statement of the code of behavior every Muslim must follow". However, these verses are not regarded by Islamic scholars as set apart from any other moral stipulations in the Qur'an, nor are they regarded as a substitute, replacement, or abrogation of some other set of commandments as found in the previous revelations.

1. **Worship only God:** Do not make with Allah another god; lest you will sit disgraced and forsaken. (Quran 17:22[1017])
2. **Be kind, honourable and humble to one's parents:** And your Lord has decreed that you not worship except Him alone, and to be good to the parents. Whether one or both of them reach old age [while] with you, say not to them [so much as], a word of disrespect, and do not repel them but speak to them a noble word. (Quran 17:23[1018]) And lower to them the wing of humility out of mercy and say, "My Lord, have mercy upon them as they brought me up [when I was] small." (Quran 17:24[1019])
3. **Be neither miserly nor wasteful in one's expenditure:** And give the relative his right, and [also] the poor and the traveler, and do not spend wastefully. (Quran 17:26[1020]) Indeed, the spendthrifts are brothers of the devil, and the devil is, to his lord, ungrateful. (Quran 17:27[1021]) And if you [must] turn away from the needy awaiting mercy from your Lord which you expect, then speak to them a gentle word. (Quran 17:28[1022]) And do not make your hand [as] chained to your neck or extend it to its utmost reach, so that you [thereby] become blamed and insolvent. (Quran 17:29[1023])
4. **Do not engage in 'mercy killings' for fear of starvation:** And do not kill your children for fear of poverty. We provide for them and for you. Indeed, their killing is ever a great sin. (Quran 17:31[1024])

5. **Do not commit adultery:** And do not approach unlawful sexual intercourse. Indeed, it is an immorality and an evil way. (Quran 17:32[1025])

6. **Do not kill unjustly:** And do not kill the soul which Allah has forbidden, except by right. And whoever is killed unjustly - We have given his heir authority, but let him not exceed limits in [the matter of] taking life. Indeed, he has been supported [by the law]. (Quran 17:33[1026])

7. **Care for orphaned children:** And do not approach the property of an orphan, except in the way that is best, until he reaches maturity...(Quran 17:34[1027])

8. **Keep one's promises:** ...fulfill (every) engagement [i.e. promise/ covenant], for (every) engagement will be questioned (on the Day of Reckoning). (Quran 17:34[1027])

9. **Be honest and fair in one's interactions:** And give full measure when you measure, and weigh with an even balance. That is the best [way] and best in result. (Quran 17:35[1028])

10. **Do not be arrogant in one's claims or beliefs:** And do not pursue that of which you have no knowledge. Indeed, the hearing, the sight and the heart - all those will be questioned. (Quran 17:36[1029]) And do not walk upon the earth exultantly. Indeed, you will never tear the earth [apart], and you will never reach the mountains in height. (Quran 17:37[1030])

Many Muslim theologians see the **Golden Rule** implicit in some verses of the Qur'an and in the Hadith. The Golden Rule was agreed 1993 also by Muslims as a central unconditional ethical norm in the Declaration Toward a Global Ethic.

Early reforms under Islam

Many reforms in human rights took place under Islam between 610 and 661, including the period of Muhammad's mission and the rule of the four immediate successors who established the Rashidun Caliphate. Historians generally agree that Muhammad preached against what he saw as the social evils of his day,[1031] and that Islamic social reforms in areas such as social security, family structure, slavery, and the rights of women and ethnic minorities improved on what was present in existing Arab society at the time.[1032,1033,1034] For example, according to Bernard Lewis, Islam "from the first denounced aristocratic privilege, rejected hierarchy, and adopted a formula of the career open to the talents." John Esposito sees Muhammad as a reformer who condemned practices of the pagan Arabs such as female infanticide, exploitation of the poor, usury, murder, false contracts, and theft.[1035] Bernard Lewis believes that the egalitarian nature of Islam "represented a very considerable advance on the practice of both the Greco-Roman and the ancient Persian world."

The Constitution of Medina, also known as the *Charter of Medina*, was drafted by Muhammad in 622. It constituted a formal agreement between Muhammad and all of the significant tribes and families of Yathrib (later known as Medina), including Muslims, Jews, and pagans.[1036] The document was drawn up with the explicit concern of bringing to an end the bitter intertribal fighting between the clans of the Aws (Aus) and Khazraj within Medina. To this effect it instituted a number of rights and responsibilities for the Muslim, Jewish and pagan communities of Medina bringing them within the fold of one community-the Ummah. The Constitution established the security of the community, freedom of religion, the role of Medina as a haram or sacred place (barring all violence and weapons), the security of women, stable tribal relations within Medina, a tax system for supporting the community in time of conflict, parameters for exogenous political alliances, a system for granting protection of individuals, a judicial system for resolving disputes, and also regulated the paying of blood-wite (the payment between families or tribes for the slaying of an individual in lieu of lex talionis).

Muhammad made it the responsibility of the Islamic government to provide food and clothing, on a reasonable basis, to captives, regardless of their religion. If the prisoners were in the custody of a person, then the responsibility was on the individual.[1037] Lewis states that Islam brought two major changes to ancient slavery which were to have far-reaching consequences. "One of these was the presumption of freedom; the other, the ban on the enslavement of free persons except in strictly defined circumstances," Lewis continues. The position of the Arabian slave was "enormously improved": the Arabian slave "was now no longer merely a chattel but was also a human being with a certain religious and hence a social status and with certain quasi-legal rights."

Esposito states that reforms in women's rights affected marriage, divorce, and inheritance. Women were not accorded with such legal status in other cultures, including the West, until centuries later.[1038] *The Oxford Dictionary of Islam* states that the general improvement of the status of Arab women included prohibition of female infanticide and recognizing women's full personhood.[1039] "The dowry, previously regarded as a bride-price paid to the father, became a nuptial gift retained by the wife as part of her personal property."[1040] Under Islamic law, marriage was no longer viewed as a "status" but rather as a "contract", in which the woman's consent was imperative. "Women were given inheritance rights in a patriarchal society that had previously restricted inheritance to male relatives." Annemarie Schimmel states that "compared to the pre-Islamic position of women, Islamic legislation meant an enormous progress; the woman has the right, at least according to the letter of the law, to administer the wealth she has brought into the family or has earned by her own work."[1041] William Montgomery Watt states that Muhammad, in the historical context of his time, can be seen as a figure who testified on behalf of women's rights and improved things considerably. Watt explains: "At the time Islam began, the conditions of women were terrible - they had no right to own property, were supposed to be the property of the man, and if the man died everything went to his sons." Muhammad, however, by "instituting rights of property ownership, inheritance, education and divorce, gave women certain basic safeguards."[1042] Haddad and Esposito state that "Muhammad granted women rights and privileges in the sphere of family life, marriage, education, and economic endeavors, rights that help improve women's status in society."[1043]

Sociologist Robert Bellah (*Beyond belief*) argues that Islam in its seventh-century origins was, for its time and place, "remarkably modern...in the high degree of commitment, involvement, and participation expected from the rank-and-file members of the community." This because, he argues, that Islam emphasized on the equality of all Muslims, where leadership positions were open to all. Dale Eickelman writes that Bellah suggests "the early Islamic community placed a particular value on individuals, as opposed to collective or group responsibility."[1044]

Environmentalism

Perhaps due to resource scarcity in most Islamic nations, there was an emphasis on limited (and some claim also sustainable) use of natural capital, i.e. producing land. Traditions of haram (site) and hima, an Arabic term meaning "protected place", and early urban planning were expressions of strong social obligations to stay within carrying capacity and to preserve the natural environment as an obligation of khalifa or "stewardship".

After Muslims established themselves in Madinah, Muhammad surveyed the natural resources in the region—the wadis (riverbeds); the rich, black volcanic soil; the high rangelands—and decreed that they be preserved and set aside as a hima.

Hadiths on agriculture and environmental philosophy were compiled in the "Book of Agriculture" of the *Sahih Bukhari*, which included the following saying:

> *There is none amongst the believers who plants a tree, or sows a seed, and then a bird, or a person, or an animal eats thereof, but it is regarded as having given a charitable gift [for which there is great recompense].*[1045]

Several such statements concerning the environment are also found in the Qur'an, such as the following:

> *And there is no animal in the earth nor bird that flies with its two wings, but that they are communities like yourselves.*[Quran 6:38][1046]

The earliest known treatises dealing with environmentalism and environmental science, especially pollution, were Arabic medical treatises written by al-Kindi, Qusta ibn Luqa, al-Razi, Ibn Al-Jazzar, al-Tamimi, al-Masihi, Avicenna, Ali ibn Ridwan, Ibn Jumay, Isaac Israeli ben Solomon, Abd-el-latif, Ibn al-Quff, and Ibn al-Nafis. Their works covered a number of subjects related to pollution such as air pollution, water pollution, soil contamination, municipal solid waste mishandling, and environmental impact assessments of certain localities. Cordoba, Al-Andalus also had the first waste containers and waste disposal facilities for litter collection.[1047]

"In order to preserve the natural environment by not polluting, plant trees, support environmentally-friendly goods and products, Muslims must rectify themselves through simplicity, contentment, resisting endless desires, and then remembering God as well as following His commands".

Politics

Many medieval Muslim thinkers pursued humanistic and rational approaches in discourses regarding values.

Democratic participation

In the early Islamic Caliphate, the head of state, the Caliph, had a position based on the notion of a successor to Muhammad's political authority, who, according to Sunnis, were ideally elected by the people or their representatives. After the Rashidun Caliphs, later Caliphates during the Islamic Golden Age had a lesser degree of democratic participation, but since "no one was superior to anyone else except on the basis of piety and virtue" in Islam, and following the example of Muhammad, later Islamic rulers often held public consultations with the people in their affairs.

Electing or appointing a Caliph

Fred Donner, in his book *The Early Islamic Conquests* (1981), argues that the standard Arabian practice during the early Caliphates was for the prominent men of a kinship group, or tribe, to gather after a leader's death and elect a leader from amongst themselves, although there was no specified procedure for this shura, or consultative assembly. Candidates were usually from the same lineage as the deceased leader, but they were not necessarily his sons. Capable men who would lead well were preferred over an ineffectual direct heir, as there was no basis in the majority Sunni view that the head of state or governor should be chosen based on lineage alone. Al-Mawardi has written that the caliph should be Qurayshi. Abu Bakr Al-Baqillani has said that the leader of the Muslims simply should be from the majority. Abu Hanifa an-Nu'man also wrote that the leader must come from the majority.

Majlis ash-Shura

Traditional Sunni Islamic lawyers agree that *shura*, loosely translated as 'consultation of the people', is a function of the caliphate. The Majlis ash-Shura advise the caliph. The importance of this is premised by the following verses of the Qur'an:Wikipedia:No original research

> "...those who answer the call of their Lord and establish the prayer, and who conduct their affairs by Shura. [are loved by God]"[42:38[1048]]

> "...consult them (the people) in their affairs. Then when you have taken a decision (from them), put your trust in Allah"[3:159[1049]]

The majlis is also the means to elect a new caliph. Al-Mawardi has written that members of the majlis should satisfy three conditions: they must be just, they must have enough knowledge to distinguish a good caliph from a bad one, and must have sufficient wisdom and judgment to select the best caliph. Al-Mawardi also said in emergencies when there is no caliphate and no majlis, the people themselves should create a majlis, select a list of candidates for caliph, then the majlis should select from the list of candidates. Some modern interpretations of the role of the Majlis ash-Shura include those by Islamist author Sayyid Qutb and by Taqiuddin al-Nabhani, the founder of a transnational political movement devoted to the revival of the Caliphate. In an analysis of the shura chapter of the Qur'an, Qutb argued Islam requires only that the ruler consult with at least some of the ruled (usually the elite), within the general context of God-made laws that the ruler must execute. Taqiuddin al-Nabhani, writes that Shura is important and part of "the ruling structure" of the Islamic caliphate, "but not one of its pillars," and may be neglected without the Caliphate's rule becoming unIslamic. Non-Muslims may serve in the majlis, though they may not vote or serve as an official.

Religious pluralism

Islamic legal framework included religious pluralism. Classical Sharia, the religious laws and courts of Christians, Jews and Hindus, were usually accommodated within the Islamic legal framework, as seen in the early Caliphate, Al-Andalus, Indian subcontinent, and the Ottoman Millet system. Non-Muslims were allowed to engage in religious practices that was usually forbidden by Islamic law. In a notable example, Zoroastrian practice of incestuous "self-marriage" where a man could marry his mother, sister or daughter, was to be tolerated according to Ibn Qayyim (1292–1350). He based his opinion on the precedent that the prophet Muhammad, who did not forbid such self-marriages among Zoroastrians despite coming in contact with them and having knowledge of their practices. Religious minorities were also free to do whatever they wished in their own homes, provided they did not publicly engage in illicit sexual activity in ways that could threaten public morals.

Freedom of expression

Citizens of the Rashidun Caliphate were also free to criticize the Rashidun Caliphs, as the rule of law was binding on the head of state just as much as it was for the citizens. In a notable incident, when Umar tried to investigate a disturbance, by entering a home without permission, he was criticized for his behavior; he was also later criticized for the judgement he gave in that case. There were also numerous other situations where citizens insulted Caliph Umar, but he tolerated the insults and simply provided them explanations. Similar situations also occurred during the time of Caliph Ali. For example, there was an occasion when he was giving a sermon and a Kharijite rudely interrupted him with insulting language. Though he was urged to punish the interrupter, Ali declined on the grounds that his "right to freedom of speech must not be imperilled."

Imad-ad-Dean Ahmad quotes a letter by a cousin of Caliph al-Ma'mun, in which he gives permission to a Christian he was attempting to convert to speak his mind freely, as evidence that in Islam even religious controversies were not exempt from open discussion.

According to George Makdisi and Hugh Goddard, "the idea of academic freedom" in universities was "modelled on Islamic custom" as practiced in the medieval Madrasah system from the 9th century. Islamic influence was "certainly discernible in the foundation of the first deliberately planned university" in Europe, the University of Naples Federico II founded by Frederick II, Holy Roman Emperor in 1224.

In a letter written by the fourth Rashidun Caliph and first cousin of the prophet Muhammad, Ali ibn Abi Talib to his governor of Egypt, Malik al-Ashtar. The Caliph advices his governor on dealings with the poor masses thus:Wikipedia:No original research

> *Out of your hours of work, fix a time for the complainants and for those who want to approach you with their grievances. During this time you should do no other work but hear them and pay attention to their complaints and grievances. For this purpose you must arrange public audience for them during this audience, for the sake of Allah, treat them with kindness, courtesy and respect. Do not let your army and police be in the audience hall at such times so that those who have grievances against your regime may speak to you freely, unreservedly and without fear. Nahjul Balaagha letter 53*[1050]

Human rights

In the field of human rights, early Islamic jurists introduced a number of advanced legal concepts which anticipated similar modern concepts in the field. These included the notions of the charitable trust and the trusteeship of property; the notion of brotherhood and social solidarity; the notions of human dignity and the dignity of labour; the notion of an ideal law; the condemnation of antisocial behavior; the presumption of innocence; the notion of "bidding unto good" (assistance to those in distress); and the notions of sharing, caring, universalism, fair industrial relations, fair contract, commercial integrity, freedom from usury, women's rights, privacy, abuse of rights, juristic personality, individual freedom, equality before the law, legal representation, non-retroactivity, supremacy of the law, judicial independence, judicial impartiality, limited sovereignty, tolerance, and democratic participation. Many of these concepts were adopted in medieval Europe through contacts with Islamic Spain and the Emirate of Sicily, and through the Crusades and the Latin translations of the 12th century.Wikipedia:No original research#Primary, secondary and tertiary sources

The concept of inalienable rights was found in early Islamic law and jurisprudence, which denied a ruler "the right to take away from his subjects certain rights which inhere in his or her person as a human being." Islamic rulers could not take away certain rights from their subjects on the basis that "they become rights by reason of the fact that they are given to a subject by a law and from a source which no ruler can question or alter." There is evidence that John Locke's formulation of inalienable rights and conditional rulership, which were present in Islamic law centuries earlier, may have also been influenced by Islamic law, through his attendance of lectures given by Edward Pococke, a professor of Islamic studies.

Early Islamic law recognized two sets of human rights. In addition to the category of civil and political rights (covered in the Universal Declaration of Human Rights), Islamic law also recognized an additional category: social, economic and cultural rights. This latter category was not recognized in the Western legal tradition until the International Covenant on Economic, Social and Cultural Rights in 1966. The right of privacy, which was not recognized in Western legal traditions until modern times, was recognized in Islamic law since the beginning of Islam. In terms of women's rights, women generally had more legal rights under Islamic law than they did under Western legal systems until the 19th and 20th centuries. For example, "French married women, unlike their Muslim sisters, suffered from restrictions on their legal capacity which were removed only in 1965." Noah Feldman, a Harvard University law professor, notes:

As for sexism, the common law long denied married women any property rights or indeed legal personality apart from their husbands. When the British applied their law to Muslims in place of Shariah, as they did in some colonies, the result was to strip married women of the property that Islamic law had always granted them — hardly progress toward equality of the sexes.

In the *North Carolina Law Review* journal, Professor John Makdisi of the University of North Carolina School of Law writes in "The Islamic Origins of the Common Law" article:

[T]he manner in which an act was qualified as morally good or bad in the spiritual domain of Islamic religion was quite different from the manner in which that same act was qualified as legally valid or invalid in the temporal domain of Islamic law. Islamic law was secular, not canonical... Thus, it was a system focused on ensuring that an individual received justice, not that one be a good person.

Count Leon Ostorog, a French jurist, wrote the following on classical Islamic law in 1927:

Those Eastern thinkers of the ninth century laid down, on the basis of their theology, the principle of the Rights of Man, in those very terms, comprehending the rights of individual liberty, and of inviolability of person and property; described the supreme power in Islam, or Califate, as based on a contract, implying conditions of capacity and performance, and subject to cancellation if the conditions under the contract were not fulfilled; elaborated a Law of War of which the humane, chivalrous prescriptions would have put to the blush certain belligerents in World War I; expounded a doctrine of toleration of non-Moslem creeds so liberal that our West had to wait a thousand years before seeing equivalent principles adopted.

Some scholars have suggested that the idea of "a charter defining the duties of a sovereign toward his subjects, as well as subjects toward the sovereign", which led to the "genesis of European legal structures" and the development of the *Magna Carta*, may have been "brought back by Crusaders who were influenced by what they had learned in the Levant about the governing system" established by Saladin. It has also been suggested that "much of the West's understanding of liberalism in law, economics and society has roots in medieval Islam."

Another influence of Islamic law on European law was the presumption of innocence, which was introduced to Europe by King Louis IX of France soon after he returned from Palestine during the Crusades. Prior to this, European legal procedure consisted of either trial by combat or trial by ordeal. In contrast, Islamic law was based on the presumption of innocence from its beginning, as declared by the Caliph Umar in the 7th century. Other freedoms and rights recognized in the Islamic legal system based on the Qur'an since the 7th century, but not recognized in the Western world until much later, include "the rights to know, to choose belief and behaviour, to read and write, the right to power, and even the right to choose government."

Rule of law

Islamic jurists anticipated the concept of the rule of law, the equal subjection of all classes to the ordinary law of the land, where no person is above the law and where officials and private citizens are under a duty to obey the same law. A Qadi (Islamic judge) was also not allowed to discriminate on the grounds of religion, race, colour, kinship or prejudice. There were also a number of cases where Caliphs had to appear before judges as they prepared to take their verdict. The following hadith established the principle of rule of law in relation to nepotism and accountability:[1051]

> *Narrated 'Aisha: The people of Quraish worried about the lady from Bani Makhzum who had committed theft. They asked, "Who will intercede for her with Allah's Apostle?" Some said, "No one dare to do so except Usama bin Zaid the beloved one to Allah's Apostle." When Usama spoke about that to Allah's Apostle Allah's Apostle said: "Do you try to intercede for somebody in a case connected with Allah's Prescribed Punishments?" Then he got up and delivered a sermon saying, "What destroyed the nations preceding you, was that if a noble amongst them stole, they would forgive him, and if a poor person amongst them stole, they would inflict Allah's Legal punishment on him. By Allah, if Fatima, the daughter of Muhammad (my daughter) stole, I would cut off her hand."*

Various Islamic lawyers do however place multiple conditions, and stipulations e.g. the poor cannot be penalised for stealing out of poverty, before executing such a law, making it very difficult to reach such a stage. It is well known during a time of drought in the Rashidun caliphate period, capital punishments were suspended until the effects of the drought passed.Wikipedia:Citation needed

According to Noah Feldman, a law professor at Harvard University, the legal scholars and jurists who once upheld the rule of law were replaced by a law governed by the state due to the codification of Sharia by the Ottoman Empire in the early 19th century:

> *How the scholars lost their exalted status as keepers of the law is a complex story, but it can be summed up in the adage that partial reforms are sometimes worse than none at all. In the early 19th century, the Ottoman empire responded to military setbacks with an internal reform movement.*

*The most important reform was the attempt to codify Shariah. This West-
ernizing process, foreign to the Islamic legal tradition, sought to transform
Shariah from a body of doctrines and principles to be discovered by the
human efforts of the scholars into a set of rules that could be looked up in
a book.*

*Once the law existed in codified form, however, the law itself was able to
replace the scholars as the source of authority. Codification took from the
scholars their all-important claim to have the final say over the content of
the law and transferred that power to the state.*

Accountability of rulers

Sunni Islamic lawyers have commented on when it is permissible to disobey,
impeach or remove rulers in the Caliphate. This is usually when the rulers
are not meeting public responsibilities obliged upon them under Islam. Al-
Mawardi said that if the rulers meet their Islamic responsibilities to the public,
the people must obey their laws, but if they become either unjust or severely
ineffective then the Caliph or ruler must be impeached via the Majlis ash-
Shura. Similarly Al-Baghdadi believed that if the rulers do not uphold justice, the ummah via the majlis should give warning to them, and if unheeded
then the Caliph can be impeached. Al-Juwayni argued that Islam is the goal
of the ummah, so any ruler that deviates from this goal must be impeached.
Al-Ghazali believed that oppression by a caliph is enough for impeachment.
Rather than just relying on impeachment, Ibn Hajar al-Asqalani obliged rebellion upon the people if the caliph began to act with no regard for Islamic law.
Ibn Hajar al-Asqalani said that to ignore such a situation is *haraam*, and those
who cannot revolt inside the caliphate should launch a struggle from outside.
Al-Asqalani used two ayahs from the Qur'an to justify this:

*"...And they (the sinners on qiyama) will say, 'Our Lord! We obeyed our
leaders and our chiefs, and they misled us from the right path. Our Lord!
Give them (the leaders) double the punishment you give us and curse them
with a very great curse'... '[33:67–68[1052]]*

Islamic lawyers commented that when the rulers refuse to step down via successful impeachment through the Majlis, becoming dictators through the support of a corrupt army, if the majority agree they have the option to launch a
revolution against them. Many noted that this option is only exercised after
factoring in the potential cost of life.

Right of revolution

According to scholar Bernard Lewis, the Qur'an and Sunnah have several points to make on governance regarding the right of revolution in Islam:

> *The Quran, for example, makes it clear that there is a duty of obedience: "Obey God, obey the Prophet, obey those who hold authority over you." And this is elaborated in a number of sayings attributed to Muhammad. But there are also sayings that put strict limits on the duty of obedience. Two dicta attributed to the Prophet and universally accepted as authentic are indicative. One says, "there is no obedience in sin"; in other words, if the ruler orders something contrary to the divine law, not only is there no duty of obedience, but there is a duty of disobedience. This is more than the right of revolution that appears in Western political thought. It is a duty of revolution, or at least of disobedience and opposition to authority. The other pronouncement, "do not obey a creature against his creator," again clearly limits the authority of the ruler, whatever form of ruler that may be.*

Medical ethics

The ethical standards of Muslim physicians was first laid down in the 9th century by Ishaq ibn 'Ali al-Ruhawi, who wrote the *Adab al-Tabib* (*Conduct of a Physician*), the first treatist dedicated to medical ethics. He regarded physicians as "guardians of souls and bodies", and wrote twenty chapters on various topics related to medical ethics, including:[1053]

- What the physician must avoid and beware of
- The manners of visitors
- The care of remedies by the physician
- The dignity of the medical profession
- The examination of physicians
- The removal of corruption among physicians

Because Islam views itself as a total system governing all areas, Islamic medical ethics view the patient as a whole. Classical texts speak more about "health", than "illness", showing an emphasis on prevention rather than cure.

Drugs

The earliest known prohibition of illegal drugs occurred under Islamic law, which prohibited the use of Hashish, a preparation of cannabis, as a recreational drug. Classical jurists in medieval Islamic jurisprudence, however, accepted the use of the Hashish drug for medicinal and therapeutic purposes, and agreed that its "medical use, even if it leads to mental derangement, remains exempt" from punishment. In the 14th century, the Islamic scholar Az-Zarkashi spoke of "the permissibility of its use for medical purposes if it is established that it is beneficial."

According to Mary Lynn Mathre, with "this legal distinction between the intoxicant and the medical uses of cannabis, medieval Muslim theologians were far ahead of present-day American law."

Medical peer review

The first documented description of a peer review process is found in the *Ethics of the Physician* by Ishaq ibn 'Ali al-Ruhawi (854–931) of al-Raha, Syria, where the notes of a practising Islamic physician were reviewed by peers and the physician could face a lawsuit from a maltreated patient if the reviews were negative.

Neuroethics

Islamic neuroethics and neurotheology hold a sympathetic attitude towards the mentally ill, as exemplified in Sura 4:5 of the Qur'an:

> *Do not give your property which God assigned you to manage to the insane: but feed and cloth the insane with this property and tell splendid words to him.*[1054]

This Quranic verse summarized Islam's attitudes towards the mentally ill, who were considered unfit to manage property but must be treated humanely and be kept under care by a guardian, according to Islamic law. This positive neuroethical understanding of mental health consequently led to the establishment of the first psychiatric hospitals in the medieval Islamic world from the 8th century, and an early scientific understanding of neuroscience and psychology by medieval Muslim physicians and psychologists, who discovered that mental disorders are caused by dysfunctions in the brain.

Military ethics

The early Islamic treatises on international law from the 9th century onwards covered the application of Islamic ethics, Islamic economic jurisprudence and Islamic military jurisprudence to international law, and were concerned with a number of modern international law topics, including the law of treaties; the treatment of diplomats, hostages, refugees and prisoners of war; the right of asylum; conduct on the battlefield; protection of women, children and non-combatant civilians; contracts across the lines of battle; the use of poisonous weapons; and devastation of enemy territory.

The Islamic legal principles of international law were mainly based on Qur'an and the Sunnah of Muhammad, who gave various injunctions to his forces and adopted practices toward the conduct of war. The most important of these were summarized by Muhammad's successor and close companion, Abu Bakr, in the form of ten rules for the Muslim army:

> *Stop, O people, that I may give you ten rules for your guidance in the battlefield. Do not commit treachery or deviate from the right path. You must not mutilate dead bodies. Neither kill a child, nor a woman, nor an aged man. Bring no harm to the trees, nor burn them with fire, especially those which are fruitful. Slay not any of the enemy's flock, save for your food. You are likely to pass by people who have devoted their lives to monastic services; leave them alone.*

Prisoners of war

After Sultan al-Kamil defeated the Franks during the Crusades, Oliverus Scholasticus praised the Islamic laws of war, commenting on how al-Kamil supplied the defeated Frankish army with food:

> *Who could doubt that such goodness, friendship and charity come from God? Men whose parents, sons and daughters, brothers and sisters, had died in agony at our hands, whose lands we took, whom we drove naked from their homes, revived us with their own food when we were dying of hunger and showered us with kindness even when we were in their power.*

Peace and justice

As in other Abrahamic religions, peace is a basic concept of Islam. The Arabic term "Islam" itself (الإسلام) is usually translated as "submission"; submission of desires to the will of God. It comes from the term *aslama*, which means "to surrender" or "resign oneself". The Arabic word *salaam* (سلام) ("peace") has the same root as the word *Islam*. One Islamic interpretation is that individual personal peace is attained by utterly submitting to Allah. The greeting "Salaam alaykum", favoured by Muslims, has the literal meaning "Peace be with you". Muhammad is reported to have said once, "Mankind are the dependents, or slaves of God, and the most beloved of them to God are those who are the most excellent to His dependents." "Not one of you believes until he loves for his brother what he loves for himself." Great Muslim scholars of prophetic tradition such as Ibn Hajar al-Asqalani and Sharafuddin al Nawawi have said[1055] that the words "his brother" mean any person irrespective of faith.

Welfare

The concepts of welfare and pension were introduced in early Islamic law as forms of *Zakat* (charity), one of the Five Pillars of Islam, since the time of the Abbasid caliph Al-Mansur in the 8th century. The taxes (including *Zakat* and *Jizya*) collected in the treasury of an Islamic government was used to provide income for the needy, including the poor, elderly, orphans, widows, and the disabled. According to the Islamic jurist Al-Ghazali (Algazel, 1058–1111), the government was also expected to store up food supplies in every region in case a disaster or famine occurs. The Caliphate was thus one of the earliest welfare states. From the 9th century, funds from the treasury were also used towards the *Waqf* (charitable trusts), often for the purpose of building of Madrassahs and Bimaristan hospitals.

Animal welfare

Concern for the treatment of animals can be found in the Qur'an and in the teachings of the Islamic Prophet Muhammad, which inspired debates over animal rights by later medieval Muslim scholars. The 10th-century work, *"Disputes Between Animals and Man"*, part of the Epistles of the Brethren of Purity, has been considered a classic in this regard. Inspired by the Qur'anic verse: "all the creatures that crawl on the earth and those that fly with their wings are communities like yourselves" (6:38), the Shafi'i jurist 'Izz al-Din Ibn 'Abd al-Salam al-Sulami (d. 1262) formulated the first full-fledged charter of the rights of livestock and animals in his legal treatise *Rules for Judgement in the Cases of Living Beings* (*Qawa'id al-ahkam fi masalih al-anam*) which was based on the stories and sayings of Muhammad.

Notes and references

References

- Aboul-Enein, H. Yousuf; Zuhur, Sherifa (2004), *Islamic Rulings on Warfare*, Strategic Studies Institute, US Army War College, Diane Publishing Co., Darby PA, ISBN 9781584871774
- Ahmad, I. A. (June 3, 2002), "The Rise and Fall of Islamic Science: The Calendar as a Case Study", *Faith and Reason: Convergence and Complementarity*[1056] (PDF), Al-Akhawayn University, archived from the original[1057] (PDF) on February 27, 2008, retrieved 2008-01-31
- Artz, F. B. (1980), *The Mind of the Middle Ages* (Third ed.), University of Chicago Press, OCLC 390600[1058]
- Badawi, Jamal A. (September 1971), "The Status of Women in Islam", *Al-Ittihad Journal of Islamic Studies*, **8** (2)

- Badr, Gamal M.; Mayer, Ann Elizabeth (Winter 1984), "Islamic Criminal Justice", *The American Journal of Comparative Law*, American Society of Comparative Law, **3 2** (1): 167–169, JSTOR 840274[1059], doi: 10.2307/840274[1060]
- Bearman, P.J.; Bianquis, Th.; Bosworth, C.E.; van Donzel, E.; Heinrichs, W.P., eds. (2009), *Encyclopaedia of Islam Online*, Brill Publishers, ISSN 1573-3912[1061]
- Becker, L.C.; Becker, C.B., eds. (1992), "Islamic Ethics", *Encyclopedia of Ethics*, New York: Routledge, ISBN 978-0-8153-0403-6
- Bekoff, Marc (2010), *Encyclopedia of animal rights and animal welfare*, ABC-CLIO, ISBN 0-313-35257-7
- Boisard, Marcel (July 1980), "On the Probable Influence of Islam on Western Public and International Law A.", *International Journal of Middle East Studies*, **11** (4): 429–50, doi: 10.1017/s0020743800054805[1062]
- Bontekoe, Ronald; Stepaniants, Mariëtta Tigranovna (1997), *Justice and Democracy*, University of Hawaii Press, ISBN 0-8248-1926-8
- Coward, Harold, ed. (1995), *Population, consumption, and the environment: religious and secular responses*, State University of New York Press, ISBN 0-7914-2671-8
- Crone, Patricia (2005), *Medieval Islamic Political Thought*, Edinburgh University Press, ISBN 0-7486-2194-6
- Donnelly, Jack (May 2007), "The Relative Universality of Human Rights"[1063] (PDF), *Human Rights Quarterly*, The Johns Hopkins University Press, **29** (2): 281–306, doi: 10.1353/hrq.2007.0016[1064]
- Feldman, Noah (March 16, 2008), "Why Shariah?"[1065], *The New York Times*, retrieved 2008-10-05
- Gallagher, Nancy (2007), "Infanticide and Abandonment of Female Children", in Joseph, Suad; Najmabadi, A., *Encyclopedia of Women & Islamic Cultures*, **II**, Brill, p. 293, ISBN 978-90-04-12818-7
- Gari, L. (November 2002), "Arabic Treatises on Environmental Pollution up to the End of the Thirteenth Century", *Environment and History*, **8** (4): 475–488, doi: 10.3197/096734002129342747[1066]
- Al-Ghamdy, Gharm Allah (April 25, 2004), "e Process of Choosing the Leader (Caliph) of the Muslims: The Muslim Khilafa"[1067], *The Muslims Internet Directory*
- Goddard, Hugh (2000), *A History of Christian-Muslim Relations*, Edinburgh University Press, ISBN 0-7486-1009-X
- Goodman, Lenn Evan (2003), *Islamic Humanism*, Oxford University Press, ISBN 0-19-513580-6
- Hamid, Shadi (August 2003), "An Islamic Alternative? Equality, Redistributive Justice, and the Welfare State in the Caliphate of Umar", *Renaissance: Monthly Islamic Journal*, **13** (8)

- Haq, S. Nomanul (2001), "Islam", in Jamieson, Dale, *A Companion to Environmental Philosophy*, Blackwell Publishing, ISBN 1-4051-0659-X
- Harper, Douglas (2001), "Islam"[1068], *Online Etymology Dictionary*, retrieved 2007-11-22
- Jackson, Sherman A. (2005), *Islam and the Blackamerican: looking toward the third resurrection*[1069], Oxford University Press, ISBN 0-19-518081-X
- Al Kawi, M. Zuheir (1997), "History of Medical Records and Peer Review", *Annals of Saudi Medicine*, **17** (3): 277–278, PMID 17369721[1070]
- Kelsay, J. (March 2003), "Al-Shaybani and the Islamic Law of War", *Journal of Military Ethics*, Routledge, **2** (1): 63–75, doi: 10.1080/15027570310000027[1071]
- Lane, Edward William, *An Arabic-English Lexicon*[1072] (PDF)
- Lewis, Bernard (May–June 2005), "Freedom and Justice in the Modern Middle East"[1073], *Foreign Affairs*, (Subscription required (help))
- Lewis, Bernard (January 21, 1988), "Islamic Revolution"[1074], *The New York Review of Books*
- Lewis, Bernard (1994), *Race and Slavery in the Middle East*[1075], Oxford University Press
- Makdisi, John A. (June 1999), "The Islamic Origins of the Common Law", *North Carolina Law Review*, **77** (5): 1704
- Martin, Richard C., ed. (2004), *Encyclopedia of Islam and the Muslim World*, vol. 1, Macmillan, ISBN 978-0-02-865604-5
- Mathre, Mary Lynn (1997), *Cannabis in Medical Practice: A Legal, Historical and Pharmacological Overview of the Therapeutic Use of Marijuana*, McFarland, ISBN 0-7864-0361-6
- Nigosian, S. A. (2004), *Islam: Its History, Teaching, and Practices*, Indiana University Press, p. 117, ISBN 978-0-253-11074-9
- Paladin, A. Vanzan (August 1998), "Ethics and neurology in the Islamic world: Continuity and change", *The Italian Journal of Neurological Sciences*, Springer-Verlag, **19** (4): 255–258, doi: 10.1007/BF02427614[1076]
- *Declaration Toward a Global Ethic*[1077] (PDF), Chicago: Parliament of the World's Religions, 4 September 1993, retrieved 2013-08-17
- Sachedina, Abdulaziz Abdulhussein (2001), *The Islamic Roots of Democratic Pluralism*, Oxford University Press, ISBN 0-19-513991-7
- Sardar, Ziauddin (2011), *Reading the Qur'an: the contemporary relevance of the sacred text of Islam*, Oxford University Press, ISBN 0-19-983674-4
- Scott, S. P. (1904), *History of the Moorish Empire in Europe*[1078], Philadelphia: J. B. Lippincott Company, OCLC 580060576[1079]
- Serjeant, R. B. (1964), "The 'Constitution of Medina'", *Islamic Quarterly*, **8** (1)

- Serjeant, R. B. (February 1978), "The Sunnah Jāmi'ah, pacts with the Yathrib Jews, and the Taḥrīm of Yathrib: analysis and translation of the documents comprised in the so-called 'Constitution of Medina'", *Bulletin of the School of Oriental and African Studies, University of London*, Cambridge University Press, **41** (1): 1–42, doi: 10.1017/S0041977X00057761[1080]
- Spier, Ray (August 2002), "The History of the Peer-Review Process", *Trends in Biotechnology*, **20** (8): 357–358, ISSN 0167-7799[1081], PMID 12127284[1082], doi: 10.1016/S0167-7799(02)01985-6[1083]
- Splichal, Slavko (2002), *Principles of Publicity and Press Freedom*, Rowman & Littlefield, ISBN 0-7425-1615-6
- Sullivan, Antony T. (January–February 1997), "Istanbul Conference Traces Islamic Roots of Western Law, Society"[1084], *Washington Report on Middle East Affairs*: 36
- Verde, Tom (November–December 2008), "A tradition of conservation"[1085], *Saudi Aramco World*, retrieved 2011-08-10
- Watt, W. Montgomery (1956), *Muhammad at Medina*, Oxford: Clarendon Press, OCLC 3456619[1086]
- Weeramantry, Christopher G. (1997), *Justice Without Frontiers: Furthering Human Rights*, Brill Publishers, ISBN 90-411-0241-8
- Youssef, Hanafy A.; Youssef, Fatma A.; Dening, T. R. (1996), "Evidence for the existence of schizophrenia in medieval Islamic society", *History of Psychiatry*, **7** (25): 55–62, PMID 11609215[1087], doi: 10.1177/0957154X9600702503[1088]

External links

- Islamic Ethics - Relationship between Pillars of Islam & Development of Excellent Moral & Character[1089]
- Islamic Human Resource Management - Islamic view of human resource management[1090]

Early social changes under Islam

Part of a series on
Muhammad

- ﷺ **Muhammad portal**
- ﷲ **Islam portal**

- v
- t
- e[1091]

Many social changes took place under Islam between 610 and 661, including the period of Muhammad's mission and the rule of his four immediate successors who established the Rashidun Caliphate.

Historians generally agree that changes in areas such as social security, family structure, slavery and the rights of women improved on what was present in existing Arab society.[1092,1093,1094,1095] For example, according to Lewis, Islam "from the first denounced aristocratic privilege, rejected hierarchy, and adopted a formula of the career open to the talents".

Advent of Islam

Bernard Lewis believes that the advent of Islam was a revolution which only partially succeeded due to tensions between the new religion and very old societies that the Muslims conquered. He thinks that one such area of tension was a consequence of what he sees as the egalitarian nature of Islamic doctrine. Islam from the first denounced aristocratic privilege, rejected hierarchy, and adopted a formula of the career open to the talents. Lewis however notes that the equality in Islam was restricted to free adult male Muslims, but even that "represented a very considerable advance on the practice of both the Greco-Roman and the ancient Iranian world".

Bernard Lewis writes about the significance of Muhammad's achievements:[1096]

"   **"**

He had achieved a great deal. To the pagan peoples of western Arabia he had brought a new religion which, with its monotheism and its ethical doctrines, stood on an incomparably higher level than the paganism it replaced. He had provided that religion with a revelation which was to become in the centuries to follow the guide to thought and count of countless millions of Believers. But he had done more than that; he had established a community and a well organized and armed state, the power and prestige of which made it a dominant factor in Arabia

Constitution of Medina

The Constitution of Medina, also known as the *Charter of Medina*, was drafted by Muhammad in 622. It constituted a formal agreement between Muhammad and all of the significant tribes and families of Yathrib (later known as Medina), including Muslims, Jews, and pagans.[1097,1098] The document was drawn up with the explicit concern of bringing to an end the bitter intertribal fighting between the clans of the Aws (Banu Aus) and Banu Khazraj within Medina. To this effect it instituted a number of rights and responsibilities for the Muslim, Jewish, and pagan communities of Medina bringing them within the fold of one community-the *Ummah*.[1099]

The precise dating of the Constitution of Medina remains debated but generally scholars agree it was written shortly after the *hijra* (622).[1100] It effectively established the first Islamic state. The Constitution established: the security of the community, religious freedoms, the role of Medina as a sacred place (barring all violence and weapons), the security of women, stable tribal relations within Medina, a tax system for supporting the community in time of conflict, parameters for exogenous political alliances, a system for granting protection of individuals, a judicial system for resolving disputes, and also regulated the paying of blood-wite (the payment between families or tribes for the slaying of an individual in lieu of *lex talionis*).

Social changes

Practices

John Esposito sees Muhammad as a reformer who condemned practices of the pagan Arabs such as female infanticide, exploitation of the poor, usury, murder, false contracts, fornication, adultery, and theft. He states that Muhammad's "insistence that each person was personally accountable not to tribal customary law but to an overriding divine law shook the very foundations of Arabian society... Muhammad proclaimed a sweeping program of religious and social reform that affected religious belief and practices, business contracts and practices, male-female and family relations". Esposito holds that the Qur'an's reforms consist of "regulations or moral guidance that limit or redefine rather than prohibit or replace existing practices." He cites slavery and women's status as two examples.

According to some scholars, Muhammad's condemnation of infanticide was the key aspect of his attempts to raise the status of women.[1101] Regarding the prevalence of this practice, we know it was "common enough among the pre-Islamic Arabs to be assigned a specific term, *wa'd*"[1102] A much cited verse the Qur'an that addresses this practice is: "When the sun shall be darkened, when the stars shall be thrown down, when the mountains shall be set moving, when the pregnant camels shall be neglected, when the savage beasts shall be mustered, when the seas shall be set boiling, when the souls shall be coupled, *when the buried infant shall be asked for what sin she was slain*, when the scrolls shall be unrolled..."[Quran 81:1[1103]]

Social security

William Montgomery Watt states that Muhammad was both a social and moral reformer. He asserts that Muhammad created a "new system of social security and a new family structure, both of which were a vast improvement on what went before. By taking what was best in the morality of the nomad and adapting it for settled communities, he established a religious and social framework for the life of many races of men."[1104]

Slavery

The Qur'an makes numerous references to slavery ([Quran 2:178[1105]], [Quran 16:75[1106]], [Quran 30:28[1107]]), regulatingWikipedia:Please clarify but thereby also implicitly accepting this already existing institution. Lewis states that Islam brought two major changes to ancient slavery which were to have far-reaching consequences. "One of these was the presumption of freedom; the other, the ban on the enslavement of free persons except in strictly defined

Figure 33: *A slave market in Islamic Yemen.*

circumstances," Lewis continues. The position of the Arabian slave was "enormously improved": the Arabian slave "was now no longer merely a chattel but
was also a human being with a certain religious and hence a social status and
with certain quasi-legal rights."[1108]

Lewis states that in Muslim lands slaves had a certain legal status and had obligations as well as rights to the slave owner, an improvement over slavery in the
ancient world.[1109] Due to these reforms the practice of slavery in the Islamic
empire represented a "vast improvement on that inherited from antiquity, from
Rome, and from Byzantium."

Although there are many common features between the institution of slavery
in the Qur'an and that of neighboring cultures, however the Qur'anic institution
had some unique new features. According to Jonathan Brockopp, professor of
History and Religious Studies, the idea of using alms for the manumission of
slaves appears to be unique to the Qur'an (assuming the traditional interpretation of verses [Quran 2:177[1110]] and [Quran 9:60[1111]]). Similarly, the practice
of freeing slaves in atonement for certain sinsWikipedia:Avoid weasel words
appears to be introduced by the Qur'an. Brockopp adds that: "Other cultures
limit a master's right to harm a slave but few exhort masters to treat their slaves
kindly, and the placement of slaves in the same category as other weak members of society who deserve protection is unknown outside the Qur'an. The

unique contribution of the Qur'an, then, is to be found in its emphasis on the place of slaves in society and society's responsibility toward the slave, perhaps the most progressive legislation on slavery in its time."[1112]

Women's rights

To evaluate the effect of Islam on the status of women, many writers have discussed the status of women in pre-Islamic Arabia, and their findings have been mixed.[1113] Some writers have argued that women before Islam were more liberated drawing most often on the first marriage of Muhammad and that of Muhammad's parents, but also on other points such as worship of female idols at Mecca. Other writers, on the contrary, have argued that women's status in pre-Islamic Arabia was poor, citing practices of female infanticide, unlimited polygyny, patrilineal marriage and others.

Valentine Moghadam analyzes the situation of women from a Marxist theoretical framework and argues that the position of women are mostly influenced by the extent of urbanization, industrialization, poletarization and political ploys of the state managers rather than culture or intrinsic properties of Islam; Islam, Moghadam argues, is neither more nor less patriarchal than other world religions especially Hinduism, Christianity and Judaism.[1114,1115]

Majid Khadduri writes that under the Arabian pre-Islamic law of status, women had virtually no rights. Sharia (Islamic law), however, provided women with a number of rights.[1116] John Esposito states that the reforms affectedWikipedia:Please clarify marriage, divorce, and inheritance.[1035] Women were not accorded with such legal status in other cultures, including the West, until centuries later.[1117] *The Oxford Dictionary of Islam* states that the general improvement of the status of Arab women included prohibition of female infanticide, and recognizing women's full personhood. Gerhard Endress states: "The social system ... build up a new system of marriage, family and inheritance; this system treated women as an individual too and guaranteed social security to her as well as to her children. Legally controlled polygamy was an important advance on the various loosely defined arrangements which had previously been both possible and current; it was only by this provision (backed up by severe punishment for adultery), that the family, the core of any sedentary society could be placed on a firm footing."[1118] One hadith records that Abu Huraira reported that a person said: Allah's Messenger, who amongst the people is most deserving of my good treatment? He said: Your mother, again your mother, again your mother, then your father, then your nearest relatives according to the order (of nearness).

Marriage

Under the Arabian pre-Islamic law, no limitations were set on men's rights to marry or to obtain a divorce. Islamic law, however, restricted polygamy ([Quran 4:3[1119]]) The institution of marriage, characterized by unquestioned male superiority in the pre-Islamic law of status, was redefined and changed into one in which the woman was somewhat of an interested partner. 'For example, the dowry, previously regarded as a bride-price paid to the father, became a nuptial gift retained by the wife as part of her personal property' Under Islamic law, marriage was no longer viewed as a "status" but rather as a "contract". The essential elements of the marriage contract were now an offer by the man, an acceptance by the woman, and the performance of such conditions as the payment of dowry. The woman's consent was imperative. Furthermore, the offer and acceptance had to be made in the presence of at least two witnesses. According to a hadith collected by Al-Tirmidhi, "You have your rights upon your wives and they have their rights upon you. Your right is that they shall not allow anyone you dislike, to trample your bed and do not permit those whom you dislike to enter your home. Their right is that you should treat them well in the matter of food and clothing."

Inheritance and wealth

'Women were given inheritance rights in a patriarchal society that had previously restricted inheritance to male relatives.' Annemarie Schimmel states that "Compared to the pre-Islamic position of women, Islamic legislation meant an enormous progress; the woman has the right, at least according to the letter of the law, to administer the wealth she has brought into the family or has earned by her own work"[1120] According to *The Oxford Dictionary of Islam*, women were also granted the right to live in the matrimonial home and receive financial maintenance during marriage and a waiting period following the death and divorce.[1039]

The status of women

Watt states that Islam is still, in many ways, a man's religion. However, he states that Muhammad, in the historical context of his time, can be seen as a figure who testified on behalf of women's rights and improved things considerably. Watt explains the historical context surrounding women's rights at the time of Muhammad: "It appears that in some parts of Arabia, notably in Mecca, a matrilineal system was in the process of being replaced by a patrilineal one at the time of Muhammad. Growing prosperity caused by a shifting of trade routes was accompanied by a growth in individualism. Men were amassing considerable personal wealth and wanted to be sure that this would be inherited by their own actual sons, and not simply by an extended family of their sisters' sons. This led to a deterioration in the rights of women. At the time Islam began, the conditions of women were terrible—they had no right to own property, were supposed to be the property of the man, and if the man died everything went to his sons." Muhammad, however, by "instituting rights of property ownership, inheritance, education and divorce, gave women certain basic safeguards".[1121]

"In the earliest centuries of Islam, the position of women was not bad at all. Only over the course of centuries was she increasingly confined to the house and was forced to veil herself." The Quran and Muhammad's example were more favorable to the security and status of women than history and later Muslim practice might suggest. For example, the Qur'an does not require women to wear veils; rather, it was a social habit picked up with the expansion of Islam. In fact, since it was impractical for working women to wear veils, "A veiled woman silently announced that her husband was rich enough to keep her idle."[1122,1123]

Haddad and Esposito state that 'although Islam is often criticized for the low status it has ascribed to women, many scholars believe that it was primarily the interpretation of jurists, local traditions, and social trends which brought about a decline in the status of Muslim women. In this view Muhammad granted women rights and privileges in the sphere of family life, marriage, education, and economic endeavors, rights that help improve women's status in society.' However, 'the Arab Bedouins were dedicated to custom and tradition and resisted changes brought by the new religion.' Haddad and Esposito state that in this view 'the inequality of Muslim women happened because of the preexisting habits of the people among whom Islam took root. The economics of these early Muslim societies were not favorable to comfortable life for women. More important, during Islam's second and third centuries the interpretation of the Qur'an was in the hands of deeply conservative scholars, whose decisions are not easy to challenge today. The Qur'an is more favorable to women than is generally realized. In principle, except for a verse or two, the Qur'an grants women equality. For example, Eve was not the delayed product of Adam's rib (as in the tradition for Christians and Jews); the two were born from a single soul Wikipedia:Citation needed. It was Adam, not Eve, who let the devil convince them to eat the forbidden fruit Wikipedia:Citation needed. Muslim women are instructed to be modest in their dress, but only in general terms. Men are also told to be modest. Many Muslims believe the veiling and seclusion are later male inventions, social habits picked up with the conquest of the Byzantine and Persian Empires.'[1124]

Part of a series on
Islam
اللّٰه
• اللّٰه **Islam portal**
• <u>v</u>
• <u>t</u>
• <u>e</u>[1125]

Children

The Qur'an rejected the pre-Islamic idea of children as their fathers' property and abolished the pre-Islamic custom of adoption.[1126]

A. Giladi holds that Quran's rejection of the idea of children as their fathers' property was a Judeo-Christian influence and was a response to the challenge of structural changes in tribal society.

The Quran also replaced the pre-Islamic custom of adoption (assimilation of an adopted child into another family in a legal sense) by the recommendation that "believers treat children of unknown origin as their brothers in the faith and clients [Quran 33:4-5[1127]], [Quran 33:37-40[1128]]. Adoption was viewed "as a lie, as an artificial tie between adults and children, devoid of any real emotional relationship, as a cause of confusion where lineage was concerned and thus a possible source of problems regarding marriage between members of the same family and regarding inheritance. But a child that was not born into a family can still be raised by a foster family but the child must retain his identity, such as his last name and lineage. The prophet has stated that a person who assists and aids an orphan, is on the same footing in heaven to the prophet himself."

Sociological changes

Sociologist Robert N. Bellah (*Beyond Belief*) argues that Islam in its 7th-century origins was, for its time and place, "remarkably modern...in the high degree of commitment, involvement, and participation expected from the rank-and-file members of the community". This because, he argues, that Islam emphasized on the equality of all Muslims. Leadership positions were open to all. However, there were restraints on the early Muslim community that kept it from exemplifying these principles, primarily from the "stagnant localisms" of tribe and kinship. Dale Eickelman writes that Bellah suggests "the early Islamic community placed a particular value on individuals, as opposed to collective or group responsibility".[1129]

The Islamic idea of community (that of *ummah*), established by Muhammad, is flexible in social, religious, and political terms and includes a diversity of Muslims who share a general sense of common cause and consensus concerning beliefs and individual and communal actions.[1130]

Moral changes

Muslims believe that Muhammad, like other prophets in Islam, was sent by God to remind human beings of their moral responsibility, and challenge those ideas in society which opposed submission to God. According to Kelsay, this challenge was directed against these main characteristics of pre-Islamic Arabia:[1131]

1. The division of Arabs into varying tribes (based upon blood and kinship). This categorization was confronted by the ideal of a unified community based upon *taqwa* (Islamic piety), an "*ummah*;"
2. The acceptance of the worship of a multitude of deities besides Allah - a view challenged by strict *Tawhid* (Islamic monotheism), which dictates that Allah has no partner in worship nor any equal;
3. The focus on achieving fame or establishing a legacy, which was replaced by the concept that mankind would be called to account before God on the *Qiyamah* (day of resurrection);
4. The reverence of and compliance with ancestral traditions, a practice challenged by Islam — which instead assigned primacy to submitting to God and following revelation.

These changes lay in the reorientation of society as regards to identity, world view, and the hierarchy of values. From the viewpoint of subsequent generations, this caused a great transformation in the society and moral order of life in the Arabian Peninsula. For Muhammad, although pre-Islamic Arabia exemplified "heedlessness", it was not entirely without merit. Muhammad approved and exhorted certain aspects of the Arab pre-Islamic tradition, such as the care for one's near kin, for widows, orphans, and others in need and for the establishment of justice. However, these values would be re-ordered in importance and placed in the context of strict monotheism.

Although Muhammad's preaching produced a "radical change in moral values based on the sanctions of the new religion, and fear of God and of the Last Judgment", the pre-Islamic tribal practices of the Arabs by no means completely died out.[1132]

Economic changes

Michael Bonner writes on poverty and economics in the Qur'an that the Qur'an provided a blueprint for a new order in society, in which the poor would be treated more fairly than before. This "economy of poverty" prevailed in Islamic theory and practice up until the 13th and 14th centuries. At its heart was a notion of property circulated and purified, in part, through charity, which illustrates a distinctively Islamic way of conceptualizing charity, generosity, and poverty markedly different from "the Christian notion of perennial reciprocity between rich and poor and the ideal of charity as an expression of community love." The Qur'an prohibits bad kind of circulation (*riba*, often understood as usury or interest) and asks for good circulation (*zakat* [legal alms giving]). Some of the recipients of charity appear only once in the Qur'an, and others—such as orphans, parents, and beggars—reappear constantly. Most common is the triad of kinsfolk, poor, and travelers.

Unlike pre-Islamic Arabian society, the Qur'anic idea of economic circulation as a return of goods and obligations was for everyone, whether donors and recipients know each other or not, in which goods move, and society does what it is supposed to do. The Qur'an's distinctive set of economic and social arrangements, in which poverty and the poor have important roles, show signs of newness. The Qur'an told that the guidance comes to a community that regulates its flow of money and goods in the right direction (from top down) and practices generosity as reciprocation for God's bounty. In a broad sense, the narrative underlying the Qur'an is that of a tribal society becoming urbanized. Many scholars, such as Charles C. Torrey and Andrew Rippin, have characterized both the Qur'an and Islam as highly favorable to commerce and to the highly mobile type of society that emerged in the medieval Near East. Muslim tradition (both *hadith* and historiography) maintains that Muhammad did not permit the construction of any buildings in the market of Medina other than mere tents; nor did he permit any tax or rent to be taken there. This expression of a "free market"—involving the circulation of goods within a single space without payment of fees, taxes, or rent, without the construction of permanent buildings, and without any profiting on the part of the caliphal authority (indeed, of the Caliph himself)—was rooted in the term *sadaqa*, "voluntary alms". This coherent and highly appealing view of the economic universe had much to do with Islam's early and lasting success. Since the poor were at the heart of this economic universe, the teachings of the Qur'an on poverty had a considerable, even a transforming effect in Arabia, the Near East, and beyond.[1133]

Civil changes

Social welfare in Islam started in the form of the construction and purchase of wells. Upon his hijra to Medina, Muhammad found only one well to be used. The Muslims bought that well, and consequently it was used by the general public. After Muhammad's declaration that "water" was a better form of *sadaqah* (charity), many of his companions sponsored the digging of new wells. During the Caliphate, the Muslims repaired many of the aging wells in the lands they conquered.[1134]

In addition to wells, the Muslims built many tanks and canals. While some canals were excluded for the use of monks (such as a spring purchased by Talhah) and the needy, most canals were open to general public use. Some canals were constructed between settlements, such as the Saad canal that provided water to Anbar, and the Abi Musa Canal to providing water to Basra.[1135]

During a famine, Umar (Umar ibn al-Khattab) ordered the construction of a canal in Egypt to connect the Nile with the Red Sea. The purpose of the canal was to facilitate the transport of grain to Arabia through a sea-route, hitherto transported only by land. The canal was constructed within a year by 'Amr ibn al-'As, and Abdus Salam Nadiv writes, Arabia was rid of famine for all the times to come."[1136]

Political changes

Arabia

Islam began in Arabia in the 7th century under the leadership of Muhammad, who eventually united many of the independent nomadic tribes of Arabia under Islamic rule.[1137,1138]

Middle East

The pre-Islamic Middle East was dominated by the Byzantine and Sassanian empires. The Roman–Persian Wars between the two had devastated the inhabitants, making the empires unpopular amongst the local tribes.

During the early Islamic conquests, the Rashidun army, mostly led by Khalid ibn al-Walid and 'Amr ibn al-'As, defeated both empires, making the Islamic state the dominant power in the region.[1139] Within only a decade, Muslims conquered Mesopotamia and Persia during the Muslim conquest of Persia and Roman Syria and Roman Egypt during the early Byzantine–Arab Wars.[1140] The Islamic conquest lowered taxes, and provided greater local autonomy and religious freedom for Jews and as well as most of the Christian Churches in the conquered areas (such as Nestorians, Monophysites, Jacobites and Copts who were deemed heretic by Christian Orthodoxy).[1141]

According to Francis Edwards Peters:

The conquests destroyed little: what they did suppress were imperial rivalries and sectarian bloodletting among the newly subjected population. The Muslims tolerated Christianity, but they disestablished it; henceforward Christian life and liturgy, its endowments, politics and theology, would be a private and not a public affair. By an exquisite irony, Islam reduced the status of Christians to that which the Christians had earlier thrust upon the Jews, with one difference. The reduction in Christian status was merely judicial; it was unaccompanied by either systematic persecution or a blood lust, and generally, though not elsewhere and at all times, unmarred by vexatious behavior.

Bernard Lewis wrote:

Some even among the Christians of Syria and Egypt preferred the rule of Islam to that of Byzantines... The people of the conquered provinces did not confine themselves to simply accepting the new regime, but in some cases actively assisted in its establishment. In Palestine the Samaritans, according to tradition, gave such effective aid to the Arab invaders that they were for some time exempted from certain taxes, and there are many other reports in the early chronicles of local Jewish and Christian assistance.

Other changes

Islam reduced the effect of blood feuds, which was common among Arabs, by encouraging compensation in money rather than blood. In case the aggrieved party insisted on blood, unlike the pre-Islamic Arab tradition in which any male relative could be slain, only the culprit himself could be executed.[1142]

The Cambridge History of Islam states that the nomadic structure of pre-Islamic Arabia had the serious moral problem of the care of the poor and the unfortunate. "Not merely did the Qur'an urge men to show care and concern for the needy, but in its teaching about the Last day it asserted the existence of a sanction applicable to men as individuals in matters where their selfishness was no longer restrained by nomadic ideas of dishonour."[1143]

Islam teaches support for the poor and the oppressed.[1144] In an effort to protect and help the poor and orphans, regular almsgiving — *zakat* — was made obligatory for Muslims. This regular alms-giving developed into a form of income tax to be used exclusively for welfare.[1145]

References

- Forward, Martin (1998). *Muhammad: A Short Biography*. Oxford: Oneworld. ISBN 1-85168-131-0.
- Lewis, Bernard (1984). *The Jews of Islam*. US: Princeton University Press. ISBN 0-691-05419-3.
- P.J. Bearman, Th. Bianquis, C.E. Bosworth, E. van Donzel and W.P. Heinrichs (Ed.), *Encyclopaedia of Islam Online*. Brill Academic Publishers. ISSN 1573-3912[1146].
- Watt, William Montgomery (1974). *Muhammad: Prophet and Statesman*. United Kingdom: Oxford University Press. ISBN 0-19-881078-4.
- Jonathan M. Bloom, Sheila S. Blair (1974). *Islam: A Thousand Years of Faith and Power*. Yale University Press. ISBN 0-300-09422-1.
- Manning, Patrick (1990). *Slavery and African Life: Occidental, Oriental, and African Slave Trades*. Cambridge University Press. ISBN 0-521-34867-6.
- Nadvi, Abdus Salam (2000). *The ways of the Sahabah*. Karachi: Darul Ishaat. Translated by Muhammad Yunus Qureshi.
- Schimmel, Annemarie (1992). *Islam: An Introduction*. US: SUNY Press. ISBN 0-7914-1327-6.
- Sonn, Tamara (2004). *A Brief History of Islam*. Blackwell Publishing. ISBN 1-4051-0900-9.

Roman law

Ancient Rome

This article is part of a series on the **politics and government of** **ancient Rome**
Periods
• **Roman Kingdom** 753–509 BC • **Roman Republic** 509–27 BC • **Roman Empire** 27 BC – AD 1453 • **Empire of Trebizond** 1204 – 1461 • Principate • Dominate • **Timeline**
Roman Constitution
• Constitution of the Kingdom • Constitution of the Republic • Constitution of the Empire • Constitution of the Late Empire • Senate • Legislative Assemblies • Executive Magistrates
Ordinary magistrates
• Consul • Praetor • Quaestor • Promagistrate • Aedile • Tribune • Censor • Governor
Extraordinary magistrates
• Dictator • Magister equitum • Consular tribune • Rex • Triumviri • Decemviri
Titles and honours

- Emperor
- Legatus
- Dux
- Officium
- Praefectus
- Vicarius
- Vigintisexviri
- Lictor
- Magister militum
- Imperator
- Princeps senatus
- Pontifex Maximus
- Augustus
- Caesar
- Tetrarch

Precedent and law

- Roman law
- Imperium
- Mos maiorum
- Collegiality
- Auctoritas
- Roman citizenship
- Cursus honorum
- Senatus consultum
- Senatus consultum ultimum

Assemblies

- Centuriate
- Curiate
- Plebeian
- Tribal

- Other countries
- Atlas

- v
- $\underline{t}$
- $\underline{e}^{1147}$

Roman law is the legal system of ancient Rome, including the legal developments spanning over a thousand years of jurisprudence, from the Twelve Tables (c. 449 BC), to the *Corpus Juris Civilis* (AD 529) ordered by Eastern Roman Emperor Justinian I. Roman law forms the basic framework for Civil law, the most used legal system today. The historical importance of Roman law is reflected by the continued use of Latin legal terminology in many legal systems influenced by it, including Common law.

After the dissolution of the Western Roman Empire, the Roman law remained in effect in the Eastern Roman Empire. From the 7th century onward, the legal language in the East was Greek.

Roman law also denoted the legal system applied in most of Western Europe until the end of the 18th century. In Germany, Roman law practice remained in place longer under the Holy Roman Empire (963–1806). Roman law thus served as a basis for legal practice throughout Western continental Europe, as well as in most former colonies of these European nations, including Latin America, and also in Ethiopia. English and Anglo American common law were influenced also by Roman law, notably in their Latinate legal glossary (for example, *stare decisis, culpa in contrahendo, pacta sunt servanda*).[1148] Eastern Europe was also influenced by the jurisprudence of the *Corpus Juris Civilis*, especially in countries such as medieval Romania (Wallachia, Moldavia, and some other medieval provinces/historical regions) which created a new system, a mixture of Roman and local law. Also, Eastern European law was influenced by the "Farmer's Law" of the medieval Byzantine legal system.

Development

Before the Twelve Tables (754–449 BC), private law comprised the Roman civil law (*ius civile Quiritium*) that applied only to Roman citizens, and was bonded to religion; undeveloped, with attributes of strict formalism, symbolism, and conservatism, e.g. the ritual practice of mancipatio (a form of sale). The jurist Sextus Pomponius said, "At the beginning of our city, the people began their first activities without any fixed law, and without any fixed rights: all things were ruled despotically, by kings". It is believed that Roman Law is rooted in the Etruscan religion, emphasising ritual.[1149]

The Twelve Tables

The first legal text is the Law of the Twelve Tables, dating from the mid-5th century BC. The plebeian tribune, C. Terentilius Arsa, proposed that the law should be written, in order to prevent magistrates from applying the law arbitrarily.[1150] After eight years of political struggle, the plebeian social class convinced the patricians to send a delegation to Athens, to copy the Laws of Solon; they also dispatched delegations to other Greek cities for like reason. In 451 BC, according to the traditional story (as Livy tells it), ten Roman citizens were chosen to record the laws (*decemviri legibus scribundis*). While they were performing this task, they were given supreme political power (*imperium*), whereas the power of the magistrates was restricted. In 450 BC, the *decemviri* produced the laws on ten tablets (*tabulae*), but these laws were regarded as unsatisfactory by the plebeians. A second decemvirate is said to have added two further tablets in 449 BC. The new Law of the Twelve Tables was approved by the people's assembly.

Modern scholars tend to challenge the accuracy of Roman historians. They generally do not believe that a second decemvirate ever took place. The decemvirate of 451 is believed to have included the most controversial points of customary law, and to have assumed the leading functions in Rome. Furthermore, the question on the Greek influence found in the early Roman Law is still much discussed. Many scholars consider it unlikely that the patricians sent an official delegation to Greece, as the Roman historians believed. Instead, those scholars suggest, the Romans acquired Greek legislations from the Greek cities of Magna Graecia, the main portal between the Roman and Greek worlds. The original text of the Twelve Tables has not been preserved. The tablets were probably destroyed when Rome was conquered and burned by the Gauls in 387 BC.

The fragments which did survive show that it was not a law code in the modern sense. It did not provide a complete and coherent system of all applicable rules or give legal solutions for all possible cases. Rather, the tables contained specific provisions designed to change the then-existing customary law. Although the provisions pertain to all areas of law, the largest part is dedicated to private law and civil procedure.

Early law and jurisprudence

Many laws include *Lex Canuleia* (445 BC; which allowed the marriage—*ius connubii*—between patricians and plebeians), *Leges Licinae Sextiae* (367 BC; which made restrictions on possession of public lands — *ager publicus* — and also made sure that one of the consuls was plebeian), *Lex Ogulnia* (300 BC; plebeians received access to priest posts), and *Lex Hortensia* (287 BC; verdicts of plebeian assemblies — *plebiscita* — now bind all people).

Another important statute from the Republican era is the *Lex Aquilia* of 286 BC, which may be regarded as the root of modern tort law. However, Rome's most important contribution to European legal culture was not the enactment of well-drafted statutes, but the emergence of a class of professional jurists (*prudentes*, sing. *prudens*, or *jurisprudentes*) and of a legal science. This was achieved in a gradual process of applying the scientific methods of Greek philosophy to the subject of law, a subject which the Greeks themselves never treated as a science.

Traditionally, the origins of Roman legal science are connected to Gnaeus Flavius. Flavius is said to have published around the year 300 BC the formularies containing the words which had to be spoken in court to begin a legal action. Before the time of Flavius, these formularies are said to have been secret and known only to the priests. Their publication made it possible for non-priests to explore the meaning of these legal texts. Whether or not this story is credible, jurists were active and legal treatises were written in larger numbers the 2nd century BC. Among the famous jurists of the republican period are Quintus Mucius Scaevola who wrote a voluminous treatise on all aspects of the law, which was very influential in later times, and Servius Sulpicius Rufus, a friend of Marcus Tullius Cicero. Thus, Rome had developed a very sophisticated legal system and a refined legal culture when the Roman republic was replaced by the monarchical system of the principate in 27 BC .

Pre-classical period

In the period between about 201 to 27 BC, we can see the development of more flexible laws to match the needs of the time. In addition to the old and formal *ius civile* a new juridical class is created: the *ius honorarium*, which can be defined as "The law introduced by the magistrates who had the right to promulgate edicts in order to support, supplement or correct the existing law."[1151] With this new law the old formalism is being abandoned and new more flexible principles of *ius gentium* are used.

The adaptation of law to new needs was given over to juridical practice, to magistrates, and especially to the praetors. A praetor was not a legislator and did not technically create new law when he issued his edicts (*magistratuum edicta*). In fact, the results of his rulings enjoyed legal protection (*actionem dare*) and were in effect often the source of new legal rules. A Praetor's successor was not bound by the edicts of his predecessor; however, he did take rules from edicts of his predecessor that had proved to be useful. In this way a constant content was created that proceeded from edict to edict (*edictum traslatitium*).

Thus, over the course of time, parallel to the civil law and supplementing and correcting it, a new body of praetoric law emerged. In fact, praetoric law was so defined by the famous Roman jurist Papinian (Amilius Papinianus—died in 212 AD): "*Ius praetorium est quod praetores introduxerunt adiuvandi vel supplendi vel corrigendi iuris civilis gratia propter utilitatem publicam*" ("praetoric law is that law introduced by praetors to supplement or correct civil law for public benefit"). Ultimately, civil law and praetoric law were fused in the *Corpus Juris Civilis*.

Classical Roman law

The first 250 years of the current era are the period during which Roman law and Roman legal science reached its greatest degree of sophistication. The law of this period is often referred to as the *classical period of Roman law*. The literary and practical achievements of the jurists of this period gave Roman law its unique shape.

The jurists worked in different functions: They gave legal opinions at the request of private parties. They advised the magistrates who were entrusted with the administration of justice, most importantly the praetors. They helped the praetors draft their edicts, in which they publicly announced at the beginning of their tenure, how they would handle their duties, and the formularies, according to which specific proceedings were conducted. Some jurists also held high judicial and administrative offices themselves.

The jurists also produced all kinds of legal punishments. Around AD 130 the jurist Salvius Iulianus drafted a standard form of the praetor's edict, which was used by all praetors from that time onwards. This edict contained detailed descriptions of all cases, in which the praetor would allow a legal action and in which he would grant a defense. The standard edict thus functioned like a comprehensive law code, even though it did not formally have the force of law. It indicated the requirements for a successful legal claim. The edict therefore became the basis for extensive legal commentaries by later classical jurists like Paulus and Ulpian. The new concepts and legal institutions developed by pre-classical and classical jurists are too numerous to mention here. Only a few examples are given here:

- Roman jurists clearly separated the legal right to use a thing (ownership) from the factual ability to use and manipulate the thing (possession). They also found the distinction between contract and tort as sources of legal obligations.
- The standard types of contract (sale, contract for work, hire, contract for services) regulated in most continental codes and the characteristics of each of these contracts were developed by Roman jurisprudence.
- The classical jurist Gaius (around 160) invented a system of private law based on the division of all material into *personae* (persons), *res* (things) and *actiones* (legal actions). This system was used for many centuries. It can be recognized in legal treatises like William Blackstone's *Commentaries on the Laws of England* and enactments like the French Code civil or the German BGB.

The Roman Republic had three different branches:

- Assemblies
- Senate
- Consuls

The Assemblies could decide whether war or peace. The Senate had complete control over the Treasury, and the Consuls were the most important.

Post-classical law

By the middle of the 3rd century, the conditions for the flourishing of a refined legal culture had become less favourable. The general political and economic situation deteriorated as the emperors assumed more direct control of all aspects of political life. The political system of the principate, which had retained some features of the republican constitution, began to transform itself into the absolute monarchy of the dominate. The existence of a legal science and of jurists who regarded law as a science, not as an instrument to achieve the political goals set by the absolute monarch, did not fit well into the new order of things. The literary production all but ended. Few jurists after the mid-3rd century are known by name. While legal science and legal education persisted to some extent in the eastern part of the Empire, most of the subtleties of classical law came to be disregarded and finally forgotten in the west. Classical law was replaced by so-called vulgar law.

Substance

Concept of Laws

- *ius civile, ius gentium, and ius naturale* – the *ius civile* ("citizen law", originally *ius civile Quiritium*) was the body of common laws that applied to Roman citizens and the *Praetores Urbani*, the individuals who had jurisdiction over cases involving citizens. The *ius gentium* ("law of peoples") was the body of common laws that applied to foreigners, and their dealings with Roman citizens. The *Praetores Peregrini* were the individuals who had jurisdiction over cases involving citizens and foreigners. *Jus naturale* was a concept the jurists developed to explain why all people seemed to obey some laws. Their answer was that a "natural law" instilled in all beings a common sense.
- *ius scriptum and ius non scriptum* – meaning written and unwritten law, respectively. In practice, the two differed by the means of their creation and not necessarily whether or not they were written down. The *ius scriptum* was the body of statute laws made by the legislature. The laws were known as *leges* (lit. "laws") and *plebiscita* (lit. "plebiscites," originating in the Plebeian Council). Roman lawyers would also include in the *ius scriptum* the edicts of magistrates (*magistratuum edicta*), the advice of the Senate (*Senatus consulta*), the responses and thoughts of jurists (*responsa prudentium*), and the proclamations and beliefs of the emperor (*principum placita*). *Ius non scriptum* was the body of common laws that arose from customary practice and had become binding over time.
- *ius commune and ius singulare* – *Ius singulare* (singular law) is special law for certain groups of people, things, or legal relations (because of which it is an exception from the general rules of the legal system), unlike general, ordinary, law (*ius commune*). An example of this is the law about wills written by people in the military during a campaign, which are exempt of the solemnities generally required for citizens when writing wills in normal circumstances.

Figure 34: *Cicero, author of the classic book The Laws, attacks Catiline for attempting a coup in the Roman Senate.*

- ***ius publicum and ius privatum*** – *ius publicum* means public law and *ius privatum* means private law, where public law is to protect the interests of the Roman state while private law should protect individuals. In the Roman law *ius privatum* included personal, property, civil and criminal law; judicial proceeding was private process (*iudicium privatum*); and crimes were private (except the most severe ones that were prosecuted by the state). Public law will only include some areas of private law close to the end of the Roman state. *Ius publicum* was also used to describe obligatory legal regulations (today called *ius cogens*—this term is applied in modern international law to indicate peremptory norms that cannot be derogated from). These are regulations that cannot be changed or excluded by party agreement. Those regulations that can be changed are called today *ius dispositivum*, and they are not used when party shares something and are in contrary.

Public law

The Roman Republic's constitution or *mos maiorum* ("custom of the ancestors") was an unwritten set of guidelines and principles passed down mainly through precedent. Concepts that originated in the Roman constitution live on in constitutions to this day. Examples include checks and balances, the separation of powers, vetoes, filibusters, quorum requirements, term limits, impeachments, the powers of the purse, and regularly scheduled elections. Even some lesser used modern constitutional concepts, such as the block voting found in the electoral college of the United States, originate from ideas found in the Roman constitution.

The constitution of the Roman Republic was not formal or even official. Its constitution was largely unwritten, and was constantly evolving throughout the life of the Republic. Throughout the 1st century BC, the power and legitimacy of the Roman constitution was progressively eroding. Even Roman constitutionalists, such as the senator Cicero, lost a willingness to remain faithful to it towards the end of the republic. When the Roman Republic ultimately fell in the years following the Battle of Actium and Mark Antony's suicide, what was left of the Roman constitution died along with the Republic. The first Roman Emperor, Augustus, attempted to manufacture the appearance of a constitution that still governed the Empire, by utilising that constitution's institutions to lend legitimacy to the Principate, e.g. reusing prior grants of greater imperium to substantiate Augustus' greater imperium over the Imperial provinces and the prorogation of different magistracies to justify Augustus' receipt of tribunician power. The belief in a surviving constitution lasted well into the life of the Roman Empire.

Private law

Stipulatio was the basic form of contract in Roman law. It was made in the format of question and answer. The precise nature of the contract was disputed, as can be seen below.

Rei vindicatio is a legal action by which the plaintiff demands that the defendant return a thing that belongs to the plaintiff. It may only be used when plaintiff owns the thing, and the defendant is somehow impeding the plaintiff's possession of the thing. The plaintiff could also institute an *actio furti* (a personal action) to punish the defendant. If the thing could not be recovered, the plaintiff could claim damages from the defendant with the aid of the *condictio furtiva* (a personal action). With the aid of the *actio legis Aquiliae* (a personal action), the plaintiff could claim damages from the defendant. *Rei vindicatio* was derived from the ius civile, therefore was only available to Roman citizens.

Status

To describe a person's position in the legal system, Romans mostly used the expression *togeus*. The individual could have been a Roman citizen (*status civitatis*) unlike foreigners, or he could have been free (*status libertatis*) unlike slaves, or he could have had a certain position in a Roman family (*status familiae*) either as the head of the family (*pater familias*), or some lower *member.*alieni iuris*-which lives by someone elses law. Two status types were Senator and Emperor.

Litigation

The history of Roman Law can be divided into three systems of procedure: that of *legis actiones*, the *formulary system*, and *cognitio extra ordinem*. The periods in which these systems were in use overlapped one another and did not have definitive breaks, but it can be stated that the legis actio system prevailed from the time of the XII Tables (c. 450 BC) until about the end of the 2nd century BC, that the formulary procedure was primarily used from the last century of the Republic until the end of the classical period (c. AD 200), and that of cognitio extra ordinem was in use in post-classical times. Again, these dates are meant as a tool to help understand the types of procedure in use, not as a rigid boundary where one system stopped and another began.[1152]

During the republic and until the bureaucratization of Roman judicial procedure, the judge was usually a private person (*iudex privatus*). He had to be a Roman male citizen. The parties could agree on a judge, or they could appoint one from a list, called *album iudicum*. They went down the list until they found a judge agreeable to both parties, or if none could be found they had to take the last one on the list.

No one had a legal obligation to judge a case. The judge had great latitude in the way he conducted the litigation. He considered all the evidence and ruled in the way that seemed just. Because the judge was not a jurist or a legal technician, he often consulted a jurist about the technical aspects of the case, but he was not bound by the jurist's reply. At the end of the litigation, if things were not clear to him, he could refuse to give a judgment, by swearing that it wasn't clear. Also, there was a maximum time to issue a judgment, which depended on some technical issues (type of action, etc.).

Later on, with the bureaucratization, this procedure disappeared, and was substituted by the so-called "extra ordinem" procedure, also known as cognitory. The whole case was reviewed before a magistrate, in a single phase. The magistrate had obligation to judge and to issue a decision, and the decision could be appealed to a higher magistrate.

Legacy

In the East

When the centre of the Empire was moved to the Greek East in the 4th century, many legal concepts of Greek origin appeared in the official Roman legislation.[1153] The influence is visible even in the law of persons or of the family, which is traditionally the part of the law that changes least. For example, Constantine started putting restrictions on the ancient Roman concept of *patria potestas*, the power held by the male head of a family over his descendents,

Figure 35: *Title page of a late 16th-century edition of the Digesta, part of Emperor Justinian's Corpus Juris Civilis*

by acknowledging that persons *in potestate*, the descendents, could have proprietary rights. He was apparently making concessions to the much stricter concept of paternal authority under Greek-Hellenistic law. The *Codex Theodosianus* (438 AD) was a codification of Constantian laws. Later emperors went even further, until Justinian finally decreed that a child *in potestate* became owner of everything it acquired, except when it acquired something from its father.

The codes of Justinian, particularly the *Corpus Juris Civilis* (529-534) continued to be the basis of legal practice in the Empire throughout its so-called *Byzantine* history. Leo III the Isaurian issued a new code, the *Ecloga*,[1154] in the early 8th century. In the 9th century, the emperors Basil I and Leo VI the Wise commissioned a combined translation of the Code and the Digest, parts of Justinian's codes, into Greek, which became known as the *Basilica*. Roman law as preserved in the codes of Justinian and in the Basilica remained the basis of legal practice in Greece and in the courts of the Eastern Orthodox Church even after the fall of the Byzantine Empire and the conquest by the Turks, and also formed the basis for much of the *Fetha Negest*, which remained in force in Ethiopia until 1931.

In the West

In the west, Justinian's political authority never went any farther than certain portions of the Italian and Hispanic peninsulas. In Law codes were issued by the Germanic kings, however, the influence of early Eastern Roman codes on some of these is quite discernible. In many early Germanic states, Roman citizens continued to be governed by Roman laws for quite some time, even while members of the various Germanic tribes were governed by their own respective codes.

The *Codex Justinianus* and the Institutes of Justinian were known in Western Europe, and along with the earlier code of Theodosius II, served as models for a few of the Germanic law codes; however, the *Digest* portion was largely ignored for several centuries until around 1070, when a manuscript of the *Digest* was rediscovered in Italy. This was done mainly through the works of glossars who wrote their comments between lines (*glossa interlinearis*), or in the form of marginal notes (*glossa marginalis*). From that time, scholars began to study the ancient Roman legal texts, and to teach others what they learned from their studies. The center of these studies was Bologna. The law school there gradually developed into Europe's first university.

The students who were taught Roman law in Bologna (and later in many other places) found that many rules of Roman law were better suited to regulate complex economic transactions than were the customary rules, which were applicable throughout Europe. For this reason, Roman law, or at least some provisions borrowed from it, began to be re-introduced into legal practice, centuries after the end of the Roman empire. This process was actively supported by many kings and princes who employed university-trained jurists as counselors and court officials and sought to benefit from rules like the famous *Princeps legibus solutus est* ("The sovereign is not bound by the laws", a phrase initially coined by Ulpian, a Roman jurist).

There have been several reasons why Roman law was favored in the Middle Ages. It was because Roman law regulated the legal protection of property and the equality of legal subjects and their wills, and because it prescribed the possibility that the legal subjects could dispose their property through testament.

By the middle of the 16th century, the rediscovered Roman law dominated the legal practice of many European countries. A legal system, in which Roman law was mixed with elements of canon law and of Germanic custom, especially feudal law, had emerged. This legal system, which was common to all of continental Europe (and Scotland) was known as *Ius Commune*. This *Ius Commune* and the legal systems based on it are usually referred to as civil law in English-speaking countries.

Only England and the Nordic countries did not take part in the wholesale reception of Roman law. One reason for this is that the English legal system was more developed than its continental counterparts by the time Roman law was rediscovered. Therefore, the practical advantages of Roman law were less obvious to English practitioners than to continental lawyers. As a result, the English system of common law developed in parallel to Roman-based civil law, with its practitioners being trained at the Inns of Court in London rather than receiving degrees in Canon or Civil Law at the Universities of Oxford or Cambridge. Elements of Romano-canon law were present in England in the ecclesiastical courts and, less directly, through the development of the equity system. In addition, some concepts from Roman law made their way into the common law. Especially in the early 19th century, English lawyers and judges were willing to borrow rules and ideas from continental jurists and directly from Roman law.

The practical application of Roman law and the era of the European *Ius Commune* came to an end, when national codifications were made. In 1804, the French civil code came into force. In the course of the 19th century, many European states either adopted the French model or drafted their own codes. In Germany, the political situation made the creation of a national code of laws impossible. From the 17th century, Roman law in Germany had been heavily influenced by domestic (common) law, and it was called *usus modernus Pandectarum*. In some parts of Germany, Roman law continued to be applied until the German civil code (Bürgerliches Gesetzbuch, BGB) came into force in 1900.

Colonial expansion spread the civil law system.[1155]

Today

Today, Roman law is no longer applied in legal practice, even though the legal systems of some countries like South Africa and San Marino are still based on the old *jus commune*. However, even where the legal practice is based on a code, many rules deriving from Roman law apply: no code completely broke with the Roman tradition. Rather, the provisions of Roman law were fitted into a more coherent system and expressed in the national language. For this reason, knowledge of Roman law is indispensable to understand the legal systems of today. Thus, Roman law is often still a mandatory subject for law students in civil law jurisdictions.

As steps towards a unification of the private law in the member states of the European Union are being taken, the old *jus commune*, which was the common basis of legal practice everywhere in Europe, but allowed for many local variants, is seen by many as a model.

References and sources

References

Sources

• Berger, Adolf, "Encyclopedic Dictionary of Roman Law"[1156], *Transactions of the American Philosophical Society*, Vol. 43, Part 2., Pp. 476. Philadelphia : American Philosophical Society, 1953. (reprinted 1980, 1991, 2002). ISBN 1-58477-142-9

Further reading

• W. W. Buckland, *A Textbook of Roman Law from Augustus to Justinian*[1157], Cambridge: *University Press*, 1921.
• Fritz Schulz, *History of Roman Legal Science*, Oxford: *Clarendon Press*, 1946.
• Peter Stein, *Roman Law in European History*. Cambridge University Press, 1999 (ISBN 0-521-64372-4).
• Andrew Borkowski and Paul Du Plessis, *Textbook on Roman law*. Oxford University Press, 3rd Ed. (ISBN 0-19-927607-2).
• Barry Nicholas, *An Introduction to Roman Law*. Rev. ed. Ernest Metzger. Clarendon Press, 2008 (ISBN 978-0-19-876063-4).
• Jill Harries, "Law and Empire in Late Antiquity" Cambridge, 1999 (ISBN 0-521-41087-8).
• Gábor Hamza, *Das römische Recht und die Privatrechtsentwicklung in Russland im modernen Zeitalter* In: Journal on European History of Law, London: STS Science Centre, Vol. 1, No. 2, pp. 20 – 26, (ISSN 2042-6402).

External links

Wikimedia Commons has media related to *Roman law*.

• An extensive collection of digital books and articles on Roman Law and History, in various languages. By professor Luiz Gustavo Kaercher[1158]
• A very good collection of resources maintained by professor Ernest Metzger[1159].
• *The Roman Law Library* by Professor Yves Lassard and Alexandr Koptev[1160]
• The Roman Law Articles of Smith's Dictionary[1161]
• Roman Legal Tradition: open access journal devoted to Roman law[1162]

Byzantine law

Byzantine culture
• Aristocracy and bureaucracy
• Army
• Art
• Architecture
• Calendar
• Coinage
• Cuisine
• Dance
• Diplomacy
• Dress
• Economy
• Gardens
• Law
• Literature
• Medicine
• Music
• Navy
• People
• Science
• $\underline{v}$ • $\underline{t}$ • $\underline{e}^{1163}$

Byzantine law was essentially a continuation of Roman law with increased Christian influence. Most sources define *Byzantine law* as the Roman legal traditions starting after the reign of Justinian I in the 6th century and ending with the Fall of Constantinople in the 15th century.

Though during and after the European Renaissance Western legal practices were heavily influenced by *Justinian's Code* (the *Corpus Juris Civilis*) and Roman law during classical times, Byzantine law nevertheless had substantial influence on Western traditions during the Middle Ages and after.

The most important work of Byzantine law was the Ecloga, issued by Leo III, the first major Roman-Byzantine legal code issued in Greek rather than Latin. Soon after the *Farmer's Law* was established regulating legal standards outside the cities. While the Ecloga was influential throughout the Mediterranean (and Europe) because of the importance of Constantinople as a trading center, the Farmer's Law was a seminal influence on Slavic legal traditions including those of Russia.

Influences and sources

Byzantium inherited its main political, cultural and social institutions from Rome. Similarly, Roman law constituted the basis for the Byzantine legal system. For many centuries, the two great codifications of Roman law, carried out by Theodosius II and Justinian respectively, were the cornerstones of Byzantine legislation. Of course, over the years these Roman codes were adjusted to the current circumstances, and then replaced by new codifications, written in Greek. However, the influence of Roman law persisted, and it is obvious in codifications, such as *Basilika*, which was based on *Corpus Juris Civilis*. In the 11th century, Michael Psellos prides himself for being acquainted with the Roman legal legacy ("Ἰταλῶν σοφία").[1164]

In accordance with the late Roman legal tradition, the main source of law (*fons legum*) in Byzantium remained the enactments of the emperors. The latter initiated some major codifications of the Roman law, but they also issued their own "new laws", the *Novels* ("Novellae", "Νεαραί"). In early Byzantine (late Roman) era the legislative interest of the emperors intensified, and laws were now regulating the main aspects of public, private, economic and social life.[1165] For example, Constantine I was the first to regulate divorce and Theodosius I intervened in faith issues, imposing a specific version of the Creed.[1166] From Diocletian to Theodosius I, namely during approximately 100 years, more than 2,000 laws were issued. Justinian alone promulgated approximately 600 laws. Gradually, the legislative enthusiasm receded, but still some of the laws of later emperors, such as Leo III's *Novels*, are of particular importance.[1167] Custom continued to play a limited role as a secondary source of law, but written legislation had a precedence.[1168]

Early Byzantine period

There is no definitively established date for when the so-called *Byzantine* period of Roman history begins. During the 4th, 5th, and 6th centuries the Empire was split and united administratively more than once. But it was during this period that Constantinople was first established and the East gained its own identity administratively; thus, it is often considered the *early* Byzantine period. Despite this, though, the legal developments during this period are typically considered part of *Roman* Law, as opposed to *Byzantine* Law, in part because legal documents during this period were still written in Latin. These developments, nevertheless, were key steps in the formation of Byzantine Law.

Codex Theodosianus

In 438, Emperor Theodosius published the Codex Theodosianus, which consisted of 16 books, containing all standing laws from the age of Constantine I till then.

Corpus Iuris Civilis

Soon after his accession in 527, Justinian appointed a commission to collect and codify existing Roman law. A second commission, headed by the jurist Tribonian, was appointed in 530 to select matter of permanent value from the works of the jurists, to edit it and to arrange it into 50 books. In 533 this commission produced the *Digesta*.

Although Law as practiced in Rome had grown up as a type of case law, this was not the "Roman Law" known to the Medieval, or modern world. Now Roman law claims to be based on abstract principles of justice that were made into actual rules of law by legislative authority of the emperor or the Roman people. These ideas were transmitted to the Middle Ages in the great codification of Roman law carried throughout by the emperor Justinian. The Corpus Iuris Civilis was issued in Latin in three parts: the Institutes, the Digest (Pandects), and the Code (Codex). It was the last major legal document written in Latin.

Two of the world's most widespread legal systems, Anglo-American common law and civil law are based on the Corpus (in, for instance, most of Europe, Asia, South America, and Africa, Scotland, Quebec and Louisiana).

Middle Byzantine period

Following Justinian's reign the Empire entered a period of rapid decline partially enabling the Arab conquests which would further weaken the Empire. Knowledge of Latin, which had been in decline since the fall of the West, virtually disappeared causing making many of the old legal codices almost inaccessible. These developments contributed to a dramatic weakening of legal standards in the Empire and a substantial drop in the standards of legal scholarship. Legal practice would become much more *pragmatic* and, as knowledge of Latin in the Empire waned, direct use of Justinian's *"Corpus Juris Civilis"* would be abandoned in favor of summaries, commentaries, and new compilations written in Greek.

Ecloga

The changes in the internal life of the empire which occurred in the years following the publication of Justinian's code called for a review of the legislation, so as for the requirements of the times should be met. Within the framework of the reforms Leo III the Isaurian, (the first Isaurian emperor), introduced, he provided also for the modification of current laws. In 726 he issued the "Ecloga", that bore his name as well as the name of his son Constantine. "Ecloga", referring to both the civil and criminal law, constituted, as was declared in the title a "rectification (of the Justinian legislation) towards a more philanthropic version". The membership of the editing committee is not known, but its primary mission, however, was, on the one hand, to modify those dispositions not in step with the times and, on the other, to provide judges with a concise legal handbook to help them dispense justice properly.

The dispositions of "Ecloga", influenced by the Christian spirit, as well as by the common law, protected and supported the institution of marriage, increased the rights of wives and legal children, and introduced the equality of all citizens before the law. On the other hand, the penalties of amputation and blindness were introduced, reflecting the Byzantine concept in this period of changesWikipedia:Citation needed. By means of his "Ecloga" Leo addressed the judges also, inviting them *"neither the poor to despise nor the ones unjust to let uncontrolled"*. Besides, in his effort to deter bribery in the execution of their duties he made their payment local and payable by the imperial treasury. "Ecloga" constituted the basic handbook of justice dispensation up to the days of the Macedonian emperors, that also assumed legislative activity, whereas later it influenced the ecclesiastic law of the Russian Orthodox Church. Formerly the researchers attributed the juridical collections *"Farmer's Law"*, *"Rhodian Sea Law"* and *"Military Laws"* to Leo III the Isaurian. These views, however, are no longer valid.

The Farmer's Laws

With the exception of a few cities, and especially Constantinople, where other types of urban economic activities were also developed, Byzantine society remained at its heart agricultural. An important source regarding law, which reflects in a particularly characteristic way the internal life of the Byzantine villages during the Middle Byzantine Era (7th – end of 12th century) is the *Nomos Georgikos*, also known as the *Lex Rustica* or *Farmer's Law*. Due to its importance, the *Farmer's Law* roused the interest of researchers from a very early stage. Ever since it has been one of the most discussed texts concerning the internal history of Byzantium. It has been suggested that, because of the major influences caused by the influx of Slavs into the Empire at the time the

Farmer's Law was established, Slavic traditions were in fact an important influence of the Farmer's Law, both in terms of why it was developed and its content.[1169]

It is a private collection, continuously enriched, and refers to specific cases relevant to rural property within the framework of the Byzantine rural "community". As evident by the dispositions of the "Law", peasants were organized in "communities" and collectively responsible for the payment of the total tax the "community" was liable for, being obliged to pay as well the amounts corresponding to indebted members of the community. As for the chronology of its writing, since the text itself bears no specific date, it is placed somewhere in between the second half of the 6th century and the middle of the 14th. Very early on, it was acknowledged as a legal handbook of great importance and greatly influenced much of the law of the Slavic countries and especially Serbia, Bulgaria and Russia.

The Sea Laws

Dating problems, similar to the ones of the *"Farmer's Law"*, presents a code of equal character, the "Rhodian Sea Law" (*Nomos Rhodion Nautikos*). Written probably between 600 and 800, it is a collection of maritime law regulations divided into three parts. The first part refers to the ratification of the "Naval Law" by the Roman emperors. The second specifies the participation of the crew in maritime profits and the regulations valid on the ship, while the third and largest refers to maritime law, as for example to the apportionment of responsibility in case of theft or damage to the cargo or the ship. The *"Naval Law"* was included in the *Basilika* of Leo VI the Wise as a complement to book 53.

Ecclesiastical law

In accordance with the model of the secular legal associations, the canons of the ecclesiastic councils concerned ecclesiastic issues and regulated the conduct of the clergy, as well as of the secular as concerned matters of belief. The "In Trullo" or "Fifth-Sixth Council", known for its canons, was convened in the years of Justinian II (691-692) and occupied itself exclusively with matters of discipline. The aim of the synod was to cover the gaps left in canon law by the previous Fifth (553)and Sixth Ecumenical Councils.

This collection of canons was divided into four parts:

a) The canons ratifying the doctrinal decisions of the first six ecumenical councils along with the teachings of the Fathers of the Church.

b) The canons specifying the obligations of the ministrational clergy.

c) The canons referring to the monks.

d) The canons referring to the secular. The influence of these canons carried on in the future and they were extensively annotated by Balsamon, Zonaras and Aristenos, the three great ecclesiastic jurists of the 12th century.

Editions

- The *Didache* from the 2nd century
- The *Apostolic Church-Ordinance*, from the third century
- The *Apostolic Constitutions*, from the 375 to 380 AD
- The *Canons of the Apostles*[1170]

AswellWikipedia:Please clarify other Ancient Church Orders not more extant in Greek. Later more scientific collections emerged like:

- The *Nomocanon* of John Scholasticus from the 6th century
- The *Nomocanon* in 14 titles of Heraclius from the 7th century
- The *Nomocanon* of Photios from the 9th century
- The *Syntagma* of Theodore Balsamon and his *Scholia* to the *Nomocanon* of Photios from the 12th century
- The *Synopsis Canonum* by Alexios Aristenos from the 12th century

All this books were compiled later by the Athonite Monk Saint Nicodemus the Hagiorite and became the basis of the Modern Eastern Orthodox Law which is his *Pedalion*.

Later Byzantine law

The following legal texts were prepared in the later Byzantine Empire:

- The *Prochiron* of Basil the Macedonian, c. 870[1171] or 872,[1172] which invalidates parts of the *Ecloga* and restores Justinians Laws, as well as Hellenising arcane Latin expressions.
- The *Epanagoge* (repetita proelectio legis), also of Basil the Macedonian, together with his sons, a second edition of the Prochiron, c.879 - 886
- The *Eisagoge* of Photios, which includes novel law, c.880
- The *Basilicae* (repurgatio veterum legum) or *Basilics* of Leo the Philosopher, together with his brother Alexander and Constantine VII, c.900 or 906-11, which attempts to synthesise 6th century commentaries and glosses on Justinians laws by headings, and remove contradictions. By the 11th century, the Basilics had replaced Justinian's laws as the primary source of Roman law.
- The *Synopsis (Basilicorum) maior*, an abridgment of the *Basilika* from the late 9th century[1173]

- The *Epitome Legum*, later known as the Epitome ad Prochiron mutata, a synthesis of Justinian and the Epanagoge, c. 920-1
- The *Epanagoge aucta*, a revision of the 9th century Epanagogue from c. 11th century.
- The *Prochiron aucta*, a revision of the 9th century Prochiron from c.13th century.
- The *Hexabiblos*, a 14th century compilation of the above books made by Konstantinos Harmenopoulos in Thessalonike
- The *Hexabiblos aucta*, a late 14th century revision of Harmenopoulos' work by Ioannes Holobolos

Other jurists (including at least one Emperor) prepared private collections of cases and commentaries, but these did not form the body of law used by jurists at large. It is held that the *113 Novels of Leo the Wise* fall into this category.

Lokin argues that while later legal texts tended to rearrange or explain the 6th century work of Justinian, rather than create new law, they did alter the locus of authority for law (*legis vigor*) from the Emperor to God. In Justinian's work, Mosaïc Law and God's authority *support* the Emperor, and are consultative, but do not temper his absolute authority. This process has already begun in the *Ecloga*, which states law is God-given by way of Isiah 8:20, and is made explicit first in the Prochiron.[1174] There was, however, 'legislative creep' over this period, where the redaction of old laws and case law created new laws in effect, although not explicitly cited as such.[1175]

Legacy

During the early Middle Ages Roman/Byzantine Law played a major role throughout the Mediterranean region and much of Europe because of the economic and military importance of the Empire.

After the Islamic conquests of the Eastern Mediterranean, the Islamic caliphates gradually codified their legal systems using Roman/Byzantine Law as an important model. It has been suggested in fact that it was the publication of the Ecloga that spurred the first major codification of Islamic imperial law.[1176]

Slavic legal traditions, including countries ranging from Bulgaria to Russia, were substantially influenced by the Farmer's Law. To a lesser extent the Ecloga and other Byzantine codices influenced these areas as well. During the 18th and 19th centuries, as Russia increased its contact with the West, Justinian's Code began to be studied thus bringing in this influence.

In Western Europe, following the fall of the Roman Empire, the influence of Roman/Byzantine law became more indirect though always significant during much of the Middle Ages. During the European Renaissance, Western scholars embraced Justinian's Code as a basis for jurisprudence, shunning many of the later legal developments of the Byzantine Empire such as the Ecloga. This was to a great extent affected by the East/West (Roman Catholic vs. Eastern Orthodox) split in the Church. The perception in the West was that Roman law that was recorded in Latin was truly *Roman* whereas later laws written in Greek was distinct and foreign.

Sources

- Cameron, Averil (2009). *The Byzantines* (in Greek). Translated by Giorgos Tzimas. Athens: Editions Psychogios. ISBN 978-960-453-529-3.
- Fine, John V. A. (1991). *The Early Medieval Balkans: A Critical Survey from the Sixth to the Late Twelfth Century*. Michigan University Press. ISBN 978-0-472-08149-3.
- Fögen, Marie Theres (1994). "Legislation in Byzantium: A Political and a Bureaucratic Technique". In Laiou, Angeliki E. *Law and Society in Byzantium*. Dumbarton Oaks. ISBN 0-88402-222-6.
- Jokisch, Benjamin (2007). *Islamic Imperial Law: Harun-Al-Rashid's Codification Project*. Walter de Gruyter GmbH. ISBN 9783110924343.
- Morris, Rosemary (1992). "Dispute Settlement in the Byzantine Provinces in the Tenth Century". In Davies, Wendy; Fouracre, Paul. *The Settlement of Disputes in Early Medieval Europe*. Cambridge University Press. ISBN 0-521-42895-5.
- Mousourakis, George (2003). *The Historical and Institutional Context of Roman Law*. Ashgate Publishing. ISBN 0-7546-2108-1.

External links

- *The Roman Law Library* by Professor Yves Lassard and Alexandr Koptev[1177]

Ancient Germanic law

Several Latin law codes of the Germanic peoples written in the Early Middle Ages (also known as *leges barbarorum* "laws of the barbarians") survive, dating to between the 5th and 9th centuries. They are influenced by Roman law, canon law, and earlier tribal customs.

Germanic law was codified in writing under the influence of Roman law; previously it was held in the memory of designated individuals who acted as judges in confrontations and meted out justice according to customary rote, based on careful memorization of precedent. Among the Franks they were called *rachimburgs*. "Living libraries, they were law incarnate, unpredictable and terrifying."[1178] When justice is oral, the judicial act is personal and subjective.Wikipedia:Manual_of_Style/ Words_to_watch#Unsupported_attributions Power, whose origins were at once said to be magical, divine and military was, according to Michel Rouche, exercised jointly by the "throne-worthy" elected king and his free warrior companions.[1179] Oral law sufficed as long as the warband was not settled in one place. Germanic law made no provisions for the public welfare, the *res publica* of Romans.

The language of all these continental codes was Latin; the only known codes drawn up in any Germanic language were the Anglo-Saxon laws, beginning with the Laws of Æthelberht (7th century). In the 13th century customary Saxon law was codified in the vernacular as the *Sachsenspiegel*.

All these laws may be described in general as codes of governmental procedure and tariffs of compositions. They all present somewhat similar features with Salic law, the best-known example, but often differ from it in the date of compilation, the amounts of fines, the number and nature of the crimes, the number, rank, duties and titles of the officers, etc.

In Germanic Europe in the Early Middle Ages, every man was tried according to the laws of his own race, whether Roman, Salian or Ripuarian Frank, Frisian, Burgundian, Visigoth, Bavarian etc.[1180]

A number of separate codes were drawn up specifically to deal with cases between ethnic Romans. These codes differed from the normal ones that covered cases between Germanic peoples, or between Germanic people and Romans. The most notable of these are the *Lex Romana Visigothorum* or *Breviary of Alaric* (506), the *Lex Romana Curiensis* and the *Lex Romana Burgundionum*.

Tacitus

Tacitus in his *Germania* gives an account of the legal practice of the Germanic peoples of the 1st century. Tacitus reports that criminal cases were put before the thing (tribal assembly). Lighter offenses were regulated with damages (paid in livestock), paid in part to the victim (or their family) and in part to the king.[1181] The death penalty was reserved for two kinds of capital offenses: military treason or desertion was punished by hanging, and corporal infamy[1182] (rape) by throwing the condemned into a bog.

The difference in punishment is explained by the idea that "glaring iniquities" must be exposed in plain sight, while "effeminacy and pollution" should best be buried and concealed.[1183]

Minor legal disputes were settled on a day-to-day basis by elected chiefs assisted by elected officials.[1184]

Principles

The Germanic law codes are designed for a clearly stratified society fixated on castes determined by descent or kinship. Legal status, and therefore freedom, was based on a person's caste, discriminating between royals and two or three successive castes of nobility, where the lower were reckoned as peasants or freemen (OE *freo man*, OHG *frīhals*), and those who are laymen, or bondmen (ON *þræll*). Accordingly, descent (nativitate) was determining who would attend the various things (house-things, local things, regional things and inter-regional or royal things). Thus the bondmen were *ipso facto* represented by their family-heads - the local nobility - on the regional things of the nobles. The same differentiation (in castes) defined who could convey and inherit property. In regulation of tribal feuds and weregeld a similar discrimination is seen.

At the head of the nobility (adalmen, eaorls, ceorls and freemen) was the king overseeing the laws, rights and privileges. Under the king came the highborn nobility (OE *æþelu*, OS *aðali*, Germ *Adel*) and the middle nobility (OE *eorl*, OS/OHG *eorl*, ON *jarl*). The lower nobility were the ordinary freemen (OE *ćeorl*, Frankish *baro*, Burgundian *leudis*). Under these ceorls (peasants or freemen) came the serfs - as in 'laymen'. Skilled serfs permitted to leave their homesteads were often called 'leysing' or 'free-men' (OE *læt*, *freolæta*, MDu *laet*, *vrilaet*, ON *leysíngr*). Otherwise common laymen were addressed as 'tjod' (OE *þēow*, OHG *diut*, OMG *deut*, ON *þjod*, Goth *þius*). As the Roman church gained political power in Europe this system was augmented by incorporating a separate class of clergy, where their bishops were to be considered of equal status as a nobleman.

The Germanic law system is in principle based on compensation rather than revenge. Any injury must be compensated according to the damage done, regardless of motive or intent. Even for capital crimes like murder, the compensation is a weregeld, a fixed amount depending on the sex and social status of the victim. The practice of paying part of the damages to the king survives in the earliest Anglo-Saxon law code (Laws of Æthelberht of Kent), under the term *drihtinbeah*, but seems to have been discontinued after Christianisation. As thralls are considered the property of their lord, crimes committed by thralls must be compensated by their masters just like damage caused by animals.

The most extreme punishment for crimes considered irredeemable seems to be outlawry, i.e. the declaration of the guilty party as beyond the protection of the law.[1185]

In most instances this may have been equivalent to a death sentence in practice, but the actual death penalty seems to have been foreseen only for very rare cases, such as sexual crimes (rape, promiscuity), religious crimes (incest) or crimes against the king (treason). Alamannic law also foresees the death penalty for plotting to assassinate the duke, and for military treason (assisting enemies or causing rebellion in the army), but in these cases the penalty may also be outlawry or a fine, depending on the judgement of the duke or the chieftains.

The weregeld was set at a basic amount of 200 shillings, which could be multiplied depending on the status (descent, caste) of the victim. In Anglo-Saxon law, the regular freeman is known as a *two-hynde man* ("a man worth 200"), and noblemen are either *six-hynde man* (threefold weregeld) or *twelve-hynde man* (sixfold weregeld). In Alamannic law, the basic weregeld for a freeman is likewise 200 shillings. Alamannic tradition is particular in doubling the fee if the victim was a woman, so that the weregeld for a free woman is 400 shillings. The weregeld for a priest is threefold, i.e. 600 shillings. Alamannic law further introduces the concept of premeditated murder (as opposed to deaths by accident or in combat), which is fined by ninefold weregeld. The Anglo-Saxon *Norðleoda laga* ("North-people's law") is unique in setting an explicit amount for a king's weregeld, at 30,000 tremisses, explaining that 15,000 tremises is for the man (the same amount as for an atheling or an archbishop) and another 15,000 for the damage to the kingdom.

Unlike Roman law, Germanic law mentions cruentation as a means to prove guilt or innocence.

Individual law codes

The principal ancient Germanic law codes are:

- *Code of Euric* (Visigoths) - c. 480
- *Lex Burgundionum* (Burgundians, Gundobad) - c. 500
- *Lex Salica* (Salian Franks, Clovis I) - c. 500
- *Pactus Alamannorum* (Alamanni) - c. 620
- *Lex Ripuaria* (Ripuarian Franks) - 630s
- *Edictum Rothari* (Lombards, Rothari) - 643
- *Lex Visigothorum* (Visigoths, Recceswinth) - 654
- *Lex Alamannorum* (Alamanni) - 730
- *Lex Bajuvariorum* (Bavarians) - c. 745
- *Lex Frisionum* (Frisians) - c. 785
- *Lex Saxonum* (Saxons) - 803
- *Lex Angliorum et Werinorum, hoc est, Thuringorum* - 9th century

Visigothic law codes

Compared with other barbarian tribes, the Goths had the longest time of contact with Roman civilization, from migration in 376 to trade interactions years beforehand. The Visigothic legal attitude held that laws were created as new offenses of justice arose, and that the king's laws originated from God and His justice-scriptural basis.[1186] Mercifulness (*clementia*) and a paternal feeling (*pietas*) were qualities of the king exhibited through the laws.[1187] The level of severity of the law was "tempered" by this mercy, specifically for the poor; it was thought that by showing paternal love in formation of law, the legislator gained the love of citizen.[1188] While the monarch's position was implicitly supreme and protected by laws, even kings were subject to royal law, for royal law was thought of as God's law.[1189] In theory, enforcement of the law was the duty of the king, and as the sovereign power he could ignore previous laws if he desired, which often led to complications.[1190] To regulate the king's power, all future kings took an oath to uphold the law.[1191] While the Visigoths' law code reflected many aspects of Roman law, over time it grew to define a new society's requirements and opinions of law's significance to a particular people.

It is certain that the earliest written code of the Visigoths dates to Euric (471). Code of Euric (*Codex Euricianus*), issued between 471 and 476, has been described as "the best legislative work of the fifth century".[1192] It was created to regulate the Romans and Goths living in Euric's kingdom, where Romans greatly outnumbered Goths. The code borrowed heavily from the Roman Theodosian Code (*Codex Theodosianus*) from the early 5th century, and its main subjects were Visigoths living in Southern France.[1193] It contained about 350 clauses, organized by chapter headings; about 276 to 336 of these clauses remain today. Besides his own constitutions, Euric included in this collection the unwritten constitutions of his predecessors Theodoric I (419-451), Thorismund (451-453), and Theodoric II (453-466), and he arranged the whole in a logical order. Of the Code of Euric, fragments of chapters 276 to 337 have been discovered in a palimpsest manuscript in the Bibliothèque Nationale at Paris (Latin coll, No. 12161), proving that the code ran over a large area. Euric's code was used for all cases between Goths, and between them and Romans; in cases between Romans, Roman law was used.

At the insistence of Euric's son, Alaric II, an examination was made of the Roman laws in use among Romans in his dominions, and the resulting compilation was approved in 506 at an assembly at Aire, in Gascony, and is known as the Breviary of Alaric, and sometimes as the *Liber Aniani*, from the fact that the authentic copies bear the signature of the *referendarius* Anian. organized by chapter headings; about 276 to 336 of these clauses remain today. In 506 CE, Alaric II, son of Euric, assembled the council of Agde to issue the Breviary of Alaric (*Lex Romana Visigothorum*), applying specifically to Hispano-Roman residents of the Iberian Peninsula,[1194] where Alaric had migrated the Visigoth population. Both the Code of Euric and Breviary of Alaric borrowed heavily from the Theodosian Code. Euric, for instance, forbade intermarriage between Goths and Romans, which was already expressed in the *Codex Theodosianus*. The *Lex Romana Visigothorum* remained a source of law in the area that later became southern France long after it had been superseded in the Iberian peninsula by the *Lex Visigothorum* (see below).

Euric's code remained in force among the Visigothic Kingdom of Hispania (the Iberian Peninsula) until the reign of Liuvigild (568-586), who made a new one, the Codex Revisus, improving upon that of his predecessor. This work is lost, and we have no direct knowledge of any fragment of it. In the 3rd codification, however, many provisions have been taken from the 2nd, and these are designated by the word *antiqua*; by means of these *antiqua* we are enabled in a certain measure to reconstruct the work of Leovigild.

After the reign of Leovigild, the legislation of the Visigoths underwent a transformation. New laws made by the kings were declared to be applicable to all subjects in the kingdom, of whatever race; in other words, they became territorial; and this principle of territoriality was gradually extended to the ancient code. Moreover, the conversion of Reccared (586-601) from Arianism to orthodox Christianity effaced the religious differences among his subjects, and all subjects, being Christians, had to submit to the canons of the councils, made obligatory by the kings.

In 643, Visigoth king Chindasuinth (642-653) proposed a new Visigothic Code, the *Lex Visigothorum* (also called the *Liber Iudiciorum* or *Forum Iudicium*), which replaced both the Code of Euric and the Breviary of Alaric. His son, Recceswinth (649-672), refined this code in its rough form and issued it officially in 654. This code applied equally to both Goths and Romans, presenting "a sign of a new society of Hispania developing in the seventh century, distinctly different from Gothic or Roman".[1195] The *Liber Iudiciorum* also marked a shift in the view of the power of law in reference to the king. It stressed that the *Liber Iudiciorum* alone is law, absent of any relation to any kingly authority, instead of the king being the law and the law merely an expression of his decisions.[1196] The lacunae in these fragments have been filled by the aid of the law of the Bavarians, where the chief Divisions are reintroduced, divided into 12 books, and subdivided into *tituli* and chapters (*aerae*). It comprises 324 constitutions taken from Leovigild's collection, a few of the laws of Reccared and Sisebur, 99 laws of Chindasuinth, and 87 of Reccasuinth. A recension of this code of Reccasuinth was made in 681 by King Erwig (680-687), and is known as the *Lex Wisigothorum renovate*; and, finally, some *additamenta* were made by Ergica (687-702).

The *Liber Iudiciorum* makes several striking differences from Roman law, especially concerning the issue of inheritance. According to the *Liber Iudiciorum*, if incest is committed, the children can still inherit, whereas in Roman law the children were disinherited and could not succeed.[1197] Title II of Book IV outlines the issue of inheritance under the newly united Visigothic Code: section 1, for instance, states that sons and daughters inherit equally if their parents die instate, section 4 says that all family members should inherit if no will exists to express the intentions of the deceased, and the final section expresses a global law of Reccesswinth, stating that anyone left without heirs has the power to do what they want with their possessions. This statement recalls the Roman right for a person to leave his possessions to anyone in his will, except this Visigothic law emphasizes males and females equally, whereas, in Roman law, only males (particularly the *pater familias*) are allowed to make a will.

Lex Burgundionum

This is the law code of the Burgundians, probably issued by king Gundobad. It is influenced by Roman law and deals with domestic laws concerning marriage and inheritance as well as regulating weregild and other penalties. Interaction between Burgundians is treated separately from interaction between Burgundians and Gallo-Romans. The oldest of the 14 surviving manuscripts of the text dates to the 9th century, but the code's institution is ascribed to king Gundobad (died 516), with a possible revision by his successor Sigismund (died

523). The *Lex Romana Burgundionum* is a separate code, containing various laws taken from Roman sources, probably intended to apply to the Burgundians' Gallo-Roman subjects. The oldest copy of this text dates to the 7th century.

Lex Salica

The exact origins of the Franks are uncertain: they were a group of Germanic peoples that settled in the lower regions of the Rhine river. They were not a unified people at the start of the 3rd century but consisted of many tribes which were loosely connected with one another. Although they were intertwined with the Roman Empire the Franks were not a part of it. "No large body of Franks was admitted into the Empire, but individuals and small groups did cross."[1198] The Romans were seen as a lower rank in Frankish society. With larger numbers the Franks over took the region of the Rhine. Latin became the secondary language to the Germanic one of the Franks and Frankish law took precedence among the people. The Romans even embraced the "Barbarians" to the north at times, making them allies to fight off the Huns.

The Franks were broken down into east and west regions. The Eastern Franks were known as the Ripuarians and those west of the Rhine were known as the Salian Franks. It was King Clovis who united the Franks under one law after defeating his rivals in 509 CE. It is during this time of unification that King Clovis developed the Salic Law.

The Lex Salica was a similar body of law to the Lex Burgundionum. It was compiled between 507 and 511 CE. The body of law deals with many different aspects of Frank society. The charges range from inheritance to murder and theft. The Salic law was used to bring order to Frank society, the main punishment for crimes being a fine with a worth designated to the type of crime. The law uses capital punishment only in cases of witchcraft and poisoning. This absence of violence is a unique feature of the Salic Law.

The code was originally brought about by the Frankish King Clovis. The code itself is a blue print for Frankish society and how the social demographics were assembled. One of the main purposes of the Salic Law is to protect a family's inheritance in the agnatic succession. This emphasis on inheritance made the Salic Law a synonym for agnatic succession, and in particular for the "fundamental law" that no woman could be king of France.

The use of fines as the main reparation made it so that those with the money to pay the fine had the ability to get away with the most heinous of crimes. "Those who commit rape shall be compelled to pay 2500 denars, which makes 63 shillings." Rape was not the only detailed violent crime. The murder of children is broken down by age and gender, and so is the murder of women.

Paying fines broke the society into economic and social demographics in that the wealthy were free to do as much as they could afford, whereas the fines themselves placed different values on the gender and ethnic demographics. This social capital is evident in the differences in the Salic Law's punishment for murder based on a woman's ability to bear children. Women who could bear children were protected by a 600 shilling fine while the fine for murdering a woman who could no longer bear children was only 200 shillings. It is also interesting that all crimes committed against Romans had lesser fines than other social classes. In the case of inheritance, it is made very clear that all property belongs to the males in the family. This also means that all debt also belongs to the males of the family.

The Salic Law outlines a unique way of securing the payment of money owed. It is called the *Chrenecruda* (or *crenecruda*, *chren ceude*, *crinnecruda*). In cases where the debtor could not pay back a loan in full they were forced to clear out everything from their home. If the debt still could not be paid off the owner could collect dust from all four corners of the house and cross the threshold. The debtor then turned and face the house with their next of kin gathered behind them. The debtor threw the dust over their shoulder. The person (or persons) that the dust fell upon was then responsible for the payment of the debt. The process continued through the family until the debt was paid. *Chrenecruda* helped secure loans within the Frankish society. It intertwined the loosely gathered tribes and helped to establish government authority. The process made a single person part of a whole group.

The Salic Law exists in two forms: the *Pactus Legis Salicae*, which is near to the original form approved by Clovis, and the *Lex Salica*, which is the edited form approved by Charlemagne. Both are published in the Monumenta Germaniae Historica's *Leges* series.

Lex Ripuaria

In the first half of the 7th century the Ripuarian Franks received the Ripuarian law, a law code applying only to them, from the dominating Salian Franks. The Salians, following the custom of the Romans before them, were mainly re-authorizing laws already in use by the Ripuarians, so that the latter could retain their local constitution.

The law of the Ripuarians contains 89 chapters and falls into three heterogeneous divisions. Chapters 1-31 consist of a scale of compositions; but, although the fines are calculated, not on the unit of 15 *solidi*, as in the Salic Law, but on that of 18 *solidi*, it is clear that this part is already influenced by the Salic Law. Chapters 32-64 are taken directly from the Salic Law; the provisions follow the same arrangement; the unit of the compositions is 15 *solidi*;

but capitularies are interpolated relating to the affranchisement and sale of immovable property. Chapters 65-89 consist of provisions of various kinds, some taken from lost capitularies and from the Salic Law, and others of unknown origin.

The compilation apparently goes back to the reign of Dagobert I (629-639)

Pactus Alamannorum and Lex Alamannorum

Of the laws of the Alamanni, who dwelt between the Rhine and the Lech, and spread over Alsace and what is now Switzerland to the south of Lake Constance, we possess two different texts.

The earlier text, of which five short fragments have come down to us, is known as the *Pactus Alamannorum*, and judging from the persistent recurrence of the expression *et sic convenit*, was most probably drawn up by an official commission. The reference to *aifranchisement in ecciesia* shows that it was composed after the conversion of the Alamanni to Christianity. There is no doubt that the text dates back at least to the reign of the Frankish king Dagobert I, i.e. to the first half of the 7th century.

The later text, known as the *Lex Alamannorum*, dates from a period when Alamannia was independent under national dukes, but recognized the theoretical suzerainty of the Frankish kings. There seems no reason to doubt the St. Gall manuscript, which states that the law had its origin in an agreement between the great Alamannic lords and Duke Lantfrid, who ruled the duchy from 709 to 730.

Leges Langobardorum

We possess a fair amount of information on the origin of the code of laws of the Lombards. The first part, consisting of 388 chapters, also known as the *Edictus Langobardorum*, and was promulgated by King Rothari at a diet held at Pavia on 22 November 643. This work, composed at one time and arranged on a systematic plan, is very remarkable. The compilers knew Roman law, but drew upon it only for their method of presentation and for their terminology; and the document presents Germanic law in its purity. Rothar's edict was augmented by his successors: Grimwald (668) added nine chapters; Liutprand (713-735), fifteen volumes, containing a great number of ecclesiastical enactments; Ratchis (746), eight chapters; and Aistulf (755), thirteen chapters. After the union of the Lombards to the Frankish kingdom, the capitularies made for the entire kingdom were applicable to Italy. There were also special capitularies for Italy, called *Capitula Italica*, some of which were appended to the edict of Rothar.

At an early date, compilations were formed in Italy for the use of legal practitioners and jurists. Eberhard, duke and margrave of Rhaetia and Friuli, arranged the contents of the edict with its successive *additamenta* into a *Concordia de singulis causis* (829-832). In the 10th century a collection was made of
the capitularies in use in Italy, and this was known as the *Capitulare Langobardorum*. Then appeared, under the influence of the school of law at Pavia,
the *Liber legis Langobardorum*, also called *Liber Papiensis* (beginning of 11th
century), and the *Lombarda* (end of 11th century), in two forms, that given in
a Monte Cassino manuscript and known as the *Lombarda Casinensis* and the
Lombarda Vulgata. In some, but not all, manuscripts of the *Liber Papiensis*
each section of the edict is accompanied by specimen pleadings setting out
the cause of action: in this way it comes near to being a treatment of substantive law as opposed to a simple tariff of penalties as found in the other *Leges
barbarorum*

There are editions of the *Edictus*, the *Concordia*, and the *Liber Papiensis* by
F. Bluhme and A. Boretius in the *Monumenta Germaniae Historica* series,
Leges (in folio) vol. iv. Bluhme also gives the rubrics of the *Lombardae*,
which were published by F. Lindenberg in his *Codex legum antiquarum* in
1613. For further information on the laws of the Lombards see J. Merkel,
Geschichte des Langobardenrechts (1850); A. Boretius, *Die Kapitularien im
Langobardenreich* (1864); and C. Kier, *Edictus Rotari* (Copenhagen, 1898).
Cf. R. Dareste in the *Nouvelle Revue historique de droit français et étranger*
(1900, p. 143).

Lombard law, as developed by the Italian jurists, was by far the most sophisticated of the early Germanic systems, and some (e.g. Frederic William Maitland) have seen striking similarities between it and early English law.[1199] It
remained living law, subject to modifications, both in the Kingdom of the
Lombards that became the Carolingian Kingdom of Italy and in the Duchy of
Benevento that became the Kingdom of Naples and continued to play a role in
the latter as late as the 18th century. The *Libri Feudorum*, explaining the distinctive Lombard version of feudalism, were frequently printed together with
the Corpus Juris Civilis and were considered the academic standard for feudal
law, influencing other countries including Scotland.

Lex Baiuvariorum

We possess an important law of the Bavarians, whose duchy was situated in the
region east of the river Lech. Parts of this law have been taken directly from the
Visigothic law of Euric and from the law of the Alamanni. The Bavarian law,
therefore, is later than that of the Alamanni. It dates unquestionably from a
period when the Frankish authority was very strong in Bavaria, when the dukes
were subjects of the Frankish kings. The law's compilation is most commonly

dated between 744 and 748, by the following argument; Immediately after the revolt of Bavaria in 743 the Bavarian Duke Odilo (died 748) was forced to submit to Pippin the Younger and Carloman, the sons of Charles Martel, and to recognize Frankish suzerainty. A little earlier, in 739, the church of Bavaria had been organized by St. Boniface, and the country divided into several bishoprics; and we find frequent references to these bishops (in the plural) in the law of the Bavarians. On the other hand, we know that the law is anterior to the reign of Duke Tassilo III (749-788). The date of compilation must, therefore, be placed between 744 and 748. Against this argument, however, it is very likely that Odilo recognized Frankish authority before 743; he took refuge at Charles Martel's court that year and married one of Martel's daughters. His "revolt" may have been in support of the claims of Pippin and Carloman's half-brother Grifo, not opposition to Frankish rule per se. Also, it is not clear that the Lex Baiuvariorum refers to multiple bishops in the duchy at the same time; when a bishop is accused of a crime, for instance, he is to be tried by the duke, and not by a council of fellow bishops as canon law required. So, it is possible that the Bavarian law was compiled earlier, perhaps between 735 (the year of Odilo's succession) and 739.

Lex Frisionum

The *Lex Frisionum* of the duchy of Frisia consists of a medley of documents of the most heterogeneous character. Some of its enactments are purely pagan, thus one paragraph allows the mother to kill her new-born child, and another prescribes the immolation to the gods of the defiler of their temple; others are purely Christian, such as those that prohibit incestuous marriages and working on Sunday. The law abounds in contradictions and repetitions, and the compositions are calculated in different moneys. From this it appears the documents were merely materials collected from various sources and possibly with a view to the compilation of a homogeneous law. These materials were apparently brought together at the beginning of the 9th century, at a time of intense legislative activity at the court of Charlemagne.

Lex Saxonum

The *Lex Saxonum* has come down to us in two manuscripts and two old editions (those of B. J. Herold and du Tillet), and the text has been edited by Karl von Richthofen in the *Mon. Germ. hist, Leges,* v. The law contains ancient customary enactments of Saxony, and, in the form in which it reached us, is later than the conquest of Saxony by Charlemagne. It is preceded by two capitularies of Charlemagne for Saxony, the *Capitulatio de partibus Saxoniae* (A. Boretius i. 68), which dates undoubtedly from 782, and is characterized by great severity, death being the penalty for every offence against the Christian religion; and the *Capitulare Saxonicum* (A. Boretius i. 71), of the 28 October 797, in which Charlemagne shows less brutality and pronounces simple compositions for misdeeds that formerly warranted death. The *Lex Saxonum* apparently dates from 803, since it contains provisions that are in the *Capitulare legi Ribuariae additum* of that year. The law established the ancient customs, at the same time eliminating anything that was contrary to the spirit of Christianity; it proclaimed the peace of the churches, whose possessions it guaranteed and whose right of asylum it recognized.

External links

> Wikisourcehas the text of a 1911 *Encyclopædia Britannica*article about ***Ancient Germanic law***.

- Leges Romanae barbarorum[1200]
- Volterra Project at UCL[1201]
- Information on the *leges Barbarorum* and the respective manuscript tradition on the *Bibliotheca legum regni Francorum manuscripta*[[*Category:Articles containing Latin-language text*[1202]] *website*], *A database on Carolingian secular law texts (Karl Ubl, Cologne University, Germany, 2012).*

Anglo-Saxon law

Anglo-Saxon law (Old English *ǽ*, later *lagu* "law"; **dōm** "decree, judgment") is a body of written rules and customs that were in place during the Anglo-Saxon period in England, before the Norman conquest. This body of law, along with early Scandinavian law and Germanic law, descended from a family of ancient Germanic custom and legal thought. However, Anglo-Saxon law codes are distinct from other early Germanic legal statements - known as the *leges barbarorum* - in part because they were written in Anglo-Saxon, instead of in Latin. The laws of the Anglo-Saxons were the second in medieval Western Europe after those of the Irish to be expressed in a language other than Latin.

Overview

Inked records of early Germanic law (*leges barbarorum*) were, in many ways, the product of Roman influence. Throughout the early middle ages, as various "Teutonic", or Germanic, tribes on the continent came into closer and

more peaceful contact with the highly institutionalized civilizations surrounding the Mediterranean – chiefly the Roman empire – it was inevitable that they
would be affected by the cultural influences emanating from the south. Many
Germanic tribes and nations subsequently began to imitate the cultural and
institutional facets of Roman civilization. Few of these imitations were so important or had such a profound impact on the nature of "barbarian" life as
the adoption of writing, a technology which spread throughout the Germanic
kingdoms hand-in-hand with Christianity, a religion based on literacy. Up to
this point, the laws, or customs, of the barbarian nations of Northern Europe
were essentially oral: they were occasionally recited publicly, and relied for
their continuation upon word-of-mouth, and the memory, perhaps capricious,
of those whose burden it was to remember them. With writing, however, it
was possible to set the ancient customs of the Northern Europeans into a lasting and more or less fixed form, using ink and parchment. It was a general
trend among the Germanic tribes of Europe that adaptation of the Roman system of writing was soon followed by the production of a national code of laws.
It was inevitable, too, that, in imitating the Roman practice of writing down
law, facets of Roman law and jurisprudence would influence these new Germanic codes. The numerous legal and customary statements which make up
the earliest written Germanic law codes from the continent are testament to the
influences of Roman language and Roman law, as each was written in Latin (a
foreign language) and was often significantly influenced by Byzantine Emperor
Justinian's great legal code.

In Britain, the situation was somewhat different, as Rome had retreated from
the island by about 400 AD, and the native inhabitants who remained were,
for a time, left relatively free of foreign influence. When, in 597 AD, strong
Roman influence again reached the island of Britain (by now in the hands of the
Anglo-Saxons), it was in the form of Christianity, the practitioners of which
brought with them the art of letters, writing, and literacy. It is significant that
it was shortly after the arrival of the first evangelical mission in England, led
by Augustine and sent by Pope Gregory I, the first Anglo-Saxon law code
appeared, issued by Æthelberht, King of Kent. The first six pronouncements
of this code deal solely with sanctions against molesting the property of the
Christian church and its officers, notably demanding twelvefold compensation
for stealing from God's house. In contrast, compensation for stealing from the
king is set at only ninefold.

Writing in the eighth century, the Venerable Bede comments that King Æthelberht, "beside all other benefits that he of wise policy bestowed upon his subjects, appointed them, with his council of wise men, judicial dooms according
to the examples of the Romans." *Iuxta exempla Romanorum* is the Latin phrase
Bede uses here; the meaning of this statement has exercised the curiosity of

historians for centuries. It was not, as with the continental Germanic tribes, that Æthelberht had the law written down in Latin; rather, without precedent, he used his own native language, Old English, to express the "dooms", or laws and judgements, which had force in his kingdom. Some have speculated that "according to the examples of the Romans" simply meant that Æthelberht had decided to cast the law in writing, whereas previously it had always been a matter of unwritten tradition and custom, handed down through generations through oral transmission, and supplemented by the edicts of kings. As such, Æthelberht's law code constitutes an important break in the tradition of Anglo-Saxon law: the body of Kentish legal customs, or at least a portion of them, were now represented by a written statement – fixed, unchanging, no longer subject to the vagaries of memory. Law was now something that could be pointed to and, significantly, disseminated with ease.

Whatever the exact motives for making oral law into written code were, King Æthelberht's law code was the first of a long series of Anglo-Saxon law codes that would be published in England for the next four and a half centuries. Almost without exception, every official version of royal law issued during the Anglo-Saxon period was written in Old English.

Divisions

The various types of secular legal pronouncements which survive from the Anglo-Saxon period can be grouped into three general categories, according to the manner of their publication:

1. Laws and collections of laws promulgated by public authority;
2. Statements of custom
3. Private compilations of legal rules and enactments

Laws and collections of laws promulgated by public authority

To the first division belong the laws of the Kentish kings, Æthelberht, Hlothhere and Eadric, Withraed; those of Ine of Wessex, of Offa (now lost), of Alfred the Great, Edward the Elder, Æthelstan (The *Judicia civitatis Lundoniae* are a guild statute confirmed by King Æthelstan), Edmund I, Edgar, Æthelred and Cnut; the treaty between Alfred and Guthrum and the so-called treaty between Edward and Guthrum.

Statements of Custom

The statements of custom included a great many of the rules entered in collections promulgated by kings; most of the paragraphs of Æthelberht's, Hlothhere's and Eadric's, and Ine's laws, are popular legal customs that have received the stamp of royal authority by their insertion in official codes. On the other hand, from Withraed's and Alfred's laws downwards, the element of enactment by central authority becomes more and more prominent. The kings endeavour, with the help of secular and clerical witan, to introduce new rules and to break the power of long-standing customs (e.g. the precepts about the keeping of holidays, the enactments of Edmund restricting private vengeance, and the solidarity of kindreds as to feuds, and the like). There are, however, no outward signs enabling us to distinguish conclusively between both categories of laws in the codes, nor is it possible to draw a line between permanent laws and personal ordinances of single sovereigns, as has been attempted in the case of Frankish legislation.

Influences

The oldest Anglo-Saxon law codes, especially from Kent and Wessex, reveal a close affinity to the laws of the North Sea peoples—those of the Saxons, Frisians, and Scandinavians. For example, one finds a division of social ranks reminiscent of the threefold gradation of nearby peoples (cf. OE *eorl* "nobleman", *ćeorl* "freeman", *þēow* "bondman", Norse *jarl*, *karl*, *þræll*, Frisian *etheling*, *friling*, *lēt*), and not of the twofold Frankish one (*baro* "freeman", *lætus* "bondman"), nor of the slight differentiation of the Upper Germans and Lombards. In subsequent history there is a good deal of resemblance between the capitularies' legislation of Charlemagne and his successors on one hand, the acts of Alfred, Edward the Elder, Æthelstan and Edgar on the other, a resemblance called forth less by direct borrowing of Frankish institutions than by the similarity of political problems and condition. Frankish law becomes a powerful modifying element in English legal history after the Conquest, when it was introduced wholesale in royal and in feudal courts. The Scandinavian invasions brought in many northern legal customs, especially in the districts thickly populated with Danes. The Domesday survey of Lincolnshire, Nottinghamshire, Yorkshire, Norfolk, etc., shows remarkable deviations in local organization and justice (lagmen, sokes), and great peculiarities as to status (socmen, freemen), while from laws and a few charters we can perceive some influence on criminal law (nidings-vaerk), special usages as to fines (lahslit), the keeping of peace, attestation and sureties of acts (faestermen), etc. But, on the whole, the introduction of Danish and Norse elements, apart from local cases, was more important owing to the conflicts and compromises it called

forth and its social results than on account of any distinct trail of Scandinavian views in English law. The Scandinavian newcomers coalesced easily and
quickly with the native population.

The direct influence of Roman law was not great during the Saxon period: we
notice neither the transmission of important legal doctrines, chiefly through the
medium of Visigothic codes, nor the continuous stream of Roman tradition in
local usage. But indirectly Roman law did exert a by no means insignificant
influence through the medium of the Church, which, for all its apparent insular character, was still permeated with Roman ideas and forms of culture. The
Old English "books" are derived in a roundabout way from Roman models,
and the tribal law of real property was deeply modified by the introduction
of individualistic notions as to ownership, donations, wills, rights of women,
etc. Yet in this respect also the Norman Conquest increased the store of Roman conceptions by breaking the national isolation of the English Church and
opening the way for closer intercourse with France and Italy.

Important features

Folk-right and privilege

The Anglo-Saxon legal system cannot be understood unless one realizes the
fundamental opposition between folk-right and privilege. Folk-right is the ag-
gregate of rules, formulated or latent but susceptible of formulation, which can
be appealed to as the expression of the juridical consciousness of the people at
large or of the communities of which it is composed. It is tribal in its origin,
and differentiated, not according to boundaries between states, but on national
and provincial lines. There may be the folk-right of West and East Saxons, of
East Angles, of Kentish men, Mercians, Northumbrians, Danes, Welshmen,
and these main folk-right divisions remain even when tribal kingdoms disap-
pear and the people are concentrated in one or two realms. The chief centres
for the formulation and application of folk-right were, in the 10th and 11th
centuries, the shire-moots, while the witan of the realm generally placed themselves on the higher ground of State expediency, although occasionally using
folk-right ideas. The older law of real property, of succession, of contracts,
the customary tariffs of fines, were mainly regulated by folk-right; the reeves
employed by the king and great men were supposed to take care of local and
rural affairs according to folk-right. The law had to be declared and applied
by the people itself in its communities, while the spokesmen of the people
were neither democratic majorities nor individual experts, but a few leading
men—the twelve eldest thanes or some similar quorum. Folk-right could, however, be broken or modified by special law or special grant, and the fountain
of such privileges was the royal power. Alterations and exceptions were, as a

matter of fact, suggested by the interested parties themselves, and chiefly by the Church. Thus a privileged land-tenure was created—bookland; the rules as to the succession of kinsmen were set at nought by concession of testamentary power and confirmations of grants and wills; special exemptions from the jurisdiction of the hundreds and special privileges as to levying fines were conferred. In process of time the rights originating in royal grants of privilege overbalanced, as it were, folk-right in many respects, and became themselves the starting-point of a new legal system—the feudal one.

Criminal justice

Anglo-Saxon England did not have a professional standing law enforcement body analogous to modern police. In general, Wikipedia:Citation needed if a crime was committed then there was a victim, and it was up to the victim – or the victim's family – to seek justice. However, after the tenth century there were some changesWikipedia:Citation needed in Anglo-Saxon England. All shires, or counties, were subdivided into hundreds. These hundreds were subdivided into tithings. The three type of division had three types of representatives as well: the tithings had a tithingman, the hundreds a hundredman and the shires a shire-reeve. They met every four weeks.Wikipedia:Citation needed The main function of this group seems to have been administrative: the king spoke to the shire-reeve, the shire-reeve spoke to the hundredmen, and the hundredmen spoke to the tithingmen when giving tasks.Wikipedia:Citation needed Examples of tasks could be, for instance, that legitimate trading was encouraged or that there was no cattle theft.Wikipedia:Citation needed They also dealt with crimes that were against a king's peace. But still the biggest powerWikipedia:Citation needed of seeking justice lay into the hand of the victim or the victim's family.

The judicial functions of the Anglo-Saxon legal system was mainly practiced-Wikipedia:Citation needed by courts. Once a charge had been brought, it had to be heard by a courtWikipedia:Citation needed which would decide whether or not a crime had been committed and, if so, what action was necessary. The hundred court met every 4 weeksWikipedia:Citation needed but the shire court only met twice a year.Wikipedia:Citation needed Lawsuits could be passed on to the shire court if the hundred court was not able to reach a judgement.Wikipedia:Citation needed

The preservation of peace

Another feature of vital importance in the history of Anglo-Saxon law is its tendency towards the preservation of peace. Society is constantly struggling to ensure the main condition of its existence—peace.Wikipedia:Citation needed Already in Æthelberht's legislation we find characteristic fines inflicted for breach of the peace of householders of different ranks—the ceorl, the eorl, and the king himself appearing as the most exalted among them. Peace is considered not so much a state of equilibrium and friendly relations between parties, but rather as the rule of a third within a certain region—a house, an estate, a kingdom. This leads on one side to the recognition of private author-ities—the father's in his family, the master's as to servants, the lord's as to his personal or territorial dependents. On the other hand, the tendency to main-tain peace naturally takes its course towards the strongest ruler, the king, and we witness in Anglo-Saxon law the gradual evolution of more and more strin-gent and complete rules in respect of the king's peace and its infringements. The codices of the early 11th century (Cnut, Aethelred) establish specific con-ditions of guaranteed peace or protection depending on particular limitations in time or place, known as grith, such as *ciric-grið* "church-grith" (right of asylum in a church) or *hand-grið* "hand-grith" (protection under the king's hand).

Legislation

In course of time the natural associations get loosened and intermixed, and this calls forth the elaborate legislation of the later Anglo-Saxon kings. Regulations are issued about the sale of cattle in the presence of witnesses. Enactments about the pursuit of thieves, and the calling in of warrantors to justify sales of chattels, are other expressions of the difficulties attending peaceful intercourse. Personal surety groups appears as a complement of and substitute for more collective responsibility. The hlaford and his hiredmen are an institution not only of private patronage, but also of supervision for the sake of laying hands on malefactors and suspected persons. The landrica assumes the same part in a territorial district. Ultimately the laws of the 10th and 11th centuries show the beginnings of the frankpledge associations, which came influence an important part of the feudal age.

Language and dialect

The English dialect in which the Anglo-Saxon laws have been handed down is in most cases a common speech derived from West Saxon. By the tenth century the West Saxons had become predominant among the Anglo-Saxon kings, and their lands were home to some of the most developed religious and monastic centres on the island. It was such centres which had the wealth, ex-pertise, and motivation, to create and to copy texts for distribution. Therefore, the dialect current in the South – and particularly that of Winchester – became the dominant literary dialect. As most of the surviving Old English law codes are only preserved in copies made during the eleventh century, the West Saxon dialect is predominant. However, traces of the Kentish dialect can be detected in codes copied out in the *Textus Roffensis*, a manuscript containing the earliest Kentish laws. Northumbrian dialectical peculiarities are also noticeable in some codes, while Danish words occur as technical terms in some documents, especially those composed in the eleventh century. With the Norman Conquest, Latin took the place of English as the language of legislation, though many technical terms from English for which Latin did not have an equivalent expression were retained.

References

Editions

- Felix Liebermann, *Die Gesetze der Angelsachsen* (Halle, 1903–1916), 3 vols. with translations, notes and commentary is indispensable. PDFs available online
  - vol. 1 (edition and translation)[1203]
  - vol. 2[1204]. Or separately, first half (dictionary)[1205] and second half (glossary)[1206]
  - vol. 3 (commentary)[1207]
- Lisi Oliver, *The Beginnings of English Law* (Toronto, 2002), text, translation, and commentary for the laws of Aethelbert, Hlohere, Eadric, and Wihtred.
- Reinhold Schmid, *Gesetze der Angelsachsen* (2nd ed., Leipzig, 1858), full glossary.
- Benjamin Thorpe, *Ancient Laws and Institutes of England* (1840), not very trustworthy.
- *Domesday Book*, i. ii. (Rec. Comm.);
- *Codex Diplomaticus Aevi Saxonici*, i.-vi. ed. J. M. Kemble (1839–1848);
- *Cartularium Saxonicum* (up to 940), ed. Walter de Gray Birch (1885–1893);
- John Earle, *A Hand-book to the Land Charters, and other Saxonic Documents.* (Oxford, 1888);
- Benjamin Thorpe, *Diplomatarium Anglicum aevi Saxonici: a collection of English charters ... with a translation of the Anglo-Saxon* (London, 1865)
- Facsimiles of Ancient Charters, edited by the Ordnance Survey and by the British Museum;
- Arthur West Haddan and William Stubbs, *Councils of Great Britain*, i.-iii. (Oxford, 1869–1878).

Modern works

- Konrad Maurer, *Über Angelsachsische Rechtsverhaltnisse, Kritische Ueberschau* (Munich, 1853 ff.), account of the history of Anglo-Saxon law;
- *Essays on Anglo-Saxon Law*, by H. Adams, H. C. Lodge, J. L. Laughlin and E. Young (1876);
- J. M. Kemble, *Saxons in England*;
- F. Palgrave, *History of the English Commonwealth*;
- William Stubbs, *Constitutional History of England*, i.;
- Pollock and Maitland, *History of English Law*, i.;
- H. Brunner, *Zur Rechtsgeschichte der römisch-germanischen Urkunde* (1880);
- Sir Frederick Pollock, *The King's Peace* (Oxford Lectures);
- Frederic Seebohm, *The English Village Community*;
- Frederic Seebohm, *Tribal Custom in Anglo-Saxon Law*;
- Heinrich Marquardsen, *Haft und Burgschaft im Angelsachsischen Recht*;
- Hermann Jastrow, *Über die Strafrechtliche Stellung der Sklaven*, Gierke's *Untersuchungen*, i.;
- J. C. H. R. Steenstrup, *Normannerne*, iv.;
- F. W. Maitland, *Domesday and Beyond* (Cambridge, 1897);
- H. M. Chadwick, *Studies on Anglo-Saxon Institutions* (1905);
- Charles E. Tucker, Jr., "Anglo-Saxon Law: Its Development and Impact on the English Legal System" (USAFA Journal of Legal Studies, 1991)
- P. Vinogradoff, "*Folcland*" in the English Historical Review, 1893;
- P. Vinogradoff, "*Romanistische Einflusse im Angelsächsischen Recht: Das Buchland*" in the Mélanges Fitting, 1907;
- P. Vinogradoff, "*The Transfer of Land in Old English Law*" in the Harvard Law Review, 1907.
- ⓦ This article incorporates text from a publication now in the public domain: Vinogradoff, Paul (1911). "Anglo-Saxon Law". In Chisholm, Hugh. *Encyclopædia Britannica*. **2** (11th ed.). Cambridge University Press. pp. 35–38.

Further reading

- Jay Paul Gates and Nicole Marafioti, eds. 2014. *Capital and Corporal Punishment in Anglo-Saxon England*. Woodbridge: Boydell & Brewer. ISBN 9781843839187.
- *Alfred the Great: Asser's life of King Alfred and other Contemporary sources* (1983) Simon Keynes and Michael Lapidge. Penguin Classics.

External links

- Medieval Sourcebook: The Anglo-Saxon Dooms, 560-975[1208]
- Medieval Sourcebook: Medieval legal history[1209]
- Laws of Alfred and Ine[1210] (georgetown.edu)
- Anglo-Saxon Law: Its Development and Impact on the English Legal System[1211] (Charles Tucker, USAFA Journal of Legal Studies)

Lex mercatoria

Lex mercatoria (from the Latin for "merchant law"), often referred to as "the Law Merchant" in English, is the body of commercial law used by merchants throughout Europe during the medieval period. It evolved similar to English common law as a system of custom and best practice, which was enforced through a system of merchant courts along the main trade routes. It functioned as the international law of commerce.[1212] It emphasised contractual freedom and alienability of property, while shunning legal technicalities and deciding cases *ex aequo et bono*. A distinct feature was the reliance by merchants on a legal system developed and administered by them. States or local authorities seldom interfered, and did not interfere a lot in internal domestic trade. Under *lex mercatoria* trade flourished and states took in large amounts of taxation.

In the last years new theories had changed the understanding of this medieval treatise considering it as proposal for legal reform or a document used for instructional purposes. These theories consider that the treatise cannot be described as a body of laws applicable in its time, but the desire of a legal scholar to improve and facilitate the litigation between merchants. The text is composed by 21 sections and an annex. The sections described procedural matters such as the presence of witnesses and the relation between this body of law and common law. It has been considered as a false statement to define this as a system exclusively based in custom, when there are structures and elements from the existent legal system, such as Ordinances and even concepts proper of the Romano-canonical procedure.

History

The *lex mercatoria* was originally a body of rules and principles laid down by merchants to regulate their dealings. It consisted of rules and customs common to merchants and traders in Europe, with some local variation. It originated from the need for quick and effective jurisdiction, administered by specialised courts. The guiding spirit of the merchant law was that it ought to derive from commercial practice, respond to the needs of the merchants, and be comprehensible and acceptable to the merchants who submitted to it. International commercial law today owes some of its fundamental principles to the *lex mercatoria*. This includes choice of arbitration institutions, procedures, applicable law and arbitrators, and the goal to reflect customs, usage and good practice among the parties.

Goods and services flowed freely during the medieval merchant law, thus generating more wealth for all involved. It is debated whether the law was uniform in nature, was spontaneous as a method of dispute resolution, or applied equally to everyone who subordinated to it. The *lex mercatoria* was also a means for local communities to protect their own markets. Local kings or lords extracted taxes and set trade restrictions. In 1303 Edward I issued the Carta Mercatoria, a charter to foreign merchants in England, which guaranteed them freedom to trade, with certain protections and exemption under the law. Although the charter was revoked by Edward II, due to complaints by English merchants, foreign merchants retained most of their rights in practice, but these would vary widely with the march of time, events and changes to state policy.

Administration

The *lex mercatoria* was the product of customs and practices among traders, and could be enforced through the local courts. However, the merchants needed to solve their disputes rapidly, sometimes on the hour, with the least costs and by the most efficient means. Public courts did not provide this. A trial before the courts would delay their business, and that meant losing money. The *lex mercatoria* provided quick and effective justice. This was possible through informal proceedings, with liberal procedural rules. The *lex mercatoria* rendered proportionate judgements over the merchants' disputes, in light of "fair price", good commerce, and equity.

Judges were chosen according to their commercial background and practical knowledge. Their reputation rested upon their perceived expertise in merchant trade and their fair-mindedness. Gradually, a professional judiciary developed through the merchant judges. Their skills and reputation would however still rely upon practical knowledge of merchant practice. These characteristics serve as important measures in the appointment of international commercial arbitrators today.

The *lex mercatoria* owed its origin to the fact that the civil law was not sufficiently responsive to the growing demands of commerce, as well as to the fact that trade in pre-medieval times was practically in the hands of those who might be termed cosmopolitan merchants, who wanted a prompt and effective jurisdiction. It was administered for the most part in special courts, such as those of the guilds in Italy, or the fair courts of Germany and France, or as in England, in courts of the Staple or Piepowder.

Legal concepts

The *lex mercatoria* was composed of such usages and customs as were common to merchants and traders in all parts of Europe, varied slightly in different localities by special peculiarities. Less procedural formality meant speedier dispensation of justice, particularly when it came to documentation and proof. Out of practical need, the medieval *lex mercatoria* originated the "writing obligatory". By this, creditors could freely transfer the debts owed to them. The "writing obligatory" displaced the need for more complex forms of proof, as it was valid as a proof of debt, without further proof of; transfer of the debt; powers of attorney; or a formal bargain for sale. The *lex mercatoria* also strengthened the concept of party autonomy: whatever the rules of the *lex mercatoria* were, the parties were always free to choose whether to take a case to court, what evidence to submit and which law to apply.

Reception

Merchant law declined as a cosmopolitan and international system of merchant justice towards the end of medieval times. This was to a large extent due to the adoption of national commercial law codes. It was also connected with an increasing modification of local customs to protect the interests of local merchants. The result of the replacement of *lex mercatoria* codes with national governed codes was the loss of autonomy of merchant tribunals to state courts. The main reason for this development was the protection of state interests.

The nationalisation of the *lex mercatoria* did not neglect the practises of merchants or their trans-border trade. Some institutions continued to function, and state judges also were appointed for their merchant expertise, just as modern commercial arbitrators. The laws of the merchants were not eradicated, but simply codified. National codes built on the principles laid down by trade commercial practise and to a large extent they embodied *lex mercatoria* substantial rules. This was for example the case in France. The Code Commercial was issued in 1807, where *lex mercatoria* rules were preserved to govern formation, performance and termination of contracts. In effect, the nation states reconstituted the *lex mercatoria* in their image.

Common law development

English courts applied merchant customs only if they were "certain" in nature, "consistent with law" and "in existence since time immemorial." English judges also required that merchant customs were proven before the court. But even as early as 1608, Chief Justice Edward Coke described *lex mercatoria* as "a part of the common law," and William Blackstone would later concur.[1213] The tradition continued especially under Lord Mansfield, who is said to be the father of English commercial law. Precepts of the *lex mercatoria* were also kept alive through equity and the admiralty courts in maritime affairs. In the US, traditions of the *lex mercatoria* prevailed in the general principles and doctrines of commercial jurisprudence.

The history of the *lex mercatoria* in England is divided into three stages: the first prior to the time of Coke, when it was a special kind of law – as distinct from the common law – administered in special courts for a special class of the community (i.e. the mercantile); the second stage was one of transition, the *lex mercatoria* being administered in the common law courts, but as a body of customs, to be proved as a fact in each individual case of doubt; the third stage, which has continued to the present day, dates from the presidency over the king's bench of Lord Mansfield (q.v.), under whom it was moulded into the mercantile law of to-day. To the *lex mercatoria* modern English law owes the fundamental principles in the law of partnership, negotiable instruments and trade marks.

Sir John Holt (Chief Justice 1689 to 1710) and Lord Mansfield (Chief Justice, 1756 to 1788) were the leading proponents of incorporating the *lex mercatoria* into the common law. Holt did not complete the task, possibly out of his own conservatism (see *Clerke v Martin*[1214]) and it was Lord Mansfield that became known as the 'founder of the commercial law of this country" (Great Britain).[1215] Whilst sitting in Guildhall, Lord Mansfield created,

> *a body of substantive commercial law, logical, just, modern in character and at the same time in harmony with the principles of the common law. It was due to Lord Mansfield's genius that the harmonisation of commercial custom and the common law was carried out with an almost complete understanding of the requirements of the commercial community, and the fundamental principles of the old law and that that marriage of idea proved acceptable to both merchants and lawyers.*[1216]

- Statute of Merchants 1285 (11 Edw I and 13 Edw I) aka "Statute of Acton Burnell"

Figure 36: *Lord Mansfield was a champion of fusing lex mercatoria with the common law.*

International commercial law and arbitration

Lex mercatoria precepts have been reaffirmed in new international mercantile law. National trade barriers are torn down in order to induce commerce. The new commercial law is grounded on commercial practice directed at market efficiency and privacy. Dispute resolution has also evolved, and functional methods like international commercial arbitration is now available. These developments have also attracted the interest of empirical sociology of law[1217]The principles of the medieval *lex mercatoria* – efficiency, party autonomy, and choice of arbitrator – are applied, and arbitrators often render judgements based on customs. The new merchant law encompasses a huge body of international commercial law.

Present and future commercial law

In summary, nation states somewhat fragmented the medieval *lex mercatoria* but it is far from destroyed. Local interests triumphed in the medieval ages, just as national interests do today. A modern variant of the *lex mercatoria* is the evolving law and dispute resolution in cyberspace. Internet traders are the fastest growing body of merchants in history. Parties can solve domain-name disputes online expeditiously and quickly. In a virtual court documents are filed and examined online, arguments are made online and decisions are published online – seldom challenged before traditional courts of law. ICANN's UDRP (and its proposals for Rapid Suspension) and Nominet's DRS are examples of this. The medieval, the modern and cyberspace merchant laws face comparable issues of enforceability. They solve the problems somewhat differently, but the reaction of the market is the main incentive to comply with a ruling.

Further, *lex mercatoria* is sometimes used in international disputes between commercial entities. Most often those disputes are decided by arbitrators which sometimes are allowed (explicitly of implied) to apply *lex mercatoria* principles.[1218] Therefore, some legal practitioners assume that there is a whole set of legal principles named "*lex mercatoria*" in international or transnational commercial law. The most recent and constantly updated set of rules are the *TransLex Principles* collected and formulated by Klaus Peter Berger (University of Cologne) and his Center for Transnational Law.

What remains of *lex mercatoria* precepts today is a qualified faith in self-regulation by merchants, and a reluctance to surrender the efficiencies of merchant practice to state confinement.

References

- JH Baker, 'The Law Merchant and the Common Law' (1979) 38 Cambridge Law Journal 295
- JS Rogers, *The Early History of the Law of Bills and Notes* (1995) chapter 1
- WH Hamilton, 'The Ancient Maxim Caveat Emptor' (1931) 50 Yale Law Journal 133, who shows that *caveat emptor* never had any place in Roman law, or civil law, or *lex mercatoria* and was probably a mistake when implemented into the common law.
- C Gross and H Hall (eds), Selden Society, *Select Cases on the Law Merchant* (1908–32)
- Basil, Bestor, Coquillette and Donahue, *Lex Mercatoria and Legal Pluralism: A Late Thirteenth Century Treatise and Its Afterlife* (1998)
- G Malynes, *Consuetudo vel lex mercatoria* (London, 1622)[1219]
- W Mitchell, *The Early History of the Law Merchant* (Cambridge, 1904)
- John William Smith, *Mercantile Law* (ed. Hart and Simey, 1905).
- Wyndham Beawes, *Lex Mercatoria: Or, A Complete Code of Commercial Law*, F. C. and J. (Rivington, 1813)

External links

- The Lex Mercatoria on-line[1220]
- The 'Law Merchant' and the Fair Court of St. Ives, 1270–1324 by Stephen Edward Sachs[1221]
- Boudreaux on Law and Legislation[1222] Podcast on law vs. legislation, including modern applications of *lex mercatoria* and economic theory. EconTalk at Econlib
- Trans-Lex, a research and codification platform for transnational law / *lex mercatoria*[1223]
- Gesa Baron: *Do the UNIDROIT Principles of International Commercial Contracts form a new lex mercatoria?*[1224]
- Bernard Audit: *The Vienna Sales Convention and the Lex Mercatoria*[1225]
- CISG (text)[1226]
- History and current implications of Lex mercatoria[1227]

Early Irish law

Early Irish law, also called **Brehon law**, comprised the statutes which governed everyday life in Early Medieval Ireland. They were partially eclipsed by the Norman invasion of 1169, but underwent a resurgence from the 13th until the 17th centuries, over the majority of the island, survived into Early Modern Ireland in parallel with English law.[1228] Early Irish law was often, although not universally, referred to within the law texts as *Fenechas*, the law of the *Feni* or free men of Gaelic Ireland mixed with Christian influence and juristic innovation. These secular laws existed in parallel, and occasionally in conflict, with canon law throughout the early Christian period.

The laws were a civil rather than a criminal code, concerned with the payment of compensation for harm done and the regulation of property, inheritance and contracts; the concept of state-administered punishment for crime was foreign to Ireland's early jurists. They show Ireland in the early medieval period to have been a hierarchical society, taking great care to define social status, and the rights and duties that went with it, according to property, and the relationships between lords and their clients and serfs.

The secular legal texts of Ireland were edited by D. A. Binchy in his six-volume *Corpus Iuris Hibernici*. The oldest surviving law tracts date from the 8th century.

Figure 37: *Redwood Castle, County Tipperary, although built by the Normans, was later occupied by the MacEgan juristic family and served as a school of Irish law under them*

Origins

Irish law represents possibly the oldest surviving codified legal system in Europe, and is believed to have Proto-Indo-European origins in common with the Hindu Laws of Manu. However, no single theory as to the origin of early Irish law is universally accepted.

Early Irish law consisted of the accumulated decisions of the Brehons, or judges, guided entirely by an oral tradition. Some of these laws were recorded in text form by Christian clerics. The earliest theory to be recorded is contained in the Prologue to the *Senchas Már*. According to that text, after a difficult case involving St. Patrick, the Saint supervised the mixing of native Irish law and the law of the church. A representative of every group came and recited the law related to that group and they were written down and collected into the *Senchas Már*, excepting that any law that conflicted with church law was replaced. The story also tells how the law transitioned from the keeping of the poets, whose speech was "dark" and incomprehensible, to the keeping of each group who had an interest in it. The story is extremely dubious as, not only is it written many centuries after the events it depicts, but it also incorrectly dates the collection of the *Senchas Már* to the time of St. Patrick while scholars have been able to determine that it was collected during the 8th century, at least three centuries after the time of St. Patrick.[1229] Some of the ideas in the tale may be correct, and it has been suggested by modern historians that the Irish jurists were an offshoot from the poetic class that had preserved the laws.

For some time, especially through the work of D. A. Binchy, the laws were held to be conservative and useful primarily for reconstructing the laws and customs of the Proto-Indo-Europeans just as linguists had reconstructed the Proto-Indo-European language. For instance, historians have seen similarities between Irish and Indian customs of fasting as a method of shaming a wrong-doer to recover a debt, or to demand the righting of a wrong.[1230] Other legal institutions prominent in early Irish law but foreign to most contemporary legal systems, such as the use of sureties, have been considered as survivals from earlier periods.[1231] More recently historians have come to doubt such attributions. While few historians argue that all Irish law comes from church influence, they are today much more wary as to what material is a survival and what has changed. A past may still be suggested for a certain legal concept based on Irish legal terms' being cognate with terms in other Celtic languages, although that information does not prove that the practice described by the legal term has not changed.[1232]

Today, the legal system is assumed to contain some earlier law influenced by the church, and adaptation through methods of reasoning the Irish jurists would have sanctioned. There is dispute, however, as to just how large a role each of these aspects may have played in creating the legal texts. The subject is an important scope for debate.[1233] There is, however, one area where scholars have found material that is clearly old. A number of legal terms have been shown to have originated in the period before the Celtic Languages split up because they are preserved in both Old Irish and in the Welsh legal texts. On the other hand, this is not regarded as unquestionable evidence that the practices described by such terms are unchanged or even have their origins in the same period as do the terms.

Another important aspect when considering the origins is that the early Irish law texts are not always consistent. Early Irish law is, like the Old Irish language, remarkably standard across an Island with no central authority. However, close examination has revealed some variations. Among these one can especially point to variations both in style and content between two of the major legal schools, as they are known; those that produced the *Bretha Nemed* and *Senchas Már* respectively.[1234]

Substantive law

Women and marriage

Women, like men, were Brehons. Brehon Laws have a reputation among modern scholars as rather progressive in their treatment of women, with some describing the law as providing for equality between the sexes. However, the Laws generally portray a patriarchal and patrilineal society in which the rules of inheritance were based on agnatic descent. It has sometimes been assumed that the patriarchal elements of the law are the result of influence by canon law or continental practice displacing an older, more egalitarian ancient Celtic tradition, but this is based mainly on conjecture and there is little hard evidence to support such claims.[1235]

Cáin Adomnáin, a Christian Law, promulgated by the Synod of Birr in 697, sought to raise the status of women of that era, although the actual effect is unknown.[1236] Regardless, although Irish society under the Brehon Laws was male-dominated, women had greater freedom, independence and rights to property than in other European societies of the time. Men and women held their property separately. The marriage laws were very complex. For example, there were scores of ways of combining households and properties and then dividing the property and its increase when disputes arose. Wikipedia:Citation needed

Divorce was provided for on a number of grounds (e.g. impotence or homosexuality on the husband's part), after which property was divided according to what contribution each spouse had made to the household. A husband was legally permitted to hit his wife to "correct" her, but if the blow left a mark she was entitled to the equivalent of her bride-price in compensation and could, if she wished, divorce him. Property of a household could not be disposed of without the consent of both spouses.

However, under Western Catholic church law, women were still largely subject to their fathers or husbands and were not normally permitted to act as witnesses, their testimony being considered "biased and dishonest".[1237]

Kingship

While scholars have discovered a fair amount of information about how Irish Kingship worked, relatively little is actually related by early Irish laws. In particular, very little material survives regarding succession practices, which have been reconstructed as the system of Tanistry. A section of the *Senchas Már* tract on status was apparently devoted to succession, although little survives. Most early material on succession was collected by Domnal O'Davoren in the 16th century.[1238] Another seemingly important omission is that the laws never mention the High King of Ireland centred at Tara.[1239] Likewise, the laws only once mention the practice of individuals being ineligible for kingship if they are blemished (a practice more widely evident elsewhere, especially in Irish mythology). However, that mention is only incidental to a regulation on the compensation for bee stings when the legal tract *Bechbretha* relates the story of Congal Cáech, who was deposed on account of being blinded by a bee.[1240]

A fair amount of the material on kings relates to their position within the Irish laws of status, which see, of which the king is ranked at the top, parallel with the Bishops and the highest level of poets. Three levels of kings are referred to in the status tracts, such as *Críth Gablach*: *rí benn*, (the king of peaks) who is identified elsewhere as the *rí túaithe* (king of a [single] *túath*), who is below the *rí buiden* (the king of bands) who is identified with the *rí túath* (king of [multiple] *túaths*) or *ruiri* (overking), who in turn is below the *rí bunaid cach cinn* (the ultimate king of every individual) who is known also as the *rí ruirech* (king of overkings) and *rí cóicid* (king of a province).[1241]

To a certain degree, kings acted as agents of the law. However, while other kings in Europe were able to promulgate law, such as Alfred the Great and his Doom book, the Irish had very little authority to do so. They could collaborate on law authored by the church. *Cáin Adomnáin* has the names of many kings attached to it who apparently enacted and enforced the law. Additionally, a king could issue a temporary law in times of emergency. But kings could not, by their own authority, issue permanent law codes.[1242] Kings also acted as judges, although the extent of their power compared to that of professional jurists has been debated. One law tract, *Gubretha Caratniad*, describes a *brithem* giving advice to a king (in this case, advice that seems flawed but is actually correct) who then gives it as judgment in a case. It is unclear, therefore, how much kings made judgments by themselves and how much they had to follow professional advice. It is clear, however, that a king had to judge in accordance with the laws. However, the kings do not appear to have stood as judges in all cases, and in some cases the professional jurists took that role.[1243]

One subject the laws *did* cover is how the king fit within the rest of the legal system. The king was not supposed to be above the law. In fact, some stipulations applied specifically to the king. However, as the king was the most powerful individual, and the one with the highest honour in an area, it was difficult to enforce the law against him. Although it might have been possible to proceed against the king as against any other, the laws also had an innovative solution to this quandary. Instead of enforcing against the king directly, a dependent of the king known as an *aithech fortha* (substitute churl) was enforced against instead, and the king was responsible for repaying the substitute churl.[1244] The laws also specified certain cases in which a king lost his honour price. These included doing the work of a commoner, moving around without a retinue, and showing cowardice in battle; again, though, it is unclear how often such stipulations were followed.

Finally, the laws commented on how the king was to arrange his life and holdings and how many individuals should be in his retinue. In particular, *Críth Gablach* gives a highly schematised and unrealistic account of how the king spends his week: Sunday is for drinking ale, Monday is for judging, Tuesday is for playing fidchell, Wednesday is for watching hounds hunt, Thursday is for sexual union, Friday is for racing horses, and Saturday is for judging (a different word from Monday, but the distinction is unclear).[1245]

Status

According to the introduction to the *Senchas Már*, the world had numerous problems before the creation of that text. Among those problems was that everyone was in a state of equality. Unequal status was of great import to early Irish Christian society and it is recorded in many places in the early Irish laws.

The Irish law texts describe a highly segmented world, in which each person had a set status that determined what legal tasks they could undertake and what recompense they could receive when a crime was committed against them. *Críth Gablach* and *Uraicecht Becc* are two of the main texts focusing on lay landholders, the latter of which also briefly covers the status of skilled individuals and of clerics.[1246] Other texts describe other groups, such as *Uraicecht na Ríar*, which focuses on the status of poets.

Much depended on status, and each rank was assigned an honour that was quantified in an honour-price to be paid to them if their honour was violated by certain crimes. The types of food one received as a guest in another's house, or while being cared for due to injury varied based on status. Lower honour-prices limited the ability to act as sureties and as witnesses. Those of higher status could "over-swear" the oaths of those of lower status.[1247]

Ecclesiastical grades

In part, the seven ecclesiastical grades originate outside Ireland (as holy orders, later subdivided into minor orders and major orders) although their position in Ireland has been shaped by local thinking. The grades are given in *Uraicecht Becc* as *liachtor* (lector), *aistreóir* (doorkeeper), *exarcistid* (exorcist), *subdeochain* (sub-deacon), *deochain* (deacon), *sacart* (priest), and *escop* (bishop)[1248] although *Bretha Déin Chécht* puts the lector in a third position. The seven grades are subsumed into the Irish law of status, but it is unclear to what degree they conformed to all of the various status stipulations. It may be noted however that, according to *Críth Gablach*, the seven grades of the church are the basis for the theoretical seven lay and poetic grades (see below). At the same time it is clear that the number seven is an insular invention, in the Eastern Church there were normally five or six grades (sometimes more), and the Western Church typically had eight or nine grades.[1249]

Although the various groups were theoretically on par with each other, the church apparently had supremacy. *Críth Gablach* states "Who is nobler, the king or the bishop? The bishop is nobler, for the king rises up before him on account of the Faith; moreover the bishop raises his knee before the king."[1250] This relative ranking is reflected elsewhere. In addition, according to *Críth Gablach* the ranking of the lay grades was modelled after the ecclesiastical grades in that there should be seven grades, a number rarely met perfectly.

Lay grades

Irish law recognised a number of classes, from unfree to king, which were ranked within the status tracts. Little space was given to the unfree, which reflects the lack of dependence upon slaves as opposed to other societies, such as Ancient Rome. However, the laws discuss slaves, both male and female, and the term for a female slave, *Cumhall*, became a broader currency term. As unfree, slaves could not be legal agents either for themselves or others.[1251] In addition to the wholly unfree, a few individuals were semi-free. The *senchléithe* (hereditary serf) was bound to work the land of his master, whereas the *fuidir* had no independent status nor land of his own, but could at least leave as he might desire.[1252]

Others might be of less than full status, based on age or origin. The status of children was based on their parents, and they could not act independently. The rights of sons increased with age, but they did not fully increase until after the death of the father. A young son just out on his own was called a *fer midboth* (a man of middle huts), apparently someone who occupied a hut on his father's land. These persons were semi-independent, but did not have the full honour-price of a free man until they reached 20.[1253] Even after a certain age, a "Son of a Living Father" was expected to be dutiful to his father and could only set up an independent household with his father's permission.[1254] In addition, those from outside a *túath* normally had a low status, as status was based not only on property but also on familial connections.[1255]

There are two main ranks of commoners, the *ócaire* (lit. young lord) and *bóaire* (cow lord), though Binchy thinks the *ócaire* is a recent offshoot of the latter, who had less property but was still a freeman. In addition are the *bóaire febsa* (a *bóaire* of quality who had an honour-price of 5 *séts*). The highest commoner was the *mruigfer* (land man). Either of the last, according to Binchy, may be the "normal *bóaire* who appears within the law texts.[1256] The three ranks of commoners, at least according to the status tract, vary in the type of clientship they undertook and the property they could hold, though it is unclear how this worked in practice. Commoners apparently had to co-operate in farming as they did not have enough property to own a whole plough-share or all the rights in a mill.

Above these are a series of lords who apparently had clients of their own—the primary factor in lordship—as well as more property and a higher honour-price. According to *Críth Gablach*, each grade of lord increase by 5 *séts* for each rank, and also increased the number of clients. In addition, when they travelled they were expected to maintain a retinue with them. A lord not only had greater ability, but also needed to take greater steps to preserve their honour, lest they lose their lordship. The order of lords varies, but in *Críth Gablach* it is as follows: *aire déso* (lord of vassals), *aire ard* (high lord), *aire tuíseo* (lord of precedence), and the *aire forgill* (lord of superior testimony).

After the normal lords was the *tánaise ríg*, who was supposed to be heir to the throne. He had higher property qualifications than the *aire forgill*, but his prime claim to higher status was that he would one day be king. Kings held the highest status that the laws describe. The basic king had an honour price of seven *cumals*, and higher kings had yet a higher status. Having the highest status, the king especially was expected to be careful to keep his honour. Cowardice, as demonstrated in flight from battle, as well as taking up manual labour might cost him his honour-price.[1257]

These grades are generally equated with the seven grades of clerics, although there is some discrepancy as to how the grades line up, with various texts doing it in different ways and selecting only certain lay grades and ignoring others.

The ranking of lay grades has been seen by many scholars as rather schematic and not reflecting realities on the ground. Some of the texts give considerable detail on diet, tools owned, number of livestock, and even the size of house a person of a given status had. Modern scholars have generally assumed such details rarely match exactly what someone of a given rank had. In addition, *Críth Gablach* contains the fee a client paid to a lord, according to rank from the lowest free man through the noble ranks, even though no noble would be another's client.[1258]

Poetic grades

Paralleling the status of the lay grades are the grades of the *filid* (poets). Each poetic rank corresponds to a particular lay (and ecclesiastical) rank, from *Bóaire* to king. In *Uraicecht na Ríar* these are given as *fochloc*, *macfuirmid*, *dos*, *cano*, *clí*, *ánruth*, and *ollam*.[1259] These are given the same status as and the same honour prices as the lay grades, and hence have effectively the same rights. The qualifications for each grade is where the difference occurs. The qualifications fit into three categories, the status of the poet's parent or grand-parent, their skill and their training. Particular number of compositions are given for each rank, with the *ollam* having 350.

In addition to the seven main ranks, variously named ranks below these seem to be names for unskilled poets, the *taman*, *drisiuc*, and *oblaires*. Their honour prices are no more than a pittance, and their poetry is apparently painful to hear.[1260]

Other grades

Other professions could give status based on the profession and the skill, but no professions besides poets could have a status as high as the bishop, king, or highest poet. For instance in one text the jurist or *brithem* had three ranks, and the highest was given an honour price only halfway up the other scales. The ranking of a *brithem* was based on his skill and whether he knew all three components of law (here: traditional law, poetry, and canon law), or fewer. A craftsman who worked with wood could have similar honour-prices but these were based on his craftsmanship. However, a physician and a blacksmith, among other ranks, had an even lower honour-price—less than half what the *brithem* could achieve, and the honour-price apparently did not vary based on skill. Other professionals, such as makers of chariots or engravers, had still lower honour-prices (less than that of a *bóaire*). Finally a few professions re-ceived only meagre ranks, as with the lowest poets, and the authors may be actively making fun of some of the professions, such as comb makers.[1261]

Change in status

Status in early Ireland was not entirely rigid and it was possible for a family to raise its status. If three consecutive generations—grandfather, father, and son—had the property qualifications of a lord, or the poetic qualifications of a higher level poet, etc., then the member of the third generation became a lord. On the other hand, the son or grandson of a lord, or a poet, etc., who did not have the proper qualifications, did not have that status. However, the grandson of a person with a certain status could have that status themselves, assuming they had the proper qualifications, even if their father did not.

This created an interesting in-between stage. A commoner who had the prop-erty qualifications but not the parentage to become a lord is variously referred to as a *flaith aithig*, (a commoner lord), a *fer fothlai* (a man of withdrawal), or an *aire iter da airig* (an *aire* [here with a broader meaning than lord] between two [types of] *aires*). According to *Críth Gablach*, these individuals had status in between a commoner and a full lord.[1262] In the case of poets, a poet with skill qualifications but who did not have proper training was a bard. (However, it has been suggested that poets who were not allied with the church were given this rank for that reason).[1263]

In addition, there were ways that, in extraordinary circumstance, an individual could achieve higher status without having parents with such qualifications. Someone who chose to become a *briugu* (hospitaller) could have twice the normal property qualifications of a lord of whatever grade (and this can extend, in theory, up to the qualifications of a king). Further, a *briugu* had to open his house to any guests. This included feeding them, no matter how large the group—he could lose his status if he ever refused a guest.[1264] Because of that stipulation, the position of *briugu* was potentially ruinous, and this outcome is portrayed in a number of tales such as in *Togail Bruidne Da Derga* and *Scela Mucce Meic Datho*. A commoner might also ascend to the status of a lord if he is a *aire échta* (lord of violence). Such a person helped individuals to avenge deaths committed in another *túath* for a limited time after the cessation of hostilities, although the details are unclear.[1265] A poet who had the skill and training of a rank, but not the proper familial qualifications received half the honour price that his skill and training otherwise earned.[1266]

Clientship

A member of the property-owning classes could advance himself by becoming a "free client" of a more powerful lord, somewhat akin to the Roman system of clientship. The lord made his client a grant of property (sometimes land, but more usually livestock) for a fixed period of time. The client owed service to his lord, and at the end of the grant period returned the grant with interest. Any increase beyond the agreed interest was his to keep. This allowed for a certain degree of social mobility as an astute free client could increase his wealth until he could afford clients of his own, thus becoming a lord.

A poorer man could become a "base client" by selling a share in his honour-price, making his lord entitled to part of any compensation due him. The lord could make him a smaller grant of land or livestock, for which the client paid rent in produce and manual labour. A man could be a base client to several lords simultaneously.

Physical injury

On account of the structure of early Irish society, all law was essentially civil and offenders had to answer only to the victim or the victim's representative. This is important to point out, as in case of serious injury it is in stark contrast to most modern legal systems.

Payment for wounding

Although early Irish law recognised a distinction between intentional and unintentional injury, any type of injury was still normally unlawful and requiring compensation. The main exception is injuries received when the victim has gone into a place where injury is likely. In all other cases an injurer was responsible for paying a fine. The legal text *Bretha Déin Chécht* "The Judgments of Dían Cécht" goes into considerable detail in describing the fines based on the location of the wound, the severity, and in some cases the type.[1267]

According to that text, the payment was decided by a physician after nine days. Prior to that, the victim was cared for by his family and a physician. Some suggest that effects of the wound would be clear to a physician at that point if not before. First, either the victim would have died if such was likely, or it would be clear that the patient was in danger. If the first was the case, the injurer had to face punishment for murder, and in the second he had to pay a heavy fine called a *crólige báis*, "blood-lying of death."[1268] If the victim had recovered but his wound was still present, it was measured and a fine paid. *Bretha Déin Chécht* describes that the wound was measured according to how many grains of a certain plant fit in the wound. The higher status one was, the smaller the grain used. Thus, there are nine grains mentioned in the text, from a grain of wheat to a bean.[1269] If the wound did not heal, and thus the physical blemish was a problem for the victim's honour, further payments were required.[1270]

Early Irish law saw certain locations, known as the "twelve doors of the soul" were considered particularly severe. It has been suggested that this is because the potential for such wounds to turn deadly, although the law texts do not suggest any reason. In such cases the physician was entitled to a greater share of the fine—one half. Similarly, if the wound is one of "the seven principal bone-breakings," or if it causes constant vomiting or bloody urine the physician also received a greater fee.

Sick maintenance

If it seemed that the patient would recover but still needed nursing, the injurer was responsible for that. This was known as sick maintenance, rendering variously *crólige*, *folog n-othrusa*, *folog*, or *othrus* in different texts. *Bretha Crólige* goes into great detail about this process, describing how the injurer had to find a suitable location and move the victim. Then the injurer had to pay for food for the victim and a retinue—which could be considerable depending on the victim's rank.[1271] The injurer also had to provide someone to fulfill the victim's duties while he was incapacitated. He also had to pay a fine for the missed opportunity for procreation if appropriate.[1272]

Bretha Crólige also goes into the importance of keeping a proper environment for the victim during his sick-maintenances. Largely this means that anything that might cause loud noise was prohibited in the vicinity. This included fights by men as well as by dogs, the playing of games and even the disciplining of children.[1273]

However, it is also clear from the law tracts that the practice of Sick Maintenance was being discarded. Thus, while *Críth Gablach* mentions some of what each individual is entitled to while being nursed according to his rank, it also mentions that the practice was no longer in use, and instead an additional fine encompassed the same provisions the injurer would have had to pay for under sick maintenance.[1274] *Bretha Crólige* does not mention anything about the practice being obsolete. However, it does mention that certain types of person could not be maintained because of the difficulty in doing so. Thus it was very hard to provision those of the highest rank and obviously impossible to find a substitute to do their work. Certain professionals could similarly be difficult. On the other hand, a number of persons could cause difficulty to the people maintaining the victim. Such troublesome individuals included the insane and women likely to cause trouble for those nursing them.[1275]

Murder and avoidance of capital punishment

Early Ireland has the distinction of being one of the first areas to shun capital punishment. While a murderer might be killed for his/her crime, this was the option of last resort. Instead the murderer typically had to pay two fines. One is the fixed *éraic* or *cró*, that is either a "body fine" or a "wergild", and the other is the *Log nEnech*, an honour price owed to the kin of the victim that varied according to the status of the kinsman to whom it was owed and the closeness of his relationship to the victim. Should the murderer be unable to pay by himself, his family was normally responsible for paying any amount the murderer could not pay. Should the family be either unable or unwilling to pay, the victim's family took custody of the murderer. At this point, the victim's family had three options. They could await payment, sell the murderer into slavery, or kill the murderer. Even then, the monetary possibilities may have discouraged capital punishment in some cases. In certain cases, though, where the murderer and victim were relatives, capital punishment could not be carried out as it would make the executioner commit *fingal* or *kin-slaying*. Wikipedia:Citation needed

Another situation where the murderer could be killed was when the murderer was at large and the fines had not been paid. The victim's family apparently was responsible to launch a blood feud.[1276] It is unclear how often capital punishment was carried out in situations where it would be licit without any records other than the legal tracts. However, it is clear that that punishment could be avoided in most cases.

The origin of this particular legal provision is as unclear as the rest of Irish law. However, the so-called "Pseudo-Historical Prologue to the Senchas Már", a late introduction to the main collection of Irish law, makes a claim on how this came about. It declares that prior to the coming of St. Patrick, Irish law demanded capital punishment in all cases of murder. However, Christianity was supposed to preach forgiveness. The two fines are apparently a compromise so that the murderer is both punished and forgiven. However, it is at least dubious whether or not this is a valid historical account, given the lateness of the story (originating hundreds of years after Patrick's time).

Kinship

Early Irish law recognised a number of degrees of agnatic kinship, based on a belief that there was common male ancestor. The closest kin group that is defined is *gelfine* (bright-kin)—descendants of a common grandfather (including the grandfather's relationships to his descendants and his children). This is followed by the *derbfine* (certain-kin)—descendants of a common great grandfather, *iarfine* (after-kin)—descendants of a common great great grandfather, and the *indfine* (end-kin), all of which contain the old Irish word for kin or family, *fine*.[1277] The *derbfine* is, by far, the kin-group most commonly mentioned.[1278]

The leader of the kin-group was known either as *ágae fine* (pillar of the family) or *cenn fine* (head [literally] of the family). He apparently was a senior member selected from the kin-group based on various qualifications. One of his main duties was to take responsibility for members of the kin-group, acting as a surety for some of the actions of members, making sure debts are paid (including for murder). If the member could not be made to pay, the fee was normally paid by members of the kin-group. He was also responsible for unmarried women after the death of their fathers.[1279]

As mentioned above, the actions of a member could require other kin to pay a fine. However, in certain cases the kin-group could refuse liabilities, although in some cases only after they been proclaimed as a non-member, which might occur if the member did not carry out his responsibilities to the kin. One particularly heinous crime in early Irish law was *fingal* (kin-slaying), because it was against a group that had some right to trust. The killer had to give up their kin-land, but was still liable for fines incurred by other members of the kin.[1280] An undutiful son might also be excluded from certain kin rights as well, especially as sons of a living father generally did not have significant rights of legal actions except as permitted by the father.[1281]

Inheritance

Early Ireland practised partitive inheritance whereby each of the sons received equal portions, and any grandsons whose father predeceased their grandfather equally split their father's portion. When the Normans entered Ireland and saw the Irish practice they called it Gavelkind, the Jute inheritance in Kent to which it seemed similar.[1282] Early Irish law typically did not distinguish between "legitimate" and "illegitimate" children, so any recognised, even those of concubines, received a portion. On the other hand, disobedient sons were automatically excluded. In addition, adopted children could receive a portion of kin land, though status as an inheritor, and the inheritance amount had to be explicitly stipulated.[1283]

The division of land is somewhat obscure. One maxim suggests that the youngest son divided the land into equal parts. The eldest chose first, followed by the second and so on until the youngest received the remaining land. The intent was to make division of land equal. Other laws suggested that the eldest son had automatic claims to the buildings. However, there are some hints that this only happened if a younger son challenged a division. The normal practice was that the eldest son both divided and chose first, but had to divide equally.[1284] More rarely, a father might divide the land for his sons in his lifetime.[1285]

While a daughter with brothers did not normally receive a portion of the inheritance in land, she could inherit movable property. However, should there be no sons, some of the law tracts allow the daughter to inherit a limited portion. However, unless her husband was a foreigner to the *túath* and had no land of his own, the land did not descend to her sons, but instead went to the other members of her agnatic kin group. However, there was apparently pressure for a woman with land to marry a relative to keep the land within the kin group.[1286]

Finally, if a man died with no children, the property was distributed between his nearest kin—first the descendants of his father, and if there were no such descendants, then between the descendants of his grandfather, and so on. Any extra land that daughters could not inherit because of female inheritance limits also went to the wider kin.[1287] The head of a kin group was entitled to extra property since he was liable for debts a kinsman could not pay.[1288]

Land rights of kin

The potential for inheritance by even distant kin meant that, in Early Irish law, those kin all had some sort of right in the land. Land that had been inherited was known as *finntiu* (kin-land). Certain rights of use of land by the owner's kin seem to have existed. Moreover, it was possible that land could be redistributed if a certain branch of the family had few descendants and hence larger shares in the land per person. In such a case, even some more distant cousins could acquire the land, though they benefited less than closer kin.[1289] Apparently because of these potential claims it could apparently be difficult to alienate kin-land. However, even when selling land that an individual had acquired separately from inheritance, a portion went to his kin.[1290]

Legal theory

Changes in the legal system

Ireland had no regular central authority capable of making new law and hence the Brehon laws were entirely in the hands of the jurists. As such some early scholars felt that the legal system was essentially unchanging and archaic.[1291] However, more recently scholars have noticed that some methods of change were laid out within the Brehon laws. In particular, *Cóic Conara Fugill* mentions five bases on which a judge must base judgment, and at least three offer some room for change: *fásach* (legal maxim), *cosmailius* (legal analogy), and *aicned* (natural law) (the other two are *roscad*, a type of legal verse jurists were trained to create to mark a statement made by someone who knows the law[1292] and *teistimin* (scriptural testimony)). However, it has not yet been studied in detail how exactly these three innovative methods were used.[1293]

Maxims

The Use and application of maxims is clearly a location where the principles of Irish law could be recorded. Any number of maxims may be found within the Early Irish Laws and perhaps the reason why we are unable to derive a coherent theory of law from them is because there are a great many different topics. Some do seem to represent a legal theory, such as the maxim in *Bechbretha* that "no-one is obliged to give something to another for nothing" and that in *Bretha Crólige* that "the misdeed of the guilty should not affect the innocent". These maxims do say more than one might think since legal systems often have problems balancing the interests of all.[1294] The majority of maxims, however, treat with more specific problems. The main problem, however, with our understanding of maxims is that while one law text tells us that they were used as a basis of judgment we know little else about them; we do not even know how exactly maxims could be used for judgment. A further complication is that we know very little about the origin of maxims (or even what the jurists thought was the origin) and similarly we do not know whether jurists were introducing new maxims regularly or whether all maxims were *supposed* to be from time immemorial.

Natural law

Early Irish law mentions in a number of places *recht aicned* or natural law. This is a concept apparently borrowed from, or at least akin with, European legal theory, and reflects a type of law that is universal and may be determined by reason and observation of natural action. Neil McLeod identifies concepts that law must accord with: *fír* (truth) and *dliged* (right or entitlement). These two terms occur frequently, though Irish law never strictly defines them. Similarly, the term *córus* (law in accordance with proper order) occurs in some places, and even in the titles of certain texts. The laws tell stories of how truth could apparently cure a person and falsehood could cause blisters. These were two very real concepts to the jurists and the value of a given judgment with respect to them was apparently ascertainable. McLeod has also suggested that most of the specific laws mentioned have passed the test of time and thus their truth has been confirmed, while other provisions are justified in other ways because they are younger and have not been tested over time.[1295]

Legal procedure

The early Irish laws are devoid of a state centred enforcement mechanism and at least some of the judges were outside the state apparatus. This did not mean that the laws were ineffective, rather the methods of enforcement of legal procedures worked in such a way to fit with the conditions of society.

Suretyship

Sureties were the prime enforcers in early Irish law. They were not government officials, but rather sureties who were appointed to enforce a contract or other legal relationship. *Berad Airechta*, the law tract that deals most with sureties, offers formulaic speeches the contractors may have recited ceremonially to appoint sureties and make the sureties swear to perform their duties properly. In addition to sureties appointed for specific contracts, relatives might be expected to act as sureties in cases where they were not specifically bound. However, there is also evidence that most sureties were either relatives or lords of the contractor.[1296]

Three types of sureties appear in Irish law. The *naidm* (and in earlier texts *macc*) refers to a surety who is expected to enforce payment from the contractor. Apparently, in standard contracts two *naidmain* (plural of *naidm*) were appointed by each party. The word *naidm*, however, might also refer to the "binding" of a contract. If the contractor whom he is appointed for defaults it is the *naidm*'s responsibility to attempt to make the contractor pay. If however he does not act or does not put in sufficient effort he loses his honour price.

In attempting to extract payment, the *naidm* had a wide range of powers. He might distrain the contractors property, imprison or even violently attack the contractor. Apparently, as with witnessing, someone could not be a *naidm* to a contract worth more than his honour-price.[1297]

The *ráth* is generally referred to as a *paying surety*. Should the contractor default, the ráth had to pay the debt from his own property. He could then attempt to extract the money from the contract. Assumedly, the ráth only paid if the naidm was unable to make the debtor pay. Since acting as a ráth could mean financial loss that might not be repaid, the law tracts apparently see the position as dangerous, as one of three "dark things of the world."[1298] However, it is clear also that the ráth, like other sureties, were paid a fee when hired, which potentially made up for the risk they undertook. Again, a person could not act as a ráth in contracts worth more than his honour-price, though it was possible that one might act as a ráth for only part of a contract, in which case they were responsible for payment only up to their honour-price.[1299]

Finally, the *aitire* is a surety who became a hostage in the case of a default. Once the hostage was in captivity, the debtor had ten days to pay the debt to have the hostage released. If the hostage was not released by then, expenses to the debtor could become exorbitant. The aitire had to pay his own ransom by paying his body-price, which was expensive, and the debtor had to pay twice that fee plus the surety's honour-price. The aitire could enforce the debt to him by himself.[1300]

Relationship to the church and church law

Brehon law was produced in the vernacular language by a group of professional jurists. The exact relationship of those jurists to the church is subject to considerable debate. However, it is clear that Brehon law at times were at odds with and at times influenced by Irish canon law.

Vernacular church law

A number of law tracts that originated from the church were written in Old Irish. The most famous of these is *Cáin Adomnáin*, which was apparently created in 697 under the influence of Adomnán and ratified by a number of ecclesiasts and kings whose names appear in the text. The idea of the law was apparently to supplement the punishments of Brehon law for crimes against women, children, and clerics. In some ways it follows the ideas embodied in Brehon law although there are differences; for instance, it uses capital punishment, which Brehon law avoids.[1301]

Canon law

More contradictions exists with Latin Canon Law, such as in the *Collectio canonum Hibernensis* (Irish Collection of Canons), than with Vernacular Church law. Brehon law allows polygyny (albeit while citing the authority of the Old Testament) and divorce, among other actions that canon law expressly forbids.[1302]

At the same time it is clear that the two legal systems have borrowed from each other. Much Latin terminology has entered into Old Irish and into the legal system, such as a type of witness *teist* from Latin *testis*. The *Collectio Canonum Hibernensis* also borrows terms found in Brehon law such as *rata* from Old Irish *rath*, a type of surety. The latter also suggests more substantive borrowing from Brehon Law into canon law.

There are a number of places where it is clear that law was borrowed in one direction or another. Large sections on the Church have been translated wholesale from the *Collectio Canonum Hibernensis* into a section of the Law tract *Bretha Nemed*. Other overlaps have been suggested, in many cases where biblical references seem to appear in the Brehon law.[1303] Where both texts cite the same rule, it is not always clear which came up with the rule first. In addition to substantive law, other legal aspects appear in both, such as the propensity towards use of analogy.

Relationship of jurists with the church

The above similarities have led scholars to ask what relationship did Brehons have with clerics. Some scholars, known as anti-nativists, have suggested that the Brehons were nothing more than clerics who had training in secular law. In addition to the similarities and evidence of borrowing from Canon law and the Bible, scholars who hold this position ask how any non Clerics could have been sufficiently literate at this period to create the texts. Other scholars, known as nativists, have asked how the differences could arise if the authors of canon and secular law were indeed the same.[1304]

Legal texts

Scholars have found over 100 distinct texts, ranging from complete texts through various degrees of partial preservation—and in some cases only as a name in a list, and even, in one case, a tract that scholars have decided must have existed. Almost all of the secular legal texts existing in various manuscripts have been printed in D.A. Binchy's six volume *Corpus Iuris Hibernici* and a few texts left out of that work made it into another book intended as a companion to the *Corpus Iuris Hibernici*.[1305]

Senchas Már

A number of the legal texts may be categorised together on account of related authorship. The largest such grouping in the *Senchas Már* a collection of at least 47 separate tracts compiled into a single group sometime in the 8th century, though individual tracts vary in date. These tracts are almost certainly written by a variety of authors, though some suggest that certain authors wrote more than one of the included tracts.[1306] The collection was apparently made somewhere in the north midlands.[1307] The Senchas Már tracts have been subjected to the greatest amount of glossing and commentary in later manuscripts. Moreover, one of the few examples of Old Irish glossing has been given to the various texts of Senchas Már. These glosses were apparently made in Munster.[1308]

The text has been arranged into thirds—three was apparently an important number to the Irish. A number of laws were grouped into threes, called *triads*—a practice also common in the Welsh. One scholar has recently suggested that there were a number of groups of six including one single tract, generally from the first third, two contiguous tracts generally in the second third, and three contiguous tracts from the third third. Each group of six is theorised as related to each other in various ways.[1309] The prologue ascribes the authorship of the book to a committee of nine appointed by St Patrick to revise the laws. It was composed of three kings, three bishops, and three professors of literature, poetry, and law. Chief among the latter was Dubthach. It became his duty to give an historical retrospect, and in doing so he exhibited, "...all the judgments of true nature which the Holy Ghost had spoken from the first occupation of this island down to the reception of the faith. What did not clash with the word of God in the written law and in the New Testament and with the consciences of believers was confirmed in the laws of the brehons by Patrick and by the ecclesiastics and chieftains of Ireland. This is the Senchus Mor."[1310]

Pseudo-historical Prologue

A few specific texts may be usefully mentioned here. The Pseudo-Historical Prologue was not an original part of the Senchas Már, but was actually a later addition that attempted to give a historical background. There is also an original introduction distinct from this text. The Pseudo-Historical Prologue was concerned with the changes in the Brehon law, which it suggested occurred with the arrival of Christianity. In effect, Saint Patrick is supposed to have blessed the mouth of the Chief Ollam of Ireland, Dubhthach moccu Lughair who then gave judgment on a particular case regarding the killing of Saint Odran an assistant and charioteer to Saint Patrick and then continued to recite the rest of the law leaving unaltered those laws acceptable to God and altering those that were not. This case is also given as the reason why Brehon law did not favour capital punishment.

While the murderer of Patrick's assistant was killed and immediately sent to heaven because he was forgiven by Patrick, future murderers were to be pardoned as Patrick would not be around to assure their forgiveness and ascent to heaven. There is, however, no reason to think that the events described actually occurred although they do provide insight into how the Brehons thought about their own law.[1311]

Cethairslicht Athgabálae

Literally the four paths of distraint, a process by which one could, under certain circumstances, seize goods owed by another. However, in Brehon law one does not immediately own the property, rather animals are taken to an intermediary land to wait in case the original owner pays the debt. As time passes, the animals are slowly forfeited. This tract deals primarily with four types of distraint, divided based on the waiting period. The waiting period apparently varies based on the circumstance although no one has yet determined what exactly those circumstances are. Other material present includes information of other aspects of legal procedure and a long section where the author asks and then answers multiple times, why the tract is called *Cethairslicht Athgabálae*.[1312]

Cáin Sóerraith and Cáin Aicillne

These two texts, "The Regulation of Noble Fief" and "Regulation of Base Clientship", deal with the structure of lord client relations. These two tracts regulate the circumstances of entering into clientship as well as setting forth what goods and services were given by the lord in return for what goods and services the client gave.[1313]

Cáin Lánamna

This tract, the "Law of Couples", deals with not only regulations for marriage but for other unions as will. It lists tens types of coupling including three types of formal marriage, five unions where there are sexual relations but no sharing of property or cohabitating, union by rape and union by two who are mentally incompetent. The text then goes on to deal with common property as well as how it is divided upon divorce.[1314]

Córus Bésgnai

The vaguely named tract *Córus Bésgnai* (or *Córus Béscnai*) has been translated as both "The Ordering of Discipline" or "The Regulation of Proper Behavior".[1315] This tract describes the relationship between the Church and the people as a contract; the people have to donate tithes and first fruits and the like, while the church must provide services such as baptism and make sure that its members must be honest, devout, and qualified.[1316] This text has been used both to show church influence on Brehon law and also to point to certain aspects that canon lawyers would disapprove of.

Sechtae

At the beginning of the second third of the Senchas Már is collection of "Heptads" or collections of seven related rules (although in some cases there are more than seven). This tract actually has no single theme, rather it is useful for what it can say about various aspects of Brehon law. The tract includes sixty five heptads, although more appear elsewhere in the Senchas Már.[1317]

Bechbretha and *Coibes Uisci Thairdne*

"Bee-Judgments" and "Kinship of Conducted Water" are two tracts some scholars believe were written by the same author.[1318] These two tracts both present legal information about relatively new animal and technological introductions to Irish law from elsewhere in Europe, Bees and Watermills. Hence they show the Brehons adapting to new legal challenges. In particular, this is one area where it is possible to see legal analogy in action.[1319]

Slicht Othrusa, *Bretha Crólige* and *Bretha Déin Chécht*

Sections on Sick-Maintenance, *Judgments of Blood-Lyings* and *Judgments of Dían Cécht* are three contiguous tracts in the third third of the Senchas Már. The first two deal with the practice of sick-maintenance (see above) and the third deals with payments for injuries. Unfortunately *Slicht Othrusa* only survives as a fragment. These tracts give us most of our knowledge on the law regarding injury, while a few other tracts cover specific situations.[1320]

Nemed texts

In addition to the school that produced the Senchas Már, scholars have detected a few other legal schools that produced texts. The next most fully formed is the *Nemed* or *Bretha Nemed* school, named after two of the texts it produced. This school, which has been referred to as *poetico-legal*, apparently was located in Munster, based on references to the King of Munster and two monasteries in Munster.[1321]

Bretha Nemed Toísech and *Bretha Nemed Déidenach*

These two texts, the "First Judgment of Privileged Ones" and the "Final Judgment of Privileged Ones" are the later scribal names of two texts written primarily in the obscure *roscad* style of poetry. The first describes the roles and status of the church, poets and various other professionals. The final primarily with the status and duties of poets although it contains other material as well.[1322] The first is also one of the few early texts scholars have assigned an author to, namely three brothers, *hua Búirecháin*, who are a bishop, a poet, and a judge.

Uraicecht Becc

The *Uraicecht Becc* ("Small primer") is a text on status and has the greatest breadth in coverage, including not only commoners, kings, churchmen and poets, but also a variety of other professional groups, including judges. However, it does not go into as much detail for each group and level as do other status tracts.[1323]

Other texts

A number of other texts have not been grouped together as coming from either the same author or from the same school. This doesn't mean no affiliation for authors of other texts exists, only that scholars have not been able to find them.

Berrad Airechta

Literally *Shearing of the Court*, Fergus Kelly suggests that this might mean more loosely "court summary" or "synopsis of court procedure."[1324] The text deals with a number of topics for judicial procedure, but most importantly on the role of the various types of sureties. Interesting, it covers the ways that sureties were appointed to their duties, and hence it is informative on the way contracts were created.[1325]

Críth Gablach

"Branched Purchase" is the title of what is perhaps the most well-known tract on status and certainly the most accessible, as a modern printed edition (though not a translation) has been published by the Dublin Institute for Advanced Studies.[1326] The text goes into details on the grades of commoners and nobility: what property should they own, how large should their house be, how should their clientship be arranged. The text however present a schema that could not have been used in actuality. For instance, it includes clientship information for even the highest nobility, who would not have acted as clients. The text also presents a certain amount of interesting information on the duties of king.

Figure 38: *Ruins of the O'Davoren law school at Cahermac-
naghten, County Clare, which was occupied in the later Middle Ages*

In addition to the main text, a poem immediately follows in the manuscript,
but there has been debate as to whether this is actually a part of the tract.[1327]

Di Astud Chor

A two part text, *On the Binding of Contracts*, deals with when contracts are
binding and when they are not. The first section deals with general rules
regarding when contracts are binding, including an analogy to the fact that
Adam's trade of an apple for access to the Garden of Eden was valid even
though it was an uneven contract because Adam knew it was such. The second half deals with cases in which a contract may be overturned. The tract is
also interesting because it is a collection of material from varying dates and
places and as such much more uneven in content than other tracts.[1328]

Uraicecht na Ríar

The "Primer of Stipulations" is a text on the status of poets. It includes information on compensation based on status, but it also includes information about
the poetic craft such as the number of type of positions one must have to be a
certain grade. It also describes the difference between a *fili* and a bard.[1329]

Later texts

While most of the legal tracts were composed during the 7th and 8th centuries, there were some independent tracts, as well as a significant amount of glossing and commentary, often written within a century of when some of the tracts were composed.

Glosses and commentary

The most voluminous legal material written after the 8th century takes the form of notes upon that earlier material. There have been numerous questions about the degree to which such glossators understood the material they worked on.[1330] However, it is also possible that in some cases jurists used the earlier material for a legitimate method of explaining how the law had come to work. This material takes two main forms: glossing between the lines of a text, and mini texts that begin with a quote from earlier legal material.

The 16th-century jurist Domnall O'Davoren created a glossary in which he quoted from many other sources. In many cases it is only text that includes certain quotes as well as information about certain whole law tracts. Its primary focus, however, is to list and define certain words, particularly legal terms, and as such has provided significant help in understanding the oldest laws.[1331]

Later legal tracts

While the majority of legal texts were written before the 9th century, a few were written later. The Middle Irish text, *The Distribution of Cró and Dibad* deals with extracting fines from a killer and dividing a dead man's property.[1332] Additionally, the legal text *Cóic Conara Fugill*(the Five Paths of Judgment) was originally written during the earliest period but received a number of subsequent recensions afterward. The text deals with how a court case should proceed based on the substance of the intended argument. It is not clear, however, what distinctions are made in this text.[1333]

Case law

Early Irish Law is almost completely lacking in case law. What exists are a few brief references in a number of texts, both legal and non-legal, which reference the laws in action. For instance *Bechbretha* mentions the case of a king who lost his throne because he was blinded by a bee.[1334] Additionally, the Latin Life of St. Columba refers to the case of a man who killed another and the subsequent punishment he was to endure.[1335]

Decline of the Brehon laws

Following the Norman invasion (from 1171), areas under Anglo-Norman control were subject to English law. One of the first changes came with the Synod of Cashel in 1172, which required single marriages to partners that were not closely related, and exempted clergy from paying their share of a family's eraic payments.

Henry II, who created the Lordship of Ireland, was also a legal reformer within his empire, and started to centralise the administration of justice and abolish local customary laws. Strongbow was assigned large parts of Leinster in 1170 under the Brehon law by his new father-in-law Dermot McMurrough that were then regranted by Henry. Landowners such as the Earl of Kildare could claim a continuous title that just predated the Lordship itself.

In the centuries that followed, a cultural and military "Gaelic revival" eventually came to cover the larger portion of the island. The majority of Norman barons eventually adopted Irish culture and language, married in with the native Irish, and adopted Irish legal custom. By the 15th century, in the areas outside of the English controlled Pale around Dublin, and some notable areas of joint tradition in northern and eastern Munster, Brehon law became the de facto legal writ.

Nevertheless, the Brehon Laws could never be adopted on an official basis by the English-controlled government of the Lordship of Ireland, although some modernised concepts have been readopted in the laws of the Republic of Ireland.Wikipedia:Please clarify The imposition of the Statutes of Kilkenny in 1367 and the policy of Surrender and regrant effectively outlawed Brehon Law. In one exceptional case, vestigial rights have been recognised in recent Irish case law, in reference to the survival of Brehon law-governed customary local fishery rights in Tyrconnell, but these also amounted to an easement under Common Law.

The Tudor conquest of Ireland in the mid-16th century, ending in the Nine Years' War (1594–1603), caused Tanistry and Gavelkind, two cornerstones of the Brehon Laws, to be specifically outlawed in 1600. The extension of English law into Ulster became possible and led in part to the Flight of the Earls in 1607.

Elements of Brehon law operated in dwindling remnants in the Gaeltacht in the west of Ireland and in the Scottish Isles, notable on the isle of Lewis. On Lewis, the chiefs of the Morrison clan (earlier, Clann mhic Amhlaigh (Macaulays) of Uig in Lewis,Wikipedia:Citation needed and Sliochd a' Bhreitheimh, later Morrison) continued to hold office as hereditary brieves (Scots for *bretheamh* or *brehon*) or judges of the MacLeod clan of Lewis into the 17th century.

"... the location of the Morisons was at Ness in Lewis, where the head of the Clan was Britheamh or Hereditary Judge long before Fifeshire colonists were heard of. It is not likely, as the late Captain Thomas put it, that any of the Brieves ever understood a word of English, and as the Scotch laws were never translated into Gaelic, it seems that the native or Brehon Laws must have been administered in this part of Scotland as late as the 17th century." (**Dan Iain Ghobha: The poems of John Morison**, cit. – Arch. Scot., Vol. V., p. 366.)::

The last Morrison to exercise the office was put down with Letter of Fire and Sword in about 1619 It is probable that it was last operative in Lewis by about 1595 or so. See the later history of Clan Morrison.

Fictional references and Ulster cycle of legends

The Brehon laws play a large role in the Sister Fidelma series of historical (7th century AD) crime books by Peter Tremayne, and in those of Cora Harrison's Mara, Brehon (investigating judge) of the Burren (early 16th century). They are also the underlying principles seen in such Irish saga as Táin Bó Flidhais and Táin Bó Cuailnge

References

Sources

Primary

- Binchy, D. A., ed. (1979) [1941]. *Críth gablach*. DIAS. ISBN 1 85500 002 4.
- Binchy, D. A., ed. (1978). *Corpus iuris Hibernici: ad fidem codicum manuscriptorum*. DIAS. Six Volumes:- Vol.I: Introduction + pages 1–337; Vol. II: 339–744; Vol. III: 745–1138; Vol. IV: 1139–1531; Vol. V: 1532–1925; Vol. VI: 1926–2343.
- Charles-Edwards, Thomas; Kelly, Fergus, eds. (1983). *Bechbretha: an Old Irish law-tract on bee-keeping*. Early Irish law. Vol.1. Dublin: Dublin Institute for Advanced Studies.
- Kelly, Fergus (1997). *Early Irish farming*. Early Irish Law. Vol.4. Dublin Institute for Advanced Studies. ISBN 1855001802.

Secondary

- Baumgarten, Rolf (1985). "The Kindred Metaphors in 'Bechbretha' and 'Coibnes Uisci Thairidne'". *Peritia*. **4**: 307–327. doi: 10.1484/J.Peri. 3.112[1336].
- Breatnach, Liam (2005). *A Companion to the Corpus Iuris Hibernici.* DIAS. ISBN 1855001845.
- Breatnach, Liam (1987). *Uraicecht na Ríar: the poetic grades in early Irish law.* Dublin Institute for Advanced Studies. ISBN 9780901282897.
- Kelly, Fergus (1988). *A Guide to Early Irish Law.* Early Irish Law Series 3. Dublin: DIAS. ISBN 0901282952.
- Jaski, Bart (June 2013). *Early Irish Kingship and Succession.* Four Courts Press. ISBN 978-1-84682-426-5.
- Kleefeld, John (2010). "From Brouhahas to Brehon Laws: Poetic Impulse in the Law" *Law and Humanities* 4(1): 21–61.[1337]
- Lyall, Andrew (2000). *Land Law in Ireland.* Roundhall Sweet & Maxwell. ISBN 9781858001999.
- MacNeill, Eoin (17 December 1923). "Ancient Irish Law: the law of status or franchise". *Proceedings of the Royal Irish Academy, Section C: Archaeology, Celtic Studies, History, Linguistics, Literature.* **36**: 265–316. JSTOR 25504234[1338]. (Subscription required (help)).
- Dáibhí Ó Cróinín (1995), *Early Medieval Ireland 400–1200*, Longman.
- Power, Patrick C. (1976). "Sex and Marriage in Ancient Ireland", Mercier.
- Katherine Simms (2004). *Gaelic military history and the later Brehon law commentaries, Unity in diversity*, 51–67.
- Katherine Simms (2007). "The poetic Brehon lawyers of early sixteenth-century Ireland" *Eiru* 57, 212–132.
- Wylie, John C.W. (2013). *Irish Land Law*, 5th ed, Bloomsbury Professional.

External links

Wikisourcehas the text of the 1911 *Encyclopædia Britannica*article **Brehon Laws**.

- Ancient laws of Ireland ... Published under direction of the commissioners for publishing the ancient laws and institutes of Ireland[1339] published 1865-1901, accessible through HathiTrust
- The Brehon Laws: A Legal Handbook[1340] by Laurence Ginnell, 1894
- The Law of the Couple[1341]: translation of an Irish legal text on marriage

- Dublin Institute for Advanced Studies – School of Celtic Studies[1342]
  Catalogue of relevant publications
- Solarguard Brehon[1343] Precis of Fergus Kelly's A Guide to Early Irish
  Law
- The Brehon Laws[1344] – Catholic Encyclopedia article
- Brehon Law Academy on YouTube[1345]

Visigothic Code

The **Visigothic Code** (*Latin*, **Forum Iudicum** or **Liber Iudiciorum**; *Spanish*, **Libro de los Jueces**, Book of the Judges), also called *Lex Visigothorum* (*English:* Law of the Visigoths) is a set of laws first promulgated by king Chindasuinth (642-653) of the Visigothic Kingdom in his second year of rule (642-643) that survives only in fragments. In 654 his son, king Recceswinth (649-672), published the enlarged law code, which was the first law code that applied equally to the conquering Goths and the general population, of which the majority had Roman roots, and had lived under Roman laws.

The code abolished the old tradition of having different laws for Romans (*leges romanae*) and Visigoths (*leges barbarorum*), and under which all the subjects of the Visigothic kingdom would stop being *romani* and *gothi* instead becoming *hispani*. In this way, all subjects of the kingdom were gathered under the same jurisdiction, eliminating social and legal differences, and allowing greater assimilation of the populations. As such, the Code marks the transition from the Roman law to Germanic law and is one of the best surviving examples of *leges barbarorum*. It combines elements of the Roman law, Catholic law and Germanic tribal customary law.

The first law codes

During the first centuries of Visigothic rule, Romans were ruled by different laws than Goths were. The earliest known visigothic laws are the Code of Euric, which were compiled by roughly 480 A.D. The first written laws of the Visigothic kingdom were compiled during the rule of king Alaric II and were meant to regulate the lives of Romans, who made up the majority of the kingdom and were based on the existing Roman imperial laws and their interpretations. The *Breviarium* (Breviary of Alaric) was promulgated during the meeting of Visigothic nobles in Toulouse on February 2, 506.[1346]

During the reign of king Leovigild an attempt was made to unite the laws regulating the lives of Goths and Romans into a revised law code, *Codex Revisus*. In 589, at the Third Council of Toledo the ruling Visigoths and Suebi, who had

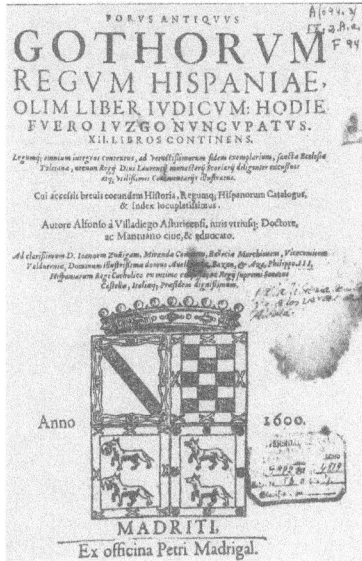

Figure 39: *The cover of an edition of the Liber Judiciorum from 1600.*

been Arians, accepted Catholicism. Now that the formerly Roman population and the Goths shared the same faith King Reccared issued laws that equally applied to both populations.[1347]

Visigothic code

The code of 654 was enlarged by the novel legislation of Recceswinth (for which reason it is sometimes called the *Code of Recceswinth*) and later kings Wamba, Erwig, Egica, and perhaps Wittiza. Recceswinth's code was edited by Braulio of Zaragoza, since Chindasuinth's original code had been hastily written and promulgated.[1348]

During the Twelfth Council of Toledo in 681, King Erwig asked that the law code be clarified and revised. Some new laws were added, out of which 28 dealt with Jews.[1349]

The laws were far-reaching and long in effect: in 10th century Galicia, monastic charters make reference to the Code.[1350] The laws govern and sanction family life and by extension political life: marriage, the transmission of property to heirs, safeguarding the rights of widows and orphans. Particularly with the Visigoth's Law Codes, women could inherit land and title, were allowed to manage land independently from their husbands or male relations, dispose

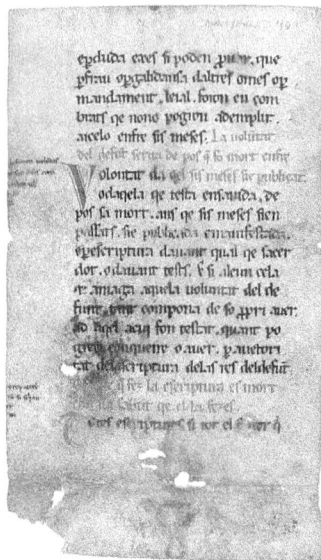

Figure 40: *Fragment of an 11th century Liber Judiciorum translation to the old Catalan language. Guarded at Santa Maria of
Montserrat Abbey on the Montserrat mountain, Catalonia (Spain).*

of their property in legal wills if they had no heirs, could represent themselves
and bear witness in court by age 14 and arrange for their own marriages by age
20 .[1351]

The laws combined the Catholic Church's Canon law, and as such have a
strongly theocratic tone.

The code is known to have been preserved by the Moors, as Christians were
permitted the use of their own laws, where they did not conflict with those of
the conquerors, upon the regular payment of Jizya tribute. Thus it may be presumed that it was the recognized legal authority of Christian magistrates while
the Iberian Peninsula remained under Muslim control. When Ferdinand III
of Castile took Córdoba in the thirteenth century, he ordered that the code be
adopted and observed by his subjects, and had it translated, albeit inaccurately,
into the Castilian language, as the Fuero Juzgo. The Catalan translation of this
document, "Llibre Jutge", is among the oldest literary texts in that language
(c. 1050).

Contents

The following is a list of the books and titles which form the Visigothic Code.

Sources

- King, P. D. "King Chindasvind and the First Territorial Law-code of the Visiogothic Kingdom." *Visigothic Spain: New Approaches*. ed. Edward James. Oxford: Clarendon Press, 1980. pp 131–157.

External links

- Lex Visigothorum[1352] - Latin text
- Visigothic Code - Forum Iudicum. 1908 English Translation of Full Text by [[Samuel Parsons Scott[1353]]]
- R. A. Fletcher, 1984. *Saint James's Catapult: The Life and Times of Diego Gelmírez of Santiago de Compostela* (Oxford University Press) (on-line text[1354])
- Information on the *Visigothic Code* as part of the *leges Visigothorum* and its manuscript tradition on the *Bibliotheca legum regni Francorum manuscripta*[[Category:Articles containing Latin-language text[1355]] website], A database on Carolingian secular law texts (Karl Ubl, Cologne University, Germany, 2012).
- Visigothic Symposia 1 'Law and Theology' - New research on the Visigothic Code[1356]

High, middle and low justice

High, middle and low justices are notions dating from Western feudalism to indicate descending degrees of judiciary power to administer justice by the maximal punishment the holders could inflict upon their subjects and other dependents.

Low justice regards the level of day-to-day civil actions, including voluntary justice, minor pleas, and petty offences generally settled by fines or light corporal punishment. It was held by many petty authorities, including many lords of the manor, who sat in justice over the serfs, unfree tenants, and freeholders on their land. Middle justice would involve full civil and criminal jurisdiction, except for capital crimes, and notably excluding the right to pass the death penalty, torture and severe corporeal punishment, which was reserved to authorities holding high justice, or the *ius gladii* ("right of the sword").

Pyramid of feudal justice

Although the terms *high* and *low* suggest a strict subordination, this was not quite the case; a case could often be brought in any of several courts, with the principle of "prevention" (in the etymological sense of Latin *praevenire*, "to come before") granting jurisdiction to the court in which the case was first filed or otherwise brought.

As a rule, each court administered justice in general (criminal cases were generally not separate from civil actions and other types of justice, while certain matters were separated such as canon law), as long as the matter was not reserved for a higher court or by virtue of some *privilegium fori* (e.g., of clerics to be judged in canon courts by other clergy, sometimes under ecclesiastical law, the origin of the English common-law concept—benefit of clergy). In addition to civil and criminal trials, the notion of justice also included *voluntary justice*, which is really the official recording of deeds (unilateral or bilateral) such as marital agreements, wills, grants, etc.

A right of appeal was not automatically available, only when explicitly established, and if so not always to a court of the superior political level and/or a higher degree of our trio. In fact, feudal justice was a labyrinth of specific customs and rules in nearly endless variation, not governed by any clear legal logic, and subject to significant historical evolution in time, though the largely customary law tended by nature to be quite conservative. In judicial matters—as in all spheres of life—feudal society did not see uniformity as either possible or necessarily desirable, each town and region having its own customs and ways of doing things, and resented attempts to interfere with them.

While the right of justice is held by many "unique" courts, relatively strong states make it a pillar of their absolutist (re)emergence to establish numerous courts to administer justice in their name in different territorial circumscriptions, such as the royal (high) sheriffs in England, and/or to impose an appeal (at least unifying the law as such) to a royal court, as to the various French provincial parlements.

High justice

High justice, also known as *ius gladii* ("right of the sword") or in German as *Blutgerichtsbarkeit*, *Blutgericht* (lit. "blood justice", "blood-court";[1357] sometimes also *Halsgericht*, lit. "neck-justice", or *peinliches Gericht*[1358]) is the highest penal authority, including capital punishment, as held by a sovereign—the sword of justice and hand of justice are regalia that symbolize it. In the early Holy Roman Empire, high justice was reserved to the king. From the 13th century, it was transferred to the king's vassals along with their

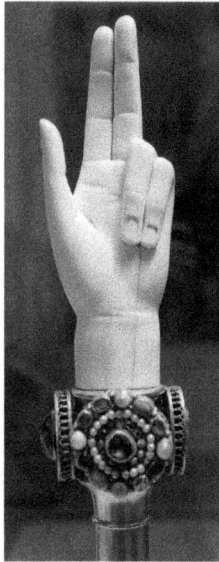

Figure 41: *Hand of justice displayed at the Louvre, Paris*

fiefs. The first codification of capital punishment was the *Halsgerichtsord-nung* passed by Maximilian I in 1499, followed in 1507 by the *Constitutio Criminalis Bambergensis*. Both codes formed the basis of the *Constitutio Criminalis Carolina* (CCC), passed in 1532 under Charles V. In the Habsburg Monarchy, all regional codes were superseded by the *Constitutio Criminalis Theresiana* in 1768.

The *Blutbanner* ("blood banner") or *Blutfahne* ("blood flag") was a solid red flag. It was presented to feudal lords as a symbol of their power of high jurisdiction (*Blutgerichtsbarkeit*) together with the heraldic banner of the fief. Some feudal houses adopted a red field symbolic of the blood banner into their coat of arms, the so-called *Regalienfeld*. The Talschaft (forest canton) of Schwyz used the blood banner as a war flag from ca. 1240, and was later incorporated into the flag of Schwyz and the flag of Switzerland.

Often it is proudly displayed, in the form of relevant status symbols. Thus permanent gallows are often erected in prominent public places; the very word for them in French, *potence*, is derived from the Latin "potentia" meaning "power".

High justice is held by all states and the highest vassals in the European type of feudal society, but may also be acquired by other authorities as part of a high degree of legal autonomy, such as certain cities; which in time often obtained other high privileges originally reserved for high nobility and sometimes high clergy. Other such privileges could include a seat in a diet or a similar feudal representative assembly, before the third estate as such even aspired to such "parliamentary" representation, or the right to mint coins. These privileges indicating its so-called *liberty* was an "equal" enclave in the territorial juris-diction of the neighboring feudal (temporal or ecclesiastical) Lord, sometimes even extending rather like a polis in Antiquity.

Not every Vogt held high justice. Up to the 18th century, for example, the blood court of much of what is now the canton of Zürich lay with Kyburg, even in the territory ruled by the counts of Greifensee. The self-administration of the blood court was an important factor of Imperial immediacy.

References

• Richard J. Evans, *Rituals of Retribution: Capital Punishment in Germany, 1600-1987*, Oxford University Press (1996).

Magna Carta

<indicator name="pp-default"> 🔒 </indicator> <indicator name="good-star"> ⊕ </indicator>

Magna Carta	

Cotton MS. Augustus II. 106, one of only four surviving exemplifications of the 1215 text	
Created	1215
Location	British Library and the cathedrals of Lincoln and Salisbury
Author(s)	John, King of England, his barons and Stephen Langton
Purpose	Peace treaty

Part of a series of articles on

Monarchy

Politics portal

- v̲
- t̲
- e̲[1359]

Magna Carta Libertatum (Medieval Latin for "the Great Charter of the Liberties"), commonly called **Magna Carta** (also *Magna Charta*; "(the) Great Charter"),[1360] The spelling *Charta* originates in the 18th century, as a restoration of classical Latin *charta* for the Medieval Latin spelling *carta*.[1361] While "Charta" remains an acceptable variant spelling it never became prevalent in English usage.[1362]</ref> is a charter agreed to by King John of England at Runnymede, near Windsor, on 15 June 1215.[1363] First drafted by the Archbishop of Canterbury to make peace between the unpopular King and a group of rebel barons, it promised the protection of church rights, protection for the barons from illegal imprisonment, access to swift justice, and limitations on feudal payments to the Crown, to be implemented through a council of 25 barons. Neither side stood behind their commitments, and the charter was annulled by Pope Innocent III, leading to the First Barons' War. After John's death, the regency government of his young son, Henry III, reissued the document in 1216, stripped of some of its more radical content, in an unsuccessful bid to build political support for their cause. At the end of the war in 1217, it formed part of the peace treaty agreed at Lambeth, where the document acquired the name Magna Carta, to distinguish it from the smaller Charter of the Forest which was issued at the same time. Short of funds, Henry reissued the charter again in 1225 in exchange for a grant of new taxes; his son, Edward I, repeated the exercise in 1297, this time confirming it as part of England's statute law.

The charter became part of English political life and was typically renewed by each monarch in turn, although as time went by and the fledgling English Parliament passed new laws, it lost some of its practical significance. At the end of the 16th century there was an upsurge in interest in Magna Carta. Lawyers and historians at the time believed that there was an ancient English constitution, going back to the days of the Anglo-Saxons, that protected individual English freedoms. They argued that the Norman invasion of 1066 had overthrown these rights, and that Magna Carta had been a popular attempt to restore them, making the charter an essential foundation for the contemporary powers of Parliament and legal principles such as *habeas corpus*. Although this historical account was badly flawed, jurists such as Sir Edward Coke used Magna Carta extensively in the early 17th century, arguing against the divine right of kings propounded by the Stuart monarchs. Both James I and his son Charles I attempted to suppress the discussion of Magna Carta, until the issue was curtailed by the English Civil War of the 1640s and the execution of Charles.

The political myth of Magna Carta and its protection of ancient personal liberties persisted after the Glorious Revolution of 1688 until well into the 19th century. It influenced the early American colonists in the Thirteen Colonies and the formation of the American Constitution in 1787, which became the supreme law of the land in the new republic of the United States.[1364] Research by Victorian historians showed that the original 1215 charter had concerned the medieval relationship between the monarch and the barons, rather than the rights of ordinary people, but the charter remained a powerful, iconic document, even after almost all of its content was repealed from the statute books in the 19th and 20th centuries. Magna Carta still forms an important symbol of liberty today, often cited by politicians and campaigners, and is held in great respect by the British and American legal communities, Lord Denning describing it as "the greatest constitutional document of all times – the foundation of the freedom of the individual against the arbitrary authority of the despot".[1365]

In the 21st century, four exemplifications of the original 1215 charter remain in existence, held by the British Library and the cathedrals of Lincoln and Salisbury. There are also a handful of the subsequent charters in public and private ownership, including copies of the 1297 charter in both the United States and Australia. The original charters were written on parchment sheets using quill pens, in heavily abbreviated medieval Latin, which was the convention for legal documents at that time. Each was sealed with the royal great seal (made of beeswax and resin sealing wax): very few of the seals have survived. Although scholars refer to the 63 numbered "clauses" of Magna Carta, this is a modern system of numbering, introduced by Sir William Blackstone in 1759; the original charter formed a single, long unbroken text. The four original 1215 charters were displayed together at the British Library for one day, 3 February 2015, to mark the 800th anniversary of Magna Carta.

Figure 42: *King John on a stag hunt*

History

13th century

Background

Magna Carta originated as an unsuccessful attempt to achieve peace between royalist and rebel factions in 1215, as part of the events leading to the outbreak of the First Barons' War. England was ruled by King John, the third of the Angevin kings. Although the kingdom had a robust administrative system, the nature of government under the Angevin monarchs was ill-defined and uncertain.[1366,1367] John and his predecessors had ruled using the principle of *vis et voluntas*, or "force and will", taking executive and sometimes arbitrary decisions, often justified on the basis that a king was above the law.[1367] Many contemporary writers believed that monarchs should rule in accordance with the custom and the law, with the counsel of the leading members of the realm, but there was no model for what should happen if a king refused to do so.[1367]

John had lost most of his ancestral lands in France to King Philip II in 1204 and had struggled to regain them for many years, raising extensive taxes on the barons to accumulate money to fight a war which ended in expensive failure in 1214.[1368] Following the defeat of his allies at the Battle of Bouvines, John had to sue for peace and pay compensation.[1369] John was already personally

Figure 43: *A contemporaneous mural of Pope Innocent III*

unpopular with many of the barons, many of whom owed money to the Crown, and little trust existed between the two sides.[1370,1371,1372] A triumph would have strengthened his position, but in the face of his defeat, within a few months after his return from France John found that rebel barons in the north and east of England were organising resistance to his rule.[1373,1374]

The rebels took an oath that they would "stand fast for the liberty of the church and the realm", and demanded that the King confirm the Charter of Liberties that had been declared by King Henry I in the previous century, and which was perceived by the barons to protect their rights.[1375,1374,1376] The rebel leadership was unimpressive by the standards of the time, even disreputable, but were united by their hatred of John;[1377] Robert FitzWalter, later elected leader of the rebel barons, claimed publicly that John had attempted to rape his daughter,[1378] and was implicated in a plot to assassinate John in 1212.[1379]

John held a council in London in January 1215 to discuss potential reforms, and sponsored discussions in Oxford between his agents and the rebels during the spring.[1380] Both sides appealed to Pope Innocent III for assistance in the dispute.[1381] During the negotiations, the rebellious barons produced an initial document, which historians have termed "the Unknown Charter of Liberties", which drew on Henry I's Charter of Liberties for much of its language; seven articles from that document later appeared in the "Articles of the Barons" and the subsequent charter.[1382,1383,1384]

It was John's hope that the Pope would give him valuable legal and moral support, and accordingly John played for time; the King had declared himself to be a papal vassal in 1213 and correctly believed he could count on the Pope for help.[1385,1381] John also began recruiting mercenary forces from France, although some were later sent back to avoid giving the impression that the King was escalating the conflict.[1380] In a further move to shore up his support, John took an oath to become a crusader, a move which gave him additional political protection under church law, even though many felt the promise was insincere.[1386,1387]

Letters backing John arrived from the Pope in April, but by then the rebel barons had organised into a military faction. They congregated at Northampton in May and renounced their feudal ties to John, marching on London, Lincoln, and Exeter.[1388] John's efforts to appear moderate and conciliatory had been largely successful, but once the rebels held London, they attracted a fresh wave of defectors from the royalists.[1389] The King offered to submit the problem to a committee of arbitration with the Pope as the supreme arbiter, but this was not attractive to the rebels.[1390] Stephen Langton, the Archbishop of Canterbury, had been working with the rebel barons on their demands, and after the suggestion of papal arbitration failed, John instructed Langton to organise peace talks.[1389,1391]

Great Charter of 1215

John met the rebel leaders at Runnymede, a water-meadow on the south bank of the River Thames, on 10 June 1215. Runnymede was a traditional place for assemblies, but it was also located on neutral ground between the royal fortress of Windsor Castle and the rebel base at Staines, and offered both sides the security of a rendezvous where they were unlikely to find themselves at a military disadvantage.[1392,1393] Here the rebels presented John with their draft demands for reform, the 'Articles of the Barons'.[1389,1391,1394] Stephen Langton's pragmatic efforts at mediation over the next ten days turned these incomplete demands into a charter capturing the proposed peace agreement; a few years later, this agreement was renamed Magna Carta, meaning "Great Charter".[1395,1391,1394] By 15 June, general agreement had been made on a text, and on 19 June, the rebels renewed their oaths of loyalty to John and copies of the charter were formally issued.[1394,1391]

Although, as the historian David Carpenter has noted, the charter "wasted no time on political theory", it went beyond simply addressing individual baronial complaints, and formed a wider proposal for political reform.[1389,1396] It promised the protection of church rights, protection from illegal imprisonment, access to swift justice, and, most importantly, limitations on taxation and other feudal payments to the Crown, with certain forms of feudal taxation requiring

Figure 44: *The Articles of the Barons, 1215, held by the British Library*

baronial consent.[1397,1373] It focused on the rights of free men—in particular the barons.[1396] However, the rights of serfs were included in articles 16, 20, and 28.[1398] Some of its articles were similar to the Runnymede Charter.[1399]</ref> Its style and content reflected Henry I's Charter of Liberties, as well as a wider body of legal traditions, including the royal charters issued to towns, the operations of the Church and baronial courts and European charters such as the Statute of Pamiers.[1400,1401]

Under what historians later labelled "clause 61", or the "security clause", a council of 25 barons would be created to monitor and ensure John's future adherence to the charter.[1402] If John did not conform to the charter within 40 days of being notified of a transgression by the council, the 25 barons were empowered by clause 61 to seize John's castles and lands until, in their judgement, amends had been made.[1403] Men were to be compelled to swear an oath to assist the council in controlling the King, but once redress had been made for any breaches, the King would continue to rule as before. In one sense this was not unprecedented; other kings had previously conceded the right of individual resistance to their subjects if the King did not uphold his obligations. Magna Carta was however novel in that it set up a formally recognised means of collectively coercing the King.[1404] The historian Wilfred Warren argues that it was almost inevitable that the clause would result in civil war, as it "was crude in its methods and disturbing in its implications".[1405] The barons were trying to force John to keep to the charter, but clause 61 was so heavily weighted against the King that this version of the charter could not survive.[1403]

John and the rebel barons did not trust each other, and neither side seriously attempted to implement the peace accord.[1402,1406] The 25 barons selected for the new council were all rebels, chosen by the more extremist barons, and many among the rebels found excuses to keep their forces mobilised.[1407,1408,1409] Disputes began to emerge between those rebels who had expected the charter to return lands that had been confiscated and the royalist faction.[1410]

Clause 61 of Magna Carta contained a commitment from John that he would "seek to obtain nothing from anyone, in our own person or through someone else, whereby any of these grants or liberties may be revoked or diminished".[1411]   Despite this, the King appealed to Pope Innocent for help in July, arguing that the charter compromised the Pope's rights as John's feudal lord.[1412,1410] As part of the June peace deal, the barons were supposed to surrender London by 15 August, but this they refused to do.[1413] Meanwhile, instructions from the Pope arrived in August, written before the peace accord, with the result that papal commissioners excommunicated the rebel barons and suspended Langton from office in early September.[1414]   Once aware of the charter, the Pope responded in detail: in a letter dated 24 August and arriving in late September, he declared the charter to be "not only shameful and demeaning but also illegal and unjust" since John had been "forced to accept" it, and accordingly the charter was "null, and void of all validity for ever"; under threat of excommunication, the King was not to observe the charter, nor the barons try to enforce it.[1415,1410,1416,1413]

By then, violence had broken out between the two sides; less than three months after it had been agreed, John and the loyalist barons firmly repudiated the failed charter: the First Barons' War erupted.[1417,1418,1410] The rebel barons concluded that peace with John was impossible, and turned to Philip II's son, the future Louis VIII, for help, offering him the English throne.[1419,1410,1420]</ ref> The war soon settled into a stalemate. The King became ill and died on the night of 18 October, leaving the nine-year-old Henry III as his heir.

Lists of participants in 1215

Great Charter of 1216

Although the Charter of 1215 was a failure as a peace treaty, it was resurrected under the new government of the young Henry III as a way of drawing support away from the rebel faction. On his deathbed, King John appointed a council of thirteen executors to help Henry reclaim the kingdom, and requested that his son be placed into the guardianship of William Marshal, one of the most famous knights in England.[1423] William knighted the boy, and Cardinal

Guala Bicchieri, the papal legate to England, then oversaw his coronation at Gloucester Cathedral on 28 October.[1424,1425,1426]

The young King inherited a difficult situation, with over half of England occupied by the rebels.[1427,1428] He had substantial support though from Guala, who intended to win the civil war for Henry and punish the rebels.[1429] Guala set about strengthening the ties between England and the Papacy, starting with the coronation itself, during which Henry gave homage to the Papacy, recognising the Pope as his feudal lord.[1430,1424] Pope Honorius III declared that Henry was the Pope's vassal and ward, and that the legate had complete authority to protect Henry and his kingdom.[1424] As an additional measure, Henry took the cross, declaring himself a crusader and thereby entitled to special protection from Rome.[1424]

The war was not going well for the loyalists, but Prince Louis and the rebel barons were also finding it difficult to make further progress.[1431,1432] John's death had defused some of the rebel concerns, and the royal castles were still holding out in the occupied parts of the country.[1433,1432] Henry's government encouraged the rebel barons to come back to his cause in exchange for the return of their lands, and reissued a version of the 1215 Charter, albeit having first removed some of the clauses, including those unfavourable to the Papacy and clause 61, which had set up the council of barons.[1434,1435] The move was not successful, and opposition to Henry's new government hardened.[1436]

Great Charter of 1217

In February 1217, Louis set sail for France to gather reinforcements.[1437] In his absence, arguments broke out between Louis' French and English followers, and Cardinal Guala declared that Henry's war against the rebels was the equivalent of a religious crusade.[1438] This declaration resulted in a series of defections from the rebel movement, and the tide of the conflict swung in Henry's favour.[1439] Louis returned at the end of April, but his northern forces were defeated by William Marshal at the Battle of Lincoln in May.[1440,1441]

Meanwhile, support for Louis' campaign was diminishing in France, and he concluded that the war in England was lost.[1442] He negotiated terms with Cardinal Guala, under which Louis would renounce his claim to the English throne; in return, his followers would be given back their lands, any sentences of excommunication would be lifted, and Henry's government would promise to enforce the charter of the previous year.[1443] The proposed agreement soon began to unravel amid claims from some loyalists that it was too generous towards the rebels, particularly the clergy who had joined the rebellion.[1444]

In the absence of a settlement, Louis remained in London with his remaining forces, hoping for the arrival of reinforcements from France.[1444] When the

Figure 45: *The Charter of the Forest, 1217, held by the British Library*

expected fleet did arrive in August, it was intercepted and defeated by loyalists at the Battle of Sandwich.[1445] Louis entered into fresh peace negotiations, and the factions came to agreement on the final Treaty of Lambeth, also known as the Treaty of Kingston, on 12 and 13 September 1217.[1445] The treaty was similar to the first peace offer, but excluded the rebel clergy, whose lands and appointments remained forfeit; it included a promise, however, that Louis' followers would be allowed to enjoy their traditional liberties and customs, referring back to the Charter of 1216.[1446] Louis left England as agreed and joined the Albigensian Crusade in the south of France, bringing the war to an end.[1442]

A great council was called in October and November to take stock of the post-war situation; this council is thought to have formulated and issued the Charter of 1217.[1447] The charter resembled that of 1216, although some additional clauses were added to protect the rights of the barons over their feudal subjects, and the restrictions on the Crown's ability to levy taxation were watered down.[1448] There remained a range of disagreements about the management of the royal forests, which involved a special legal system that had resulted in a source of considerable royal revenue; complaints existed over both the implementation of these courts, and the geographic boundaries of the royal forests.[1449] A complementary charter, the Charter of the Forest, was created, pardoning existing forest offences, imposing new controls over the forest

Figure 46: *The 1225 version of Magna Carta is-*
sued by Henry III, held in the National Archives

courts, and establishing a review of the forest boundaries.[1449] To distinguish
the two charters, the term *magna carta libertatum*, "the great charter of liberties", was used by the scribes to refer to the larger document, which in time
became known simply as Magna Carta.[1450,1451]

Great Charter of 1225

Magna Carta became increasingly embedded into English political life during Henry III's minority.[1452] As the King grew older, his government slowly
began to recover from the civil war, regaining control of the counties and beginning to raise revenue once again, taking care not to overstep the terms of
the charters.[1453] Henry remained a minor and his government's legal ability
to make permanently binding decisions on his behalf was limited. In 1223,
the tensions over the status of the charters became clear in the royal court,
when Henry's government attempted to reassert its rights over its properties
and revenues in the counties, facing resistance from many communities that
argued—if sometimes incorrectly—that the charters protected the new arrangements.[1454,1455] This resistance resulted in an argument between Archbishop
Langton and William Brewer over whether the King had any duty to fulfil the
terms of the charters, given that he had been forced to agree to them.[1456] On
this occasion, Henry gave oral assurances that he considered himself bound

by the charters, enabling a royal inquiry into the situation in the counties to progress.[1457]

Two years later, the question of Henry's commitment to the charters re-emerged, when Louis VIII of France invaded Henry's remaining provinces in France, Poitou and Gascony.[1458,1459] Henry's army in Poitou was under-resourced, and the province quickly fell.[1460] It became clear that Gascony would also fall unless reinforcements were sent from England.[1461] In early 1225, a great council approved a tax of £40,000 to dispatch an army, which quickly retook Gascony.[1462,1463] In exchange for agreeing to support Henry, the barons demanded that the King reissue Magna Carta and the Charter of the Forest.[1464,1465] The content was almost identical to the 1217 versions, but in the new versions, the King declared that the charters were issued of his own "spontaneous and free will" and confirmed them with the royal seal, giving the new Great Charter and the Charter of the Forest of 1225 much more authority than the previous versions.[1466,1465]

The barons anticipated that the King would act in accordance with these char-ters, subject to the law and moderated by the advice of the nobility. Uncer-tainty continued, and in 1227, when he was declared of age and able to rule independently, Henry announced that future charters had to be issued under his own seal.[1467,1468] This brought into question the validity of the previous charters issued during his minority, and Henry actively threatened to overturn the Charter of the Forest unless the taxes promised in return for it were actually paid.[1467,1468] In 1253, Henry confirmed the charters once again in exchange for taxation.[1469]

Henry placed a symbolic emphasis on rebuilding royal authority, but his rule was relatively circumscribed by Magna Carta.[1470,1426] He generally acted within the terms of the charters, which prevented the Crown from taking ex-trajudicial action against the barons, including the fines and expropriations that had been common under his father, John.[1470,1426] The charters did not address the sensitive issues of the appointment of royal advisers and the distribution of patronage, and they lacked any means of enforcement if the King chose to ig-nore them.[1471] The inconsistency with which he applied the charters over the course of his rule alienated many barons, even those within his own faction.[1426]

Despite the various charters, the provision of royal justice was inconsistent and driven by the needs of immediate politics: sometimes action would be taken to address a legitimate baronial complaint, while on other occasions the prob-lem would simply be ignored.[1472] The royal courts, which toured the country to provide justice at the local level, typically for lesser barons and the gentry claiming grievances against major lords, had little power, allowing the major barons to dominate the local justice system.[1473] Henry's rule became lax and

careless, resulting in a reduction in royal authority in the provinces and, ultimately, the collapse of his authority at court.[1473,1426]

In 1258, a group of barons seized power from Henry in a *coup d'état*, citing
the need to strictly enforce Magna Carta and the Charter of the Forest, creating
a new baronial-led government to advance reform through the Provisions of
Oxford.[1474] The barons were not militarily powerful enough to win a decisive
victory, and instead appealed to Louis IX of France in 1263–1264 to arbitrate
on their proposed reforms. The reformist barons argued their case based on
Magna Carta, suggesting that it was inviolable under English law and that the
King had broken its terms.[1475]

Louis came down firmly in favour of Henry, but the French arbitration failed to
achieve peace as the rebellious barons refused to accept the verdict. England
slipped back into the Second Barons' War, which was won by Henry's son,
Prince Edward. Edward also invoked Magna Carta in advancing his cause,
arguing that the reformers had taken matters too far and were themselves acting
against Magna Carta.[1476] In a conciliatory gesture after the barons had been
defeated, in 1267 Henry issued the Statute of Marlborough, which included a
fresh commitment to observe the terms of Magna Carta.[1477]

Witnesses in 1225

Great Charter of 1297: statute

King Edward I reissued the Charters of 1225 in 1297 in return for a new
tax.[1479] It is this version which remains in statute today, although with most
articles now repealed.

The *Confirmatio Cartarum* (Confirmation of Charters) was issued in Norman
French by Edward I in 1297.[1480] Edward, needing money, had taxed the nobility, and they had armed themselves against him, forcing Edward to issue his
confirmation of Magna Carta and the Forest Charter to avoid civil war. The
nobles had sought to add another document, the *De Tallagio*, to Magna Carta.
Edward I's government was not prepared to concede this, they agreed to the issuing of the *Confirmatio*, confirming the previous charters and confirming the
principle that taxation should be by consent,[1479] although the precise manner
of that consent was not laid down.[1481]

A passage mandates that copies shall be distributed in "cathedral churches
throughout our realm, there to remain, and shall be read before the people two
times by the year",[1482] hence the permanent installation of a copy in Salisbury
Cathedral. In the Confirmation's second article, it is confirmed that

> *if any judgement be given from henceforth contrary to the points of the*
> *charters aforesaid by the justices, or by any other our ministers that hold*

Figure 47: *1297 version of the Great Charter, on display in the National Archives Building in Washington, D.C.*

plea before them against the points of the charters, it shall be undone, and holden for nought.

With the reconfirmation of the Charters in 1300, an additional document was granted, the *Articuli super Cartas* (The Articles upon the Charters).[1483] It was composed of 17 articles and sought in part to deal with the problem of enforcing the Charters. Magna Carta and the Forest Charter were to be issued to the sheriff of each county, and should be read four times a year at the meetings of the county courts. Each county should have a committee of three men who could hear complaints about violations of the Charters.[1484]

Pope Clement V continued the papal policy of supporting monarchs (who ruled by divine grace) against any claims in Magna Carta which challenged the King's rights, and annulled the *Confirmatio Cartarum* in 1305. Edward I interpreted Clement V's papal bull annulling the *Confirmatio Cartarum* as effectively applying to the *Articuli super Cartas*, although the latter was not specifically mentioned.[1485] In 1306 Edward I took the opportunity given by the Pope's backing to reassert forest law over large areas which had been "disafforested". Both Edward and the Pope were accused by some contemporary chroniclers of "perjury", and it was suggested by Robert McNair Scott that Robert the Bruce refused to make peace with Edward I's son, Edward II, in

1312 with the justification: "How shall the king of England keep faith with me, since he does not observe the sworn promises made to his liege men..."[1486,1487]

Magna Carta's influence on English medieval law

The Great Charter was referred to in legal cases throughout the medieval period. For example, in 1226, the knights of Lincolnshire argued that their local sheriff was changing customary practice regarding the local courts, "contrary to their liberty which they ought to have by the charter of the lord king".[1488] In practice, cases were not brought against the King for breach of Magna Carta and the Forest Charter, but it was possible to bring a case against the King's officers, such as his sheriffs, using the argument that the King's officers were acting contrary to liberties granted by the King in the charters.[1489]

In addition, medieval cases referred to the clauses in Magna Carta which dealt with specific issues such as wardship and dower, debt collection, and keeping rivers free for navigation.[1490] Even in the 13th century, some clauses of Magna Carta rarely appeared in legal cases, either because the issues concerned were no longer relevant, or because Magna Carta had been superseded by more relevant legislation. By 1350 half the clauses of Magna Carta were no longer actively used.[1491]

14th–15th centuries

During the reign of King Edward III six measures, later known as the *Six Statutes*, were passed between 1331 and 1369. They sought to clarify certain parts of the Charters. In particular the third statute, in 1354, redefined clause 29, with "free man" becoming "no man, of whatever estate or condition he may be", and introduced the phrase "due process of law" for "lawful judgement of his peers or the law of the land".[1492]

Between the 13th and 15th centuries Magna Carta was reconfirmed 32 times according to Sir Edward Coke, and possibly as many as 45 times.[1493,1494] Often the first item of parliamentary business was a public reading and reaffirmation of the Charter, and, as in the previous century, parliaments often exacted confirmation of it from the monarch.[1494] The Charter was confirmed in 1423 by King Henry VI.

By the mid-15th century, Magna Carta ceased to occupy a central role in English political life, as monarchs reasserted authority and powers which had been challenged in the 100 years after Edward I's reign.[1495] The Great Charter remained a text for lawyers, particularly as a protector of property rights, and became more widely read than ever as printed versions circulated and levels of literacy increased.[1496]

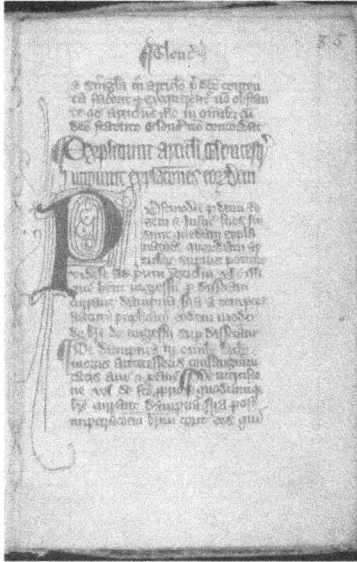

Figure 48: *Magna carta cum statutis angliae (Great Charter with English Statutes), early 14th-century*

16th century

During the 16th century, the interpretation of Magna Carta and the First Barons' War shifted.[1497] Henry VII took power at the end of the turbulent Wars of the Roses, followed by Henry VIII, and extensive propaganda under both rulers promoted the legitimacy of the regime, the illegitimacy of any sort of rebellion against royal power, and the priority of supporting the Crown in its arguments with the Papacy.[1498]

Tudor historians rediscovered the Barnwell chronicler, who was more favourable to King John than other 13th-century texts, and, as historian Ralph Turner describes, they "viewed King John in a positive light as a hero struggling against the papacy", showing "little sympathy for the Great Charter or the rebel barons".[1499] Pro-Catholic demonstrations during the 1536 uprising cited Magna Carta, accusing the King of not giving it sufficient respect.[1500]

The first mechanically printed edition of Magna Carta was probably the *Magna Carta cum aliis Antiquis Statutis* of 1508 by Richard Pynson, although the early printed versions of the 16th century incorrectly attributed the origins of Magna Carta to Henry III and 1225, rather than to John and 1215, and accordingly worked from the later text.[1501,1502,1503] An abridged English-language edition was published by John Rastell in 1527. Thomas Berthelet, Pynson's

Figure 49: *A version of the Charter of 1217, produced between 1437 and c. 1450*

successor as the royal printer during 1530–1547, printed an edition of the text along with other "ancient statutes" in 1531 and 1540.[1504] In 1534, George Ferrers published the first unabridged English-language edition of Magna Carta, dividing the Charter into 37 numbered clauses.[1505]

At the end of the 16th century, there was an upsurge in antiquarian interest in England.[1500] This work concluded that there was a set of ancient English customs and laws, temporarily overthrown by the Norman invasion of 1066, which had then been recovered in 1215 and recorded in Magna Carta, which in turn gave authority to important 16th century legal principles.[1506,1500,1507] Modern historians note that although this narrative was fundamentally incorrect—many refer to it as a "myth"—it took on great importance among the legal historians of the time.[1507,1508,1509,1510,1511,1512]</ref>

The antiquarian William Lambarde, for example, published what he believed were the Anglo-Saxon and Norman law codes, tracing the origins of the 16th-century English Parliament back to this period, albeit misinterpreting the dates of many documents concerned.[1506] Francis Bacon argued that clause 39 of Magna Carta was the basis of the 16th-century jury system and judicial processes.[1513] Antiquarians Robert Beale, James Morice, and Richard Cosin argued that Magna Carta was a statement of liberty and a fundamental, supreme law empowering English government.[1514] Those who questioned

Figure 50: *Jurist Edward Coke made extensive political use of Magna Carta.*

these conclusions, including the Member of Parliament Arthur Hall, faced sanctions.[1515,1516]

17th–18th centuries

Political tensions

In the early 17th century, Magna Carta became increasingly important as a political document in arguments over the authority of the English monarchy.[1517] James I and Charles I both propounded greater authority for the Crown, justified by the doctrine of the divine right of kings, and Magna Carta was cited extensively by their opponents to challenge the monarchy.[1510]

Magna Carta, it was argued, recognised and protected the liberty of individual Englishmen, made the King subject to the common law of the land, formed the origin of the trial by jury system, and acknowledged the ancient origins of Parliament: because of Magna Carta and this ancient constitution, an English monarch was unable to alter these long-standing English customs.[1510,1517,1518,1519] Although the arguments based on Magna Carta were historically inaccurate, they nonetheless carried symbolic power, as the charter had immense significance during this period; antiquarians such as Sir Henry Spelman described it as "the most majestic and a sacrosanct anchor to English Liberties".[1510,1517,1507]

Figure 51: *John Lilburne criticised Magna Carta*
as an inadequate definition of English liberties.

Sir Edward Coke was a leader in using Magna Carta as a political tool during this period. Still working from the 1225 version of the text—the first printed copy of the 1215 charter only emerged in 1610—Coke spoke and wrote about Magna Carta repeatedly.[1507] His work was challenged at the time by Lord Ellesmere, and modern historians such as Ralph Turner and Claire Breay have critiqued Coke as "misconstruing" the original charter "anachronistically and uncritically", and taking a "very selective" approach to his analysis.[1510,1520] More sympathetically, J. C. Holt noted that the history of the charters had already become "distorted" by the time Coke was carrying out his work.[1521]

In 1621, a bill was presented to Parliament to renew Magna Carta; although this bill failed, lawyer John Selden argued during Darnell's Case in 1627 that the right of *habeas corpus* was backed by Magna Carta.[1522,1523] Coke supported the Petition of Right in 1628, which cited Magna Carta in its preamble, attempting to extend the provisions, and to make them binding on the judiciary.[1524,1525] The monarchy responded by arguing that the historical legal situation was much less clear-cut than was being claimed, restricted the activities of antiquarians, arrested Coke for treason, and suppressed his proposed book on Magna Carta.[1523,1526] Charles initially did not agree to the Petition of Right, and refused to confirm Magna Carta in any way that would reduce his independence as King.[1527,1528]

England descended into civil war in the 1640s, resulting in Charles I's execution in 1649. Under the republic that followed, some questioned whether Magna Carta, an agreement with a monarch, was still relevant.[1529] An anti-Cromwellian pamphlet published in 1660, *The English devil*, said that the nation had been "compelled to submit to this Tyrant Nol or be cut off by him; nothing but a word and a blow, his Will was his Law; tell him of Magna Carta, he would lay his hand on his sword and cry Magna Farta".[1530] In a 2005 speech the Lord Chief Justice of England and Wales, Lord Woolf, repeated the claim that Cromwell had referred to Magna Carta as "Magna Farta".

The radical groups that flourished during this period held differing opinions of Magna Carta. The Levellers rejected history and law as presented by their contemporaries, holding instead to an "anti-Normanism" viewpoint.[1531] John Lilburne, for example, argued that Magna Carta contained only some of the freedoms that had supposedly existed under the Anglo-Saxons before being crushed by the Norman yoke.[1532] The Leveller Richard Overton described the charter as "a beggarly thing containing many marks of intolerable bondage".[1533] Both saw Magna Carta as a useful declaration of liberties that could be used against governments they disagreed with.[1534] Gerrard Winstanley, the leader of the more extreme Diggers, stated "the best lawes that England hath, [viz., the Magna Carta] were got by our Forefathers importunate petitioning unto the kings that still were their Task-masters; and yet these best laws are yoaks and manicles, tying one sort of people to be slaves to another; Clergy and Gentry have got their freedom, but the common people still are, and have been left servants to work for them."[1535,1536]

Glorious Revolution

The first attempt at a proper historiography was undertaken by Robert Brady,[1537] who refuted the supposed antiquity of Parliament and belief in the immutable continuity of the law. Brady realised that the liberties of the Charter were limited and argued that the liberties were the grant of the King. By putting Magna Carta in historical context, he cast doubt on its contemporary political relevance;[1538] his historical understanding did not survive the Glorious Revolution, which, according to the historian J. G. A. Pocock, "marked a setback for the course of English historiography."[1539]

According to the Whig interpretation of history, the Glorious Revolution was an example of the reclaiming of ancient liberties. Reinforced with Lockean concepts, the Whigs believed England's constitution to be a social contract, based on documents such as Magna Carta, the Petition of Right, and the Bill of Rights.[1540] The *English Liberties* (1680, in later versions often *British Liberties*) by the Whig propagandist Henry Care (d. 1688) was a cheap polemical book that was influential and much-reprinted, in the American colonies as well

Figure 52: *A 1733 engraving of the Charter of 1215 by John Pine*

as Britain, and made Magna Carta central to the history and the contemporary legitimacy of its subject.[1541]

Ideas about the nature of law in general were beginning to change. In 1716, the Septennial Act was passed, which had a number of consequences. First, it showed that Parliament no longer considered its previous statutes unassailable, as it provided for a maximum parliamentary term of seven years, whereas the Triennial Act (1694) (enacted less than a quarter of a century previously) had provided for a maximum term of three years.[1542]

It also greatly extended the powers of Parliament. Under this new constitution, monarchical absolutism was replaced by parliamentary supremacy. It was quickly realised that Magna Carta stood in the same relation to the King-in-Parliament as it had to the King without Parliament. This supremacy would be challenged by the likes of Granville Sharp. Sharp regarded Magna Carta as a fundamental part of the constitution, and maintained that it would be treason to repeal any part of it. He also held that the Charter prohibited slavery.[1542]

Sir William Blackstone published a critical edition of the 1215 Charter in 1759, and gave it the numbering system still used today.[1543] In 1763, Member of Parliament John Wilkes was arrested for writing an inflammatory pamphlet, *No. 45, 23 April 1763*; he cited Magna Carta continually.[1544] Lord Camden denounced the treatment of Wilkes as a contravention of Magna Carta.

Figure 53: *Magna Carta replica and display in the rotunda of the United States Capitol, Washington, D.C.*

Thomas Paine, in his *Rights of Man*, would disregard Magna Carta and the Bill of Rights on the grounds that they were not a written constitution devised by elected representatives.

Use in the Thirteen Colonies and the United States

When English colonists left for the New World, they brought royal charters that established the colonies. The Massachusetts Bay Company charter, for example, stated that the colonists would "have and enjoy all liberties and immunities of free and natural subjects." The Virginia Charter of 1606, which was largely drafted by Sir Edward Coke, stated that the colonists would have the same "liberties, franchises and immunities" as people born in England.[1545] The Massachusetts Body of Liberties contained similarities to clause 29 of Magna Carta; when drafting it, the Massachusetts General Court viewed Magna Carta as the chief embodiment of English common law.[1546] The other colonies would follow their example. In 1638, Maryland sought to recognise Magna Carta as part of the law of the province, but the request was denied by Charles I.[1547]

In 1687, William Penn published *The Excellent Privilege of Liberty and Property: being the birth-right of the Free-Born Subjects of England*, which contained the first copy of Magna Carta printed on American soil. Penn's comments reflected Coke's, indicating a belief that Magna Carta was a fundamental law.[1548] The colonists drew on English law books, leading them to an anachronistic interpretation of Magna Carta, believing that it guaranteed trial by jury and *habeas corpus*.[1549]

The development of parliamentary supremacy in the British Isles did not constitutionally affect the Thirteen Colonies, which retained an adherence to English common law, but it directly affected the relationship between Britain and the colonies.[1550] When American colonists fought against Britain, they were fighting not so much for new freedom, but to preserve liberties and rights that they believed to be enshrined in Magna Carta.

In the late 18th century, the United States Constitution became the supreme law of the land, recalling the manner in which Magna Carta had come to be regarded as fundamental law. The Constitution's Fifth Amendment guarantees that "no person shall be deprived of life, liberty, or property, without due process of law", a phrase that was derived from Magna Carta. In addition, the Constitution included a similar writ in the Suspension Clause, Article 1, Section 9: "The privilege of the writ of habeas corpus shall not be suspended, unless when in cases of rebellion or invasion, the public safety may require it."

Each of these proclaim that no person may be imprisoned or detained without evidence that he or she committed a crime. The Ninth Amendment states that "The enumeration in the Constitution, of certain rights, shall not be construed to deny or disparage others retained by the people." The writers of the U.S. Constitution wished to ensure that the rights they already held, such as those that they believed were provided by Magna Carta, would be preserved unless explicitly curtailed.[1551,1552]

The Supreme Court of the United States has explicitly referenced Lord Coke's analysis of Magna Carta as an antecedent of the Sixth Amendment's right to a speedy trial.

Figure 54: *A romanticised 19th-century recre-
ation of King John signing Magna Carta*

19th–21st centuries

Interpretation

Initially, the Whig interpretation of Magna Carta and its role in constitutional
history remained dominant during the 19th century. The historian William
Stubbs's *Constitutional History of England*, published in the 1870s, formed
the high-water mark of this view.[1553] Stubbs argued that Magna Carta had
been a major step in the shaping of the English nation, and he believed that the
barons at Runnymede in 1215 were not just representing the nobility, but the
people of England as a whole, standing up to a tyrannical ruler in the form of
King John.[1553,1554]

This view of Magna Carta began to recede. The late-Victorian jurist and historian Frederic William Maitland provided an alternative academic history in
1899, which began to return Magna Carta to its historical roots.[1555] In 1904,
Edward Jenks published an article entitled "The Myth of Magna Carta", which
undermined the traditionally accepted view of Magna Carta.[1556] Historians
such as Albert Pollard agreed with Jenks in concluding that Edward Coke had
largely "invented" the myth of Magna Carta in the 17th century; these historians argued that the 1215 charter had not referred to liberty for the people at
large, but rather to the protection of baronial rights.[1557]

This view also became popular in wider circles, and in 1930 Sellar and Yeat-man published their parody on English history, *1066 and All That*, in which they mocked the supposed importance of Magna Carta and its promises of universal liberty: "Magna Charter was therefore the chief cause of Democracy in England, and thus a *Good Thing* for everyone (except the Common People)".[1558,1559]

In many literary representations of the medieval past, however, Magna Carta remained a foundation of English national identity. Some authors used the medieval roots of the document as an argument to preserve the social status quo, while others pointed to Magna Carta to challenge perceived economic injustices.[1555] The Baronial Order of Magna Charta was formed in 1898 to promote the ancient principles and values felt to be displayed in Magna Carta. The legal profession in England and the United States continued to hold Magna Carta in high esteem; they were instrumental in forming the Magna Carta Society in 1922 to protect the meadows at Runnymede from development in the 1920s, and in 1957, the American Bar Association erected the Magna Carta Memorial at Runnymede.[1560,1561] The prominent lawyer Lord Denning described Magna Carta in 1956 as "the greatest constitutional document of all times – the foundation of the freedom of the individual against the arbitrary authority of the despot".[1562]

Repeal of articles and constitutional influence

Radicals such as Sir Francis Burdett believed that Magna Carta could not be repealed,[1563] but in the 19th century clauses which were obsolete or had been superseded began to be repealed. The repeal of clause 36 in 1829, by the Offences against the Person Act 1828 (9 Geo. 4 c. 31 s. 1), was the first time a clause of Magna Carta was repealed. Over the next 140 years, nearly the whole of Magna Carta (1297) as statute was repealed, leaving just clauses 1, 9, and 29 still in force (in England and Wales) after 1969. Most of the clauses were repealed in England and Wales by the Statute Law Revision Act 1863, and in modern Northern Ireland and also in the modern Republic of Ireland by the Statute Law (Ireland) Revision Act 1872.

Many later attempts to draft constitutional forms of government trace their lineage back to Magna Carta. The British dominions, Australia and New Zealand,[1564] Canada[1565] (except Quebec), and formerly the Union of South Africa and Southern Rhodesia, reflected the influence of Magna Carta in their laws, and the Charter's effects can be seen in the laws of other states that evolved from the British Empire.[1566]

Figure 55: *The Magna Carta Memorial at Runnymede, designed by Sir Edward Maufe and erected by the American Bar Association in 1957. The memorial stands in the meadow known historically as Long Mede: it is likely that the actual site of the sealing of Magna Carta lay further east, towards Egham and Staines.*[1392]

Modern legacy

Magna Carta continues to have a powerful iconic status in British society, being cited by politicians and lawyers in support of constitutional positions.[1562,1567] Its perceived guarantee of trial by jury and other civil liberties, for example, led to Tony Benn's reference to the debate in 2008 over whether to increase the maximum time terrorism suspects could be held without charge from 28 to 42 days as "the day Magna Carta was repealed". Although rarely invoked in court in the modern era, in 2012 the Occupy London protestors attempted to use Magna Carta in resisting their eviction from St. Paul's Churchyard by the City of London. In his judgment the Master of the Rolls gave this short shrift, noting somewhat drily that although clause 29 was considered by many the foundation of the rule of law in England, he did not consider it directly relevant to the case, and the two other surviving clauses actually concerned the rights of the Church and the City of London.

Magna Carta carries little legal weight in modern Britain, as most of its clauses have been repealed and relevant rights ensured by other statutes, but the historian James Holt remarks that the survival of the 1215 charter in national life is a "reflexion of the continuous development of English law and administration" and symbolic of the many struggles between authority and the law over the

Figure 56: *The plan for four surviving original copies of Magna Carta to be brought together in 2015, at the British Library in collaboration with Lincoln Cathedral and Salisbury Cathedral and supported by the law firm Linklaters*

centuries.[1568] The historian W. L. Warren has observed that "many who knew little and cared less about the content of the Charter have, in nearly all ages, invoked its name, and with good cause, for it meant more than it said".[1569]

It also remains a topic of great interest to historians; Natalie Fryde characterised the charter as "one of the holiest of cows in English medieval history", with the debates over its interpretation and meaning unlikely to end.[1554] In many ways still a "sacred text", Magna Carta is generally considered part of the uncodified constitution of the United Kingdom; in a 2005 speech, the Lord Chief Justice of England and Wales, Lord Woolf, described it as the "first of a series of instruments that now are recognised as having a special constitutional status".[1570]

The document also continues to be honoured in the United States as an antecedent of the United States Constitution and Bill of Rights. In 1976, the UK lent one of four surviving originals of the 1215 Magna Carta to the United States for their bicentennial celebrations and also donated an ornate display case for it. The original was returned after one year, but a replica and the case are still on display in the United States Capitol Crypt in Washington, D.C.

Celebration of the 800th anniversary

The 800th anniversary of the original charter occurred on 15 June 2015, and organisations and institutions planned celebratory events. The British Library brought together the four existing copies of the 1215 manuscript in February

2015 for a special exhibition. British artist Cornelia Parker was commissioned to create a new artwork, *Magna Carta (An Embroidery)*, which was shown at the British Library between May and July 2015. The artwork is a copy of an earlier version of this Wikipedia page (as it appeared on the document's 799th anniversary, 15 June 2014), hand-embroidered by over 200 people.

On 15 June 2015, a commemoration ceremony was conducted in Runnymede at the National Trust park, attended by British and American dignitaries.

The copy held by Lincoln Cathedral was exhibited in the Library of Congress in Washington, D.C., from November 2014 until January 2015. A new visitor centre at Lincoln Castle will also be opened for the anniversary. The Royal Mint released two commemorative two-pound coins.

In 2014, Bury St Edmunds in Suffolk celebrated the 800th anniversary of the barons' Charter of Liberties, said to have been secretly agreed there in November 1214.

Content

Physical format

Numerous copies, known as exemplifications, were made of the various charters, and many of them still survive.[1571] The documents were written in heavily abbreviated medieval Latin in clear handwriting, using quill pens on sheets of parchment made from sheep skin, approximately 15 by 20 inches (380 by 510 mm) across.[1572,1573] They were sealed with the royal great seal by an official called the spigurnel, equipped with a special seal press, using beeswax and resin.[1574,1573] There were no signatures on the charter of 1215, and the barons present did not attach their own seals to it.[1575] The charters were not numbered or divided into paragraphs or separate clauses at the time; the numbering system used today was introduced by the jurist Sir William Blackstone in 1759.[1543]

Exemplifications

1215 exemplifications

At least 13 original copies of the 1215 charter were issued by the royal chancery at the time, seven in the first tranche distributed on 24 June and another six later; they were sent to county sheriffs and bishops, who would probably have been charged for the privilege.[1576] Variations would have existed between each of these copies and there was probably no single "master copy".[1577] Of these documents, only four survive, all held in the UK—two in the British Library, one by Lincoln Cathedral, and one in Salisbury Cathedral.[1578] Each of these

Figure 57: *1225 charter, held in the British
Library, with the royal great seal attached*

versions is slightly different in size and text, and each is considered by historians
to be equally authoritative.[1579]

The two 1215 charters held by the British Library, known as Cotton MS. Au-
gustus II.106 and Cotton Charter XIII.31a, were acquired by the antiquarian
Sir Robert Cotton in the 17th century.[1580] One of these was originally found by
Humphrey Wyems, a London lawyer, who may have discovered it in a tailor's
shop.[1581] The other was found in Dover Castle in 1630 by Sir Edward Dering.
The Dering charter is usually identified as the copy originally sent to the Cinque
Ports in 1215.[1582] (In 2015 it was announced that David Carpenter had found
Dering's copy to be identical to a 1290s transcription made from Canterbury
Cathedral's 1215 copy and so he suggests that the Dering copy's destination
was the Cathedral rather than the Cinque Ports.) This copy was damaged in
the Cotton library fire of 1731, when its seal was badly melted. The parchment
was somewhat shrivelled but otherwise relatively unscathed, and an engraved
facsimile of the charter was made by John Pine in 1733. In the 1830s, however, an ill-judged and bungled attempt at cleaning and conservation rendered
the manuscript largely illegible to the naked eye.[1583] This is, nonetheless, the
only surviving 1215 copy still to have its great seal attached.[1584,1585]

Lincoln Cathedral's original copy of the 1215 charter has been held by the
county since 1215; it was displayed in the Common Chamber in the cathedral

before being moved to another building in 1846.[1578] Between 1939 and 1940 the copy was displayed in the British Pavilion at the 1939 World Fair in New York City, and at the Library of Congress. When the Second World War broke out, Winston Churchill wanted to gift the charter to the American people, hoping that this would encourage the United States, then neutral, to enter the war against the Axis powers, but the cathedral was unwilling and the plans were dropped.[1586] After December 1941, the copy was stored in Fort Knox, Kentucky for safety, before being put on display again in 1944 and returned to Lincoln Cathedral in early 1946.

The copy was put on display in 1976 as part of the cathedral's medieval library. It was subsequently displayed in San Francisco, and was taken out of display for a time to undergo conservation in preparation for another visit to the United States, where it was exhibited in 2007 at the Contemporary Art Center of Virginia and the National Constitution Center in Philadelphia. The document returned to New York to be displayed at the Fraunces Tavern Museum during 2009.

The fourth copy, owned by Salisbury Cathedral, was first given in 1215 to its predecessor, Old Sarum Cathedral. Rediscovered by the cathedral in 1812, it has remained in Salisbury throughout its history, except when being taken off-site for restoration work.[1587] It is possibly the best preserved of the four, although small pin holes can be seen in the parchment from where it was once pinned up. The handwriting on this version is different from that of the other three, suggesting that it was not written by a royal scribe but rather by a member of the cathedral staff, who then had it exemplified by the royal court.[1587,1571]

Later exemplifications

Other early versions of the charters survive today. Only one exemplification of the 1216 charter survives, held in Durham Cathedral.[1588] Four copies of the 1217 charter exist; three of these are held by the Bodleian Library in Oxford and one by Hereford Cathedral.[1588] Hereford's copy is occasionally displayed alongside the Mappa Mundi in the cathedral's chained library and has survived along with a small document called the *Articuli super Cartas* that was sent along with the charter, telling the sheriff of the county how to observe the conditions outlined in the document. One of the Bodleian's copies was displayed at San Francisco's California Palace of the Legion of Honor in 2011.

Four exemplifications of the 1225 charter survive: the British Library holds one, which was preserved at Lacock Abbey until 1945; Durham Cathedral also holds a copy, with the Bodleian Library holding a third. The fourth copy of the 1225 exemplification was held by the museum of the Public Record Office and is now held by The National Archives.[1589] The Society of Antiquaries also holds a draft of the 1215 charter (discovered in 2013 in a late 13th-century

Figure 58: *A 1297 copy of Magna Carta, owned by the Australian Government and on display in the Members' Hall of Parliament House, Canberra*

register from Peterborough Abbey), a copy of the 1225 third re-issue (within an early 14th-century collection of statutes) and a roll copy of the 1225 reissue.

Only two exemplifications of Magna Carta are held outside England, both from 1297. One of these was purchased in 1952 by the Australian Government for £12,500 from King's School, Bruton, England. This copy is now on display in the Members' Hall of Parliament House, Canberra. The second was originally held by the Brudenell family, earls of Cardigan, before they sold it in 1984 to the Perot Foundation in the United States, which in 2007 sold it to U.S. businessman David Rubenstein for US$21.3 million. Rubenstein commented "I have always believed that this was an important document to our country, even though it wasn't drafted in our country. I think it was the basis for the Declaration of Independence and the basis for the Constitution". This exemplification is now on permanent loan to the National Archives in Washington, D.C.[1590] Only two other 1297 exemplifications survive, one of which is held in the UK's National Archives.

Seven copies of the 1300 exemplification by Edward I survive, in Faversham, Oriel College, Oxford, the Bodleian Library, Durham Cathedral, Westminster Abbey, the City of London (held in the archives at the London Guildhall) and Sandwich (held in the Kent County Council archives). The Sandwich copy was rediscovered in early 2015 in a Victorian scrapbook in the town archives of Sandwich, Kent, one of the Cinque Ports. In the case of the Sandwich and

Figure 59: *A silver King John penny; much of Magna Carta concerned how royal revenues were raised*

Oriel College exemplifications, the copies of the Charter of the Forest originally issued with them also survive.

Clauses

Most of the 1215 charter and later versions sought to govern the feudal rights of the Crown over the barons.[1591] Under the Angevin kings, and in particular during John's reign, the rights of the King had frequently been used inconsistently, often in an attempt to maximise the royal income from the barons. Feudal relief was one way that a king could demand money, and clauses 2 and 3 fixed the fees payable when an heir inherited an estate or when a minor came of age and took possession of his lands.[1591] Scutage was a form of medieval taxation; all knights and nobles owed military service to the Crown in return for their lands, which theoretically belonged to the King, but many preferred to avoid this service and offer money instead; the Crown often used the cash to pay for mercenaries.[1592] The rate of scutage that should be payable, and the circumstances under which it was appropriate for the King to demand it, was uncertain and controversial; clauses 12 and 14 addressed the management of the process.[1591]

Figure 60: *King John holding a church, painted c. 1250–59 by Matthew Paris*

The English judicial system had altered considerably over the previous century, with the royal judges playing a larger role in delivering justice across the country. John had used his royal discretion to extort large sums of money from the barons, effectively taking payment to offer justice in particular cases, and the role of the Crown in delivering justice had become politically sensitive among the barons. Clauses 39 and 40 demanded due process be applied in the royal justice system, while clause 45 required that the King appoint knowledgeable royal officials to the relevant roles.[1593]   Although these clauses did not have any special significance in the original charter, this part of Magna Carta became singled out as particularly important in later centuries.[1593] In the United States, for example, the Supreme Court of California interpreted clause 45 in 1974 as establishing a requirement in common law that a defendant faced with the potential of incarceration be entitled to a trial overseen by a legally trained judge.[1594]

Royal forests were economically important in medieval England and were both protected and exploited by the Crown, supplying the King with hunting grounds, raw materials, and money.[1595,1596] They were subject to special royal jurisdiction and the resulting forest law was, according to the historian Richard Huscroft, "harsh and arbitrary, a matter purely for the King's will".[1595] The size of the forests had expanded under the Angevin kings, an unpopular development.[1597]

The 1215 charter had several clauses relating to the royal forests; clauses 47 and 48 promised to deforest the lands added to the forests under John and investigate the use of royal rights in this area, but notably did not address the forestation of the previous kings, while clause 53 promised some form of redress for those affected by the recent changes, and clause 44 promised some relief from the operation of the forest courts.[1598] Neither Magna Carta nor the subsequent Charter of the Forest proved entirely satisfactory as a way of managing the political tensions arising in the operation of the royal forests.[1598]

Some of the clauses addressed wider economic issues. The concerns of the barons over the treatment of their debts to Jewish moneylenders, who occupied a special position in medieval England and were by tradition under the King's protection, were addressed by clauses 10 and 11.[1599] The charter concluded this section with the phrase "debts owing to other than Jews shall be dealt with likewise", so it is debatable to what extent the Jews were being singled out by these clauses.[1600] Some issues were relatively specific, such as clause 33 which ordered the removal of all fishing weirs—an important and growing source of revenue at the time—from England's rivers.[1598]

The role of the English Church had been a matter for great debate in the years prior to the 1215 charter. The Norman and Angevin kings had traditionally exercised a great deal of power over the church within their territories. From the 1040s onwards successive popes had emphasised the importance of the church being governed more effectively from Rome, and had established an independent judicial system and hierarchical chain of authority.[1601] After the 1140s, these principles had been largely accepted within the English church, even if accompanied by an element of concern about centralising authority in Rome.[1602,1603]

These changes brought the customary rights of lay rulers such as John over ecclesiastical appointments into question.[1602] As described above, John had come to a compromise with Pope Innocent III in exchange for his political support for the King, and clause 1 of Magna Carta prominently displayed this arrangement, promising the freedoms and liberties of the church.[1591] The importance of this clause may also reflect the role of Archbishop Langton in the negotiations: Langton had taken a strong line on this issue during his career.[1591]

Clauses in detail

Clauses remaining in English law

Only three clauses of Magna Carta still remain on statute in England and Wales.[1567] These clauses concern 1) the freedom of the English Church, 2) the "ancient liberties" of the City of London (clause 13 in the 1215 charter, clause 9 in the 1297 statute), and 3) a right to due legal process (clauses 39 and 40 in the 1215 charter, clause 29 in the 1297 statute).[1567] In detail, these clauses (using the numbering system from the 1297 statute) state that:

- *I. FIRST, We have granted to God, and by this our present Charter have confirmed, for Us and our Heirs for ever, that the Church of England shall be free, and shall have all her whole Rights and Liberties inviolable. We have granted also, and given to all the Freemen of our Realm, for Us and our Heirs for ever, these Liberties under-written, to have and to hold to them and their Heirs, of Us and our Heirs for ever.*
- *IX. THE City of London shall have all the old Liberties and Customs which it hath been used to have. Moreover We will and grant, that all other Cities, Boroughs, Towns, and the Barons of the Five Ports, as with all other Ports, shall have all their Liberties and free Customs.*
- *XXIX. NO Freeman shall be taken or imprisoned, or be disseised of his Freehold, or Liberties, or free Customs, or be outlawed, or exiled, or any other wise destroyed; nor will We not pass upon him, nor condemn him, but by lawful judgment of his Peers, or by the Law of the land. We will sell to no man, we will not deny or defer to any man either Justice or Right.*

Bibliography

- Aurell, Martin (2003). *L'Empire de Plantagenêt, 1154–1224* (in French). Paris, France: Tempus. ISBN 978-2-262-02282-2.
- Barnes, Thomas Garden (2008). *Shaping the Common Law: From Glanvill to Hale, 1188–1688*[1606]. Stanford University Press. ISBN 978-0804779593.
- Black, Charles (1999). *A New Birth of Freedom: Human Rights, Named and Unnamed*. New Haven, US: Yale University Press. ISBN 978-0300077346.
- Breay, Claire (2010). *Magna Carta: Manuscripts and Myths*. London, UK: The British Library. ISBN 978-0-7123-5833-0.
- Breay, Claire; Harrison, Julian, eds. (2015). *Magna Carta: Law, Liberty, Legacy*. London: The British Library. ISBN 978-0-7123-5764-7.
- Browning, Charles Henry (1898). "The Magna Charta Described"[1607]. *The Magna Charta Barons and Their American Descendants with the Pedigrees of the Founders of the Order of Runnemede Deduced from the Sureties for the Enforcement of the Statutes of the Magna Charta of King John*[1608]. Philadelphia. OCLC 9378577[1609].
- Burdett, Francis (1810). *Sir Francis Burdett to His Constituents*[1610]. R. Bradshaw.

- Carpenter, David A. (1990). *The Minority of Henry III*. Berkeley, US and Los Angeles, US: University of California Press. ISBN 978-0413623607.
- Carpenter, David (1996). *The Reign of Henry III*. London, UK: Hambledon Press. ISBN 9781852851378.
- Carpenter, David A. (2004). *Struggle for Mastery: The Penguin History of Britain 1066–1284*. London, UK: Penguin. ISBN 978-0-14-014824-4.
- Clanchy, Michael T. (1997). *Early Medieval England*. The Folio Society.
- Clark, David (2000). "The Icon of Liberty: The Status and Role of Magna Carta in Australian and New Zealand Law"[1611]. *Melbourne University Law Review*. **24** (3).
- Cobbett, William; Howell, Thomas Bayly; Howell, Th. J.; Jardine, William (1810). *Cobbett's Complete Collection of State Trials and Proceedings for High Treason and Other Crimes and Misdemeanors from the Earliest Period to the Present Time*[1612]. Bagshaw.
- Crouch, David (1996). *William Marshal: Court, Career and Chivalry in the Angevin Empire 1147–1219*. Longman. ISBN 978-0582037861.
- Danziger, Danny; Gillingham, John (2004). *1215: The Year of Magna Carta*[1613]. Hodder Paperbacks. ISBN 978-0340824757.
- Davis, G. R. C. (1963). *Magna Carta*. The British Library Publishing Division. ISBN 978-0712300148.
- Davis, John Paul (2013). *The Gothic King: A Biography of Henry III*. London, UK: Peter Owen. ISBN 978-0-7206-1480-0.
- Drew, Katherine F. (2004). *Magna Carta*. Greenwood Press. ISBN 978-0313325908.
- Edwards, J. G. (1943). "Confirmatio Cartarum and Baronial Grievances in 1297". *The English Historical Review*. **58** (231): 273–300. JSTOR 554340[1614]. doi: 10.1093/ehr/lviii.ccxxxi.273[1615].
- Eele, Caroline (2013). *Perceptions of Magna Carta: Why has it been seen as significant?*[1616] (PDF) (Thesis). 2014 Magna Carta 2015 Committee. Retrieved 18 November 2014.
- Fryde, Natalie (2001). *Why Magna Carta? Angevin England Revisited*. Munster, Germany: LiT. ISBN 978-3825856571.
- Fritze, Ronald; Robison, William (2002). *Historical Dictionary of Late Medieval England 1272–1485*. Greenwood Press. ISBN 978-0313291241.
- Galef, David (1998). *Second Thoughts: Focus on Rereading*. Detroit, US: Wayne State University Press. ISBN 978-0814326473.
- Goodman, Ellen (1995). *The Origins of the Western Legal Tradition: From Thales to the Tudors*[1617]. Federation Press. ISBN 978-1862871816.
- Greenberg, Janelle (2006). *The Radical Face of the Ancient Constitution: St Edward's 'Laws' in Early Modern Political Thought*. Cambridge, UK: Cambridge University Press. ISBN 978-0521024884.

- Hallam, Elizabeth M.; Everard, Judith A. (2001). *Capetian France, 987–1328* (2nd ed.). Harlow, UK: Longman. ISBN 978-0-582-40428-1.
- Hazeltine, H. D. (1917). "The Influence of Magna Carta on American Constitutional Development". In Malden, Henry Elliot. *Magna Carta commemoration essays*. BiblioBazaar. ISBN 978-1116447477.
- Hewit, H. J. (1929). *Mediaeval Cheshire*. Manchester, UK: Manchester University Press.
- Hill, Christopher (2006). *Winstanley 'The Law of Freedom' and Other Writings*[1618]. Cambridge University Press. ISBN 978-0521031608.
- Hillaby, Caroline (2013). *The Palgrave Dictionary of Medieval Anglo-Jewish History*[1619]. Palgrave Macmillan. ISBN 978-1137308153.
- Hindley, Geoffrey (1990). *The Book of Magna Carta*. London, UK: Constable. ISBN 978-0094682405.
- Holt, James C. (1992a). *The Northerners: A Study in the Reign of King John*. Oxford, UK: Oxford University Press. ISBN 978-0198203094.
- Holt, James C. (1992b). *Magna Carta*. Cambridge, UK: Cambridge University Press. ISBN 978-0521277785.
- Holt, James C. (2015). *Magna Carta* (3rd ed.). Cambridge, UK: Cambridge University Press. ISBN 9781107093164.
- Holt, James C. (2008) [1993]. *The Ancient Constitution in Medieval England*[1620] (PDF). Liberty Fund. ISBN 978-0865977099.
- Howard, A. E. Dick (2008). "Magna Carta Comes To America". *Fourscore*. **58** (4).
- Huscroft, Richard (2005). *Ruling England, 1042–1217*. Harlow, UK: Pearson. ISBN 978-0-582-84882-5.
- Jobson, Adrian (2012). *The First English Revolution: Simon de Montfort, Henry III and the Barons' War*. London, UK: Bloomsbury. ISBN 978-1-84725-226-5.
- Kennedy, William Paul McClure (1922). *The Constitution of Canada*. Oxford, UK: Oxford University Press.
- Kewes, Paulina (2006). *The Uses of History in Early Modern England*. Berkeley, US: University of California Press. ISBN 978-0873282192.
- Lewis, Suzanne (1987). *The Art of Matthew Paris in the Chronica Majora*[1621]. University of California Press. ISBN 9780520049819.
- Linebaugh, Peter (2009). *The Magna Carta Manifesto: Liberties and Commons for All*[1622]. Berkeley, US: University of California Press. ISBN 978-0520260009.
- Mayr-Harting, Henry (2011). *Religion, Politics and Society in Britain, 1066–1272*. Harlow, UK: Longman. ISBN 978-0-582-41413-6.
- McGlynn, Sean (2013). *Blood Cries Afar: The Forgotten Invasion of England, 1216*. London, UK: Spellmount. ISBN 978-0752488318.

- Menache, Sophia (2003). *Clement V*. Cambridge, UK: Cambridge University Press. ISBN 978-0521521987.
- Pocock, J. G. A. (1987). *The Ancient Constitution and the Feudal Law: A Study of English Historical Thought in the Seventeenth Century*. Cambridge, UK: Cambridge University Press. ISBN 978-0521316439.
- Pollard, Albert Frederick (1912). *The history of England; a study in political evolution*[1623]. H. Holt.
- Poole, Austin Lane (1993) [1951]. *From Domesday Book to Magna Carta 1087–1216* (2nd ed.). Oxford, UK: Oxford University Press.
- Powicke, F. M. (1929). "The Bull 'Miramur Plurimum' and a Letter to Archbishop Stephen Langton, 5 September 1215". *English Historical Review*. **44**: 87–93. doi: 10.1093/ehr/xliv.clxxiii.87[1624].
- Powicke, Frederick Maurice (1963). *The Thirteenth Century 1216–1307*. Oxford, UK: Oxford University Press. ISBN 978-0198217084.
- Prestwich, Michael (1997). *Edward I*. New Haven, US: Yale University Press. ISBN 978-0300071573.
- Ridgeway, Huw W. (2004). "Henry III (1207–1272)"[1625]. *Oxford Dictionary of National Biography, online edition*. Oxford University Press (published September 2010). doi: 10.1093/ref:odnb/12950[1626]. Archived from the original[1627] on 3 August 2013. Retrieved 17 August 2013.
- Rothwell, Harry (1975). *English Historical Documents 1189–1327*. London, UK: Eyre & Spottiswoode. ISBN 0413233006.
- Russell, Conrad (1990). *Unrevolutionary England, 1603–1642*. Continnuum-3PL. ISBN 978-1852850258.
- Scott, Robert McNair (2014). *Robert The Bruce: King Of Scots*[1628]. Canongate Books. ISBN 9781847677464.
- Simmons, Clare A. (1998). "Absent Presence: The Romantic-Era Magna Charta and the English Constitution". In Shippey, Richard; Utz, Tom. *Medievalism in the Modern World. Essays in Honour of Leslie J. Workman*. Brepols Publishers.
- Stimson, Frederick Jessup (2004). *The Law Of The Federal And State Constitutions Of The United States*. Lawbook Exchange Ltd. ISBN 978-1584773696.
- Tatton-Brown, Tim (July 2015). "Magna Carta at 800: Uncovering its Landscape Archaeology". *Current Archaeology* (304): 34–37.
- Thompson, Faith (1948). *Magna Carta—Its Role In The Making Of The English Constitution 1300–1629*. Minneapolis, US: University of Minnesota Press. ISBN 978-1299948686.
- Turner, Ralph V. (2003a). "The Meaning of Magna Carta since 1215"[1629]. *History Today*. **53** (9).
- Turner, Ralph (2003b). *Magna Carta:Through the Ages*. Routledge. ISBN 978-0582438262.

- Turner, Ralph (2009). *King John: England's Evil King?*. Stroud, UK: History Press. ISBN 978-0-7524-4850-3.
- Vincent, Nicholas (2012). *Magna Carta: A Very Short Introduction*. Oxford, UK: Oxford University Press. ISBN 978-0-19-958287-7.
- Vincent, Nicholas (2015). "From World War to World Heritage: Magna Carta in the Twentieth Century". In Vincent, Nicholas. *Magna Carta: The Foundation of Freedom, 1215–2015*. London, UK: Third Millennium Publishing. pp. 154–169. ISBN 9781908990488.
- Warren, W. Lewis (1990). *King John*. London, UK: Methuen. ISBN 978-0413455208.
- Weiler, Björn K. U. (2012). *Henry III of England and the Staufen Empire, 1216–1272*. Paris, France: Royal Historical Society: Boydell Press. ISBN 978-0-86193-319-8.
- White, Albert Beebe (1915). "The Name Magna Carta"[1630]. *The English Historical Review*. **XXX** (CXIX): 472–475. doi: 10.1093/ehr/XXX.CXIX.472[1631].
- White, Albert Beebe (1917). "Note on the Name Magna Carta"[1632]. *The English Historical Review*. XXXII (CXXVIII): 545–555. doi: 10.1093/ehr/XXXII.CXXVIII.554[1633].
- Woolwrych, Austin Herbert (2003). Smith, David Lee, ed. *Cromwell and Interregnum: The Essential Readings*[1634]. Wiley-Blackwell. ISBN 978-0631227250.
- Wright, Herbert G. (1919). *The Life And Works Of Arthur Hall Of Grantham, Member Of Parliament, Courtier And First Translator Of Homer Into English*. Book on Demand.
- Wright, Patrick (1990). *The River: A Thames Journey*. London, UK: BBC Books. ISBN 978-0563384786.

Further reading

- Ambler, S. T. (August 2015). "Magna Carta: Its Confirmation at Simon de Montfort's Parliament of 1265". *English Historical Review*. **CXXX** (545): 801–30. doi: 10.1093/ehr/cev202[1635].
- McKechnie, William Sharp (1914). *Magna Carta: A Commentary on the Great Charter of King John with an Historical Introduction*[1636] (PDF). Glasgow, UK: James Maclehose and Sons.
- Sandoz, Ellis (2008). *Roots of Liberty: Magna Carta, Ancient Constitution and the Anglo-American Tradition of Rule of Law*[1637]. Liberty Fund Inc. ISBN 978-0865977099.
- Blick, Andrew (2015). *Magna Carta and contemporary constitutional change*[1638]. History & Policy.

- Royal Holloway University of London. "The Magna Carta and its Legacy, free online course"[1639].
- Ruddick, Andrea (15 June 2015). "The English Church shall be Free!"[1640]. *Church Society*. Retrieved 26 July 2016.

External links

Wikisourcehas original text related to this article:
Magna Carta

Latin Wikisourcehas original text related to this article:
Magna Carta

Wikimedia Commons has media related to *Magna Carta*.

Wikiquote has quotations related to: *Magna Carta*

Government Magna Carta websites

- British Library[1641]
- National Archives United Kingdom[1642]
- British Parliament[1643]
- Library of Congress USA[1644]
- National Archives USA[1645]

Texts

- Text of the Magna Carta 1297[1646] as in force today (including any amendments) within the United Kingdom, from legislation.gov.uk
- *Magna Carta Libertatum*[1647] Latin and English text of the 1215 charter
- Text of Magna Carta[1648] English translation, with introductory historical note. From the Internet Medieval Sourcebook.
- Glossary of terms in Magna Carta[1649]
- Interactive, high-resolution view[1650] of a copy from 1297, owned by David Rubenstein and on permanent loan to the US National Archives
- Timeline of 13th Century Magna Carta Events[1651] National Archives-UK
- ◄) *Magna Carta*[1652] public domain audiobook at LibriVox

Video

- Magna Carta[1653] at BBC Radio 4, 2015
- BBC Anniversary Lecture[1654] Professor Linda Colley 25 Nov 2014
  Guildhall London, England
- *Magna Carta's Legal Legacy*[1655] US Chief Justice John Roberts and Lord
  Igor Judge Former Lord Chief Justice of England and Wales 14 Nov 2014
- *The Relevance of the Magna Carta to the 21st Century*[1656] Sir Robert
  Worcester 29 Nov 2012

Schwabenspiegel

The *Schwabenspiegel* is a legal code, written in ca. 1275 by a Franciscan friar
in Augsburg. It deals mainly with questions of land ownership and fiefdom,
and it is based on the Pentateuch, Roman law as well as Canon law. It draws
on the early 13th century *Sachsenspiegel*, and is immediately dependent on the
Deutschenspiegel code.

The name "mirror of the Swabians" is also taken from the *Sachsenspiegel*
("mirror of the Saxons"). Since the code is not prescriptive but descriptive,
i.e. it records current legal practice, it does not impose any new laws, it was
metaphorically compared to a mirror in which to perceive right and wrong.

External links

- (fragment)[1657]

Napoleonic Code

Napoleonic Code	
 First page of the 1804 original edition.	
Original title	*Code civil des Français* *Code Napoléon*
Date effective	21 March 1804 (frequently amended)

The **Napoleonic Code** (French: *Code Napoléon*; officially **Code civil des Français**, referred to as **(le) Code civil**) is the French civil code established under Napoléon I in 1804.

It was drafted by a commission of four eminent jurists and entered into force on 21 March 1804.[1658] The Code, with its stress on clearly written and accessible law, was a major step in replacing the previous patchwork of feudal laws. Historian Robert Holtman regards it as one of the few documents that have influenced the whole world.

The Napoleonic Code was not the first legal code to be established in a European country with a civil legal system; it was preceded by the Codex Maximilianeus bavaricus civilis (Bavaria, 1756), the Allgemeines Landrecht (Prussia, 1794), and the West Galician Code (Galicia, then part of Austria, 1797). It was, however, the first modern legal code to be adopted with a pan-European scope, and it strongly influenced the law of many of the countries formed during and after the Napoleonic Wars. The Napoleonic Code influenced developing countries outside Europe, especially in the Middle East, attempting to modernize their countries through legal reforms.

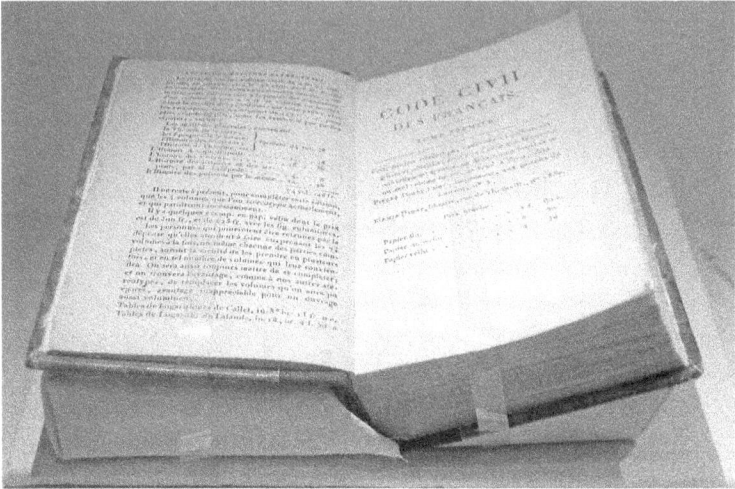

Figure 61: *The Napoleonic Code in the His-*
torical Museum of the Palatinate in Speyer

History

The categories of the Napoleonic Code were not drawn from the earlier French laws, but instead from Justinian's sixth-century codification of Roman law, the *Corpus Juris Civilis* and within it, the *Institutes*. The *Institutes* divide law into the law of:

1. persons
2. things
3. actions.

Similarly, the Napoleonic Code divided law into law of:

1. persons
2. property
3. acquisition of property
4. civil procedure (moved into a separate code in 1806).

Napoleonic reforms

Napoleon set out to reform the French legal system in accordance with the ideas of the French Revolution, because the old feudal and royal laws seemed confusing and contradictory. Before the Napoleonic Code, France did not have a single set of laws; law consisted mainly of local customs, which had sometimes been officially compiled in "customals" (*coutumes*), notably the

Custom of Paris. There were also exemptions, privileges, and special charters granted by the kings or other feudal lords. During the Revolution, the last vestiges of feudalism were abolished.

Specifically, as to civil law, the many different bodies of law used in different parts of France were replaced by a single legal code. Jean-Jacques Régis de Cambacérès led this drafting process. His drafts of 1793 (for which he had been given a one-month deadline), 1794, and 1799, however, were adopted only piecemeal by a National Convention more concerned about the turmoil resulting from the various wars and strife with other European powers.

A fresh start was made after Napoleon came to power in 1799. A commission of four eminent jurists was appointed in 1800, including Louis-Joseph Faure and chaired by Cambacérès (now Second Consul), and sometimes by the First Consul, Napoleon himself. The Code was complete by 1801, after intensive scrutiny by the Council of State, but was not published until 21 March 1804. It was promulgated as the "Civil Code of the French" (*Code civil des Français*), but was renamed "the Napoleonic Code" (*Code Napoléon*) from 1807 to 1815, and once again after the Second French Empire.

The process developed mainly out of the various customals, but was inspired by Justinian's sixth-century codification of Roman law, the *Corpus Iuris Civilis* and, within that, Justinian's Code (*Codex*). The Napoleonic Code, however, differed from Justinian's in important ways: it incorporated all kinds of earlier rules, not only legislation; it was not a collection of edited extracts, but a comprehensive rewrite; its structure was much more rational; it had no religious content; and it was written in the vernacular.

The development of the Napoleonic Code was a fundamental change in the nature of the civil law system, making laws clearer and more accessible. It also superseded the former conflict between royal legislative power and, particularly in the final years before the Revolution, protests by judges representing views and privileges of the social classes to which they belonged. Such conflict led the Revolutionaries to take a negative view of judges making law.

This is reflected in the Napoleonic Code provision prohibiting judges from deciding a case by way of introducing a general rule (Article 5), since the creation of general rules is an exercise of legislative and not of judicial power. In theory, there is thus no case law in France. However, the courts still had to fill in the gaps in the laws and regulations and, indeed, were prohibited from refusing to do so (Article 4). Moreover, both the code and legislation have required judicial interpretation. Thus a vast body of case law has come into existence. There is no rule of *stare decisis* (binding precedent) in French law, but decisions by important courts have become more or less equivalent to case law (see jurisprudence constante).

Contents of the Napoleonic Code

The preliminary article of the Code established certain important provisions regarding the rule of law. Laws could be applied only if they had been duly promulgated, and then only if they had been published officially (including provisions for publishing delays, given the means of communication available at the time). Thus, no secret laws were authorized. It prohibited *ex post facto* laws (i.e. laws that apply to events that occurred before their introduction). The code also prohibited judges from refusing justice on grounds of insufficiency of the law, thereby encouraging them to interpret the law. On the other hand, it prohibited judges from passing general judgments of a legislative value (see above).

With regard to family, the Code established the supremacy of the man over the wife and children, which was the general legal situation in Europe at the time. A woman was given fewer rights than a minor. Divorce by mutual consent was abolished in 1804.[1659]

Other French codes of Napoleon's era

Military code

The Draft on Military Code was presented to Napoleon by the Special Commission headed by Pierre Daru in June 1805; however, as the War Against the Third Coalition progressed, the Code was put aside and never implemented.

Criminal code

In 1791, Louis Michel le Peletier de Saint-Fargeau presented a new criminal code to the national Constituent Assembly. He explained that it outlawed only "true crimes", and not "phony offenses created by superstition, feudalism, the tax system, and [royal] despotism".[1660] He did not list the crimes "created by superstition". The new penal code did not mention blasphemy, heresy, sacrilege, witchcraft or homosexuality, which led to these former offences being swiftly decriminalized. In 1810, a new criminal code was issued under Napoleon. As with the Penal Code of 1791, it did not contain provisions against religious crimes.

Code of civil procedure

As the entire legal system was being overhauled, the code of civil procedure was adopted in 1806.

Commercial code

The commercial code (*code de commerce*) was adopted in 1807.[1661] The kernel of the commercial code is the BOOK III[1662], "Of The Different Modes Of Acquiring Property", of the Napoleonic Code. It is a norm about the contracts and transactions.

Code of criminal instruction

In 1808, a code of criminal instruction (*code d'instruction criminelle*) was published. This code laid out criminal procedure. The *parlement* system, from before the Revolution, had been guilty of much abuse, while the criminal courts established by the Revolution were a complex and ineffective system, subject to many local pressures. The genesis of this code resulted in much debate. The resulting code is the basis of the modern so-called "inquisitorial system" of criminal courts, used in France and many civil law countries, though significantly changed since Bonaparte's day (especially with regard to the expansion of the rights of the defendant).

The French Revolution's Declaration of the Rights of Man and of the Citizen declared that suspects were presumed to be innocent until they had been declared guilty by a court. A concern of Bonaparte's was the possibility of arbitrary arrest, or excessive remand (imprisonment prior to a trial). Bonaparte remarked that care should be taken to preserve personal freedoms, especially when the case was before the Imperial Court: "these courts would have a great strength, they should be prohibited from abusing this situation against weak citizens without connections." However, remand still was the usual procedure for defendants suspected of serious crimes such as murder.

The possibility of lengthy remand periods was one reason why the Napoleonic Code was criticized for its *de facto* presumption of guilt, particularly in common law countries. Another reason was the combination of magistrate and prosecutor in one position. However, the legal proceedings did not have *de jure* presumption of guilt; for instance, the juror's oath explicitly required that the jury not betray the interests of the defendants and not ignore the means of defense.

The rules governing court proceedings, by today's standards, gave significant power to the prosecution; however, criminal justice in European countries in those days tended to side with repression. For instance, it was only in 1836 that prisoners charged with a felony were given a formal right to counsel, in England. In comparison, article 294 of the Napoleonic Code of Criminal Procedure allowed the defendant to have a lawyer before the Court of Assizes (judging felonies), and mandated the court to appoint a lawyer for the defendant if the defendant did not have one (failure to do so rendered the proceedings null).

Whether or not the Cour d'assisess, whose task was to judge severe crimes, were to operate with a jury was a topic of considerable controversy. Bonaparte supported jury trials (or petit jury), and they were finally adopted. On the other hand, Bonaparte was opposed to the indictment jury ("grand jury" of common law countries), and preferred to give this task to the criminal division of the Court of Appeals. Some special courts were created to judge of criminals who could intimidate the jury.

Bonaparte also insisted that the courts judging civil and criminal cases should be the same, if only to give them more prestige.

The French codes in the 21st century

The French codes, now more than 60 in number, are frequently amended, as well as judicially re-interpreted. Therefore, for over a century all of the codes in force have been documented in the annually revised editions published by Dalloz (Paris). These editions consist of thorough annotations, with references to other codes, relevant statutes, judicial decisions (even if unpublished), and international instruments. The "small (*petit*)" version of the Civil Code in this form is nearly 3,000 pages, available in print and online. Additional material, including scholarly articles, is added in the larger "expert (*expert*)" version and the still larger "mega (*méga*)" version, both of which are available in print and on searchable CD-ROM. By this stage, it has been suggested, the Civil Code has become "less a book than a database".

The sheer number of codes, together with digitisation, led the Commission supérieure de codification to reflect in its annual report for 2011:

> The Commission observes that the age of drawing up new codes is probably reaching its end. The aim of a nearly complete codification of the law is no longer pursued, for three reasons: firstly, the technical developments by which texts are provided in non-physical form offer to users modes of access that are comparable in many ways to those available through a code; secondly, the creation of new codes encounters a kind of law of diminishing returns in that, the more progress that is made in the development of new codes, the trickier it becomes to determine in which code particular provisions should be located; and, finally, it is clear that certain kinds of provision [...] are unsuitable for codification, since codification makes sense only when it involves provisions that possess sufficient generality.[1663]

A year later, the Commission recommended that, after its current codification projects were completed, there should not be any further codes; an additional reason was government delay in publishing reforms that the Commission had completed.[1664] The government responded encouragingly in March 2013, but the Commission complains that this has not been followed through; in particular, that the government has abandoned its plan for a public service code (*code général de la fonction publique*).[1665]

Codes in other countries

Even though the Napoleonic Code was not the first civil code and did not represent the whole of his empire, it was one of the most influential. It was adopted in many countries occupied by the French during the Napoleonic Wars, and thus formed the basis of the private law systems of Italy, the Netherlands, Belgium, Spain, Portugal (and their former colonies), and Poland (1808–1946). In the German regions on the west bank of the Rhine (Rhenish Palatinate and Prussian Rhine Province), the former Duchy of Berg and the Grand Duchy of Baden, the Napoleonic Code was in use until the introduction of the Bürgerliches Gesetzbuch in 1900 as the first common civil code for the entire German Empire.

A number of factors have been shown by Arvind and Stirton to have had a determinative role in the decision by the German states to receive the Code, including territorial concerns, Napoleonic control and influence, the strength of central state institutions, a feudal economy and society, rule by liberal (enlightened despotism) rulers, nativism (local patriotism) among the governing elites, and popular anti-French sentiment.

A civil code with strong Napoleonic influences was also adopted in 1864 in Romania, and remained in force until 2011. The Code was also adopted in Egypt as part of the system of mixed courts introduced in Egypt after the fall of Khedive Ismail. The Code was translated into Arabic from the French by Youssef Wahba Pasha between 1881 and 1883. Other codes with some influence in their own right were the Swiss, German, and Austrian codes, but even therein some influence of the French code can be felt, as the Napoleonic Code is considered the first successful codification.

Thus, the civil law systems of the countries of modern continental Europe, with the exception of Russia and the Scandinavian countries have, to different degrees, been influenced by the Napoleonic Code. The legal systems of the United Kingdom other than Scotland, as well as Ireland and the Commonwealth, are derived from English common law rather than from Roman roots.

Scots law, though also a civil law system, is uncodified; it was strongly influenced by Roman-Dutch legal thought, and after the Act of Union 1707, by English law.

In the Persian Gulf Arab states of the Middle East, the influence of the Napoleonic Code mixed with hints of Islamic law is clear, even in Saudi Arabia (which abides more towards Islamic law). In Kuwait, for example, property rights, women's rights, and the education system can be seen as Islamic reenactments of the French civil code. Some of these aspects can be seen in other Persian Gulf Arab states (although less pronounced than in Kuwait), this primarily being due to the relatively democratic nature of Kuwait, rather than the absolutist nature of many other Persian Gulf nations. Wikipedia:Citation needed

The term "Napoleonic Code" is also used to refer to legal codes of other jurisdictions that are influenced by the *French Code Napoléon*, especially the *Civil Code of Lower Canada* (replaced in 1994 by the *Civil Code of Quebec*), mainly derived from the *Coutume de Paris*, which the British continued to use in Canada following the Treaty of Paris in 1763. Most of the laws in Latin American countries are also heavily based on the Napoleonic Code, e.g. the Chilean Civil Code and the Puerto Rican Civil Code.

In the United States, whose legal system is largely based on English common law, the state of Louisiana is unique in having a strong influence from Napoleonic Code and Spanish legal traditions on its civil code (Spanish and French colonial forces quarreled over Louisiana during most of the 1700s, with Spain ultimately ceding the territory to France in 1800, which in turn sold the territory to the United States in 1803). Examples of the practical legal differences between Louisiana and the other states include the bar exam and legal standards of practice for attorneys in Louisiana being significantly different from other states; Louisiana being the only American state to practice forced heirship of a deceased person's estate; and some of Louisiana's laws clashing with the Uniform Commercial Code practiced by the other 49 states.[1666]

In fiction

- The Napoleonic Code is mentioned by *Stanley Kowalski* in *A Streetcar Named Desire*, in an effort to ensure he could benefit from any inheritance his wife Stella might share with her sister Blanche DuBois.

References

Notes

- G. Levasseur, "Napoléon et l'élaboration des codes répressifs" in *Mélanges en hommage à Jean Imbert* (Paris, PUF, 1989) p. 371
- *Code Pénal* and *Code d'Instruction Criminelle* - Original French Texts and other old legislation[1667]

External links

> Wikisourcehas the text of the 1911 *Encyclopædia Britannica*article *Code Napoléon*.

- Code civil (France), French Wikipedia
- English Translation of the Original Text[1668]
- *The Code Napoleon, or the French Civil Code; Literally Translated from the Original and Official Edition, Published at Paris, in 1804 by A Barrister at the Inner Temple*[1669] (1 ed.). London: Printed for Charles Hunter Booksellers. Retrieved 30 November 2016 – via Internet Archive.
- Beginnings of Napoleonic Code[1670]
- Current French Text: Légifrance[1671]
- The "Other" Little Red Book[1672] Interview with legal historian Jean-Louis Halpérin in *France Magazine*.

Bürgerliches Gesetzbuch

The **Bürgerliches Gesetzbuch** (German: [ˈbʏʁɡɐlɪçəs ɡəˈzɛtsbuːx]), abbreviated **BGB**, is the civil code of Germany. In development since 1881, it became effective on January 1, 1900, and was considered a massive and groundbreaking project.

The BGB served as a template for the regulations of several other civil law jurisdictions, including Estonia, Latvia, Taiwan (the Republic of China), Japan, Thailand, South Korea, the People's Republic of China, Brazil, Greece and Ukraine. It also had a major influence on the 1907 Swiss civil code, the 1942 Italian civil code, the 1966 Portuguese civil code, and the 1992 reformed Dutch civil code

Figure 62: *Publication in the Reich Law Gazette on August 24, 1896*

History

German Empire

The introduction in German of the Napoleonic code in 1804 created in Germany a similar desire for obtaining a civil code (despite the opposition of the Historical School of Law of Friedrich Carl von Savigny), which would systematize and unify the various heterogeneous laws that were in effect in the country. However, the realization of such an attempt during the life of the German Confederation was difficult because the appropriate legislative body did not exist.

However, in 1871, most of the various German states were united into the German Empire. In the beginning, civil law legislative power was held by the individual states, not the Empire (*Reich*) that was composed of those states. An amendment to the constitution passed in 1873 (called "Lex Miquel-Lasker" referring to the amendment's sponsors, representatives Johannes von Miquel and Eduard Lasker) transferred this legislative authority to the Reich. Various committees were then formed to draft a bill that was to become a civil law codification for the entire country, replacing the civil law systems of the states.

A first draft code, in 1888, did not meet with favour. A second committee of 22 members, comprising not only jurists but also representatives of financial interests and of the various ideological currents of the time, compiled a second draft. After significant revisions, the BGB was passed by the Reichstag in 1896. It was put into effect on January 1, 1900 and has been the central codification of Germany's civil law ever since.

Nazi Germany

In Nazi Germany, there were plans to replace the BGB with a new codification that was planned to be entitled "Volksgesetzbuch" ("people's code"), which was meant to reflect Nazi ideology better than the liberal spirit of the BGB, but these plans did not become reality. However, some general principles of the BGB such as the doctrine of good faith (§ 242 BGB, *Grundsatz von Treu und Glauben*) were used to interpret the BGB in a Nazi-friendly way. Therefore, the political 'need' to draft a completely new code to match the Nazis expectations subsided, and instead the many flexible doctrines and principles of the BGB were re-interpreted to meet the (legal) spirit of that time. Especially through the good faith doctrine in § 242 BGB (see above) or the *contra bonos mores* doctrine in § 138 BGB (*sittenwidriges Rechtsgeschäft*), voiding transactions perceived as being *contra bonos mores*, i.e. against public policy or morals, the Nazis and their willing judges and lawyers were able to direct the law in a way to serve their nationalist ideology.

Germany from 1945

When Germany was divided into a democratic capitalist state in the West and a socialist state in the East after World War II, the BGB continued to regulate the civil law in both parts of Germany. Over time, however, the BGB regulations were replaced in East Germany by new laws, beginning with a family code in 1966 and ending with a new civil code (*Zivilgesetzbuch*) in 1976 and a contract act in 1982. Since Germany's reunification in 1990, the BGB has again been the codification encompassing the civil law of Germany.

In western and reunited Germany, the BGB has been amended many times since it came into existence. The most significant changes were made in 2002, when the Law of Obligations, one of the BGB's five main parts, was extensively reformed. Despite its status as a civil code, legal precedent does play a limited role; the way the courts construe and interpret the regulations of the code has changed in many ways, and continues to evolve and develop, due particularly to the high degree of abstraction throughout. In recent years lawmakers have tried to bring some outside legislation "back into the BGB". For example, aspects of tenancy legislation, which had been transferred to separate laws like the *Miethöhengesetz* ("Rental Rate Act") are once again covered by the BGB.

The BGB continues to be the centerpiece of the German legal system. Other legislation builds on principles defined in the BGB. The German Commercial

Code, for example, contains only those rules relevant to merchant partnerships and limited partnerships, as the general rules for partnerships in the BGB also apply.

The BGB is typical of 19th century legislation and has been criticized from its very beginnings for its lack of social responsibility. Lawmakers and legal practice have improved the system over the years to adapt the BGB in this respect with more or less success. Recently, the influence of EU legislation has been quite strong and the BGB has seen many changes as a result.

Structure

The BGB follows a modified pandectist structure, derived from Roman law: like other Roman-influenced codes, it regulates the law of persons, property, family and inheritance, but unlike e.g. the French Code civil or the Austrian Civil Code, a chapter containing generally applicable regulations is placed first. Consequently, the BGB contains five main parts (or "books"):

- the general part (*allgemeiner Teil*), articles 1 through 240, comprising regulations that have effect on all the other four parts, such as person-hood and civil status, contractual capacity, declarations of will, rescission, formation of contracts, limitation of actions, and agency
- law of obligations (*Schuldrecht*), art. 241 through 853, describing contractual obligations and other civil obligations, including torts and unjust enrichment
- property law (*Sachenrecht*), art. 854 through 1296, describing possession, ownership, other property rights (e.g. servitudes, security interests), and how those rights can be transferred
- family law (*Familienrecht*), art. 1297 through 1921, describing marriage and other legal relationships among family members
- inheritance law (*Erbrecht*), which regulates what happens to a deceased's estate, as well as the law of wills.

Abstract system of alienation

One of the BGB's fundamental components is the doctrine of abstract alienation of property (German: *Abstraktionsprinzip*), and its corollary, the separation doctrine (*Trennungsprinzip*). Derived from the works of the pandectist scholar Friedrich Carl von Savigny, the Code draws a sharp distinction between obligationary agreements (BGB, Book 2), which create enforceable obligations, and "real" or alienation agreements (BGB, Book 3), which transfer property rights. In short, the two doctrines state: the owner having an obligation to transfer ownership does not make you the owner, but merely gives you the right to *demand* the transfer of ownership. The opposite system, the causal system, is in effect in France and other legal jurisdictions influenced by French law, under which an obligationary agreement is sufficient to transfer ownership; no subsequent conveyance is needed. The German system thus mirrors the English common law differentiation between *in rem* rights and *in personam* rights.

The separation doctrine states that obligationary agreements for alienation and conveyances that effect that alienation must be treated separately and follow their own rules. Also, under the abstract system, alienation does not depend on the validity of the underlying causa of the obligationary contract; in other words, a conveyance is *sine causa* (without legal consideration). From this differentiation it follows that a mere obligationary agreement, such as for the sale of property, does not transfer ownership if and until a separate legal instrument, the conveyance, has been drawn up and goes into effect; conversely, the alienation of property based on an invalid obligationary agreement may give rise to a restitutionary obligation for the transferee to restore the property (e.g. unjust enrichment), but until the property is re-conveyed, again by way of a conveyance, the transferred property is not affected.

Under the BGB, a sales contract alone, for example, would not lead to the buyer acquiring ownership, but merely impose an obligation on the seller to transfer ownership of the sold property. The seller is then contractually obligated to form another, and separate, agreement to transfer the property. Only once this second agreement is formed, the buyer acquires ownership of the purchased property. Consequently, these two procedures are regulated differently: the contracting parties' obligations are regulated by art. 433, whereas real contracts alienating movable property are provided for under art. 929. The payment of the purchase price (or valuable consideration) is treated likewise.

In day-to-day business, this differentiation is not needed, because both types of contract would be formed simultaneously by exchanging the property for payment of money. Although the abstract system can be seen as overly technical and contradicting the usual common-sense interpretation of commercial transactions, it is undisputed among the German legal community. The main advantage of the abstract system is its ability to provide a secure legal construction to nearly any financial transaction, however complicated this transaction may be.

A good example is retention of title. If someone buys something and pays the purchase price in installments, there are two conflicting interests at play: the buyer wants to have the purchased property immediately, whereas the seller wants to secure full payment of the purchase price. Under the abstract system, the BGB has a simple answer: the sales contract obligates the buyer to pay the full price and requires the seller to transfer property upon receipt of the last installment. As the sale obligations and the actual conveyance of ownership are embodied in two separate agreements, it is quite simple to secure both parties' interests. The seller maintains ownership of the property until the last payment, while the buyer merely possesses the property. If the buyer defaults, the seller may repossess the property just like any other owner.

Another advantage is that should the sales contract be found defective due to some vitiating factor (e.g. fraud, mistake, or undue influence), this would not affect the seller's ownership, thereby making it unnecessary to resell the property for the sake of transferring ownership back to the original seller. Instead, under the rules of unjust enrichment, the buyer is obligated to transfer the property back if possible or otherwise pay compensation.

Template for other jurisdictions

- In 1896, the Japanese government established a civil code based on a draft of the *Bürgerliches Gesetzbuch*; with post–World War II modifications, the code remains in effect.

Trivia

- No other German law has a larger number of sections: The BGB ends with sec. 2385.
- Sec. 923 (1) BGB is a perfect hexameter:

Steht auf der Grenze ein Baum, so gebühren die Früchte und, wenn der Baum gefällt wird, auch der Baum den Nachbarn zu gleichen Teilen ("Where there is a tree standing on the boundary, the fruits and, if the tree is felled, the tree itself belong to the neighbours in equal shares.").

- Sec. 923 (3) BGB rhymes:

  Diese Vorschriften gelten auch | für einen auf der Grenze stehenden Strauch ("These provisions also apply to a bush standing on the boundary.")

- Although several other laws are meant to deal with specific legal questions deemed to be outside the scope of a general civil code, the highly specialised *Bienenrecht* (law of bees) is found within the property law chapter of the BGB (sections 961–964). This results from the fact that, in legal terms, bees become wild animals as soon as they leave their hive. As wild animals can't be owned by anyone, the said sections provide for the former owner to keep his claim over that swarm. But sections 961–964 are usually described as the least cited regulations in German law, with not a single decision of any higher court pertaining thereto since the BGB entered into force.

External links

- English translation of the BGB (German Civil Code)[1673]
- German BGB[1674] (in German) by the German Ministry of Justice, Books 1, 2, & 3[1675] (in English)
- Search the BGB[1676] (in German)
- BGB-Informationspflichten-Verordnung[1677] (in German)
- Civil law overview[1678] by the German Ministry of JusticeWikipedia:Link rot
- Commentary on the BGB[1679] (in German)

English law

English law is the common law legal system governing England and Wales, comprising criminal law and civil law.

English law has no formal codification: the essence of English common law is that it is made by judges sitting in courts applying statute, and legal precedent (*stare decisis*) from previous cases. A decision of the Supreme Court of the United Kingdom, the highest civil appeal court of the United Kingdom, is binding on every other court.

Some rulings are derived from legislation; others, known as common law, are based on rulings of previous courts. For example, murder is a common law crime rather than one established by an Act of Parliament. Common law can be amended or repealed by Parliament; murder, for example, now carries a mandatory life sentence rather than the death penalty.

Statute law

Statutory framework

The first schedule of the Interpretation Act 1978, defines the following terms: "British Islands", "England", and "United Kingdom". The use of the term "British Isles" is virtually obsolete in statutes and, when it does appear, it is taken to be synonymous with "British Islands". For interpretation purposes, England includes a number of specified elements:

- Wales and Berwick Act 1746, section 3 (entire Act now repealed) formally incorporated Wales and Berwick-upon-Tweed into England. But section 4 Welsh Language Act 1967 provided that references to England in future Acts of Parliament should no longer include Wales (see now Interpretation Act 1978, Schedule 3, part 1). But Dicey & Morris say

Figure 63: *The Royal Courts of Justice on the Strand in London is the seat of the High Court of Justice and the Court of Appeal.*

(at p28) "It seems desirable to adhere to Dicey's [the original] definition for reasons of convenience and especially of brevity. It would be cumbersome to have to add "or Wales" after "England" and "or Welsh" after "English" every time those words are used."

* the "adjacent islands" of the Isle of Wight and Anglesey are a part of England and Wales by custom, while *Harman v Bolt* (1931) 47 TLR 219 expressly confirms that Lundy is a part of England.
* the "adjacent territorial waters" by virtue of the Territorial Waters Jurisdiction Act 1878 and the Continental Shelf Act 1964 as amended by the Oil and Gas Enterprise Act 1982.

"Great Britain" means England, Wales, Scotland, their adjacent territorial waters and the islands of Orkney and Shetland, the Hebrides and, by virtue of the Island of Rockall Act 1972, Rockall. "United Kingdom" means Great Britain and Northern Ireland and their adjacent territorial waters, but not the Isle of Man, nor the Channel Islands, whose independent status was discussed in *Rover International Ltd. v Canon Film Sales Ltd.* (1987) 1 WLR 1597 and *Chloride Industrial Batteries Ltd. v F. & W. Freight Ltd.* (1989) 1 WLR 823. "British Islands" – but not "British Isles" – means the United Kingdom, the Isle of Man and the Channel Islands.

Types of statute law

- Acts of the Old Irish Parliament
- Acts of the Scottish Parliament
- Acts of the United Kingdom Parliament
- Measures of the Northern Ireland Assembly
- Measures of the National Assembly for Wales
- Acts of the National Assembly for Wales
- Ministerial Order
- Northern Ireland Statutory Rules
- UK Statutory Instruments

Citation style

Statutory law is referred to as "*Title of Act* **Year**",[1680] where the title is the "short title", and ends in "Act", as in "Interpretation Act 1978". Compare with American convention, which includes "of", as in "Civil Rights Act *of* 1964".

This became the usual way to refer to Acts in the second half of the 19th century, starting in the 1840s; previously Acts were referred to by their long title together with the regnal year of the parliamentary session in which they received Royal Assent, and the chapter number. For example, the Pleading in English Act 1362 was referred to as *36 Edw. III c. 15,* meaning "36th year of the reign of Edward III, chapter 15", though in the past this was all spelt out, together with the long title.

Common law

Description

Common law is a term with historical origins in the legal system of England. It denotes, in the first place, the judge-made law that developed from the early Middle Ages as described in a work published at the end of the 19th century, *The History of English Law before the Time of Edward I,*[1681] in which Pollock and Maitland expanded the work of Coke (17th century) and Blackstone (18th century). Specifically, the law developed in England's Court of Common Pleas and other common law courts, which became also the law of the colonies settled initially under the crown of England or, later, of the United Kingdom, in North America and elsewhere; and this law as further developed after those courts in England were reorganised by the Supreme Court of Judicature Acts passed in the 1870s, and developed independently, in the legal systems of the United States and other jurisdictions, after their independence from the United Kingdom, before and after the 1870s. The term is used, in the second place, to denote the law developed by those courts, in the same periods (pre-colonial, colonial and post-colonial), as distinct from within the jurisdiction, or former jurisdiction, of other courts in England: the Court of Chancery, the ecclesiastical courts, and the Admiralty court.

In the Oxford English Dictionary (1933) "common law" is described as "The unwritten law of England, administered by the King's courts, which purports to be derived from ancient usage, and is embodied in the older commentaries and the reports of abridged cases", as opposed, in that sense, to statute law, and as distinguished from the equity administered by the Chancery and similar courts, and from other systems such as ecclesiasical law, and admiralty law.[1682] For usage in the United States the description is "the body of legal doctrine which is the foundation of the law administered in all states settled from England, and those formed by later settlement or division from them".[1683]

Early development

Since 1189, English law has been described as a common law rather than a civil law system; in other words, no major codification of the law has taken place and judicial precedents are binding as opposed to persuasive. This may be a legacy of the Norman conquest of England, when a number of legal concepts and institutions from Norman law were introduced to England. In the early centuries of English common law, the justices and judges were responsible for adapting the system of writs to meet everyday needs, applying a mixture of precedent and common sense to build up a body of internally consistent law. An example is the Law Merchant derived from the "Pie-Powder" Courts, named from a corruption of the French *pieds-poudrés* ("dusty feet") implying ad hoc marketplace courts. As the Parliament of England became ever more established and influential, legislation gradually overtook judicial law-making such that today, judges are only able to innovate in certain very narrowly defined areas.

In 1276, the concept of "time immemorial" often applied in common law was defined as being any time before 6 July 1189 (i.e. before Richard I's accession to the English throne).

Precedent

One of the major challenges in the early centuries was to produce a system that was certain in its operation and predictable in its outcomes. Too many judges were either partial or incompetent, acquiring their positions only by virtue of their rank in society. Thus, a standardised procedure slowly emerged, based on a system termed stare decisis which roughly means "let the decision stand". The doctrine of precedent which requires similar cases to be adjudicated in a like manner, falls under the principle of *stare decisis*. Thus, the ratio decidendi (reason for decision) of each case will bind future cases on the same generic set of facts both horizontally and vertically in the court structure. The highest appellate court in the UK is the Supreme Court of the United Kingdom and its decisions are binding on every other court in the hierarchy which are obliged to apply its rulings as the law of the land. The Court of Appeal binds the lower courts, and so on.

Overseas influences

The influences are two-way.

* England exported English Common law and English Statute law to most parts of the British Empire, and many aspects of that system have survived after Independence or otherwise cessation of British rule. "English law" prior to the American Revolutionary Wars (American War of Independence) is still an influence on United States law, and provides the basis for many American legal traditions and policies. Many jurisdictions that have maintained the use of English Common law continue to incorporate modern developments of the Common law in England, and decisions from England are in many jurisdictions usually considered persuasive. The common law as taken or received from England has developed within each jurisdiction, and in that context, "common law" has been described as a body of judge-made law enforced and developed by the courts which *includes* equity and admiralty law, but has always been "unintelligible without reference to statute". After the colonial period, the common law was developed within each jurisdiction under its final court of appeal: for a time in jurisdictions remaining under the British crown, it was the Judicial Committee of the Privy Council, while from the founding of the United States each state has its own supreme court with final appellate jurisdiction, and in respect of federal law the US Supreme Court has the final appellate jurisdiction.[1684]
* For a number of jurisdictions within the Commonwealth of Nations, the Judicial Committee of the Privy Council in Britain remains the ultimate court of appeal in place of a local Supreme Court. The decisions of the committee made before the change of jurisdiction remain binding legal precedent.
* Britain is a dualist in its relationship with international law, i.e., international obligations have to be formally incorporated into English law before the courts are obliged to apply supranational laws. For example, the European Convention on Human Rights and Fundamental Freedoms was signed in 1950 and Britain allowed individuals to directly petition the European Commission on Human Rights from 1966. Now s6(1) Human

Rights Act 1998 (HRA) makes it unlawful "... for a public authority to act in a way which is incompatible with a convention right", where a "public authority" is any person or body which exercises a public function, expressly including the courts but expressly excluding Parliament. Although the European Convention has begun to be applied to the acts of non-state agents, the HRA does not make the Convention specifically applicable between private parties. Courts have taken the Convention into account in interpreting the common law. They also must take the Convention into account in interpreting Acts of Parliament, but must ultimately follow the terms of the Act even if inconsistent with the Convention (s3 HRA).

- Similarly, because Britain remains a strong international trading nation, international consistency of decision making is of vital importance, so Admiralty Law is strongly influenced by Public International Law and the modern commercial treaties and conventions regulating shipping.

Application to Wales

Unlike Scotland and Northern Ireland, Wales is not a separate jurisdiction within the United Kingdom. The customary laws of Wales within the Kingdom of England were abolished by King Henry VIII's Laws in Wales Acts which brought Wales into legal conformity with England. While Wales now has a devolved Assembly, any legislation which that Assembly passes is enacted in particular circumscribed policy areas defined by the Government of Wales Act 2006, other legislation of the British Parliament, or by Orders in Council given under the authority of the 2006 Act.

Between 1746 and 1967, any reference to England in legislation was deemed to include Wales. This ceased with the enactment of the Welsh Language Act 1967 and the jurisdiction is now commonly referred to as "England and Wales". Although devolution has accorded some degree of political autonomy to Wales in the National Assembly for Wales, it did not have the ability to pass primary legislation until the Government of Wales Act 2006 came into force after the 2007 Welsh general election. That said, the Welsh legal system remains English common law, in that the legal system administered through both civil and criminal courts remains unified throughout England and Wales. This is different from the situation of Northern Ireland, for example, which did not cease to be a distinct jurisdiction when its legislature was suspended (see Northern Ireland (Temporary Provisions) Act 1972). A major difference is also the use of the Welsh language, as laws concerning it apply in Wales and not in the rest of the United Kingdom. The Welsh Language Act 1993 is an Act of the Parliament of the United Kingdom, which put the Welsh language on an equal footing with the English language in Wales with regard to the public sector. Welsh may also be spoken in Welsh courts.

Subjects and links

Criminal law

English criminal law derives its main principles from the common law. The main elements of a crime are the *actus reus* (doing something which is criminally prohibited) and a *mens rea* (having the requisite criminal state of mind, usually intention or recklessness). A prosecutor must show that a person has caused the offensive conduct, or that the culprit had some pre-existing duty to take steps to avoid a criminal consequence. The types of different crimes range from those well known ones like manslaughter, murder, theft and robbery to a plethora of regulatory and statutory offences. It is estimated that in the UK, there are 3,500 classes of criminal offence. Certain defences may exist to crimes, which include self-defence, intention, necessity, duress, and in the case of a murder charge, under the Homicide Act 1957, diminished responsibility, provocation and, in very rare cases, survival of a suicide pact. It has often been suggested that England and Wales should codify its criminal law in an English Criminal Code, but there has been no overwhelming support for this in the past.

Family law

- Alimony
- Residence in English family law
- Bastard

Property

- Chose

Evidence

- Hearsay
- *Ladd v Marshall*

Miscellaneous

- Alcohol licensing laws of the United Kingdom
- Costs

References

- Beale, Joseph H. (1935) *A Treatise on the Conflict of Laws*. ISBN 1-58477-425-8
- Dicey & Morris (1993). *The Conflict of Laws* 12th edition. London: Sweet & Maxwell Ltd. ISBN 0-420-48280-6
- Slapper, Gary; David Kelly (2008-07-15). *The English Legal System*. London: Routledge-Cavendish. ISBN 978-0-415-45954-9.
- Barnett, Hilaire (2008-07-21). *Constitutional & Administrative Law*. London: Routledge-Cavendish. ISBN 978-0-415-45829-0.

Further reading

- Milsom, S.F.C., *A Natural History of the Common Law*. Columbia University Press (2003) ISBN 0231129947
- Milsom, S.F.C., *Historical Foundations of the Common Law* (2nd ed.). Lexis Law Publishing (Va), (1981) ISBN 0406625034

External links

- *The History of English Law before the Time of Edward I, 2 vols.*, on line, with notes, by [[S. F. C. Milsom[1685]], originally published in Cambridge University Press's 1968 reissue.]

Appendix

References

[1] Budge. *The Gods of the Egyptians* Vol. 1 p. 418.

[2] John Romer, *"Testament"*, pp. 41-42, Guild Publishing, 1988.

[3] *"Religion and Cultural Memory: Ten Studies"*, Jan Assmann, Translated by Rodney Livingstone, p. 34, Stanford University Press, 2006, .

[4] Black, p. 130

[5] Black, p. 131

[6] Black, p. 132

[7] Black, p. 157

[8] Hieroglyphs can be found in (Collier and Manley pp. 27, 29, 154)

[9] Budge *The Gods of the Egyptians* Vol. 1 p. 416

[10] "The Oxford Encyclopedia of Ancient Egypt" Vol. 2 p. 320

[11] *"The Oxford Essential Guide to Egyptian Mythology"*, Edited by Donald B. Redford, p. 190, Berkeley, 2003,

[12] "Reflections on Osiris", John D. Ray, p. 64, Profile books,2002, ; An inscription of Hatshepsut reads *'I have made bright the truth which he [Amun-Re] loved, [I] know that he liveth by it the truth[Maat]; it is my bread, I eat of its brightness"* (Breasted Records, V2, p. 123)

[13] *"The Essential Guide to Egyptian Mythology:The Oxford Guide"*, p. 190, Berkeley Reference, 2003,

[14] Budge *The Gods of the Egyptians* Vol. 1 pp. 418-20

[15] http://www.shemtaia.com/diss.shtml

[16] //en.wikipedia.org/w/index.php?title=Template:Ancient_Near_East_topics&action=edit

[17] Conduct of a Physician, Adab al-Tabib, by Ishāq ibn 'Alī al-Ruhāwī

[18] https://web.archive.org/web/20080509192326/http://eawc.evansville.edu/anthology/hammurabi.htm

[19] //en.wikipedia.org/w/index.php?title=Template:Slavery&action=edit

[20] //en.wikipedia.org/w/index.php?title=Babylonian_law&action=edit

[21] http://avalon.law.yale.edu

[22] Sandys 1911, p. 501.

[23] Carey 1998, p. 93.

[24] Carey 1998, p. 95.

[25] Carey 1998, p. 96.

[26] Carey 1998, p. 99.

[27] Andrewes, pp. 381–382.

[28] Carey 1998, p. 106.

[29] Forsdyke 2008, p. 6.

[30] Gagarin 2003, p. 204.

[31] Hamel 2003, pp. 141–142.

[32] Hamel 2003, p. 142.

[33] Hamel 2003, p. 143.

[34] Gagarin 2003, pp. 198–199.

[35] Gagarin 2003, p. 206.

[36] //doi.org/10.1093%2Fcq%2F48.1.93

[37] //doi.org/10.1353%2Fapa.2003.0015

[38] //en.wikipedia.org/w/index.php?title=Template:Tanakh_OT&action=edit

[39] Gorman, pp. 4–5, 14–16

[40] Wenham, p. 8 ff.

[41] Gerstenberger, p. 4

[42] Watts (2013), pp. 104–07

[43] Grabbe (1998), p. 92

[44] Wenham, pp. 3–4

[45] Hartley, pp. vii–viii
[46] Milgrom (1991), pp. v–x
[47] Watts (2013), pp. 12–20
[48] Grabbe (2006), p. 208
[49] Kugler, Hartin, p. 82
[50] Kugler, Hartin, pp. 82–83
[51] Kugler, Hartin
[52] Kugler, Hartin, p. 83
[53] Kugler, Hartin, pp. 83–84
[54] Kugler, Hartin, p. 84
[55] Newsom, p.26
[56] Levine (2006), p. 11
[57] Houston, p. 102
[58] Houston, pp. 102–03
[59] Milgrom (2004), pp. 8–16.
[60] Milgrom (1991), pp. 704–41.
[61] Watts (2013), pp. 40–54.
[62] Balentine (1999) p. 150
[63] Grabbe (2006), p. 211
[64] Grabbe (2006), p. 211 (fn. 11)
[65] Houston, p. 110
[66] Davies, Rogerson, p. 101
[67] Marx, p. 104
[68] Balentine (2002), p. 8
[69] Gorman, pp. 10–11
[70] Houston, p. 106
[71] Houston, p. 107
[72] Knierim, p. 114
[73] Rodd, p. 7
[74] Brueggemann, p. 99
[75] Rodd, p. 8
[76] Clines, p.56
[77] Watts (2013), p. 10
[78] Wenham, p. 65
[79] Watts (2013), pp. 77–86
[80] http://www.biblegateway.com/passage/?search=Leviticus+1&version=NIV
[81] https://books.google.com/books?id=A399uVxU_RUC
[82] https://books.google.com/books?id=6xs258sZfcUC
[83] https://books.google.com/books?id=RwSMl8od4yAC
[84] https://books.google.com/books?id=wCRYl9Ikk6EC&pg=PA105&lpg=PA105&dq=Grabbe+ Leviticus+Oxford#v=onepage&q=Grabbe%20Leviticus%20Oxford&f=false
[85] https://books.google.com/?id=PgovQQAACAAJ&dq=hartley+leviticus
[86] https://books.google.com/books?id=2Vo-11umIZQC&pg=PA101&dq=Eerdmans+Leviticus+ Walter+J+Houston#v=onepage&q&f=false
[87] https://books.google.com/?id=pTgRPQAACAAJ&dq=Leviticus+-+Concordia+ Commentary++by+Kleinig,+John+W.
[88] http://www.nebraskapress.unl.edu/product/JPS-Torah-Commentary-Leviticus,675358.aspx
[89] http://yalepress.yale.edu/yupbooks/book.asp?isbn=9780300139402
[90] https://books.google.com/books/about/Leviticus.html?id=ep3XiyuinhMC
[91] https://books.google.com/?id=2SY0nwEACAAJ&dq=Watts+leviticus+1-10
[92] https://books.google.com/books?id=9SKlbar7-SkC
[93] https://books.google.com/books?id=k94UhKBRbtQC&printsec=frontcover&dq=The+ Torah%27s+vision+of+worship++Samuel+Eugene+Balentine#v=onepage&q&f=false
[94] https//books.google.com
[95] https://books.google.com/books?id=dBJQ71RIpdMC&printsec=frontcover&dq=theological+ handbook+of+Old+Testament+themes#v=onepage&q&f=false

[96] https://books.google.com/?id=cwhICpcHBsQC&pg=PR3&dq=Sources+of+the+bible#v=onepage&q=Sources%20of%20the%20bible&f=false

[97] https://books.google.com/books?id=Z45ullcFRG8C&printsec=frontcover&dq=Clines+Theme+of+the+Pentateuch#v=onepage&q&f=false

[98] https//books.google.com

[99] https://books.google.com/books?id=UX9RsDHKp7wC&printsec=frontcover&dq=Introduction+to+the+Bible+Gregory+W.+Dawes#v=onepage&q&f=false

[100] https://books.google.com/books?id=q9XUv3KAVIUC&printsec=frontcover&dq=A+Complete+Introduction+to+the+Bible+Christopher+Gilbert#v=onepage&q&f=false

[101] https://books.google.com/books?id=7Vh1Ozo3QHMC&printsec=frontcover&dq=The+Book+of+Leviticus:+Composition+and+Reception#v=onepage&q&f=false

[102] https://books.google.com/books?id=nE-xfAGv3ScC&pg=PA381&dq=Knierim+Numbers#v=onepage&q&f=false

[103] https://books.google.com/books?id=L8WbXbPjxpoC&printsec=frontcover&dq=Robert+Kugler,+Patrick+Hartin#v=onepage&q&f=false

[104] https://books.google.com/books?id=Dkr7rVd3hAQC&printsec=frontcover&dq=Reading+the+Pentateuch:+a+historical+introduction#v=onepage&q&f=false

[105] https//books.google.com

[106] https://books.google.com/?id=4YQwycUTJ-IC&printsec=frontcover&dq=nihan+priestly+torah#v=onepage&q=nihan%20priestly%20torah&f=false

[107] https://books.google.com/books?id=UvjCgYtcmMgC&printsec=frontcover&dq=Glimpses+of+a+strange+land:+studies+in+Old+Testament+ethics#v=onepage&q&f=false

[108] https://books.google.com/books?id=EFle13pCS0wC&printsec=frontcover&dq=Genesis+1-11+John+William+Rogerson#v=onepage&q&f=false

[109] https://books.google.com/books?id=owwhpmIVgSAC&printsec=frontcover&dq=The+Hebrew+Bible+today:+an+introduction+to+critical+issues#v=onepage&q&f=false

[110] https://books.google.com/books?id=7cdy67ZvzdkC&printsec=frontcover&dq=Introduction+to+reading+the+Pentateuch+Jean+Louis+Ska#v=onepage&q&f=false

[111] https//books.google.com

[112] http://www.mgketer.org/mikra/3/1/1

[113] http://www.mechon-mamre.org/e/et/et0301.htm

[114] http://bible.ort.org/books/pentd2.asp?ACTION=displaypage&BOOK=3&CHAPTER=1

[115] http://www.chabad.org/article.asp?aid=8162

[116] http://www.mechon-mamre.org/p/pt/pt0301.htm

[117] http//www.catholicrevelations.com

[118] http://www.gospelhall.org/bible/bible.php?passage=Leviticus+1

[119] http://bible-book.org/en/pentateuch/leviticus

[120] http://bible.oremus.org/?ql=56782100

[121] http://bible.oremus.org/?ql=56782135

[122] https//librivox.org

[123] http://jewishencyclopedia.com/view.jsp?artid=301&letter=L&search=Leviticus

[124] http://chaver.com/Torah/The%20Literary%20Structure%20of%20Leviticus%20(TBH).pdf?artid=301&letter=L&search=Leviticus

[125] http://www.vts.edu/ftpimages/95/download/download_group10629_id370999.pdf

[126] *Peake's commentary on the Bible*, Revised Edition (1962), ad

[127] S. M. Jauss, *Kasuistik – Systematik – Reflexion über Recht*, in Journal for Ancient Near Eastern and Biblical Law 21, 2015, 185 pp.

[128] http://www.fordham.edu/halsall/ancient/1650nesilim.html

[129] http://irisonline.org.uk/index.php/features/features-archive/197-voting-in-ancient-athens

[130] According to some sources, part of the agora was roped-off, according to others it was temporarily immured with wooden planks.

[131] http://www.perseus.tufts.edu/hopper/text?doc=Perseus%3Atext%3A2008.01.0009%3Achapter%3D7%3Asection%3D5 Life of Aristides 7.5

[132] http://www.attalus.org/translate/philochorus.html See n. 30

[133] Plutarch, *Life of Cimon* 17.2–6 http://www.perseus.tufts.edu/hopper/text.jsp?doc=Perseus:text:1999.01.0182:text=Cim.:chapter=17.

[134] Broneer, Oscar. "Excavations on the North Slope of the Acropolis, 1937". *Hesperia*, 1938. pp. 228-243.

[135] See Surikov, pp. 284–294

[136] //en.wikipedia.org/wiki/Ostracism#endnote_Oration

[137] Aristotle, Athenian Constitution 22.3 http://www.perseus.tufts.edu/hopper/text.jsp?doc= Perseus:text:1999.01.0046:chapter=22

[138] Lysias 14.39

[139] Mabel Lang, (1990). *Ostraka*: 3–6, Athens.

[140] Plutarch, Life of Pericles 11 http://www.perseus.tufts.edu/hopper/text.jsp?doc=Perseus:text: 1999.01.0182:text=Per.:chapter=11–, 14 http://www.perseus.tufts.edu/hopper/text.jsp?doc= Perseus:text:1999.01.0182:text=Per.:chapter=14.

[141] Plutarch, Life of Aristides 7.7 http://www.perseus.tufts.edu/hopper/text.jsp?doc=Perseus:text: 1999.01.0182:text=Arist.:chapter=7

[142] see Surikov, pp. 121–122.

[143] see Surikov, pp. 73–80, and references therein.

[144] Williams, K. 2001. Ostracism: The Power of Silence. New York: Guilford Press. p. ix

[145] Williams, K. 2001. Ostracism: The Power of Silence. New York: Guilford Press. pp. 2-18.

[146] Douglas, K. 2008. 'Antisocial Communication on Electronic Mail and the Internet'. In: A. Konjin, M. Tanis, S. Utz, and S Barnes (eds.) Mediated Interpersonal Communication. (200-214). New York: Routledge. p.203.

[147] Wesselmann, E. and Williams, K. 2013. 'Ostracism and Stages of Coping'. In: C. Dewall (ed.) Oxford Handbook of Social Exclusion. (20-30). Oxford: Oxford University Press. p.21.

[148] J. Rose, *The Literary Churchill* (Yale 2015) p. 233

[149] Williams, K. 2001. Ostracism: The Power of Silence. New York: Guilford Press. pp. 195.

[150] Brown, A.J. (ed) 2008. Whistling While They Work. Canberra: ANU Press. p. 129.

[151] https//books.google.com

[152] U.S. News Health Care, Dr. Kambiz Behzadi, MD http://health.usnews.com/doctors/kambiz-behzadi-1166

[153] J. Rose, The Literary Churchill (Yale 2015) p. 233

[154] https//books.google.com

[155] http://www.commisceo-global.com/country-guides/iran-guide

[156] *Gender Relationships in Iran* http://www.cultureofiran.com/gender_relations_in_iran.html

[157] Treatise On Rights (Risalat al-Huquq) https://www.al-islam.org/treatise-rights-risalat-al-huquq-imam-zain-ul-abideen

[158] *Iran: At War with History*, by John Limbert, pub. 1987 ppg 37-38https:// books.google.com/books?id=rXS3DAAAQBAJ&pg=PA37&lpg=PA37&dq=qahr +iranian+behavior&source=bl&ots=oT1PRsnIAA&sig=givEDjpjh1QgCDLtP2-FzTZPrcg&hl=en&sa=X&ved=0ahUKEwinzO_lorfPAhXH7SYKHWADBAIQ6AEIJzAD#v=onepage&q=% 20iranian%20behavior&f=false

[159] *Iran: At War with History*, by John Limbert, pub. 1987 ppg 37-38

[160] Repentancehttp://sunnahonline.com/library/purification-of-the-soul/175-repentance

[161] Koran 66:8http://understandquran.com/how-repentance-can-draw-you-nearer-to-allah-swt.html

[162] http://islam.ru/en/content/story/what-dua

[163] http://www.perseus.tufts.edu/hopper/text.jsp?doc=Perseus:text:1999.01.0046:chapter=22

[164] http://www.attalus.org/translate/philochorus.html#30

[165] http://www.perseus.tufts.edu/hopper/text.jsp?doc=Perseus:text:1999.01.0182:text=Per.: chapter=11

[166] http://www.perseus.tufts.edu/hopper/text.jsp?doc=Perseus:text:1999.01.0182:text=Per.: chapter=14

[167] http://www.perseus.tufts.edu/hopper/text.jsp?doc=Perseus:text:1999.01.0182:text=Arist.: chapter=7

[168] http://www.perseus.tufts.edu/hopper/text.jsp?doc=Perseus:text:1999.01.0182:text=Cim.: chapter=17

[169] http://www.perseus.tufts.edu/hopper/text.jsp?doc=Plut.+Alc.+13&fromdoc=Perseus% 3Atext%3A1999.01.0182

[170] http://www.perseus.tufts.edu/hopper/text.jsp?doc=Plut.+Nic.+11&fromdoc=Perseus%3Atext%3A1999.01.0182

[171] http://www.csun.edu/~hcfll004/ostracis.html

[172] http://www.ancient.eu/Ostracism/

[173] http://www.livius.org

[174] http://www.livius.org/on-oz/ostracism/ostracism.html

[175] //en.wikipedia.org/w/index.php?title=Template:Hindu_scriptures&action=edit

[176] Manusmriti http://oxfordindex.oup.com/view/10.1093/acref/9780195134056.013.0539, The Oxford International Encyclopedia of Legal History (2009), Oxford University Press, , See entry for Manusmriti

[177] Flood (1996), page 56

[178] P Bilimoria (2011), The Idea of Hindu Law, Journal of the Oriental Society of Australia, Volume 43, pages 103-130

[179] Steven Collins (1993), The discourse of what is primary, Journal of Indian philosophy, Volume 21, pages 301-393

[180] Patrick Olivelle (2005), Manu's Code of Law, Oxford University Press, , pages 3-4

[181] Robert Lingat (1973), The Classical Law of India, University of California Press, , page 77

[182]

[183] For composition between 200 BCE and 200 CE see: Avari, p. 142. For dating of composition "between the second century BCE and third century CE" see: Flood (1996), p. 56. For dating of Manu Smriti in "final form" to the 2nd century CE, see: Keay, p. 103. For dating as completed some time between 200 BCE and 100 CE see: Hopkins, p. 74. For probable origination during the 2nd or 3rd centuries AD, see: Kulke and Rothermund, p. 85. For the text as preserved dated to around the 1st century BCE. see:

[184] *Glimpses of Indian Culture*, Dinkar Joshi, p.51

[185] Patrick Olivelle (2005), Manu's Code of Law, Oxford University Press, , pages 24-25

[186]

[187] John Bowker (2012), The Message and the Book: Sacred Texts of the World's Religions, Yale University Press, , pages 179-180

[188] Patrick Olivelle (1999), Dharmasutras - the law codes of ancient India, Oxford University Press, , pages xxiv-xxv, 280-314

[189] Patrick Olivelle (2005), *Manu's Code of Law https://books.google.com/books?id=PnHo02RtONMC*, Oxford University Press, , pages 7-8

[190] Patrick Olivelle (2005), Manu's Code of Law, Oxford University Press, , pages 25-27

[191] Patrick Olivelle (2005), Manu's Code of Law, Oxford University Press, , pages 9-10

[192] Patrick Olivelle (2005), Manu's Code of Law, Oxford University Press, , pages 9-10, 87-92

[193] The Laws of Manu 2.6 with footnotes https://archive.org/stream/lawsofman00manu#page/n173/mode/2up George Bühler (Translator), The Sacred Books of the East, Vol. 25, Oxford University Press

[194] Brian Smith and Wendy Doniger (1992), The Laws of Manu, Penguin, , pages 17-18

[195] David Levinson (2002), Encyclopedia of Crime and Punishment, Volume 1, SAGE Publications, , page 829

[196] Werner Menski, *Hindu Law: Beyond Tradition and Modernity* (Delhi: Oxford UP, 2003), p. 126 and Domenico Francavilla, *The Roots of Hindu Jurisprudence: Sources of Dharma and Interpretation in Mīmāṃsā and Dharmaśāstra*. Corpus Iuris Sanscriticum. Vol. 7 (Torino: CESMEO, 2006), pp.165–76.

[197] Patrick Olivelle (2005), Manu's Code of Law, Oxford University Press, , pages 10-15, 154-205

[198] Patrick Olivelle (2005), Manu's Code of Law, Oxford University Press, , pages 16, 8-14, 206-207

[199] Patrick Olivelle (2005), Manu's Code of Law, Oxford University Press, , pages 16-17, 208-229

[200] Patrick Olivelle (2005), Manu's Code of Law, Oxford University Press, , pages 237-350, 914-982

[201]

[202] Robert Lingat (1973), The Classical Law of India, University of California Press, , page 86

[203] The Laws of Manu 12.125 https://archive.org/stream/lawsofman00manu#page/n655/mode/2up George Bühler (Translator), The Sacred Books of the East, Vol. 25, Oxford University Press, page 513

[204] Patrick Olivelle (2005), Manu's Code of Law, Oxford University Press, , page 41

[205]

[206] The Laws of Manu 6.75 https://archive.org/stream/lawsofman00manu#page/n355/mode/2up George Bühler (Translator), The Sacred Books of the East, Vol. 25, Oxford University Press, page 212

[207] J Duncan M Derrett (1975), Bharuci's commentary on the Manusmrti, Schriftenreihe des Sudasien-Instituts der Universitat Heidelberg, , page 23

[208] The Laws of Manu 10.63 https://archive.org/stream/lawsofman00manu#page/n559/mode/2up George Bühler (Translator), The Sacred Books of the East, Vol. 25, Oxford University Press, page 416

[209] Patrick Olivelle (2005), Manu's Code of Law, Oxford University Press, , pages 208-214, 337

[210] Patrick Olivelle (2005), Manu's Code of Law, Oxford University Press, , page 275

[211] The Laws of Manu 4.204 https://archive.org/stream/lawsofman00manu#page/n303/mode/2up George Bühler (translator), The Sacred Books of the East, Vol. 25, Oxford University Press, page 160-161

[212] J Duncan M Derrett (1975), Bharuci's commentary on the Manusmrti, Schriftenreihe des Sudasien-Instituts der Universitat Heidelberg, , pages 30, 439-440

[213] Patrick Olivelle (2005), Manu's Code of Law, Oxford University Press, , pages 31-32

[214] Patrick Olivelle (2005), Manu's Code of Law, Oxford University Press, , page 97

[215] Patrick Olivelle (2005), Manu's Code of Law, Oxford University Press, , page 140

[216] Patrick Olivelle (2005), Manu's Code of Law, Oxford University Press, , pages 31-32, 138-147, 558-593

[217] Robert Lingat (1973), The Classical Law of India, University of California Press, , page 84

[218] Patrick Olivelle (2005), Manu's Code of Law, Oxford University Press, , pages 190-207, 746-809

[219] Patrick Olivelle (2005), Manu's Code of Law, Oxford University Press, , pages 31-32, 108-123, 138-147

[220] Patrick Olivelle (2005), Manu's Code of Law, Oxford University Press, , pages 98, 146-147

[221] Patrick Olivelle (2005), Manu's Code of Law, Oxford University Press, , page 111

[222] Sanskrit: यत्र नार्यस्तु पूज्यन्ते रमन्ते तत्र देवता: । यत्रैतास्तु न पूज्यन्ते सर्वास्तत्राफला: क्रिया:
The Laws of Manu 3.55-3.56 https://archive.org/stream/lawsofman00manu#page/n227/mode/2up George Bühler (Translator), The Sacred Books of the East, Vol. 25, Oxford University Press, page 85

[223] Patrick Olivelle (2005), Manu's Code of Law, Oxford University Press, , page 146

[224] Patrick Olivelle (2005), Manu's Code of Law, Oxford University Press, , pages 31-32, 194-207, 755-809

[225] Robert Lingat (1973), The Classical Law of India, University of California Press, , pages 83-84

[226] Patrick Olivelle (2005), Manu's Code of Law, Oxford University Press, , pages 182-193, 659-706

[227] Patrick Olivelle (2005), Manu's Code of Law, Oxford University Press, , pages 200-201, 746-809

[228]

[229] Abdullahi Ahmed An-Na'im (2010), Islam and the Secular State, Harvard University Press, , pages 149, 289

[230]

[231]

[232]

[233] Arun Kumbhare (2009), Women of India: Their Status Since the Vedic Times, , page 56

[234]

[235]

[236] Mahatma Gandhi, Hinduism According to Gandhi, Orient Paperbacks (2013 Reprint Edition), , page 129

237 Kane, P. V., History of Dharmaśāstra, (Poona: Bhandarkar Oriental Research Institute, 1975), Volume I, Part I, 566.

238 Olivelle, Patrick, "Dharmaśāstra: A Literary History", page 29.

239 J Duncan M Derrett (1975), Bharuci's commentary on the Manusmrti, Schriftenreihe des Sudasien-Instituts der Universitat Heidelberg,

240 J Duncan J Derrett (1977), Essays in Classical and Modern Hindu Law, Brill Academic, , pages 10-17, 36-37 with footnote 75a

241 Kane, P. V., History of Dharmaśāstra, (Poona: Bhandarkar Oriental Research Institute, 1975), Volume I, Part II, 583.

242

243 Visvanath Narayan Mandlik (1886), Manavadharmaśastram, 5 volumes,

244 David Buxbaum (1998), Family Law and Customary Law in Asia: A Contemporary Legal Perspective, Springer Academic, , page 204

245 Donald Davis (2010), The Spirit of Hindu Law, Cambridge University Press, , page 14

246 Werner Menski (2009), Hindu Law: Beyond Tradition and Modernity, Oxford University Press, , Chapters 2 & 4

247 Donald R Davis Jr (2005), Intermediate Realms of Law: Corporate Groups and Rulers in Medieval India, Journal of the Economic and Social History of the Orient, Volume 48, Issue 1, pages 92–117

248 Tomothy Lubin et al (2010), Hinduism and Law: An Introduction (Editors: Lubin and Davis), Cambridge University Press, , Chapter 1

249 Michael Anderson (1995), Institutions and Ideologies: A SOAS South Asia Reader (Studies in Asian Topics, Editors: David Arnold, Peter Robb), Routledge, , Chapter 10;
K Ewing (1988), Sharia and ambiguity in South Asian Islam, University of California Press,

250 Abdullahi Ahmed An-Na'im (2010), Islam and the Secular State, Harvard University Press, , pages 149-150

251 A digest of Moohummudan law on the subjects to which it is usually applied by British courts of justice in India https://archive.org/stream/digestmoohummud00bailgoog#page/n7/mode/2up Neil Baillie, Smith, Elder & Co. London

252 Ludo Rocher, "Hindu Law and Religion: Where to draw the line?" in *Malik Ram Felicitation Volume*. ed. S.A.J. Zaidi (New Delhi, 1972), 190–1.

253 J.D.M. Derrett, *Religion, Law, and the State in India* (London: Faber, 1968), 96; For a related distinction between religious and secular law in Dharmaśāstra, see

254

255

256 For reviews of the British misappropriations of Dharmaśāstra, see: and

257

258 Victor Lieberman (2014), Burmese Administrative Cycles, Princeton University Press, , pages 66-68; Also see discussion of 13th-century Wagaru Dhamma-sattha / 11th century Manu Dhammathat manuscripts discussion

259 On Laws of Manu in 14th-century Thailand's Ayuthia kingdom named after Ayodhya, see David Wyatt (2003), Thailand: A Short History, Yale University Press, , page 61;
Robert Lingat (1973), The Classical Law of India, University of California Press, , pages 269-272

260 M Rama Jois (2004), Legal and Constitutional History of India, Universal Law Publishing, , pages 19-34

261 M Rama Jois (2004), Legal and Constitutional History of India, Universal Law Publishing, , page 31

262 M Rama Jois (2004), Legal and Constitutional History of India, Universal Law Publishing, , pages 31-32

263 M Rama Jois (2004), Legal and Constitutional History of India, Universal Law Publishing, , page 32

264 For objections to the work by feminists, see: Avari, pp. 142-143.

265

266

[267] For Manu Smriti as one of the first Sanskrit texts noted by the British and translation by Sir William Jones in 1794, see: Flood (1996), p. 56.

[268] For British interest in Dharmashastras due to administrative needs, and their misinterpretation of them as legal codes rather than as social and ritual texts, see: Thapar (2002), pp. 2-3.

[269] Friedrich Nietzsche, *The Antichrist* (1888), 56-57.

[270] Daniel Conway (1997), "Nietzsche and the Political", Routledge, , page 36

[271] Julian Young (2010), "Friedrich Nietzsche: A Philosophical Biography", Cambridge University Press, , page 515

[272] Nietzsche: The Anti-Christ, Ecce Homo, Twilight of the Idols: And Other Writings, Aaron Ridley, Cambridge University Press, P.58

[273] Walter Kaufmann (2013), Nietzsche: Philosopher, Psychologist, Antichrist, Princeton University Press, , pages 225-226

[274] Walter Kaufmann (1980), From Shakespeare to Existentialism, Princeton University Press, , page 215

[275] Revolution and Counter-Revolution in India http://www.ambedkar.org/ambcd/19A. Revolution%20and%20Counter%20Rev.in%20Ancient%20India%20PART%20I.htm

[276] Romila Thapar, *Aśoka and the Decline of the Mauryas*, Oxford University Press (1960) p. 200.

[277] John Marshall, "An Historical and Artistic Description of Sanchi", from *A Guide to Sanchi*, citing p. 11. Calcutta: Superintendent, Government Printing (1918). Pp. 7-29 on line, Project South Asia. http://projectsouthasia.sdstate.edu/docs/archaeology/primarydocs/Sanchi/HistArt. htm

[278] K. V. Rao, *Socialism, Secularism, and Democracy in India*, pp. 28-30. Nagendra K. Singh, *Enforcement of Human Rights in Peace and War and the Future of Humanity*, p. 35. Martinus Nijhoff (1986)

[279] The Light of Truth, Chapter 4

[280] Friedrich Nietzsche, *The Will to Power*, vol. 1.

[281] https//books.google.com

[282] http://www.sacred-texts.com/hin/manu.htm

[283] https://books.google.com/books/about/Manusmr%CC%A5ti.html?id=dzAJAAAAIAAJ

[284] https://www.wisdomlib.org/hinduism/book/manusmriti-with-the-commentary-of-medhatithi

[285] //en.wikipedia.org/w/index.php?title=Template:Hindu_scriptures&action=edit

[286] Patrick Olivelle 2006, p. 176 with note 24.

[287] Patrick Olivelle 2005, p. 20.

[288] Patrick Olivelle 2006, p. 188.

[289] Robert Lingat 1973, p. 98.

[290] Timothy Lubin, Donald R. Davis Jr & Jayanth K. Krishnan 2010, pp. 59-72.

[291] Mandagadde Rama Jois 1984, p. 31.

[292] Robert Lingat 1973, p. 97.

[293] Mandagadde Rama Jois 1984, pp. 31-32.

[294] Patrick Olivelle suggests the latter part of this timeframe, while PV Kane favored an earlier date.

[295] Winternitz 1986, pp. 599-600.

[296] Mandagadde Rama Jois 1984, p. 300.

[297] Robert Lingat 1973, pp. 97-98.

[298] Ludo Rocher 2014, pp. 22-24.

[299] Timothy Lubin, Donald R. Davis Jr & Jayanth K. Krishnan 2010, p. 44.

[300] Timothy Lubin, Donald R. Davis Jr & Jayanth K. Krishnan 2010, p. 51.

[301] Timothy Lubin, Donald R. Davis Jr & Jayanth K. Krishnan 2010, p. 45.

[302] SC Vidyarnava (1938), Yajnavalkya Smriti https://archive.org/stream/yajnavalkyasmrit00yj# page/162/mode/2up, Book 1, verse III.LXXXII, page 163

[303] Olivelle, "Literary History," p. 21

[304] Timothy Lubin, Donald R. Davis Jr & Jayanth K. Krishnan 2010, pp. 45-46.

[305] Mandagadde Rama Jois 1984, pp. 300-302.

[306] Olivelle, "Literary History," p. 22

[307] Mandagadde Rama Jois 1984, p. 32.

[308] John Mayne 1991, pp. 21-22.

[309] https://books.google.com/books?id=V552bAz5xFAC

[310] https://books.google.com/books?id=Sauo8iSIj7YC

[311] https://books.google.com/books?id=MtuhClbfL7EC

[312] https://archive.org/stream/atreatiseonhind02mayngoog#page/n86/mode/2up

[313] //www.worldcat.org/oclc/561697663

[314] https://books.google.com/books?id=efaOR_-YsIcC

[315] https://books.google.com/books?id=gnVxqvPg9a0C

[316] https://books.google.com/books?id=PnHo02RtONMC

[317] https://books.google.com/books?id=dziNBAAAQBAJ

[318] https://archive.org/stream/yajnavalkyasmrit00yj#page/n7/mode/2up

[319] https//archive.org

[320] //en.wikipedia.org/w/index.php?title=Template:Hindu_scriptures&action=edit

[321] , **Quote:** "(...) is classically expressed in Indian literature in the Arthashastra of Kautilya";
, **Quote:** "The paper develops value based management guidelines from the famous Indian treatise on management, Kautilya's Arthashastra.";
, **Quote:** "(...) the doctrines and ideas from the ancient Indian scriptures like Vedanta, Bhagavad Gita, Kautilya's Arthashastra etc (...).";
, **Quote:** "This article compares the ancient Indian text the Arthashastra with the famous animal fables of the Panchatantra and (...).";
, **Quote:** "This paper explores the Arthashastra of Kaultilya, an ancient Indian literature (4th Century B.C.); and (...)"

[322] Olivelle 2013, pp. 1-5.

[323] Olivelle 2013, pp. 24–25, 31.

[324] Olivelle 2013, pp. 1, 34-35.

[325] : "References to the work in other Sanskrit literature attribute it variously to , and . The same individual is meant in each case. The *Pañcatantra* explicitly identifies Chanakya with ."

[326] Olivelle 2013, pp. 31-38.

[327] ;
"while in his character as author of an *arthaśāstra* he is generally referred to by his *gotra* name, ;"
"T. Burrow... has now shown that Cāṇakya is also a *gotra* name, which in conjunction with other evidence makes it clear that we are dealing with distinct persons, the minister Cāṇakya of legend and Kautilya the compiler of *Arthaśāstra.*

[328] : "The confident initial assertion that the text's author was 'the famous Brahman Kautilya, also named Vishnugupta, and known from other sources by the patronymic Chanakya', and that the text was written at the time of the foundation of the Maurya dynasty, has of course been considerably eroded over the course of the twentieth century."

[329] Olivelle 2013, pp. 30-31.

[330] Olivelle 2013, pp. 14, 330: "The title Arthaśāstra is found only in the colophons, in three verses 5.6.47, 7.10.38 and 7.18.42", (page 14) and "Prosperity and decline, stability and weakening, and vanquishing — knowing the *science of politics* [अर्थशास्त्र, *arthaśāstra*], he should employ all of these strategies." (page 330)

[331] Olivelle 2013, pp. 1-62, 179-221.

[332] Sen, R.K. and Basu, R.L. 2006. *Economics in Arthashastra.* New Delhi: Deep & Deep Publications.

[333] Thomas Trautmann (2012), Arthashastra: The Science of Wealth, Penguin, , pages xxv-27

[334] , **Quote:** During the same period, an ancient **Hindu text (the Arthashastra)** included a recipe...";
; **Quote:** "Arthasastra, the major surviving **Hindu text on polity,** attributed to Chanakya (also known as Kautilya)..."
, **Quote:** The most important single text in **Hindu political philosophy is Kautilya's Arthasastra** (...)

[335] Olivelle 2013, pp. 122-175.

[336] Olivelle 2013, pp. 101, 228-229, 286-287.

[337] Olivelle 2013, pp. 29, 52.

[338] Olivelle 2013, pp. 1–2.

[339] Trautmann 1971, p. 1.

[340] Olivelle 2013, pp. ix, xiii, xiv-xvii.
[341] Olivelle 2013, Introduction.
[342] Olivelle 2013, pp. 3–4.
[343] Olivelle 2013, pp. 49-51, 99-108, 277-294, 349-356, 373-382.
[344] Olivelle 2013, pp. 4–5.
[345] ;
: "the very last verse of the work...is the unique instance of the personal name rather than the *gotra* name in the *Arthaśāstra*.
[346] Olivelle 2013, pp. 24-25, 31.
[347] RP Kangle (1969, Reprinted in 2010), Arthaśāstra, Part 3, Motilal Banarsidass, , pages 1-2
[348]
[349] Arvind Sharma (1999), The Puruşārthas: An Axiological Exploration of Hinduism, The Journal of Religious Ethics, Vol. 27, No. 2 (Summer, 1999), pp. 223-256
[350] Steven Rosen (2006), Essential Hinduism, Praeger, , page 34-45
[351] John Bowker (2003), The Oxford Dictionary of World Religions, Oxford University Press, , pages 650-651
[352] Olivelle 2013, pp. vii–xxvii.
[353] Olivelle 2013, pp. 66-69.
[354] Arthashastra https://archive.org/stream/Arthasastra_English_Translation/Arthashastra_of_Chanakya_-_English#page/n7/mode/2up R Shamasastry (Translator), pages 8-9
[355] JS Rajput (2012), Seven Social Sins: The Contemporary Relevance, Allied, , pages 28-29
[356] Olivelle transliterates this word as *Vārttā*, translates it as "roughly economics", and notes that Kautilya placed the knowledge of economics at the heart of king's education; See: Olivelle<ref name="FOOTNOTEOlivelle201343">Olivelle 2013, p. 43.
[357] Kangle transliterates this word as *Anviksiki* , and states that this term may be better conceptualized as science of reasoning rather than full philosophy, in ancient Indian traditions; See: Kangle's Part III<ref name="FOOTNOTEKangle196999-100">Kangle 1969, pp. 99-100.
[358] Kangle 1969, p. 130.
[359]
[360] Olivelle 2013, pp. 68-69.
[361] Sanskrit Original: कौटिलीय अर्थशास्त्र, Arthashastra http//sanskritdocuments.org Book 1, Kautilya, page 5
[362] Rangarajan 1992, pp. 121-122.
[363] Olivelle 2013, pp. 70-72.
[364]
[365] Olivelle 2013, pp. xx, xxii, 69-221.
[366] Olivelle 2013, pp. 69-70.
[367] Olivelle 2013, pp. 72-74.
[368] Olivelle 2013, pp. 72-75.
[369] Olivelle 2013, pp. 74-75.
[370] Sanskrit Original: कौटिलीय अर्थशास्त्र, Arthashastra http//sanskritdocuments.org Book 1, Kautilya, pages 7-8
[371] Olivelle 2013, pp. 75-76.
[372] Olivelle 2013, pp. 72-76.
[373] Sanskrit Original: कौटिलीय अर्थशास्त्र, Arthashastra http//sanskritdocuments.org Book 1, Kautilya, pages 5-7
[374] Olivelle 2013, pp. 290-291.
[375]
[376] Sanskrit Original: कौटिलीय अर्थशास्त्र, Arthashastra http//sanskritdocuments.org Book 3, Kautilya, page 80;
Archive 2: KAZ03.1.41 - KAZ03.1.43 Transliterated Arthashastra http://gretil.sub.uni-goettingen.de/gretil/1_sanskr/6_sastra/5_artha/kautil_u.htm Muneo Tokunaga (1992), Kyoto University, Archived at University of Goettingen, Germany
[377] Olivelle 2013, pp. 181-182.

[378] Thomas Trautmann (2012), Arthashastra: The Science of Wealth, Penguin, , pages 136-137, for context see 134-139

[379] Olivelle 2013, pp. 112-117.

[380] Thomas Trautmann (2012), Arthashastra: The Science of Wealth, Penguin, , page xx

[381] Sanskrit Original: कौटिलीय अर्थशास्त्र, Arthashastra http//sanskritdocuments.org Book 4, Kautilya, pages 110-111

[382]

[383] The girl, notes Olivelle (2013), may marry a man of equal status or any status (no mention of caste, the original Sanskrit text does not use the word *Varna* or any other related to caste). See: Olivelle<ref name="FOOTNOTEOlivelle2013248">Olivelle 2013, p. 248.

[384] Rangarajan (1992), however, translates the verse to "same varna or another varna". See: Rangarajan<ref name="FOOTNOTERangarajan199249, 364">Rangarajan 1992, pp. 49, 364.

[385] Olivelle 2013, p. 248.

[386] Olivelle 2013, p. 189.

[387] Sanskrit Original: कौटिलीय अर्थशास्त्र, Arthashastra http//sanskritdocuments.org Book 3, Kautilya, pages 84-85

[388] Sanskrit Original: कौटिलीय अर्थशास्त्र, Arthashastra http//sanskritdocuments.org Book 3, Kautilya, pages 81-82

[389] Rangarajan 1992, p. 366.

[390] Boesche 2002, pp. 18-19.

[391] Olivelle 2013, pp. 140-142, 44-45.

[392] Olivelle 2013, pp. 127-130.

[393] Olivelle 2013, pp. 122-126, 130-135.

[394] Olivelle 2013, pp. 139-140.

[395] Olivelle 2013, pp. 140-141.

[396] Olivelle 2013, pp. 142-143.

[397] Olivelle 2013, pp. 143-147.

[398] Olivelle 2013, pp. 147-151.

[399] Olivelle 2013, pp. 152-156.

[400] Olivelle 2013, pp. 157-159.

[401] Olivelle 2013, pp. 160-162.

[402] Olivelle 2013, pp. 162-170.

[403] Olivelle 2013, p. 172.

[404] Olivelle 2013, pp. 171-175.

[405] Olivelle 2013, pp. 173-175, 78-90.

[406] Sanskrit Original: कौटिलीय अर्थशास्त्र, Arthashastra http//sanskritdocuments.org Book 11, Kautilya, pages 206-208

[407] Olivelle 2013, pp. 42-47, 78-80, 98, 112-117, 231-234, 261-263, 407-414, 476-483.

[408] Olivelle 2013, pp. xv-xvi, 42-43, 78-82, 98, 260.

[409] Olivelle 2013, pp. 42-43.

[410] Olivelle 2013, pp. 78-83.

[411] Olivelle 2013, pp. 42–47, 78–83, 260–261.

[412]

[413] Olivelle 2013, p. 261.

[414] Olivelle 2013, p. 294.

[415] Olivelle 2013, pp. 294-297.

[416] Olivelle 2013, pp. 277-278.

[417] Rangarajan 1992, p. 530.

[418] Olivelle 2013, pp. 273-274.

[419]

[420] Torkel Brekke (2009), The Ethics of War in Asian Civilizations: A Comparative Perspective, Routledge, , pages 121-138

[421] Olivelle 2013, pp. 43-44.

[422] Olivelle 2013, pp. 44-45.

[423] K Thanawala (2014), Ancient Economic Thought (Editor: Betsy Price), Routledge, , page 50

[424] Boesche 2002, p. 72.

[425] Charles Waldauer et al. (1996), Kautilya's Arthashastra: A Neglected Precursor to Classical Economics, Indian Economic Review, Vol. XXXI, No. 1, pages 101-108

[426] Joseph Spengler (1971), Indian Economic Thought, Duke University Press, , pages 72-73

[427] Olivelle 2013, pp. 43-44, 101, 228-229, 286-287.

[428] K Thanawala (2014), Ancient Economic Thought (Editor: Betsy Price), Routledge, , page 52

[429] Olivelle 2013, pp. 99-111.

[430] Olivelle 2013, p. 140.

[431] Olivelle 2013, pp. 40-45, 99-110, 136-137, 150-153, 173-174, 536-545, 556-557, 572-580, 646-647.

[432] Olivelle 2013.

[433]

[434] MV Krishna Rao (1958, Reprinted 1979), Studies in Kautilya, 2nd Edition, , , pages 13-14, 231-233

[435] Max Weber, *Politics as a Vocation* (1919). This translation is from *Weber: Selections in Translation*, ed. W. G. Runciman, trans. Eric Matthews (Cambridge: Cambridge University Press, 1978), pp. 212–25 (p. 220); see also this translation http://www.ne.jp/asahi/moriyuki/abukuma/weber/lecture/politics_vocation.html.

[436] A Kumar (2005), The Structure and Principles of Public Organization in Kautilya's Arthashastra https://www.jstor.org/stable/41856143, The Indian Journal of Political Science, Vol. 66, No. 3, pages 463-488

[437] S Set (2015), Ancient Wisdom for the Modern World: Revisiting Kautilya and his Arthashastra in the Third Millennium, Strategic Analysis, Volume 39, Issue 6, pages 710-714

[438] Patrick Olivelle states that the Kangle edition has problems as it incorrectly relied on a mistaken text as commentary; he has emended the corrections in his 2013 translation. See: Olivelle<ref name="FOOTNOTEOlivelle2013xv-xvii">Olivelle 2013, pp. xv-xvii.

[439] Boesche 2002, pp. 1-7.

[440] Boesche 2002, pp. 7-8.

[441] Thomas Trautmann (2012), Arthashastra: The Science of Wealth, Penguin, , pages 116-139

[442] Boesche 2002, p. 7.

[443] Boesche 2002, pp. 15-16.

[444]

[445] Thomas Trautmann (2012), Arthashastra: The Science of Wealth, Penguin, , pages 134-138

[446] J Gonda (1957), Ancient Indian Kingship from the Religious Point of View (Continued and Ended) https://www.jstor.org/stable/3269370, Journal: Numen, Vol. 4, Fasc. 2, page 159

[447] Timothy Starzl and Krishna Dhir (1986), Strategic Planning 2300 Years Ago: The Strategy of Kautilya https://www.jstor.org/stable/40227819, Management International Review, Vol. 26, No. 4, pages 70-77

[448] BS Sihag (2004), Kautilya on the scope and methodology of accounting, organizational design and the role of ethics in ancient India, The Accounting Historians Journal, Vol 31, Number 2, pages 125-148

[449] //www.jstor.org/stable/597102

[450] //doi.org/10.2307%2F597102

[451] https://books.google.com/books?id=6MlgU0oQb4sC

[452] https://books.google.com/books?id=h0_xhdCScQkC&pg=PA164

[453] https://archive.org/details/Arthasastra_English_Translation

[454] //en.wikipedia.org/w/index.php?title=Template:Hindu_scriptures&action=edit

[455] John Bowker (2012), The Message and the Book: Sacred Texts of the World's Religions, Yale University Press, , pages 179–180

[456] Pandurang Vaman Kane mentions over 100 different Dharmasastra texts were known by the Middle Ages in India, but most of these are lost to history and their existence is inferred from quotes and citations in bhasya and digests that have survived.<ref>Kane, P.V. *History of the Dharmaśāstras* Vol. 1 p. 304

[457] James Lochtefeld (2002), "Dharma Shastras" in The Illustrated Encyclopedia of Hinduism, Vol. 1: A-M, Rosen Publishing, , pages 191–192

[458] Patrick Olivelle 1999, pp. xxiii–xxv.

[459] Robert Lingat 1973, p. 73.

[460] Patrick Olivelle 2006, pp. 173, 175–176, 183.

[461] Patrick Olivelle, *Manu's Code of Law: A Critical Edition and Translation of the Mānava-Dharmaśāstra* (New York: Oxford UP, 2005), 64.

[462] Ludo Rocher, "Hindu Law and Religion: Where to draw the line?" in *Malik Ram Felicitation Volume*, ed. S.A.J. Zaidi. (New Delhi, 1972), pp.167–194 and Richard W. Lariviere, "Law and Religion in India" in *Law, Morality, and Religion: Global Perspectives*, ed. Alan Watson (Berkeley: University of California Press), pp.75–94.

[463] Patrick Olivelle (2005), Manu's Code of Law, Oxford University Press, , pages 31–32, 81–82, 154–166, 208–214, 353–354, 356–382

[464] Donald Davis (2010), The Spirit of Hindu Law, Cambridge University Press, , page 13–16, 166–179

[465] Werner Menski (2003), Hindu Law: Beyond tradition and modernity, Oxford University Press, , Chapter 1

[466] Patrick Olivelle 1999, pp. xxii.

[467] Robert Lingat 1973, pp. 7–8.

[468] Robert Lingat 1973, p. 12.

[469] Patrick Olivelle 1999, pp. xxiv–xxv.

[470] Robert Lingat 1973, pp. 19–22, Quote: The dharma-sutra of Apastamba suggests that a rich literature on dharma already existed. He cites ten authors by name. (...).

[471] Patrick Olivelle 2006, pp. 178, see note 29 for a list of 17 cited ancient scholars in different Dharmasutras.

[472] Patrick Olivelle 2006, p. 178.

[473] Patrick Olivelle 1999, pp. xxiv.

[474] Robert Lingat 1973, p. 18.

[475] Patrick Olivelle 2006, p. 185.

[476] Robert Lingat 1973, p. 19.

[477] Robert Lingat 1973, pp. 19–20.

[478] Patrick Olivelle 2006, p. 46.

[479] Patrick Olivelle 1999, pp. xxvi.

[480] Patrick Olivelle 1999, p. 325.

[481] Patrick Olivelle 1999, pp. xxxi.

[482] Patrick Olivelle 2006, p. 178 with note 28.

[483] Patrick Olivelle 1999, pp. xxvii.

[484] Patrick Olivelle 1999, pp. xxviii.

[485] Patrick Olivelle 1999, pp. xxxiv.

[486] Patrick Olivelle 1999, pp. xxxv.

[487] Patrick Olivelle 1999, pp. xxxvi.

[488] Patrick Olivelle 1999, pp. xxxvii.

[489] Patrick Olivelle 1999, pp. xxxviii–xxxix.

[490] Patrick Olivelle 1999, pp. xxxviii–xxxix, 27–28.

[491] Patrick Olivelle 1999, pp. xxxix.

[492] Patrick Olivelle 1999, pp. xl.

[493] Patrick Olivelle 1999, pp. xli.

[494] Patrick Olivelle 2006, pp. 180.

[495] Robert Lingat 1973, p. 69.

[496] Patrick Olivelle 1999, pp. 100–101.

[497] Baudhayana, in verses 1.1.5–6, provides a complete definition of śiṣṭa as "Now, śiṣṭa are those who are free from envy and pride, who possess just a jarful of grain, who are without greed, and who are free from hypocrisy, arrogance, greed, folly and anger."<ref name="FOOTNOTEPatrick Olivelle2006181">Patrick Olivelle 2006, p. 181.

[498] Patrick Olivelle 1999, pp. xlii.

[499] Patrick Olivelle 1999, pp. xlii.

[500] Robert Lingat 1973, pp. 73–77.

[501] Patrick Olivelle 2006, pp. 169–170.

[502] Timothy Lubin, Donald R. Davis Jr & Jayanth K. Krishnan 2010, p. 57.

[503] Patrick Olivelle (2005), Manu's Code of Law, Oxford University Press, , pages 24–25

[504] See Flood 1996: 56 and Olivelle 2005.

[505] Steven Collins (1993), The discourse of what is primary, Journal of Indian philosophy, Volume 21, pages 301–393

[506] Patrick Olivelle 2005, pp. 3–4.

[507] Robert Lingat 1973, p. 77.

[508] Lingat 1973: 98

[509] Timothy Lubin, Donald R. Davis Jr & Jayanth K. Krishnan 2010, pp. 59–72.

[510] Robert Lingat 1973, p. 98.

[511] Lariviere 1989: ix

[512] Olivelle 2007: 149–150.

[513] Robert Lingat 1973, p. 277.

[514] Numerous Dharmasastras are known, but most are lost to history and only known from them being mentioned or quoted in other surviving texts. For example, Dharmasastras by Atri, Harita, Ushanas, Angiras, Yama, Apastamba, Samvartha, Katyayana, Brihaspati, Parasara, Vyasa, Sankha, Likhita, Daksha, Gautama, Satatapa, Vasistha, Prachetas, Budha, Devala, Sumantu, Jamadgni, Visvamitra, Prajapati, Paithinasi, Pitamaha, Jabala, Chhagaleya, Chyavana, Marichi, Kasyapa, Gobhila, Risyasrimaga and others.<ref name="FOOTNOTEMandagadde Rama Jois198422">Mandagadde Rama Jois 1984, pp. 22.

[515] Robert Lingat 1973, pp. 195–198.

[516] Robert Lingat 1973, p. 104.

[517] Patrick Olivelle 2006, p. 188.

[518] Robert Lingat 1973, pp. 14, 109–110, 180–189.

[519] Robert Lingat 1973, p. 97.

[520] Robert Lingat 1973, pp. 98, 103–106.

[521] Robert Lingat 1973, pp. 130–131.

[522] Robert Lingat 1973, p. 6.

[523] Patrick Olivelle 2006, pp. 173–174.

[524] Patrick Olivelle 2006, pp. 175–178, 184–185.

[525] Patrick Olivelle 2006, pp. 176–177.

[526] Robert Lingat 1973, p. 22.

[527] Patrick Olivelle (2005), Manu's Code of Law, Oxford University Press, , pages 353–354, 356–382

[528] G Srikantan (2014), Entanglements in Legal History (Editor: Thomas Duve), Max Planck Institute: Germany, , page 123

[529] Robert Lingat 1973, pp. 129–131.

[530] P.V. Kane, *History of Dharmaśāstra: (ancient and mediaeval, religious and civil law)*. (Poona: Bhandarkar Oriental Research Institute, 1962 – 1975).

[531] Robert Lingat 1973, pp. 158–159.

[532] Robert Lingat 1973, p. 103, 159.

[533] Patrick Olivelle 2006, p. 172.

[534] Patrick Olivelle 2006, pp. 172–173.

[535] Robert Lingat 1973, pp. 14–16.

[536] Robert Lingat 1973, p. 285.

[537] Patrick Olivelle 2006, pp. 186–188.

[538] Robert Lingat 1973, pp. 149–150.

[539] On this topic, see Olivelle, Patrick, *Language, Tests, and Society: Explorations in Ancient Indian Culture and Religion.* p. 174

[540] Robert Lingat 1973, pp. 98–99.

[541] Patrick Olivelle 2006, pp. 195–198 with footnotes.

[542] Kane, P.V. *History of the Dharmaśāstras* Vol. 4 p. 38, 58

[543] Robert Lingat 1973, pp. 54–56.

[544] Robert Lingat 1973, p. 55.

[545] Robert Lingat 1973, p. 107.

[546] J Duncan J Derrett (1977), Essays in Classical and Modern Hindu Law, Brill Academic, , pages 10–17, 36–37 with footnote 75a

[547] Kane, P. V., History of Dharmaśāstra, (Poona: Bhandarkar Oriental Research Institute, 1975), Volume I, Part II, 583.
[548] Patrick Olivelle 2005, pp. 367–369.
[549] Robert Lingat 1973, p. 116.
[550] Robert Lingat 1973, p. 117.
[551] Donald R. Davis, Jr 2010, pp. 47–49.
[552] Kisori Lal Sarkar, *The Mimansa Rules of Interpretation as applied to Hindu Law*. Tagore Law Lectures of 1905 (Calcutta: Thacker, Spink, 1909).
[553] Ludo Rocher 2008, p. 112.
[554] Mandagadde Rama Jois 1984, pp. 3, 469–481.
[555] Tomothy Lubin et al (2010), Hinduism and Law: An Introduction (Editors: Lubin and Davis), Cambridge University Press, , Chapter 1
[556] Ludo Rocher, "Hindu Law and Religion: Where to draw the line?" in *Malik Ram Felicitation Volume*. ed. S.A.J. Zaidi (New Delhi, 1972), 190–1.
[557] J.D.M. Derrett, *Religion, Law, and the State in India* (London: Faber, 1968), 96; For a related distinction between religious and secular law in Dharmaśāstra, see
[558] https://books.google.com/books?id=RGPSEuNsPLEC
[559] https://www.wisdomlib.org/hinduism/book/manusmriti-with-the-commentary-of-medhatithi
[560] http://www.sacred-texts.com/hin/manu.htm
[561] http://www.sacred-texts.com/hin/sbe02/index.htm
[562] http://www.sacred-texts.com/hin/sbe14/index.htm
[563] http://www.sacred-texts.com/hin/sbe07/index.htm
[564] http://www.sacred-texts.com/hin/sbe33/index.htm
[565] https://books.google.com/books?id=9oEhAwAAQBAJ
[566] https://books.google.com/books?id=V552bAz5xFAC
[567] https://books.google.com/books?id=MtuhClbfL7EC
[568] https://books.google.com/books?id=Sauo8iSIj7YC
[569] https://books.google.com/books?id=gnVxqvPg9a0C
[570] https://books.google.com/books?id=PnHo02RtONMC
[571] https://books.google.com/books?id=efaOR_-YsIcC
[572] https://books.google.com/books?id=SKBxa-MNqA8C
[573] http://hdl.handle.net/2027/mdp.35112105134516
[574] http://hdl.handle.net/2027/mdp.35112105134524
[575] https://mywebspace.wisc.edu/drdavis/web/hindulaw/
[576] http://www.payer.de/dharmashastra/dharmash00.htm/
[577] http://is1.mum.edu/vedicreserve/smriti/smriti_complete.pdf
[578] //en.wikipedia.org/w/index.php?title=Template:Hinduism&action=edit
[579] Rocher, Rosane *The Creation of Anglo-Hindu Law*
[580] Hacker, Paul. 2006. pp. 484
[581] Davis, Jr. Donald R. *The Spirit of Hindu Law*. Chapter 1.
[582] Davis, Jr. Donald R. 2005
[583] Davis, Jr. Donald R. Ch. 1. pp. 2
[584] Davis, Jr. Donald R. Ch. 7
[585] Coburn, Thomas B. 1984. pp. 439.
[586] Jho, Chakradhar. 1986. pp. 59
[587] Jho, Chakradhar. 1986. pp. 60
[588] Davis, Jr. Donald R. Ch. 1, pp. 2.
[589] Lingat, Robert. 1973. Ch. 1, pp. 9-10.
[590] Davis, Jr. Donald R. Ch. One
[591] Hacker, Paul. 2006. pp. 484
[592] Davis, Jr. Donald R. Ch. Seven
[593] Davis, Jr. Donald R. Ch. Seven
[594] Olivelle, Patrick. 2004. *The Law Code of Manu*. 2.6.
[595] Davis, Jr. Donald R. Ch. 1, pp. 6.
[596] Lingat, Robert. 1973. Ch. 1, pp. 6.
[597] Davis:*The Spirit of Hindu Law*

[598] Lingat: 1973

[599] Davis:*The Spirit of Hindu Law*

[600] Lingat: 1973

[601] Davis

[602] Davis:2005 http://www.ingentaconnect.com/content/brill/sho/2005/00000048/00000001/art00003

[603] Davis:2005

[604] Olivelle:2004, xl

[605] yājñavalkya, vijñāneśvara

[606] yājñavalkya I.323

[607] Davis: *The Spirit of Hindu Law*

[608] Das: 1977. 93-127.

[609] Kaul:1993. 136-37.

[610] Kaul:1993. 149-155.

[611] Das:1977. 93-127.

[612] //en.wikipedia.org/w/index.php?title=Template:Hinduism&action=edit

[613] William Musyoka (2010), A Casebook on the Law of Succession, , page 12

[614] Werner Menski (2003), Hindu Law: Beyond tradition and modernity, Oxford University Press, , Chapter 1

[615] P Bilimoria (2011), The Idea of Hindu Law http://search.informit.com.au/documentSummary;dn=377009149672171;res=IELHSS, Journal of the Oriental Society of Australia, Volume 43, pages 103-130

[616]

[617]

[618] For reviews of the British misappropriations of Dharmaśāstra, see: Richard W. Lariviere, "Justices and Paṇḍitas: Some Ironies in Contemporary Readings of the Hindu Legal Past," in *Journal of Asian Studies* 48 (1989), pp. 757–769, and Ludo Rocher, "Law Books in an Oral Culture: The Indian Dharmaśāstras," *Proceedings of the American Philosophical Society* 137 (1993), pp. 254–267.

[619] John Griffith (1986), What is legal pluralism?, The Journal of Legal Pluralism and Unofficial Law, Volume 18, Issue 24, pages 1-55

[620] John H. Mansfield (2005), "The Personal Laws or a Uniform Civil Code?" in Robert D. Baird, ed., Religion and Law in Independent India, , pages 139-177

[621] TN Madan (1987), Secularism in Its Place, The Journal of Asian Studies, Volume 46, Issue 04, pages 747-759

[622]

[623] Dharma, The Columbia Encyclopedia, 6th Ed. (2013), Columbia University Press, Gale,

[624]

[625]

[626] yuktatA http://spokensanskrit.de/index.php?tinput=yuktatA&direction=SE&script=HK&link=yes&beginning=0 Sanskrit-English Dictionary, Koeln University, Germany

[627] prasaMvidA http://spokensanskrit.de/index.php?tinput=prasaMvidA&direction=SE&script=HK&link=yes&beginning=0 Sanskrit-English Dictionary, Koeln University, Germany

[628] vivAdayati&direction=SE&script=HK&link=yes&beginning=0 vivAdayati http://spokensanskrit.de/index.php?tinput= Sanskrit-English Dictionary, Koeln University, Germany

[629] NyAya http://www.sanskrit-lexicon.uni-koeln.de/scans/MWScan/tamil/index.html and other words, Cologne Digital Sanskrit Lexicon, Koeln University, Germany

[630] lawyer http://spokensanskrit.de/index.php?script=HK&beginning=0+&tinput=lawyer&trans=Translate&direction=AU Sanskrit-English Dictionary, Koeln University, Germany

[631]

[632] Werner Menski (2003), Hindu Law: Beyond tradition and modernity, Oxford University Press, , pages 547-549

[633] JDM Derrett (1999), Law Religion and the State in India, Oxford University Press, , Chapter 2

[634] Malcolm Voyce (2010), Law and Anthropology: Current Legal Issues (Editors: Freeman and Napier), Oxford University Press, , page 554 with footnote 27

[635] Axel Michaels (2010), Hinduism and Law: An Introduction (Editors: Lubin and Davis), Cambridge University Press, , Chapter 3 and pages 58-73 with footnotes

[636] Donald Davis (2010), The Spirit of Hindu Law, Cambridge University Press,

[637] Donald R. Davis, Jr., *The Boundaries of Hindu Law: Tradition, Custom, and Politics in Medieval Kerala*. Corpus Iuris Sanscriticum et Fontes Iuris Asiae Meridianae et Centralis. Vol. 5. Ed. Oscar Botto (Torino (Italy): CESMEO, 2004).

[638] Elisa Freschi (2012): The Vedas are not deontic authorities in absolute sense and may be disobeyed, but still recognized as an epistemic authority in Hindu dharma;<ref>Elisa Freschi (2012), Duty, Language and Exegesis in Prabhakara Mimamsa, BRILL, , page 62

[639] James Lochtefeld (2002), "Smrti", The Illustrated Encyclopedia of Hinduism, Vol. 2: N–Z, Rosen Publishing, , pages 656 and 461

[640] A Smriti is a derivative work, has less epistemic authority than the Vedas, and does not have any deontic authority in Hindu dharma.<ref>Tomothy Lubin (2010), Hinduism and Law: An Introduction (Editors: Lubin and Davis), Cambridge University Press, , pages 137-143

[641]

[642] The Laws of Manu 2.6 with footnotes https://archive.org/stream/lawsofman00manu#page/n173/mode/2up George Bühler (Translator), The Sacred Books of the East, Vol. 25, Oxford University Press

[643] Brian Smith and Wendy Doniger (1992), The Laws of Manu, Penguin, , pages 17-18

[644]

[645] Bilimoria, Purushottama (2011), The idea of Hindu law, Journal of Oriental Society of Australia, Vol. 43, pages 103-130

[646] Donald R. Davis, Jr., "On Ātmastuṣṭi as a Source of *Dharma*," *Journal of the American Oriental Society* 127:3 (2007), pages 279–96

[647] Werner Menski, *Hindu Law: Beyond Tradition and Modernity* (Delhi: Oxford UP, 2003), p. 126 and Domenico Francavilla, *The Roots of Hindu Jurisprudence: Sources of Dharma and Interpretation in Mīmāṃsā and Dharmaśāstra*. Corpus Iuris Sanscriticum. Vol. 7 (Torino: CESMEO, 2006), pp.165–76.

[648] John Dawson Mayne (1910), , Stevens and Hynes, Harvard Law Library Series

[649]

[650] KL Seshagiri Rao (1997), Practitioners of Hindu Law: Ancient and Modern http://heinonline.org/HOL/LandingPage?handle=hein.journals/flr66&div=60&id=&page=, Fordham Law Review, vol. 66, pages 1185-1191

[651] Terence Day (1982), The Conception of Punishment in Early Indian Literature, Wilfrid Laurier University Press, , Chapters 2 & 3

[652]

[653] MB Hooker (1978), The Indian-derived law texts of Southeast Asia, The Journal of Asian Studies, volume 37, number 2, pages 201-219

[654] Hooker 1986.

[655] Creese 2009a, 2009b.

[656] Tomothy Lubin et al (2010), Hinduism and Law: An Introduction (Editors: Lubin and Davis), Cambridge University Press, , Chapter 1

[657] Scott Kugle (2001), Framed, Blamed and Renamed: The Recasting of Islamic Jurisprudence in Colonial South Asia, Modern Asian Studies, 35(2), pages 257-313

[658] Ludo Rocher, "Hindu Law and Religion: Where to draw the line?" in *Malik Ram Felicitation Volume*. ed. S.A.J. Zaidi (New Delhi, 1972), 190–1.

[659] J.D.M. Derrett, *Religion, Law, and the State in India* (London: Faber, 1968), 96; For a related distinction between religious and secular law in Dharmaśāstra, see Timothy Lubin, "Punishment and Expiation: Overlapping Domains in Brahmanical Law," http://papers.ssrn.com/sol3/papers.cfm?abstract_id=1084716 *Indologica Taurinensis* 33 (2007): 93–122.

[660] K Ewing (1988), Sharia and ambiguity in South Asian Islam, University of California Press,

[661] A digest of Moohummudan law on the subjects to which it is usually applied by British courts of justice in India https://archive.org/stream/digestmoohummud00bailgoog#page/n7/mode/2up Neil Baillie, Smith, Elder & Co. London

[662] Michael Anderson (1995), Institutions and Ideologies: A SOAS South Asia Reader (Studies in Asian Topics, Editors: David Arnold, Peter Robb), Routledge, , Chapter 10

[663] Rosie Llewellyn-Jones (2007), The Great Uprising in India: 1857-58, Boydell & Brewer, , pages 111-112

[664] David Cook (2005), Understanding Jihad, University of California Press, ISBN, pages 80-83

[665] JDM Derrett (1968), Religion, Law and State in India, Faber and Faber, London,

[666]

[667] Kunal Parker (Editor: Gerald James Larson, 2001), Religion and Personal Law in Secular India: A Call to Judgment, Indiana University Press, , pages 184-199

[668] Chandra Mallampalli (2004), Christians and Public Life in Colonial South India: 1863-1937, Routledge, , pages 59-64

[669] Seshagiri Rao, K.L. (1997–1998). Practitioners of Hindu Law: Ancient and Modern. Fordham Law Review, 66, Retrieved 15 October 2008

[670] Singh, Pritam. 2005. "Hindu Bias in India's 'Secular' Constitution: probing flaws in the instruments of governance." *Third World Quarterly*. 26:6, 909–926.

[671] Donald E Smith (2011), India as a Secular State, Princeton University Press,

[672] Gerald James Larson (2001), Religion and Personal Law in Secular India: A Call to Judgment, Indiana University Press,

[673]

[674] //www.jstor.org/stable/25165079

[675] //doi.org/10.1007%2Fs10781-004-8651-4

[676] https://dx.doi.org/10.1023/A:1026483519342

[677] https://dx.doi.org/10.1007/s10781-006-9002-4

[678] https://www.wisdomlib.org/hinduism/book/manusmriti-with-the-commentary-of-medhatithi

[679] http://papers.ssrn.com/sol3/papers.cfm?abstract_id=1084716

[680] http://heinonline.org/HOL/LandingPage?handle=hein.journals/hastlj29&div=57&id=&page=

[681] https://dx.doi.org/10.1017/S0026749X00008714

[682] https://dx.doi.org/10.1017/S0010417500001213

[683] http://heinonline.org/HOL/LandingPage?handle=hein.journals/flr66&div=60&id=&page=

[684] https://books.google.com/books?id=vFEZAAAAYAAJ&pg=PAPA109

[685] https://dx.doi.org/10.1093/jaarel/lfm004

[686] Johnson, Wallace and Denis Twitchett (1993), "Criminal Procedure in T'ang China", *Asia Major* 3rd series, 6.2, 137.

[687] https://books.google.com/?id=w68uObIhx9MC&printsec=frontcover#v=onepage&q&f=false

[688] http://kuscholarworks.ku.edu/dspace/handle/1808/3608

[689] http://reference.allrefer.com/country-guide-study/china/china343.html

[690] http://pages.stern.nyu.edu/~wstarbuc/ChinCtrl.html

[691] http://ancientchinaonline.com/ancient-china-law/

[692] //en.wikipedia.org/w/index.php?title=Template:Chinese_Political_Realism&action=edit

[693] Gernet (1996), 244 https://books.google.com/books?id=jqb7L-pKCV8C&printsec= frontcover&source=gbs_summary_r&cad=0#PPA244,M1. • Jianfu Chen (1960) p.9., Chinese Law: Context and Transformation: Revised and Expanded Edition, https://books.google.com/books?id=Q2xyDAAAQBAJ&pg=PA9

[694] Gernet (1996), 244-245 https://books.google.com/books?id=jqb7L-pKCV8C&printsec= frontcover&source=gbs_summary_r&cad=0#PPA245,M1.

[695] Gernet (1996), 244 https://books.google.com/books?id=jqb7L-pKCV8C&printsec= frontcover&source=gbs_summary_r&cad=0#PPA244,M1.

[696] Jacques Gernet, *A History of Chinese Civilization*, p. 245 https://books.google.com/books?id= jqb7L-pKCV8C&printsec=frontcover&source=gbs_summary_r&cad=0#PPA245,M1.

[697] Johnson and Twitchett (1993), 135.

[698] Johnson and Twitchett (1993), 125-126.

[699] Johnson and Twitchett (1993), 128-129.

[700] The Tang Code translated by Wallace Johnson volume II, article 482

[701] Johnson and Twitchett (1993), 128.

[702] https://books.google.com/books?id=jqb7L-pKCV8C

[703] Chinese: 《大清律例》 ; pinyin: *Da Qing lü li*; Manchu: ⟡⟡⟡⟡⟡⟡ ⟡⟡⟡⟡⟡ ⟡

□□□□□
□
□□□□□
□□□□□ Wylie: Daitsing gurun i fafun i pitghe kauli, Möllendorff *Daicing gurun-i fafun-i bithe kooli*

[704] S.P. Ong, Jurisdictional Politics in Canton and the First English Translation of the Qing Penal Code (1810), Winner of the 2nd Sir George Staunton Award, 20 J. ROYAL ASIATIC SOC'Y GR. BRIT. & IR. 141, 148-51 (2010)

[705] https://kuscholarworks.ku.edu/dspace/handle/1808/3635

[706] https://books.google.com/books?id=gaQBAAAAQAAJ&printsec=frontcover&source=gbs_ge_summary_r&cad=0#v=onepage&q&f=false

[707] https://books.google.com/books?id=smYuAQAAIAAJ&printsec=frontcover&source=gbs_ge_summary_r&cad=0#v=onepage&q&f=false

[708] The Secret History of the Mongols

[709] Nişanyan - Türkçe Etimolojik Sözlük

[710] http://www.coldsiberia.org/webdoc9.htm

[711] https://web.archive.org/web/20060112130533/http://www.geocities.com/Athens/Pantheon/3055/yasa.htm

[712] http://www.nisanyansozluk.com/search.asp?w=yasa&x=0&y=0

[713] //en.wikipedia.org/w/index.php?title=Template:Catholic_canon_law&action=edit

[714] Dr. Edward N. Peters, CanonLaw.info http://www.canonlaw.info, accessed Jul-1-2013

[715] Manual of Canon Law, pg. 13, #8

[716] Paul Fournier and Gabriel Le Bras, *Histoire des Collections Canoniques en Occident depuis les Fausses Décrétales jusqu'au Décret de Gratien*, 2 vols. (Paris, 1931), vol I, pp. 16-17

[717] On the controversial date of the Dionysian collections, see E. Wirbelauer, ed., *Zwei Päpste in Rom: der Konflikt zwischen Laurentius und Symmachus (498–514)*, Studien und Texte, Quellen und Forschungen zur antiken Welt 16 (Munich, 1993), p. 121.

[718] David N. Dumville, "Ireland, Brittany and England: Transmission and Use of the *Collectio canonum Hibernensis*", in Catherine Laurent and Helen Davis (eds.), *Irlande et Bretagne : vingt siècles d'histoire*, Actes du colloque de Rennes, 29-31 mars 1993 (Rennes, 1994), pp. 84-85.

[719] M. Elliot, *Canon Law Collections in England ca 600–1066: The Manuscript Evidence*, unpubl. PhD dissertation (University of Toronto, 2013).

[720] Fournier and Le Bras, *Histoire des Collections Canoniques en Occident*, vol I, pp. 51-62.

[721] Law and Revolution, pg. 116

[722] Law and Revolution, pg. 240

[723] NYTimes.com, *Neighbors and Wives* book review https://www.nytimes.com/1988/11/13/books/neighbors-and-wives.html of Nov-13-1988, accessed 27 June 2013

[724] Catholic Encyclopedia http://www.newadvent.org/cathen/06730a.htm

[725] Europe in the High Middle Ages, pp. 127–128

[726] Europe in the High Middle Ages, pg. 116

[727] Dr. Kenneth J. Pennington, Ph.D., CL701, CUA School of Canon Law, "History of Canon Law, Day 1" https://www.youtube.com/watch?v=EVwHMzCUx4k&index=27&list=PLIyjmpcCSGmbeqoESo25a9Rg6YH0BQVnc, around 0:25:30, accessed 8-15-2014

[728] Harold J. Berman, "Law and Revolution: The Formation of the Western Legal Tradition", pg. 254

[729] John XXIII, allocution *Questa festiva* (25 Jan. 1959), AAS 51 (1959) pp. 68-69

[730] CanonLaw.info, "Legislative History of the 1983 Code of Canon Law" http://canonlaw.info/canonlaw_LegisHistory.htm; accessed June-7-2013

[731] Berman, *Law and Revolution*, pg. 605

[732]

[733] Edward N. Peters, "1917 Code of Canon Law" (San Francisco: Ignatius Press, 2001), pg. 6 (Card. Gasparri's Preface to 1917 CIC)

[734] Benedict XV, Ap. Const. *Providentissima Mater Ecclesia* of 27 May 1917

[735] Coriden, *The Code of Canon Law*, pg. 948

[736] John Paul II, Ap. Const. *Sacrae Disciplinae Leges*

[737] 1983 Code, canon 6 §1, 1°

[738] John Paul II, *Ad Tuendam Fidem* http://w2.vatican.va/content/john-paul-ii/en/motu_proprio/documents/hf_jp-ii_motu-proprio_30061998_ad-tuendam-fidem.html, accessed 16 July 2015

[739] Benedict XVI, *Omnium in Mentem* http://w2.vatican.va/content/benedict-xvi/en/apost_letters/documents/hf_ben-xvi_apl_20091026_codex-iuris-canonici.html, accessed 16 July 2015.

[740] Pope Francis reforms Church law in marital nullity trials http://en.radiovaticana.va/news/2015/09/08/pope_francis_reforms_church_law_in_marital_nullity_trials/1170336, Vatican Radio, accessed 8 September 2015

[741] //en.wikipedia.org/w/index.php?title=Template:Catholic_canon_law&action=edit

[742] Black's Law Dictionary, 5th Edition, pg. 771: "Jus canonicum"

[743] Della Rocca, *Manual of Canon Law*, pg. 3

[744] Berman, Harold J. *Law and Revolution*, pg. 86 & pg. 115

[745] Canon 331 http://www.vatican.va/archive/ENG1104/__P16.HTM, 1983 Code of Canon Law

[746]

[747] Manual of Canon Law, pg. 49

[748] 1983 Code of Canon Law http://www.intratext.com/IXT/ENG0017/_P2.HTM

[749] St. Joseph Foundation newsletter, Vol. 30 No. 7 https://stjosephcanonlaw.com/sites/default/files/newsletter-preview-pdfs/christifidelis30.7.pdf, pg. 3

[750] Black's Law Dictionary, 5th Edition, pg. 187: "Canonist"

[751] Berman, *Law and Revolution*, pg. 288

[752] Berman, *Law and Revolution*, pg. 202.

[753] Berman, *Law and Revolution*, pg. 253

[754] Smith, *Elements of Ecclesiastical Law*, Vol. I (9th ed.), pg. 9 https://archive.org/stream/elementsofeccles01smituoft#page/9/mode/1up. Internet Archive, accessed 28 March 2016.

[755] Rev. James Socias (gen. edit.), *Our Moral Life in Christ*. (Chicago: Midwest Theological Forum, 2003), 84.

[756] Della Rocca, Fernando, *Manual of Canon Law* (Milwaukee: The Bruce Publishing Company, 1959) trans. The Rev. Anselm Thatcher, O.S.B., pg. 9.

[757] Canon 832 as found in http://www.vatican.va/archive/ENG1104/__P2Q.HTM

[758] Berman, *Law and Revolution*, pg. 199

[759] Mylne, *The Canon Law*, pg. 22.

[760] Manual of Canon Law, pg. 13, #8

[761] Blessed John Paul II, Ap. Const. Sacri Canones https://archive.org/stream/ApostolicConstitutionSacriCanonesJohnPaulIi1990/Sacri_Canones_Apostolic_Constitution_John_Paul_II_1990#page/n7/mode/2up

[762]

[763] Manual of Canon Law, pg. 14

[764] Law and Revolution, pg. 116

[765] Law and Revolution, pg. 240

[766] Dr. Kenneth J. Pennington, Ph.D., CL701, CUA School of Canon Law, "History of Canon Law, Day 1" https://www.youtube.com/watch?v=EVwHMzCUx4k&index=27&list=PLIyjmpcCSGmbeqoESo25a9Rg6YH0BQVnc, around 0:25:30, accessed 8-15-2014

[767] Rommen, *Natural Law*, pg. 38-39

[768] NYTimes.com, *Neighbors and Wives* book review https://www.nytimes.com/1988/11/13/books/neighbors-and-wives.html of Nov-13-1988, accessed 27 June 2013

[769] Dr. Edward N. Peters, A suggestion for reordering the major divisions of canonical history http://www.canonlaw.info/ten_drhistory.htm, accessed 16 May 2013

[770] CanonLaw.info http://canonlaw.info/masterpage1917.htm, accessed Jan-19-2013

[771] John XXIII, allocution *Questa festiva* (25 Jan. 1959), AAS 51 (1959) pp. 68-69

[772] CanonLaw.info, "Legislative History of the 1983 Code of Canon Law" http://canonlaw.info/canonlaw_LegisHistory.htm; accessed June-7-2013

[773] NYTimes.com, " New Canon Law Code in Effect for Catholics https://www.nytimes.com/1983/11/27/us/new-canon-law-code-in-effect-for-catholics.html", 27-Nov-1983, accessed June-25-2013

[774] Britannica "Canon Law" http://www.britannica.com/EBchecked/topic/92870/canon-law/67236/The-new-Code-of-Canon-Law, accessed 6-24-2013

[775] Can. 1, 1983 CIC ("The Canons of this code regard only the Latin Church.")

[776] Rommen, Heinrich A., *Natural Law*, pg. 114

[777] Friedman, Lawrence M., *American Law*, pg. 70

[778] NYTimes.com, "Pope to Codify Canon Law" https://query.nytimes.com/mem/archive-free/pdf?res=F20A11F93B5913738DDDA80894DC405B848CF1D3, 1-Apr-1904, accessed 25-June-2013

[779] McCormick, Anne O'Hare. *Vatican Journal*, pg. 44

[780] Comparative Legal Traditions, pg. 43

[781] TheFreeDictionary.com http://legal-dictionary.thefreedictionary.com/Inquisitorial+System, accessed June-28-2013

[782] Wormser, *The Story of the LAW*, pg. 189

[783] Dr. Edward Peters, CanonLaw.info http://www.canonlaw.info/masterpageEastern.htm, accessed June-9-2013

[784] Code of Canons of the Eastern Churches, Latin-English Edition, New English Translation (Canon Law Society of America, 2001), page xxv
Cf. *Pastor Bonus* n. 2

[785] 1983 Code, canon 7.

[786] Catholic Encyclopedia 1913, "Words (In Canon Law)"

[787] J. Budziszewski, The Architecture of Law According to Thomas Aquinas http://www.undergroundthomist.org/the-architecture-of-law-according-to-thomas-aquinas; accessed 14 March 2016

[788] Blackfriars *Summa Theologiæ* Vol. 28, pg. 16 [notes by Thomas Gilby O.P. on *Summa* Ia-IIæ, q. 90, a. 4]

[789] Exegetical Commentary on the Code of Canon Law, Vol. I, pg. 261-262 (commentary on 1983 CIC, Book I, Title I)

[790] Errázuriz, "Justice in the Church", pg. 71

[791] Ladislas Orsy, "Towards a Theological Conception of Canon Law" (published in Jordan Hite, T.O.R., & Daniel J. Ward, O.S.B., "Readings, Cases, Materials in Canon Law: A Textbook for Ministerial Students, Revised Edition" (Collegeville, MN: The Liturgical Press, 1990), pg. 11

[792] Errázuriz M., *Fundamental Theory*, 3

[793] Errázuriz M., *Fundamental Theory*, xvii.

[794] Errázuriz M., *Fundamental Theory*, 59 et seq.

[795] Errázuriz M., *Fundamental Theory*, 62

[796] 1983 CIC, can. 252 §3

[797] 1983 CIC, can. 1420 §4

[798] 1983 CIC, can. 1421 §3

[799] 1983 CIC, can. 1435

[800] 1983 CIC, can. 1483

[801] 1983 CIC, can. 478 §1

[802] 1983 CIC, can. 378 §1 °5

[803] http://www.canonlaw.info

[804] http://www.vatican.va/archive/ENG0015/_INDEX.HTM

[805] https://web.archive.org/web/20080220062727/http://www.vatican.va/archive/ENG1104/_INDEX.HTM

[806] https//web.archive.org

[807] http://www.iuscangreg.it/diritto_universale.php?lang=EN

[808] http://www.ahereford.org/canonlaw

[809] http://www.intratext.com/X/LAT0010.HTM

[810] http://www.intratext.com/IXT/ENG0017/_INDEX.HTM

[811] http://www.intratext.com/X/LAT0758.HTM

[812] http://www.intratext.com/X/ENG1199.HTM

[813] http://www.intratext.com/X/LAT0813.HTM

[814] http://catho.org/9.php?d=fn

[815] //en.wikipedia.org/w/index.php?title=Template:Islam&action=edit

[816] //en.wikipedia.org/w/index.php?title=Template:Basic_forms_of_government&action=edit

[817] Vikør 2014.

[818] Calder 2009.

[819] John L. Esposito, Natana J. DeLong-Bas (2001), *Women in Muslim family law https: //books.google.com/books?id=MOmaDq8HKCgC&pg=PA2#v=onepage&q&f=false*, p. 2. Syracuse University Press, . Quote: "[...], by the ninth century, the classical theory of law fixed the sources of Islamic law at four: the *Quran*, the *Sunnah* of the Prophet, *qiyas* (analogical reasoning), and *ijma* (consensus)."

[820] Otto 2008, p. 19.

[821] Mayer 2009.

[822] While the advocacy of *hudud* punishments has gained symbolic importance, and in theory often involved rejection of the stringent traditional restrictions on their application, in practice, in those few countries where they have been reintroduced, they have often been used sparingly or not at all. Their application has varied depending on local political climate.<ref name="FOOTNOTEVikør2014">Vikør 2014.

[823] Otto 2008, p. 20.

[824] Rabb 2009.

[825] Staff (January 3, 2003). "Analysis: Nigeria's Sharia Split" http://news.bbc.co.uk/2/hi/africa/ 2632939.stm. BBC News. Retrieved September 19, 2011. "Thousands of people have been killed in fighting between Christians and Muslims following the introduction of sharia punishments in northern Nigerian states over the past three years".

[826] Harnischfeger, Johannes (2008). p. 16. "When the Governor of Kaduna announced the introduction of Sharia, although non-Muslims form almost half of the population, violence erupted, leaving more than 1,000 people dead." p. 189. "When a violent confrontation loomed in February 200, because the strong Christian minority in Kaduna was unwilling to accept the proposed sharia law, the sultan and his delegation of 18 emirs went to see the governor and insisted on the passage of the bill."

[827] Otto 2008, pp. 18–20.

[828] Stahnke, Tad and Robert C. Blitt (2005), "The Religion-State Relationship and the Right to Freedom of Religion or Belief: A Comparative Textual Analysis of the Constitutions of Predominantly Muslim Countries." Georgetown Journal of International Law, volume 36, issue 4; also see Sharia Law profile by Country http://www.law.emory.edu/ifl/index2.html, Emory University (2011)

[829] Al-Suwaidi, J. (1995). *Arab and western conceptions of democracy; in Democracy, war, and peace in the Middle East* (Editors: David Garnham, Mark A. Tessler), Indiana University Press, see Chapters 5 and 6;

[830] Calder & Hooker 2007, p. 321.

[831] Otto 2008, pp. 9–10.

[832] Calder & Hooker 2007, p. 323.

[833] Calder & Hooker 2007, p. 326.

[834] Abdal-Haqq, Irshad (2006). *Understanding Islamic Law – From Classical to Contemporary* (edited by Aminah Beverly McCloud). Chapter 1 *Islamic Law – An Overview of its Origin and Elements*. AltaMira Press. p. 4.

[835]

[836] Ullmann, M. (2002), Wörterbuch der griechisch-arabischen Übersetzungen des neunten Jahrhunderts, Wiesbaden, p. 437. Rom. 7: 22: 'συνήδομαι γὰρ τῷ νόμῳ τοῦ θεοῦ' is translated as 'أني أفرح بشريعة الله'

[837] Calder & Hooker 2007, p. 322.

[838] Jokisch 2015.

[839] Ziadeh 2009.

[840] Rabb 2009b.

[841] Lapidus 2014, p. 125.

[842] Hallaq 2009, pp. 31–35.

[843] Lapidus 2014, p. 130.

[844] Schneider 2014.

[845] Hallaq 2009, p. 15.

[846] Kamali 1999, pp. 121–22.

[847] Hallaq 2009, pp. 16–18.

[848] Hallaq 2009, pp. 16-18.

[849] Hallaq 2009, pp. 21–22.

[850] Kamali 1999, p. 146.

[851] Hallaq 2009, pp. 23–24.

[852] Rabb 2009c.

[853] Hallaq 2009, p. 20.

[854] Duderija 2014, pp. 2–6.

[855] Brown 2009.

[856] Gleave 2012.

[857] Opwis 2007, p. 65.

[858] Opwis 2007, pp. 66–68.

[859] Opwis 2007, pp. 68–69.

[860] //en.wikipedia.org/w/index.php?title=Template:Fiqh&action=edit

[861] Hallaq 2009, pp. 28-30.

[862] Ziadeh 2009c.

[863] Hallaq 2009, pp. 10-11.

[864] Hussin 2014.

[865] //en.wikipedia.org/w/index.php?title=Template:Islamism_sidebar&action=edit

[866] Marshall Hodgson, *The Venture of Islam Conscience and History in a World Civilization Vol 3*. University of Chicago, 1958, pp. 105–08.

[867] Marshall Hodgson, *The Venture of Islam Conscience and History in a World Civilization Vol 3*. University of Chicago, 1958, pp. 176–77.

[868] Sarah Ansari, *The Cambridge Illustrated History of the Islamic World edited by Francis Robinson*. Cambridge University Press, 1996, p. 90.

[869] Marshall Hodgson, *The Venture of Islam Conscience and History in a World Civilization Vol 3*. University of Chicago, 1958, pp. 366–67.

[870] Ansari, Sarah. *The Cambridge Illustrated History of the Islamic World edited by Francis Robinson*. Cambridge University Press, 1996, pp. 103–11.

[871] Hodgson, Marshall. *The Venture of Islam Conscience and History in a World Civilization Vol 3*. University of Chicago, 1958, pp. 384–86.

[872] Amanat & Griffel (2007), *Shari'a: Islamic Law in the Contemporary Context*, Stanford University Press,

[873] Khadduri & Liebesny 1955, p. Wikipedia:Citing sources.

[874]

[875] Otto 2010, p. 28.

[876] Otto 2010, pp. 29–33.

[877] Taher, Abul (September 14, 2008). Revealed: UK's first official sharia courts. *The Sunday Times*

[878] Inside Britain's Sharia courts http://www.telegraph.co.uk/news/uknews/law-and-order/9975937/Inside-Britains-Sharia-courts.html Jane Corbin, *The Telegraph* (April 7, 2013)

[879] *muṭawi'in*; variant English spellings: mutawwain, muttawa, mutawallees, mutawa'ah, mutawi', mutawwa' most literally means "volunteers" in the Arabic language, *Dictionary of Modern Written Arabic* by Hans Wehr, edited by J. M. Cowan, 4th edition (1994,), p. 670.

[880] Fealy & White (2008), *Regional Sharia Regulations in Indonesia: Anomaly or Symptom?*, Chapter: Expressing Islam: Religious life and politics in Indonesia,

[881] SK Moore (2012), Military Chaplains as Agents of Peace, Rowman & Littlefield, , p. 169, Quote: "The Department of the Promotion of Virtue and Prevention of Vice enforced their version of Sharia Law. A woman could not appear in public without being accompanied by a male relative. The burkha remains a symbol of oppression in Afghan society... women resisting these arcane restrictions were beaten publicly by the Taliban clothes police whose mandate it was to patrol city streets in search of malcontents, enforcing their version of Sharia law."

[882] * Taliban from department of Amro bil mahroof (Promotion of Virtue and Prevention of Vice, Taliban religious police) http://rawa.org/beating.htm RAWA, Afghanistan (2001), Quote: "It shows two Taliban from department of Amro bil mahroof (Promotion of Virtue and Prevention of Vice, Taliban religious police) beating a woman in public because she has dared to remove her burqa

in public"; Taliban mistreat women http://www.rawa.org/women4.htm, Associated Press, Quote: "a woman described how her 8-year-old sister had been caught outside without a burqa and beaten by religious police."

[883] Sami Zubaida (2005), Law and Power in the Islamic World, , pp. 58–60

[884] Lorenzo Vidino (2013), Hisba in Europe? http://www.css.ethz.ch/publications/pdfs/Hisba_in_ Europe.pdf, European Foundation for Democracy, Switzerland

[885] Michael Cook: *Commanding right and forbidding wrong in Islamic thought*. Cambridge University Press. Cambridge 2000.

[886] , ,

[887] Nancy Gallagher (2005), Apostasy, Encyclopedia of Women and Islamic Cultures: Family, Law and Politics, Editors: Suad Joseph and Afsāna Naǧmābād, , pp. 7–9

[888] Helmi Noman (2013), "In the name of God – Faith based internet censorship in majority Muslim countries", in *Routledge Handbook of Media Law* (Editors: Monroe E. Price, et al.), Routledge, , Chapter 14

[889] SK Moore (2012), Military Chaplains as Agents of Peace, Rowman & Littlefield, , p. 169

[890] Islamic Law – Legal Literature And Institutions, Jurisprudence: The "Sources" of the Law, The Modern Period http://science.jrank.org/pages/7816/Law-Islamic.html.

[891] *Saudi Arabia Basic Industries Corp. v. Mobil Yanbu Petrochemical Co.*, Supreme Court of Delaware, January 14, 2005 p. 52 http://caselaw.findlaw.com/data2/delawarestatecases/493-2003.pdf. "The Saudi law system differs in critically important respects from the system of legal thought employed by the common law countries, including the United States. Perhaps most significant is that Islamic law does not embrace the common law system of binding precedent and *stare decisis*. In Saudi Arabia, judicial decisions are not in themselves a source of law, and with minor exceptions, court decisions in Saudi Arabia are not published or even open to public inspection."

[892] Tetley (1999), Mixed Jurisdictions: Common Law v. Civil Law (Codified and Uncodified), La. Law Review, 60, 677

[893] Fortna, Benjamin C. (March 2011). "Education and Autobiography at the End of the Ottoman Empire". *Die Welt des Islams*. New Series, Vol. 41, Issue 1. p. 131. "the literacy rate in the Ottoman Empire in 1900 was between five and ten percent".

[894] Antoinette Vlieger (2012), Domestic Workers in Saudi Arabia and the Emirates, , Chapter 4

[895] Tahir Wasti (2009), The Application of Islamic Criminal Law in Pakistan, Brill Academic, , pp. 126–27

[896] Etannibi E. O. Alemika (2005), "Human Rights and Shariah Penal Code in Northern Nigeria", *UN Human Rights Monitor*, pp. 110–27

[897] Mohamed S. El-Awa (1993), Punishment In Islamic Law, American Trust Publications, , pp. 1–68

[898] Philip Reichel and Jay Albanese (2013), Handbook of Transnational Crime and Justice, SAGE publications, , pp. 36–37

[899] Otto 2008, p. 663.

[900] Otto 2008, p. 31.

[901] Ajijola, Alhaji A.D. (1989). *Introduction to Islamic Law*. Karachi: International Islamic Publishers. p. 133.

[902] http://www.perseus.tufts.edu/hopper/text?doc=Perseus%3Atext%3A2002.02.0006%3Asura% 3D2%3Averse%3D282

[903]

[904] Timur Kuran (2012), The Long Divergence: How Islamic Law Held Back the Middle East, Princeton University Press, , pp. 246–49 and Chapter 12

[905] "Explaining the Economic Trajectories of Civilizations – Musings on the Systemic Approach" http://www.usc.edu/schools/college/crcc/private/ierc/conference_registration/papers/Kuran. pdf. pp. 7, 10.

[906] Lippman, Matthew Ross; McConville, Seán; Yerushalmi, Mordechai (1988). *Islamic Criminal Law and Procedure – An Introduction*. New York City: Praeger Publishers. p. 71.

[907] Frank, Michael J. (April 2006). "Trying Times – The Prosecution of Terrorists in the Central Criminal Court of Iraq". *Florida Journal of International Law*.

[908] M Kar (2005), Encyclopedia of Women and Islamic Cultures: Family, Law and Politics (Ed: Suad Joseph, Afsāna Naǧmābādī), Brill, , pp. 406–07

[909]

[910] State Department of the U.S. Government (2012), SAUDI ARABIA 2012 INTERNATIONAL RELIGIOUS FREEDOM REPORT https://www.state.gov/documents/organization/208622. pdf, p. 4

[911] Human Rights Watch (2004), Migrant Communities in Saudi Arabia https://www.hrw.org/reports/2004/saudi0704/4.htm#_ftn54

[912] Saudi Arabia https://www.state.gov/j/drl/rls/irf/2011/nea/192905.htm BUREAU OF DEMOC-RACY, HUMAN RIGHTS, AND LABOR, US State Department, 2011 Report on International Religious Freedom Report (2011)

[913] Stence 2013, p. 48.

[914] Jonathan A.C. Brown, Misquoting Muhammad, p. 131.

[915] Killing for religion is justified, say third of Muslim students http://www.telegraph.co.uk/news/religion/2461830/Killing-for-religion-is-justified-say-third-of-Muslim-students.html The Telegraph (July 26, 2008)

[916] Michael Broyde's Faculty Profile http://law.emory.edu/faculty-and-scholarship/faculty-profiles/broyde-profile.html

[917] Horrie & Chippindale 1991, p. 4.

[918] Horrie & Chippindale 1991, p. 100.

[919] Bernard Lewis (with Buntzie Ellis Churchill) 'Islam: The Religion and the People' (2008). Pearson Prentice Hall. p. 151

[920] Bernard Lewis (with Buntzie Ellis Churchill) 'Islam: The Religion and the People' (2008). Pearson Prentice Hall p. 153

[921] Controversial preacher with 'star status' http://news.bbc.co.uk/2/hi/uk_news/3874893.stm BBC article, by agdi Abdelhadi on 7 July 2004

[922]

[923] Ira Lapidus, *The Cambridge Illustrated History of the Islamic World edited by Francis Robinson*. Cambridge University Press, 1996, pp. 297–98 see Bibliography for Conclusion.

[924] http://www.cbc.ca/news/canada/montreal/quebec-gives-thumbs-down-to-shariah-law-1. 535601

[925] Otto 2008, p. 30.

[926] Khan, L. Ali. *A Theory of Universal Democracy: Beyond the End of History*, The Hague, Kluwer Law International, 2003, .

[927] Mogahed, D. (2006), Islam and democracy http://arsiv.setav.org/ups/dosya/48531.pdf, Washington: The Gallup Center for Muslim Studies

[928] Hearing of the European Court of Human Rights http://www.echr.coe.int/NR/rdonlyres/29AC6DBD-C3F8-411C-9B97-B42BE466EE7A/0/2004__Wildhaber_Cancado_Trindade_BIL__opening_legal_year.pdf , January 22, 2004 (PDF)

[929] Christian Moe (2012), Refah Revisited: Strasbourg's Construction of Islam, in Islam, Europe and emerging legal issues (editors: W. Cole Durham Jr. et al.), , pp. 235–71

[930] David P. Forsythe (2009), Encyclopedia of Human Rights: Vol. 1, Oxford University Press, pp. 239–45

[931] Anver M. Emon, Mark Ellis, Benjamin Glahn (2012), Islamic Law and International Human Rights Law, Oxford University Press,

[932] Paul Kurtz, Austin Dacey, and Tom Flynn. "Defaming Human Rights". *Free Inquiry*. February/March 2009, Vol. 29, No. 2.

[933] Glenn, H. Patrick (2014), pp. 199–205

[934] Siraj Khan, Blasphemy against the Prophet, in Muhammad in History, Thought, and Culture (Editors: Coeli Fitzpatrick and Adam Hani Walker), , pp. 59–67

[935] R Ibrahim (2013), Crucified Again, , pp. 100–01

[936] Ibn Taymiyyah (a Salafi, related to Hanbali school), *al-Sārim al-Maslūl 'ala Shātim al-Rasūl* (or, A ready sword against those who insult the Messenger), Published in 1297 AD in Arabic, Reprinted in 1975 and 2003 by Dar-ibn Hazm (Beirut), the book is on blasphemy/insulting Muhammad and the punishment per sharia

[937] Jerusha Lamptey (2014), Never Wholly Other: A Muslima Theology of Religious Pluralism, Oxford University Press, Chapter 1 with footnotes 28, 29 p. 258

[938] Carl Ernst (2005), "Blasphemy: Islamic Concept", Encyclopedia of Religion (Editor: Lindsay Jones), Vol 2, Macmillan Reference,

[939] Harun Omer, "The Invented Islam – 'Punishment for Blasphemy'" http://thesharia.com/the-invented-islam-punishment-for-blasphemy/, *TheSharia.com*, 2015

[940] An Anti-Blasphemy Measure Laid to Rest http://www.nationalreview.com/articles/263450/anti-blasphemy-measure-laid-rest-nina-shea Nina Shea, National Review (MARCH 31, 2011)

[941] Brian Winston (2014), The Rushdie Fatwa and After: A Lesson to the Circumspect, Palgrave Macmillan, , p. 74, Quote: "(In the case of blasphemy and Salman Rushdie) the death sentence it pronounced was grounded in a jurisprudential gloss on the Surah al-Ahzab (33:57)"

[942] Bad-mouthing: Pakistan's blasphemy laws legitimise intolerance https://www.economist.com/news/asia/21635070-pakistans-blasphemy-laws-legitimise-intolerance-bad-mouthing The Economist (November 29, 2014)

[943] Blasphemy: Dangerous words https://www.economist.com/blogs/prospero/2015/01/johnson-blasphemy The Economist (January 7, 2015)

[944] Which countries still outlaw apostasy and blasphemy? http://www.pewresearch.org/fact-tank/2014/05/28/which-countries-still-outlaw-apostasy-and-blasphemy/ Pew Research Center, United States (May 2014)

[945] ABDULLAHI AHMED AN-NA'IM, ISLAM AND THE SECULAR STATE: NEGOTIATING THE FUTURE OF SHARI'A 14 (2008)

[946] Freedom of Religion, Apostasy and Islam by Abdullah Saeed and Hassan Saeed (Mar 30, 2004),

[947] Shafi'i: Rawda al-talibin, 10.7, Hanafi: Ibn 'Abidin: Radd al-muhtar 3.287, Maliki: al-Dardir: al-Sharh al-saghir, 4.435, and Hanbali: al-Bahuti: Kashshaf al-qina', 6.170 (see The Struggle to Constitute and Sustain Productive Orders: Vincent Ostrom's Quest to Understand Human Affairs), Mark Sproule-Jones et al (2008), Lexington Books,)

[948] RAHIM, ABDUR. The Principles of Muhammadan Jurisprudence According to the Hanafi, Maliki, Shafi'i, and Hanbali Schools (1911), Westport CT, Hyperion Press, see 1981 Reprint

[949] Khadduri 1955, p. Wikipedia:Citing sources.

[950] al-Zuhayli, Wahbah *Al-Fiqh, al-Islami wa Adillatuhu*, 8 vols., 3rd edition, Dar al-Fikr, Damascus (1989)

[951] Saeed, Abdullah, and Hassan Saeed, eds. Freedom of religion, apostasy and Islam. Ashgate Publishing, 2004.

[952] Salhi and Grami (2011), Gender and Violence in the Middle East and North Africa, Florence (Italy), European University Institute http://www.eui.eu/DepartmentsAndCentres/RobertSchumanCentre/Research/InternationalTransnationalRelations/MediterraneanProgramme/MRM/MRM2011/ws04.aspx

[953] Horrie & Chippindale 1991, p. 49.

[954] http://www.perseus.tufts.edu/hopper/text?doc=Perseus%3Atext%3A2002.02.0006%3Asura%3D4%3Averse%3D12

[955] http://www.perseus.tufts.edu/hopper/text?doc=Perseus%3Atext%3A2002.02.0006%3Asura%3D4%3Averse%3D11

[956] • Bernard Lewis (2002), What Went Wrong?, , pp. 82–83; • Brunschvig. 'Abd; Encyclopedia of Islam, Brill, 2nd Edition, Vol 1, pp. 13–40.

[957] (,)

[958] Slavery in Islam http://www.bbc.co.uk/religion/religions/islam/history/slavery_1.shtml BBC Religions Archives

[959] Ali, K. (2010). Marriage and slavery in early Islam. Harvard University Press.

[960] Sikainga, Ahmad A. (1996). Slaves Into Workers: Emancipation and Labor in Colonial Sudan. University of Texas Press.

[961] Tucker, Judith E.; Nashat, Guity (1999). Women in the Middle East and North Africa. Indiana University Press.

[962] "Why the Middle East Is Economically Underdeveloped – Historical Mechanisms of Institutional Stagnation" http://pubs.aeaweb.org/doi/pdfplus/10.1257/0895330042162421.

[963] https://web.archive.org/web/20140116094053/http://www.law.emory.edu/aannaim/pdfiles/dwnld15.pdf

[964] http://www.oxfordislamicstudies.com/article/opr/t236/e0514

[965] http://referenceworks.brillonline.com/entries/encyclopaedia-of-islam-2/sharia-COM_1040

[966] http://www.oxfordislamicstudies.com/article/opr/t236/e0473

[967] https://dx.doi.org/10.1163/1573-3912_islam_SIM_8809

[968] //doi.org/10.1163%2F1573-3912_islam_SIM_8809

[969] http://www.oxfordreference.com/view/10.1093/acref:oiso/9780199739356.001.0001/acref-9780199739356-e-0416

[970] http://www.oxfordhandbooks.com/view/10.1093/oxfordhb/9780199679010.001.0001/oxfordhb-9780199679010-e-12

[971] //www.worldcat.org/oclc/647084498

[972] //www.worldcat.org/oclc/578890367

[973] http://www.oxfordislamicstudies.com/article/opr/t236/e0473#e0473-s5

[974] https://openaccess.leidenuniv.nl/bitstream/handle/1887/20694/Sharia%20and%20national%20Law%20in%20Muslim%20countries.pdf

[975] http://www.oxfordislamicstudies.com/article/opr/t236/e0473#e0473-s6

[976] http://www.oxfordreference.com/view/10.1093/acref/9780195305135.001.0001/acref-9780195305135-e-1150

[977] http://www.oxfordreference.com/view/10.1093/acref/9780195305135.001.0001/acref-9780195305135-e-0354

[978] http://www.oxfordreference.com/view/10.1093/acref:oiso/9780199739356.001.0001/acref-9780199739356-e-0171

[979] http://bridgingcultures.neh.gov/muslimjourneys/items/show/226

[980] http://www.oxfordreference.com/view/10.1093/acref/9780195305135.001.0001/acref-9780195305135-e-0831

[981] http://www.oxfordislamicstudies.com/article/opr/t236/e0170

[982] http://www.sfb-governance.de/publikationen/working_papers/wp54/SFB-Governance-Working-Paper-54.pdf

[983] https://www.worldcat.org/search?fq=x0:jrnl&q=n2:1863-6896

[984] https://www.worldcat.org/oclc/742018517

[985] https://www.worldcat.org/oclc/35673415

[986] http://nbn-resolving.de/urn:nbn:de:0159-2011112127

[987] http://www.oxfordislamicstudies.com/print/opr/t125/e1107

[988] https://web.archive.org/web/20140903142056/https://www.unaa.org.au/brunei-implements-sharia-law.html

[989] http://yulr.org/sharia-law-in-the-international-legal-sphere/

[990] http://bostonreview.net/john-bowen-private-arrangements-sharia-England

[991] http://www.quraanicstudies.com/no-error-in-qur-an-division-of-inheritance-according-to-quran/

[992] http://www.wdl.org/en/item/6895

[993] //en.wikipedia.org/w/index.php?title=Template:Fiqh&action=edit

[994] //en.wikipedia.org/w/index.php?title=Template:Islam&action=edit

[995] Fiqh http://www.britannica.com/EBchecked/topic/207723/fiqh Encyclopædia Britannica

[996] Glasse, Cyril, *The New Encyclopedia of Islam*, Altamira, 2001, p.141

[997] Calder 2009.

[998] Schneider 2014.

[999] Levy (1957). Page 150.

[1000] El-Gamal, *Islamic Finance*, 2006: p.30-1

[1001] Weiss, Bernard G. (2002) *Studies in Islamic Legal Theory*, edited by Bernard G. Weiss, (Leiden: E. J. Brill, 2002. pp.3, 161.)

[1002] Weiss, Bernard G. (2002), *Studies in Islamic Legal Theory*, edited by Bernard G. Weiss, (Leiden: E. J. Brill, 2002. p.162.

[1003] Nyazee, Imran Ahsan Khan (2000). *Islamic Jurisprudence (UsulAI-Fiqh)*. Islamabad: Islamic Research Institute Press.

[1004] *Al-Muwatta* of Imam Malik Ibn Anas, translated by Aisha Bewley (Book #5, Hadith #5.9.23) (Book #16, Hadith #16.1.1)(Book #17, Hadith #17.24.43)(Book #20, Hadith #20.10.40)(Book #20, Hadith #20.11.44)(Book #20, Hadith #20.32.108)(Book #20, Hadith #20.39.127)(Book

#20, Hadith #20.40.132)(Book #20, Hadith #20.49.167) (Book #20, Hadith #20.57.190)(Book #26, Hadith #26.1.2)(Book #29, Hadith #29.5.17)(Book #36, Hadith #36.4.5) Al-Muwatta' http://bewley.virtualave.net/muwcont.html

[1005] //en.wikipedia.org/w/index.php?title=Template:Islam_scholars_diagram&action=edit

[1006] Nahj ul Balagha Letter 54

[1007] Najeebabadi, Akbar Shah (2001). The History of Islam V.2. Riyadh: Darussalam. pp. 110.

[1008] Nahj al-Balagha Sermon 71, Letter 27, Letter 34, Letter 35

[1009] Muawiya Restorer of the Muslim Faith By Aisha Bewley Page 68

[1010] El-Gamal, *Islamic Finance*, 2006: p.32

[1011] http://iugc.yolasite.com/resources/Reference%20Book%2004%20-%20Islamic%20finance, %20law%20economics%20and%20practice,%20M.%20El%20Gamal.pdf

[1012] //www.jstor.org/stable/3312162

[1013] //doi.org/10.2307%2F3312162

[1014] http://nbn-resolving.de/urn:nbn:de:0159-2011112127

[1015] //en.wikipedia.org/w/index.php?title=Template:Islam&action=edit

[1016] http://www.perseus.tufts.edu/hopper/text?doc=Perseus%3Atext%3A2002.02.0006%3Asura% 3D7%3Averse%3D172

[1017] http://www.perseus.tufts.edu/hopper/text?doc=Perseus%3Atext%3A2002.02.0006%3Asura% 3D17%3Averse%3D22

[1018] http://www.perseus.tufts.edu/hopper/text?doc=Perseus%3Atext%3A2002.02.0006%3Asura% 3D17%3Averse%3D23

[1019] http://www.perseus.tufts.edu/hopper/text?doc=Perseus%3Atext%3A2002.02.0006%3Asura% 3D17%3Averse%3D24

[1020] http://www.perseus.tufts.edu/hopper/text?doc=Perseus%3Atext%3A2002.02.0006%3Asura% 3D17%3Averse%3D26

[1021] http://www.perseus.tufts.edu/hopper/text?doc=Perseus%3Atext%3A2002.02.0006%3Asura% 3D17%3Averse%3D27

[1022] http://www.perseus.tufts.edu/hopper/text?doc=Perseus%3Atext%3A2002.02.0006%3Asura% 3D17%3Averse%3D28

[1023] http://www.perseus.tufts.edu/hopper/text?doc=Perseus%3Atext%3A2002.02.0006%3Asura% 3D17%3Averse%3D29

[1024] http://www.perseus.tufts.edu/hopper/text?doc=Perseus%3Atext%3A2002.02.0006%3Asura% 3D17%3Averse%3D31

[1025] http://www.perseus.tufts.edu/hopper/text?doc=Perseus%3Atext%3A2002.02.0006%3Asura% 3D17%3Averse%3D32

[1026] http://www.perseus.tufts.edu/hopper/text?doc=Perseus%3Atext%3A2002.02.0006%3Asura% 3D17%3Averse%3D33

[1027] http://www.perseus.tufts.edu/hopper/text?doc=Perseus%3Atext%3A2002.02.0006%3Asura% 3D17%3Averse%3D34

[1028] http://www.perseus.tufts.edu/hopper/text?doc=Perseus%3Atext%3A2002.02.0006%3Asura% 3D17%3Averse%3D35

[1029] http://www.perseus.tufts.edu/hopper/text?doc=Perseus%3Atext%3A2002.02.0006%3Asura% 3D17%3Averse%3D36

[1030] http://www.perseus.tufts.edu/hopper/text?doc=Perseus%3Atext%3A2002.02.0006%3Asura% 3D17%3Averse%3D37

[1031] Alexander (1998), p.452

[1032] Watt (1974), p.234

[1033] Robinson (2004) p.21

[1034] Haddad, Esposito (1998), p. 98

[1035] Esposito (2005) p. 79

[1036] Firestone (1999) p. 118

[1037] Maududi (1967), Introduction of Ad-Dahr, "Period of revelation", pg. 159

[1038] Jones, Lindsay. p.6224

[1039] Esposito (2004), p. 339

[1040] Khadduri (1978)

[1041] Schimmel (1992) p.65

[1042] Maan, McIntosh (1999)

[1043] Haddad, Esposito (1998) p.163

[1044] McAuliffe (2005) vol. 5, pp. 66-76. "Social Sciences and the Qur'an"

[1045] *Sahih Bukhari* 3:513

[1046] http://www.perseus.tufts.edu/hopper/text?doc=Perseus%3Atext%3A2002.02.0006%3Asura%3D6%3Averse%3D38

[1047] (cf. References http://www.1001inventions.com/index.cfm?fuseaction=main.viewSection&intSectionID=441 , 1001 Inventions)

[1048] http://www.perseus.tufts.edu/hopper/text?doc=Perseus%3Atext%3A2002.02.0006%3Asura%3D42%3Averse%3D38

[1049] http://www.perseus.tufts.edu/hopper/text?doc=Perseus%3Atext%3A2002.02.0006%3Asura%3D3%3Averse%3D159

[1050] http://www.al-islam.org/nahjul/letters/letter53.htm

[1051] Sahih Bukhari, Volume 4, Book 56, Number 681

[1052] http://www.perseus.tufts.edu/hopper/text?doc=Perseus%3Atext%3A2002.02.0006%3Asura%3D33%3Averse%3D67

[1053] Islamic Science, the Scholar and Ethics http://www.muslimheritage.com/topics/default.cfm?ArticleID=570, Foundation for Science Technology and Civilisation.

[1054] Qur'an, Sura 4:5

[1055] Fath al-Bari and sharh sahih bukhari by Imam Al Nawawi

[1056] https://web.archive.org/web/20080227095928/http://images.agustianwar.multiply.com/attachment/0/RxbYbQoKCr4AAD%40kzFY1/IslamicCalendar-A-Case-Study.pdf

[1057] http://images.agustianwar.multiply.com/attachment/0/RxbYbQoKCr4AAD@kzFY1/IslamicCalendar-A-Case-Study.pdf

[1058] //www.worldcat.org/oclc/390600

[1059] //www.jstor.org/stable/840274

[1060] //doi.org/10.2307%2F840274

[1061] //www.worldcat.org/issn/1573-3912

[1062] //doi.org/10.1017%2Fs0020743800054805

[1063] http://www.sph.umich.edu/symposium/2010/pdf/donnelly1.pdf

[1064] //doi.org/10.1353%2Fhrq.2007.0016

[1065] https://www.nytimes.com/2008/03/16/magazine/16Shariah-t.html?ei=5070&em=&en=5c1b8de536ce606f&ex=1205812800&pagewanted=all

[1066] //doi.org/10.3197%2F096734002129342747

[1067] http://www.2muslims.com/directory/Detailed/225505.shtml

[1068] http://www.etymonline.com/index.php?search=islam&searchmode=none

[1069] https://books.google.com/?id=nprKYM8sleYC&pg=PA144&dq=ankiha+fasida#v=onepage&q

[1070] //www.ncbi.nlm.nih.gov/pubmed/17369721

[1071] //doi.org/10.1080%2F15027570310000027

[1072] http://www.studyquran.org/LaneLexicon/Volume4/00000137.pdf

[1073] https://www.foreignaffairs.com/articles/middle-east/2005-05-01/freedom-and-justice-modern-middle-east

[1074] http://www.nybooks.com/articles/4557

[1075] http://www.fordham.edu/halsall/med/lewis1.html

[1076] //doi.org/10.1007%2FBF02427614

[1077] http://www.weltethos.org/1-pdf/10-stiftung/declaration/declaration_english.pdf

[1078] https://archive.org/details/historyofmoorish01scotuoft

[1079] //www.worldcat.org/oclc/580060576

[1080] //doi.org/10.1017%2FS0041977X00057761

[1081] //www.worldcat.org/issn/0167-7799

[1082] //www.ncbi.nlm.nih.gov/pubmed/12127284

[1083] //doi.org/10.1016%2FS0167-7799%2802%2901985-6

[1084] http://www.washington-report.org/backissues/0197/9701036.htm

[1085] http://www.saudiaramcoworld.com/issue/200806/a.tradition.of.conservation.htm

[1086] //www.worldcat.org/oclc/3456619

[1087] //www.ncbi.nlm.nih.gov/pubmed/11609215

[1088] //doi.org/10.1177%2F0957154X9600702503

[1089] http://www.learndeen.org/cms/english-blog/tazkiya-an-nafs/pillars-of-islam-ethics-1

[1090] https://www.scribd.com/doc/4958488/Islamic-Human-Resource-Management

[1091] //en.wikipedia.org/w/index.php?title=Template:Muhammad&action=edit

[1092] Watt (1974), p.234

[1093] Robinson (2004) p.21

[1094] Esposito (1998), p. 98

[1095] "Akhlāk", *Encyclopaedia of Islam Online*

[1096] Bernard Lewis, *Arabs in History*, p.45-46

[1097] See: • Firestone (1999) p. 118; • "Muhammad", *Encyclopaedia of Islam Online*

[1098] Watt. Muhammad at Medina and R. B. Serjeant "The Constitution of Medina." *Islamic Quarterly* 8 (1964) p.4.

[1099] R. B. Serjeant, *The Sunnah Jami'ah, pacts with the Yathrib Jews, and the Tahrim of Yathrib: Analysis and translation of the documents comprised in the so-called "Constitution of Medina."* Bulletin of the School of Oriental and African Studies, University of London, Vol. 41, No. 1. 1978), page 4.

[1100] Watt. *Muhammad at Medina*. pp. 227-228 Watt argues that the initial agreement was shortly after the hijra and the document was amended at a later date specifically after the battle of Badr. Serjeant argues that the constitution is in fact 8 different treaties which can be dated according to events as they transpired in Medina with the first treaty being written shortly after Muhammad's arrival. R. B. Serjeant. "The Sunnah Jâmi'ah, Pacts with the Yathrib Jews, and the Tahrîm of Yathrib: Analysis and Translation of the Documents Comprised in the so called 'Constitution of Medina'." in *The Life of Muhammad: The Formation of the Classical Islamic World*: Volume iv. Ed. Uri Rubin. Brookfield: Ashgate, 1998, p. 151 and see same article in BSOAS 41 (1978): 18 ff. See also Caetani. *Annali dell'Islam, Volume I*. Milano: Hoepli, 1905, p. 393. Julius Wellhausen. *Skizzen und Vorabeiten*, IV, Berlin: Reimer, 1889, p 82f who argue that the document is a single treaty agreed upon shortly after the hijra. Wellhausen argues that it belongs to the first year of Muhammad's residence in Medina, before the battle of Badr in 2/624. Wellhausen bases this judgement on three considerations; first Muhammad is very diffident about his own position, he accepts the pagan tribes within the *Ummah*, and maintains the Jewish clans as clients of the Ansars see Wellhausen, Excursus, p. 158. Even Moshe Gil a skeptic of Islamic history argues that it was written within 5 months of Muhammad's arrival in Medina. Moshe Gil. "The Constitution of Medina: A Reconsideration." *Israel Oriental Studies* 4 (1974): p. 45.

[1101]

[1102] Donna Lee Bowen, Encyclopaedia of the Qur'an, Infanticide

[1103] http://www.perseus.tufts.edu/hopper/text?doc=Perseus%3Atext%3A2002.02.0006%3Asura%3D81%3Averse%3D1

[1104] Watt (1961), p. 229

[1105] http://www.perseus.tufts.edu/hopper/text?doc=Perseus%3Atext%3A2002.02.0006%3Asura%3D2%3Averse%3D178

[1106] http://www.perseus.tufts.edu/hopper/text?doc=Perseus%3Atext%3A2002.02.0006%3Asura%3D16%3Averse%3D75

[1107] http://www.perseus.tufts.edu/hopper/text?doc=Perseus%3Atext%3A2002.02.0006%3Asura%3D30%3Averse%3D28

[1108] Bernard Lewis, Race and Slavery in the Middle East, Oxford Univ Press 1994, chapter 1 http://www.fordham.edu/halsall/med/lewis1.html

[1109] Bernard Lewis, (1992), pp. 78-79

[1110] http://www.perseus.tufts.edu/hopper/text?doc=Perseus%3Atext%3A2002.02.0006%3Asura%3D2%3Averse%3D177

[1111] http://www.perseus.tufts.edu/hopper/text?doc=Perseus%3Atext%3A2002.02.0006%3Asura%3D9%3Averse%3D60

[1112]

[1113] Turner, Brian S. *Islam* (). Routledge: 2003, p77-78 https://books.google.com/books?id= zOAo9VvT4FEC&pg=PA77&dq=%22pre-islamic+arabia%22+women&sig=IiMFAyu6P3-rNii4QQmN_q3mXQQ#PPA78,M1.

[1114] Unni Wikan, review of *Modernizing Women: Gender and Social Change in the Middle East*, American Ethnologist, Vol. 22, No. 4 (Nov., 1995), pp. 1078-1079

[1115] Valentine M. Moghadam. *Modernizing Women: Gender and Social Change in the Middle East.* (Lynne Rienner Publishers, USA, 1993) p. 5

[1116] Majid Khadduri, *Marriage in Islamic Law: The Modernist Viewpoints*, American Journal of Comparative Law, Vol. 26, No. 2, pp. 213-218

[1117] Encyclopedia of Religion, second edition, Lindsay Jones, p.6224,

[1118] Gerhard Endress, *Islam: An Introduction to Islam*, Columbia University Press, 1988, p.31

[1119] http://www.perseus.tufts.edu/hopper/text?doc=Perseus%3Atext%3A2002.02.0006%3Asura%3D4%3Averse%3D3

[1120] Annemarie Schimmel, *Islam-: An Introduction*, p.65, SUNY Press, 1992

[1121] Interview: William Montgomery Watt http://www.alastairmcintosh.com/articles/2000_watt. htm , by Bashir Maan & Alastair McIntosh (1999). A paper using the material on this interview was published in The Coracle, the Iona Community, summer 2000, issue 3:51, pp. 8-11.

[1122] Bloom and Blair (2002) p.46-47

[1123] Michael J. Perry, *The Idea of Human Rights: Four Inquiries*, p.78, Oxford University Press US

[1124] Yvonne Yazbeck Haddad, John L. Esposito, *Islam, Gender, and Social Change*, Oxford University Press US, 2004, p.163

[1125] //en.wikipedia.org/w/index.php?title=Template:Islam&action=edit

[1126] Encyclopaedia of Islam, *saghir* http://dx.doi.org/10.1163/1573-3912_islam_COM_0969

[1127] http://www.perseus.tufts.edu/hopper/text?doc=Perseus%3Atext%3A2002.02.0006%3Asura%3D33%3Averse%3D4-5

[1128] http://www.perseus.tufts.edu/hopper/text?doc=Perseus%3Atext%3A2002.02.0006%3Asura%3D33%3Averse%3D37-40

[1129] "Social Sciences and the Qur'an," in Encyclopaedia of the Qur'an, vol. 5, ed. Jane Dammen McAuliffe. Leiden: Brill, pp. 66-76.

[1130] "Community and Society in the Qur'an," in Encyclopaedia of the Qur'an, vol. 1, ed. Jane Dammen McAuliffe. Leiden: Brill, pp. 385.

[1131] *Islamic ethics*, Encyclopedia of Ethics

[1132] Encyclopaedia of Islam Online, *Akhlaq* http://dx.doi.org/10.1163/1573-3912_islam_COM_0035

[1133]

[1134] Nadvi (2000), pg. 403-4

[1135] Nadvi (2000), pg. 405-6

[1136] Nadvi (2000), pg. 407-8

[1137] *Cambridge History of Islam, Vol. 1A* (1977), p.57

[1138] Hourani (2003), p.22

[1139] Sonn, pg.24-6

[1140] Esposito, Islam: The Straight Path, extended edition, p.35

[1141] Esposito, Islam: The Straight Path, extended edition, p.36

[1142] Bloom and Blair (2002) p.46

[1143] *The Cambridge History of Islam* (1970), p. 34

[1144] Nasr (2004), *The Heart of Islam: Enduring Values for Humanity*, p. 104, .

[1145] Minou Reeves (2000), *Muhammad in Europe*, New York University Press, p. 42.

[1146] https://www.worldcat.org/search?fq=x0:jrnl&q=n2:1573-3912

[1147] //en.wikipedia.org/w/index.php?title=Template:Politics_of_ancient_Rome&action=edit

[1148] In Germany, Art. 311 BGB

[1149] Jenő Szmodis: *The Reality of the Law—From the Etruscan Religion to the Postmodern Theories of Law*; Ed. Kairosz, Budapest, 2005.; http://www.jogiforum.hu/publikaciok/231.

[1150] "A Short History of Roman Law", Olga Tellegen-Couperus pp. 19–20.

[1151] Cf. Berger, Adolf. Encyclopedic Dictionary of Roman Law. The American Philosophical Society. 1953. p 529.

[1152] Jolowicz, H. F. Historical Introduction to the Study of Roman Law. Cambridge University Press. 1967.

[1153] "A Short History of Roman Law" By Olga Tellegen-Couperus, Tellegen-Couper

[1154] http://www.britannica.com/EBchecked/topic/178179/Ecloga

[1155] " Civil law (Romano-Germanic) http://www.britannica.com/EBchecked/topic/119271/civil-law". Encyclopædia Britannica.

[1156] https://books.google.com/books?id=or0LAAAAIAAJ&printsec=frontcover

[1157] https://books.google.com/books?id=l5U8xwaGxb0C&printsec=frontcover

[1158] http://www.jusromanum.com.br/

[1159] http://www.iuscivile.com/

[1160] http://droitromain.upmf-grenoble.fr/

[1161] http://penelope.uchicago.edu/Thayer/E/Roman/Texts/secondary/SMIGRA/Law/home.html

[1162] http://www.romanlegaltradition.org/

[1163] //en.wikipedia.org/w/index.php?title=Template:Byzantine_culture&action=edit

[1164] A. Cameron, *The Byzantines*, p. 153; G. Mousourakis, *Context of Roman Law*, p. 397.

[1165] M.T. Fögen, "Legislation in Byzantium", pp. 53–54; R. Morris, "Dispute Settlement", 126; G. Mousourakis, *Context of Roman Law*, pp. 399–400.

[1166] M.T. Fögen, "Legislation in Byzantium", pp. 56, 59.

[1167] A. Cameron, *The Byzantines*, p. 153; M.T. Fögen, "Legislation in Byzantium", pp. 53–54.

[1168] R. Morris, "Dispute Settlement", 126; G. Mousourakis, *Context of Roman Law*, pp. 401–402.

[1169] J. Fine, *The Early Medieval Balkans: A Critical Survey from the Sixth to the Late Twelfth Century*, pp. 90-91

[1170] Pitra, Jean Baptiste Francois (1864). Juris ecc. Græcorum historia et monumenta. I. Rome.

[1171] Lambert Mears, Analysis of M. Ortolan's Institutes of Justinian, pp. 64-66

[1172] Laiou and Simon (eds), Law and Society in Byzantium: Ninth-twelfth Centuries, p. 71

[1173] G. Mousourakis, Roman Law and the Origins of the Civil Law Tradition, p. 226

[1174] Laiou and Simon (eds), Law and Society in Byzantium: Ninth-twelfth Centuries, p. 77

[1175] Laiou and Simon (eds), Law and Society in Byzantium: Ninth-twelfth Centuries, p. 85

[1176] B. Jokisch, *Islamic Imperial Law: Harun-Al-Rashid's Codification Project*, pp. 484-485.

[1177] https://web.archive.org/web/20120831060912/http://web.upmf-grenoble.fr/Haiti/Cours/Ak/

[1178] Rouche, "Private life conquers state and society", in Paul Veyne, ed. *A History of Private Life: I. From Pagan Rome to Byzantium* (Harvard University Press) 1987:421ff. This paragraph follows Rouche.

[1179] Rouche 1987:421.

[1180] As Agobard of Lyons put it, pleading for a unified legal system in the Frankish Empire, "Of five men sitting or walking together none will have the same law as his fellow."

[1181] "In lighter transgressions too the penalty is measured by the fault, and the delinquents upon conviction are condemned to pay a certain number of horses or cattle. Part of this mulct accrues to the King or the community, part to him whose wrongs are vindicated, or to his next kindred." (trans. Gordon)

[1182] *ignavos et imbelles at corpore infames*. Gordon translates *corpore infames* as "unnatural prostitutes", another interpretation is "corporal infamation" (rape). Thus Tacitus may refer to rape, even though scholars have speculated that "corporal infamation" could refer to the catholic view of male homosexuality. See David F. Greenberg, *The construction of homosexuality*, p. 242 f. Consequently some scholars have speculated that the later Germanic concept of Old Norse *argr*, Langobardic *arga*, may combine the meanings "effeminate, cowardly, homosexual", see Jaan Puhvel, 'Who were the Hittite *hurkilas pesnes*?' in: A. Etter (eds.), *O-o-pe-ro-si* (FS Risch), Walter de Gruyter, 1986, p.154.

[1183] "In the assembly it is allowed to present accusations, and to prosecute capital offences. Punishments vary according to the quality of the crime. Traitors and deserters they hang upon trees. Cowards, and sluggards, and unnatural prostitutes they smother in mud and bogs under an heap of hurdles. Such diversity in their executions has this view, that in punishing of glaring iniquities, it behoves likewise to display them to sight; but effeminacy and pollution must be buried and concealed." (trans. Gordon)

[1184] "In the same assemblies are also chosen their chiefs or rulers, such as administer justice in their villages and boroughs. To each of these are assigned an hundred persons chosen from amongst the populace, to accompany and assist him, men who help him at once with their authority and their counsel." (trans. Gordon)

[1185] e.g. Laws of Alfred, paragraph 6, "As if he fight and wound any one, let him be liable in his wer. If he fell a man to death, let him then be an outlaw, and let every one of those seize him with hearm who desire right. And if he so do that any one kill him, for that he resisted God's law or the kings, if that be proved true, let him lie uncompensated. "

[1186] King, Law and Society in the Visigothic Kingdom (Cambridge University Press) 1972:36-37

[1187] King, Law and Society in the Visigothic Kingdom (Cambridge University Press) 1972:38-39

[1188] King, Law and Society in the Visigothic Kingdom (Cambridge University Press) 1972:39

[1189] King, Law and Society in the Visigothic Kingdom (Cambridge University Press) 1972:44-45.

[1190] King, Law and Society in the Visigothic Kingdom (Cambridge University Press) 1972:45-46

[1191] King, Law and Society in the Visigothic Kingdom (Cambridge University Press) 1972:45

[1192] King, Law and Society in the Visigothic Kingdom (Cambridge University Press) 1972:7

[1193] Carr, Vandals to Visigoths (University of Michigan Press) 2002:36

[1194] Carr, Vandals to Visigoths (University of Michigan Press) 2002:29

[1195] Heather, The Visigoths from the Migration Period to the Seventh Century (Boydell Press) 1999:261

[1196] Heather, The Visigoths from the Migration Period to the Seventh Century (Boydell Press) 1999:268

[1197] Heather, The Visigoths from the Migration Period to the Seventh Century (Boydell Press) 1999:189

[1198] (Katherine Fischer Drew, The laws of the Salian Franks (Pactus legis Salicae), Philadelphia: University of Pennsylvania Press (1991).

[1199] Pollock and Maitland, *History of English Law before the Time of Edward I* vol. 1 p. 77.

[1200] https://web.archive.org/web/20120831060912/http://web.upmf-grenoble.fr/Haiti/Cours/Ak/

[1201] https://web.archive.org/web/20110105083519/http://www.ucl.ac.uk/history2/volterra/eml.htm

[1202] http://www.leges.uni-koeln.de/en/lex/

[1203] https://archive.org/details/diegesetzederang01liebuoft

[1204] https://archive.org/details/diegesetzederang02liebuoft

[1205] https://archive.org/details/p1diegesetzedera02greauoft

[1206] https://archive.org/details/p2diegesetzedera02greauoft

[1207] https://archive.org/details/diegesetzederang03liebuoft

[1208] http://www.fordham.edu/halsall/source/560-975dooms.html

[1209] http://www.fordham.edu/halsall/sbook-law.html

[1210] https://web.archive.org/web/20071217131452/http://www8.georgetown.edu/departments/medieval/labyrinth/library/oe/texts/prose/laws.html#cap42#cap42

[1211] https://www.academia.edu/5013232/Anglo-Saxon_Law_Its_Development_and_Impact_on_the_English_Legal_System

[1212] Sealy and Hooley (2008) 14

[1213] James Brown Scott, *Law, the State, and the International Community* https://books.google.com.ph/books?id=o2ItplkkogIC&pg=PA259&, p. 259, Columbia University Press, (1939)

[1214] (1702) 2 Ld Raym 757

[1215] *Lickbarrow v Mason* (1787) 2 Term Rep 63, 73, Buller J

[1216] CM Schmitthoff, 'International Business Law, A New Law Merchant' in *Current Law and Social Problems* (1961) 137

[1217] cf. Volkmar Gessner/Ali Cem Budak, eds., Emerging Legal Certainty: Empirical Studies on the Globalization of Law. Ashgate: Dartmouth 1998

[1218] Some examples of such arbitral awards: Collected by Trans-Lex.org http://www.trans-lex.org/000011

[1219] http://www.trans-lex.org/104970

[1220] http://www.jus.uio.no/lm/

[1221] http://www.stevesachs.com/papers/paper_thesis.html

[1222] http://www.econtalk.org/archives/2006/12/boudreaux_on_la.html

[1223] http://www.trans-Lex.org

[1224] http://www.cisg.law.pace.edu/cisg/biblio/baron.html

[1225] http://www.cisg.law.pace.edu/cisg/biblio/audit.html

[1226] http://translex.uni-koeln.de/500100

[1227] https://www.trans-lex.org/the-lex-mercatoria-and-the-translex-principles_ID8

[1228] Lyall 2000

[1229] John Carey, "An Edition of the Pseudo-historical Prologue to the Senchas Már", Ériu 45 (1994) 1–32.

[1230] D.A. Binchy, "Irish History and Irish Law", *Studia Hibernica* 15 (1975)

[1231] D.A. Binchy, "Celtic Suretyship, a Fossilized Indo-European Institution?" *Indo-European and Indo-Europeans*, ed. Hoenigswald and Senn Cardona

[1232] Kelly 1988, pp.231–232

[1233] Kelly 1988, pp.232 forward.

[1234] Kelly 1988, pp.242 forward.

[1235] C. E. Meek and K. Simms, *The Fragility of Her Sex: Medieval Irish Women in their European Context*, page 25, 'Marriage Laws in the Early Middle Ages.' Historian Bart Jaski compares the earlier Pagan marriage law to early Roman 'manus' marriage, implying an improvement in the status of Irish women over time.

[1236] Kelly 1988, p. 79

[1237] Kelly 1988, p. 207 quoting and translating Binchy 1978, p.45 l.3 and p.1421 l.30

[1238] Jaski 2013, Appendices 1 and 2.

[1239] Kelly 1988, p.18

[1240] Kelly 1988, p. 19

[1241] Binchy 1979, 104–105

[1242] Kelly 1988, p. 21–22

[1243] Kelly 1988, pp. 23–25, 52

[1244] Kelly 1988, pp. 25–26

[1245] Binchy 1979 pp. 21, 37, 105

[1246] MacNeill 1923 gives a translation of these two texts

[1247] Kelly 1988, various pages.

[1248] MacNeill 1923

[1249] Breatnach 1987, p. 85–86

[1250] Binchy 1979 line 604–606. Partially translated by Kelly 1988, p. 41

[1251] Kelly 1988, pp. 95, 112–113

[1252] Kelly 1988, p. 11

[1253] Kelly 1988, p. 82

[1254] Kelly 1988, p. 81–82

[1255] Kelly 1988, pp. 5–6

[1256] Binchy 1979, pp. 76–77, 101–102

[1257] Kelly 1988, pp. 18–19

[1258] Binchy 1979, p. xix

[1259] Breatnach 1987, p. 81 ff

[1260] Breatnach 1987, p. 113

[1261] Kelly 1988, p. 52 forward

[1262] Kelly 1988, p. 28

[1263] Liam Breatnach, *Uraiccecht na Ríar*

[1264] Kelly 1988, pp. 36–37

[1265] Binchy 1979, pp. 70–72

[1266] Liam Breatnach, *Uraiccecht na Ríar*, pp96–97.

[1267] Kelly 1988, pp. 131 ff

[1268] Kelly 1988, pp. 129–130.

[1269] D.A. Binchy, *Bretha Déin Chécht*, pp 22–23.

[1270] Kelly 1988, pp. 132.

[1271] Binchy 1979, pp. 91–92.

[1272] Kelly 1988, pp. 131.

[1273] Kelly 1988, pp. 130.

[1274] Binchy 1979 page 93.

[1275] Kelly 1988, pp. 133.

[1276] Kelly 1988, p. 125–127

[1277] Baumgarten 1985. It should be mentioned that the translation of the last name is uncertain in the *Dictionary of the Irish Language*.Wikipedia:Accuracy dispute#Disputed statement

[1278] Kelly 1988, 12

[1279] Kelly 1988, 13–14

[1280] Kelly 1988, 13.

[1281] Kelly 1988, pp.80–81

[1282] Lyall 2000

[1283] Kelly 1988, pp. 102–105

[1284] Jaski 2013, 115

[1285] Kelly 1997, 412–413

[1286] Kelly 1997, 416–417

[1287] Kelly 1997 p. 413–414

[1288] Jaski 2013, 119–120

[1289] Baumgarten 1985, pp 312–313

[1290] Kelly 1997, pp. 399–400

[1291] D.A. Binchy, "Linguistic and Historical Value of the Irish Law Tracts", in *Celtic Law Papers*, (Aberystwyth, 1971) p, 93.

[1292] Robin Chapman Stacey, *Dark Speech: the Performance of Law in Early Ireland*

[1293] Kelly 1988, p. 196–197, which does give some examples of what may be meant by each

[1294] Kelly 1988, p. 236

[1295] Neil McLeod, *The Concept of Law in Ancient Irish Jurisprudence*, in "Irish Jurist" 17 (1982)

[1296] Binchy 1979, p. 70

[1297] Kelly 1988, p. 171–172.

[1298] Kelly 1988, p 169

[1299] Kelly 1988, p. 168–171.

[1300] Kelly 1988, p. 172–173.

[1301] Kelly 1988, pp 234–235, 281 and elsewhere.

[1302] Binchy 1978, p ix

[1303] Donnchadh Ó Corráin *et al.*, "The Laws of the Irish" in *Peritia* 3 (1984)

[1304] Kelly 1988, p. 232 forward discusses the outlines of this argument

[1305] Breatnach 2005, Appendices 2 – 7.

[1306] Charles-Edwards and Kelly 1983, pp 27 and forward

[1307] Kelly 1988, pp 242–243

[1308] Breatnach 2005, p. 344

[1309] Neil McLeod "A True Companion to the Corpus Iuris Hibernici", *Peritia* 19 (2005)

[1310] Senchus Mor, Rolls ed. pages 5–16.

[1311] John Carey, *The two laws in Dubthach's judgment*, in *Cambridge Medieval Celtic Studies*, (1990) number 19 and Kim McCone, "Dubthach maccu Lugair and a Matter of Life and Death in the Pseudohistorical Prologue to the Senchas Már" in *Peritia* 5 (1986)

[1312] Breatnach 2005, 286–287; Kelly 1988, pp. 178 and forward.

[1313] Kelly 1988, p. 29 and forward.

[1314] Kelly 1988, p. 70, 93. Bart Jaski, Translation of *Cáin Lánamna* at http://www2.let.uu.nl/Solis/keltisch/CL-translation.htm

[1315] Breatnach 2005 and Kelly 1988 respectively. The text can be found in D.A. Binchy, ed., *Corpus Iuris Hibernici*, vol. 1: 90.33 – 93.30; vol. 2: 520.1 – 536.27; vol. 3: 903.37 – 905.5; 411–1479; vol. 5: 1812.33 – 1821.27; vol. 6: 2045.37 – 2046.28, 2045.37 – 2046.28

[1316] Kelly 1988, p. 42

[1317] Breatnach 2005, p. 291

[1318] Charles-Edwards and Kelly 1983, pp. 27–28

[1319] Charles-Edwards and Kelly 1983, pp. 32 forward

[1320] Breatnach 2005, p. 303

[1321] Kelly 1988, p. 246

[1322] Kelly 1988, 268–269

[1323] Breatnach 2005, pp. 316–317

[1324] Kelly 1988, p. 278

[1325] Robin Chapman Stacey, *The Road to Judgment: From Custom to Court in Medieval Ireland and Wales*

[1326] Binchy 1979. The only reliable translation of the text is Mac Neill 1923 pp. 265–316

[1327] Breatnach 2005, pp 242–243. This poem is translated at ancienttexts.org http://www. ancienttexts.org/library/celtic/ctexts/crith.html, where it is misleadingly termed the Crith Gablach, and the translation attributed to D.Binchy.

[1328] Neil McLeod, *Early Irish Contract Law*

[1329] Breatnach 1987

[1330] Kelly 1988, p. 251

[1331] Breatnach 2005, pp 100 forward

[1332] Kelly 1988, p. 279.

[1333] Kelly 1988, p. 280

[1334] Charles-Edwards and Kelly 1983, p. 68

[1335] Richard Sharpe, ed., *Life of St. Columba*, p. 189 forward

[1336] //doi.org/10.1484%2FJ.Peri.3.112

[1337] http://ssrn.com/abstract=1937496

[1338] //www.jstor.org/stable/25504234

[1339] http://catalog.hathitrust.org/Record/001624978

[1340] http://www.libraryireland.com/Brehon-Laws/Contents.php

[1341] http://www.ucc.ie/celt/published/T102030/index.html

[1342] http://www.celt.dias.ie/publications/cat/cat_f.html

[1343] http://www.webcitation.org/query?url=http://www.geocities.com/solarguard/celtic/irlaw. html&date=2009-10-26+02:56:13

[1344] http://www.newadvent.org/cathen/02753a.htm

[1345] https://www.youtube.com/channel/UCwm3xPB2m81uwquNLmLAISA

[1346] Visigothic Spain 409 - 711 https//books.google.lv

[1347] Law and Society in the Visigothic Kingdom https//books.google.lv

[1348] King, 148–149.

[1349] Law and Society in the Visigothic Kingdom https//books.google.lv

[1350] Fletcher 1984, ch. 1, note 56

[1351] Klapisch-Zuber, Christine; A History of Women: Book II Silences of the Middle Ages, The Belknap Press of Harvard University Press, Cambridge, Massachusetts, London, England. 1992, 2000 (5th printing). Chapter 6, "Women in the Fifth to the Tenth Century" by Suzanne Fonay Wemple, pg 74. According to Wemple, Visigothic women of the Iberian Peninsula and the Aquitaine could inherit land and title and manage it independently of their husbands, and dispose of it as they saw fit if they had no heirs, and represent themselves in court, appear as witnesses (by the age of 14), and arrange their own marriages by the age of twenty

[1352] http://mdz1.bib-bvb.de/~db/bsb00000852/images/index.html?id=00000852&nativeno=3

[1353] http://libro.uca.edu/vcode/visigoths.htm

[1354] http://libro.uca.edu/sjc/sjc1.htm

[1355] http://www.leges.uni-koeln.de/en/lex/leges-visigothorum/

[1356] https://visigothicsymposia.org/symposia

[1357] "blood-court" is a literal of ; The *Dictionary of the English and German Languages* by Christoph Friedrich Grieb (1863) translates the term simply as "a criminal court".

[1358] Halsgericht http://lexika.digitale-sammlungen.de/adelung/lemma/bsb00009132_3_0_452 in Adelung, *Grammatisch-kritisches Wörterbuch der Hochdeutschen Mundart* (1774–1786).

[1359] //en.wikipedia.org/w/index.php?title=Template:Monarchism&action=edit

[1360] The document's Latin name is spelled either *Magna Carta* or *Magna Charta*, (the pronunciation is the same) and, in English, with or without the definite article "the". Latin does not have a definite article equivalent to "the". The Oxford English Dictionary recommends usage without the definite article.<ref>

[1361] Du Cange s.v. 1 carta http://ducange.enc.sorbonne.fr/charta#CHARTA1

[1362] "The usual—and the better—form is *Magna Carta*. [...] *Magna Carta* does not take a definite article". *Magna Charta* is the recommended spelling in German-language literature. (Duden online http://www.duden.de/rechtschreibung/Magna_Charta)

1363 Within this article, dates before 14 September 1752 are in the Julian calendar. Later dates are in the Gregorian calendar. In the Gregorian calendar, however, the date would have been 22 June 1215.

1364 The United States (US) Constitution was written in 1787, went into effect in 1788, after ratification by nine of the 13 states, and the US Federal government started operation in 1789.

1365 Danziger & Gillingham 2004, p. 268.

1366 Carpenter 1990, p. 8.

1367 Turner 2009, p. 149.

1368 Carpenter 1990, p. 7.

1369 Danziger & Gillingham 2004, p. 168.

1370 Turner 2009, p. 139.

1371 Warren 1990, p. 181.

1372 Carpenter 1990, pp. 6–7.

1373 Carpenter 1990, p. 9.

1374 Turner 2009, p. 174.

1375 Danziger & Gillingham 2004, pp. 256–58.

1376 McGlynn 2013, pp. 131–32.

1377 McGlynn 2013, p. 130.

1378 Danziger & Gillingham 2004, p. 104.

1379 Danziger & Gillingham 2004, p. 165.

1380 Turner 2009, p. 178.

1381 McGlynn 2013, p. 132.

1382 Holt 1992a, p. 115.

1383 Poole 1993, pp. 471–72.

1384 Vincent 2012, pp. 59–60.

1385 Turner 2009, p. 179.

1386 Warren 1990, p. 233.

1387 Danziger & Gillingham 2004, pp. 258–59.

1388 Turner 2009, pp. 174, 179–80.

1389 Turner 2009, p. 180.

1390 Holt 1992a, p. 112.

1391 McGlynn 2013, p. 137.

1392 Tatton-Brown 2015, p. 36.

1393 Holt 2015, p. 219.

1394 Warren 1990, p. 236.

1395 Turner 2009, pp. 180, 182.

1396 Turner 2009, p. 182.

1397 Turner 2009, pp. 184–85.

1398 The Runnymede Charter of Liberties did not apply to Chester, which at the time was a separate feudal domain. Earl Ranulf granted his own Magna Carta of Chester.<ref name="FOOTNOTEHewit19299">Hewit 1929, p. 9.

1399 Holt 1992b, pp. 379–80.

1400 Vincent 2012, pp. 61–63.

1401 Carpenter 2004, pp. 293–94.

1402 Turner 2009, p. 189.

1403 Danziger & Gillingham 2004, pp. 261–62.

1404 Goodman 1995, pp. 260–61.

1405 Warren 1990, pp. 239–40.

1406 Poole 1993, p. 479.

1407 Turner 2009, pp. 189–91.

1408 Danziger & Gillingham 2004, p. 262.

1409 Warren 1990, pp. 239, 242.

1410 Carpenter 1990, p. 12.

1411 Carpenter 1996, p. 13.

1412 Turner 2009, p. 190–91.

1413 Turner 2009, p. 190.

[1414]Warren 1990, pp. 244–45.

[1415]Rothwell 1975, pp. 324–26.

[1416]Warren 1990, pp. 245–46.

[1417]Holt 1992a, p. 1.

[1418]Crouch 1996, p. 114.

[1419]Carpenter 2004, pp. 264–67.

[1420]Louis' claim to the English throne, described as "debatable" by the historian David Carpenter, derived from his wife, Blanche of Castile, who was the granddaughter of King Henry II of England. Louis argued that since John had been legitimately deposed, the barons could then legally appoint him king over the claims of John's son Henry.<ref name="FOOTNOTECarpenter199012">Carpenter 1990, p. 12.

[1421]Holt 1992b, pp. 478–80:the list in the collection of law tracts is at British Library, Harley MS 746, fol. 64; the Reading Abbey list is at Lambeth Palace Library, MS 371, fol. 56v.

[1422]Powicke 1929.

[1423]Carpenter 1990, pp. 14–15.

[1424]Carpenter 1990, p. 13.

[1425]McGlynn 2013, p. 189.

[1426]Ridgeway 2004.

[1427]Weiler 2012, p. 1.

[1428]Carpenter 1990, p. 1.

[1429]Mayr-Harting 2011, pp. 259–60.

[1430]Mayr-Harting 2011, p. 260.

[1431]Carpenter 2004, p. 301.

[1432]Carpenter 1990, pp. 19–21.

[1433]Aurell 2003, p. 30.

[1434]Carpenter 1990, pp. 21–22, 24–25.

[1435]Powicke 1963, p. 5.

[1436]Carpenter 1990, p. 25.

[1437]Carpenter 1990, p. 27.

[1438]Carpenter 1990, pp. 28–29.

[1439]Carpenter 1990, pp. 127–28.

[1440]Carpenter 1990, pp. 36–40.

[1441]McGlynn 2013, p. 216.

[1442]Hallam & Everard 2001, p. 173.

[1443]Carpenter 1990, p. 41–42.

[1444]Carpenter 1990, p. 42.

[1445]Carpenter 1990, p. 44.

[1446]Carpenter 1990, pp. 41, 44–45.

[1447]Carpenter 1990, p. 60.

[1448]Carpenter 1990, pp. 60–61.

[1449]Carpenter 1990, pp. 61–62.

[1450]White 1915, pp. 472–75.

[1451]White 1917, pp. 545–55.

[1452]Carpenter 1990, p. 402.

[1453]Carpenter 1990, pp. 333–35, 382–83.

[1454]Carpenter 1990, pp. 295–96.

[1455]Jobson 2012, p. 6.

[1456]Carpenter 1990, pp. 296–97.

[1457]Carpenter 1990, p. 297.

[1458]Hallam & Everard 2001, p. 176.

[1459]Weiler 2012, p. 20.

[1460]Carpenter 1990, pp. 371–73.

[1461]Carpenter 1990, pp. 374–75.

[1462]Carpenter 1990, pp. 376, 378.

[1463]Hallam & Everard 2001, pp. 176–77.

[1464]Carpenter 1990, p. 379.

[1465] Carpenter 2004, p. 307.

[1466] Carpenter 1990, p. 383.

[1467] Clanchy 1997, p. 147.

[1468] Davis 2013, p. 71.

[1469] Davis 2013, p. 174.

[1470] Carpenter 1996, pp. 76, 99.

[1471] Carpenter 1990, p. 3.

[1472] Carpenter 1996, pp. 26, 29, 37, 43.

[1473] Carpenter 1996, p. 105.

[1474] Davis 2013, pp. 195–97.

[1475] Jobson 2012, p. 104.

[1476] Davis 2013, p. 224.

[1477] Jobson 2012, p. 163.

[1478] Holt 1992b, pp. 510–11.

[1479] Prestwich 1997, p. 427.

[1480] Edwards 1943.

[1481] Prestwich 1997, p. 434.

[1482] Cobbett et al. 1810, p. 980.

[1483] Holt 2008, p. 62.

[1484] Fritze & Robison 2002, pp. 34–35.

[1485] Prestwich 1997, pp. 547–48.

[1486] Menache 2003, pp. 253–55.

[1487] Scott 2014.

[1488] Holt 2008, pp. 44–45.

[1489] Holt 2008, pp. 45–46.

[1490] Holt 2008, p. 56.

[1491] Holt 2008, pp. 56–57.

[1492] Turner 2003b, p. 123.

[1493] Thompson 1948, pp. 9–10.

[1494] Turner 2003a.

[1495] Turner 2003b, p. 132.

[1496] Turner 2003b, p. 133.

[1497] Hindley 1990, pp. 185–187.

[1498] Hindley 1990, pp. 185–86.

[1499] Turner 2003b, p. 138.

[1500] Hindley 1990, p. 188.

[1501] Thompson 1948, p. 146.

[1502] Warren 1990, p. 324.

[1503] Hindley 1990, p. 187.

[1504] *Magna Carta, cum aliis antiquis statutis ...* London: Thomas Berthelet, 1531 Beale S9; STC 9271 http://digitalspecialcollections.law.umn.edu/magnacarta/1531_s9.php. Magna carta cvm aliis antiqvis statvtis, qvorvm catalogvm, in fine operis reperies. London: Thomas Berthelet, 1540. Beale S12; STC 9274 http://digitalspecialcollections.law.umn.edu/magnacarta/1540_s12_s22.php. revised edition by Thomas Marshe (1556), *Magna Carta et cetera antiqua statuta nunc nouiter per diuersa exemplaria examinata et summa diligentia castigata et correcta cui adiecta est noua tabula valde necessaria.* .

[1505] Thompson 1948, pp. 147–49.

[1506] Turner 2003b, p. 140.

[1507] Danziger & Gillingham 2004, p. 280.

[1508] Among the historians to have discussed the "myth" of Magna Carta and the ancient English constitution are Claire Breay, Geoffrey Hindley, James Holt, John Pocock, Danny Danziger, and John Gillingham.<ref name="FOOTNOTEDanzigerGillingham2004280">Danziger & Gillingham 2004, p. 280.

[1509] Hindley 1990, p. 183.

[1510] Breay 2010, p. 46.

[1511] Pocock 1987, p. 124.

[1512] Holt 1992b, p. 9.
[1513] Eele 2013, p. 20.
[1514] Thompson 1948, pp. 216–30.
[1515] Pocock 1987, p. 154.
[1516] Wright 1919, p. 72.
[1517] Hindley 1990, pp. 188–89.
[1518] Pocock 1987, p. 300.
[1519] Greenberg 2006, p. 148.
[1520] Turner 2003b, p. 148.
[1521] Holt 1992b, pp. 20–21.
[1522] Turner 2003b, p. 156.
[1523] Hindley 1990, p. 189.
[1524] Hindley 1990, pp. 189–190.
[1525] Turner 2003b, p. 157.
[1526] Danziger & Gillingham 2004, pp. 280–81.
[1527] Russell 1990, p. 41.
[1528] Hindley 1990, p. 190.
[1529] Danziger & Gillingham 2004, p. 271.
[1530] Woolwrych 2003, p. 95.
[1531] Pocock 1987, p. 127.
[1532] Kewes 2006, p. 279.
[1533] Kewes 2006, p. 226.
[1534] Danziger & Gillingham 2004, pp. 281–82.
[1535] Hill 2006, pp. 111–22.
[1536] Linebaugh 2009, p. 85.
[1537] Pocock 1987, pp. 182–228.
[1538] Turner 2003b, p. 165.
[1539] Pocock 1987, p. 228.
[1540] Turner 2003b, pp. 169–70.
[1541] Breay & Harrison 2015, pp. 110–11, 134.
[1542] Linebaugh 2009, pp. 113–14.
[1543] Turner 2003b, pp. 67–68.
[1544] Fryde 2001, p. 207.
[1545] Howard 2008, p. 28.
[1546] Hazeltine 1917, p. 194.
[1547] Hazeltine 1917, p. 195.
[1548] Turner 2003b, p. 210.
[1549] Turner 2003b, p. 211.
[1550] Hazeltine 1917, pp. 183–84.
[1551] Stimson 2004, p. 124.
[1552] Black 1999, p. 10.
[1553] Turner 2003b, pp. 199–200.
[1554] Fryde 2001, p. 1.
[1555] Simmons 1998, pp. 69–83.
[1556] Galef 1998, pp. 78–79.
[1557] Pollard 1912, pp. 31–32.
[1558] Barnes 2008, p. 23.
[1559] Danziger & Gillingham 2004, p. 283.
[1560] Wright 1990, p. 167.
[1561] Holt 1992b, p. 2–3.
[1562] Danziger & Gillingham 2004, p. 278.
[1563] Burdett 1810, p. 41.
[1564] Clark 2000.
[1565] Kennedy 1922, p. 228.
[1566] Drew 2004, pp. pxvi–pxxiii.
[1567] Breay 2010, p. 48.

[1568] Holt 1992b, p. 2.
[1569] Warren 1990, p. 240.
[1570] Holt 1992b, p. 21.
[1571] Breay 2010, p. 37.
[1572] Breay 2010, pp. 37–38.
[1573] Hindley 1990, p. 143.
[1574] Breay 2010, pp. 38–39.
[1575] Browning 1898, p. 50.
[1576] Breay 2010, pp. 34–35.
[1577] Breay 2010, p. 34.
[1578] Breay 2010, p. 35.
[1579] Breay 2010, pp. 34–36.
[1580] Breay 2010, pp. 35–36.
[1581] Breay 2010, p. 36.
[1582] Turner 2003b, p. 65.
[1583] Breay & Harrison 2015, pp. 66, 216–19.
[1584] Breay 2010, pp. 36–37.
[1585] Davis 1963, p. 36.
[1586] Vincent 2012, p. 107.
[1587] Vincent 2012, p. 104.
[1588] Vincent 2012, p. 106.
[1589] Lewis 1987, p. 494.
[1590] Vincent 2015, p. 160.
[1591] Breay 2010, p. 28.
[1592] Poole 1993, pp. 16–17.
[1593] Breay 2010, p. 29.
[1594] *Gordon v. Justice Court*, 12 Cal. 3d 323 http://online.ceb.com/calcases/C3/12C3d323.htm (1974).
[1595] Huscroft 2005, p. 97.
[1596] Poole 1993, pp. 29–30.
[1597] Poole 1993, p. 29.
[1598] Breay 2010, p. 32.
[1599] Poole 1993, pp. 353, 474.
[1600] Hillaby 2013, p. 23.
[1601] Huscroft 2005, p. 190.
[1602] Huscroft 2005, p. 189.
[1603] Turner 2009, p. 121.
[1604] Breay 2010, pp. 49–54.
[1605] Hindley 1990, p. 201.
[1606] https//books.google.com
[1607] https://books.google.com/books?vid=0XPZLx6VcMoY1KO0KO&id=hTUfAAAAMAAJ&pg=PA501
[1608] https://books.google.com/?id=hTUfAAAAMAAJ
[1609] //www.worldcat.org/oclc/9378577
[1610] https//books.google.com
[1611] http://www.austlii.edu.au/au/journals/MULR/2000/34.html
[1612] https//books.google.com
[1613] https://books.google.com/?id=av1pjnpVRNAC&pg=PA271&lpg=PA271&dq=Cromwell+Magna+Carta#v=onepage&q=Cromwell%20Magna%20Carta&f=false
[1614] //www.jstor.org/stable/554340
[1615] //doi.org/10.1093%2Fehr%2Flviii.ccxxxi.273
[1616] http://magnacarta800th.com/wp-content/uploads/2011/08/Perceptions-of-Magna-Carta-C-Eele-Dissertation.pdf
[1617] https://books.google.com/books?id=bB_0M9oviBQC&pg=PA260
[1618] https//books.google.com
[1619] https//books.google.com

[1620] http://lf-oll.s3.amazonaws.com/titles/2180/Sandoz1470_LFeBk.pdf
[1621] https//books.google.com
[1622] https//books.google.com
[1623] https://archive.org/details/historyenglanda00pollgoog
[1624] //doi.org/10.1093%2Fehr%2Fxliv.clxxiii.87
[1625] https://www.webcitation.org/6Iak4PVrC?url=http://www.oxforddnb.com/view/printable/12950
[1626] //doi.org/10.1093%2Fref%3Aodnb%2F12950
[1627] http://www.oxforddnb.com/view/printable/12950
[1628] https//books.google.com
[1629] http://www.historytoday.com/ralph-v-turner/meaning-magna-carta-1215
[1630] http://ehr.oxfordjournals.org/content/XXX/CXIX/472.citation
[1631] //doi.org/10.1093%2Fehr%2FXXX.CXIX.472
[1632] http://ehr.oxfordjournals.org/content/XXXII/CXXVIII/554.citation
[1633] //doi.org/10.1093%2Fehr%2FXXXII.CXXVIII.554
[1634] https://books.google.com/books?id=sW8ycm-sC9cC&printsec=frontcover#v=onepage&q&f=false
[1635] //doi.org/10.1093%2Fehr%2Fcev202
[1636] http://lf-oll.s3.amazonaws.com/titles/338/0032_Bk.pdf
[1637] http://oll.libertyfund.org/titles/2180
[1638] http://www.historyandpolicy.org/policy-papers/papers/magna-carta-and-contemporary-constitutional-change
[1639] https://www.royalholloway.ac.uk/aboutus/newsandevents/events/magnacarta/magnacartamooc.aspx
[1640] http://churchsociety.org/crossway/page/the_english_church_shall_be_free
[1641] http://www.bl.uk/magna-carta
[1642] http://www.nationalarchives.gov.uk/education/medieval/magna-carta/
[1643] http://www.parliament.uk/about/living-heritage/evolutionofparliament/originsofparliament/birthofparliament/overview/magnacarta/
[1644] http://www.loc.gov/exhibits/magna-carta-muse-and-mentor/
[1645] https://www.archives.gov/exhibits/featured-documents/magna-carta/
[1646] http://www.legislation.gov.uk/aep/Edw1cc1929/25/9/contents
[1647] http://www.orbilat.com/Languages/Latin/Texts/06_Medieval_period/Legal_Documents/Magna_Carta.html
[1648] http://legacy.fordham.edu/halsall/source/magnacarta.asp
[1649] http://www.magnacartaplus.org/magnacarta/definitions.htm
[1650] https://www.nytimes.com/interactive/2007/09/24/nyregion/20070924_MAGNA_GRAPHIC.html
[1651] http://nationalarchives.gov.uk/documents/education/magna-carta-timeline.pdf
[1652] https//librivox.org
[1653] http://www.bbc.co.uk/programmes/b04y6wdt/episodes/guide
[1654] https://www.youtube.com/watch?v=cFTDUtK2a6Y
[1655] https://www.youtube.com/watch?v=45Y7bN7ZwaY
[1656] https://www.youtube.com/watch?v=5B6neLohOCM/
[1657] http://web.uni-marburg.de/hosting//zfda/pic_prguen_xiii5_1v2r.jpg
[1658] Robert B. Holtman, *The Napoleonic Revolution* (Baton Rouge: Louisiana State University Press, 1981)
[1659] "The *Code Napoléon*: French Legislation on Divorce," *Exploring the European Past: Texts & Images*, Second Edition, ed. Timothy E. Gregory (Mason: Thomson, 2007), 62-64.
[1660] "ces délits factices, créés par la superstition, la féodalité, la fiscalité et le despotisme" (id., p 325).
[1661] Code de commerce http://www.legifrance.gouv.fr/rechCodeArticle.do?reprise=true&page=1 Retrieved 2011-12-30
[1662] http://www.napoleon-series.org/research/government/code/book3/c_title03.html
[1663] Commission supérieure de codification, *Vingt et unième rapport annuel 2010* http://www.legifrance.gouv.fr/Droit-francais/Codification/Rapports-annuels-de-la-CSC (Paris, 2011), 13; quoted and translated,

[1664] Commission supérieure de codification, *Vingt-deuxième rapport annuel 2011* http://www.
legifrance.gouv.fr/Droit-francais/Codification/Rapports-annuels-de-la-CSC (Paris, 2012), 21.

[1665] Commission supérieure de codification, *Vingt-quatrième rapport annuel 2013* http://www.
legifrance.gouv.fr/Droit-francais/Codification/Rapports-annuels-de-la-CSC (Paris, 2014),
6-7.

[1666] Engber, Daniel. Is Louisiana Under Napoleonic Code? http://www.slate.com/articles/news_
and_politics/explainer/2005/09/louisianas_napoleon_complex.html Slate.com, retrieved 11
September 2014

[1667] http://ledroitcriminel.free.fr/la_legislation_criminelle/anciens_textes.htm

[1668] http://www.napoleon-series.org/research/government/c_code.html

[1669] https://archive.org/stream/codenapoleonorf00statgoog#page/n4/mode/2up

[1670] http://www.cambaceres.org/vie-poli/code-civ/cod-civi.htm

[1671] http://www.legifrance.gouv.fr/affichCode.do?cidTexte=
LEGITEXT000006070721&dateTexte=20080121

[1672] http://www.francemagazine.org/articles/issue70/article94.asp?issue_id=70&article_id=94

[1673] http://www.gesetze-im-internet.de/englisch_bgb/

[1674] http://bundesrecht.juris.de/bundesrecht/bgb/index.html

[1675] http://bundesrecht.juris.de/englisch_bgb/index.html

[1676] https://web.archive.org/web/20060208020806/http://www.lumrix.de/bgb.php

[1677] http://bundesrecht.juris.de/bundesrecht/bgb-infov/index.html

[1678] https://web.archive.org/web/20101223112315/http://www.bmj.bund.de/Themen/Zivilrecht_
108.html

[1679] http://www.jusline.de/BGB.html

[1680] There was originally a comma after the name of the Act, as is usual to separate a qualifier, but
this has been dropped, yielding the more abrupt current form.

[1681] *The History of English Law before the Time of Edward I, 2 vols.*, on line, with notes, by
Professor S. F. C. Milsom, originally published in Cambridge University Press's 1968
reissue.http://oll.libertyfund.org/titles/pollock-the-history-of-english-law-before-the-time-
of-edward-i-2-vols

[1682] OED, 1933 edition: citations supporting that description, before Blackstone, are from the 14th
and 16th centuries.

[1683] OED, 1933 edition: citations supporting that description are two from 19th century sources.

[1684] Liam Boyle, *An Australian August Corpus: Why There is Only One Common Law in Australia*,
Bond Law Review, Volume 27, 2015.http://epublications.bond.edu.au/cgi/viewcontent.cgi?
article=1473&context=blr

[1685] http://oll.libertyfund.org/titles/pollock-the-history-of-english-law-before-the-time-of-
edward-i-2-vols

Article Sources and Contributors

The sources listed for each article provide more detailed licensing information including the copyright status, the copyright owner, and the license conditions.

Maat *Source:* https://en.wikipedia.org/w/index.php?oldid=806186834 *License:* Creative Commons Attribution-Share Alike 3.0 *Contributors:* A. Parrot, AbigailAbernathy, Alexlange, Alxndr, Andrew Lancaster, Andrewman327, AnnekeBart, Aritmaat, Aroni the pony, Batternut, BedrockPerson, Bender235, Bgwhite, Big blue cookie, Bobbywashere, Callinus, Cecerevigh, Chandra,Eye of Ma'at, Closerange897, ClueBot NG, DVdm, DavidLeighEllis, Dawnseeker2000, Discospinster, DocWatson42, Donner60, Doug Weller, Draymusa, Drewmutt, Egsan Bacon, Excirial, Favonian, FeanorStar7, Fearless5forever6, Flyer22 Reborn, Fraggle81, Gareth Griffith-Jones, Ginsuloft, GorillaWarfare, Guest2625, HMSLavender, Haploidavey, Harmakheru, Home Lander, I dream of horses, Iamleel, Ian.thomson, InverseHypercube, Iry-Hor, Ithinkicahn, JHICBCGC, Jeraphine Gryphon, Jhirschberg13, Jim1138, K6ka, KemetMaat, Khruner, Klilidiplomus, KyZan, LlywelynII, Lor, Lugia2453, Lunazagor, Magioladitis, MarianaSF, Materialscientist, Me, Myself, and I are Here, Miket341, Mimihitam, Mindmatrix, Minimac, Mr.Z-man, Myasuda, Nathaniel360, Nephiliskos, NewEnglandYankee, Niceguyedc, Nihiltres, Nikodaimos, Nsaa, Oiophron∼enwiki, Omnipaedista, Pastmasterdan, Peacedance, Pitbullhanee, RA0808, Rebekahw7, RenamedUser01302013, Richardjdonald, Ronhjones, RusudanGulaziani, Sander123, Sesh84, Sigmundur, Slightsmile, Some jerk on the Internet, SquillTheSquid9, Stephenb, Tahir mq, Talost, TheLateDentarthurdent, Tlxxxviii, Tom Morris, Troy the intellect, Usb10, Vernel22, WadeSimMiser, Werieth, Widr, Wikipelli, XxEnder GamerxX, Yomangani, Yosri, Yourmajezty, Yt95, Zytigon, 183 anonymous edits 3

Babylonian law *Source:* https://en.wikipedia.org/w/index.php?oldid=795468360 *License:* Creative Commons Attribution-Share Alike 3.0 *Contributors:* ANE.Scholar, Accedie, Akerbeltz, AndrewHowse, Angel ivanov angelov, Aude, BD2412, Beetstra, Bob Burkhardt, Bobblehead, Bobo192, Bornintheguz, BotMultichill, Branddobbe, Burzmali, Castanea dentata, Categorystuff, Chameleon, Charles Matthews, Clicketyclack, ClueBot NG, Codex Sinaiticus, Cvaneg, D Namtar, DavidBrooks, DavidBrooks-AWB, Dbachmann, DeluxNate, Devieeeeeeee, Donner60, Dorpater, DragonessEclectic, Dreadstar, Dream of Nyx, Eaqq, Eastlaw, Ed Poor, Edward, EliasAlucard, Ellmist, Eve Teschlemacher, Ewlyahoocom, Favonian, Flying Saucer, Francs2000, Fratrep, Greenrd, Gurch, Gw2005, Hao2lian, Hapsiainen, IansAwesomePizza, J04n, Jagged 85, JamesAM, Jc37, Juansidious, Junglecat, Klbrain, Materialscientist, Mattmayo, Mauron∼enwiki, Mike65535, Mongo83, Ms2ger, MusikAnimal, Natg 19, NatusRoma, Ogress, Onel5969, Oxymoron83, PBS-AWB, PM Poon, Pyrotle, R'n'B, Randy Kryn, RapidReferenceWriter, Raylu, Rich Farmbrough, Rich257, Rknasc, Rktect, Rupert loup, ShelfSkewed, Sintaku, SiobhanHansa, SoxBot III, Squids and Chips, Sshah, StAnselm, SteinbDJ, Sweetmoose6, Tachs, Tbacksha, Thaurisil, Til Eulenspiegel, Torchiest, Vishruth, Whitejay251, WikHead, Woohookitty, Zaledin, Zvika, Zymurgy, ∼riley, Šarukinu, 112 anonymous edits 12

Ancient Greek law *Source:* https://en.wikipedia.org/w/index.php?oldid=805045032 *License:* Creative Commons Attribution-Share Alike 3.0 *Contributors:* 3 of Diamonds, A Raider Like Indiana, AdjustShift, Aldux, Angel ivanov angelov, Anne drew Andrew and Drew, Antandrus, Arjayay, AvalerionV, Azazyel, Bwpach, Caeciliusinhorto, CalJW, Can't sleep, clown will eat me, Chitrapa, ClueBot NG, DARTH SIDIOUS 2, DarthShrine, DavidBrooks-AWB, Davidiad, Dawn Bard, Dcirovic, Deadbeef, Derusa, Donner60, Dragon6329, DragonflySixtyseven, E-Soter, Erud, Favonian, FlagFlayer, Flauto Dolce, Florian Blaschke, Gilliam, Gillyweed, Grover cleveland, HMSLavender, I Feel Tired, I dream of horses, IW.HG, Igoldste, Ionesco, J.delanoy, JForget, Katolophyromai, Knjaz Aranath, KoshVorlon, KylieTastic, Library Guy, Materialscientist, Michael Devore, Mr.Z-man, Niceguyedc, Non-dropframe, Northamerica1000, Novusuna, O.Koslowski, Omnipaedista, Oshwah, Paladinwannabe2, PaulHanson, Philip Trueman, Pimpdaddybiprincess, Primaryspace, Quenhitran, Qzd, RandomAct, Rjwilmsi, Sardanaphalus, Scytha, Serols, Snake01, Snow Blizzard, Stambouliote, Staszek Lem, Sven nestle2, Tachs, Telecineguy, Tls, Twospoonfuls, Tyler22321, Wenli, White Shadows, Winterst, Zymurgy, 185 anonymous edits 32

Book of Leviticus *Source:* https://en.wikipedia.org/w/index.php?oldid=804899007 *License:* Creative Commons Attribution-Share Alike 3.0 *Contributors:* Alephb, Alexb102072, Amitorit, Awien, Awilley, Beetstra, Beland, Belchfire, Bellerophon5685, Bender235, Bgwhite, Bo Basil, BobKilcoyne, Carteki, Casswenze, Chicagoveter, Cjcollom, ClueBot NG, Damiens.rf, Dark T Zeratul, Darth Vader7, Davidonline, Dentalplanlisa, Dimadick, Dkennamer210, DocWatson42, Doug Weller, Drsmoo, EamonnPKeane, Eat me, I'm an azuki, Emmanuel678, EncycloPetey, Eugensokolov, FFD14, Flyer22 Reborn, Frip the bip!, Gilliam, Greenshed, Hadarot, Hbprof, Hebrides, Hypopopo, IZAK, ItsZippy, JTWaggoner, JasonAQuest, Jbribeiro1, JesseAlanGordon, Jheald, Jim1138, Joe Decker, Johanna, John, John "Hannibal" Smith, JohnThorne, JudeccaXIII, Kelisi, Kevinmcalvey, Koavf, Kylelehman2009, Laura Aten, Lipsquid, Lotje, MJ94, Macedonian, MagicatthemovieS, Magioladitis, Makecat, Malerooster, MamaTattletail, Mark Arsten, Matanya, Mean as custard, Meshach, Monochrome Monitor, Moshe Yehudi, MrX, Muppetchump, Musdan77, Mx. Granger, N43618, Naamatt2, Neilham, Neo-Jay, Niceguyedc, North Atlanticist Usonian, ObtuseAngle, Omnipaedista, Peter1c, PiCo, Pinnerup, Plastikspork, PrimeHunter, R'n'B, Revdyl, Robertgreer, Robin klein, Roy Brumback, Rupert loup, Serols, Snow Blizzard, Socialservice, Srich32977, StAnselm, Str1977, SugarvilleMom, The Rambling Man, TheTruthiness, Trusilver, Vanished user ewfisn2348tui2f8n2fio2utjfeoi210r39jf, Vee Ate, Vejlefjord, Vieque, WereSpielChequers, Widr, Will Pittenger, Xlxfjh, 153 anonymous edits 36

Hittite laws *Source:* https://en.wikipedia.org/w/index.php?oldid=736397491 *License:* Creative Commons Attribution-Share Alike 3.0 *Contributors:* Angel ivanov angelov, Artaxiad, Categorystuff, Chris8155, ClueBot NG, Dbachmann, Donner60, Dungodung, Epbr123, Gwil, Haymaker, Izzedine, J.delanoy, Jorditessa, Kruttlefish, Lugia2453, Magioladitis, Meaghan, Mx. Granger, Newman Luke, Niceguyedc, Od Mishehu, Pax:Vobiscum, Petroalbion, Rich Farmbrough, Rjwilmsi, Runcorn, Sphilbrick, Sumerophile, Sweetmoose6, Til Eulenspiegel, ددم, 23 anonymous edits 50

Ostracism *Source:* https://en.wikipedia.org/w/index.php?oldid=796581033 *License:* Creative Commons Attribution-Share Alike 3.0 *Contributors:* 28bytes, ABF, Aarktica, Abcqwery, Abstractrabbit, AeAnBr, Aec is away, Aitias, Amit A., Andonic, Andycjp, Anonymous from the 21st century, Apparition11, Armadillo35, Arrow storm, Asmith44, Astatine, Baileypalblue, Bazuz, Bismaela, Bogdangiusca, BreakfastJr, C.l.schwab, Caeciliusinhorto, CanadianLinuxUser, Carlossuarez46, Carnildo, Catalographer, Ccreitz, Chealer, ClueBot NG, Coastside, Collins719, Crusoe8181, Cyberbot II, Davidiad, DeadEyeArrow, Dia^, Dimboukas, Doktordoris, Dominus, DopefishJustin, Dorieo, Dorieo21, DrStrauss, Drmies, Ekantik, Ekko, Epbr123, Eric Drexler, Erik Kennedy, Excirial, Flounderer, G.dallorto, Gangsta242, Genuflectivity, Gloladin00, Grakirby, GrinBot∼enwiki, HLwiKi, Hao16, Histree, Hmains, Hmainsbot1, I dream of horses, Indubitably, IronGargoyle, J S Ayer, JMK, JWNoctis, Jacobisq, Jakec, Jamessmithpage, Jarble, Jcbutler, Jim1138, John, Joseph Solis in Australia, Joshtaco, Joshualouie711, Joz3d, K6ka, Kane5187, Katieh5584, Khan5342, King of Hearts, Kree, La goutte de pluie, Leszek Jańczuk, Lowi82, Magd1722, Magioladitis, Maqs, Marco.natalino, Marcocapelle, Materialscientist, Me, Myself, and I are Here, Michael Hardy, Misheu, Mmh, Modal Jig, Mro, Myrvin, NebY, Neddyseagoon, Nev1, Nihil novi, Nsaa, Octane, Off Break King, Oiophron, Omnipaedista, Openflower, Pedant, Penbat, Pol098, Popo le Chien, Presteign, Ptbotgourou, R'n'B, RadiX, Reedy, Richard75, RickinBaltimore, Rjwilmsi, Rmperry77, Ryker-Smith, SP612, Sai2020, Saile, Shiggity, Shindo9Hikaru, Simetrical, Sionus, SkyWalker, Sowlos, SpikeTorontoRCP, Spondoolicks, SpuriousQ, Srednuas Lenoroc, SummerWithMorons, Sv1xv, Syko, TaBOT-zerem, Taintain, Tawkerbot2, Tentinator, Tesseran, The Legend of Julie Egbert, The Parting Glass, TheCatalyst31, Tickle me, TimBentley, Tupsumato, Twthmoses, Ucanlookitup, Uruiamme, Vistor, Wareh, Wavelength, Weetoddid, Wl219, Woer$, Wolfdog, WriteinEnglish, XxZanthamonxX, Zappa12341234, 182 anonymous edits 52

Manusmriti *Source:* https://en.wikipedia.org/w/index.php?oldid=805318942 *License:* Creative Commons Attribution-Share Alike 3.0 *Contributors:* AMuraliKumar, Aadhini, Abecedare, Abhishek.arya, AddWittyNameHere, Anadimishra2, Ankitamehta2, Ankush 89, Anonymous from the 21st century, Averruncus, BD2412, Bender235, Billinghurst, BishuYadav, Bladesmulti, Bo99, Capitals00, Casliber, Chitrada, ChrisGualtieri, Cksridhar, ClueBot NG, Compfreak7, Cpt.a.haddock, DaGizza, Dbachmann, Dcirovic, Deepcruze, Deepp213, DiscantX, Doubtysmurf, El C, Faizhaider, Fconaway, Floyd Chaterji, Geunineart, Gilliam, Harsh.dev, Hsarpotdar1, Human3015, Huon, InverseHypercube, Iridescent, Iztwoz, Jessicapierce, Jim1138, Jobas, Jonathansammy, Jsp98806, Just granpa, Katyare, Kautilya3, Keithh, Lawgra, Lifelessboy, Magioladitis, Manujune, Materialscientist, Me, Myself, and I are Here, Metalello, Mogism, Mojo Hand, Ms Sarah Welch, Neelkamala, Oshwah, PCWren&HMartin, Parijaatd, Pawyilee, Peter1c, Pinethicket, PlyrStar93, Poems of borns, Polyesterthought, Powstini, Profitt23, Rahulgedam, Rao Ravindra, Rashkeqamar, Raviv4877, Riteshmmec, Rjwilmsi, SDC, Satyamjha2410, SchreiberBike, Sdebbad, Shemaroo, Smaines, SmrutiakaMemories, Solomon7968, SpacemanSpiff, Squids and Chips, Sreejiraj, Srz92, Sudhirkbhargava, Tbhotch, Titodutta, Tony Tan, Topbanana, Ugog Nizdast, Vanisaac, Vanished user zm34pq51mz, Vegetarianra025, Vensco, Vish4urwish, Wiki-uk, Wikiscout30, Wjhonson, Work2win, Worldbruce, Xoloitzcuintle, Zompist, संदेश हिवाळे, 95 anonymous edits 62

Yājñavalkya Smṛti *Source:* https://en.wikipedia.org/w/index.php?oldid=792310880 *License:* Creative Commons Attribution-Share Alike 3.0 *Contributors:* Anastomoses, AvicAWB, Dbachmann, GoingBatty, IBW3, Jcwent, Mack2, Ms Sarah Welch, Oiophron∼enwiki, Ostensibly1, Pawyilee, Ruzulo, Solomon7968, Tallahassle, Titodutta, Verbum Veritas, Woohookitty, Zerokitsune, 3 anonymous edits 79

Arthashastra *Source:* https://en.wikipedia.org/w/index.php?oldid=805576882 *License:* Creative Commons Attribution-Share Alike 3.0 *Contributors:* Aditya soni, AgniKalpa, Ajcheema, Alansohn, Alfons2, Altruism, Aman Zaidi, Amitrochates, Anoptimistix, Aoidh, Aryavartveer, AshokSrinath, Astynax, Avantiputra7, AxelBoldt, Baking Soda, Barek, Bellerophon5685, Bender235, Bgwhite, Bilasai, BreakfastJr, Capankajsmilyo, Chowbok, Citation bot 1, ClueBot NG, CommonsDelinker, Cpt.a.haddock, Debastein, DocWatson42, DuncanHill, Eastlaw, Edit suggested, Effulgence108, Esszet, Ghatus, Gnbgv∼enwiki, GoingBatty, GoldCoastPrior, I dream of horses, ISoham, ImproveWIKI**article, Jakshay006, Jasonanaggie, Joseph2302, Kautilya3, Kbir1, Kethrus, Knight1993, Krishateja007, Krishnachandranvn, Kww, Lakun.patra, LilHelpa, Lilboox, Maimai009, Materialscientist, Miniapolis, Minimac's Clone, Mogism, Mohitmusaddi, MrBill3, Ms Sarah Welch, N6EpBa7Q, Neddyseagoon, NehalDaveND, Nightbat, NittyG, Ohconfucius, Omnipaedista, Pawyilee, Pochsad, Prashanthns, Prithika roy, Psmith fan, Ptbotgourou, Qasim Arif Sethi, Quuxplusone, R'n'B, Randy Kryn, Regstuff, Rosarino, Saddhiyama, Salamurai, Serols, Shreevatsa, Shyamsunder, Skcpublic, Solomon7968, Sonal nandeesh, Sriram Vikram, SumanaKoundinya, Svabhiman, The Utahraptor, Titodutta, Uncle Milty, Utcursch, Vanisaac, Vanished user sdij4rtltkjasdk3, Vycl1994, WestCoastMusketeer, Wtmitchell, Wujastyk, Yamaguchi先生 , Yorkshirian, Zuggernaut, अनुनाद सिंह, 126 anonymous edits 84

Dharmaśāstra *Source:* https://en.wikipedia.org/w/index.php?oldid=804912556 *License:* Creative Commons Attribution-Share Alike 3.0 *Contributors:* Abecedare, Anelson4, Astynax, BOTarate, Badgerblueliner, Bgwhite, Bhawani Gautam, Bladesmulti, Bless sins, BoH, CanisRufus, Cardreader, Carlossuarez46, Chris the speller, Cminard, Dalitsreligion, Dangerous-Boy, Despentes, Drdj, Dthomsen8, Esantaksri, Gurubrahma, Haida19, Harivishwanathan, Hmains, Hypnosadist, Hz.tiang, I am One of Many, IBW3, Iztwoz, Jcwent, Jerry teps, John of Reading, Joy1963, KahnJohn27, Keithh, Kirankumars 21, Kjginther, Kkm010, Koavf, Langdell∼enwiki, Leaflord, Lotje, Lotus in the hills, Machaon, Mamgeorge, Mild Bill Hiccup, MrOllie, Ms Sarah Welch, Nat Krause, NawlinWiki, Nocowardsoulismine, Ntennis, Ntrikha, Oleaster, Paul 012, Pawyilee, R'n'B, Rama's Arrow, Remuel, Rjwilmsi, SadieBean, Skinsmoke, Sokoljan, Solomon7968, Spicemix, Srisharmaa, Tgeorgescu, Thaimoon, Thiseye, Uanfala, Ugog Nizdast, Utcursch, Vinod2988, Wiki-uk, Will Beback, Worldbruce, Xoloitzcuintle, Yajnavalkaya, Yoddha123, Zerokitsune, 43 anonymous edits 102

Classical Hindu law *Source:* https://en.wikipedia.org/w/index.php?oldid=786151293 *License:* Creative Commons Attribution-Share Alike 3.0 *Contributors:* Amrit Ghimire Ranjit, ClaretAsh, Dbachmann, Drdj, Editor2020, Joshua Issac, LilHelpa, Munci, Nks9242, PBNY, Pawyilee, Plv620, T@nn, Thinnan, 6 anonymous edits 117

Classical Hindu law in practice *Source:* https://en.wikipedia.org/w/index.php?oldid=786749333 *License:* Creative Commons Attribution-Share Alike 3.0 *Contributors:* ClaretAsh, Colonies Chris, Courcelles, Editor2020, George Burgess, GoingBatty, Grafen, Jacklee, John, Joshua Issac, Khazar2, LilHelpa, Lotus in the hills, Nick Number, Nks9242, PBNY, PCWren&HMartin, Pawyilee, Sadads, Soap, T@nn, The Man in Question, Verbum Veritas, Δ, 5 anonymous edits 120

Hindu law *Source:* https://en.wikipedia.org/w/index.php?oldid=805632876 *License:* Creative Commons Attribution-Share Alike 3.0 *Contributors:* Abecedare, AkhilKumarPal, Alansohn, Anelson4, Aymatth2, BD2412, Badgerblueliner, BetsyBetsyBetsy, Bhadani, Bless sins, Briangotts, BryantR77, CanadianLinuxUser, ClueBot NG, Dangerous-Boy, Darth Panda, Davecrosby uk, Dbachmann, Dewritech, Dpr, Drdj, Eastlaw, Editor2020, EricWesBrown, Foreverarear, G upadhyay, Gaurav.shukla360, Gilliam, Good Olfactory, Gopalan evr, Grampion76, Gurubrahma, Haida19, Harperhere, Headbomb, Helpsome, Hodag15, Imc, Indian.advocate, Indianstar, Iph, Itaqallah, JaconaFrere, Januarythe18th, Jb-hindu, Jcwent, Jeff G., Kira22, Knife-in-the-drawer, LadyofShalott, LilHelpa, Lotus in the hills, Magioladitis, Matt Fitzpatrick, Mattmuelle, MelbourneStar, Ms Sarah Welch, NawlinWiki, Nks9242, Ohconfucius, Oranjelo100, PBNY, Patricksullivan2332, Patsully2332, Pearle, Philip Trueman, Plv620, Prhartcom, Rama's Arrow, Rjsandler, Rohitde, Rsteenholdt, Sadalmelik, SadieBean, Salamurai, Santoshchandra Chitrapu, Seanlope, Shreshth91, Shyamsunder, Signalhead, SkyMachine, Smaines, Solomon7968, Space-Age Meat, SteveMcCluskey, TheRingess, Thinnan, Tide rolls, Tigercompanion25, Timothy Lubin, Tom Radulovich, Tom.Reding, Toussaint, VoABot II, Who.was.phone, Woohookitty, Worldbruce, Xoloitzcuintle, Yaris678, Zarcadia, Zerokitsune, Zumbiz, 111 anonymous edits 128

Traditional Chinese law *Source:* https://en.wikipedia.org/w/index.php?oldid=796087362 *License:* Creative Commons Attribution-Share Alike 3.0 *Contributors:* Abigailgem, Acroterion, Ahoerstemeier, Alai, Alexius08, Amys eye, Anna Roy, Balthazarduju, Bathrobe, BehdadN, Bernard Ee, Boomur, Bridgeplayer, Bunser, CAPTAIN RAJU, CWH, Chris the speller, ClueBot NG, DVdm, Davidcannon, Dcirovic, Dpr, Eastlaw, Everyking, Filthybutter, Flyer22 Reborn, FourLights, Fram, Geistcj, HRW in 1899, Hadoooookin, Handsomelyian, Incrassate, Instantnood, Jackson2002, JamesAM, Jfruh, Jiang, John24343543, JustAGal, K6ka, Kaihsu, Keahapana, Kharkiv07, Ksyrie, Levellend, Mais oui!, Mboverload, Mild Bill Hiccup, Miss Madeline, Misterx2000, Morningstar1814, MusikAnimal, Nbarth, Niohe, Nsae Comp, Oxymoron83, Philg88, Qeny, Quinton Feldberg, Rickyrab, Roadrunner, SchmuckyTheCat, Shell Kinney, SimmeD, Sweetmoose6, Visik, Wiae, Wikiain, Woohookitty, YURiN, Yeu Ninje, Yingzi99, 64 anonymous edits 140

Tang Code *Source:* https://en.wikipedia.org/w/index.php?oldid=795578788 *License:* Creative Commons Attribution-Share Alike 3.0 *Contributors:* Barbequeue, CWH, Ceyockey, ClueBot NG, Confuzion, Eastlaw, Entranced98, Felix Wan, Fixer88, FourLights, Frietjes, Frosty, Ginsuloft, Hmainsbot1, HongQiGong, Housegeek224, Jonesey95, Keahapana, Killy-the-frog∼enwiki, Lockley, Madalibi, Malik Shabazz, Mathias-S, MusikAnimal, Nbarth, Nlu, Philg88, Serols, Shanghainese.ua, Tachyon01, The Thing That Should Not Be, Yeu Ninje, Yug, Zmam, 損齋, 26 anonymous edits 150

Great Qing Legal Code *Source:* https://en.wikipedia.org/w/index.php?oldid=794779934 *License:* Creative Commons Attribution-Share Alike 3.0 *Contributors:* 7Sidz, Absconditus, Abstrakt, Archenok, Arjayay, Asdnhk, Bender235, Benjwong, Benlisquare, Billposer, Chevymontecarlo, ChrisGualtieri, Confuzion, Csmth, Davidcannon, Difference engine, Douglas the Comeback Kid, Eastlaw, Evecurid, FourLights, GagHalfrunt, Georgebaily, Gwern, Hoising, ImreK, Incrassate, JNZ, Jjfadd, Jusjih, Kaihsu, Keahapana, Kvasir, Laca, Lao Wai, Levellend, Madalibi, Mansasakura, Milesli, Niohe, PalaceGuard008, Philg88, Rjwilmsi, ShelfSkewed, Shell Kinney, Srnec, Tassedethe, TranquilHope, Welsh, Woohookitty, Île flottante, 32 anonymous edits 153

Yassa *Source:* https://en.wikipedia.org/w/index.php?oldid=788334651 *License:* Creative Commons Attribution-Share Alike 3.0 *Contributors:* Aelfthrytha, Agbdavis, Alai, AlefZet, Alvin Seville, Aqwis, Athomeinkobe, Autoalchemy, Baeda735, Benlisquare, Bestlyriccollection, Boneyard90, Bookinvestor, Breno, Caerwine, ClueBot NG, ColRad85, Crom daba, Dberndtd, Dhartung, DocWatson42, DragonflySixtyseven, Dthomsen8, Eastlaw, Enerelt, Epicgenius, Eteru, Ezeu, Fainites, Faizan, Favonian, Gavleson, Ghirlandajo, Greatpopcorn, Grutness, Gxlarson, Hakeem.gadi, Hinio, Inluminetuovidebimuslumen, IronMaidenRocks, Johnlacrosse, Jumperwd, Karl-Henner, Kordas, Lao Wai, Latebird, Makecat, Mani1, MatthewDBA, MichaelvonHorde, MikeTango, Mmoople, Muhends, NetRolller 3D, Neutrality, Nihiltres, Niteowlneils, Nyttend, Rdsmith4, Rockrogue, Ryuch, Sovmen, Tawkerbot2, Toddintr, Walt.roth, Wikidea, Woohookitty, Yastanovog, 94 anonymous edits 158

Legal history of the Catholic Church *Source:* https://en.wikipedia.org/w/index.php?oldid=787000467 *License:* Creative Commons Attribution-Share Alike 3.0 *Contributors:* Alekol, BD2412, Bgwhite, Bostonbetty, CanonLawJunkie, Carriearchdale, Elizium23, Eltheodigraeardgesece, Iridescent, JamesP, JoeHebda, Josve05a, Magioladitis, Mogism, Wikiain 167

Canon law of the Catholic Church *Source:* https://en.wikipedia.org/w/index.php?oldid=797648602 *License:* Creative Commons Attribution-Share Alike 3.0 *Contributors:* BD2412, Bender235, BoBoMisiu, CanonLawJunkie, Chicbyaccident, Clivemacd, ClueBot NG, CommonsDelinker, Dewritech, Elizium23, Hmains, Jennica, JoeHebda, Jujutsuan, Materialscientist, NDSteve10, Soupforone, StAnselm, StarryGrandma, SteveMcCluskey, VladGerp, Wtmitchell, Xanzzibar, Zfish118, Zymurgy, 20 anonymous edits 175

Sharia *Source:* https://en.wikipedia.org/w/index.php?oldid=801837405 *License:* Creative Commons Attribution-Share Alike 3.0 *Contributors:* Acroterion, Ahmed A S, Ahpook, Al-Andalus, Alarob, Azarapat8, BillyPreset, Bkonrad, Blozier2006, BoogaLouie, CambridgeBayWeather, Cherdchai Iamwongsrikul, Chicbyaccident, ClueBot NG, Dan Koehl, David A, David.moreno72, Dfoofnik, Display name 99, Don4of4, El C, El cid, el campeador, Eperoton, Faisal2380, Fatass-Negro, Fixuture, Frndlyy, Gilo1969, Hayman30, Home Lander, I dream of horses, Ian.thomson, Iridescent, JB KKH, JahlilMA, Jaycech3n, Jim1138, Johnuniq, Joshualouie711, Keniac0320, Knightablaze, Labtek00, Literaturegeek, Magioladitis, Materialscientist, Md Belal Noor, Mean as custard, Mikael Häggström, MohammedMohammed, Muhammad Abul Fazal, Narky Blert, NeilN, Noto.wiki, Octoberwoodland, Oddfox, Oshwah, Penskins, Philip Trueman, Pragueclock, Qzd, RainFall, Rebecca.stones82, Rendichoda, Rupert loup, Sadsaque, Seraphimblade, Shaded0, Srich32977, There'sNoTime, Tobby72, Turturkk, UmarMayKnow, Vicky Ankara 2017, Webmgr, Wegesrand, Wikiain, Woodlot, Wtmitchell, Xenophrenic, Zymurgy, 112 anonymous edits 190

Fiqh *Source:* https://en.wikipedia.org/w/index.php?oldid=802565913 *License:* Creative Commons Attribution-Share Alike 3.0 *Contributors:* AdRock, Agent AX, Alan Liefting, AliJaana, Andrew Reynolds, Anggoro, Auric, Averroist, Babitaarora, Bender235, Bihco, Billposer, BoogaLouie, Braincricket, CLCStudent, Carmichael, CasualObserver'48, Child Star Grown Up, Chris the speller, ChrisGualtieri, Chumwa, Citation bot 1, ClueBot NG, Cntras, Coffeepusher, Cyberbot II, DamlaAziz, DeCausa, Delta 51, Dmvjjvmd, Don4of4, Download, Edgarde, Emir of Wikipedia, Enver62, Eperoton, Epicgenius, Eyrryds, Faizan, Fraggle81, FreeatlastChitchat, Frietjes, Frosted14, Gilliam, Giraffedata, Good Olfactory, Gugganij, Herr Lennartz, Hjonjon, Htonl, HyperGaruda, Ibn kathir, Iridescent, IslamMeansPeace, Jagged 85, JahlilMA, Jim1138, John of Reading, Johnleeds1, Johnuniq, Josve05a, Joy, Kamran the Great, Klilidiplomus, Kuru, Kwamikagami, LilHelpa, Lockesdonkey, Lotje, Mahmudmasri, Makyen, Marcussundberg, MarnetteD, MartinKassemJ120, Materialscientist, Mato, Md iet, Mehdi ghaed, MezzoMezzo, Middayexpress, Missyis21, Mogism, Muhandes, NAMASAYAZAIDI, NeilN, Neutron Jack, Nilli, North Atlanticist Usonian, Obradovic Goran, Octoberwoodland, Ohnoitsjamie, Omnipaedista, OpTioNiGhT, Passionpersian, Peaceworld111, PhnomPencil, Quebec99, R'n'B, RL0919, Rafeeque A Ansari, Raprchju, Redheylin, Rich Farmbrough, Rinneganmaster, Robert1054, Rursus, Sam Sailor, Sardanaphalus, SariaMuh, Sasajid, Sct72, Seattle Skier, Sirmylesnagopaleentheda, Sobreira, Soleado, Syncategoremata, TAnthony, The wub, Thomas Blomberg, Tom Dawkes, Turaab84, Ueutyi, Underlying lk, Urduboy, W.Kaleem, WereSpielChequers, WhisperToMe, Whoop whoop pull up, Wiki id2, Wiqi55, Wtmitchell, Xezbeth, Yacheen, YdhaW, Yohoyo, Уральский Кот, 145 anonymous edits 224

Islamic ethics *Source:* https://en.wikipedia.org/w/index.php?oldid=803634580 *License:* Creative Commons Attribution-Share Alike 3.0 *Contributors:* AA, AAA765, AKS.9955, Al-Andalusi, Alan Liefting, Alansohn, Alexis Ivanov, Anaselshamy, Anupam, Arrow740, AsceticRose, AtticusX, Aua, Azeemrags, BD2412, Bddrey, Beit Or, Bender235, Bihco, Billinghurst, Bless sins, Bluetd, Brandmeister, BritishWatcher, CBM, Charist, Charlesdrakew, Chris the speller, Citation bot 1, ClueBot NG, Diamondbuster, Download, Dsp13, Editor2020, Eeekster, Epbr123, Eperoton, Explicit, Gaius Cornelius, Gibbja, Harishseyal, Hhaaf000, Hmains, Horseless Headman, Ian Pitchford, Imnotminkus, Itaqallah, J.delanoy, J8079s, JackFarrington, Jagged 85, Jamesx12345, Jayjg, John of Reading, Johnuniq, Jonesey95, Jtamad, Jusdafax, Kadaveri, Karam.Anthony.K, Karl Meier, Koavf, Lenny Kaufman, Lobotoja, Luna Santin, MacHardy, Mahmagin, Mark Ironie, Materialscientist, Mogism, Morgankevinj huggle, Mpatel, Msin10, Muhammad Hamza, Niceguyedc, Nick Number, Nobody60, NuclearWarfare, Nurg, Ohnoitsjamie, Pharaoh of the Wizards, Presearch, Proabivouac, Prof.akbar, R'n'B, RandomP, Rich Farmbrough, Rich257, Riddleme, Rjwilmsi, Rsrikanth05, Rupert loup, Sa.vakilian, SamuelTheGhost, Scarian, Sharif Uddin, Shellwood, SimonP, Sionus, Sir192, Sodicadl, Syeda ujala, Syncategoremata, Teammm, Telpardec, Truthspreader, Turaab84, Unauthored, Vice regent, Viiiccc, WRK, Wavelength, Wbm1058, Wiki-uk, William M. Connolley, Woohookitty, Worldbruce, Yahel Guhan, Zikrullah, Zortwort, 101 anonymous edits 236

Early social changes under Islam *Source:* https://en.wikipedia.org/w/index.php?oldid=806011455 *License:* Creative Commons Attribution-Share Alike 3.0 *Contributors:* AAA765, Alefbe, Altetendekrabbe, Aminullah, Anaxial, Animum, Anythingcouldhappen, Arrow740, BD2412, Babloyi, Bddrey, Bender235, BhaiSaab, Bless sins, CLCStudent, CaliphoShah, CambridgeBayWeather, Chris the speller, ClueBot NG, DavidYork71, Dawn Bard, Diaa abdelmoneim, Dialectric, Domfurrlong, Eperoton, Gaius Cornelius, Gibbja, Gun Powder Ma, GünniX, Harishseyal, Ibrahim ebi, Iluvatar, Itsmejudith, J.delanoy, Jagged 85, JustAnIdea, Khazar2, Kuffsuk, Kwamikagami, Lamoonia, Lenny Kaufman, LindsayH, Marcocapelle, Materialscientist, Me, Myself, and I are Here, Miss Madeline, Mma mma2, Mpatel, Muon, Netscott, Nielswik, Octoberwoodland, Opiner, Patstuart, Philip Trueman, Ptbotgourou, Qzd, Redvers, Rileybo, Rjwilmsi, Robdurbar, RockyAlley, Samin096, Something Wrong, Stenen Bijl, Str1977, Striver, Supertouch, Swingoswingo, Tariqabjotu, Theseawolf, Thine Antique Pen, Thiseye, Truthspreader, WRK, WereSpielChequers, William M. Connolley, Woohookitty, 74 anonymous edits 256

Roman law *Source:* https://en.wikipedia.org/w/index.php?oldid=805945050 *License:* Creative Commons Attribution-Share Alike 3.0 *Contributors:* A. Parrot, ASHaber, Ahmedi490, Albany NY, Alexeynemov4, Altaïr, Andrew19960719, Andy Dingley, Barjimoa, Bear-rings, Bender235, Blobscar,

Image Sources, Licenses and Contributors

The sources listed for each image provide more detailed licensing information including the copyright status, the copyright owner, and the license conditions.

Image *Source:* https://en.wikipedia.org/w/index.php?title=File:Maat.svg *License:* Creative Commons Attribution-Share Alike *Contributors:* User:Jeff Dahl ... 3
Figure 1 *Source:* https://en.wikipedia.org/w/index.php?title=File:Winged_Maat_(KV11).jpg *License:* Public Domain *Contributors:* Dutertre, Tresea ... 4
Figure 2 *Source:* https://en.wikipedia.org/w/index.php?title=File:Maat.jpg *License:* Public Domain *Contributors:* JMCC1, Lunazagor, Petri Krohn, Tonycaffrey~commonswiki, Vassil, 1 anonymous edits ... 6
Figure 3 *Source:* https://en.wikipedia.org/w/index.php?title=File:BD_Weighing_of_the_Heart.jpg *License:* Public Domain *Contributors:* A. Parrot, Darekk2, Eunostos, JMCC1, Luna92 ... 9
Image *Source:* https://en.wikipedia.org/w/index.php?title=File:Babylonlion.JPG *License:* Public Domain *Contributors:* Attar-Aram syria, Chaos, Hama Rock, Jarekt, Jbribeiro1, Meno25, Slowking4, Thiotrix, Wst ... 12
Image *Source:* https://en.wikipedia.org/w/index.php?title=File:IJzeren_voetring_voor_gevangenen_transparent_background.png *License:* Creative Commons Attribution-Sharealike 3.0 *Contributors:* Chatsam, Ies, RaphaelQS ... 16
Image *Source:* https://en.wikipedia.org/w/index.php?title=File:Wikisource-logo.svg *License:* Creative Commons Attribution-Sharealike 3.0 *Contributors:* ChrisiPK, Guillom, INeverCry, Jarekt, JuTa, Leyo, Lokal Profil, MichaelMaggs, NielsF, Rei-artur, Rocket000, Romaine, Steinsplitter ... 31
Figure 4 *Source:* https://en.wikipedia.org/w/index.php?title=File:Constitution_of_Athens_BL_Papyrus_131.jpg *Contributors:* DopefishJustin, Helical gear, Primaler ... 32
Image *Source:* https://en.wikipedia.org/w/index.php?title=File:Aleppo_Codex_Joshua_1_1.jpg *License:* Public Domain *Contributors:* see en:Aleppo Codex; scanned by http://www.aleppocodex.org ... 36
Figure 5 *Source:* https://en.wikipedia.org/w/index.php?title=File:Book_of_Leviticus,_Mikraot_Gdolot,_Warsaw_edition,_1860,_Page_1.jpg *License:* Creative Commons Attribution-Sharealike 3.0 *Contributors:* User:Bo Basil ... 39
Figure 6 *Source:* https://en.wikipedia.org/w/index.php?title=File:Tabernacle_Camp.jpg *License:* Public Domain *Contributors:* Gover ... 41
Figure 7 *Source:* https://en.wikipedia.org/w/index.php?title=File:William_Holman_Hunt_-_The_Scapegoat.jpg *License:* Public Domain *Contributors:* Berrucomons, BotMultichill, Bukk, Dmitry Rozhkov, Flominator, Ham II, Hekerui, Hystrix, JalalV, Judithcomm, Kersti Nebelsiek, M0tty, Mattes, Shakko, Taivo, Thierry Caro, Wst, 2 anonymous edits ... 42
Figure 8 *Source:* https://en.wikipedia.org/w/index.php?title=File:Blake_The_Blasphemer.jpg *License:* Public Domain *Contributors:* Dauster, Jed, Wheeke ... 44
Figure 9 *Source:* https://en.wikipedia.org/w/index.php?title=File:Sacrifice_of_the_Old_Covenant_Rubens.jpg *License:* Public Domain *Contributors:* Ariely, BotMultichillT, Never covered, Vincent Steenberg ... 45
Image *Source:* https://en.wikipedia.org/w/index.php?title=File:Commons-logo.svg *License:* logo *Contributors:* Anomie, Callanecc, CambridgeBayWeather, Jo-Jo Eumerus, RHaworth ... 48
Image *Source:* https://en.wikipedia.org/w/index.php?title=File:Wikiquote-logo.svg *License:* Public Domain *Contributors:* Rei-artur ... 48
Image *Source:* https://en.wikipedia.org/w/index.php?title=File:Speaker_Icon.svg *License:* Public Domain *Contributors:* User:Mobius ... 49
Figure 10 *Source:* https://en.wikipedia.org/w/index.php?title=File:Hittite_Cuneiform_Tablet-_Legal_Deposition(?).jpg *License:* Creative Commons Zero *Contributors:* User:Mr. Granger ... 51
Figure 11 *Source:* https://en.wikipedia.org/w/index.php?title=File:Athen_Stoa_Ostrakismos_2.jpg *License:* Public Domain *Contributors:* –Xocolatl 09:29, 15 April 2008 (UTC) ... 55
Image *Source:* https://en.wikipedia.org/w/index.php?title=File:Om_symbol.svg *License:* Public Domain *Contributors:* User:Rugby471 ... 62
Image *Source:* https://en.wikipedia.org/w/index.php?title=File:Dr._Bhim_Rao_Ambedkar.jpg *License:* Public Domain *Contributors:* David Levy, Human3015, Magog the Ogre, Roland zh, Terabar, संदेश हिवाळे, 1 anonymous edits ... 75
Image *Source:* https://en.wikipedia.org/w/index.php?title=File:MKGandhi.jpg *Contributors:* - ... 75
Figure 12 *Source:* https://en.wikipedia.org/w/index.php?title=File:Chanakya_artistic_depiction.jpg *License:* Public Domain *Contributors:* Capankajsmilyo, Roland zh, Titodutta, Utcursch ... 91
Figure 13 *Source:* https://en.wikipedia.org/w/index.php?title=File:Maurya_Empire,_c.250_BCE_2.png *License:* Creative Commons Attribution-Sharealike 3.0 *Contributors:* User:Avantiputra7 ... 97
Figure 14 *Source:* https://en.wikipedia.org/w/index.php?title=File:Copper_plate_Malla.jpg *License:* Public Domain *Contributors:* J. Burgess, W. Abraham ... 103
Figure 15 *Source:* https://en.wikipedia.org/w/index.php?title=File:Oriya_land_grant.jpg *License:* Public Domain *Contributors:* J. Beames ... 110
Image *Source:* https://en.wikipedia.org/w/index.php?title=File:Aum_Om_red.svg *Contributors:* Cathy Richards, Ms Sarah Welch, Sarang ... 117
Image *Source:* https://en.wikipedia.org/w/index.php?title=File:It-□.png *License:* Public Domain *Contributors:* Arlas! it ... 150
Image *Source:* https://en.wikipedia.org/w/index.php?title=File:PD-icon.svg *License:* Public Domain *Contributors:* Alex.muller, Anomie, Anonymous Dissident, CBM, Jo-Jo Eumerus, MBisanz, PBS, Quadell, Rocket000, Strangerer, Timotheus Canens, 1 anonymous edits ... 157
Image *Source:* https://en.wikipedia.org/w/index.php?title=File:Scale_of_justice,_canon_law.svg *License:* Creative Commons Attribution-Sharealike 3.0 *Contributors:* User:Ktr101 ... 167
Image *Source:* https://en.wikipedia.org/w/index.php?title=File:046CupolaSPietro.jpg *License:* Creative Commons Attribution-Sharealike 3.0 *Contributors:* MarkusMark ... 167
Figure 16 *Source:* https://en.wikipedia.org/w/index.php?title=File:Extract_from_Burchard_of_Worms'_Decretum.jpg *License:* Public Domain *Contributors:* Dbachmann, Felix Folio Secundus, G.dallorto, Jbribeiro1, Jheald, Jkelly ... 178
Figure 17 *Source:* https://en.wikipedia.org/w/index.php?title=File:Graciano.jpg *License:* Public Domain *Contributors:* Albert Krantz, Bibi Saint-Pol, Davepape, Dodo, G.dallorto, Libertad y Saber, Yakoo ... 179
Figure 18 *Source:* https://en.wikipedia.org/w/index.php?title=File:Pietro_Gasparri.jpg *License:* Public Domain *Contributors:* BotMultichill, BotMultichillT, Fex1993, Massimo Macconi, Mef.ellingen, Paul.Matthies, Steinsplitter, Väsk ... 181
Figure 19 *Source:* https://en.wikipedia.org/w/index.php?title=File:Roman_Rota.jpg *License:* Public Domain *Contributors:* Adam sk~commonswiki, NeverDoING, OgreBot 2 ... 183
Figure 20 *Source:* https://en.wikipedia.org/w/index.php?title=File:SummaTheologiae.jpg *License:* Public Domain *Contributors:* Bibi Saint-Pol, Longbow4u, Markus Mueller~commonswiki, Martynas Patasius, Tomisti ... 184
Image *Source:* https://en.wikipedia.org/w/index.php?title=File:Flag_of_Côte_d'Ivoire.svg *License:* Public Domain *Contributors:* User:Jon Harald Søby ... 185
Image *Source:* https://en.wikipedia.org/w/index.php?title=File:Flag_of_Cameroon.svg *License:* Public Domain *Contributors:* (of code) cs:User:-xfi- 185
Image *Source:* https://en.wikipedia.org/w/index.php?title=File:Flag_of_the_Democratic_Republic_of_the_Congo.svg *Contributors:* User:Nightstallion ... 185
Image *Source:* https://en.wikipedia.org/w/index.php?title=File:Flag_of_Canada.svg *License:* Public Domain *Contributors:* Anomie, Jo-Jo Eumerus 185
Image *Source:* https://en.wikipedia.org/w/index.php?title=File:Flag_of_Mexico.svg *License:* Public Domain *Contributors:* Alex Covarrubias, 9 April 2006 Based on the arms by Juan Gabino. ... 185
Image *Source:* https://en.wikipedia.org/w/index.php?title=File:Flag_of_the_United_States.svg *License:* Public Domain *Contributors:* Anomie, Jo-Jo Eumerus, MSGJ, Mr. Stradivarius ... 185
Image *Source:* https://en.wikipedia.org/w/index.php?title=File:Flag_of_Argentina.svg *Contributors:* Government of Argentina ... 185
Image *Source:* https://en.wikipedia.org/w/index.php?title=File:Flag_of_Brazil.svg *License:* Public Domain *Contributors:* Anomie, Jo-Jo Eumerus 185
Image *Source:* https://en.wikipedia.org/w/index.php?title=File:Flag_of_Colombia.svg *License:* Public Domain *Contributors:* SKopp ... 185
Image *Source:* https://en.wikipedia.org/w/index.php?title=File:Flag_of_India.svg *License:* Public Domain *Contributors:* Anomie, Jo-Jo Eumerus, Mifter ... 186
Image *Source:* https://en.wikipedia.org/w/index.php?title=File:Flag_of_Lebanon.svg *License:* Public Domain *Contributors:* Traced based on the CIA World Factbook with some modification done to the colours based on information at Vexilla mundi ... 186
Image *Source:* https://en.wikipedia.org/w/index.php?title=File:Flag_of_the_Philippines.svg *License:* Public Domain *Contributors:* User:Achim1999 186

463

464

License

Index

Hindu culture, 73
Hinduism, 62, 79, 102, 109, 117, 128, 129, 243, 260
Hindu law, 62, 117, **128**
Hindu texts, 62, 79, 84, 102
Hippias (tyrant), 56
Hippocrates, 55
Hisbah, 205
Hisham ibn Urwah, 227
Hispania, 295
Historical Museum of the Palatinate, 394
Historical revisionism, 195
Historiography, 371
History, 281, 409
History of Hinduism, 117, 128
History of Mithila, 81
History of the Middle East, 13
Hittite Empire, 50
Hittite language, 12, 50
Hittite laws, **50**
Hittite mythology, 13
Hittites, 12
Hittite texts, 13
Hlothhere, 304
H. M. Chadwick, 310
Holiness code, 38, 40
Holy of holies, 40
Holy orders, 322
Holy Roman Empire, 270, 350
Holy See, 172
Homage (feudal), 360
Homer, 32
Homilies dOrganyà, 346
Honorarium, 17
Honour, 322, 328
Horse racing, 322
Hostage, 250
Hound, 322
House of Stuart, 354
How to Read Egyptian Hieroglyphs, 11
H. Patrick Glenn, 214, 220
H. Radau, 31
Hudud, 192, 200, 204, 207
Hukm, 225
Humane, 250
Humanistic, 242
Human rights, 193, 256
Human Rights Act 1998, 412
Human skin color, 247
Hundred (county division), 307
Hungary, 186
Hunger strike, 319
Huns, 297
Hurrian language, 12
Hurrians, 12
Husbandman, 20

Hussein ibn Ali, 229
Hygiene in Islam, 233
Hyperbolos, 56, 57
Hyperbolus, 55

IAST, 79, 84
Ibadah, 192, 231
Ibadi, 202, 232, 234
Iberian Peninsula, 295
Ibn Al-Jazzar, 242
Ibn al-Nafis, 242
Ibn Batuta, 158
Ibn Hajar al-Asqalani, 248, 251
Ibn Hanbal, 195
Ibn Jumay, 242
Ibn Khaldun, 225
Ibn Qayyim, 243
Ibn Taymiyyah, 439
Ignac Goldziher, 195
Igor Judge, 392
Ijma, 192, 196, 197, 226, 229–231
Ijtihad, 192, 196, 225, 228
Illiberal democracy, 191
Imad-ad-Dean Ahmad, 244
Impartiality, 245
Impeachment, 248, 276
Imperator, 270
Imperial immediacy, 352
Imperialism, 56
Imperium, 270
Important civil codes, 399
Inalienable rights, 245
Incest, 27, 243, 301
Incipit, 14
Income tax, 268
India, 136, 186, 234
Indiana University, 254
Indian subcontinent, 233
Indictment, 398
Individual freedom, 245
Individualism, 261
Indonesia, 63, 109, 204, 217, 234
Industrial relations, 245
Ine of Wessex, 304
Infidel, 216
Informal value transfer system, 234
Inheritance, 240, 404
In naturalia, 17
Inns of Court, 235, 281
Inquisitorial system, 140, 182, 397
Insane, 328
Inscription, 13
Institut Catholique de Paris, 186
Institute of European History, 222, 236
Institutes of Justinian, 280, 285
Institution, 234, 303